D1601884

ALL·IN·ONE

CompTIA
Linux+™/LPIC-1 Certification

EXAM GUIDE

Second Edition

ABOUT THE AUTHOR

Robb H. Tracy (CNA, CNE, CNI, CompTIA A+, CompTIA Network+, CompTIA Security+, CompTIA Linux+) has been a professional technology instructor and courseware developer since 1996. He has designed and implemented technical training products and curricula for major hardware and software vendors including Novell, Micron Technology, TestOut, Messaging Architects, and Motorola. Robb previously served on CompTIA's Network+ Advisory Committee, where he helped define the objectives that make up the CompTIA Network+ certification. He is a cofounder of Nebo Technical Institute, Inc., a leading provider of information technology training and consulting. Robb is the author of *Novell Certified Linux Engineer (Novell CLE) Study Guide* (Novell Press, 2005), *Novell Certified Linux Engineer 9 (CLE 9) Study Guide* (Novell Press, 2006), *Linux+ Certification Study Guide* (McGraw-Hill Education, 2008), *LPIC-1/CompTIA Linux+ Certification Exam Guide* (McGraw-Hill Education, 2011), *CompTIA Network+ Certification Practice Exams* (McGraw-Hill Education, 2012), and *LPI Linux Essentials Certification All-in-One Exam Guide* (McGraw-Hill Education, 2013).

About the Technical Editor

Brian Barber (CompTIA Linux+, MCSE, MCSA, MCP+I, MCNE, CNE, CNA-GW) is the Manager of Monitoring and Reporting Systems with the Canada Deposit Insurance Corporation (CDIC). He first started using Linux at home with Red Hat 5.1, and since then he has been a staunch advocate of open source software in both commercial and residential settings. He has belonged to the Ottawa Canada Linux User Group (OCLUG) since 2001. His primary areas of interest are operating systems, multiplatform integration, directory services, and enterprise messaging. In the past he has held the positions of Principal Consultant with Sierra Systems Group, Senior Technical Coordinator with LGS Group (now a part of IBM Global Services), and Senior Technical Analyst with MetLife Canada. Brian has been a lead or contributing author as well as a technical editor for 18 technology books, including the previous edition of this book and Robb's *Linux+ Certification Study Guide* (McGraw-Hill Education, 2008).

ALL · IN · ONE

CompTIA
Linux+™/LPIC-1
Certification

EXAM GUIDE

Second Edition

(Exams LX0-103 & LX0-104/101-400 & 102-400)

Robb H. Tracy

Mc
Graw
Hill
Education

New York • Chicago • San Francisco
Athens • London • Madrid • Mexico City
Milan • New Delhi • Singapore • Sydney • Toronto

Library of Congress Cataloging-in-Publication Data

Tracy, Robb H.
  CompTIA Linux+/LPIC-1 certification : exam guide / Robb H. Tracy. — Second edition.
       pages   cm
  ISBN 978-0-07-184168-9 (set : alk. paper) — ISBN 978-0-07-184170-2 (CD) — ISBN 978-0-07-184169-6 (book) — ISBN 0-07-184168-7 (set) — ISBN 0-07-184169-5 (book : alk. paper) — ISBN 0-07-184170-9 (CD)
  1. Linux—Examinations—Study guides   2. Operating systems (Computers)—Examinations—Study guides.
  3. Computer networks—Examinations—Study guides.   4. Electronic data processing personnel—Certification.
  I. Title.
  QA76.774.L46T73   2015
  005.4'46—dc23
                                                                                      2015014913

McGraw-Hill Education books are available at special quantity discounts to use as premiums and sales promotions, or for use in corporate training programs. To contact a representative, please visit the Contact Us pages at www .mhprofessional.com.

CompTIA Linux+™/LPIC-1 Certification All-in-One Exam Guide, Second Edition (Exams LX0-103 & LX0-104/101-400 & 102-400)

2 3 4 5 6 7 8 9 10   DOC   20 19 18 17 16

ISBN: Book p/n 978-0-07-184169-6 and CD p/n 978-0-07-184170-2
of set 978-0-07-184168-9

MHID: Book p/n 0-07-184169-5 and CD p/n 0-07-184170-9
of set 0-07-184168-7

Sponsoring Editors	**Technical Editor**	**Production Supervisor**
Jeff Kellum	Brian Barber	Jean Bodeaux
Meghan Riley Manfre	**Copy Editor**	**Composition**
Editorial Supervisor	Bart Reed	Cenveo Publisher Services
Patty Mon	**Proofreader**	**Illustration**
Project Manager	Paul Tyler	Cenveo Publisher Services
Namita Gahtori,	**Indexer**	**Art Director, Cover**
Cenveo® Publisher Services	Ted Laux	Jeff Weeks
Acquisitions Coordinator		
Amy Stonebraker		

This book is dedicated to all the individuals who have made a difference in my life. To my Dad, for instilling in me a love of teaching and of all things mechanical. To my Mom, for teaching me the value of hard work and devotion. To my mentor, Dennis Simmons, for teaching me to strive for excellence in all I do. To my wife and best friend, for supporting and loving me through the process of writing this book.

—Robb H. Tracy

Becoming a CompTIA Certified IT Professional Is Easy

It's also the best way to reach greater professional opportunities and rewards.

Why Get CompTIA Certified?

Growing Demand

Labor estimates predict some technology fields will experience growth of more than 20 percent by the year 2020. (Source: CompTIA 9th Annual Information Security Trends study: 500 U.S. IT and Business Executives Responsible for Security.) CompTIA certification qualifies the skills required to join this workforce.

Higher Salaries

IT professionals with certifications on their résumé command better jobs, earn higher salaries, and have more doors open to new multi-industry opportunities.

Verified Strengths

Ninety-one percent of hiring managers indicate CompTIA certifications are valuable in validating IT expertise, making certification the best way to demonstrate your competency and knowledge to employers. (Source: CompTIA Employer Perceptions of IT Training and Certification.)

Universal Skills

CompTIA certifications are vendor neutral—which means that certified professionals can proficiently work with an extensive variety of hardware and software found in most organizations.

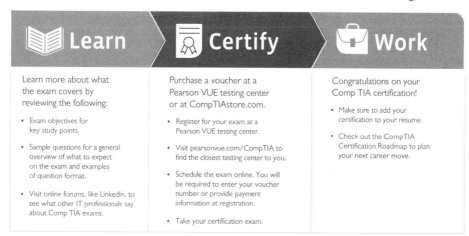

Learn

Learn more about what the exam covers by reviewing the following:

- Exam objectives for key study points.

- Sample questions for a general overview of what to expect on the exam and examples of question format.

- Visit online forums, like LinkedIn, to see what other IT professionals say about Comp TIA exams.

Certify

Purchase a voucher at a Pearson VUE testing center or at CompTIAstore.com.

- Register for your exam at a Pearson VUE testing center.

- Visit pearsonvue.com/CompTIA to find the closest testing center to you.

- Schedule the exam online. You will be required to enter your voucher number or provide payment information at registration.

- Take your certification exam.

Work

Congratulations on your Comp TIA certification!

- Make sure to add your certification to your resume.

- Check out the CompTIA Certification Roadmap to plan your next career move.

To learn more, visit Certification.CompTIA.org/ linuxplus.

Content Seal of Quality

This courseware bears the seal of CompTIA Approved Quality Content. This seal signifies this content covers 100 percent of the exam objectives and implements important instructional design principles. CompTIA recommends multiple learning tools to help increase coverage of the learning objectives.

The logo of the CompTIA Approved Quality Content (CAQC) program and the status of this or other training material as "Approved" under the CompTIA Approved Quality Content program signify that, in CompTIA's opinion, such training material covers the content of CompTIA's related certification exam.

The contents of this training material were created for the CompTIA Linux+ exams covering CompTIA certification objectives that were current as of the date of publication.

CompTIA has not reviewed or approved the accuracy of the contents of this training material and specifically disclaims any warranties of merchantability or fitness for a particular purpose. CompTIA makes no guarantee concerning the success of persons using any such "Approved" or other training material in order to prepare for any CompTIA certification exam.

Disclaimer

CONTENTS AT A GLANCE

CONTENTS

Congratulations on your decision to become Linux+/LPIC-1 certified! By purchasing this book, you've taken the first step toward earning one of the hottest certifications around. Being Linux+/ LPIC-1 certified provides you with a distinct advantage in today's IT job market. When you obtain your Linux+/LPIC-1 certification, you prove to your employer, your coworkers, and yourself that you truly know your stuff with Linux.

This is a big issue. Over the years, I've had the opportunity to interview a number of job applicants for open positions in my organization. I learned early on that you can't rely on the Skills and Knowledge section of an applicant's résumé to get an accurate picture of what the applicant can and can't do. Case in point: Several years ago, my group had a position open that required an exceptionally strong technology background. The job posting listed "extensive background with computer hardware and networking" as one of the requirements for the position.

One of the candidates I interviewed claimed in her résumé to have an extensive background in these areas. In fact, during the interview this person claimed to be an expert in the field. I have to admit, the résumé did look impressive.

However, as the interview progressed I began to have some doubts. This person just didn't speak or act like a true techie, so I decided to administer a little test during the interview. I asked her to connect a storage device to a workstation. A pretty easy task for an "expert," right? Well, the applicant couldn't do it. In fact, she didn't even know where to begin.

To make a long story short, upper management eventually hired this applicant in spite of my concerns. It wasn't a good situation. She didn't have the background required and subsequently performed very poorly on the job and eventually quit after only a year. The key problem in this situation was conflicting definitions of a "computer hardware and networking expert." My team needed someone who could install expansion cards, hard drives, and operating systems as well as set up a computer network.

This applicant, on the other hand, had a very different definition of a "computer hardware and networking expert." She considered herself to be an expert because she knew how to use Microsoft Word, Excel, and PowerPoint. She also knew how to log in to a network using a username and password. In essence, she was an expert *end user,* but she was not an expert *system administrator,* which was what we were looking for.

This situation could have been avoided if my company had listed specific certifications in the job requirements instead of just asking for an "extensive background with computer hardware and networking." Certifications help everyone involved in the hiring process. By requiring applicants to have their Linux+/LPIC-1 certification, prospective employers can weed out applicants who really don't have the skills and knowledge required for a particular position. Having your Linux+/ LPIC-1 certification also helps you demonstrate to potential employers that you truly have the Linux background you claim on your résumé, giving you an advantage over other job applicants who aren't certified.

The goal of this book is to help you reach this state of certification nirvana. The Linux+/LPIC-1 certification is the perfect place to start. By merging two popular, widely respected industry certifications together (CompTIA Linux+ and LPIC-1), CompTIA has created the ideal entry-level Linux certification. Linux+/LPIC-1 is the first stepping stone on the path to total Linux mastery. After gaining some real-life experience on the job with your Linux+/LPIC-1 certification, you can further enhance your skills and reputation by gaining the LPIC-2 and the coveted LPIC-3 certifications.

Let's get started on Level 1!

ACKNOWLEDGMENTS

The title page of this book lists Robb H. Tracy as its author. However, this attribution is deceiving. By no means was this a one-person job. Behind every book is a team of individuals who rarely get the credit they deserve. They are the unsung heroes who make sure the job gets done.

First, I would like to acknowledge the efforts of the production team behind this book. These folks were the glue that kept everything together. Thanks to Timothy Green for giving me the opportunity to write this book. I appreciate your confidence in me! Thanks to Stephanie Evans and Meghan Manfre for managing the development process. No matter the time of day, they were always there with the information I needed. Thanks also to Bart Reed for helping me through the final review process. His experienced eyes are the reason this title looks good.

Finally, a huge thank you to Brian Barber. Brian reviewed each and every word and exercise step in this book for technical accuracy. His efforts kept me honest and were absolutely invaluable, dramatically increasing the overall quality of this title. Brian spent many late nights testing the lab exercises in this book, ensuring that you have a successful experience. Thanks, Brian!

INTRODUCTION

We first need to introduce you to the nuts and bolts of this book and the Linux+/LPIC-1 certification program. Let's take a look at the following:

- Who this book is for
- How this book is organized
- Special features of the All-in-One Certification series
- The Linux+/LPIC-1 certification exams
- Tips for succeeding on the Linux+/LPIC-1 certification exams

Let's begin by discussing whom this book is for.

Who This Book Is For

Before you start this book, you need to be aware that I have two primary goals in mind as I write:

- To help you prepare for and pass the Linux+/LPIC-1 exams offered by CompTIA
- To provide you with the extra skills and knowledge you need to be successful on the job after you are certified

Essentially, when we're done here I want you to be able to do more than just recite facts. I want you to be able to walk the walk and talk the talk. I want you to be able to actually do the job once hired.

To accomplish this, we're going to focus heavily on the core Linux knowledge and skills in this book required by the Linux+/LPIC-1 certification. You need to already have a strong computing background before starting, including

- **Managing computer hardware** You should be able to install new peripheral devices, configure system resources, and troubleshoot basic hardware-related problems. For example, if someone were to hand you several memory modules and ask you to install them in a PC system, you should know exactly what to do. You should be familiar with the following:
  - PC cases and power supplies
  - Motherboards
  - Expansion slots and expansion boards
  - CPUs and memory
  - Storage devices such as hard drives, optical drives, and USB drives

- Video boards and monitors
- Peripheral devices such as printers, scanners, and digital cameras
- **Implementing and managing computer networks**   You should be able to set up a network switch, install and configure network interface cards, and connect everything together with cabling. I'm going to assume you are familiar with the following:
  - Common networking topologies, such as star, bus, and ring
  - Common networking components, such as NICs, cables, routers, and hubs/switches
  - Common networking protocols, such as IP, TCP, and UDP
  - Common networking services, such as FTP servers, web servers, and mail servers

If possible, CompTIA recommends that you have your CompTIA A+ and CompTIA Network+ certifications under your belt (or have equivalent experience in the field) before starting this book. These two certification programs will provide you with the hardware and networking background you need to be successful in your Linux+/LPIC-1 certification program.

If you have this background, you're ready to roll! Let's next discuss how this book is organized to accomplish its two main goals.

How This Book Is Organized

I love CompTIA certification programs. They go the extra mile to make sure their certifications truly reflect current trends in the information technology industry, and the Linux+/LPIC-1 certification is no exception. Working in partnership with the Linux Professional Institute (LPI), CompTIA has defined the Linux+ certification by publishing objectives that list the skills and knowledge that a certified person should have.

These objectives, as currently published, are organized by topic. They aren't organized into a logical instructional flow. As you read through this book, you'll quickly notice that I don't address the Linux+/LPIC-1 objectives in the same order as they are published by CompTIA. All of the objectives are covered; however, I've reorganized them such that we start with the most basic Linux concepts first. Then, as we progress through the course, we'll address increasingly more advanced Linux+ objectives, building on the skills and knowledge covered in preceding chapters.

Special Features of the All-in-One Certification Series

To make our exam guides more useful and a pleasure to read, we have designed the All-in-One Certification series to include several conventions.

Icons

To alert you to an important bit of advice, a shortcut, or a pitfall, you'll occasionally see Notes, Tips, Cautions, and Exam Tips peppered throughout the text.

NOTE Notes offer nuggets of especially helpful stuff, background explanations, and information. They also define terms occasionally.

 TIP Tips provide suggestions and nuances to help you learn to finesse your job. Take a tip from us and read the Tips carefully.

 CAUTION When you see a Caution, pay special attention. Cautions appear when you have to make a crucial choice or when you are about to undertake something that may have ramifications you might not immediately anticipate. Read them now so that you don't have regrets later.

 EXAM TIP Exam Tips give you special advice or may provide information specifically related to preparing for the exam itself.

End-of-Chapter Reviews and Questions

An important part of this book comes at the end of each chapter, where you will find a brief review of the high points, along with a series of questions followed by the answers to those questions. Each question is in multiple-choice format. The answers provided also include a small discussion explaining why the correct answer choice actually is the correct answer.

The questions are provided as a study aid to you, the reader and prospective Linux+/LPIC-1 exam taker. We obviously can't guarantee that if you answer all of our questions correctly you will absolutely pass the certification exams. Instead, what we can guarantee is that the questions will provide you with an idea about how ready you are for the exams.

The DVD

This book comes complete with a DVD containing even more questions and their answers to help you prepare for the exams. It also contains virtual machine files that you can use to set up your very own Linux system to practice with. Read more about the companion DVD in Appendix B.

The Linux+/LPIC-1 Certification Exams

Now that you understand how this book is organized, it's time for you to become familiar with the Linux+/LPIC-1 certification program and its associated exams. Let's review the following:

- About the Linux+/LPIC-1 certification
- Taking the Linux+/LPIC-1 exams
- Exam makeup

About the Linux+/LPIC-1 Certification

The Linux+/LPIC-1 certification is an excellent program! It is a vendor-neutral certification designed and administered by the Computing Technology Industry Association, affectionately known as CompTIA. The current version was developed by merging two very popular and well-respected Linux certifications together: CompTIA's Linux+ certification and LPI's LPIC-1 certification. Because they are basically the same certification now, you'll see me use the term "Linux+/LPIC-1 certification" throughout this book. In fact, if you pass your CompTIA Linux+ exams, you can also receive your LPIC-1 certification by simply submitting your results to LPI.

The Linux+/LPIC-1 certification is considered "vendor neutral" because the exams aren't based on one particular vendor's hardware or software. This is somewhat unique in the information technology industry. Many IT certification programs are centered on one particular vendor's hardware or software, such as those from Microsoft, Cisco, and Red Hat.

The Linux+/LPIC-1 certification, on the other hand, is designed to verify your knowledge and skills with the Linux operating system in general, not on any one particular distribution. The following is according to CompTIA:

> *CompTIA Linux+ Powered by LPI is a high-stakes, vendor-neutral certification that validates the fundamental knowledge and skills required of junior Linux administrators.... Candidate job roles include junior Linux administrator, junior network administrator, systems administrator, Linux database administrator and web administrator. Companies such as Dell, HP, IBM, Lenovo and Xerox recommend or require CompTIA Linux+.*

To verify your knowledge, CompTIA requires you to take two exams to earn your certification: LX0-103 and LX0-104. The LX0-103 exam covers the following general knowledge areas:

- Linux system architecture
- Linux installation and package management
- GNU and UNIX commands
- Hardware devices
- Linux file systems and the Filesystem Hierarchy Standard

The LX0-104 exam covers the following general knowledge areas:

- Shells
- Scripting and data management
- User interfaces and desktops
- Administrative tasks
- Essential system services
- Networking fundamentals
- Security

CompTIA has published sets of objectives for both exams that together define the Linux+/LPIC-1 certification. These objectives specify what a junior Linux system admin should know and be able to do. You can view the Linux+/LPIC-1 objectives at http://certification.comptia.org/. All of the items on the CompTIA Linux+ exams are based on these objectives. If you're going to be Linux+/LPIC-1 certified, you have to be able to do the tasks contained in these objectives. As we go through this book, you'll see that the complete list of Linux+/LPIC-1 objectives is quite extensive.

In the latest version of the Linux+/LPIC-1 certification, you have the option of forwarding your exam results to the Linux Professional Institute (LPI). Passing both the LX0-103 and LX0-104 exams allows you to become LPIC level 1 certified as well as CompTIA Linux+ certified.

Let's talk about the exams in a little more detail.

Taking the Linux+/LPIC-1 Exams

The Linux+/LPIC-1 exams are timed exams delivered electronically on a computer. Each exam is composed of 60 questions, and you will have 90 minutes per exam to complete them.

 NOTE You may actually see more than 60 questions on your exams. If this happens, it's because CompTIA has slipped a few beta test items into your exam to evaluate them. In this situation, you should be automatically given extra time on the exam to accommodate the extra items.

The exam interface is fairly straightforward. Items are displayed one at a time on the screen. You are presented with a question along with a series of responses. You mark the appropriate response and then go to the next question.

Each exam is composed primarily of multiple-choice items. This testing format presents you with a question and asks you to mark the correct answer from a list of choices. Most of the multiple-choice questions require only one answer; however, some will require you to select multiple correct responses from the list displayed. If this is the case, the test question will end with the text "(Choose x.)," where x is the number of responses you should mark.

After you complete your exam, the computer will immediately evaluate it and your score will be printed out. To pass, you need a minimum score of 500 points out of a possible 800. Hopefully, you will pass your exams on the first try. However, if you don't, your score printout will list the objectives where you missed questions. You can use this information to review and prepare yourself to retake the exam.

To make the exams globally available, CompTIA administers the Linux+/LPIC-1 exams through its testing partner, Pearson VUE (www.vue.com).

To sign up for the Linux+/LPIC-1 exams, visit the LPI website (www.lpi.org) and purchase an exam voucher. Then visit the Pearson VUE website and locate a testing center near you. Most community and technical colleges are authorized testing centers. Just specify the exam you want to take and your locale information. You will then be provided with a list of testing centers near you, as shown in Figure 1.

You can then use the Pearson VUE website to schedule your exams and pay your fees. You can also call the test provider directly and schedule your exams over the phone. Be aware that they will need to verify your identity before they can sign you up, so be prepared to share your Social

Test Center Search

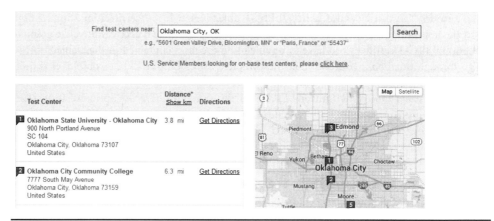

Figure I   Locating a testing center near you

Security number when you call or log on. The test provider will send you a confirmation e-mail listing the date, time, and location of your exam.

On the day of the test, be sure you allow adequate travel time. You never know when you will run into a traffic jam or have a mechanical failure. (I've actually had this happen to me. It's very stressful!) In addition, you should try to show up early enough to find a parking spot and walk to the testing center. If you're taking your exams at a community college, you may find that you have to walk a very long distance to get from the parking lot to the building where the exams are delivered. The last thing you need right before your exam is to feel rushed and stressed!

When you check in at the testing center, you will be required to show two forms of identification, one of which must have your photo on it. The following are acceptable forms of ID:

- Driver's license
- Social Security card
- Credit card
- Student ID card
- Military ID card
- State-issued ID card

Be forewarned that, when you check in, you must surrender your phone, iPod, tablet, laptop, or any other electronic devices to the test proctor. The last testing center I visited wouldn't even allow hats, so be prepared to show the world your hat-hair. You're not allowed to take any reference materials into the exam room, including blank paper. Most testing centers will provide you with note-taking materials that must remain in the room where the test is being administered. Some testing centers will provide you with paper and a pencil; others may provide a small whiteboard slate with an erasable pen.

Let's now look at the composition of the Linux+/LPIC-1 exams.

Exam Makeup

Each exam is divided into several categories, which CompTIA calls "domains." The first exam is number LX0-103. The knowledge domains covered on the first exam are shown in Table 1. The knowledge domains covered on the second exam, LX0-104, are shown in Table 2.

Table 1 LX0-103 Exam Domains	Domain	% of Exam
	101 System Architecture	14
	102 Linux Installation and Package Management	18
	103 GNU and UNIX Commands	43
	104 Devices, Linux File systems, Filesystem Hierarchy Standard	25
	Total	100

Table 2 LX0-104 Exam Domains	Domain	% of Exam
	105 Shells, Scripting, and Data Management	17
	106 User Interfaces and Desktops	8
	107 Administrative Tasks	20
	108 Essential System Services	17
	109 Networking Fundamentals	23
	110 Security	15
	Total	100

As you can see in the tables, some domains are tested more heavily than others. When studying, be sure to pay special attention to those domains with the highest percentage of exam questions! With this in mind, let's now discuss how to prepare for the Linux+/LPIC-1 exams.

Tips for Succeeding on the Linux+/LPIC-1 Certification Exams

I'll never forget the first time I took an IT certification exam back in the early 1990s. I was so nervous that I almost couldn't function. Fortunately, the exam went very well and I passed it handily. Over the last decade, I've helped a lot of folks prepare themselves for a variety of certification exams. I've even written a number of industry certification exams myself. As a result, I've learned a number of things that you can do to increase the likelihood that you will pass your exam. We'll discuss the following here:

- Preparing for the exams
- Taking the exams

Let's begin by learning how you can prepare yourself for the Linux+/LPIC-1 exams.

Preparing for the Exams

The most important thing you can do to prepare for your Linux+/LPIC-1 exams is to thoroughly study. No tip, no trick, no strategy can compensate for a lack of study. The goal is to move the information you need to pass the exams into your long-term memory. Following are some study tips that can help you prepare for your certification exams.

One to Two Months Before Your Exams

- Schedule your Linux+/LPIC-1 exams. Ideally, you should schedule them to take place about 30–60 days after you begin this book. If you don't give yourself a deadline, you probably will never "get around" to studying for and taking the exams.

- Pace yourself. Don't try to cram for the exams the night before. This is a very common mistake made by many students. (I did this myself in college.) Cramming rarely works, because your short-term memory can only hold a limited amount of information. All that stuff you're trying to cram into your short-term memory gets lost. Instead, successful test-takers spend a good deal of time loading information into their long-term memory. You can do this by setting a goal to read a certain number of pages or chapters each day and sticking to it.

- Take notes! As you read each chapter, write down important information that stands out to you. Writing this down helps reinforce the information, moving it from short-term memory into long-term memory in your brain. It also provides you with a valuable review resource.

- Do the lab exercises, even the simple ones. Doing the lab exercises helps you learn the practical implementation of the conceptual skills and knowledge presented in each chapter.

- Tackle the end-of-chapter questions for each chapter. After you read a chapter, get a blank piece of paper and run through the questions, recording your responses on the paper. (Don't write in the book! You'll want it to be pristine for later study sessions.) Check your answers and review the topics you missed.

- Review the "Summary" and "Accelerated Review" sections after you complete each chapter.

Two to Three Days Before Your Exam

- Review your notes.

- Review the questions at the end of each chapter. Review any topics you are still struggling with.

- Repeat the lab exercises for each chapter. This time, however, try to complete the exercises without looking at the steps in the book.

The Night Before Your Exam

- Relax! Being well rested is key to performing well on your exams. Don't get so worked up and nervous that you can't sleep the night before your exams. Get to bed at a reasonable hour.

- Review your notes.

- Review the "Summary" and "Accelerated Review" sections again for each chapter. Repetition is the key to retention!

The Morning of Your Exam

- Eat a good breakfast. Your brain requires a tremendous amount of calories to operate. Give it what it needs!

- Review your notes.

- Review the "Summary" and "Accelerated Review" sections once again for each chapter. Did I mention that repetition is the key to retention?

- Run through the questions one more time for each chapter.

- Allow yourself plenty of time to get to the testing center. Don't get stressed out by being late.

What we're trying to do is upload the information you need to pass your tests into your long-term memory through repetition and practice. Then, shortly before the exams, we're exercising the brain by retrieving that stored information and bringing it to the forefront of your thoughts (kind of like loading data from a hard drive into system RAM) so that it is ready and available when you take the test.

With this in mind, let's review some of the key "gotchas" certification candidates have observed about the Linux+/LPIC-1 exams:

- The exams have a reputation for being nit-picky on command options. In fact, some candidates have criticized the exams for focusing too much on vague or obscure command options that aren't used often. We've tried to cover the commands options that we think you'll be tested on in this book. However, we obviously don't have access to the exam banks, so we can't guarantee that all of the command options you'll see on the exams are addressed here. Covering all options for all the commands isn't realistic, as it would easily double the page count of this book (and put you to sleep). Therefore, I *strongly* recommend that you review the man pages for all the commands we've covered in this book and review their various options.

- You must know both RPM and Debian package management systems for your Linux+/ LPIC-1 exams. In earlier versions of the certification, you could pick which one you wanted to be tested on. Not so now. You are expected to be familiar with both.

- There's some debate about whether it's best to take your exams one at a time or together all at once. The general consensus is that the first exam is the more difficult of the two. Accordingly, my recommendation is that you take the exams separately and that you take the first exam first. Don't be alarmed if you have to retake the first exam to pass it. The reality is that not many candidates pass it the first time. However, after passing the first exam, many candidates report that the second exam is noticeably less difficult. You must take both exams within five years of each other in order to be certified.

- The average score on the Linux+/LPIC-1 exams is around 480. Remember that a 500 score is required to pass. This statistic should tell you that these are very difficult exams! A lot of candidates (about half) fail. According to the LPI website, this is done deliberately. Their goal is to weed out less experienced Linux admins from those who know their stuff.

EXAM TIP From my observations, Linux+/LPIC-1 certification candidates who study their shell commands and associated options (especially some of the more obscure ones) are the candidates who pass!

Next, let's talk about some strategies you should keep in mind when actually taking the exams.

Taking the Exams

As I mentioned earlier, I've written a number of industry certification exams in addition to developing training materials for them. Because I've done this, I have some insights as to what goes on inside the devious minds of exam developers. I'm going to share them with you here:

- *Carefully read the text of each question (called the stem).* Some of the information in the stem is superfluous and intended to distract you. However, the question stem usually contains one or two critical pieces of information that influence the correct answer. If your testing center provides you with writing materials (and they should), I suggest you quickly jot down the key points from the stem.

- *Carefully read each response.* Don't just skim them. Exam authors deliberately include responses that are *almost* correct, but not quite. (We call them *red herrings.*) The intent is to distract you away from the real answer. I know it sounds sneaky, but the intent is to make the exam such that you can't divine the correct answer without really knowing your stuff.

- *Eliminate responses that are obviously wrong.* Each item will have one or more responses that are blatantly wrong. (Usually, it's because the exam author couldn't think of anything better to include as a response.) Eliminate these answers and focus only on the responses that could be correct.

- *Make your best choice and move on.* My experience has been that your first impression is usually the correct one. If you agonize over the answers, you can over-think the question and end up picking the wrong response. You also waste valuable time. After carefully reading the question and each response, go with your intuition and then go on to the next item.

- *If you get stuck on a particularly difficult item, don't waste a lot of time trying to figure out the right answer.* You can skip the item and come back to it later. Many students get obsessed with finding the right answer to a particularly difficult question and end up with insufficient time to answer the rest of the items on the exam. Answer the questions that you can and then come back to the difficult questions that will require more time.

After you finish your exams, your results will be automatically printed out for you. The report will be embossed by your test proctor to certify the results. Don't lose this report; it's the only hard copy you will receive! I've heard of candidates who've had to send a paper copy of their exam report back to CompTIA when technical problems prevented their test results from being transmitted correctly.

The report will display your performance on each section of the exams. The Linux+/LPIC-1 exams are pass/fail. If you score 500 or better, you pass! A candidate with a score of 577 is every bit as certified as a candidate with a score of 798.

If you didn't pass, you can use the information on your report to identify the areas where you need to study. You can retake the exams immediately, if you wish. However, there are two things you need to keep in mind before you do this:

- You have to pay full price for the retake.

- The retake exam probably won't be the same as the first. CompTIA publishes multiple forms of the Linux+/LPIC-1 exams.

However, if you don't pass again, you must wait at least 14 days before you will be allowed to take the exam a third time.

If you fail, I suggest that you step back, take a deep breath, go home, and study up on the items you missed. Then schedule your retake within a day or two. If you wait any longer than that, your mind will probably go "cold" and you may need to go through the entire preparation process again from scratch.

Objective Map

The following table has been constructed to allow you to cross-reference the official exam objectives with the objectives as they are presented and covered in this book. References have been provided for each objective exactly as the exam vendor presents it, the section of the exam guide that covers that objective, and a chapter and page reference.

Exam LX0-103

Official Exam Objective	All-in-One Coverage	Chapter No.	Page No.
101 System Architecture			
101.1 Determine and configure hardware settings.			
Enable and disable integrated peripherals.	Managing Hardware Under Linux	12	434
Configure systems with or without external peripherals such as keyboards.	Managing Hardware Under Linux	12	436
Differentiate between the various types of mass storage devices.	Managing Hardware Under Linux	12	420

Official Exam Objective	All-in-One Coverage	Chapter No.	Page No.
Know the differences between cold-plug and hot-plug devices.	Managing Hardware Under Linux	12	446
Determine hardware resources for devices.	Managing Hardware Under Linux	12	430
Tools and utilities to list various hardware information (lsusb, lspci, etc.).	Managing Hardware Under Linux	12	439
Tools and utilities to manipulate USB devices.	Managing Hardware Under Linux	12	442
Conceptual understanding of sysfs, udev, and dbus.	Managing Hardware Under Linux	12	447
The following is a partial list of the files, terms, and utilities used: • /sys • /proc • /dev • modprobe • lsmod • lspci • lsusb	Managing Hardware Under Linux	12	436
101.2 Boot the system,			
Provide common commands to the boot loader and options to the kernel at boot time.	Managing the Linux Boot Process	6	182
Demonstrate knowledge of the boot sequence from BIOS to boot completion.	Managing the Linux Boot Process	6	169
Understanding of SysVinit and systemd.	Managing the Linux Boot Process	6	196
Awareness of Upstart.	Managing the Linux Boot Process	6	206
Check boot events in the log file.	Managing the Linux Boot Process	6	171
The following is a partial list of the files, terms, and utilities used: • dmesg • initramfs • BIOS • init • bootloader • SysVinit • kernel • System	Managing the Linux Boot Process Securing Linux	6 17	169 671
101.3 Change runlevels or boot targets and shut down or reboot system.			
Set the default runlevel or boot target.	Managing the Linux Boot Process	6	192, 206
Change between runlevels or boot targets, including single user mode.	Managing the Linux Boot Process	6	200, 207
Shut down and reboot from the command line.	Managing the Linux Boot Process	6	209

Official Exam Objective	All-in-One Coverage	Chapter No.	Page No.
The following is a partial list of the files, terms, and utilities used: • menu.lst, grub.cfg, and grub.conf • grub-install • grub-mkconfig • MBR			176
102.3 Manage shared libraries.			
Identify shared libraries.	Managing Linux Software	8	299
Identify the typical locations of system libraries.	Managing Linux Software	8	300
Load shared libraries.	Managing Linux Software	8	300
The following is a partial list of the files, terms, and utilities used: • ldd • ldconfig • /etc/ld.so.conf • LD_LIBRARY_PATH	Managing Linux Software	8	300
102.4 Use Debian package management.			
Install, upgrade, and uninstall Debian binary packages.	Managing Linux Software	8	290
Find packages containing specific files or libraries that may or may not be installed.	Managing Linux Software	8	293
Obtain package information such as version, content, dependencies, package integrity, and installation status (whether or not the package is installed).	Managing Linux Software	8	293
The following is a partial list of the files, terms, and utilities used: • /etc/apt/sources.list • apt-get • dpkg • apt-cache • dpkg-reconfigure • aptitude	Managing Linux Software	8	291
102.5 Use RPM and YUM package management.			
Install, reinstall, upgrade, and remove packages using RPM and YUM.	Managing Linux Software	8	270, 280
Obtain information on RPM packages such as version, status, dependencies, integrity, and signatures.	Managing Linux Software	8	276
Determine what files a package provides, as well as find which package a specific file comes from.	Managing Linux Software	8	277

Official Exam Objective	All-in-One Coverage	Chapter No.	Page No.
The following is a partial list of the files, terms, and utilities used: • rpm • rpm2cpio • /etc/yum.conf • /etc/yum.repos.d/ • yum • yumdownloader	Managing Linux Software	8	270
103 GNU and UNIX Commands			
103.1 Work on the command line.			
Use single shell commands and one-line command sequences to perform basic tasks on the command line.	Working with the Linux Shell	2	22
Use and modify the shell environment, including defining, referencing, and exporting environment variables.	Working with the Linux Shell	2	40
Use and edit command history.	Working with the Linux Shell	2	27
Invoke commands inside and outside the defined path.	Working with the Linux Shell	2	23
The following is a partial list of the files, terms, and utilities used: • bash • echo • env • export • pwd • set • unset • man • uname • history • .bash_history	Working with the Linux Shell Managing Linux Files and Directories	2 4	24 100
103.2 Process text streams using filters.			
Send text files and output streams through text utility filters to modify the output using standard UNIX commands found in the GNU textutils package.	Writing Shell Scripts	14	514
The following is a partial list of the files, terms, and utilities used: • cat • cut • expand • fmt • head • od • join • nl • paste • pr • sed • sort • split • tail • tr • unexpand • uniq • wc	Managing Linux Files and Directories Writing Shell Scripts	4 14	100 514

Official Exam Objective	All-in-One Coverage	Chapter No.	Page No.
Monitor active processes.	Managing Linux Processes	13	465
Select and sort processes for display.	Managing Linux Processes	13	467
Send signals to processes.	Managing Linux Processes	13	479
The following is a partial list of the files, terms, and utilities used: • • top • bg • free • fg • uptime • jobs • pgrep • kill • pkill • nohup • killall • ps • screen	Managing Linux Processes	13	467
103.6 Modify process execution priorities.			
Know the default priority of a job that is created.	Managing Linux Processes	13	474
Run a program with higher or lower priority than the default.	Managing Linux Processes	13	474
Change the priority of a running process.	Managing Linux Processes	13	474
The following is a partial list of the files, terms, and utilities used: • nice • ps • renice • top	Managing Linux Processes	13	474
103.7 Search text files using regular expressions.			
Create simple regular expressions containing several notational elements.	Managing Linux Files and Directories	4	112
Use regular expression tools to perform searches through a file system or file content.	Managing Linux Files and Directories	4	112
The following is a partial list of the files, terms, and utilities used: • grep • egrep • fgrep • sed • regex(7)	Managing Linux Files and Directories	4	111
103.8 Perform basic file editing operations using vi.			
Navigate a document using vi.	Using the vi Text Editor	3	72
Use basic vi modes.	Using the vi Text Editor	3	73
Insert, edit, delete, copy, and find text.	Using the vi Text Editor	3	72

Official Exam Objective	All-in-One Coverage	Chapter No.	Page No.
The following is a partial list of the files, terms, and utilities used: • vi • /, ? • h, j, k, l • i, o, a • c, d, p, y, dd, yy • ZZ, :w!, :q!, :e!	Using the vi Text Editor	3	77
104 Devices, Linux File Systems, Filesystem Hierarchy Standard			
104.1 Create partitions and file systems.			
Manage MBR partition tables.	Managing Linux File Systems	10	342
Use various mkfs commands to create various file systems such as • ext2/ext3/ext4 • XFS • VFAT	Managing Linux File Systems	10	350
Awareness of ReiserFS and Btrfs.	Managing Linux File Systems	10	134, 352
Basic knowledge of gdisk and parted with GPT.	Managing Linux File Systems	10	346
The following is a partial list of the files, terms, and utilities used: • fdisk • gdisk • parted • mkfs • mkswap	Managing Linux File Systems	10	342, 346
104.2 Maintain the integrity of file systems.			
Verify the integrity of file systems.	Managing Linux File Systems	10	363
Monitor free space and inodes.	Managing Linux File Systems	10	361
Repair simple file system problems.	Managing Linux File Systems	10	363
The following is a partial list of the files, terms, and utilities used: • du • mke2fs • df • debugfs • fsck • dumpe2fs • e2fsck • tune2fs • xfs tools (such as xfs_metadump and xfs_info)	Managing Linux File Systems	10	361

Official Exam Objective	All-in-One Coverage	Chapter No.	Page No.
104.6 Create and change hard and symbolic links.			
Create links.	Managing Linux Files and Directories	4	109
Identify hard and/or soft links.	Managing Linux Files and Directories	4	109
Copying versus linking files.	Managing Linux Files and Directories	4	109
	Managing the Linux Boot Process	6	196
Use links to support system administration tasks.	Managing Linux Files and Directories	4	109, 196
The following is a partial list of the files, terms, and utilities used: • ln • ls	Managing Linux Files and Directories	4	109
104.7 Find system files and place files in the correct location.			
Understand the correct locations of files under the FHS.	Managing Linux Files and Directories	4	88
Find files and commands on a Linux system.	Managing Linux Files and Directories	4	96
Know the location and purpose of important files and directories as defined in the FHS.	Managing Linux Files and Directories	4	88
The following is a partial list of the files, terms, and utilities used: • find • which • locate • type • updatedb • /etc/updatedb.conf • whereis	Managing Linux Files and Directories	4	96

Exam LX0-104

Official Exam Objective	All-in-One Coverage	Chapter No.	Page No.
105 Shells, Scripting, and Data Management			
105.1 Customize and use the shell environment.			
Set environment variables (e.g. PATH) at login or when spawning a new shell.	Working with the Linux Shell	2	44

Official Exam Objective	All-in-One Coverage	Chapter No.	Page No.
Write BASH functions for frequently used sequences of commands.	Writing Shell Scripts	14	527
Maintain skeleton directories for new user accounts.	Managing Linux Users and Groups	9	327
Set the command search path with the proper directory.	Working with the Linux Shell	2	23
The following is a partial list of the files, terms, and utilities used: • Source • /etc/bash.bashrc • /etc/profile • env • export • set • unset • ~/.bash_profile • ~/.bash_login • ~/.profile • ~/.bashrc • ~/.bash_logout • function • alias • lists	Working with the Linux Shell	2	45

105.2 Customize or write simple scripts.

Official Exam Objective	All-in-One Coverage	Chapter No.	Page No.
Use standard sh syntax (loops, tests).	Writing Shell Scripts	14	508
Use command substitution.	Writing Shell Scripts	14	526
Test return values for success or failure or other information provided by a command.	Writing Shell Scripts	14	529
Perform conditional mailing to the superuser.	Writing Shell Scripts	14	528
Correctly select the script interpreter through the shebang (#!) line.	Writing Shell Scripts	14	504
Manage the location, ownership, execution, and suid-rights of scripts.	Writing Shell Scripts	14	504
The following is a partial list of the files, terms, and utilities used: • for • while • test • if • read • seq • exec	Writing Shell Scripts	14	505

105.3 SQL data management.

Official Exam Objective	All-in-One Coverage	Chapter No.	Page No.
Use of basic SQL commands.	Managing Network Services on Linux	16	625
Perform basic data manipulation.	Managing Network Services on Linux	16	627

Official Exam Objective	All-in-One Coverage	Chapter No.	Page No.
The following is a partial list of the files, terms, and utilities used: • insert • where • update • group by • select • order by • delete • join • from	Managing Network Services on Linux	16	628
106 User Interfaces and Desktops			
106.1 Install and configure XII.			
Verify that the video card and monitor are supported by an X server.	Managing the Graphical Environment	7	229
Awareness of the X font server.	Managing the Graphical Environment	7	239
Basic understanding and knowledge of the X Window configuration file.	Managing the Graphical Environment	7	230
The following is a partial list of the files, terms, and utilities used: • /etc/XI1/xorg.conf • xhost • DISPLAY • xwininfo • xdpyinfo • X	Managing the Graphical Environment Using Encryption Working with the Linux Shell	7 18 2	230 717
106.2 Set up a display manager.			
Basic configuration of LightDM.	Managing the Graphical Environment	7	243
Turn the display manager on or off.	Managing the Graphical Environment	7	243
Change the display manager greeting.	Managing the Graphical Environment	7	244
Awareness of XDM, KDM, and GDM.	Managing the Graphical Environment	7	243
The following is a partial list of the files, terms, and utilities used: • lightdm • /etc/lightdm/	Managing the Graphical Environment	7	243
106.3 Accessibility.			
Basic knowledge of keyboard accessibility settings (AccessX).	Managing the Graphical Environment	7	247
Basic knowledge of visual settings and themes.	Managing the Graphical Environment	7	251
Basic knowledge of assistive technology (ATs).	Managing the Graphical Environment	7	246

Official Exam Objective	All-in-One Coverage	Chapter No.	Page No.
The following is a partial list of the files, terms, and utilities used: • ~/.forward • sendmail emulation layer commands • newaliases • mail • mailq • postfix • sendmail • exim • qmail	Managing Network Services on Linux	16	616-624
108.4 Manage printers and printing.			
Basic CUPS configuration (for local and remote printers).	Managing Network Services on Linux	16	594
Manage user print queues.	Managing Network Services on Linux	16	602
Troubleshoot general printing problems.	Managing Network Services on Linux	16	605
Add and remove jobs from configured printer queues.	Managing Network Services on Linux	16	603
The following is a partial list of the files, terms, and utilities used: • CUPS configuration files, tools, and utilities • /etc/cups • lpd legacy interface (lpr, lprm, lpq)	Managing Network Services on Linux	16	594-606
109 Networking Fundamentals			
109.1 Fundamentals of Internet protocols.	Managing Linux Network Settings	15	540
Demonstrate an understanding of network masks and CIDR notation.	Managing Linux Network Settings	15	549
Knowledge of the differences between private and public "dotted quad" IP addresses.	Managing Linux Network Settings	15	547
Knowledge about common TCP and UDP ports (20, 21, 22, 23, 25, 53, 80, 110, 123, 139, 143, 161, 162, 389, 443, 465, 514, 636, 993, 995).	Managing Linux Network Settings	15	544
Knowledge about the differences and major features of UDP, TCP, and ICMP.	Managing Linux Network Settings	15	542
Knowledge of the major differences between IPv4 and IPv6.	Managing Linux Network Settings	15	552
Knowledge of the basic features of IPv6.	Managing Linux Network Settings	15	552

Official Exam Objective	All-in-One Coverage	Chapter No.	Page No.
Understand the role of TCP wrappers.	Securing Linux	17	686
The following is a partial list of the files, terms, and utilities used: • /etc/nologin • /etc/passwd • /etc/shadow • /etc/xinetd.d/* • /etc/xinetd.conf • /etc/inetd.d/* • /etc/inetd.conf • /etc/inittab • /etc/init.d/* • /etc/hosts.allow • /etc/hosts.deny	Managing Linux Users and Groups Securing Linux	9 17	648-689
110.3 Securing data with encryption.			
Perform basic OpenSSH 2 client configuration and usage.	Using Encryption	18	709
Understand the role of OpenSSH 2 server host keys.	Using Encryption	18	710
Perform basic GnuPG configuration, usage, and revocation.	Using Encryption	18	723
Understand SSH port tunnels (including X11 tunnels).	Using Encryption	18	715
The following is a partial list of the files, terms, and utilities used: • ssh • ssh-keygen • ssh-agent • ssh-add • ~/.ssh/id_rsa and id_rsa.pub • ~/.ssh/id_dsa and id_dsa.pub • /etc/ssh/ssh_host_rsa_key and ssh_host_rsa_key.pub • /etc/ssh/ssh_host_dsa_key and ssh_host_dsa_key.pub • ~/.ssh/authorized_keys • /etc/ssh_known_hosts • gpg • ~/.gnupg/*	Using Encryption	18	709-731

An Introduction to Linux

In this chapter you will learn about:

- The role of an operating system
- How Linux came to be
- GNU and Linux
- Linux distributions
- Common Linux implementations

The introduction and adoption of Linux has been an interesting drama to observe. When Linux was first introduced back in the early 1990s, it largely went unnoticed. Professionals in the information technology industry were focused on the big operating systems of the day, including Microsoft Windows, Novell NetWare, Mac OS, and UNIX. At the time, Linux was considered experimental; something you would play with in the lab but never actually dare to implement in production.

Since that time, however, things have changed dramatically. Linux has become a mainstay in the server room for many major organizations around the world. Using the wide variety of network services available for Linux, it can be configured to perform just about any networking role that competing server operating systems can perform.

In addition to the server room, Linux has made huge inroads into the mobile device market in the form of the Android operating system, in many cases replacing mobile operating systems from Microsoft and Apple. In addition, Linux can be deployed on desktop systems. Many Linux desktop applications are available (most of them free of charge) that allow end users to perform their day-to-day work, including the use of word processing, database, spreadsheet, and presentation applications.

As you can see, Linux has evolved from an after-hours hobby for computer geeks to a major force for change in the information technology industry.

As such, there is a growing demand for network administrators who can implement, maintain, and support the Linux operating system. If you've had any experience with Linux, you know that it is very different from the operating systems most users are familiar with, such as Microsoft Windows. Migrating to Linux requires a degree of expertise. By the time you're done with this book, you will have the knowledge and skills required to make this happen.

The Role of an Operating System

Before we begin, you must understand the role Linux plays in a computer system. Linux is an *operating system,* not an application. All operating systems, including Linux, provide five key functions in a computer system:

- **Application platform** An operating system provides a platform where applications can run, managing their access to the CPU and system memory.

- **Hardware moderator** The operating system also serves as a mediator between running applications and the system hardware. Most applications are not written to directly address a computer's hardware. Instead, they include prewritten code that can be called from an application to access system hardware, such as memory, hard drives, and communication ports. This feature makes life much easier for programmers. Instead of having to write code for completing these tasks in each and every program, they can simply reuse this existing code provided by the operating system. The operating system also manages access to the system hardware. For example, two of its key roles are to ensure that one application running on the system doesn't try to use memory already in use by another application and to ensure that applications don't use an inordinate amount of CPU time.

- **Data storage** The operating system is also responsible for providing an efficient and reliable means for storing information. Usually this is done using some type of storage device, such as a hard disk drive or flash memory that has been formatted with a particular type of file system that organizes the information in an easily retrievable format.

- **Security** The operating system is responsible for providing a degree of security for the data stored on it. The system administrator can create rules that determine who can access what information.

- **Connectivity** The operating system manages connectivity between computer systems using a variety of network media and interfaces, including Bluetooth, Ethernet, RS-232, 802.11x (Wi-Fi) wireless, NFC, and even mobile broadband wireless.

The Linux operating system is composed of the following components:

- **The Linux kernel** This is the heart of Linux (hence its name). The kernel is the actual operating system itself. It's the component that fulfills the key operating system duties just listed.

- **Libraries** Prewritten code elements that application programmers can use in their programs, which can be a huge time saver. Libraries can be used to incorporate functionality into an application without having to write the code from scratch.

- **Utilities** Linux includes a wide variety of utilities you can use to complete operating system management tasks, such as maintaining the file system, editing text files, managing running processes, and installing new software packages.

- **User interface** Of course, the end user needs some means of interacting with the operating system. Linux includes both a command-line interface (CLI) and an optional graphical user interface (GUI). We'll explore both of these interfaces in Chapter 2.

How Linux Came to Be

Linux is somewhat of an anomaly in the software development industry. Most software products, whether they are applications or operating systems, are developed as a part of a well-organized design and development effort. I've worked for many years in the software development industry, and I've seen how it works firsthand. Here's what usually happens:

- The organization identifies a customer need.

- A design team is put together, which hashes out a product requirements document (PRD) that specifies exactly what the product will do.

- The tasks identified in the PRD are assigned to teams of programmers who write their assigned code elements.

- When complete, the code is checked in and the product is run through a series of testing cycles.

- When the product has its bugs worked out (or at least most of them), the finished product is shipped to the customer.

- The customer uses the product for a period of time and usually identifies bugs that were missed during the initial testing. In addition, they usually identify new features and functionality that they would like to see added.

- The software company receives feedback from the customers, and the cycle begins all over again.

Interestingly, Linux didn't conform to this cycle when it was originally developed. Instead, a graduate student at the University of Helsinki in Finland named Linus Torvalds developed the Linux kernel. In the early 1990s, Torvalds became interested in a minimal freeware operating system called *Minix*. Dr. Andrew S. Tanenbaum, a university professor who taught computer programming in the Netherlands, developed Minix as a clone of the commercial UNIX operating system. At one point in time, the source code to the UNIX operating system had been made available to universities for educational purposes. However, in the late 1980s, this practice had been stopped, leaving Tanenbaum without an effective tool to teach his students about the inner workings of an operating system. Undaunted, Tanenbaum decided to make his own operating system to use in class and developed a small clone of the UNIX kernel, which he called Minix. His goal was to provide students with a real operating system and its accompanying source code. Tanenbaum even included the source code to Minix in his textbook, *Operating Systems: Design and Implementation* (Prentice Hall, 1987).

Inspired by Tanenbaum and Minix, Torvalds developed his own UNIX clone in 1991, which he dubbed *Linux*. This first version of Linux was very minimal in nature; it wasn't a full-blown operating system complete with applications and utilities. Instead, Linux version 0.02, released on October 5, 1991, consisted of only the Linux kernel and three basic utilities:

- **bash**   A command-line interface

- **update**   A utility for flushing file system buffers

- **gcc**   A C++ compiler

In an unprecedented move, Torvalds posted the source code for his Linux operating system on the Internet and made it freely available to anyone who wanted to download it. With that, the corporate software development model had been completely broken. Torvalds even took things one step further. He invited other programmers to modify his Linux source code and enhance it. Linux took on a life of its own and became a worldwide collaborative development project. No secrecy, no tightly guarded copyrights. Access to the Linux source code was open to anyone who wanted it.

This collaborative development project on Linux continued for several years. In 1994, Linux version 1.0 was ready for release. The results since have been nothing short of amazing.

GNU and Linux

So why did Torvalds "give away" Linux to anyone who wanted it? Why didn't he follow the standard corporate development model and try to make a mountain of money? To understand this, you need to be familiar with the GNU's Not UNIX (GNU) movement. In the early 1980s, a programmer named Richard Stallman at the Massachusetts Institute of Technology proposed an alternative to the standard corporate software development model. He objected to the proprietary nature of the process and the product.

In 1983, Stallman launched the GNU Project, centered on the idea that the source code for applications and operating systems should be freely distributable to anyone who wants it. He felt that the source code for programs should be free from all restrictions that prevent copying, modification, and redistribution. Stallman hoped that allowing programmers around the world to modify an application's source code would result in higher-quality software. Software developed under GNU is frequently referred to as *free software*. A variation on the free software concept is called *open source* software.

The GNU Project slowly took hold. Many useful utilities, such as the GNU C Compiler (gcc), were developed under GNU. Torvalds was heavily influenced by the GNU Project and released the source code for his Linux operating system kernel to the world as a result.

Linux itself is licensed under the GNU General Public License (GPL). The key point to remember about the GPL is that it requires the source code to remain freely available to anyone who wants it. As a result, you can download the Linux kernel's source code, modify it, recompile it, and run it. You can even create your own custom version, or distribution, of Linux.

Linux Distributions

The philosophy of GNU software leads us directly to a discussion of Linux distributions. The concept of a *distribution* can be confusing to many new to Linux. To help you navigate the myriad Linux distributions currently available, we will discuss the following topics in this part of the chapter:

- What is a distribution?
- Commonly used distributions
- The life cycle of a Linux distribution

What Is a Distribution?

Perhaps the best way to think of a distribution is to compare Linux to ice cream. Ice cream comes in a variety of flavors; however, the basic formula for the ice cream itself is the same. Most ice cream is made from the following ingredients:

- Cream
- Milk
- Sugar
- Eggs

Companies that sell ice cream take this basic ice cream recipe and customize it by adding additional ingredients, such as chocolate, vanilla, fruit, cookies, nuts, and candy. By doing this, they create their own flavors of ice cream.

Linux distributions work in much the same way: the kernel source code is comparable to the basic recipe for ice cream. Because the Linux kernel source code—the core of the operating system around which everything else runs—is freely distributable, software vendors are free to download it. Just as ice cream companies add additional ingredients to the basic ice cream recipe, software vendors can then modify and enhance the Linux source code and create a customized kernel. They can also add specialized tools, utilities, and applications to the operating system to enhance its usefulness. The result is a Linux distribution.

You may already be aware that there are many different Linux distributions available. This is yet another unique characteristic of Linux that differentiates it from other operating systems. Nearly every other operating system is developed and marketed by a single vendor. For example, the only vendor who develops and sells OS X is Apple, Inc. You can't go to Microsoft for their version of the Mac OS.

With Linux, however, many different software developers have taken the basic Linux kernel and modified it to suit some particular purpose. They may have also bundled many powerful applications with it. Some distributions may be customized to provide high-end network services to remote end users. Others may be customized to provide excellent productivity applications on end users' desktops. Either way, the result is a customized Linux distribution.

Commonly Used Distributions

Today, literally hundreds of different distributions are available. Some are freely available, and some require you to pay a fee. Some of the more popular Linux distributions include the following:

- openSUSE Linux
- Ubuntu Linux
- Fedora Linux
- Mint Linux
- Debian Linux
- Mageia Linux
- Arch Linux
- elementary Linux
- CentOS

NOTE   A great table providing an overview and comparison of most Linux distributions is available at http://en.wikipedia.org/wiki/Comparison_of_ Linux_distributions. The http://distrowatch.com/ website is also a great resource for information on all available Linux distributions.

So which distribution is best? That is a dangerous question. Pacifists can come to blows while debating it. That's because the distribution that works the best for you may not meet the needs of someone else. The key is to try out several distributions and pick the one you like.

Personally, I have grown to love openSUSE, and it has become my Linux distribution of choice. You can download a copy of this distribution from opensuse.org. I also really like Fedora from Red Hat as well as Ubuntu. You can download a copy of Fedora from fedora.redhat.com and a copy of Ubuntu from ubuntu.com. For security testing, I also like the Knoppix and Kali (formerly BackTrack) Linux distributions.

When downloading your Linux distribution, be sure you select the correct architecture for your system's CPU. For years, this was really a non-issue because we really only worked with a single architecture: Intel's 32-bit x86 architecture. Although most early distributions were available for the x86 and the Alpha CPU architectures, the average system administrator didn't have many Alpha machines. Instead, most of the systems we worked with ran on some variation of the x86 architecture.

Today, however, we have many more hardware options available to us. We still have the venerable x86 architecture, but we also have the newer 64-bit x86 architecture. In addition, Intel produces the IA-64 architecture used by their Itanium CPUs. Each of these architectures requires a different version of Linux. In fact, many Linux distributions have even been ported to run on the Power PC (PPC) architecture from Apple Computer. Other distributions are available for the iSeries, pSeries, and RS/6000 servers from IBM.

The important point is to be sure that you select the appropriate architecture for your distribution. For example, if you are going to install Linux on an older system with a 32-bit CPU, then you need the x86 (32-bit) version of your distribution. If your hardware uses a 64-bit CPU, you need the x86-64 (64-bit) version of the distribution. If you pick the wrong one, most Linux installers will generate an error and you won't be able to complete the installation.

The Life Cycle of a Linux Distribution

Let's look at the life cycle of a typical Linux distribution. Understand that nothing lasts forever, including Linux distributions. Eventually newer, better versions of a Linux distribution will be released, making older versions obsolete. Essentially, a Linux distribution goes through the same life cycle as any other software:

- **Design**   During this phase, the goal or purpose of the distribution is identified, features or functions are defined, and roles are assigned. Typically, this phase involves determining what didn't work so well in the previous version of the distribution and how the problems can be fixed. It also usually involves determining what new functionality needs to be added to the distribution.

- **Develop** The distribution is created according to the plans made during the design phase. The way this is carried out depends on the development model employed. It may use a tightly controlled, cathedral-style development process, or it could be a wild free-for-all over the Internet using the bazaar-style development process. Usually some form of testing and validation is employed to ensure the distribution is as "bug free" as possible.

- **Deploy** The completed distribution is released and end users begin deploying it in a variety of environments.

- **Manage** The deployed distribution is managed on a day-to-day basis. Because it is used in such a diversity of environments, inevitably a host of bugs are discovered that eluded the developers in the develop phase. As a result, interim updates need to be released to fix these bugs. The frequency of update releases in Linux is typically much faster than in commercial operating systems and applications, usually every few months.

- **Retire** Distributions typically remain supported for a period of time, called the *support life cycle*. However, the length of the support life cycle will vary greatly from distribution to distribution. For example, Red Hat Linux currently provides a 10-year life cycle (although it can be extended to 13 years). By way of contrast, Debian only provides a three-year life cycle. Once the support life cycle ends, the distribution is obsolete and must be retired. When the distribution reaches this state, it should be removed from your production environment.

During this process, new versions of the given Linux distribution may be released before the end of the support life cycle of earlier versions. The developers don't typically wait for the retirement of a distribution before releasing a new one. Therefore, it's possible for multiple versions of a given Linux distribution to be supported at the same time; however, they will all be at different points in the support life cycle.

Common Linux Implementations

Because Linux is distributed under the GPL, software vendors have been able to tweak and customize the operating system to operate in a variety of roles. Although the number of these roles is virtually limitless, you should be familiar with the following roles:

- Using Linux on the desktop
- Using Linux on the server
- Using Linux on mobile devices
- Using Linux for virtualization
- Using Linux with cloud computing
- Using embedded Linux

Linux on the Desktop

Linux can be optimized to function extremely well as a desktop system. However, Linux has been somewhat slow to make inroads into this market. As of 2014, Linux had garnered only about 2 percent of the desktop market share, while Windows occupies over 90 percent. There are two important reasons for this.

First, there has been a historical lack of desktop productivity applications available for Linux. Users need word processing, spreadsheet, and presentation software on their desktops to do their day-to-day work. Fortunately, many productivity applications are available today that make Linux a viable option for the desktop, including the following:

- OpenOffice.org
- LibreOffice

The second (and most vexing) issue is the fact that the average end user tends to find Linux intimidating. For "techies" like you and me, this isn't a problem. We're comfortable with new applications and operating systems. We can learn them quickly and use them effectively. Unfortunately, the average end user in most organizations probably first learned how to use a computer using some version of Windows. That's what they are most comfortable with, and they tend to be resistant to learning a new operating system. The key to making Linux viable on the desktop is as follows:

- Provide users with the applications they need to get their work done.
- Make the user interface easy and intuitive such that a migration from Windows to Linux is as painless as possible.

 TIP　Because Linux can be intimidating to the average end user, if you plan to roll out Linux desktops in your organization, you should consider implementing an extensive training program as an integral part of your overall deployment plan.

Many vendors have been working on desktop-oriented Linux distributions that seek to do just this. They've optimized Linux to run efficiently and fast as a desktop system. They've also bundled application suites such as OpenOffice or LibreOffice with their distributions. Additionally, they've optimized their Linux window managers to provide the end user with an easy-to-use graphical interface. Some of the more popular desktop Linux distributions include the following:

- Ubuntu Desktop Edition
- openSUSE
- Fedora Desktop Edition

Linux on the Server

Linux works great as a server. In fact, Linux has experienced widespread acceptance in the server room, much more so than on the desktop. Depending on the services provided, Linux occupies between 40 and 97 percent of the server market share. This is because Linux can assume a variety of server roles and perform them extremely well, including the following:

- **File server**   Using the Network File System (NFS) or Samba services, you can configure Linux to provide network storage of users' files. NFS works great for Linux or UNIX client systems, but it doesn't work as well for Windows clients. Samba is a better choice for Windows client systems. Using Samba, your Linux server can even be configured to function as a Windows domain controller.

- **Print server**   Using the Common UNIX Printing System (CUPS) and Samba services together, you can configure Linux to provide shared printing for network users.

- **Database server**   Linux can be configured as a powerful database server. There are a variety of database services available for Linux, including MySQL, MariaDB, NoSQL, and PostgreSQL.

- **Web server**   Linux has been widely deployed as a web server. In fact, the most popular web service currently used on Linux is the Apache web server.

- **E-mail server**   There are a variety of e-mail services available for Linux that can turn your system into an enterprise-class mail server.

- **Super computer**   Linux is the preferred operating system for deploying high-powered super computers.

The widespread popularity of Linux as a server is due to a number of reasons. First of all, Linux is extremely stable. Simply put, a Linux server rarely crashes. It just keeps running and running. Other server operating systems have had a notorious reputation for crashing on a regular basis.

Second, Linux servers are very fast. Many benchmark tests have been run pitting Linux servers against other server operating systems. Each time, Linux servers have performed as well as, if not much better than, comparable operating systems running similar services under a similar workload.

Third, Linux servers tend to be less expensive to own. Most server operating systems charge expensive per-seat licensing fees, making them very expensive to deploy in large organizations. Most Linux distributions do not. In fact, depending on the distribution you choose, you may only need to pay for your server hardware, your support contract, and staff to manage the system.

Although you can configure almost any Linux distribution to provide network services, you should use a distribution specifically optimized to function as a server if you are going to deploy a Linux server in a large organization. Red Hat offers the Red Hat Enterprise Linux Server distribution, which has a proven track record as enterprise-class server. Likewise, you can also use the SUSE Linux Enterprise Server (SLES) and Ubuntu Server distributions, which are also optimized for the server role.

Mobile Linux

Linux has nearly taken over the mobile device market in the form of the Android operating system provided by Google. Android is really a specially optimized Linux distribution. As late as 2009, Android was installed on only about 3 percent of all the mobile devices (smartphones and tablets) in the world. However, that market share has currently increased to almost 50 percent. You can even download and install a special version of Android, called Android-x86, that will run on standard PC hardware. The reason Android is so popular is three-fold:

- **Price**   Because Android is based on the Linux kernel, it is much less expensive than other mobile device operating systems, such as iOS and Windows RT.
- **Performance**   Android performs extremely well on mobile devices.
- **App support**   A plethora of apps are available for Android devices, allowing these devices to provide the same functionality as more expensive devices from Apple and Microsoft.

Linux and Virtualization

Virtualization is an aspect of information technology that is gaining a great deal of momentum in the industry. To understand how virtualization works, you first need to understand how operating systems are traditionally deployed on computer hardware.

In the traditional model, one operating system was installed on one hardware device. For example, if you were installing a new system, you would go out and purchase your system hardware and then install the Linux operating system on that hardware. In this scenario, the installed operating system has full reign over all the resources in the system, including the following:

- RAM
- Processor time
- Storage devices
- Network interfaces

Now, this is how we have typically deployed systems in the past. However, this model is very inefficient because the operating system doesn't fully utilize all system resources all of the time, especially on server systems. In fact, much of the time your computing resources are woefully underutilized. This means computing capacity is available but remains unused and is therefore wasted.

For example, suppose you have three servers, each installed on their own physical hardware. The CPU utilization on each system usually hovers around 8 to 9 percent, with occasional spikes up to 50 percent. The system RAM, storage, and network devices are utilized in the same manner. You don't actually need this much processing power in this scenario. About 90 percent of each server's capacity goes unused most of the time.

Virtualization offers an alternative deployment model. Virtualization pools multiple operating system instances onto the same physical hardware and allows them to run concurrently. To do this, virtualization uses a mediator called a *hypervisor* to manage access to system resources.

Each operating system instance is installed into a *virtual machine* instead of onto physical hardware. Each virtual machine is allocated CPU time, an area of RAM to work in, a storage device, and its own virtual network interface. Each virtual machine appears and functions just like a physical host.

One of the key benefits of virtualization is the fact that it uses system resources more efficiently. The available computing capacity of the system hardware is allocated among all of the virtual machines running on the system.

Another benefit of virtualization is the fact that it allows multiple platforms to run at the same time on the same hardware, including Windows and Linux. This is a huge benefit for software developers and testers, making it much easier to test how an application in development performs on different platforms.

Virtualization also allows you to implement thin clients in your organization. In this configuration, you run multiple desktops on same virtualization server. All of your end-user desktops are provided as virtual machines on the server. This can save a ton of cash because it allows you to deploy very minimal, low-end workstations for your users. The wimpy workstations are simply used to display (using a network connection) the desktop environment running as a virtual machine on the server.

Several high-performance virtualization platforms are available for Linux, including the following:

- Xen (open source)

- VMware Workstation, Player, ESX, and ESXi (proprietary)

- VirtualBox (open source)

- KVM (open source)

When you install one of these hypervisors, you turn your Linux system into a hypervisor that can run virtual machines. Note that ESX and ESXi use a special Linux distribution from VMware as their foundation and can't be used with any other flavor of Linux.

Linux and Cloud Computing

Virtualization is a key component of *cloud computing,* where the hardware, software, and/or network resources we historically implemented locally onsite are moved offsite and delivered to you over a network connection. Many cloud-computing providers even offer their services through the Internet. For example, let's suppose you need to deploy an additional Linux server in your organization. Traditionally, you would purchase new hardware, pick a distribution, install it, and configure it to work in your network.

With cloud computing, on the other hand, a provider on the Internet could deploy a new Linux virtual machine on a hypervisor at their site. You then pay a fee to access this virtual server through your organization's network connection. The provider assumes all the costs of implementing, maintaining, and protecting the server. This model is referred to *Infrastructure as a Service (IaaS).*

In addition to IaaS, there are several other cloud computing models:

- **Software as a Service (SaaS)**   Provides access to software and data through the cloud

- **Network as a Service (NaaS)**   Provides network connectivity through the cloud

- **Storage as a Service (STaaS)**   Provides access to storage devices through the cloud

- **Desktop as a Service (DaaS)**   Provides access to desktop operating systems through the cloud

- **Platform as a Service (PaaS)**   Provides access to a full solution suite to accomplish a computing task, including networking, infrastructure, storage, and software

In fact, you can use Linux and virtualization to create your own private cloud, offering on-demand computing resources through a network connection to other users in your organization.

Embedded Linux

One of the great benefits of Linux is the fact that it can be optimized down to a very small foot-print, which allows it to run on very minimal hardware to perform a very specific set of tasks. As such, it is ideal for embedding within intelligent devices, including the following:

- Automation and control equipment used in industry
- Networking devices
- Video game systems
- Smart TVs
- Smartphones and tablets

To do this, the operating system is customized to provide just the essential functions required by the device. All of the remaining unnecessary elements of Linux are removed, and then the operating system is embedded in flash memory chips within the given device. This allows the device to run an operating system and use its programming intelligence to control the device's operations.

Chapter Review

In this chapter, you were introduced to the Linux operating system. We first discussed what an operating system is and the components that compose the Linux operating system. I emphasized the fact that modern computer systems and operating systems are modular. You can install Linux on any compatible computer.

We then spent some time reviewing the historical development of Linux. We went over the typical corporate software development model and related how Linux was developed outside this norm. We talked about GNU and the GPL and the fact that Linux is developed under the GPL, thus allowing anyone free access to the source code. We then discussed the open source software movement and identified how it is related to GNU. I related that open source offers free software whose source code must remain publicly available.

We ended this chapter by reviewing how Linux distributions are created and listed several of the more popular distributions. We also discussed the different roles that Linux can play in a typical organization, including servers, desktops, mobile platforms, hypervisors, and cloud computing.

Accelerated Review

- Linux is an operating system.
- Operating systems provide four key functions:
  - Application platform
  - Hardware moderator
  - Data storage
  - Security

- Linux is composed of the following components:
  - Kernel
  - Libraries
  - Utilities
  - User interfaces
- Linus Torvalds first developed Linux in the early 1990s.
- Linux is licensed under the GPL.
- Anyone can download and modify the Linux kernel source code.
- Different software companies develop unique Linux flavors called *distributions.*
- You should determine the role of the system and its processor architecture before selecting a distribution.
- Systems used in a production environment should provide technical support.
- You should verify that your software applications will run on your selected distribution before deploying it.
- Linux can function as a server, desktop, or hypervisor in a computer network.

Questions

1. Which of the following represents the actual operating system component within a Linux system?
   A. Libraries
   B. Kernel
   C. Desktop environment
   D. The bash shell functions

2. Which of the following provides prewritten code elements that programmers can call when writing Linux programs?
   A. The kernel
   B. Kernel modules
   C. Libraries
   D. The bash shell profiles

3. What was the name of the UNIX clone written by Andrew Tanenbaum?
   A. CPM
   B. DR-DOS
   C. Linux
   D. Minix
   E. Solaris

4. What did Linus Torvalds do with the source code for Linux?

   A. He sold it to IBM.

   B. He gave it to Microsoft for free.

   C. He developed Minix.

   D. He patented and copyrighted it.

   E. He posted it on the Internet for anyone who wanted a copy.

5. Who initiated the GNU Project?

   A. Richard Stallman

   B. Andrew Tanenbaum

   C. Linus Torvalds

   D. Richard Berkley

6. You are a computer programmer. Your supervisor wants you to download the source code for the latest Linux kernel and modify it to support a custom application your company is developing for use in-house. Can you do this?

   A. No, the source code for Linux is no longer available on the Internet.

   B. No, the copyright on the source code won't permit it.

   C. Yes, but you must pay a royalty to the GNU Project.

   D. Yes, you can create a new Linux flavor and even redistribute it as long as the source code remains freely available.

7. You have been tasked with setting up an e-mail server for your organization of 150 people. You're considering using Linux to do this. Is this possible?

   A. Yes, Linux can be configured to provide e-mail services.

   B. No, although Linux can be configured to provide e-mail services, it's not recommended for more than 25 users.

   C. Yes, but you'll have to purchase special e-mail software that's compatible with Linux.

   D. No currently available commercial groupware software suite has been ported to run on Linux.

8. Which Linux services can be used to configure shared network printing on a Linux server for both Linux and Windows client workstations? (Choose two.)

   A. MySQL

   B. NFS

   C. CUPS

   D. Samba

   E. NIS

   F. OpenPrint

9. Which service can be used to configure shared file storage on a Linux server for network users using Windows workstations?

   A. MySQL

   B. NFS

   C. PostgreSQL

   D. Samba

   E. NIS

   F. FileManager

10. You're installing a new Linux server that will be used to host mission-critical database applications. This server will be heavily utilized by a large number of users every day. Which distributions would be the best choice for this deployment? (Choose two.)

    A. Red Hat Enterprise Linux Server

    B. Red Hat Enterprise Linux Desktop

    C. Ubuntu Server

    D. SUSE Linux Enterprise Desktop

11. You're planning to install Fedora on an older system that uses a Pentium 4 hyperthreading CPU. Which distribution architecture should you download?

    A. IA-64

    B. x86-Celeron

    C. x86-64

    D. x86

    E. PPC

12. You're planning to install Fedora on a system that uses a 64-bit quad-core CPU. Which distribution architecture should you download?

    A. IA-64

    B. x86-64

    C. x86

    D. PPC

Answers

1. **B.** The Linux kernel is the component that handles operating system functions.

2. **C.** Libraries contain prewritten code that programmers can reuse in their applications.

3. **D.** Andrew Tanenbaum wrote the Minix operating system when universities were no longer allowed access to the UNIX source code.

4. **E.** Linus Torvalds posted the source code for his Linux kernel on the Internet and invited other programmers to modify and enhance it.

5. **A.** Richard Stallman championed the freely distributable source code concept behind GNU.

6. **D.** Under the GPL, you are free to download the Linux source code and modify it.

7. **A.** A variety of powerful e-mail packages are available for Linux that make it highly suitable for large organizations.

8. **C, D.** The CUPS service provides network printing to other Linux systems. When combined with Samba, network printing can be extended to Windows systems (as well as any other operating system that supports Samba, including Linux and Mac OS X).

9. **D.** The Samba service can be used to support Samba-compatible clients, including Windows, Mac OS X, and Linux systems.

10. **A, C.** These distributions are optimized for high-demand network servers.

11. **D.** The Pentium 4 hyperthreading CPU uses the Intel x86 architecture.

12. **B.** The 64-bit AMD CPU uses a 64-bit x86 architecture.

Working with the Linux Shell

In this chapter you will learn about:
- How the Linux shell works
- Using the shell prompt
- Getting help for Linux shell commands
- Working with environment variables
- Working with aliases
- Using redirection and piping

For an operating system to be useful, it must provide some means for the user to communicate with it. Users need a way to tell the operating system what tasks it needs to complete, such as running a program, copying a file, and shutting the system down. These commands are given through a *user interface*. Linux provides two types of user interfaces:

- **Command-line interface (CLI)**   With the command-line interface, the user communicates with the Linux operating system by typing commands at a command prompt.
- **Graphical user interface (GUI)**   In addition to a command-line interface, Linux also offers users an easy-to-use graphical user interface, which allows them to interact with the Linux kernel using a mouse.

In this chapter, we'll focus on working with the Linux CLI. Use and configuration of the Linux GUI will be addressed in Chapter 7.

How the Linux Shell Works

Although graphical user interfaces are generally easier to use, many of the tasks you must perform to administer and support a Linux system must be done from the command line. Basically, end users use the GUI; administrators use the command line.

EXAM TIP On the Linux+ and LPIC-1 exams, you will be tested very heavily on your ability to use the Linux CLI to manage the system.

Therefore, we will spend a great deal of time working with the Linux command-line interface in this book. We will discuss the following topics:

- Linux shells
- Managing shell configuration files

Let's begin by discussing commonly used Linux shells.

Linux Shells

To fully understand how the command-line interface works under Linux, you need to understand the concept of a shell. A *shell* is a command interpreter that allows you to type commands at the keyboard that are sent to the operating system kernel.

Linux enables you to choose from a variety of shells. As with many other aspects of Linux, you can try out several different command-line shells and choose the one that you like the best. Here's a list of some of the more popular shells:

- **sh (Bourne Shell)**   The sh shell was the earliest shell, being developed for UNIX back in the late 1970s. Although not widely used on Linux systems, it is still frequently used on UNIX systems.
- **bash (Bourne-Again Shell)**   The bash shell is an improved version of the sh shell and is one of the most popular shells today. In fact, it's the shell used by default on most Linux distributions. If you're using the command-line interface on a Linux system, more than likely you're using the bash shell.
- **csh (C Shell)**   The csh shell was originally developed for BSD UNIX. It uses a syntax that is very similar to C programming.
- **tsch**   The tsch shell is an improved version of the C Shell. It is the default shell used on FreeBSD systems.
- **zsh (Z Shell)** The Z Shell is an improved version of the bash shell.

When you first boot your Linux system and log in, your default shell is loaded. You can identify which shell you're using by entering **echo $SHELL** at the command prompt. The echo command is used to display text on the screen. Adding $SHELL to the echo command tells echo to display the contents of the SHELL environment variable for the currently logged-in user. An example is shown here, where the bash shell is set to be the default shell for the rtracy user account:

```
rtracy@openSUSE:~> echo $SHELL
/bin/bash
```

However, you're not stuck with the default shell. If you want to switch to a different shell, simply enter the shell's command name at the prompt. For example, if you are currently using the bash shell and want to use zsh instead, simply enter **zsh** at the prompt. To stop using the new shell and revert back to the original shell, enter **exit**.

EXAM TIP You can also specify the default shell to use by modifying your user account details. We'll discuss how to do this in Chapter 9. The Linux+ and LPIC-1 exams require you only to be familiar with the bash shell. Therefore, only bash will be addressed in this chapter.

Linux is capable of running multiple shell sessions at once. Each session can run its own programs, all simultaneously. This can be very useful if you have one program running and then need access to the command prompt. With many distributions, such as openSUSE, you simply press ALT-F*x* (where *x* is a number from 2 to 6) to open a new session. For example, to switch to the third alternate console screen, press ALT-F3. You can then return to your original session by pressing ALT-F1.

NOTE Some distributions, such as Ubuntu, require you to press CTRL-ALT-F*X* to open a new session.

As with Windows, you can also run terminal sessions within the Linux GUI. This is done by running a terminal program such as Konsole or GNOME Terminal. To run multiple command-line sessions, simply open two or more terminal windows. Each shell session runs its programs independently of the other sessions.

This can also be accomplished in a second way. While you're within the Linux GUI, press CTRL-ALT-F*x* (where *x* is a number from 1 to 6). This will switch you to a text-based shell prompt. To switch back to your GUI environment, press ALT-F7 (on most distributions).

Exercise 2-1: Working with Linux Shells

In this exercise, you learn how to access the shell prompt, change shells, and access alternate console screens. You can perform this exercise using the virtual machine that comes with this book. Run snapshot 2-1 for the correctly configured environment.

VIDEO Please watch the Exercise 2-1 video for a demonstration on how to perform this task.

Complete the following:

1. Boot your Linux system.

2. Log in as the user **student** with a password of **student**; then press CTRL-ALT-F1.

3. At your login prompt, authenticate to the system as the user **student** with a password of **student**.

4. View your default shell by entering **echo $SHELL** at the prompt. Your default shell is displayed. On most systems, this will be /bin/bash.

5. Open an alternate console window by pressing ALT-F2. A new login prompt is displayed.

6. Authenticate again to the system.

7. Return to the first console screen by selecting ALT-F1.

8. Load the sh shell by entering **sh** at the prompt.

9. Return to your default shell by entering **exit** at the prompt.

10. Enter **logout**.

11. Return to the graphical environment by pressing ALT-F7.

Now that you know how to access your bash shell, let's talk about how you configure it.

Managing Shell Configuration Files

You can customize your bash shell environment using several configuration files. The files actually used to configure the shell depend on whether you are using a *login shell* or a *non-login shell*. A login shell is in use if your Linux system boots to a text-based login screen and you use the CLI to log in to the system. An example of this type of shell is shown in Figure 2-1.

 NOTE A login shell is what you are using if your system boots to runlevel 3. We'll discuss runlevels in detail in Chapter 6.

Even if your system is configured to boot into a graphical environment (runlevel 5), a login shell is still created at boot time; you just don't see it. However, if you open a terminal window within your desktop environment, you are *not* using a login shell. Instead, you are running a non-login shell. This is shown in Figure 2-2.

This distinction is important because the type of shell you're using dictates what configuration files are used to customize your shell environment. These files are text-based shell scripts that contain specific commands to be run. When the configuration file is run, all of the commands in the file are run in the order they appear in the file.

 NOTE A shell script is similar to a batch file on other operating systems.

Commonly used shell configuration files are listed in Table 2-1.

Figure 2-1
Using a login shell

Ubuntu 14.04.1 LTS Ubuntu tty1

Ubuntu login: _

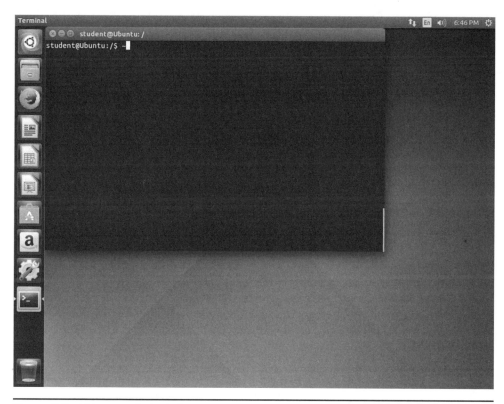

Figure 2-2   Using a non-login shell

bash Configuration File	Type of Shell	Function
/etc/bashrc or /etc/bash .bashrc	Non-login shells	Contains shell system-wide functions and aliases
~/.bashrc	Non-login shells (Although login shells on many distributions use this file as well. It is frequently called from one of the configuration files listed next.)	Stores user-specific functions and aliases
/etc/profile and the files in /etc/profile.d	Login shells	Contains system-wide shell environment configuration parameters
~/.bash_profile	Login shells	Stores user-specific shell preferences
~/.bash_login	Login shells	Stores user-specific shell preferences
~/.profile	Login shells	Stores user-specific shell preferences
~/.bash_logout	Login shells	Stores user-specific shell preferences

Table 2-1   bash Shell Configuration Files

If you're using a non-login shell, things are pretty straightforward. The bash shell simply runs /etc/bashrc for system-wide functions and aliases, and then it runs ~/.bashrc from the user's home directory for user-specific customizations.

If you're using a login shell, bash first runs /etc/profile and applies the configurations specified in that file. After that, however, things get a little more complex. As you may have noticed in Table 2-1, several of the files listed sound like they do exactly the same thing. You're right, they do. The issue here is that no distribution uses *all* of these files. For example, a Fedora system uses ~/.bashrc, ~/.bash_profile, and ~/.bash_logout. Alternatively, openSUSE and Ubuntu systems use ~/.bashrc and ~/.profile.

When a login shell is run, the bash shell program searches for configuration files in the following order:

1. ~/.bash_profile
2. ~/.bash_login
3. ~/.profile

It uses the first file it finds and ignores all of the rest. This isn't much of an issue on SUSE and Fedora. Remember that .bashrc is not read by bash when loading a login shell (although it may be called by .bash_profile or .profile). Therefore, after reading /etc/profile, the bash shell reads .bash_profile on a Fedora system. Likewise, on an openSUSE system bash reads .profile after reading /etc/profile.

CAUTION If you want to make a change to the bash shell environment that will be applied to all users on a Linux system whenever a login shell is opened, you can make the change to the /etc/profile file. However, there is a chance that any changes you make could be lost if an update is applied to the operating system. Most distributions will recommend that you make the change to the /etc/profile. local file to prevent this from happening.

The .bash_logout file is used only when you log out of a login shell. Most distributions don't include this file in users' home directories by default. However, most distributions do allow individual users to create their own .bash_logout file and customize it with their own commands to be run at logout.

Now that you understand the role and function of the shell, you are ready to learn how to use it to run programs.

Using the Shell Prompt

In this part of the chapter, you will learn how to do the following:

- Enter commands at the shell prompt
- Use command history
- Use tab completion

Let's begin by discussing how to enter commands at the shell prompt.

Entering Commands at the Shell Prompt

Running a program or command from the shell prompt is relatively easy. It is done in the same manner as within a Command window in Windows. You simply type the command, script filename, or program filename at the shell prompt and press ENTER. In this example, the **ls** command has been entered at the shell prompt:

```
rtracy@openSUSE:~> ls
bin         Downloads  Public        schedule.txt  widget_project.doc
Desktop     Music      public_html   Templates
Documents   Pictures   resources.odp Videos
```

The ls command is equivalent to the DIR command within the Windows command prompt. It displays a listing of files and directories within the current directory on the screen.

There is one issue here you need to be aware of when using the shell prompt. In fact, this is one of the key issues that I see new Linux admins struggle with the most. This is the fact that Linux handles the path to the executable you want to run in a different manner than other operating systems.

For example, within a Windows Command window, the command interpreter first looks in the current directory for the executable filename you entered at the prompt. If the file isn't located in the current directory, the command interpreter reads the PATH environment variable. It searches each directory listed in the PATH variable, looking for the executable filename that was entered at the command prompt. If the file is found, it will then run the executable. If not, an error message is displayed on the screen for the user.

Linux also employs a PATH environment variable. However, Linux does *not* check the current directory. This can be very confusing to new Linux administrators and users. They expect to be able to switch to the directory where an executable resides and run it from the command line.

Under Linux, this doesn't work. Instead, Linux only searches for the file being run within the directories in the current user's PATH variable. A typical Linux PATH environment variable is shown in this example:

```
rtracy@openSUSE:~> echo $PATH
/usr/lib/mpi/gcc/openmpi/bin:/home/rtracy/bin:/usr/local/bin:/usr/bin:/bin:/
usr/bin/X11:/usr/X11R6/bin:/usr/games
```

 EXAM TIP You can also view the current user's PATH variable by entering **env** at the command prompt.

Notice that the PATH environment variable contains a list of directories separated by colons (:).

Even if the executable in question resides in the current directory, Linux won't be able to find it if the current directory is not in the PATH variable. Instead, the shell will return an error. In the following example, an executable script file named runme.sh is located in the home directory of the rtracy user. This has been verified using the ls command.

```
rtracy@openSUSE:~> ls
bin         Downloads  Public        runme.sh      Videos
Desktop     Music      public_html   schedule.txt  widget_project.doc
```

```
Documents  Pictures   resources.odp  Templates
rtracy@openSUSE:~> runme.sh
If 'runme.sh' is not a typo you can use command-not-found to look up the
package that contains it, like this:
    cnf runme.sh
```

As you can see, when runme.sh is entered at the shell prompt, the shell can't find the file. This is because rtracy's home directory (/home/rtracy) is not listed within the PATH environment variable.

There are three ways to deal with this. First, you can enter the full path to the executable file. For the example just shown, you could enter **/home/rtracy/runme.sh** at the shell prompt to execute the file.

Second, you can switch to the directory where the executable file resides. Then add **./** to the beginning of the command. In the preceding example, you would first verify that the current directory is /home/rtracy; then you could enter **./runme.sh** at the shell prompt. The ./ characters specify the current directory. By adding them to the beginning of a command, you tell the shell to look for the specified file in the command in the current directory.

Finally, you could add the directory where the executable resides to the list of directories in the PATH environment variable. We'll talk about how to do this later on in this chapter.

In addition to path issues, you also need to be aware of the fact that Linux filenames and directory names are case sensitive! This means Linux commands are also case sensitive. If the executable file you are going to run is named runme.sh, then you must enter runme.sh at the shell prompt. Entering Runme.sh, RUNME.SH, or Runme.SH won't work. The shell interprets each of those names as different files.

This rule applies to directory names as well. If you're calling **/home/rtracy/runme.sh**, then you must enter the command using the exact case. /Home/Rtracy/Runme.sh will point the shell to a completely different place in the file system.

As you gain experience with Linux, you'll discover that it includes some very powerful commands and utilities that you will use over and over. Some of these include the following:

- **halt**   This command shuts down the operating system but can be run only by the root user.
- **reboot**   This command shuts down and restarts the operating system. It also can be run only by root.
- **init 0**   This command also shuts down the operating system and can be run only by your root user.
- **init 6**   This command also shuts down and restarts the operating system. It also can be run only by root.
- **shutdown**   This command can be used by root to shut down or reboot the system.
- **exit**   This command terminates the currently running process, including the current shell session. For example, if you open a terminal session within the Linux GUI and enter **exit** at the shell prompt, the terminal session is closed. Likewise, if you are working in the CLI and enter **exit**, the current shell session is ended and you are logged out.

- **su**   This command switches from the current user to a new user account. For example, if you're logged in as rtracy and need to change to user account dcoughanour, you can enter **su dcoughanour** at the shell prompt. This command is most frequently used to switch to the superuser root account. In fact, if you don't supply a username, this utility assumes that you want to change to the root account. If you enter **su –**, you will switch to the root user account and have all of root's environment variables applied. When you're done, enter **exit** to return to the original user account.

TIP   Many think "su" stands for "superuser." It doesn't. It stands for "substitute user."

- **env**   This command displays the environment variables for the currently logged-in user.
- **echo**   This command is used to echo a line of text on the screen. It's frequently used to display environment variables. For example, if you wanted to see the current value of the PATH variable, you could enter **echo $PATH**.
- **top**   This command is a very useful command that displays a list of all applications and processes currently running on the system. You can sort them by CPU usage, memory usage, process ID number, and which user owns them.
- **which**   This command is used to display the full path to a shell command or utility. For example, if you wanted to know the full path to the ls command, you would enter **which ls**.
- **whoami**   This command displays the username of the currently logged-in user.
- **netstat**   This command displays the status of the network, including current connections, routing tables, and so on.
- **route**   This command is used to view or manipulate the system's routing table.
- **ifconfig**   This command is used to manage network boards installed in the system. It can be used to display or modify your network board configuration parameters. This command can be run only by the root user.
- **uname**   This command returns information about your Linux system using several different options, including the following:
  - **-s**   Displays the Linux kernel's name
  - **-n**   Displays the system's hostname
  - **-r**   Displays the Linux kernel's release number
  - **-v**   Displays the Linux kernel's version number
  - **-m**   Displays the system's hardware architecture (such as x86_64)
  - **-p**   Displays the processor type
  - **-i**   Displays the hardware platform
  - **-o**   Displays the operating system
  - **-a**   Displays all of this information

NOTE The list of commands presented here is only intended to acquaint you with common Linux commands and utilities. You will need to be very familiar with these and many other commands for your Linux+ and LPIC-1 exams. Additional commands and utilities will be covered in later chapters in this book.

In addition to running a command directly from the shell prompt, you can also use the **exec** command to run a program. For example, if you had a Linux application whose executable filename was myapp, you could execute it by entering **exec myapp** at the shell prompt (assuming the path to the myapp file is included in your PATH environment variable).

This command isn't actually used that often because it is usually just as easy to run the command directly from the shell prompt, as already discussed.

However, the exec command does have a useful feature. To use this feature, you first need to understand that when you execute a command directly from the shell prompt (without using exec), the new process created by the command runs alongside the shell process. However, if you execute a command using exec, the new process created by the command actually *replaces* the shell process from which it was launched. When you exit out of the application, it is as if the shell itself was terminated. For example, if you enter **exec vi** at the shell prompt, the vi text editor is loaded. Then, when you exit out of the vi editor, the entire session terminates because the shell process was replaced by the editor's process.

Let's practice using common Linux commands in the following exercise.

Exercise 2-2: Using Linux Commands

In this exercise, you will learn how to use common Linux commands from the shell prompt. You can perform this exercise using the virtual machine that comes with this book. Run snapshot 2-1 for the correctly configured environment.

 VIDEO Please watch the Exercise 2-2 video for a demonstration on how to perform this task.

Complete the following:

1. Boot your Linux system to a shell prompt.
2. If your system booted into a graphical system, log in as the **student** user with a password of **student** and then press CTRL-ALT-F1.
3. At the login prompt, authenticate to the system as **student** with a password of **student**.
4. At the shell prompt, determine your current directory by entering **pwd**. What is the current working directory?
5. Determine the current user by entering **whoami**. Who is the current user?
6. Create a directory listing of the files in the current directory by entering **ls**.
7. Get more information about the ls utility by entering **man ls** at the shell prompt.
8. Use the PGDN key to scroll through the man page. Which option can you use with ls to use a long listing format?

9. Press Q.

10. Create a long listing with the ls command by entering **ls –l** at the shell prompt.

11. Enter **logout** and then press ALT-F7.

Using Command History

The bash shell supports command history. Every time you enter a command at the shell prompt, that command is saved in the ~/.bash_history file in your home directory. This file is just a simple (hidden) text file that contains all of your previously entered shell commands, one on each line. This file is continually updated each time you enter a shell command. You can display the contents of the .bash_history file by entering **history** at the shell prompt. An example is shown here:

```
rtracy@openSUSE:~> history
    1   echo $SHELL
    2   ls -al
    3   ls
    4   touch ./resources.odp
    5   touch ./schedule.txt
    6   touch ./widget_project.doc
    7   ls
    8   echo $PATH
    9   vi ./runme.sh
   10   chmod 666 ./runme.sh
   11   ls
   12   ls -l
   13   chmod 766 ./runme.sh
   14   ls
   15   runme.sh
   16   history
```

If you press the UP ARROW key at the shell prompt, bash will read this file and display the last command you entered. If you press the UP ARROW key repeatedly, you can scroll through a list of your last-used commands. When you arrive at the one you want, simply press ENTER to execute the command. I love this feature, especially if I need to retype a very long, complex command. Just hit the UP ARROW key until the desired command is displayed and then press ENTER!

If you don't want to arrow through all of your past commands to find the one you want, you can also enter a part of the command you need and then press CTRL-R. The bash shell will search through your command history and display the most recent matching command.

You can manage the entries in your history file using the following environment variables:

- **HISTSIZE** or **HISTFILESIZE** Configures the size of your history file. On most distributions, this is set to 1,000 entries. You can customize the size of your history file by changing the value of this variable.

- **HISTCONTROL** Controls how your command history is stored. You can set this variable to a value of ignoredups, ignorespace, ignoreboth, or erasedups. A value of ignorespace tells the shell to ignore commands in the history that start with spaces. A value of ignoredups tells the shell to ignore duplicate commands in the history. A value of ignoreboth specifies both ignorespace and ignoredups. You can also set this variable to a value of erasedups to remove all duplicate entries in the history file.

NOTE We'll discuss environment variables in more depth later in this chapter.

Let's practice using command history in the following exercise.

Exercise 2-3: Using Command History

In this exercise, you will practice using command history in the bash shell. You can perform this exercise using the virtual machine that comes with this book. Run snapshot 2-1 for the correctly configured environment.

VIDEO Please watch the Exercise 2-3 video for a demonstration on how to perform this task.

Complete the following:

1. Boot your Linux system to a shell prompt. If your system booted into a graphical system, log in as the **student** user with a password of **student** and then press CTRL-ALT-F1.

2. Authenticate to your system as the **student** user with a password of **student**.

3. At the shell prompt, enter **ls –l /var/log**.

4. At the shell prompt, enter **pwd**.

5. At the shell prompt, enter **whoami**.

6. Run the ls command in step 3 again by pressing the UP ARROW key three times and then pressing ENTER.

7. Use the UP ARROW key to run the pwd command again.

8. Use the UP ARROW key to run the whoami command again.

9. Enter **logout** and then press ALT-F7.

In addition to command history, the bash shell also offers command completion. Let's talk about this feature next.

Using Command Completion

In addition to command history, I also love the command completion feature offered by the bash shell. This feature is extremely helpful when you need to enter a very long filename in a command line. The command completion feature allows you to simply press the TAB key while entering a command at the shell prompt. When you do, the bash shell "guesses" what it is you want to type and then automatically completes the command for you.

For example, suppose a file named vmware-linux-tools.tar.gz exists in the /tmp directory. I need to extract this tarball archive so I can install the application it contains. If I wanted to, I could type out the full command **tar –zxvf /tmp/vmware-linux-tools.tar.gz** at the shell prompt and tar would extract the file for me. (We'll discuss how the tar command works in more detail in Chapter 10.)

However, if you're like me, your fingers don't always do what you tell them to do. I tend to make a lot of typos when I'm entering commands, especially when dealing with long filenames, as in this example. To prevent this, I can use command completion to take care of the typing for me. In this example, I would enter **tar –zxvf /tmp/vmw** at the shell prompt and then press the TAB key. When I do, the bash shell looks at the files in the /tmp directory that begin with **vmw** and determines that I probably am referring to the vmware-linux-tools.tar.gz file. It then tacks this filename on to the end of the command. All I then have to do is press ENTER. Command completion is great!

Let's practice using command completion in the following exercise.

Exercise 2-4: Using Command Completion

In this exercise, you will practice using command completion in the bash shell. You can perform this exercise using the virtual machine that comes with this book. Run snapshot 2-1 for the correctly configured environment.

VIDEO   Please watch the Exercise 2-4 video for a demonstration on how to perform this task.

Complete the following:

1. Boot your Linux system to a shell prompt. If your system booted into a graphical system, log in as **student** with a password of **student** and then press CTRL-ALT-F1.

2. Authenticate to your system as **student** with a password of **student**.

3. Change to your root user account by entering **su –** followed by a password of **student**.

4. At the shell prompt, type **tail /var/log/m**, but don't press ENTER yet.

5. Press the TAB key twice. A list of all files in /var/log/ that start with *m* should be displayed.

6. Add an **e** to the command, but don't press ENTER yet. Your command prompt should display **tail /var/log/me**.

7. Press the TAB key. The command should automatically display **tail /var/log/messages**.

8. Press ENTER to execute the command.

9. Enter **logout** and then press ALT-F7.

Getting Help for Linux Shell Commands

One of the great things about Linux is that documentation and help information are abundantly available for your use. Pick any Linux operating system task or utility and you can probably find documentation that will teach you how to accomplish what you need to do. In this chapter, we're going to look at how to use two excellent resources for getting help when using Linux.

However, before doing so, there are a few key things about Linux documentation materials you need to understand. First of all, the vendor who provided your Linux distribution probably provides some kind of general system documentation for you to use. However, this system documentation is probably quite minimal. (For some distributions, it may be nonexistent.)

This is because each service or application you install on a Linux distribution usually includes documentation for that particular program. If you think about all the different packages distributed with Linux, you can see that it would be an extremely daunting task for a Linux vendor to try to develop their own documentation describing how to use all of these packages. Instead, they rely on others in the open source community to document all the various applications and services that can be used on Linux.

This brings us to the second point you need to keep in mind when working with Linux documentation: the programmer who wrote a particular service or utility is probably the person who wrote the associated documentation. Only some of the Linux software documentation is actually written by professional technical writers. This means there are wide variations in the quality of the documentation from one piece of software to another. Some programmers are quite good at writing documentation. They write well and they understand how to structure information in a fashion that is easy to understand.

Unfortunately, other programmers aren't very good at writing documentation. In fact, they can be absolutely terrible at documenting their software. The key mistake they make is that they assume the reader has the same knowledge level as they do. (This presents a contradiction of sorts. If the reader has the same knowledge level as the author, then he or she wouldn't need the documentation, right?) This kind of documentation tends to be incomplete and generally unhelpful.

NOTE If you encounter this situation and have some extra time to spare, most programmers would love to have someone volunteer to help write documentation for their products. As you'll see later in this chapter, most Linux help sources include a contact e-mail address that you can use to contact the author.

The third point you need to keep in mind is that most Linux documentation sources are not print based. Back in the early days of Linux, many distributions did include a thick printed manual. The first Linux distribution I installed back in 1995 (Caldera OpenLinux version 1.0) included just such a manual. Today, however, printed manuals are a rarity. As you can imagine, printing manuals of this size is very expensive and uses up a lot of paper. Therefore, nearly all current documentation sources for your Linux distribution are made available in an electronic format.

EXAM TIP Knowing how to get help when working with Linux is a critical part of a Linux admin's job role. When a problem happens, you need to be able to find an answer fast. Therefore, on the Linux+ and LPIC-1 exams, you need to be able to demonstrate that you know how to use the various tools available for finding help. You need to be very familiar with using man and info to find information. You need to know how to launch the utilities, navigate through the information displayed, and exit.

In this part of the chapter, you are introduced to the various sources for getting help when working with Linux. The following topics will be covered:

- Using man pages
- Using info

Let's begin by discussing how to use man to get help with your Linux system.

Using man Pages

One of the primary ways to maintain Linux system documentation is through the use of manual (man) pages. These manual pages contain documentation about the operating system itself as well as any applications installed on the system. These man pages are viewed using a utility called **man**.

The man utility was original developed and used by the UNIX operating system. It has been ported to Linux and provides the same functionality as on a UNIX system. It can be used to display a manual page for a particular Linux command, utility, or file.

The man utility is an extremely useful tool when managing a Linux system. If you think about it, a lot of commands and utilities are available on even the most basic Linux system. Some of the commands and utilities are used frequently; others are used very rarely. It's very difficult for the average Linux admin to remember the syntax and options used by every possible command and utility, especially those you don't use frequently.

The man utility is a real lifesaver. If you ever find yourself at a loss when working with a particular command or utility, you can use man to display the appropriate man page and remind yourself of how it's used. I love man!

In addition to system commands and utilities, man pages are also maintained for most of the packages on your system. Whenever you install a package on Linux, the man pages containing the documentation for the software are also installed. This allows you to use man to view documentation for these packages as well.

In this part of the chapter, we'll review the following man-related topics:

- The man directory structure
- Manual sections
- Using man to view documentation

The man Directory Structure

The actual pages displayed by man are maintained in several directories beneath the directory specified in the MANPATH environment variable. On a 64-bit openSUSE Linux system, the MANPATH variable is set to the /usr/lib64/mpi/gcc/openmpi/share/man, /usr/local/man, and /usr/share/man directories.

You can check the value of the MANPATH variable on your system by entering **echo $MAN-PATH** at a shell prompt. When you do, a list of environment variables is displayed. The MANPATH variable lists the directories containing man pages, each separated by a colon, as shown here:

```
rtracy@openSUSE:~> echo $MANPATH
/usr/lib/mpi/gcc/openmpi/share/man:/usr/local/man:/usr/share/man
```

```
# ----------------------------------------------------------------------
# set up PATH to MANPATH mapping
# ie. what man tree holds man pages for what binary directory.
#
#                 *PATH*           ->           *MANPATH*
#
MANPATH_MAP      /bin                          /usr/share/man
MANPATH_MAP      /usr/bin                      /usr/share/man
MANPATH_MAP      /sbin                         /usr/share/man
MANPATH_MAP      /usr/sbin                     /usr/share/man
MANPATH_MAP      /usr/local/bin                /usr/local/man
MANPATH_MAP      /usr/local/bin                /usr/local/share/man
MANPATH_MAP      /usr/local/sbin               /usr/local/man
MANPATH_MAP      /usr/local/sbin               /usr/local/share/man
MANPATH_MAP      /usr/X11R6/bin                /usr/X11R6/man
MANPATH_MAP      /usr/bin/X11                  /usr/X11R6/man
MANPATH_MAP      /usr/games                    /usr/share/man
MANPATH_MAP      /opt/bin                      /opt/man
MANPATH_MAP      /opt/sbin                     /opt/man
# ----------------------------------------------------------------------
```

Figure 2-3   Configuring man directories on Fedora in the /etc/man_db.conf file

It's important to note that the man utility can be implemented in different ways on different Linux distributions. For example, the Fedora distribution doesn't use the MANPATH environment variable by default. Instead, it uses the MANPATH_MAP directive in the /etc/man_db.conf file to specify the directories where man pages are stored. An example of this configuration file is shown in Figure 2-3.

Beneath the directories specified in the MANPATH variable or in the MANPATH_MAP directive in the /etc/man_db.conf file is a series of directories denoted by man1, man2, man3, and so on, as shown here:

```
rtracy@openSUSE:/usr/share/man> ls
ar            cs       et            gd   ja    man1p  man9  pa      sk   ug
ast           cy       eu            gl   kk    man2   mann  pl      sl   uk
be            da       fa            he   km    man3   ml    ps      sq   uz
bg            de       fi            hi   ko    man3p  ms    pt      sr   vi
bn            el       fo            hr   ku    man4   my    pt_BR   sv   zh
bo            en_AU    fr            hu   lt    man5   nb    ro      ta   zh_CN
bs            en_GB    fr.ISO8859-1  id   lv    man6   nl    ru      te   zh_HK
ca            eo       fr.UTF-8      io   man0p man7   nn    shn     th   zh_TW
ca@valencia   es       fy            it   man1  man8   oc    si      tr
```

Some of the directories aren't used for manual sections. Directories such as hu, it, and jp are used for man pages that have been localized into a language other than English.

The MANPATH variable is not set by default on Ubuntu distributions either. The path can be displayed on Ubuntu using the **man –w** command.

Manual Sections

All of the man pages contained in the various man directories together compose the *manual.* Each of the directories just shown represents a *section* of the manual. The standards used by man page authors divide the manual into the sections shown in Table 2-2.

Section	Content
1	Programs and shell commands that can be used by any user
2	System functions provided by the Linux kernel
3	Library functions
4	Special files found in /dev
5	File format descriptions and conventions
6	Games
7	Miscellaneous conventions
8	Administrative utilities used by the root user
9	Kernel routine documentation

Table 2-2 Sections Used in man Pages

Manual pages are categorized and stored in the appropriate directory, depending on the type of software they are associated with. Many of the man pages you will use in this book will be stored in Section 1: Shell Commands and Section 8: Administrative Utilities.

Using man to View Documentation

Using man to look up information is really easy. All you have to do is enter **man** followed by the name of the utility you need information about.

For example, the ls command is a very useful shell command you can use to display a list of files in a directory. It can be used with a variety of options that customize how it works and how the data it returns is displayed. How do you know what these options are and how to use them? You use the man utility to display the manual page for the ls command. To do this, simply enter **man ls** at a shell prompt. When you do, the screen shown in Figure 2-4 is displayed.

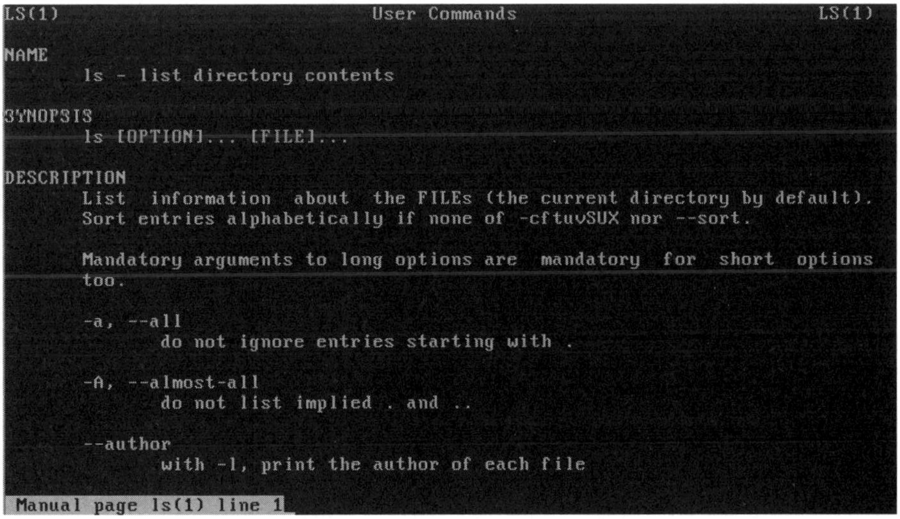

```
LS(1)                          User Commands                          LS(1)

NAME
       ls - list directory contents

SYNOPSIS
       ls [OPTION]... [FILE]...

DESCRIPTION
       List  information  about  the FILEs (the current directory by default).
       Sort entries alphabetically if none of -cftuvSUX nor --sort.

       Mandatory arguments to long options are  mandatory  for  short  options
       too.

       -a, --all
              do not ignore entries starting with .

       -A, --almost-all
              do not list implied . and ..

       --author
              with -l, print the author of each file

Manual page ls(1) line 1
```

Figure 2-4 Viewing the man page for the ls utility

A given man page consists of several elements, as shown in Figure 2-4. Some man pages will include many sections; others will include only a few. Most man pages will include the following:

- **Title**   The title section is the first line of the man page. It lists the name of the utility, command, or file discussed in the man page followed by the section number. In Figure 2-4, notice that the first line reads LS(1). This indicates the man page describes the ls utility and is located in Section 1 of the manual. Remember from Table 2-2 that Section 1 of the manual contains manual pages for commands and utilities that all users on the Linux system can use.

- **NAME**   The NAME section simply displays the name of the command, file, or utility and a short abstract about what it does. In Figure 2-4, the NAME section indicates that the ls utility is used to list directory contents.

- **SYNOPSIS**   The SYNOPSIS section provides a brief description of the syntax for using a particular command or utility. If the manual page documents a configuration file, such as smb.conf, the SYNOPSIS section provides a brief overview of what the file is used for. In Figure 2-4, the SYNOPSIS section of the man page for the ls utility displays the syntax for using the command from the shell prompt. It tells you that you can enter **ls** followed by a list of possible options and filenames.

- **DESCRIPTION**   The DESCRIPTION section provides the meat of the manual page. This section describes how the command, file, or utility works in detail. It also provides a list of options that can be used. For example, in Figure 2-4, the man page specifies that you can use the –a or --all option with the ls utility to display hidden directories and files along with normal files and directories in the file system. Without a man page, you probably would have never known that you could use the –a option with ls!

 EXAM TIP   The names of hidden Linux files and directories begin with a period.

- **AUTHOR**   The AUTHOR section displays the name of the programmer who wrote the command, utility, or service referenced in the man page. This is shown for the ls utility in Figure 2-5.

- **REPORTING BUGS**   The REPORTING BUGS section provides an e-mail address you can use to report any bugs you discover in the utility or the documentation, as shown in Figure 2-5.

- **COPYRIGHT**   The COPYRIGHT section provides you with details about who owns the copyright to the command, utility, or service referenced in the man page. It also provides you with redistribution information, as shown in Figure 2-5.

- **SEE ALSO**   The SEE ALSO section provides you with a list of man pages or other resources that are related to the current man page. For example, in Figure 2-5, the SEE ALSO section directs the user to use info to view the complete documentation for the ls command.

- **Version Number and Revision Date**   The very last line of the man page displays the version number of the program and the revision date.

```
AUTHOR
        Written by Richard M. Stallman and David MacKenzie.

REPORTING BUGS
        Report ls bugs to bug-coreutils@gnu.org
        GNU coreutils home page: <http://www.gnu.org/software/coreutils/>
        General help using GNU software: <http://www.gnu.org/gethelp/>
        Report ls translation bugs to <http://translationproject.org/team/>

COPYRIGHT
        Copyright © 2010 Free Software Foundation, Inc.   License  GPLv3+:  GNU
        GPL version 3 or later <http://gnu.org/licenses/gpl.html>.
        This  is  free  software:  you  are free to change and redistribute it.
        There is NO WARRANTY, to the extent permitted by law.

SEE ALSO
        The full documentation for ls is maintained as a  Texinfo  manual.   If
        the  info and ls programs are properly installed at your site, the com-
        mand

                info coreutils 'ls invocation'

        should give you access to the complete manual.

 Manual page ls(1) line 224/250 99%
```

Figure 2-5   Viewing additional man page sections for the ls utility

All sections other than NAME are optional. Authors are free to add new sections not shown in the preceding list if their particular program requires them. You may see man pages for other utilities or services that contain sections such as OPTIONS, FILES, ENVIRONMENT, and DIAGNOSTICS.

As you use man to display a manual page, a status indicator is shown at the very bottom of the display. This status indicator tells you what manual page is being displayed, the current line displayed, and how far into the document you are. This status indicator is shown in Figure 2-5. In this example, the status indicator shows that the ls(1) manual page is being displayed. It also indicates that line 224 is the top line currently displayed and that the current text displayed resides about 99 percent of the way through the entire document.

With a man page displayed, you can use the keystrokes shown in Table 2-3 to navigate around within the page.

Keystroke	Function
DOWN ARROW	Scrolls down one line in the page
UP ARROW	Scrolls up one line in the page
PAGE DOWN	Scrolls down 14 lines in the page
PAGE UP	Scrolls up 14 lines in the page
SPACEBAR	Scrolls down 26 lines in the page
HOME	Moves you to the beginning of the page
END	Moves you to the end of the page
Q	Unloads the current man page and exits the man utility

Table 2-3   Keystrokes Used in man Pages

Some man pages are short and concise; others are quite long and extensive. When working with a man page, you may need to search for a specific term within the page itself.

For example, if you're using the ls command, you may need to view extended information about files and directories in your file system. Notice in Figure 2-4 that by default ls displays only the names of the files or directories within the current directory. What if you need to view extended information, such as permissions, ownership, file size, or modification dates? This is called the *long listing format*. Which ls option can format the output in this manner?

You can search for specific information within a man page by entering a forward slash (/) followed by the term you want to search for. For example, to find out how to obtain a long listing format from ls, load the man page for ls by entering **man ls**. Then, enter **/long** to search for the text string "long" in the man page. This is shown in Figure 2-6.

When you press ENTER, the first instance of "long" is located in the man page. To find the next instance, simply press N. After you press N several times, the instance you wanted to find is located, as shown in Figure 2-6. As you can see, using the –l option with the ls utility will display its output in long format, which shows permissions, ownership, size, and modification dates for files and directories.

Many times, you will need to search for information in a man page for a utility, but you can't quite remember exactly how the command is spelled. Remember that man requires you to know the name of the command, utility, or file to view its associated manual page. If, for some reason, you can't remember, you can use two different tools to search across man pages:

- **man –k** Using the –k option with man allows you to search across all manual page names and descriptions to find a specific keyword. For example, suppose you wanted to remove a directory from your file system, but you can't remember which utility is used to do it. You can enter **man –k "remove empty"** at the shell prompt to view a list of man pages that include the phrase "remove empty," as shown next:

```
rtracy@openSUSE:~> man -k "remove empty"
rmdir (1)              - remove empty directories
```

  Also notice that the rmdir command can be used to remove a directory. Now that you know the name of the command, you can enter **man rmdir** to learn how to use it.

- **apropos** The apropos utility does basically the same thing as the man –k command. You can use this utility to search across man page names and descriptions to locate a text string. For example, to search for man pages that have the string "remove" in their text, you would enter **apropos remove**.

With this in mind, let's practice using man in the following exercise.

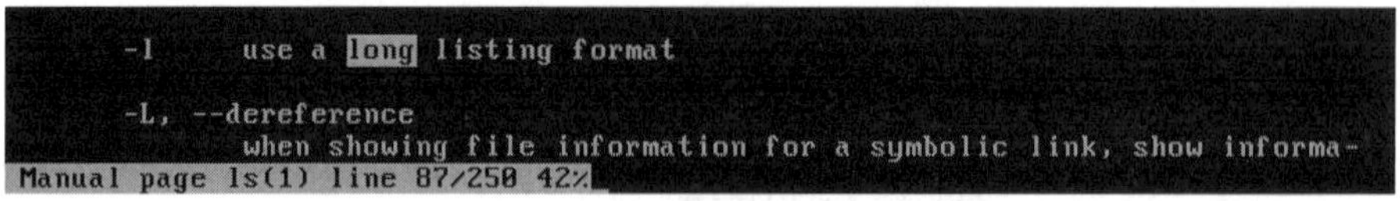

Figure 2-6   Searching for the text string "long" in a man page

Exercise 2-5: Using man Pages

In this exercise, you will practice using the man utility to view manual pages for Linux utilities. You can perform this exercise using the virtual machine that comes with this book. Run snapshot 2-1 for the correctly configured environment.

 VIDEO   Please watch the Exercise 2-5 video for a demonstration on how to perform this task.

Complete the following:

1. Boot your Linux system to a shell prompt. If your system booted into a graphical environment, log in as **student** with a password of **student** and then press CTRL-ALT-F1.

2. Authenticate as **student** with a password of **student**.

3. At the shell prompt, enter **man cp**.

4. Answer the following questions:
   - What does the cp utility do?
   - What does the –r option do when used with cp?
   - Who wrote the cp utility?
   - To what e-mail address can you send any bugs you discover?
   - In what man section does the cp page reside?
   - If you wanted the cp utility to prompt you before overwriting an existing file, what option would you use?

5. Close man by pressing Q.

6. Enter **logout** and then press ALT-F7.

Using the info Utility

In addition to man, you can also use the info utility to view documentation for commands, utilities, services, and files on your Linux system. You might be asking, "Why do I need info if I've already got man?" The two utilities do serve a similar purpose; however, they do it in different ways.

The man utility is a "down-and-dirty" reference utility. Man pages are packed with information, but they aren't really instructional in nature. Essentially, man says, "Here's the utility and its syntax. You go figure out how to use it."

The info utility, on the other hand, is more of a learning utility. Most info nodes contain the same information as a man page. However, info nodes are usually more verbose and can actually teach you how to use a particular Linux tool.

 NOTE   Instead of calling them *pages,* we refer to units of information displayed by the info utility as *nodes.* You'll see why they are called nodes later in this chapter.

Launching info is done in much the same manner as man. You simply enter **info** followed by the name of the command, utility, service, or file you need to learn about. For example, earlier in this chapter, you used man to view information about the ls utility. To use info to learn about the ls utility, you simply enter **info ls**. When you do, the information in Figure 2-7 is displayed.

Right away, you'll notice several differences between man and info. The information available in the ls man page is fairly minimal. Conversely, the information available in info is much more verbose. The info node explains what the ls utility does and what you can expect when you use it.

Notice in Figure 2-7 that the top line of the info display shows information about the current page. The file that contains the information is named coreutils.info. Within the coreutils.info file, the ls invocation node is currently being displayed. The next node in the file is named dir invocation.

One of the key differences between info and man is the fact that info divides the information into nodes, whereas man displays all information related to the particular utility or command on a single page. You can use the keystrokes listed in Table 2-4 to navigate within the info interface and between nodes.

Just as you can search for information using the man utility, you can also search for information using info. If you want to search for information within the node displayed, press CTRL-S. When you do, the **I–search** prompt is displayed, as shown in Figure 2-8. At the I-search prompt, enter the text you want to search for and press ENTER. The first instance of the text you entered after your current cursor location is displayed. Pressing CTRL-S again will jump to the next instance of the string you entered.

Let's practice using info in the following exercise.

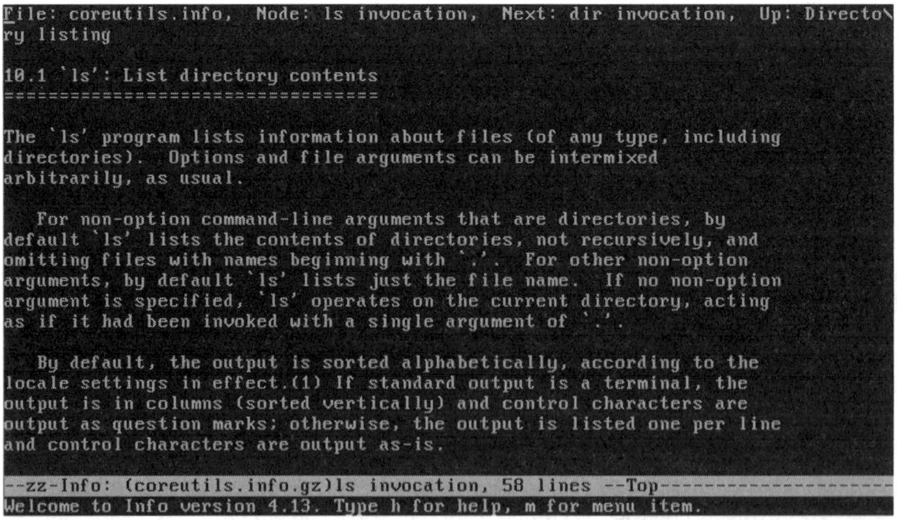

Figure 2-7   Using info to view information about the ls utility

Keystroke	Function
DOWN ARROW	Scrolls down one line at a time
UP ARROW	Scrolls up one line at a time
PAGE DOWN	Scrolls down one page at a time
PAGE UP	Scrolls up one page at a time
SPACEBAR	Scrolls down one page at a time
DEL or BACKSPACE	Scrolls up one page at a time
HOME	Moves you to the beginning of the node
END	Moves you to the end of the node
N	Takes you to the next node
P	Takes you to the previous node
Q	Unloads the current node and exits the info utility

Table 2-4   Keystrokes for Navigating in info

Exercise 2-6: Using info

In this exercise, you will practice using the info utility to view documentation for your Linux system. You can perform this exercise using the virtual machine that comes with this book. Run snapshot 2-1 for the correctly configured environment.

 VIDEO   Please watch the Exercise 2-6 video for a demonstration on how to perform this task.

Complete the following:

1. If you haven't done so already, boot your Linux system and log in.

2. If necessary, start a terminal session.

3. At the shell prompt, enter **info rm**.

4. Answer the following questions:

   • What does the rm utility do?

   • What does the –v option do when used with rm?

   • In which node does the rm documentation reside?

   • What node comes before the current node?

```
`-B'
`--ignore-backups'
--zz-Info: (coreutils.info.gz)Which files are listed, 94 lines --Top-----------
Regexp I-search:
```

Figure 2-8   Searching for information in an info node

- What node comes after the current node?

- If you want the rm utility to prompt you before deleting each file, which option would you use?

- If you want to be sure a deleted file cannot be recovered, would rm be the right utility to use?

5. Close info by pressing Q.

Now that you know how to use the bash shell, let's talk about some of the tasks you need to know how to complete with it. The next topic covers working with environment variables.

Working with Environment Variables

Whenever you start a bash shell, several different variables are used to define critical parameters the shell needs to run properly. Because these variables define the shell environment, they are called *environment variables.* In this part of this chapter, we're going to spend some time discussing environment variables. Specifically, we're going to cover the following topics:

- What are environment variables?

- Managing environment variables

- Creating user-defined variables

Let's begin by reviewing what environment variables are.

What Are Environment Variables?

Before you can understand what an environment variable is, you must first understand what a variable itself is. The best way to describe variables is to envision a bucket in which a variety of substances can be stored. This bucket has a name, such as "MyStuff," and you can fill it with sand, rocks, water, soil, and so on. If the bucket is already full of a particular substance, such as sand, you must empty it before you can fill it with another substance, such as rocks.

That's essentially how a variable in a Linux system works. It's an area in your system's RAM that's reserved to store whatever values you want to put in it. Essentially, it's like a "bucket" in memory. Just as you must empty out a real bucket before you can pour a new substance in, you must also empty out a variable before you can assign a new value to it. On your Linux system, you can define and use two different types of variables:

- User-defined variables

- Environment variables

User-defined variables are just that. They are "buckets" in memory that you create yourself. You can assign user-defined variables with a name of your choice. You can also assign whatever contents you want to them. User-defined variables can be very useful when working with shell scripts, discussed later in Chapter 14.

Environment variables, on the other hand, are initially created, named, and populated by the operating system itself. As the name implies, environment variables are used to configure the system's computing environment. Environment variables are frequently accessed and used by programs you run from the shell prompt. Using the information stored in these variables makes these programs much more flexible and robust.

For example, suppose you were to enter the **cd ~** command at the shell prompt. This command will switch the current directory in the shell to the user's home directory, no matter what user is currently logged in.

For example, suppose I were logged in to my Linux system with the rtracy user account. By default, my home directory would be /home/rtracy. If I were to enter the **cd ~** command while logged in as rtracy, the current directory would be changed to /home/rtracy. Notice that nowhere in the command did I specify the path /home/rtracy. The cd command just "knew" that ~ pointed to /home/rtracy. If I were logged in as the ksanders user, however, the same cd ~ command would not take me to /home/rtracy. Instead, the current directory would be changed to /home/ksanders.

The question is, how does the cd command know what directory in the file system to switch to? The cd command checked the value of an environment variable named HOME. As you can see here, the value of the HOME environment variable is set to the home directory path of the current user:

```
rtracy@openSUSE:~> echo $HOME
/home/rtracy
```

Because rtracy is currently logged in, the value of HOME is set to /home/rtracy. If, however, I were to log in as a user named ksanders, the value of the HOME environment variable is changed by the system to /home/ksanders. This is shown next:

```
ksanders@openSUSE:~> echo $HOME
/home/ksanders
```

Your Linux system defines a number of environment variables like the HOME variable we just looked at. Some of the more pertinent environment variables commonly used on most Linux distributions are listed in Table 2-5.

Now that you know what environment variables are and the names of variables commonly used on a Linux system, let's next discuss how you go about managing your environment variables.

Managing Environment Variables

For the most part, the values assigned to your environment variables by the system are usually sufficient for most tasks. However, there are occasions when you will need to manipulate the values assigned to your environment variables. To do this, you need to know how to manage them. In this section, we'll discuss how to do just that. The following topics will be addressed:

- Viewing variables and their values
- Setting the value of a variable
- Making variables persistent

Environment Variable	Stores	Default Value
BASH and SHELL	The full path to the shell executable	/bin/bash
CPU	The type of CPU installed in the system	Depends on your system. An Intel Pentium IV computer would have a value of i686.
DISPLAY	The location where your X Window display should be sent	0.0 (The local video card and monitor.)
ENV	The name of the file bash read to configure its environment	/etc/bash.bashrc
EUID	The user ID (UID) of the current user	The UID number of the current user.
HISTFILE	The path to the bash command history file	~/.bash_history
HISTSIZE	The number of commands saved in the command history file	1000
HOME	The path to the current user's home directory	The current user's home directory.
HOST and HOSTNAME	The hostname of the system	The hostname you assigned when you installed the system.
LOGNAME	The username of the current user	The username of the current user.
MAIL	The path to the current user's mailbox file	/var/spool/mail/*username* or /var/mail/*username*.
MANPATH	The path to your system's man program	Depends on the distribution.
OLDPWD	The path to the prior current directory	Depends on what your prior current directory was.
OSTYPE	The type of operating system currently being run	Linux.
PATH	A list of directories to be searched when running a command from the shell prompt	Depends on your distribution.
PS1	The characters used to create the shell prompt	Depends on your distribution.
PWD	The path to the current working directory	Depends on what your current directory is.

Table 2-5 Commonly Used Environment Variables

Let's begin by discussing how to view the value of a variable.

Viewing Variables and Their Values

If you need to see the value assigned to a variable on your system, you can use a variety of different commands from the shell prompt. If you need to see the value of a single variable, you can use the echo command. The syntax is **echo $*variable***. For example, if I wanted to view the value of the PATH variable, I would enter **echo $PATH** at the shell prompt. This is shown next:

```
ksanders@openSUSE:~> echo $PATH
/usr/lib/mpi/gcc/openmpi/bin:/home/rtracy/bin:/usr/local/bin:/usr/bin:/bin:/
usr/bin/X11:/usr/X11R6/bin:/usr/games
```

As you can see, the contents of the PATH variable are displayed on the screen. Notice that when you use the echo command you *must* place **$** before the name of the variable. This is very important. The $ character tells the echo command that the text that follows is not a literal string but is instead the name of a variable and that echo should retrieve the value of the variable and display it on the screen. If you omit the $ character, the echo command will display your variable name on the screen. For example, if you were to enter **echo PATH** at the shell prompt, the echo command will simply display "PATH" on the screen. That's because it didn't know that "PATH" was the name of a variable. The echo command thought you wanted the text string "PATH" displayed. Therefore, don't forget the $ character when using echo with variables!

As you just saw, the echo command works great for displaying the contents of a variable on the screen. However, it can only display the variables you specify. That means you have to know the name of the variables you want to view. What if you don't know the exact name of the variable? What if you want to view all of your variables at once?

In these situations you can use other shell commands to view your variables and their associated values. One of these is the set command. If you enter **set** at the shell prompt, all of your variables, including environment and user-defined variables, are displayed on the screen. Because the output of set can be very long, you should use **| more** with set to pause the output displayed one page at a time. (We'll discuss redirection later in this chapter.) For example, in Figure 2-9, the **set | more** command has been issued at the shell prompt.

As you can see, each variable is displayed along with its associated value. In addition to the set command, you can also use the **env** command to view your system's environment variables. As with set, the output of env can be very long, so you should append **| more** to the command to pause the display one page at a time. In Figure 2-10, the **env** command has been issued.

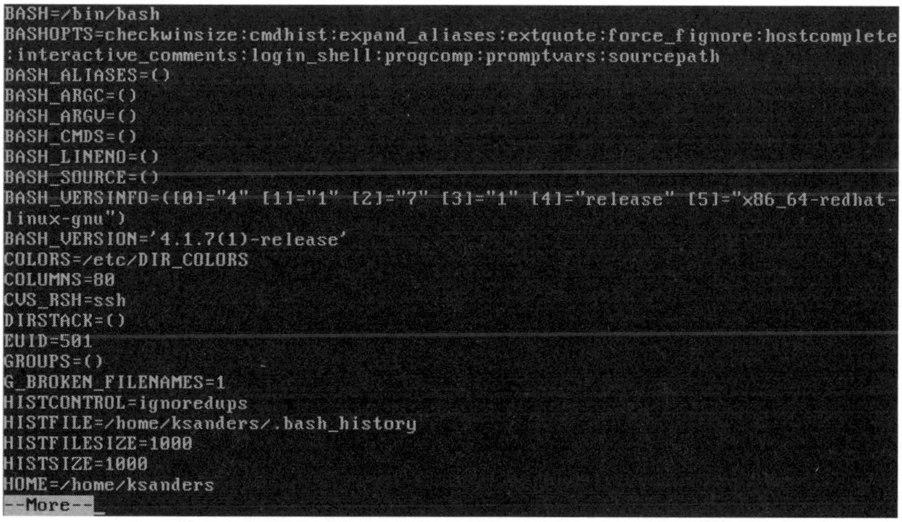

```
BASH=/bin/bash
BASHOPTS=checkwinsize:cmdhist:expand_aliases:extquote:force_fignore:hostcomplete
:interactive_comments:login_shell:progcomp:promptvars:sourcepath
BASH_ALIASES=()
BASH_ARGC=()
BASH_ARGV=()
BASH_CMDS=()
BASH_LINENO=()
BASH_SOURCE=()
BASH_VERSINFO=([0]="4" [1]="1" [2]="7" [3]="1" [4]="release" [5]="x86_64-redhat-
linux-gnu")
BASH_VERSION='4.1.7(1)-release'
COLORS=/etc/DIR_COLORS
COLUMNS=80
CVS_RSH=ssh
DIRSTACK=()
EUID=501
GROUPS=()
G_BROKEN_FILENAMES=1
HISTCONTROL=ignoredups
HISTFILE=/home/ksanders/.bash_history
HISTFILESIZE=1000
HISTSIZE=1000
HOME=/home/ksanders
--More--
```

Figure 2-9   Using set to view environment variables and their values

```
MAIL=/var/spool/mail/ksanders
PATH=/usr/lib64/qt-3.3/bin:/usr/lib64/ccache:/usr/local/bin:/bin:/usr/bin:/usr/l
ocal/sbin:/usr/sbin:/sbin:/home/ksanders/bin
PWD=/home/ksanders
LANG=en_US.UTF-8
KDE_IS_PRELINKED=1
KDEDIRS=/usr
SSH_ASKPASS=/usr/libexec/openssh/gnome-ssh-askpass
HISTCONTROL=ignoredups
SHLVL=1
HOME=/home/ksanders
LOGNAME=ksanders
QTLIB=/usr/lib64/qt-3.3/lib
CVS_RSH=ssh
LESSOPEN=|/usr/bin/lesspipe.sh %s
G_BROKEN_FILENAMES=1
_=/bin/env
[ksanders@fs3 ~]$
```

Figure 2-10 Using env to view environment variables and their values

As with set, the env command displays each variable and its current value. However, notice that env doesn't sort the variables. The set command actually sorts the variables alphabetically, which I really like!

These commands—echo, set, and env—all can be used to show you variables and their values. However, what if you need to change the value assigned to a variable? Let's talk about how this is done next.

Setting the Value of a Variable

As we discussed earlier, most of the environment variables used on a Linux system work great using the values assigned to them by the system. In fact, there are many environment variables that you should not change! For example, changing the value of the HOSTNAME variable could cause problems with many services running on your system.

However, there are times when you will need to change the value assigned to an environment variable. For example, you may need to add an additional directory to the end of the PATH variable. This can be a handy way to make life easier for your users (and for you as well). In addition, you may need to edit the DISPLAY variable to configure your X Window System to send its display to a remote computer. Likewise, you may want to alter the shell prompt to display different information.

To do these tasks, you need to change the value of an environment variable. This is relatively easy to do. Simply enter *variable=value* at the shell prompt. For example, suppose you installed an application in /var/opt/mydb named myapp. This path doesn't currently exist in your PATH variable, and you want to add it so that you won't have to use the full path when you want to run the program. To do this, you can enter **PATH=$PATH:/var/opt/mydb** at the shell prompt.

Note that I specified **$PATH** in the variable assignment. This includes the current value of the PATH variable in the new value assignment. I then tacked on **:/var/opt/mydb** to the end of the existing list of paths. If you don't include $PATH in your reassignment, then the current directories in your PATH variable will be *erased* and replaced by the new path you specify in the command! When this happens, your system will start to experience a host of problems!

NOTE Remember that setting the value of an environment variable will erase its current contents. If you want to preserve the current contents, use the technique just shown. If you do actually want to erase the contents of the variable and replace it with a new value, you can simply enter *variable=value* at the shell prompt.

However, we still have one more task to complete. We've assigned the value of PATH to include an additional directory. However, the new value of the PATH variable applies only to the current shell session. If I open up another terminal session, the change that I made to PATH will not be applied.

To make the assignment apply to all shells, I need to export the new value of the variable. To do this, I enter **export *variable*** at the shell prompt. In this example, I need to enter **export PATH** at the shell prompt. After I do so, the new value assigned to PATH is made available to all other shells, including any subshells created by the current shell.

Making Variables Persistent

One problem you will encounter in this process, however, is the fact that any new value you add to an environment variable will be lost after the system reboots. If the change you made needs to be persistent across system restarts, then you need to edit one of your bash configuration files, discussed at the beginning of the chapter, and add the variable assignment command to the file.

In the preceding example, I probably want my new PATH variable value assignment to be automatically made each time the system restarts. I don't want to have to manually set the value of PATH and export it each time the system reboots.

To do this, I can use the command to set the value of PATH to include /var/opt/mydb as well as the command to export the PATH variable to one of the following bash configuration files:

- ~/.bashrc
- /etc/profile
- ~/.bash_profile
- ~/.bash_login
- ~/.profile

TIP Adding the commands to a global bash configuration file such as /etc/profile will cause the change to be applied to all users. If you want to apply the change to only a single user, you should use the appropriate bash configuration file found in that user's home directory.

You need to determine which files your particular distribution uses. For example, you could modify the following commands in the ~/.bash_profile file in the ksanders user's home directory:

```
PATH=$PATH:$HOME/bin:/var/opt/mydb
export PATH
```

Now, whenever the system boots and ksanders logs in, the /var/opt/mydb path is automatically added to his PATH environment variable. Because we added the command to the ~/. bash_profile file in the ksanders user's home directory, it will not be added to any other user's PATH variable.

Let's practice working with environment variables in the following exercise.

Exercise 2-7: Working with Environment Variables

In this exercise, you will practice working with environment variables in the bash shell. You can perform this exercise using the virtual machine that comes with this book. Run snapshot 2-1 for the correctly configured environment.

 VIDEO Please watch the Exercise 2-7 video for a demonstration on how to perform this task.

Complete the following:

1. If you haven't done so already, boot your Linux system and log in.

2. If necessary, start a terminal session.

3. Change to your root user account by entering **su** – followed by your root password.

4. At the shell prompt, view the value of the following environment variables by entering the following commands:

   echo $PWD
   echo $HOME
   echo $EUID
   echo $PATH
   echo $PS1

5. Change your shell prompt to display the currently logged-in user, the name of the Linux host, the current time, the full path to the current working directory, and a colon by doing the following:

   a. At the shell prompt enter **PS1="[\u@\h \t \w]:"**. The prompt should immediately change.

   b. At the shell prompt, enter **export PS1**.

   c. At your shell prompt, enter **ls ~ –a**. Which file would you edit on your particular distribution if you wanted to make the changes to your PS1 environment variable persistent?

With this in mind, let's now talk about creating user-defined variables.

Creating a User-Defined Variable

In the preceding topic, we focused on working with environment variables. These variables are automatically defined for you each time the system boots. However, you can actually create your own customized variables as well. This is done in exactly the same way as when managing environment variables. Simply enter *variable=value* at the shell prompt.

For example, suppose I wanted to create a variable named ME and set it to a value of "Robb Tracy." I can do this by entering **ME="Robb Tracy"** at the shell prompt. Once I do this, a variable named ME is added to my system and is set to a value of Robb Tracy. You can use the echo command to view the value of the ME variable, as shown here:

```
rtracy@openSUSE:~> ME="Robb Tracy"
rtracy@openSUSE:~> echo $ME
Robb Tracy
rtracy@openSUSE:~>
```

Like an environment variable, a user-defined variable is available only to the current instance of the shell. To make it available to other shells, including subshells created by the current shell, you need to export it with the export command. In this example, I would enter **export ME** at the shell prompt to do this. In addition to echo, you can also use **set** or **env** to view user-defined variables just as you did with environment variables.

As with an environment variable, you can make a user-defined variable persistent by adding the appropriate commands to one of the bash configuration files discussed previously. When creating user-defined variables, keep the following rules in mind:

- Variable names can contain letters or numbers, but they may not begin with a number.

- Variable names may contain hyphens (-) or underscore characters (_).

- Although not required, you should try to use all uppercase characters when naming your variables. Notice when you enter **set** or **env** that all of your system's environment variables use uppercase names. You should do the same.

The next topic we need to address is that of aliases. Let's discuss how aliases work next.

Working with Aliases

Aliases are really cool. An *alias* is basically a shortcut to a different file or command on your Linux system. When your system boots, a series of aliases is automatically created for you. You can view these by entering **alias** at the shell prompt. An example is shown here:

```
rtracy@openSUSE:~> alias
alias +='pushd .'
alias -='popd'
alias ..='cd ..'
alias ...='cd ../..'
alias beep='echo -en "\007"'
alias cd..='cd ..'
alias dir='ls -l'
alias egrep='egrep --color=auto'
alias fgrep='fgrep --color=auto'
alias grep='grep --color=auto'
alias l='ls -alF'
alias la='ls -la'
alias ll='ls -l'
alias ls='_ls'
alias ls-l='ls -l'
alias md='mkdir -p'
alias o='less'
```

```
alias rd='rmdir'
alias rehash='hash -r'
alias unmount='echo "Error: Try the command: umount" 1>&2; false'
alias you='if test "$EUID" = 0 ; then /sbin/yast2 online_update ;
 else su - -c "/sbin/yast2 online_update" ; fi'
```

Notice that the series of commands listed aren't really commands at all. Instead, they are aliases that point to real shell commands. For example, if you type **dir** at the shell prompt, the output from alias tells you that the **ls –l** shell command is actually run. Likewise, typing **..** will actually execute the **cd ..** command.

You can create your own aliases too. To do this, just enter **alias *name*="*command*"** at the shell prompt. For example, suppose you want to be able to enter **ldir** at the shell prompt to view a long listing of a directory. You could enter **alias ldir="ls –l"** at the shell prompt, as shown here:

```
rtracy@openSUSE:~> alias ldir="ls -l"
rtracy@openSUSE:~> alias
...
alias dir='ls -l'
alias l='ls -alF'
alias la='ls -la'
alias ldir='ls -l'
...
```

Now, if you enter **ldir** at the shell prompt, the **ls –l** command is executed and its output is displayed on screen, as shown here:

```
rtracy@openSUSE:~> ldir
total 40
drwxr-xr-x 2 rtracy users 4096 2011-01-19 10:41 bin
drwxr-xr-x 2 rtracy users 4096 2011-01-19 10:42 Desktop
drwxr-xr-x 2 rtracy users 4096 2011-01-19 10:42 Documents
drwxr-xr-x 2 rtracy users 4096 2011-01-19 10:42 Downloads
drwxr-xr-x 2 rtracy users 4096 2011-01-19 10:42 Music
drwxr-xr-x 2 rtracy users 4096 2011-01-19 10:42 Pictures
drwxr-xr-x 2 rtracy users 4096 2011-01-19 10:42 Public
drwxr-xr-x 2 rtracy users 4096 2011-01-19 10:41 public_html
drwxr-xr-x 2 rtracy users 4096 2011-01-19 10:42 Templates
drwxr-xr-x 2 rtracy users 4096 2011-01-19 10:42 Videos
```

You can include multiple commands within a single alias. To do this, separate the commands in the alias command line with a semicolon (;). For example, if you wanted to create an alias that would mount a DVD inserted in your optical drive and then generate a long listing of the files it contains, you could enter the following at the shell prompt:

```
alias mntdvd="mount -t iso9660 /dev/sr0 /media/dvd;ls -l /media/dvd"
```

After doing so, you can enter **mntdvd** at the shell prompt to mount the DVD and generate a listing of its files.

As with variables, any aliases you define with the alias command are not persistent. If you reboot the system, they will be gone when the system comes back up. As with variables, you can make your aliases persistent by adding them to one of the bash configuration files (either system-wide or specific to a user).

Let's practice working with aliases in the following exercise.

Exercise 2-8: Working with Aliases

In this exercise, you will practice creating aliases in the bash shell. You can perform this exercise using the virtual machine that comes with this book. Run snapshot 2-1 for the correctly config-ured environment.

 VIDEO Please watch the Exercise 2-8 video for a demonstration on how to perform this task.

Do the following:

1. If necessary, boot your Linux system and log in as a standard user.

2. Open a terminal session and change to your root user account by entering **su –**. Then enter your root password when prompted.

3. Create an alias named **log** that will display the last few lines of your /var/log/messages file by entering **alias log="tail /var/log/messages"** at the shell prompt.

4. At the shell prompt, enter **alias** and verify that the alias has been created.

5. Test your alias by entering **log** at the shell prompt.

6. Verify that the last few lines of your /var/log/messages file are displayed.

7. At your shell prompt, enter **ls ~ –a**. Which file would you edit on your particular distribution if you wanted to make the alias persistent?

Now that you know how to manage variables, it's time to discuss how to redirect output from shell commands. Let's do that next.

Using Redirection and Piping

The bash shell (as well as most other Linux shells) is extremely powerful and flexible. One of the features that makes it this way is its ability to manipulate command input and output. In this part of this chapter, we're going to explore how to do this. Specifically, we're going to cover the following:

- Standard bash file descriptors
- Redirecting output and input for shell commands
- Piping information

Let's begin by reviewing bash shell file descriptors.

Figure 2-11
bash shell file
descriptors

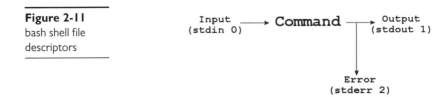

Standard bash File Descriptors

Before you can learn how to redirect or pipe outputs from a bash command, you must first understand bash shell *file descriptors.* Three file descriptors are available for every command you enter at a shell prompt (as shown in Figure 2-11):

- **stdin** This file descriptor stands for *standard input,* which is the input provided to a particular command to process. The stdin for a command is represented by the number 0.

- **stdout** This file descriptor stands for *standard output,* which is simply the output from a particular command. For example, the directory listing generated by the ls command is its stdout. The stdout for a command is represented by the number 1.

- **stderr** This file descriptor stands for *standard error,* which is the error code generated, if any, by a command. The stderr for a command is represented by the number 2.

Not all commands will use all three of these descriptors, but many do. Let's take a look at some examples. Suppose I display the contents of a file in my home directory by entering **cat ~/test2 .txt**, as shown here:

```
rtracy@openSUSE:~> cat ~/test2.txt
This is a text file named test2.txt.
```

The cat command displays the contents of the file on the screen. This is the stdout of the cat command. Now suppose I enter the same command but specify a file that doesn't exist, as shown here:

```
rtracy@openSUSE:~> cat ~/test1.txt
cat: /home/rtracy/test1.txt: No such file or directory
```

Because the file doesn't exist, the cat command generates an error. This is the stderr of the cat command. Knowing these descriptors, you can redirect where each one goes when the command is executed. Let's discuss how this is done next.

Redirecting Output and Input for Shell Commands

Using the three descriptors you can manipulate where a command gets its input from and where it sends its outputs. In this part of this chapter, we're going to review how you can do this from the command line. We'll discuss the following:

- Redirecting output
- Redirecting input

Let's begin by discussing how to redirect outputs.

Redirecting Output

The bash shell allows you to manipulate where the output from a command goes after it is generated. By default, it is displayed on the screen. However, you can specify that it be sent elsewhere. For example, it is very common to redirect output of a command from the screen to a text file in the file system, especially if the output from the command is very long.

Redirection is accomplished using the **>** character on the command line. The syntax for redirecting output is **command output> filename_or_device**. For example, suppose we want to use the tail command to view the last few lines of our system log file /var/log/messages and we want to save the output to a file named lastmessages in the current directory. We could do this by entering **tail /var/log/messages 1> lastmessages**. This tells the shell to redirect the stdout (1) to a file named lastmessages. The output from the command is truly redirected. It isn't displayed on the screen at all. All stdout text is sent to the file specified, as shown here:

```
openSUSE:~ # tail /var/log/messages 1>lastmessages
openSUSE:~ # cat lastmessages
2014-10-13T19:14:58.719210-06:00 linux su: pam_unix(su-l:auth): authentication
failure; logname=rtracy uid=1000 euid=0 tty=pts/0 ruser=rtracy rhost=  user=root
2014-10-13T19:15:01.106998-06:00 linux /usr/sbin/cron[23401]:
pam_unix(crond:session): session opened for user root by (uid=0)
…
```

If you don't enter a file descriptor number in the command, the shell will assume that you want to redirect only the stdout from the command. In this example, you could enter **tail /var/log/messages > lastmessages** and get the same result.

You can use the same technique to redirect stderr from the screen to a file. For example, if I were to use the cat command to try to display a file that doesn't exist, I can redirect any error messages generated to a file by entering **cat myfiles.odt 2> errorfile**. Because the file doesn't exist, the cat command generates an error message (stderr) instead of regular output (stdout). This is shown next:

```
openSUSE:~ # cat myfiles.odt 2>errorfile
openSUSE:~ # cat errorfile
cat: myfiles.odt: No such file or directory
```

This command specifies that the stderr (2) from the cat command be redirected to a file named errorfile in the current directory. Because it's redirected, the stderr output is not displayed on the screen but is instead written to the specified file.

When you redirect output to a file that doesn't exist, the bash shell will automatically create it for you. This is what happened in the preceding examples. However, if the file already exists, be warned that the shell will erase the existing file and replace it with the new output by default. If you want to append the new output to an existing file without erasing its contents, you should use **>>** instead of **>**. For example, if you wanted to write the stdout from the ps command to a file named myprocesses without overwriting the existing contents of that file, you would enter **ps 1>> myprocesses**.

You can even redirect both stderr and stdout to text files at the same time. To do this, you add two redirection instructions to the command—one for the stdout and one for the stderr. The syntax for doing this is **command 1> stdout_filename 2> stderr_filename**. This will send stdout to one file and stderr to a different file. For example, if you wanted to write the stdout from the mount command to a file named mntok and the stderr to a file named mnterr, you would enter **mount 1> mntok 2> mnterr**.

You can also send both outputs to the same file. To do this, use the syntax of ***command* 1> *filename* 2> &1**. This syntax causes the stdout first to be sent to the specified file, and then stderr (2) output is redirected to the stdout output (&1). If you're going to use this option, it's very important to remember to use the **&** symbol before the 1. This tells the shell that the character that follows is a file descriptor and not a filename. If you omit this character, the shell will write stderr output to a separate file named 1.

Now that you know how to redirect outputs from a command, we next need to discuss how to redirect command inputs.

Redirecting Input

Just as you can specify where output from a command is sent, you can also specify where a command's inputs (stdin) come from. To do this, you simply reverse the character we used previously for redirecting output. The syntax you use is ***command* < *input_text_or_file***.

For example, I could enter **tail < /var/log/messages** at the shell prompt. This sends the text string "/var/log/messages" to the tail command as an input. For most commands, however, this isn't a terribly useful option. In the preceding example, it would probably be easier to simply enter **tail /var/log/messages**. Where this option really shines is when you need to send a lot of text to a command that is expecting it.

For example, you can send a list of words from a text file to the sort command and have it sort them for you. I've used a text editor to create a file named **words** that contains several lines of text:

```
rtracy@openSUSE:~> cat words
Who
What
Why
Where
How
```

With this file created, I can specify that it be used as an input with the sort command. This is done by entering **sort < words** at the shell prompt. The sorted output is then displayed on the screen, as shown here:

```
rtracy@openSUSE:~> sort < words
How
What
Where
Who
Why
```

Let's practice working with redirection in the following exercise.

Exercise 2-9: Redirecting Input and Output

You can perform this exercise using the virtual machine that comes with this book. Run snapshot 2-1 for the correctly configured environment.

 VIDEO Please watch the Exercise 2-9 video for a demonstration on how to perform this task.

In this exercise, you will practice redirecting input and output. Complete the following:

1. If necessary, boot your Linux system and log in as a standard user.

2. Change to your root user account by entering **su –** followed by your root password.

3. Use tail to view the last lines of your /var/log/messages file and then redirect the standard output to a text file in your home directory by entering **tail /var/log/messages 1> lastlines**.

4. Enter **ls l*** and verify that the lastlines file was created.

5. Use the cat command to view the lastlines file by entering **cat lastlines** at the shell prompt.

6. Append the last lines of the content of your /var/log/firewall log file to lastlines by entering **tail /var/log/firewall 1>\> lastlines** at the shell prompt.

7. Use the cat command to view the lastlines file again by entering **cat lastlines** at the shell prompt. You should see the lines from the firewall log file added to the end of the file.

8. Send standard error to a log file by entering **tail /var/log/mylog 2> errorout** at the shell prompt.

9. View the errorout file by entering **cat errorout** at the shell prompt. Why was an error generated by the preceding command?

10. Send the lastlines file to the stdin of the sort command by entering **sort < lastlines** at the shell prompt. The sort command should send the words from the file to the stdout (the screen) in alphabetical order.

In addition to redirecting input or output from a command, you can also pipe outputs. Let's discuss how this is done next.

Piping Information

Redirection is great, but it has one weakness. It only allows us to redirect to or from a file in the file system or a system device. What if you needed to redirect the output from one command to the input of another command? Can this be done? You bet it can! This is done using *pipes*. This part of the chapter explains how this is done.

Pipes are extremely useful when you're working at the shell prompt. For example, I mentioned earlier in this chapter that you can use **| more** with the set and env commands. The pipe character (|) used in the command tells the shell to take the output of the first command and send it to the input of the second program specified.

For example, if I enter **cat /var/log/messages | more** at the shell prompt, the cat command reads the contents of the /var/log/messages file and sends it to the stdout. Normally, this would be displayed on the screen. However, because we are using a pipe, the shell knows that it should not display the stdout from cat on the screen. Instead, it takes the stdout from cat and sends it as the stdin for the next command listed—in this case, the more command. The more command then takes the output from cat and performs its manipulations on it, which is to display the text on the screen one page at a time.

Pipes can be used with any commands that produce output of some sort and accept input of some sort. A great example is the grep command. You can use grep alone at the command line, of course. However, it's very handy when used in a pipe in conjunction with another command. The syntax of the command is ***command*** | **grep** *expression*. Doing this pipes the output of the first command to the input of grep, which then searches for information that matches the specified expression.

For example, suppose you are using the cat command to display the contents of the /var/log/ messages file on the screen. You're only interested in displaying log file entries created when the network interfaces in the system were brought up. You could filter out the output of cat by piping it to grep and searching for the expression "ifup" in the output of cat. To do this, you would enter **cat /var/log/messages | grep ifup**, as shown here:

```
openSUSE:~ # cat /var/log/messages | grep ifup
2014-10-13T15:31:01.402528-06:00 linux ifup[2493]: Service
network not started -> skipping
2014-10-13T15:31:12.448163-06:00 linux ifup[3225]:      lo
2014-10-13T15:31:12.744951-06:00 linux ifup[3225]:      lo
2014-10-13T15:31:12.762301-06:00 linux ifup[3225]: IP address: 127.0.0.1/8
2014-10-13T15:31:12.776442-06:00 linux ifup[3225]:
2014-10-13T15:31:13.537806-06:00 linux systemd[1]: Starting
ifup managed network interface eno16777736...
```

Notice that only the entries in the output of cat that match the expression "ifup" are displayed on the screen by grep.

 NOTE   Remember that when you are piping information, only the last command in the pipe actually displays output on the screen. The output from all the other commands is redirected to the input of the next command in the pipe and is not displayed on the screen.

In this example, there are actually too many matching entries to fit on a single screen. What can you do? You can actually include multiple commands within a pipe. In this situation, we need to use cat to generate the initial output, then filter it through grep to find only those entries that have "ifup" in them, and then send the output of grep to the more command so that the display is paused one screen at a time. To do this, you would enter **cat /var/log/messages | grep ifup | more** at the shell prompt.

Occasionally, you may need the output from a command to be displayed on the screen *and* written to a file at the same time. This can be done using the **tee** command. The syntax for using tee is ***command*** | **tee** *file_name*. For example, if I wanted to output the stdout from the ls –l command to be displayed on the screen and written to a file named output.txt, I could use the following command:

```
ls -l | tee output.txt
```

Let's practice working with pipes in the following exercise.

Exercise 2-10: Using Pipes

In this exercise, you will practice using pipes to send stdout from one command to the stdin of another. You can perform this exercise using the virtual machine that comes with this book. Run snapshot 2-1 for the correctly configured environment.

 VIDEO Please watch the Exercise 2-10 video for a demonstration on how to perform this task.

Complete the following:

1. If necessary, boot your Linux system and log in as a standard user.

2. If necessary, open a terminal session.

3. Change to your root user account by entering **su –** followed by your root password.

4. View all entries in your system log that contain the word "kernel" by piping the output from cat to grep. Enter **cat /var/log/messages | grep kernel** at the shell prompt to do this.

5. The output from the preceding command was probably very long. Pipe the output from cat to grep to more by entering **cat /var/log/messages | grep kernel | more** at the shell prompt.

6. Send the output from the preceding command to the screen and to a file named kernel. txt in your home directory by entering **cat /var/log/messages | grep kernel | tee ~/kernel.txt** at the shell prompt.

7. Verify the information was written to kernel.txt by entering **cat ~/kernel.txt** at the shell prompt.

 EXAM TIP You can use the unset command to remove a value assigned to a variable. Simply enter **unset variable_name** at the shell prompt.

Chapter Review

This chapter started by reviewing the two user interfaces provided by most Linux distributions: the command-line interface and the graphical user interface. I discussed the bash configuration files. I pointed out that there are two types of shells on a Linux system:

- Login shells
- Non-login shells

When a login shell is run, /etc/profile is read first to initially configure the shell environment. The shell then searches for the following files in the user's home directory in the following order:

- .bash_profile
- .bash_login
- .profile

The shell will read the first of these files found and use it to configure the shell environment for the current user. Different distributions will use different bash configuration files.

I then discussed the command history function of the bash shell. Using command history, you can press the UP ARROW key to scroll through a list of previously entered commands. These commands are saved in the .bash_history file in each user's home directory.

The bash shell also offers command completion. Using command completion, you can enter part of a command and then press the TAB key to automatically finish the command for you.

Next, I discussed how to get help when working with the Linux shell. I first reviewed how to use the man utility to view manual pages. I related that most commands and utilities on your Linux system have a man page associated with them that contains information about what they do and how to use them. I discussed the fact that all of the man pages together compose the manual. The manual is divided into sections according to the functionality of the utility or command. The files that compose the manual are stored in the directory specified by the MANPATH variable or the MANPATH directive in the /etc/man_db.conf file.

To use man, you simply enter **man** followed by the name of the command, utility, file, or service that you need to learn more about. I reviewed the different sections used in most man pages. I also reviewed the keystrokes you can use to navigate within a man page.

I also discussed how to search man pages. I pointed out that you can enter / followed by a text string to search for a word within a single man page. You can also enter **man –k** or use the apropos utility to search for text across man pages.

After discussing the man utility, we turned our attention to the info utility. I pointed out that info contains more extensive documentation than the man utility. To view information about a command or utility, you enter **info** followed by the name of the utility you want to learn about. I also discussed the keystrokes you can use to navigate within and between info nodes. I pointed out that you can search info nodes for a string of text by pressing CTRL-S and entering a search pattern.

At this point in the chapter, I turned to a discussion of environment variables. Environment variables are used to configure the shell environment. These variables are automatically populated when the bash shell is started, but you can modify many of them if needed. You can view the value of an environment variable using the following utilities:

- echo
- set
- env

To set the value of a variable, you can enter *variable_name=value*. After assigning a new value to an environment variable, you can enter **export *variable_name*** at the shell prompt to make the new value available to other shells, including subshells launched by the current shell.

It's important to remember that any change you make to an environment variable is not persistent. To make it persistent, you need to edit one of the bash configuration files discussed in this chapter to make the value assignment to the variable each time a shell is started.

I also pointed out that you can create your own variables from the shell prompt. This is done using the same technique as described for environment variables. Like environment variables, user-defined variables have to be exported in order for them to be available to other shells.

I then turned our discussion to aliases. An alias is a shortcut to commands on your Linux system. Many aliases are usually defined automatically when a shell is started by most distributions. You can view these using the alias command. You can also define your own aliases by entering **alias** *alias_name=*"*commands*" at the shell prompt. Like variables, alias definitions aren't persistent. To make them persistent, you need to add the appropriate commands to one of your bash configuration files.

I then shifted gears and addressed the issue of managing the inputs and outputs of shell commands. Most shell commands have three file descriptors:

- stdin (0)
- stdout (1)
- stderr (2)

You can redirect stdout and stderr output from a command to a file by adding **1>** *filename* or **2>** *filename* to any command. If the specified file doesn't exist, the shell will create it. If it does exist, its contents will be overwritten. If you want to preserve the existing contents of the file, use >> instead of >. You can also send input from a file to a command's stdin using the < character.

In addition to redirecting to a file, you can also use a pipe to redirect stdout from one command to the stdin of another. This is done by entering **command | command** at the shell prompt. In fact, you can include many different commands in the same pipe.

Accelerated Review

- Linux offers both command-line and graphical user interfaces.
- The Linux command-line interface is created by shells.
- The bash shell is the default shell for most distributions.
- Linux shells do not search the current directory when running a file from the command prompt.
- Shells used to log in to the system are login shells.
- Shells opened after the user has logged in are non-login shells.
- The .bashrc file is used to configure non-login shells.
- The /etc/profile file is the first file read when creating a login shell.

- After the /etc/profile file is read, the bash shell looks for one of the following configuration files in the user's home directory:
  - .bash_profile
  - .bash_login
  - .profile
- The first of these files found is the one used to configure the user's shell environment.
- The bash shell saves your command history in .bash_history.
- Pressing the UP ARROW key displays the last commands entered at the shell prompt.
- The bash shell offers command completion using the TAB key.
- Using manual (man) pages is one of the primary means for maintaining documentation on a Linux system.
- Manual pages are viewed using the man utility.
- Manual pages are maintained for most commands, utilities, services, and configuration files on your system.
- The location of the man pages in your file system is stored in the MANPATH environment variable or in the MANPATH directive in the /etc/man.config file.
- All of the man pages together compose the manual.
- The manual is divided into the following sections:
  - Section 1: User programs and shell commands
  - Section 2: Kernel functions
  - Section 3: Library functions
  - Section 4: Special files found in /dev
  - Section 5: File format descriptions and conventions
  - Section 6: Games
  - Section 7: Miscellaneous conventions
  - Section 8: Utilities used by root
  - Section 9: Kernel routines
- Some of the more commonly used man page sections include the following:
  - NAME
  - SYNOPSIS
  - DESCRIPTION
  - AUTHOR
  - REPORTING BUGS
  - COPYRIGHT
  - SEE ALSO

- To search for text within a man page, you enter **/** followed by the text you want to search for.

- To search for text across man pages, you can use one of the following:

  - man –k

  - apropos

- In addition to man, you can also use the info utility to view system documentation.

- The info utility displays more in-depth information than the man utility.

- The information displayed by the info utility is called a node.

- To use info, enter **info** at the shell prompt followed by the name of the command, utility, or configuration file you need to learn about.

- To search for information in info, press CTRL-S and enter the term you want to search for.

- Environment variables are used to define the shell environment.

- You can view the values of your environment variables using the echo, set, and env shell commands.

- You must use a $ when referencing an environment variable to specify that the text is a variable name, not a string.

- You can set the value of an environment variable by entering *variable_name=value* at the shell prompt.

- After setting the value of a variable, you must export it using the export command.

- The value you assign to an environment variable is not persistent.

- To make a variable assignment persistent, you need to add the appropriate commands to one of your bash configuration files.

- You can also create user-defined variables in the same manner as environment variables.

- User-defined variables need to be exported in order for them to be used by other shells.

- You can create aliases on your system to create shortcuts to commands.

- You can view existing aliases using the alias command.

- You can define a new alias by entering **alias** *alias_name=command*.

- Aliases are not persistent. You must add the appropriate commands to one of your bash configuration files to make them persistent.

- Most Linux shell commands have three standard file descriptors:

  - stdin (0)

  - stdout (1)

  - stderr (2)

- You can redirect output (stdout and stderr) from the screen to a file using the > character after the command.

- Using 1> *filename* redirects stdout to the specified file.

- Using 2>*filename* redirects stderr to the specified file.
- Using > causes the specified file to be created if it doesn't exist. If it does exist, the file's contents will be overwritten.
- Using >> will cause the specified file's existing contents to be preserved and the new output appended to the end.
- You can use < to specify a file to be used as the stdin for a command.
- Using pipes allows you to move the stdout from one command to the stdin of another command.
- The syntax for using pipes is *command1 | command2*.
- You can use multiple commands within a single pipe.

Questions

1. Which shell is the default shell for most Linux distributions?

   A. sh

   B. csh

   C. bash

   D. zsh

2. You are working at the bash shell in a CLI-only environment on an openSUSE Linux system. You have a program currently running when you discover that you need to access to the shell prompt to perform another task. You don't want to halt the first program to do this. What can you do?

   A. Nothing, you must halt the first program to access the shell prompt.

   B. You can press CTRL-PAUSE on the keyboard. This will pause the running program while you access the shell prompt.

   C. You can press ALT-F2 to open an alternate console screen and access a new shell session.

   D. Press CTRL-SHIFT-F6. This will automatically open a new shell session without pausing the running program.

3. You've copied down an executable file named runupdate.sh from your company's server to the /tmp directory on your Linux system. You change to the /tmp directory at the shell prompt. When you enter **runupdate.sh**, the shell indicates that it can't find the file. What can you do?

   A. Enter the filename in all capital letters.

   B. Add **./** before the filename when entering it at the prompt.

   C. Enter the filename without the .sh extension.

   D. Move the file to your home directory and then execute it.

4. You need to find out what directories in the Linux file system are included in the path. What command can you use? (Choose two.)

    A. env

    B. show $PATH

    C. man path

    D. echo $PATH

    E. writeln PATH

5. You've copied an executable file named update1.sh from your company's server to /tmp on your Linux system. You open a shell and change to the /tmp directory. When you enter **./Update1.sh**, the shell indicates that it can't find the file. What can you do?

    A. Enter the filename in all lowercase letters.

    B. Add .\ before the filename when entering it at the prompt.

    C. Enter the filename without the .sh extension.

    D. Move the file to your home directory and then execute it.

6. Which Linux utility can be used to display a list of all running processes on your system?

    A. env

    B. procman

    C. processes

    D. top

    E. echo $PROCESSES

7. Which Linux utility can be used to display your network board configuration?

    A. netstat

    B. route

    C. ifconfig

    D. ipconfig

    E. echo $NETWORK_CONFIG

8. Which Linux utility can be used to change to a different user account at the shell prompt?

    A. user

    B. chuser

    C. swuser

    D. su

9. Which configuration file is read when a non-login bash shell is run?

   A. .bashrc

   B. .bash_profile

   C. .bash_login

   D. .profile

10. Which configuration file is the first file read when a login bash shell is run?

    A. ~/.bashrc

    B. ~/.bash_profile

    C. ~/.bash_login

    D. ~/.profile

    E. /etc/profile

11. Which file contains a list of your most recently entered shell commands?

    A. ~/.history

    B. ~/.bash_history

    C. /etc/bash_history

    D. ~/.bash_commands

12. Which keystroke is used for the command completion feature of bash?

    A. ENTER

    B. FI

    C. TAB

    D. UP ARROW

13. Which utility is used to view manual pages?

    A. man

    B. manual

    C. gman

    D. Kwrite

14. Which environment variable contains the directory where man page files are located?

    A. MANUAL

    B. MANUALPATH

    C. MANPAGEPATH

    D. MANPATH

15. Which file can be used to configure the path to the man page files?

    A. /etc/man_db.conf

    B. /etc/man.conf

    C. /etc/man.txt

    D. /etc/manual.conf

16. Which of the following manual sections contains man pages for administrative utilities used by the root user?

    A. 1

    B. 3

    C. 8

    D. 9

17. Which of the following manual sections contains man pages for utilities and commands that can be used by any user?

    A. 9

    B. 1

    C. 3

    D. 7

18. You need to learn about the options available for the mkdir utility. Which command will display its manual page?

    A. gman mkdir

    B. cat mkdir | man

    C. manual mkdir

    D. man mkdir

19. You need to learn about the options available for the chmod utility. Which command will display its manual page?

    A. gman chmod

    B. manual chmod

    C. man chmod

    D. man display chmod

20. Which section in a man page provides a brief review of the syntax used for a particular command or utility?

    A. REVIEW

    B. SYNOPSIS

    C. DESCRIPTION

    D. SYNTAX

21. Which section in a man page provides a list of man pages or other resources related to the particular command or utility?

   A. DESCRIPTION

   B. VERSION

   C. SEE ALSO

   D. REFERENCES

22. You're using man to view the man page for the chown utility. Which keystroke will unload the current man page and exit man?

   A. CTRL-U

   B. X

   C. CTRL-X

   D. Q

23. You're using man to view the man page for the Samba daemon. Which keystrokes can you use to search for the term "password" in the man page?

   A. /"password"

   B. CTRL-S

   C. /password

   D. CTRL-F

24. After searching for a term within a man page, you need to jump to the next instance of the term in the page. Which keystroke will do this?

   A. Q

   B. P

   C. N

   D. S

25. You need to search for man pages that relate to the Samba daemon. Which command will do this?

   A. man –s samba

   B. man –k samba

   C. search samba | man

   D. which samba

26. You need to search for man pages that relate to the PAM service. Which command will do this?

   A. which pam

   B. man –s pam

   C. search pam | man

   D. apropos pam

27. You need to use info to view information about using the smbpasswd utility. Which command will do this?

    A. info /smbpasswd

    B. info "smbpasswd"

    C. show info smbpasswd

    D. info smbpasswd

28. While viewing an info node, which keystroke can you use to navigate to the next node?

    A. /next

    B. P

    C. N

    D. L

29. While viewing an info node, which keystroke can you use to navigate to the previous node?

    A. P

    B. /prev

    C. N

    D. /up

30. While viewing an info node, which keystroke can you use to navigate to the beginning of the node?

    A. B

    B. /top

    C. HOME

    D. T

31. You want to add the ~/temp directory to your system's PATH environment variable. You want to be sure you don't overwrite the existing directories in your path, so you enter **PATH=PATH:~/temp** at your shell prompt. Did you do this correctly?

    A. Yes, this command will work correctly.

    B. No, you must first export the variable before you set it.

    C. No, you must use a $ before each PATH variable name in the command.

    D. No, you must use a $ before the second PATH variable name in the command.

32. Which commands can you use to view the values currently assigned to your environment variables? (Choose two.)

    A. set

    B. display

    C. var

    D. show

    E. env

33. You want to view a list of the aliases currently defined on your Linux system. What command can you issue at the shell prompt to do this?

   A. alias

   B. alias –l

   C. alias –a

   D. env alias

34. Which file descriptor refers to the text a command displays on the screen after the command has finished processing? (Choose two.)

   A. stdin

   B. stdout

   C. stdisplay

   D. stdoutput

   E. stderr

35. You want to send the standard output and the standard error from the tail /var/log/ firewall command to a file named lastevents in the current directory. Which command will do this?

   A. tail /var/log/firewall 1> lastevents 2> lastevents

   B. tail /var/log/firewall > lastevents

   C. tail /var/log/firewall 1> lastevents 2> &1

   D. tail /var/log/firewall 1&2> lasteventss

36. You want to send the contents of the logfile.txt file in the current directory to the sort command to sort them alphabetically and display them on the screen. Which command will do this?

   A. sort < ./logfile.txt

   B. sort –i ./logfile.txt

   C. sort < ./logfile.txt –d "screen"

   D. sort < ./logfile.txt > screen

Answers

   1. **C.** bash is the default shell used with most Linux distributions.

   2. **C.** Pressing ALT-F2 will open an alternate console. You can use this console to perform other tasks without stopping the program running in the first console screen. You can switch back by pressing ALT-F1.

   3. **B.** Adding ./ before the filename tells the shell that the file resides in the current directory.

   4. **A, D.** Both env and echo can be used to print the PATH environment variable on the screen.

5. **A.** Linux is case-sensitive. The command in the question uses an uppercase *U*.

6. **D.** The top utility displays running processes.

7. **C.** The ifconfig command is used to view and modify your network board configuration.

8. **D.** The su command can be used to change to a different user account at the shell prompt. The syntax is **su *username*.** If you omit the username, the su command assumes you want to switch to the root superuser account.

9. **A.** A non-login shell reads the ~/.bashrc file to define the user's shell environment.

10. **E.** The /etc/profile file is read when a bash login shell is first opened.

11. **B.** The ~/.bash_history file contains a list of your most recent shell commands.

12. **C.** The TAB key is used with command completion.

13. **A.** The man utility is used to view man pages. If an info node isn't available for a particular command or utility, then info may actually display a man page as well.

14. **D.** The MANPATH environment variable stores the path to the man pages on most Linux distributions.

15. **A.** You can use the /etc/man_db.conf file to specify the path to the man files on some Linux distributions.

16. **C.** Section 8 of the manual contains man pages for utilities and commands used by root.

17. **B.** Section 1 of the manual contains man pages for commands that can be used by any user.

18. **C.** The **man mkdir** command will display the man page for mkdir.

19. **C.** The **man chmod** command will display the man page for chmod.

20. **B.** The SYNOPSIS section of a man page provides a review of the syntax used for a command or utility.

21. **C.** The SEE ALSO section of a man page provides a list of related resources.

22. **D.** Pressing Q will exit man.

23. **C.** To search for the expression "password" in a man page, you enter **/password**.

24. **C.** After entering a search term, pressing N will take you to the next instance of that term in a man page.

25. **B.** Entering **man –k samba** will search across man pages for the term "samba."

26. **D.** Entering **apropos pam** will search across man pages for the term "pam."

27. **D.** Entering **info smbpasswd** will cause info to display information about the smbpasswd utility.

28. **C.** Pressing N will jump to the next node.

29. **A.** Pressing P will jump to the previous node.

30. **C.** Pressing the HOME key will take you to the first line in an info node.

31. **D.** You must reference the PATH variable using $PATH after the = sign. Otherwise, PATH will be interpreted as a literal string of text.

32. **A** and **E.** You can use the set command or the env command to view your variables.

33. **A.** The alias command is used to view your system's aliases.

34. **B** and **E.** The stdout and stderr file descriptors represent output displayed onscreen (by default) by most commands.

35. **C.** The **tail /var/log/firewall 1> lastevents 2> &1** command will send both stdout and stderr to the same file.

36. **A.** The **sort < ./logfile.txt** command will send the file to the stdin of the sort command.

Using the vi Text Editor

In this chapter, you will learn about:
- The role and function of the vi text editor
- Editing text files in vi

One of the key skills you will need when working with any Linux system (and for your Linux+ and LPIC-1 exams) is the ability to use a text editor effectively. Most system-configuration tasks in Linux are completed using a text editor to edit a text file, whether you're configuring the operating system itself or configuring a service running on the system.

This represents a significant difference between Linux and other operating systems such as Windows. Under Windows, most of your configuration settings are stored in a database called the *Registry*. This information is stored in logical sections called *keys*. These keys are stored in a hierarchy; a given key can contain a number of subkeys. These keys contain values that store the system's configuration information.

The Registry is a good concept, but one of the "key" problems with it is that it isn't designed with the end user in mind. Although a Registry editor named Regedit.exe is supplied with Windows, you are discouraged from manually editing values in the Registry. Instead, you're supposed to let the operating system along with applications installed on the system make any and all changes to the Registry.

Linux, on the other hand, doesn't use a central database of all system configuration information like the Windows Registry. Instead, all of your configuration information is stored in text files. Most of these files are stored in the /etc directory in your Linux file system.

Instead of discouraging you from manually editing these configuration files, as Windows does with the Registry, Linux *expects* you to know how to edit these files to customize the way your system runs. Therefore, you must know how to use Linux text editors to manage your system.

The Role and Function of the vi Text Editor

At this point, you may be thinking, "I know how to use text editors on other operating systems. I can use Notepad on Windows. Why are you devoting an entire chapter to text editors in this book?" There are two reasons:

- Knowing how to use a text editor is absolutely critical to being able to manage a Linux system. If you can't use a text editor, you will struggle with the topics presented throughout the rest of this book.

- Linux editors, frankly, are difficult for most new users to learn how to use, especially if you're coming from a Windows background.

 EXAM TIP For your Linux+ and LPIC-1 exams, you need to be familiar with only the vi text editor. Therefore, you should pay special attention to vi. You need to be very familiar with how to open a file in vi, edit it, and save your changes.

Therefore, in this chapter, we're going to spend a significant amount of time learning how to use a variety of Linux text-editing tools. Be aware, however, that front ends are frequently available that allow you to make changes to your configuration files without directly editing a configuration file with a text editor. One of the best front ends currently available, in my opinion, is Yet another Setup Tool (YaST), which is installed with openSUSE Linux. The YaST front end is shown in Figure 3-1.

Using YaST, you can install software, manage hardware settings, partition hard drives, configure bootloaders, configure network boards, configure users and groups, and configure settings for the services running on your system.

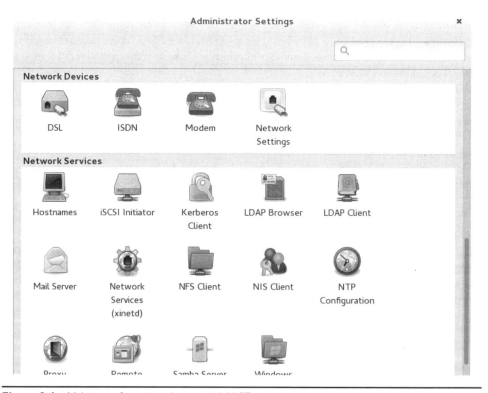

Figure 3-1 Making configuration changes with YaST

Many other distributions also use configuration front ends. For example, Fedora provides several different utilities that can be used to configure system settings, network settings, services, and users.

Admittedly, I like using these graphical front ends. In the early days of Linux, however, these tools didn't exist. Every configuration change made had to be done with a text editor. As these tools have matured and become more pervasive, more and more Linux administrators are starting to use them as an alternative to manually editing configuration files.

Why, then, are we spending an entire chapter discussing text manipulation tools? The reason is twofold:

- The Linux+ and LPIC-1 exams don't cover these graphical configuration utilities. If you want to pass these exams, you've got to be familiar with the text-based configuration files and the text editors used to manage them.

- Most Linux administrators use graphical front ends only for convenience. They don't rely on them. In other words, a good Linux admin should be intimately familiar with the configuration text files behind the graphical interface, not just with the interface itself.

With this in mind, let's dig in and start learning about text editors. For your Linux+ and LPIC-1 exams, you need to be familiar with the vi text editor. The vi editor is a very basic program that can be used to edit text files on a Linux system. The vi editor has been around for quite some time, and I dare say that it is one of the more widely used text editors by Linux administrators.

There are actually two versions of vi. The older version is called simply vi. The newer version is called vim (Vi IMproved). On older systems, you may be actually using vi when you enter **vi** at a shell prompt. However, on most modern Linux distributions, you are probably using the newer vim version of vi.

The executable for the vi program is a file on your system's hard drive called vim. On most distributions, the vim executable is located in the /bin directory. A symbolic link file named vi is placed in your /usr/bin directory that points to the /bin/vim executable, which is shown here:

```
openSUSE:/usr/bin # ls -al vi*
lrwxrwxrwx 1 root root      8 Nov  6  2013 vi -> /bin/vim
lrwxrwxrwx 1 root root      3 Nov  6  2013 view -> vim
lrwxrwxrwx 1 root root      8 Nov  6  2013 vim -> /bin/vim
lrwxrwxrwx 1 root root      3 Nov  6  2013 vimdiff -> vim
```

Notice that there is also a file named vim in /usr/bin that is only a symbolic link that points to the /bin/vim executable file.

NOTE A *symbolic link* is a shortcut file that points to another file elsewhere in the file system. We'll discuss symbolic links in depth in Chapter 4.

The result is that no matter what command you type at the shell prompt (**vi** or **vim**), the vim editor is loaded. For example, in Figure 3-2, the vi command has been entered at a shell prompt of a Fedora system. Notice, however, that the vim editor has been loaded, as shown in the welcome screen.

With this in mind, let's discuss how to edit text files in vi.

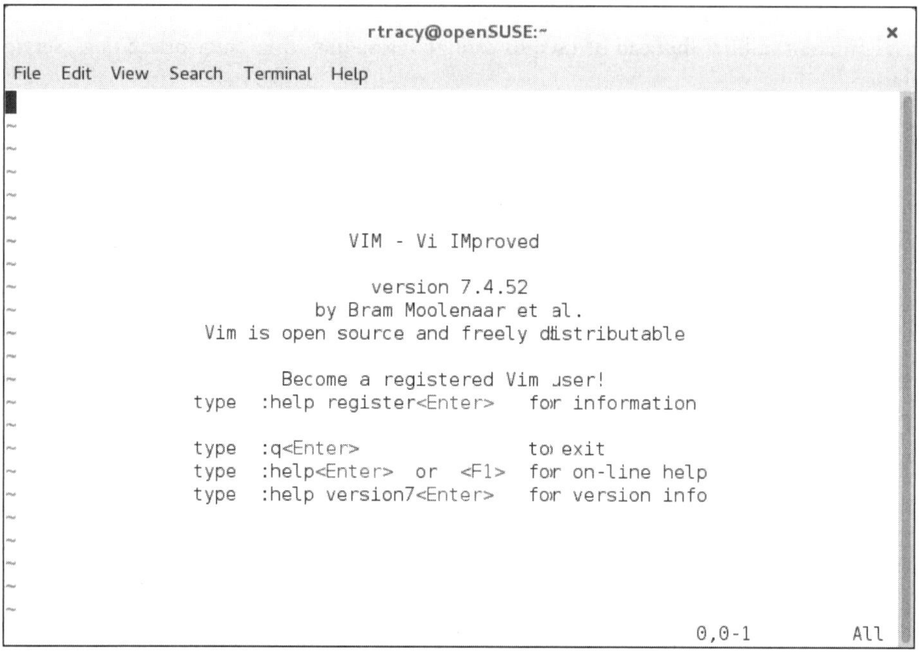

```
                          rtracy@openSUSE:~                              ×

 File   Edit   View   Search   Terminal   Help
█
~
~
~
~
~
~
~
~                       VIM - Vi IMproved
~
~                          version 7.4.52
~                      by Bram Moolenaar et al.
~             Vim is open source and freely distributable
~
~                   Become a registered Vim user!
~          type  :help register<Enter>    for information
~
~          type  :q<Enter>                to exit
~          type  :help<Enter>  or  <F1>   for on-line help
~          type  :help version7<Enter>    for version info
~
~
~
~
~
~
~
~
~
~
~                                           0,0-1          All
```

Figure 3-2   Using vim

Editing Text Files in vi

The first time you run vi, you'll notice right away that its user interface is very different than what you may be used to with other text editors. To familiarize you with vi, we'll discuss the following topics here:

- Opening files in vi
- The vi modes
- Working in insert mode
- Working in command-line mode
- Working in command mode

Opening Files in vi

To open a file from the shell prompt to manipulate in vi, simply enter **vi** *filename*. For example, suppose there is a file named myfile.txt in your user's home directory. If the file resides in the current directory, you can simply enter **vi myfile.txt** at the shell prompt to load this file into the vi editor. If the file resides in a directory other than the current directory, you then need to include the full path to the file. For example, if your current directory is /tmp and you need to open the /home/rtracy/myfile.txt file in vi, you would enter **vi /home/rtracy/myfile.txt** at the shell prompt.

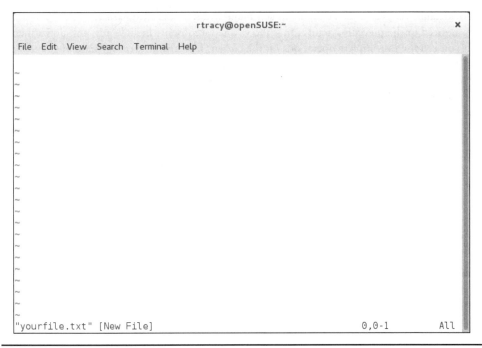

Figure 3-3 Creating a new file with vi

It's also possible to create a new text file using vi. To do this, simply enter **vi** followed by the name of the file you wish to create at the shell prompt. If you don't include a path with the filename, the file will be created in the current directory. If you specify a path, the file will be created in that directory.

For example, in Figure 3-3, the current directory is /home/rtracy and the command **vi yourfile .txt** has been entered at the shell prompt. Notice that a blank file has been opened in the vi editor interface, as indicated by the "[New File]" text at the bottom of the screen. It's important to note that when you're creating a new file with vi, the file isn't actually created on disk until you save the file. Until then, all the lines of text you enter in the vi interface are saved only in a memory buffer. If you don't save the file, you will lose it!

Now, let's discuss vi modes.

The vi Modes

So far, so good, right? Most of the students I teach vi to can handle opening a file in vi or creating a new file. However, once the file is opened, things start to get a little confusing. That's because vi uses four different operating modes:

- Command mode
- Command-line mode
- Insert mode
- Replace mode

By default, vi opens or creates a file in command (sometimes called *normal*) mode. You probably noticed in the preceding figures that the vi interface doesn't include any pull-down menus that you can use to complete operations on the current file, such as writing, searching, and closing. Instead, you must use commands in command (and command-line) mode to accomplish these tasks.

The confusing part for most of my students is the fact that, while in command or command-line mode, you can't actually edit the file! Unless you happen to hit the right key, nothing happens on the screen if you try to change the text of the file. To do this, you must first enter insert mode. To enter insert mode, you can press any one of the following keys on the keyboard:

- I
- INSERT
- S
- O
- A

After pressing one of these keys, you can then actually edit the text of the file. You can tell you're in insert mode by the "--INSERT--" text displayed at the bottom of the vi interface. This is shown in Figure 3-4.

Pressing INSERT a second time will cause vi to switch to replace mode. Insert mode is analogous to using a word processor in insert mode. Any text you type is inserted wherever the cursor is located in the file. All text that may already exist after the cursor is moved down a space for each character typed.

Replace mode, on the other hand, is analogous to overtype mode. When you type in new characters, the new characters overwrite any existing characters. You can toggle back to insert mode by pressing INSERT again.

While in insert mode, you can add text, change text, or delete text from the file. However, you can't perform any file operations. For example, if you make changes to a file and want to save them, you can't do so while in insert mode. To do this, you must first switch back to command mode. This is done by pressing ESC. In Figure 3-5, we've switched from insert mode back into command mode by pressing ESC.

In command mode, you can enter a variety of different commands to delete lines of text or search the file for particular words. You can also enter command mode, where you can save the current file or exit the editor. We'll review these commands later in this section. To switch back to insert mode, just press I, INSERT, or S.

```
~
~
~
-- INSERT --                                               0,1              All
```

Figure 3-4 The vi editor in insert mode

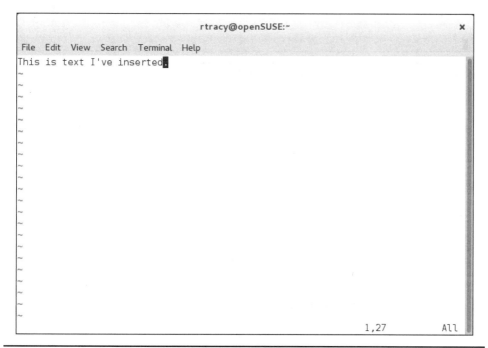

Figure 3-5 Switching back to command mode in vi

Now that you know how to open a file in vi and how to switch between modes, let's discuss how you edit text in insert mode.

Working in Insert Mode

Once you have opened a file in vi and entered insert mode, you can edit the text as you would with any other text editor. Note that, on the left side of the screen, you see several lines of tildes (~). These characters aren't actually in the file. These characters simply indicate that these lines don't exist in the file. After adding lines to the file, you'll see that the tildes disappear one at a time.

You can navigate around to different insertion points in the file by pressing the arrow keys as well as the PAGE UP, PAGE DOWN, HOME, and END keys. You can add text by simply typing characters on the keyboard. You can remove text by pressing DELETE or BACKSPACE.

Once you're done editing the text, you can then switch back to command mode by pressing ESC. From command mode, you can also enter command-line mode. Let's discuss what you can do in command-line mode next.

Working in Command-Line Mode

As we discussed earlier, the vi editor doesn't provide menus to accomplish common file tasks. Instead, you have to enter commands in command-line mode. In this topic, we're going to review some of the commands you can use and what they do.

Figure 3-6 The vi command-line mode command prompt

To enter command-line mode in vi, you must first enter command mode (if you were previously in insert mode) and then enter a colon (:). When you do, a command prompt is displayed at the bottom of the screen, as shown in Figure 3-6.

You can then enter commands at this prompt to accomplish file-related tasks. Obviously, one of the most important tasks you'll need to complete in command mode is to write the file to disk. This is done by entering **w** at the command prompt. Be sure to press ENTER after entering the command. After entering **w** at the command prompt, you'll see a message at the bottom of the screen indicating that the file has been written to disk, as shown in this example:

```
"yourfile.txt" [New] 1L, 28C written                    1,26            All
```

Entering **w** *filename* at the command prompt will write the file to a different filename. You can also enter these other commands at the command-line prompt:

- **exit** Writes the current file and then closes vi.

- **wq** Also writes the current file to disk and closes vi.

- **q** Closes vi without saving the current file. This can be used only if the file hasn't been changed. If the file has been changed, you must enter **q!**.

- **w!** Overwrites the current file.

- **e!** Forgets changes since the last write.

Another helpful feature of the vi editor is that it provides a very useful syntax checker. This feature can be a real lifesaver when you're writing scripts or editing a configuration file. There's nothing more frustrating than having a script or daemon not work because you forgot a semicolon or closing parenthesis somewhere. The syntax checker can be enabled or disabled using the syntax command-line command. Press ESC to enter command mode, and then enter **:syntax on | off**. For example, to enable the syntax checker, you would enter the following:

```
:syntax on
```

When you do, different elements in the script or configuration file are denoted with different colors. If you make a syntax error, the mistake will be highlighted with an alternate color, making it easy for you to spot. An example of using the vi syntax checker while editing a daemon's configuration file is shown in Figure 3-7.

In addition to commands that are entered at the command-line prompt, you can also enter commands in command mode. Let's discuss these commands next.

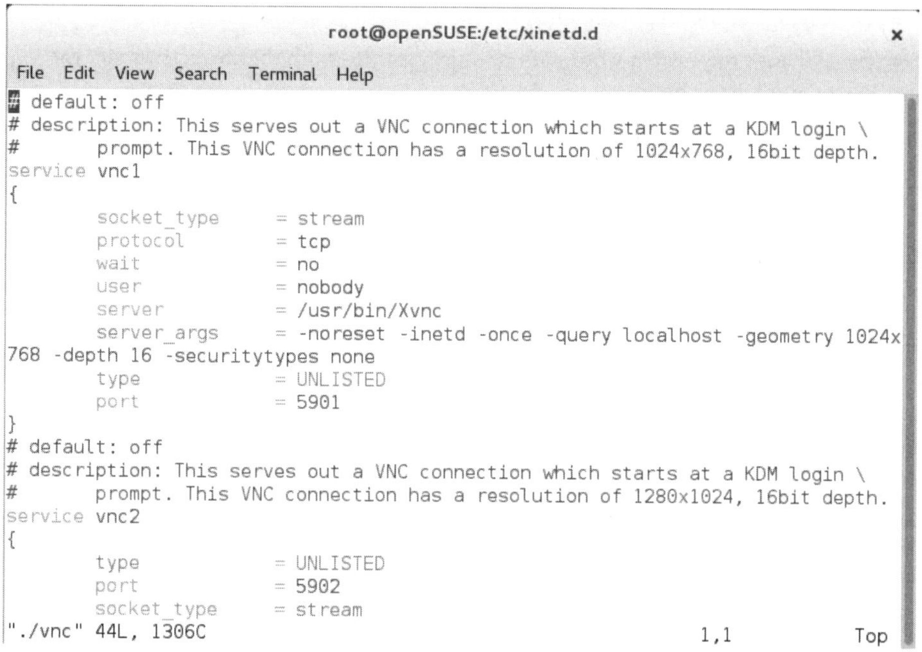

```
                        root@openSUSE:/etc/xinetd.d                          x

File  Edit  View  Search  Terminal  Help
# default: off
# description: This serves out a VNC connection which starts at a KDM login \
#       prompt. This VNC connection has a resolution of 1024x768, 16bit depth.
service vnc1
{
        socket_type     = stream
        protocol        = tcp
        wait            = no
        user            = nobody
        server          = /usr/bin/Xvnc
        server_args     = -noreset -inetd -once -query localhost -geometry 1024x
768 -depth 16 -securitytypes none
        type            = UNLISTED
        port            = 5901
}
# default: off
# description: This serves out a VNC connection which starts at a KDM login \
#       prompt. This VNC connection has a resolution of 1280x1024, 16bit depth.
service vnc2
{
        type            = UNLISTED
        port            = 5902
        socket_type     = stream
"./vnc" 44L, 1306C                                      1,1              Top
```

Figure 3-7   Using the vi syntax checker

Working in Command Mode

Command-mode commands aren't entered at the command prompt. Instead, these commands are entered *without* entering a colon (:) first. If you are in insert mode, press ESC to return to command mode. Then you can enter the following commands:

- **dw**   Deletes the word that comes immediately after the cursor, including the space following the word. The text is saved in a memory buffer.

- **de**   Deletes the word that comes immediately after the cursor, not including the space. The text is saved in a memory buffer.

- **d$**   Deletes from the insertion point to the end of the line. The text is saved in a memory buffer.

- **dd**   Deletes the entire current line. The text is saved in a memory buffer.

- **p**   Inserts the text deleted in the last deletion operation after the current cursor location.

- **u**   Undoes the last action.

- **D**   Deletes the rest of the current line from the cursor position.

- **yy**   Copies the line in which the cursor is located to the buffer.

- **a**   Append after cursor.

- **A**   Append after line.

- **C**   Change to the end of the line.

- **cw**   Change the current word with new text, starting with the character under the cursor, until ESC is hit.

- **cc**   Change the whole line.

- **ZZ**   Saves the current file and ends vi.

- **h**   Moves the cursor left one character.

- **j**   Moves the cursor down one line.

- **k**   Moves the cursor up one line.

- **l**   Moves the cursor right one character.

- **0**   Moves the cursor to the start of the current line.

- **CTRL-G**   Displays a status line at the bottom of the interface. This displays the name of the file, the status of the file, the total number of lines in the file, and the current cursor location. The result is shown in this example:

  ```
  "yourfile.txt" [Modified] 2 lines --100%--                    2,29          All
  ```

- **/search_term**   Searches for the next instance of the term specified. For example, entering **/init** searches for the next instance of the text "init" after the cursor. Pressing N after executing a search will search for the next instance of the search term. In Figure 3-8, the **/5901** command has been entered while in command mode. The first instance of 5901 has been highlighted as a result.

- **?/search_term**   Searches for the previous instance of the term specified.

```
                          root@openSUSE:/etc/xinetd.d                              ✕

 File  Edit  View  Search  Terminal  Help
# default: off
# description: This serves out a VNC connection which starts at a KDM login \
#        prompt. This VNC connection has a resolution of 1024x768, 16bit depth.
service vnc1
{
        socket_type      = stream
        protocol         = tcp
        wait             = no
        user             = nobody
        server           = /usr/bin/Xvnc
        server_args      = -noreset -inetd -once -query localhost -geometry 1024x
768 -depth 16 -securitytypes none
        type             = UNLISTED
        port             = 5901
}
# default: off
# description: This serves out a VNC connection which starts at a KDM login \
#        prompt. This VNC connection has a resolution of 1280x1024, 16bit depth.
service vnc2
{
        type             = UNLISTED
        port             = 5902
        socket_type      = stream
/5901                                                13,10-27        Top
```

Figure 3-8   Searching for text in vi

As you can see, vi is a simple, yet fairly powerful text editor. The only complaint I have about vi is that its user interface can be difficult to learn. However, once you've used vi for a while, it will become second nature to you. Therefore, let's spend some time practicing with vi in the following exercise.

Exercise 3-1: Using the vi Editor

In this exercise, you will practice using the vi editor to create and manipulate text files. You can perform this exercise using the virtual machine that comes with this book. Run snapshot 3-1 for the correctly configured environment.

 VIDEO   Please watch the Exercise 3-1 video for a demonstration on how to perform this task.

Complete the following:

1. If not already done, boot your Linux system and log in as **student** with a password of **student**.

2. If necessary, open a terminal session.

3. The current directory should be your user's home directory. You can check this by entering **pwd** at the shell prompt. In this example, the user account is named rtracy, so the current directory is displayed as /home/rtracy:

    ```
    rtracy@openSUSE:~> pwd
    /home/rtracy
    ```

4. At the shell prompt, enter **vi test.txt**. The vi editor should run with test.txt open as a new file.

5. Press the INSERT key on your keyboard. You should now be in insert mode.

6. Enter the following text in the file:

    ```
    Usu agam legere delicata ut, per democritum scriptorem an. Nec
    te zzril possim tincidunt, at qui probo mucius quberqren. Ea mei
    paulo cetero oportere, at pertinax liberavisse pri.
    ```

7. Save your file by completing the following:

    a. Press ESC to return to command mode.

    b. Enter **:w**. You should see a message indicating that the file was written.

8. Exit vi by entering **:exit**.

9. Reload test.txt in vi by entering **vi test.txt** at the shell prompt.

10. Display the status line by pressing CTRL-G while in command mode.

11. Use the arrow keys to move the cursor to the beginning of the first word in the first line of the file.

12. Search for all occurrences of the text "at" by completing the following:

   a. While in command mode, enter **/at**. The first instance should be highlighted.

   b. Find the next instance by pressing the N key.

   c. Find the remaining instance by pressing N until you reach the end of the file.

13. Practice deleting text by doing the following:

   a. While in command mode, use the arrow keys to place the cursor on the first letter of the word *legere.*

   b. Delete the word *legere* and the space that follows it by pressing **dw**.

   c. Use the arrow keys to move the cursor to the period at the end of the last line.

   d. Put the contents of the memory buffer after the period by entering **p**.

14. Exit the file without saving your changes by entering **:q!**.

You now have sufficient skills to use vi to manage a typical Linux system!

Chapter Review

In this chapter, you learned how to use the vi text editor. I first emphasized the important role text editors play in Linux system management. Unlike other operating systems that use a database to store system and application settings, Linux stores this information in text files. Therefore, to configure a Linux system, you need to know how to edit these files.

Normally we wouldn't spend much time learning how to use text editors. However, because the vi text editor is a little harder to use than text editors on other operating systems, we spent some extra time learning how to operate it. I pointed out that there are a variety of graphical front ends now available to make system-configuration tasks easier. However, I also pointed out that a good system administrator needs to understand the underlying configuration files being manipulated by these utilities. To do that, you need to know how to use a text editor.

The most commonly used Linux text editor (and the one you will be tested on in the Linux+ and LPIC-1 exams) is the vi editor. Although vi is a relatively simple editor, it is small, it doesn't require a graphical environment, and it can fit on a floppy diskette. This makes it ideal for use in emergency repair situations when you need to boot a malfunctioning system from a floppy.

To run vi, simply enter **vi** at a shell prompt. To run vi and load a file, enter **vi** *filename* at a shell prompt. If the filename you specify doesn't exist, vi will create a new file for you.

I then discussed the four different modes that vi can operate in. In command mode, you can't directly edit the text of the file. To do this, you need to switch to insert mode or replace mode by pressing the INSERT, s, o, or i key. To return to command mode, you just press the ESC key. Once in insert mode or replace mode, you can edit the text file just as you would with most typical word processors.

I then discussed the commands you can enter to perform file-related operations in command-line mode. To enter command-line mode, you first switch to command mode (if necessary) and then enter a colon (:). This causes a command-line prompt to be displayed that you can use to enter vi commands, including the following:

- **w**   Writes the current file to disk.
- **exit**   Writes the current file to disk and then closes vi.
- **wq**   Also writes the current file to disk and closes vi.
- **q**   Closes vi without saving the current file.
- **q!**   Closes vi without saving the current file, even if the file has been modified.
- **w!**   Overwrites the current file.
- **e!**   Forgets changes since the last write.

We then discussed the text-manipulation commands that you can enter in command mode. These commands are entered without entering a colon (:). You can enter the following:

- **dw**   Deletes the word that comes immediately after the cursor, including the space following the word.
- **de**   Deletes the word that comes immediately after the cursor, but not the following space.
- **d$**   Deletes from the insertion point to the end of the line.
- **dd**   Deletes the entire current line.
- **p**   Inserts deleted text after the current cursor location.
- **u**   Undoes the last action.
- **/term**   Searches for the specified term in the file.
- **D**   Deletes the rest of the current line from the cursor position.
- **yy**   Copies the line in which the cursor is located to the buffer.
- **a**   Append after cursor.
- **A**   Append after line.
- **C**   Change to the end of the line.
- **cc**   Change the whole line.
- **ZZ**   Saves the current file and ends vi.
- **h**   Moves the cursor left one character.
- **j**   Moves the cursor down one line.
- **k**   Moves the cursor up one line.
- **l**   Moves the cursor right one character.
- **0**   Moves the cursor to the start of the current line.

Accelerated Review

- You must be able to use a text editor to manage a Linux system.

- Linux uses text files to store operating system and application-configuration settings.

- Most of your configuration files reside in /etc.

- Many graphical configuration utilities are now available for most Linux distributions; however, you still need to be familiar with manually editing configuration files with a text editor.

- The vi editor is one of the most commonly used Linux text editors.

- The older version of vi was called *vi*; the newest version is called *vim* (Vi IMproved).

- You can open a file with vi by entering **vi *filename***. If the file doesn't exist, a new file will be created.

- The vi editor opens in command mode by default.

- You can't directly edit files in vi when you are in command mode.

- To switch to insert mode, press I, S, or INSERT.

- In insert mode, you can directly edit the text of a file.

- Pressing INSERT while in insert mode will cause vi to switch to replace mode.

- To switch back to command mode, press ESC.

- From within command mode, you can enter a colon (:) to switch to command-line mode.

- In command-line mode, you can enter file-related commands:

  - Entering **:w** will write the current file to disk.

  - Entering **:exit** will write the current file to disk and exit vi.

  - Entering **:q** will exit vi.

  - Entering **:q!** will exit vi without saving changes to a modified file.

- You can enter text-manipulation commands from within command mode in vi:

  - Entering **dw** deletes the word that comes immediately after the cursor, including the space following the word.

  - Entering **de** deletes the word that comes immediately after the cursor, not including the space.

  - Entering **d$** deletes from the insertion point to the end of the line.

  - Entering **dd** deletes the entire current line.

  - Entering **p** inserts the text deleted in the last deletion operation after the cursor.

  - Entering **u** undoes the last action.

- Pressing CTRL-G displays a status line at the bottom of the interface.

- Entering **/*search_term*** or ?**search_term** searches for the term specified.

Questions

1. How are operating system and application configuration parameters stored on a Linux system?

    A. In text files

    B. In the Registry

    C. In .ini files

    D. In the system database

2. Where are most configuration files stored in the Linux file system?

    A. /boot

    B. /var

    C. /usr

    D. /etc

3. Where can you find the vi symbolic link file on most Linux distributions?

    A. /usr/bin

    B. /usr

    C. /sys

    D. /sbin

4. Which command-line command can be used to enable syntax checking of a script while editing it in the vi editor?

    A. :syntax_checking on

    B. :syntax=enabled

    C. :syntax=script

    D. :syntax on

5. You have a terminal window open on your Linux system, and the current directory is /tmp. You need to use vi to edit a text file named vnc in the /etc/xinetd.d directory on your system. Which of the following commands will do this?

    A. vi vnc

    B. vi /tmp/vnc

    C. vi /etc/xinetd.d/vnc

    D. vi /etc/xinetd.d

6. You have a terminal window open on your Linux system, and the current directory is your user's home directory. You need to create a new file in your home directory named resources.txt using vi. Which of the following commands will do this?

    A. vi resources.txt –new

    B. vi resources

    C. vi ~/resources

    D. vi resources.txt

7. Which mode does vi open in by default?

   A. Command-line mode

   B. Insert mode

   C. Command mode

   D. Replace mode

8. You've opened a text file named list.txt in vi. You move the cursor using the arrow keys to the point in the file where you need to make several changes. You try to type, but nothing happens. Why is this happening?

   A. The vi editor is in insert mode. You need to switch to command mode.

   B. The vi editor is in command mode. You need to switch to insert mode.

   C. The vi editor is in insert mode. You need to switch to replace mode.

   D. The text file is corrupt.

9. Which keystroke will switch vi from command mode to insert mode? (Choose two.)

   A. DELETE

   B. ESC

   C. INSERT

   D. S

   E. FI

10. You're using vi to edit a text file in insert mode. Because of the nature of the changes you're making to the file, you need to switch to replace mode. Which keystroke will do this?

    A. ESC

    B. CTRL-X CTRL-R

    C. :

    D. INSERT

11. You're using vi to edit a file in insert mode. You need to switch back to command mode. Which keystroke will do this?

    A. INSERT

    B. :

    C. ESC

    D. BACKSPACE

12. You're using vi to edit a file in command mode. You try to use the BACKSPACE key to delete a word, but nothing happens. What's wrong with the system?

    A. You need to switch to normal mode.

    B. You need to press CTRL-BACKSPACE.

    C. Nothing is wrong. BACKSPACE doesn't work in command mode.

    D. You need to switch to command-line mode.

13. You've created a new file using vi and now need to save the file without exiting the editor. Which command will do this?

   A. :s

   B. :w

   C. :save

   D. :exit

14. You've created a new file using vi and need to save the file to disk and exit the program. Which command will do this? (Choose two.)

   A. :w

   B. :e!

   C. :wq

   D. :exit

   E. :q

15. You've made several changes to a configuration file using vi. You realize that you've made a myriad of mistakes and want to quit without saving the changes so that you can start over. Which command will do this?

   A. :q!

   B. :exit

   C. :q

   D. :exit!

16. You're working with a file in vi in command mode. You locate a word in the file that needs to be deleted and place your cursor at the beginning of that word. Which command will delete this word without deleting the space that follows the word?

   A. dw

   B. de

   C. d$

   D. dd

17. You're viewing a configuration file in vi in command mode. You need to locate a directive named **server** in the file. However, the file is very long and you don't want to scan through it line by line. What command can you use in command mode to search for this term?

   A. /server

   B. search=server

   C. /"server"

   D. find "server"

Answers

1. **A.** Linux uses text files to store configuration parameters for both the operating system and applications or services running on the system.

2. **D.** Most Linux configuration files are stored in the /etc directory or in a subdirectory of /etc.

3. **A.** Depending on your distribution, either the vi program itself or a symbolic link to the vim program will be stored in /usr/bin.

4. **D.** The **:syntax on** command is used to turn syntax checking on in the vi editor.

5. **C.** Because the file to be loaded doesn't reside in the current directory, you have to provide the full path to the file along with its filename when starting vi.

6. **D.** Because you haven't specified a path, vi will create the file in the current directory, which is what you want.

7. **C.** By default, vi opens in command mode.

8. **B.** The vi editor opens by default in command mode. You must press INSERT to switch to insert mode to start editing the file.

9. **C, D.** Pressing INSERT or s switches vi from command mode to insert mode.

10. **D.** Pressing INSERT while in insert mode will switch vi to replace mode.

11. **C.** Pressing ESC while in insert mode switches vi to command mode.

12. **C.** The BACKSPACE key doesn't work in command mode. You must first switch to insert or replace mode.

13. **B.** Entering **:w** will save the current memory buffer to disk without exiting the editor.

14. **C, D.** Entering **:exit** will cause vi to save the current file and exit the program, as will entering **:wq**.

15. **A.** Entering **:q!** will exit vi without saving changes to the current file.

16. **B.** Entering **de** in command mode will cause vi to delete the word without deleting the space that follows the word.

17. **A.** Entering **/server** in command mode will search for the expression "server" in the file.

Managing Linux Files and Directories

In this chapter, you will learn about:

- Understanding Linux file systems and the Filesystem Hierarchy Standard (FHS)
- Finding files in the Linux file system
- Managing directories from the command line
- Managing files from the command line
- Working with link files
- Finding content within files

It's time to dig in and start working with Linux files and directories! If you're coming to Linux from a Windows background, this chapter may be challenging for you. The Linux file system is similar to the file systems used by other operating systems in many ways, but it is radically different in many others. My experience has been that there are just enough similarities to give you a false sense of security when you initially start working with the file system. Then, as you dig deeper and start looking at more advanced tasks, the frustration starts.

Hopefully, I can make things as easy to understand as possible as we work through this chapter. If I could emphasize one thing that will make your life easier, it would be to remember that Linux file and directory names are case sensitive! New Linux users tend to really struggle with this aspect of the Linux file system. When you see a command or filename in an example or exercise in this book, remember that you must use the correct case; otherwise, you won't get the same results!

EXAM TIP   Be prepared to be tested heavily on this chapter in your LPIC-1/ Linux+ exam. When you take your exam, you may be presented with a hypothetical scenario and asked to supply the correct command to complete the required task. You must be familiar enough with the contents of this chapter to respond instantly. The only way to do this is to practice, practice, practice!

Understanding Linux File Systems and the Filesystem Hierarchy Standard (FHS)

In this part of the chapter, we're going to discuss the Linux file system in general. Specifically, we're going to review the following:

- The role of the Linux file system
- The hierarchical structure of the Linux file system
- Linux file types

Let's begin by discussing the role of the file system.

The Role of the Linux File System

So what exactly is the role of the file system? On a Linux system (or any other operating system, for that matter) the file system stores information on a storage device in such a manner that

- data can be saved in a persistent manner,
- data is organized and can be easily located,
- data can be quickly retrieved for use at a later point in time, and
- data integrity is preserved.

In other words, if you save a file to a storage device, you should be able to find it later on and retrieve it, all the while assured that its contents will be exactly the same as when it was saved. It doesn't matter whether you're saving data to a floppy diskette, a hard drive, or a USB drive; the goals are the same. To accomplish this, you must use some type of file system to manage stored data.

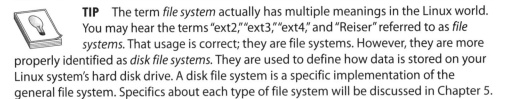

TIP   The term *file system* actually has multiple meanings in the Linux world. You may hear the terms "ext2," "ext3," "ext4," and "Reiser" referred to as *file systems*. That usage is correct; they are file systems. However, they are more properly identified as *disk file systems*. They are used to define how data is stored on your Linux system's hard disk drive. A disk file system is a specific implementation of the general file system. Specifics about each type of file system will be discussed in Chapter 5.

Let's review how the Linux file system organizes the data to make it easily locatable and retrievable using the Filesystem Hierarchy Standard (FHS).

The Hierarchical Structure of the Linux File System

The Linux file system uses a hierarchical structure to organize and store data. This is shown in Figure 4-1.

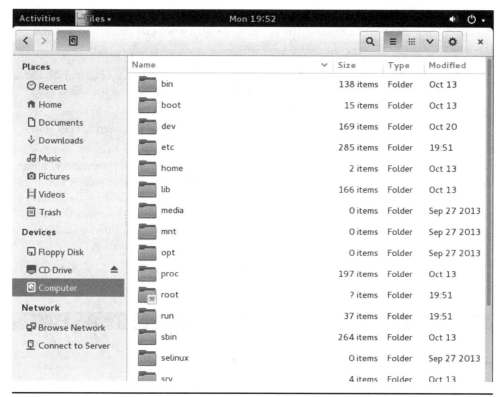

Figure 4-1   The hierarchical structure of the Linux file system

The topmost directory in the structure is the / directory, also called the *root* directory, which by the way has nothing to do with your root user account. It simply indicates that this is the topmost directory (the "root") of your hierarchical file system tree.

Beneath the root directory are many subdirectories. Specifications for how these directories are to be named are contained in the Filesystem Hierarchy Standard (FHS). The FHS provides Linux software developers and system administrators with a standard directory structure for the file system, ensuring consistency between systems and distributions. Can you imagine the mess if every distribution used its own proprietary file system structure? What a disaster! You wouldn't be able to find anything.

NOTE   You can view more information about the FHS at www.pathname .com/fhs/.

Fortunately, we have the FHS to keep everyone in line. The FHS defines the directories that should appear under the root directory (/) as well as the directories that should appear under the /usr and /var directories. These include the following:

- **/bin** This directory contains the executable files necessary to manage and run the Linux system, including shells (such as bash) and file system management utilities such as cp and rm.

- **/boot** This directory contains your bootloader files, which are required to boot your system.

- **/dev** This directory contains special files that are used to represent the various hardware devices installed in the system. For example, the first hard disk drive in your system is called sda, the second is called sdb, and so on. The partitions on each drive are identified by an additional number added to the end of the disk filename. For example, the first partition on the first hard drive in the system is sda1, the second partition is sda2, and so on. The files that represent these devices are stored in /dev, as shown in Figure 4-2. Notice in the figure that two kinds of device files are stored in /dev:

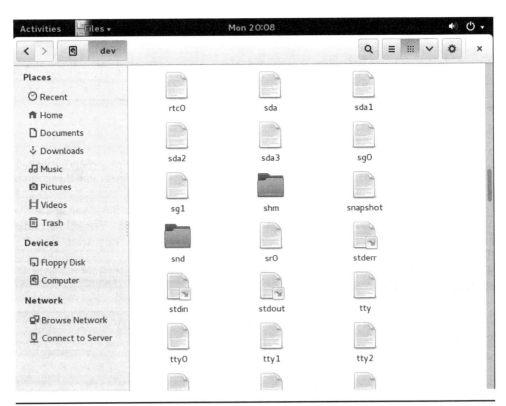

Figure 4-2 Addressing hardware devices with files in /dev

- **Character-oriented device files** These files are used for devices that send or receive data sequentially one character at a time, such as a printer, mouse, or tape drive. These devices usually don't support random access to the data they manage.

- **Block-oriented device files** These files are used for devices that manage data in blocks, such as floppy disks and hard drives. Block devices usually support random access to the data they manage.

Many types of hardware devices are represented by device files in /dev. A sampling is shown in Table 4-1. The key thing to understand is the fact that the physical hardware in a Linux system is addressed by applications and services running on the system through the files in /dev. Need to save a file to disk? It goes through the appropriate file in /dev. Need to send a print job to a printer? It goes through a file in /dev. Need to open a file from a DVD? It comes in through a file in /dev.

TIP Device files in /dev can also be used to access system resources that have no connection to any physical hardware device, such as random-number generators (/dev/random).

- **/etc** This directory contains text-based configuration files used by the system, as well as services running on the system. You can edit these files with a text editor to customize how Linux behaves. Some of the more important files in this directory include those shown in Table 4-2.

- **/home** This directory contains subdirectories that serve as home directories for each user account on your Linux system.

- **/lib** This directory contains code libraries used by programs in /bin and /sbin. Your kernel modules are also stored in the modules subdirectory of /lib.

- **/media** This directory is used by some Linux distributions (such as openSUSE and Fedora) to mount external devices, including optical drives and USB drives.

- **/mnt** This directory is used by some Linux distributions to mount external devices, including optical drives and \USB drives. As with the /media directory on other distributions, a series of subdirectories are used to do this.

- **/opt** This directory contains files for some programs you install on the system.

- **/proc** This directory is a little different from the other directories in this list. /proc doesn't actually exist in the file system. Instead, it's a pseudo–file system that is dynamically created whenever it is accessed. It's used to access process and other system information from the Linux kernel.

Table 4-1

Hardware Represented by Files in /dev

Device	Device File in /dev
Floppy drive	/dev/fd0
Optical drive	/dev/scd0 or /dev/sr0
Serial port	/dev/ttyS0
Parallel port	/dev/lp0

File	Function
/etc/aliases	Contains a table used to redirect mail to local recipients.
/etc/exports	Configures file systems to be exported to remote NFS clients.
/etc/fstab	Lists the partitions and file systems that will be automatically mounted when the system boots.
/etc/ftpusers	Controls user access to the FTP service running on the system.
/etc/group	Contains local group definitions.
/etc/hosts	Contains a list of hostname-to–IP address mappings the system can use to resolve hostnames.
/etc/inittab	Contains configuration parameters for the init process.
/etc/init.d/	A subdirectory that contains startup scripts for services installed on the system. On a Fedora or Red Hat system, these are located in /etc/rc.d/init.d.
/etc/nsswitch.conf	Configures which services are to be used to resolve hostnames and to store users, groups, and passwords.
/etc/passwd	Contains your system user accounts.
/etc/resolv.conf	Specifies the DNS server and domain suffix used by the system.
/etc/services	Maps port numbers to named services on the system.
/etc/shadow	Contains encrypted passwords for your user accounts.
/etc/X11/	Contains X Window configuration files.

Table 4-2   Some of the Configuration Files in /etc

Within /proc are a number of different subdirectories, as shown in Figure 4-3. Notice that each of these subdirectories is identified with a number, not a name. These numbers correspond to the process ID (PID) number of the associated software process running on the system. In Figure 4-4, the top program is being run to display the running processes on the system.

The PID column, on the far-left side of the display, lists the PID number of each software process. The actual name of the command that was run to create the process is displayed in the far-right column of the display. For example, the process associated with the top program itself has a PID of 2632. Therefore, if you were to look in the /proc/2632 directory, you could view information about the top process running on the system, as shown in Figure 4-5.

- **/root**   This directory is the root user's home directory. Notice that it is located separately from the home directories for other users in /home.

- **/sbin**   This directory contains important system management and administration files, such as fdisk, fsck, ifconfig, init, mkfs, shutdown, and halt.

- **/srv**   This directory contains subdirectories where services running on the system (such as httpd and ftpd) save their files.

- **/sys**   This directory contains information about the hardware in your system.

- **/tmp**   This directory contains temporary files created by you or by the system.

```
                              root@openSUSE:/proc                              ✕

 File  Edit  View  Search  Terminal  Help
openSUSE:/proc # ls
1      1884  2035   2170   3      5411     dma            mpt
10     1889  2047   22     30     544      dri            mtrr
107    1892  2052   22640  30152  560      driver         net
108    1893  2054   23     310    6195     execdomains    pagetypeinfo
11     1896  2060   2412   311    6408     fb             partitions
12     1897  2063   2419   312    6410     filesystems    sched_debug
13     19    2064   25     31488  7        fs             schedstat
14     1917  20808  2518   31580  75       interrupts     scsi
15     1936  20839  255    32123  8        iomem          self
16     1939  20849  2579   32124  9        ioports        slabinfo
17     1940  2087   2580   32209  96       irq            softirqs
1704   1947  20876  26     35     97       kallsyms       stat
1709   1949  20877  2631   36     99       kcore          swaps
175    1958  20906  2632   3602   acpi     key-users      sys
176    1963  20953  2634   3620   asound   kmsg           sysrq-trigger
177    1967  20961  2655   38     buddyinfo kpagecount    sysvipc
18     1970  20976  26616  487    bus      kpageflags     timer_list
1807   1977  21     27     491    cgroups  latency_stats  timer_stats
1812   1979  21035  2704   492    cmdline  loadavg        tty
1815   1986  21036  2732   493    config.gz locks         uptime
1837   1990  2115   28     5      consoles mdstat         version
1838   2     212    2823   503    cpuinfo  meminfo        vmallocinfo
1840   20    21219  286    504    crypto   misc           vmstat
```

Figure 4-3 Subdirectories of /proc

```
                              root@openSUSE:/proc                              ✕

 File  Edit  View  Search  Terminal  Help
top - 20:22:29 up  5:18,  3 users,  load average: 0.07, 0.29, 0.38
Tasks: 136 total,   2 running, 134 sleeping,   0 stopped,   0 zombie
%Cpu(s):  9.0 us,  3.3 sy,  0.0 ni, 87.0 id,  0.7 wa,  0.0 hi,  0.0 si,  0.0 st
KiB Mem:   1025360 total,   904168 used,   121192 free,    42492 buffers
KiB Swap:  1541116 total,     6536 used,  1534580 free,   417624 cached

  PID USER      PR  NI    VIRT    RES    SHR S  %CPU  %MEM     TIME+ COMMAND
 1709 root      20   0   71896  20880   7684 S 5.956 2.036   0:45.51 Xorg
 1990 root      20   0  587376 225012  41092 S 4.633 21.94   1:07.18 gnome-she+
 2412 root      20   0  211400  25840  18468 S 0.993 2.520   0:08.47 nautilus
  544 root      20   0   41936   3236   2772 S 0.662 0.316   1:58.10 vmtoolsd
 2063 root      20   0   34968  14228  11660 S 0.331 1.388   0:05.16 vmtoolsd
 2518 root      20   0  157768  18044  12872 S 0.331 1.760   0:01.23 gnome-ter+
 2632 root      20   0    4888   1276    928 R 0.331 0.124   0:00.07 top
    1 root      20   0    6184   3156   2120 S 0.000 0.308   0:07.08 systemd
    2 root      20   0       0      0      0 S 0.000 0.000   0:00.07 kthreadd
    3 root      20   0       0      0      0 S 0.000 0.000   0:01.61 ksoftirqd+
    5 root       0 -20       0      0      0 S 0.000 0.000   0:00.00 kworker/0+
    7 root      rt   0       0      0      0 S 0.000 0.000   0:00.01 migration+
    8 root      -2   0       0      0      0 S 0.000 0.000   0:11.21 rcuc/0
    9 root      -2   0       0      0      0 S 0.000 0.000   0:00.00 rcub/0
   10 root      20   0       0      0      0 R 0.000 0.000   0:09.19 rcu_preem+
   11 root      20   0       0      0      0 S 0.000 0.000   0:00.00 rcu_bh
   12 root      20   0       0      0      0 S 0.000 0.000   0:00.00 rcu_sched
```

Figure 4-4 Using top to display running processes

```
openSUSE:/proc/2632 # ls
attr             cpuset   limits      ns              sched       syscall
autogroup        cwd      loginuid    numa_maps       schedstat   task
auxv             environ  maps        oom_adj         sessionid   wchan
cgroup           exe      mem         oom_score       smaps
clear_refs       fd       mountinfo   oom_score_adj   stack
cmdline          fdinfo   mounts      pagemap         stat
comm             io       mountstats  personality     statm
coredump_filter  latency  net         root            status
```

Figure 4-5   Viewing information about the top process in /proc

TIP   The system will periodically delete old files out of the /tmp directory. Don't save anything in /tmp that you want to keep!

- **/usr**   This directory contains application files. In fact, most of the application files used on your system are stored in a subdirectory of /usr. These subdirectories include those shown in Table 4-3.
- **/var**   This directory contains variable data, including your system log files. Some of the typical subdirectories contained in /var are shown in Table 4-4.

With this structure in mind, let's next discuss the types of files used by the Linux file system.

Types of Files Used by Linux

When working with Linux, you need to be aware of the fact that there are a number of different file types used by the file system. This is another area where the Linux file system differs significantly from the Windows file system. With a Windows file system you basically have two entry types in the file system:

- Directories
- Files

Granted, you can have normal files, hidden files, shortcut files, word processing files, executable files, and so on. However, these are all simple variations of the basic file type.

Subdirectory	Contents
bin	Most of your executable programs
lib	Library files
lib64	64-bit library files
local	Locally installed software that you created yourself (used to prevent it from being overwritten during a system update)
sbin	System administration programs
share	Documentation and man page files

Table 4-3   Subdirectories of /usr

Subdirectory	Contents
lib	Library files created by various services and applications running on the system
log	Log files from your system and from services running on the system
spool	Print queues

Table 4-4   Subdirectories of /var

On Linux, however, there are a variety of different file types used by the file system. These include the file types listed in Table 4-5.

With this introduction to the Linux file system in mind, you're ready to start learning how to complete common file system tasks. Just as with any other operating system, you need to be able to create, copy, and move files and directories in the Linux file system. In the next part of this chapter, we're going to spend some time reviewing how this is done.

If you have any experience working with the command line in other operating systems, you may be thinking that these tasks are trivial in nature. Believe it or not, these tasks can be difficult for many of my students when they are first learning how to use Linux. The key mistake I see is students trying to use Windows commands when working with the file system at the Linux shell prompt.

I even catch myself doing this on occasion. I was presenting a demo for students recently and needed to copy some files on a Linux system. Without thinking, I entered **copy** instead of **cp** at the shell prompt and, of course, it didn't work. Boy was I was red-faced! My students had a great time reminding me of my mistake for the rest of the class!

As with Windows, you can perform file system manipulation tasks either from the shell prompt or from within the Linux GUI. Many who are coming to Linux from a Windows background are tempted to perform these tasks solely using the GUI utilities provided with most distributions.

Although these graphical utilities are handy and easy to use, you still need to learn how to do these tasks from the shell prompt. I realize that this goes against standard practice with Windows systems. I've worked with many Windows users who don't know the command prompt even exists

File Type	Description
Regular files	These files are similar to those used by the file systems of other operating systems—for example, executable files, word processing files, images, text files, and so on.
Links	These files are pointers that point to other files in the file system.
FIFOs	FIFO stands for *First In, First Out*. These are special files used to move data from one running process on the system to another. A FIFO file is basically a queue where the first chunk of data added to the queue is the first chunk of data removed from the queue. Data can only move in one direction through a FIFO.
Sockets	Sockets are similar to FIFOs in that they are used to transfer information between processes. Unlike FIFOs, however, sockets can move data bidirectionally.

Table 4-5   Linux File Types

on their systems. With Linux, however, you need to first become proficient with shell commands and then use the GUI utilities for convenience. I say this for the following reasons:

- Most employers and coworkers won't take you seriously as a Linux administrator if you can't manage the system from the shell prompt. It just goes with the territory.

- Many Linux systems, especially those deployed as servers, don't run a GUI. Running a GUI environment requires a lot of CPU overhead. Many server admins prefer to allocate those CPU cycles to system services instead of moving the mouse cursor on the screen or running a screensaver. In this situation, you need to know how to do things from the shell prompt.

- You need to know how to complete these tasks from the shell prompt to pass your LPIC-1/Linux+ exam.

 EXAM TIP For your exam, you must be proficient with a large number of file system manipulation commands. You need to be able to navigate the file system, manage files and directories, run executable files, and search the file system from the shell prompt.

Let's begin by learning how to find files in the file system using shell prompt commands.

Finding Files in the Linux File System

One of the great weaknesses in my life is the fact that I have a terrible memory. You can call me on the phone and relate some bit of important information and I am pretty much guaranteed to forget what you told me by the time I hang up. This problem can be very embarrassing when I run into someone I've known and worked with for years and find myself unable to recall that person's name.

This fallibility, unfortunately, carries over into my work life. I can't tell you how many times I've created a file, saved it, and then promptly forgot where I saved it. To help people like me, Linux includes utilities that can be used to search for files in the file system. In this part of the chapter, you'll learn the following:

- Using find
- Using locate
- Using which
- Using whereis
- Using type

Let's begin by learning how to use the find utility.

Using find

The find utility is a fantastic tool that you can use to search the Linux file system. To use find, simply enter **find** *path* **–name** "*filename*" at the shell prompt. Replace *path* with the place in the file system where you want to start looking. Replace *filename* with the name of the file you want to search for.

TIP Don't forget to use quotation marks!

You can use regular expressions such as * to broaden your search results. For example, suppose you wanted to find all of the log files stored in your file system that have a .log extension. You could enter **find / –name "*.log"**. The find utility would then locate all files with an extension of .log starting in the root directory of the file system and searching all subdirectories. This is shown in Figure 4-6.

The find utility is flexible. You can also use the **–user** "*username*" option to search for files owned by a specific user, or use the **–size** "*size*" option to search for files of a specified size. You can use a + sign before the size value to search for files larger than the specified size, or a – sign before the size value to search for files smaller than the specified size. The find utility has many other options. You can use the man page for find to see everything it has to offer.

In addition to find, you can also use the locate utility to search for files in the file system.

Using locate

The locate utility functions in much the same manner as find. However, it has one distinct advantage over find. Here's the issue: whenever you run a search with find, it manually walks through each directory in the path you specify in the command looking for matching files. This process can take a really long time, especially if you're doing a top-down search from the root of the file system.

The locate utility, on the other hand, works in a much more efficient way. Instead of walking the file system each time you run a search, it builds an index of the files in the file system. Then, when you run a search, locate simply queries the index. It doesn't actually search the file system directly. The result is that locate runs *much* faster than find in most situations.

Figure 4-6
Using the find utility to search for files

```
openSUSE:/ # find / -name "*.log"
/root/.local/share/gvfs-metadata/home-80886715.log
/root/.local/share/gvfs-metadata/root-39c8511e.log
/root/.mozilla/firefox/c5h6kt54.default/marionette.log
/var/log/YaST2/mkinitrd.log
/var/log/YaST2/config_diff_2013_11_06.log
/var/log/YaST2/y2start.log
/var/log/YaST2/internet-test/ip_addr.log
/var/log/YaST2/internet-test/ip_route.log
/var/log/YaST2/internet-test/curl_0.log
/var/log/YaST2/config_diff_2014_10_13.log
/var/log/alternatives.log
/var/log/wpa_supplicant.log
/var/log/gdm/:0.log
/var/log/Xorg.0.log
/var/log/pbl.log
/var/log/boot.log
/var/log/pm-powersave.log
/home/rtracy/.local/share/gvfs-metadata/home-587e6e95.log
/home/rtracy/.local/share/gvfs-metadata/root-019127d2.log
```

To use locate, you must first install the findutils-locate package on your system. With the package installed, an index (named locatedb) of all the files in your file system will be created in /var/log. This index will be updated each day with the latest changes to the file system. However, you can also manually update the index using the **updatedb** command from the shell prompt. Be aware that updatedb does all the legwork for the locate utility; it can take some time to complete and will use up a lot of system resources in the process.

With the index updated, you can search for files by simply entering **locate** *filename* at the shell prompt. For example, if you wanted to search for a file named snmp.conf, you could enter **locate snmp.conf**, as shown here:

```
openSUSE:/ # locate snmp.conf
/etc/cups/snmp.conf
/usr/share/man/man5/cups-snmp.conf.5.gz
```

Notice that locate found two files that had the text string "snmp-.conf" somewhere in the filename.

 TIP The /etc/udatedb.conf file is used to configure the behavior of the updatedb utility. You can set the PRUNEFS variable in this file to the file system type(s) you don't want updatedb to scan. You can also set the PRUNEPATHS variable in this file to a list of directories in your file system you want updatedb to skip when scanning.

With this in mind, let's next discuss how to use which.

Using which

The which command is used to display the full path to a shell command or utility. For example, if you wanted to know the full path to the ls command, you would enter **which ls** at the shell prompt. When you do, the full path to ls is displayed on screen, as shown here:

```
openSUSE:/ # which ls
/bin/ls
```

In addition to which, you can also use whereis. Let's talk about how to use this utility next.

Using whereis

The whereis command locates the source code, binary files, and manuals pages for specified files. The **–b** option returns the location of the binaries for the specified command. The **–m** option returns the location of the command's manual pages. To see the location of the command's source code, use the **–s** option with the whereis command. If no option is used, all information is returned.

For example, if you enter **whereis –b ls** at the shell prompt, the location of the ls command's binary executable file is returned. An example is shown here:

```
openSUSE:/ # whereis -b ls
ls: /bin/ls
```

Likewise, entering the **whereis –m ls** command returns the location of the ls command's man page file, as shown next:

```
openSUSE:/ # whereis -m ls
ls: /usr/share/man/man1p/ls.1p.gz /usr/share/man/man1/ls.1.gz
```

Using type

The type command returns what type of command is executed when you enter it. The values returned will be one of the following:

- **A command that is hard-coded into the shell itself**   For example, the **cd** command is a built-in shell command:

  ```
  openSUSE:/ # type cdcd is a shell builtin
  ```

- **An external command that is called by the shell**   If the command has been run recently in the shell, the output of **type** says that the command is *hashed,* which indicates the location of the external command in the file system has been stored in the shell's hash table. If you run the same command again, the shell will execute it without searching for it in the directories in the PATH environment variable. An example is shown here:

  ```
  openSUSE:/ # type cat
  cat is hashed (/bin/cat)
  ```

- **An alias**   An alias is essentially a shortcut to another file in the Linux file system. Aliases are frequently used for commonly used commands, such as the ls command. This is shown in the following example:

  ```
  openSUSE:/ # type ls
  ls is aliased to 'ls $LS_OPTIONS'
  ```

- **A function**   The bash shell allows you to create new internal commands by defining your own shell functions.

You can also use the **–a** option with the type command. This option causes type to return all instances of the specified command in the file system. For example, entering the **type –a ip** command shows that there are two executables named ip:

```
openSUSE:/ # type -a ip
ip is /sbin/ip
ip is /bin/ip
```

Let's practice using Linux search tools in the following exercise.

Exercise 4-1: Using Linux Search Tools

In this exercise, you will practice using Linux search tools. You can perform this exercise using the virtual machine that comes with this book. Run snapshot 4-1 for the correctly configured environment.

VIDEO   Please watch the Exercise 4-1 video for a demonstration on how to perform this task.

Complete the following:

1. Verify that you are logged in to your Linux system as **student** with a password of **student**.

2. If necessary, open a terminal session.

3. Change to your root user account by entering **su –** at the shell prompt and entering a password of **student**.

4. Search for a file named inittab by entering **find / –name "resolv.conf"** at the shell prompt. Where is this file located?

5. Perform the same search using locate by entering **locate resolve.conf** at the shell prompt.

6. Find the location of the init executable by entering **which init** at the shell prompt. Where is it located?

7. Enter **whereis init** at the shell prompt. Where is the file that contains the manual sections for the init command located?

8. At the shell prompt, display the last few lines of your messages log file by entering **tail /var/log/messages**.

9. At the shell prompt, see if the tail command is now hashed by the shell session by entering **type tail**. Is it? What does this mean?

Managing Directories from the Command Line

Now that you understand how the Linux file system is structured as well as how to search for files, you're ready to start managing the file system. In this part of the chapter, we're going to focus on managing directories from the shell prompt. The following topics are addressed:

- Navigating the file system
- Viewing directory contents
- Creating new directories
- Copying, moving, and deleting directories

Let's begin by discussing how to navigate the file system from the shell prompt.

Navigating the File System

As you work with the Linux file system from the shell prompt, one of the most common tasks you will complete is to move around between the different directories on your storage devices. Your Linux system provides the following shell commands that you can use to do this:

- pwd
- cd

Let's start by learning how to use the pwd command.

Using the pwd Command

The pwd command is a relatively simple utility. The name of the command, *pwd*, stands for *Print Working Directory*. This command simply displays the current directory on the screen.

This utility can be useful if your shell profile hasn't been configured to display the current directory as a part of the shell prompt. To use pwd, simply enter **pwd** at the shell prompt, as shown here:

```
rtracy@openSUSE:~> pwd
/home/rtracy
```

In this example, you can see that the current directory is set to /home/rtracy.

 TIP The ~ character in the shell prompt points to the current user's home directory. Because I'm logged in as the rtracy user in the preceding example, ~ points to the /home/rtracy directory.

If you use the **–P** option with the pwd command, pwd will display the physical directory without symbolic links. We'll discuss link files later in this chapter.

At this point, you know how to identify what directory you're in. Frequently, you're going to need to change to a different directory in the file system. Let's discuss how to do this next.

Using the cd Command

The cd command is used from the Linux shell prompt to change directories in the file system. To use this command, simply enter **cd** followed by the name of the directory you want to switch to. There are two ways you can do this. If you enter **cd** and then the name of a directory *without* specifying the full path to the directory, cd will assume that the directory is a subdirectory of the current directory. In the example that follows, the **cd Documents** command has been issued:

```
rtracy@openSUSE:~> cd Documents/
rtracy@openSUSE:~/Documents>
```

Because the command was issued from /home/rtracy, cd changed directories to /home/rtracy/Documents. This is called using a *relative path*. The path specified with the command is relative to some other point in the file system—in this case, the /home/rtracy directory.

You can also use *absolute paths* with the cd command. When you use an absolute path, you specify the full path, starting from /, to the directory you want to change to, as in the following example:

```
rtracy@openSUSE:~> cd /var/log
rtracy@openSUSE:/var/log>
```

Because we specified an absolute path (/var/log), the cd command knew that the /var/log directory didn't exist in the current directory. Instead, the path was determined from the root directory (/) and the current directory was changed to it.

 TIP If you enter **cd** at the shell prompt without specifying a path, it will automatically change to the home directory of the currently logged-in user.

You can also use the cd command to move up the file system hierarchy. You can do this by entering **cd ..**, which will change the current directory to the next directory higher in the hierarchy. Consider the following example:

```
rtracy@openSUSE:/var/log> cd ..
rtracy@openSUSE:/var>
```

In this example, the **cd ..** command has been issued, changing from /var/log to the /var directory. To go up two directories, you can enter the cd ../.. command at the shell prompt:

```
rtracy@openSUSE:/var/log> cd ../..
rtracy@openSUSE:/>
```

 TIP You can also use the .. alias to move up one level in the hierarchy and the ... alias to move up two levels. Most distributions define these aliases automatically for you in one of your bash configuration files.

Let's next look at the ls command.

Viewing Directory Contents

To this point, you've learned how to view the current directory and change to other directories in the file system. Now you need to learn how to list the files and subdirectories that may exist within a directory. This is done using the ls command. If you enter **ls** at the shell prompt, the contents of the current directory are listed on the screen, as shown here:

```
rtracy@openSUSE:~> ls
bin       Documents  Music     Public        Templates  test.txt  words
Desktop   Downloads  Pictures  public_html   test2.txt  Videos    yourfile.txt
```

As with the cd command, you can also provide an absolute path when using ls. This will cause ls to display the contents of the directory you specify. Consider this example:

```
rtracy@openSUSE:~> ls /var/log
acpid       cups          mail            ntp                Xorg.0.log.old
apparmor    faillog       mail.err        pk_backend_zypp    YaST2
audit       firewall      mail.info       pm-powersave.log   zypp
boot.log    gdm           mail.warn       samba              zypper.log
boot.msg    krb5          messages        warn
boot.omsg   lastlog       NetworkManager  wtmp
ConsoleKit  localmessages news            Xorg.0.log
```

In this example, the **ls /var/log** command has been issued, causing the contents of /var/log to be displayed. When working with ls, you can use a variety of options to customize how it works. Here are some of these options:

- **−a** Displays all files, including hidden files. In the next example, the **ls −a** command has been issued in the /home/rtracy directory:

```
rtracy@openSUSE:~> ls -a
.                 .esd_auth         .inputrc          test2.txt
..                .fontconfig       .local            test.txt
.bash_history     .fonts            .mozilla          .themes
.bashrc           .gconf            Music             .thumbnails
bin               .gconfd           .nautilus         Videos
.cache            .gnome2           Pictures          .viminfo
.config           .gnome2_private   .profile          .vimrc
.dbus             .gstreamer-0.10   Public            words
Desktop           .gtk-bookmarks    public_html       .xim.template
.dmrc             .gvfs             .pulse            .xinitrc.template
Documents         .hplip            .pulse-cookie     .xsession-errors
Downloads         .ICEauthority     .recently-used.xbel  .xsession-errors.old
.emacs            .icons            Templates         yourfile.txt
```

- **–l**   Displays a long listing of the directory contents. This is a very useful option. You can use it to see the filenames, ownership, permissions, modification dates, and sizes. A sample is shown here:

```
rtracy@openSUSE:~> ls -l
total 56
drwxr-xr-x 2 rtracy users 4096 2011-01-19 10:41 bin
drwxr-xr-x 2 rtracy users 4096 2011-01-19 10:42 Desktop
drwxr-xr-x 2 rtracy users 4096 2011-01-19 10:42 Documents
drwxr-xr-x 2 rtracy users 4096 2011-01-19 10:42 Downloads
drwxr-xr-x 2 rtracy users 4096 2011-01-19 10:42 Music
drwxr-xr-x 2 rtracy users 4096 2011-01-19 10:42 Pictures
drwxr-xr-x 2 rtracy users 4096 2011-01-19 10:42 Public
drwxr-xr-x 2 rtracy users 4096 2011-01-19 10:41 public_html
drwxr-xr-x 2 rtracy users 4096 2011-01-19 10:42 Templates
-rw-r--r-- 1 rtracy users   37 2011-01-20 11:04 test2.txt
-rw-r--r-- 1 rtracy users  182 2011-01-21 11:48 test.txt
drwxr-xr-x 2 rtracy users 4096 2011-01-19 10:42 Videos
-rw-r--r-- 1 rtracy users   23 2011-01-20 11:32 words
-rw-r--r-- 1 rtracy users  121 2011-01-21 11:46 yourfile.txt
```

- **–R**   Displays directory contents recursively; that is, it displays the contents of the current directory as well as the contents of all subdirectories. Depending on the number of entries in the directory, you may want to append **| more** after using this option. This will cause the more utility to pause the display one page at a time.

Most distributions define several aliases that you can use for the ls command. For example, on openSUSE the dir or ll alias runs the ls –l command, the l alias runs the ls –alF command, and the la alias runs the ls –la command.

This list is only a sampling of the different options you can use with ls. You can view the ls man page or info node to learn more.

Let's practice navigating the file system in the following exercise.

Exercise 4-2: Navigating the File System

In this exercise, you will practice using shell commands to navigate the Linux file system. You can perform this exercise using the virtual machine that comes with this book. Run snapshot 4-1 for the correctly configured environment.

VIDEO Please watch the Exercise 4-2 video for a demonstration on how to perform this task.

Complete the following:

1. Boot your Linux system and log in as the **student** user with a password of **student**.

2. If necessary, open a terminal session.

3. Determine your current working directory by entering **pwd** at the shell prompt. What's the current directory?

4. Change directories to /etc by entering **cd /etc** at the shell prompt.

5. Generate a listing of the current directory by entering **ls**.

6. Generate a long listing of the current directory by entering **ls –l**.

7. Generate a long list and pause the output a page at a time by entering **ls –l | more**. Page your way through the listing.

8. Switch back to your home directory by entering **cd ~**.

9. Enter **ls**.

10. View the hidden files in your user's home directory by entering **ls –a**. Which files are displayed by ls –a that are not displayed by ls?

Let's now shift gears and discuss shell commands that you can use to manage directories in the Linux file system. Let's first look at how you create new directories.

Creating New Directories

You can use shell commands to create new directories. This is done using the mkdir command. You enter **mkdir** from the shell prompt followed by the name of the directory you want to create. In the next example, the **mkdir MyFiles** command has been issued from the home directory of the rtracy user:

```
rtracy@openSUSE:~> mkdir MyFiles
rtracy@ openSUSE:~> ls
bin        Downloads  Pictures     Templates  Videos
Desktop    Music      Public       test2.txt  words
Documents  MyFiles    public_html  test.txt   yourfile.txt
```

Notice in the output from the ls command that a new directory named MyFiles was created in /home/rtracy. Of course, you could use an absolute path with the directory name if you wanted to create it somewhere other than the current directory. For example, if you wanted to create a new directory named backup in the /tmp directory, you would enter **mkdir /tmp/backup** at the shell prompt.

On many distributions, an alias named md is defined in a shell configuration file that runs the mkdir –p command. The –p option specifies that the entire directory path specified in the command be created if it doesn't exist. For example, **md ~/temp/backups/daily** would create the temp and backups directories, if they didn't already exist, before creating the daily directory.

Copying, Moving, and Deleting Directories

In addition to creating and viewing directories in the Linux file system, you can also copy, move, or delete them using shell commands. You use the following utilities to accomplish these tasks:

- **cp**   This utility is used to copy entire directory structures from one location in the file system to another.

  To copy an entire directory structure, you need to include the –R option, which specifies that the directory contents be recursively copied. In the example that follows, the **cp –R ~/MyFiles ~/backup** command was issued in the rtracy user's home directory. This caused the MyFiles directory and all of its files and subdirectories to be copied to the backup directory in the user's home directory. Because cp *copies* the directory, the original directory is left intact.

  ```
  rtracy@ openSUSE:~> cp -R ~/MyFiles ~/backup
  rtracy@ openSUSE:~> ls
  backup    Documents  MyFiles   public_html  test.txt   yourfile.txt
  bin       Downloads  Pictures  Templates    Videos
  Desktop   Music      Public    test2.txt    words
  ```

- **mv**   The mv command is used much like cp. However, it copies the specified directory to the new location in the file system and then *deletes* the original. For example, to move a directory named backup from my home directory to /tmp, I would enter **mv ~/backup /tmp**. The mv command can also be used to rename directories. Simply enter **mv** followed by the directory to be renamed and then the new directory name. For example, to rename the backup directory in the home directory to temp, you would enter **mv ~/backup ~/temp**.

- **rmdir**   This utility can be used to delete an existing directory. To use it, simply enter **rmdir *directory_name***—for example, **rmdir MyFiles**. Be aware, however, that rmdir requires that the directory be empty before it will delete it. On many distributions, an alias named rd is defined by one of your shell configuration files that *runs* the rmdir command.

- **rm**   The rm utility is a more powerful deletion utility that can be used to delete a populated directory. To delete a directory, enter **rm –r *directory_name***.

So, that's how you manage directories from the shell prompt. With this in mind, we need to discuss how to manage files within those directories from the shell prompt. Let's do that next.

Managing Files from the Command Line

In addition to managing directories in the file system, there will be many occasions when you need to manage the files they contain. In this part of the chapter, you will learn how to complete the following tasks:

- Creating files
- Viewing file contents

- Deleting files
- Copying and moving files
- Determining the file type

Let's first look at how to create new files in your file system.

Creating New Files

From time to time, you will need to create new files in your Linux file system. Creating a new file can be accomplished using the touch command from the shell prompt. To use touch, enter **touch** followed by the name of the file you want to create. In the next example, the command **touch myfile.txt** was issued from within the home directory of the rtracy user:

```
rtracy@ openSUSE:~> touch myfile.txt
rtracy@ openSUSE:~> ls -l my*
-rw-r--r-- 1 rtracy users 0 2011-02-01 11:36 myfile.txt
```

After touch was entered, the ls command was entered. You can see that a 0-byte file was created named myfile.txt in /home/rtracy. If you wanted to create the file elsewhere in the file system, you would use an absolute path with the filename.

Viewing File Contents

As we discussed earlier, your Linux system and the services that run on it are configured using simple text files stored in (usually) the /etc directory in the file system. In addition, many of your system log files are saved as text files. Because Linux uses text files to configure and manage just about everything, you will frequently need to view the contents of files.

In the preceding chapter, you learned how to use text editors to open a file for viewing and editing. This works very well. However, there will be many occasions when you simply want to quickly view a text file on screen and don't need or want to load up a text editor. Linux provides you with a variety of command-line tools that you can use to do this. These include the following:

- **cat**   The **cat** *filename* command will display the specified text file on screen. For example, if you needed to view the /etc/xinetd.conf configuration file, you would enter **cat /etc/xinetd.conf** at the shell prompt.

 TIP   The cat command doesn't pause the output, so if you use it to view a long file you may need to pipe it to the more program (**| more**) to pause the output a page a time.

- **less**   The **less** *filename* command can also be used to display the specified text file on screen, much like cat. However, the less command automatically pauses a long text file one page at a time. You can use the SPACEBAR, PAGE UP, PAGE DOWN, and ARROW keys to navigate around the output.

- **head**   The **head** *filename* command is used to display the first couple of lines of a text file on the screen.

- **tail** The **tail** *filename* command is used to display the last couple of lines of a text file onscreen. The tail command is particularly useful when displaying a log file onscreen. When viewing a log file, you usually only need to see the end of the file. You probably don't care about log entries made several days or weeks ago. You can use tail to see just the last few log entries added to the end of the file.

The tail command also includes the –f option, which is very useful. You can use it to monitor the file specified in the command. If new content is added to the end of the file (such as a log file), the new lines will be displayed onscreen. In Figure 4-7, the **tail –f /var/log/messages** command has been issued to monitor the file for new entries.

Using –f with the tail command can be very helpful when troubleshooting a misbehaving service or configuration problem on the system. When you're done, you can break out of tail by pressing CTRL-C.

In addition to creating and viewing files, you will also need to know how to delete existing files. Let's discuss how this is done next.

Deleting Files

As with directories, there will be times when you will need to delete an existing file from the Linux file system. Deleting files can be accomplished with the rm command. This is the same command we used previously to delete directories. The rm utility is a powerful deletion utility that can be used to delete either a file or a populated directory. To delete a file, simply enter **rm** *filename*. In the next example, the myfile.txt file is deleted using the rm command:

```
rtracy@openSUSE:~> rm myfile.txt
rtracy@openSUSE:~>
```

You need to be very careful when using the rm utility! As you can see in the preceding example, it doesn't prompt you to confirm a deletion operation. It assumes that you really meant to delete

```
openSUSE:/ # tail -f /var/log/messages
2014-10-28T19:38:44.586183-06:00 linux ifup[4070]: eno16777736 DHCP6 continues in backg
round
2014-10-28T19:38:44.607193-06:00 linux ifup-dhcp[4159]:      eno16777736 DHCP6 continues
 in background
2014-10-28T19:38:45.186547-06:00 linux systemd[1]: Started ifup managed network interfa
ce eno16777736.
2014-10-28T19:38:45.296665-06:00 linux network[3638]: ..done..doneSetting up service ne
twork    .   .   .   .   .   .   .   .   .   ...done
2014-10-28T19:38:45.307283-06:00 linux systemd[1]: Started LSB: Configure network inter
faces and set up routing.
2014-10-28T19:45:01.078673-06:00 linux /usr/sbin/cron[5915]: pam_unix(crond:session): s
ession opened for user root by (uid=0)
2014-10-28T19:45:01.140646-06:00 linux systemd[1]: Starting Session 30 of user root.
2014-10-28T19:45:01.145664-06:00 linux systemd[1]: Started Session 30 of user root.
2014-10-28T19:45:01.450926-06:00 linux /USR/SBIN/CRON[5915]: pam_unix(crond:session): s
ession closed for user root
2014-10-28T19:51:50.678645-06:00 linux gdm-password]: gkr-pam: unlocked login keyring
```

Figure 4-7   Using tail with the –f option to monitor a log file

the file or directory and does the deed. And by the way, the deleted file doesn't get moved to the Recycle Bin. If you delete a file or directory with rm, it is gone! If you want rm to prompt you before deleting a file or directory, include the –i option.

Let's next review how you can copy and move files from the shell prompt.

Copying and Moving Files

In addition to creating and deleting files in the Linux file system, you can also copy or move them. You use the same utilities that you used to manage directories to copy or move files:

- **cp** This utility is used to copy files from one location in the file system to another. For example, to copy a file named /tmp/schedule.txt to your home directory, you would enter **cp /tmp/schedule.txt ~**. Remember, cp makes a copy of the file, so the original file is left intact. You can use the –R option with cp to copy files recursively.

- **mv** The mv command copies a file to the new location in the file system and then deletes the original. For example, to move a file named mylog.txt from /tmp to /var/log, you would enter **mv /tmp/mylog.txt /var/log**.

As with directories, the mv command can also be used to rename files. Simply enter **mv** followed by the file to be renamed and then the new filename. For example, to rename schedule.txt to schedule.old, you would enter **mv schedule.txt schedule.old**.

Determining the File Type

You can use the file command at the shell prompt to determine a file's type. Understand that, on Linux, file extensions (such as .txt) are not necessary. Therefore, it may not be immediately obvious from a file's name what kind of file you are looking at.

The file command can be used at the shell prompt to get information about a file. The output of the command will not only tell you the general file type (such as directory, named pipe, link, and so on), but it can also provide you with detailed information about your files. To do this, it compares the file you specify in the command with file signatures contained in /usr/share/misc/magic, /usr/share/misc/magic.mgc, and /etc/magic.

In the next example, you can see that the file command has identified the **words** file in my home directory as an ASCII text file while the **resources** file is an OpenOffice.org document:

```
rtracy@openSUSE:~> ls
bin         Downloads          MyFiles    public_html  Templates   Videos
Desktop     hs_err_pid7458.log Pictures   resources    test2.txt   words
Documents   Music              Public     temp                     test.txt  yourfile.txt
rtracy@fs2:~> file words
words: ASCII text
rtracy@fs2:~> file resources
resources: OpenDocument Text
```

Thus far, we've been working primarily with files, directories, and aliases in the Linux file system. However, there's a fourth type of Linux file that is used a lot and that you need to be familiar with. These files are called *links*. Let's discuss how they work next.

Working with Link Files

As we discussed earlier in this chapter, the Linux file system supports a file type called a *link file*. Link files don't contain content in the way that regular files do. Instead, they are redirectors that point you to a different file or directory in the file system. On Linux you can create two different types of link files:

- **Hard**   A hard link is a file that points directly to the inode of another file. An *inode* stores basic information about a file in the Linux file system, including its size, device, owner, and permissions. Because the two files use the same inode, you can't actually tell which file is the pointer and which is the pointee after the hard link is created. It is as if the two files were the same file, even though they may exist in different locations in the file system.

- **Symbolic**   A symbolic link file also points to another file in the file system. However, a symbolic link has its own inode. Because the pointer file has its own inode, the pointer and the pointee in the file system can be easily identified. For example, in the preceding chapter, you saw that the /usr/bin/vi file is actually a symbolic link that points to the /bin/vim file. This is shown in the following example:

```
openSUSE:/usr/bin # ls -l vi
lrwxrwxrwx 1 root root 8 Jan 19 10:24 vi -> /bin/vim
```

To create a link file, you use the ln command. The syntax is **ln *pointee_file pointer_file***. Using ln without any options creates a hard link. If you want to create a symbolic link, you use the **–s** option. In the example that follows, the ln command has been used to create a symbolic link between a file named myapp in the bin subdirectory of my user's home directory and an executable file named myapp located in /var/opt:

```
rtracy@ openSUSE:~/bin> ln -s /var/opt/myapp myapp
rtracy@ openSUSE:~/bin> ls -l
total 0
lrwxrwxrwx 1 rtracy users 14 2011-02-01 13:15 myapp -> /var/opt/myapp
rtracy@fs2:~/bin>cd ..
rtracy@fs2:~> myapp
This is my new executable script file.
```

Using the **ls –l** command, you can see that myapp actually points to the /var/opt/myapp executable file. This can be a useful trick if the /var/opt/myapp program is one that you need to use frequently. Because the /var/opt directory is not in my user's PATH environment variable, I would need to supply the full path to the myapp executable each time I wanted to run it (or switch to the /var/opt directory first). However, the bin subdirectory of my home directory is automatically added to the PATH environment variable by my bash configuration files. By placing the symbolic link in this directory, I can run the /var/opt/myapp executable by simply entering **myapp** at the shell prompt. The symbolic link file redirects the shell to the appropriate file in /var/opt and runs it from there. This is shown in the preceding example.

NOTE   In Chapter 6, we'll discuss the vital role symbolic links play when the init process initializes your Linux system.

Let's practice managing files in the following exercise.

Exercise 4-3: Managing Files and Directories

In this exercise, you will practice managing files and directories using shell commands. You can perform this exercise using the virtual machine that comes with this book. Run snapshot 4-1 for the correctly configured environment.

 VIDEO   Please watch the Exercise 4-3 video for a demonstration on how to perform this task.

Complete the following:

1. With your Linux system running and authenticated as the **student** user, open a terminal session and switch to your home directory by entering **cd** at the shell prompt.

2. Create a new directory in your home directory by entering **mkdir MyFiles**.

3. Enter **ls** and verify that the new directory exists.

4. Create a new file in the MyFiles directory called myfile.txt by entering **touch ~/MyFiles/ myfile.txt**.

5. Enter **ls ~/MyFiles** and verify that the file exists.

6. Change to your root user account by entering **su –** and entering a password of **student**.

7. View your system log file by entering **cat /var/log/messages | more**.

8. Page through a few pages of the file and then press CTRL-C to break out to the shell prompt.

9. View the last few entries in the log file by entering **tail /var/log/messages**.

10. Monitor your /var/log/messages log file while you stop and start services by doing the following:

    a. At the shell prompt, enter **tail –f /var/log/messages**. You should see that the log file is now being monitored by tail.

    b. Open a new terminal window and switch to your root user account using the **su –** command and your root user's password.

    c. Disable your system's network card by entering **ifdown enp0s3** at the shell prompt.

    d. Switch to the terminal session where tail is running. You should see new lines added to the file as the network board is disabled.

    e. Switch back to the second shell prompt and enter **systemctl restart network**. Again, you should see new lines added to the file as the network board is re-enabled in the first terminal window.

    f. Enter **exit** twice to close the second terminal window.

    g. Switch to the terminal session where tail is running and press CTRL-C to break out of tail.

11. Switch back to your regular user account by entering **exit**.

12. Delete the MyFiles directory in your home directory by entering **rm –r ~/MyFiles**.

13. Enter **ls** and verify that the directory and its contents are gone.

14. Make a copy of your home directory files and subdirectories in /tmp by entering **cp –R ~ /tmp**.

15. View the contents of /tmp by entering **ls /tmp**. Verify that your home directory was copied.

16. Work with symbolic links by doing the following:

    a. Create a symbolic link from a directory named docs in your home directory to the /usr/share/doc directory by entering **ln –s /usr/share/doc/ ~/docs**.

    b. Enter **ls –l**. Verify that the docs file points to /usr/share/doc/.

    c. Enter **cd docs**.

    d. Enter **pwd**. What directory are you in?

    e. Enter **ls**. You should see the contents of the /usr/share/doc/ directory even though you are still in ~/docs.

Finding Content within Files

Earlier in this chapter, we discussed shell commands that can be used to search for files in the file system. However, Linux also provides a utility called grep that you can use to search for specific content *within* a file. The grep utility is extremely useful; in fact, I dare say that most Linux admins use it on a daily basis. Using grep, you can search through a file for a particular text string. This can come in handy when you want to search a very large log file for a specific message or when you need to find a specific directive within a configuration file. You can even use grep to search through multiple files at once to locate a particular expression.

To use grep, you enter **grep *search_expression file_name*** at the shell prompt. For example, let's suppose you want to search through your /var/log/messages file for any log entries related to the VNC service running on your Linux system. You would enter **grep vnc /var/log/messages**. The grep utility would then display each line from the file that contained your search term, as shown here:

```
openSUSE:~ # grep vnc /var/log/messages
Feb  1 13:47:25 fs2 xinetd[7134]: Reading included configuration file:
/etc/xinetd.d/vnc [file=/etc/xinetd.d/vnc] [line=15]
```

Likewise, if you needed to find a line in your /etc/ntp.conf file that contains the directive "server," you could enter **grep server /etc/ntp.conf** at the shell prompt. This is shown in the next example:

```
openSUSE:~ # grep server /etc/ntp.conf
# server 127.127.8.0 mode 5 prefer
server 127.127.1.0
## # rcntp addserver <yourserver>
server bigben.cac.washington.edu iburst
```

```
# key (7) for accessing server variables
# controlkey 15          # key (6) for accessing server variables
```

When working with grep at the command line, you can use the following options:

- **−i** Ignores case when searching for the text.
- **−l** Displays only the names of the files that contain the matching text. It doesn't display the actual matching line of text.
- **−n** Displays matching line numbers.
- **−r** Searches recursively through subdirectories of the path specified.
- **−v** Displays all lines that *do not* contain the search string.

The grep utility works great when you need to search for a specific text string within a file. However, there may be times when you need to search for more complex patterns. In this situation, you can use the egrep command instead.

NOTE The egrep command is the same as using the grep –E command.

The key advantage of egrep is that it can search files for extended *regular expressions,* which are strings consisting of metacharacters and literals. *Literals* are regular letters (A–Z, a–z) and numerals. *Metacharacters* are characters that do not represent themselves but instead represent other characters. They can also be used to specify a character's location within a text string. Some commonly used regular expressions are listed in Table 4-6. See the regex(7) man page for more information.

In addition to egrep, you can also use the fgrep (fixed-string grep) utility to search for content within files. The fgrep utility searches files for lines that match a fixed string. Unlike egrep, it does not perform searches for regular expressions. Instead, fgrep uses direct string comparisons to find matching lines of text in the input. The syntax is **fgrep *pattern filename***. For example, running the **fgrep server *.c** command searches for the string "server" in all files in the current directory whose filename has a ".c" extension.

NOTE Running fgrep is the same as running grep –F. When using regular expressions, including text with the * or ? wildcard characters (such as "*.c") is called a *file globbing pattern.*

Let's practice using Linux search tools in the following exercise.

Exercise 4-4: Using grep

In this exercise, you will practice using Linux search tools. You can perform this exercise using the virtual machine that comes with this book. Run snapshot 4-1 for the correctly configured environment.

Metacharacter	Function	Example
*	Matches any number of any characters	**Myfile*** would match Myfile1, Myfile2, Myfiles, Myfiles23, and so on.
.	Matches a single character	**Myfile.** would match Myfile1, Myfile2, and Myfiles, but would not match Myfiles23.
^	Matches an expression if it appears at the beginning of a line	**^server** would match any instance of "server" as long as it appears at the beginning of a line.
$	Matches an expression if it appears at the end of a line	**server$** would match any instance of "server" as long as it appears at the end of a line.
|	Matches the expressions on either side of the pipe character	**Server|server** would match either "Server" or "server."
[nnn]	Matches any one character between the braces	**[xyz]** would match any one of "x," "y," or "z."
[^nnn]	Matches an expression that does not contain any one of the characters specified	**[^aei]** would not match the characters "a," "e," and "i."
[n-n]	Matches any single character in the range	**[1-5]** would match any number between 1 and 5.

Table 4-6   Regular Expressions

 VIDEO   Please watch the Exercise 4-4 video for a demonstration on how to perform this task.

Complete the following:

1. With your Linux system running and authenticated as the **student** user, switch to root by entering **su –** followed by a password of **student** at the shell prompt.

2. Locate references to the inittab file in your system log file by entering **grep ifup /var/log messages**. What can you learn about ifup from the output of grep?

3. Use egrep to find information about the systemd daemon in your system log file by entering **egrep systemd /var/log/messages** at the shell prompt.

4. Use egrep again to find information about all the Ethernet interfaces installed in your system by entering **egrep enp0s[0-3] /var/log/messages** at the shell prompt.

5. Find all lines in your system log file that end with "Enabled" by entering **egrep Enabled$ /var/log/messages** at the shell prompt.

You are now a file system pro! You have to be humble when you know this much!

Chapter Review

In this chapter, we reviewed a variety of topics related to managing the Linux file system. I began this chapter by introducing you to the Linux file system. I first differentiated between a general file system and a specific disk file system such as Reiser or ext4. I then pointed out that the role of the Linux file system is to organize data such that it can be easily located and retrieved as well as reliably preserved.

I then related that Linux uses a hierarchical file system. The topmost directory of this hierarchy is the root directory (/). We discussed the role of the various standard directories used in a typical Linux system as specified in the Filesystem Hierarchy Standard (FHS). These include the following:

- /bin
- /boot
- /dev
- /etc
- /home
- /lib
- /media
- /mnt
- /opt
- /proc
- /root
- /sbin
- /srv
- /sys
- /tmp
- /usr
- /var

We also discussed the four different types of files used on a Linux system: regular files, links, FIFOs, and sockets.

With this background information in hand, we turned our attention to common Linux file system tasks. I emphasized that, although most of these tasks can be performed using graphical utilities, the LPIC-1/Linux+ exam expects you to know how to complete them from the shell prompt.

We first discussed utilities that you can use to search for files or directories in the Linux file system. We reviewed how to use the find and locate commands to find specific files or directories. I pointed out that find manually walks the file system hierarchy to conduct its searches, which can be somewhat slow. As an alternative, the locate utility creates a database of files in the file system. When you search with locate, it queries its database instead of walking the file system hierarchy, which is much faster.

I also pointed out that you can use the which command to find out where the executables for system utilities, such as ls, cp, and man, reside in the file system. We also looked at the whereis command, which displays information such as executable file, source file, and man page file locations for a particular shell command. We also reviewed how to use the file command to determine a file's type. We also discussed how you can use the type command to determine what type of command is executed when you enter it at the command line.

We next reviewed how to navigate through the Linux file system using the pwd and cd commands. We then discussed how to manage files and directories. I pointed out that you can create new files using the touch command. You can also create new directories using the mkdir command.

We also reviewed the utilities you can use to delete files and directories, including rmdir and rm. To copy and move files and directories, you can use the cp and mv utilities. I pointed out that mv can also be used to rename files or directories. We also discussed link files. I mentioned that link files point to other files or directories in the file system, and I related that you can create either hard links or symbolic links using the ln command.

We then discussed utilities you can use to view the contents of text files onscreen. I pointed out that you can use cat, less, head, or tail to do this. I also pointed out that you can use the –f option with tail to monitor changes to a text file, such as a log file, as they are made. We ended the chapter by discussing how to use grep to find content within text files.

Accelerated Review

- The role of the file system is to store and organize data such that it can be easily located and retrieved.
- The file command displays a file's type.
- The type command identifies the type of command entered at the command line.
- The file system must also keep data intact.
- Linux uses a hierarchical file system.
- The Linux file system hierarchy is based on the Filesystem Hierarchy Standard (FHS).
- The topmost directory is /.
- Other standard directories are created beneath / and serve functions defined in the FHS.
- The Linux file system uses regular files, links, FIFOs, and sockets.
- Most file system management tasks can be completed using either graphical or command-line tools.
- You can use the find utility to locate files or directories in the file system.
- The find utility manually walks the file system hierarchy to search for files.
- You can use locate to search for files or directories.
- The locate utility maintains a database of all files in the file system.
- When locate conducts a search, it searches the database instead of the file system.
- The which command is used to display the location of files in the file system.

- The whereis command displays information about a command's executable file, source code file, and man page file.
- The type command displays a file's type.
- The pwd command is used to display the current directory.
- The cd command is used to change directories.
- The ls command is used to display directory contents.
- Using ls with the –l option displays additional details about files and directories.
- Using ls with the –R option displays directory contents recursively.
- The touch command is used to create new files.
- The mkdir command is used to create new directories.
- You can use cat to view a text file onscreen.
- You can also use less to view a text file onscreen.
- The less command pauses the display one line at a time.
- The head command can be used to display the first few lines of a text file.
- The tail command can be used to display the last few lines of a text file.
- The tail command used with the –f option can monitor a text file for changes.
- You can use rmdir to delete an empty directory.
- You can use rm to delete populated directories or files.
- The cp command is used to copy files.
- The mv command is used to move files.
- The Linux file system allows you to create link files that point to other files or directories in the file system.
- Hard links point directly to the inode of another file.
- Symbolic links have their own inode.
- Links are created using the ln command.
- You can use grep to search for text within a file.

Questions

1. Which of the following are roles of the Linux file system? (Choose two.)

   A. Create automatic backups of system data.

   B. Make data easily locatable.

   C. Preserve data integrity.

   D. Provide the user with a command-line interface.

   E. Provide the user with a graphical user interface.

2. Which directory contains file system management utilities such as cp and rm?

   A. /bin

   B. /dev

   C. /var

   D. /usr

3. Which directory is a pseudo–file system that is dynamically created when it is accessed?

   A. /var

   B. /opt

   C. /proc

   D. /srv

4. Which directory does the ~ character represent when used with file system commands?

   A. /var

   B. The current directory

   C. The current user's home directory

   D. The root user's home directory

5. You need to generate a listing of files and directories within the /var directory, including files in subdirectories. Which command will do this?

   A. ls /var

   B. ls –l /var

   C. ls –f /var

   D. ls –R /var

6. You need to view the last few lines of your /var/xinetd.log file. Which is the best command to do this?

   A. tail /var/xinetd.log

   B. cat /var/xinetd.log |more

   C. head /var/xinetd.log

   D. less /var/xinetd.log

7. You need to delete the Temp directory within your user's home directory. Given that Temp has files in it, which is the best command to do this?

   A. rmdir Temp

   B. rmdir ~/Temp

   C. rm Temp

   D. rm –r ~/Temp

8. You need to copy the Documents directory within your user's home directory to the /tmp directory. Given that Documents has files and subdirectories within it, which is the correct command to do this?

   A. cp ~/Documents /tmp

   B. cp –R ~/Documents /tmp

   C. cp ~/Documents ~/tmp

   D. cp –R ~/Documents ~/tmp

9. You want to create a symbolic link in your home directory that will link the manual file to the /usr/share/doc/manual directory. Which is the correct command to do this?

   A. ln –s /usr/share/doc/manual ~/manual

   B. ln /usr/share/doc/manual ~/manual

   C. ln –s ~/manual /usr/share/doc/manual

   D. ln ~/manual /usr/share/doc/manual

10. You need to find a file named myfile.txt somewhere in your Linux file system. Which is the correct command to do this?

    A. find / –name "myfile.txt"

    B. find "myfile.txt"

    C. find / –n myfile.txt

    D. find –name "myfile.txt"

11. You need to find all entries in your /var/log/messages file that contain the term "scsi." Which is the correct command to do this?

    A. grep /var/log/messages "scsi"

    B. grep -find "scsi" /var/log/messages

    C. grep /var/log/messages scsi

    D. grep scsi /var/log/messages

Answers

1. **B** and **C**. The role of the file system is to make data easily locatable and to preserve its integrity.

2. **A**. File system utilities are located in /bin.

3. **C**. The /proc file system is a pseudo–file system.

4. **C**. The ~ character points to the home directory of the current user.

5. **D**. The ls –R /var command will generate a listing of /var and its subdirectories.

6. **A**. The tail utility is the best choice to display the last few lines of the file.

7. **D.** The rm –r command will delete the Temp directory and its contents.

8. **B.** The cp –R ~/Documents /tmp command copies data recursively from the Documents directory within your user's home directory to the /tmp directory.

9. **A.** The ln –s /usr/share/doc/manual ~/manual command creates a symbolic link from the manual file in your home directory to the /usr/share/doc/manual directory.

10. **A.** The find / –name "myfile.txt" command uses the correct syntax.

11. **D.** The grep scsi /var/log/messages command uses the correct syntax.

Installing Linux

In this chapter, you will learn about:
- Designing a Linux installation
- Installing Linux
- Configuring locale settings
- Configuring time zone settings

To be LPIC-1/Linux+ certified, you need to know how to perform a clean installation of a Linux distribution. Linux is extremely flexible and can fill a wide variety of roles in your organization. Therefore, you need to make a number of important decisions as the operating system is installed. Most Linux distributions expect you to have a solid understanding of the Linux system before you start installing.

Linux has become dramatically easier to install in the last few years. The distributions available in the mid-1990s could be quite challenging to install. Hardware support was limited; the installation wizard, if one existed at all, was very primitive. The first time I installed a Linux distribution in the mid-1990s, I was ready to put my foot through the monitor before it was done. It required two full days to work through all the quirks.

Fortunately, most modern Linux distributions employ an easy-to-use graphical installation wizard to facilitate the installation process.

To install Linux properly, you need to spend some time planning the installation *before* you actually start the installation process. Therefore, we will begin this chapter discussing how to plan a new Linux system.

Designing a Linux Installation

If you're reading this book, you're probably a *techie*. You love computers and you're not intimidated by new technologies. You love to investigate new innovations in hardware and software and experiment with them. The brightest spot in your week is when the big brown delivery truck arrives at your place of work to drop off a load of new hardware. You happily work overtime for days on end getting everything set up and running with a big grin on your face. Been there, my friend; I share your glee.

Linux Installers and the LPIC-1/Linux+ Exam

Because there is a right way and a wrong way to implement a new Linux system, you will be expected to be very familiar with Linux installation topics on the LPIC-1/Linux+ exam. Roughly 20 percent of the exam will be composed of Linux installation and package management questions. The exam will expect you to be familiar with deployment planning topics, not just the installation process itself.

One of the problems encountered by CompTIA and LPIC is the wide variety of installers used by the various Linux distributions. There's no way for the LPIC-1/Linux+ exam to address them all. It's not reasonable for the exam to expect you to be familiar with them all either. There are just too many distributions. Therefore, you need to be familiar with generic installation concepts and tasks that are common to all distributions.

We don't have time and space in this book to cover installing all distributions either. What a nightmare that would be to write! So, I'm going to pick just one distribution and focus on installing openSUSE. However, the principles you learn here by installing openSUSE can be transferred to other distributions without much difficulty.

Being a techie can be a lot of fun. However, techies are notorious for sharing a common set of traits, including the following:

- *Techies never read the documentation for anything.* It's much more fun to experiment and figure it out on our own. Besides, we already know what we're doing, right?

- *Techies hate to plan out anything on paper, especially a hardware or software deployment.* It takes the fun out of playing with all that cool new stuff. Besides, it's all in our heads anyway, right?

- *Techies hate to document anything.* We'll remember what we did three years down the road when something breaks, right?

When deploying Linux (or any other system, for that matter), you must overcome these tendencies and do things the right way. If you don't change your ways, you'll be spending a lot of time fixing your mistakes later. If you keep it up long enough, you'll also be spending a lot of time working on your résumé.

If you're working on a test system at home or in a lab environment, you can usually get away with implementing Linux the techie way. There's probably no real risk in making mistakes. In fact, it can be a great learning experience. I highly recommend it when time permits because you can really learn a lot.

However, when you're deploying systems that will be used in your organization's production environment, the techie approach is completely unacceptable. Mistakes on your part will lead to system outages. Outages cost your organization time and money and will probably cost you your job.

Instead of deploying systems in a haphazard, unstructured manner, you should develop a deployment plan *before* you start buying hardware and installing software. Doing so will help you prevent costly errors (and probably save your job).

Being a confessed techie myself, I know how painful this process can be. When tasked with deploying new Linux systems, your first impulse is to get on your hardware vendor's site and start ordering. Resist this urge! If you will instead follow the process laid out in this chapter and actually *plan* the implementation before you start ordering hardware and software, life will be good for you and for those who will follow in your footsteps.

Let me give you an example of what I'm talking about. Years ago, I worked for a major networking software vendor. One of the functional groups in my department wanted to implement a new application that would make their jobs easier. When reviewing the system requirements, they found that the software required a specific version of the Windows server software—one that we didn't currently have. Implementing the application would first require a new server to be installed. Rather than develop a plan for the new server deployment, the individuals in this group completely winged it. They ordered a new server and set up the software themselves without telling anyone.

Not a big deal, you think? Consider this: all of the critical data from that group as well as the group I worked for was saved on this server. This data represented thousands of hours of work and was worth millions of dollars. No one on my team gave it a second thought until several years later when we discovered that our company's Information Systems team had no idea that server even existed on the network. No one had ever run a single backup of the data on that server. No one had attached an uninterruptible power supply (UPS) to it. No one was responsible for patching the operating system. No one managed the security of the system. (They left it sitting in an unoccupied cubicle.) Millions of dollars' worth of information was completely unprotected. One simple power spike coming in through the power lines could have completely destroyed everything we'd been working on for years with no way to recover it. In addition, only one person had the password for the administrative user account. If he had quit or been laid off, we would have lost administrative access to the system as well.

Where was the point of failure in this story? No implementation plan was developed for this new server. Had someone planned the deployment, they would have noted these issues before the server was installed and planned for them accordingly.

In this part of the chapter, we'll discuss how to go about planning a Linux installation. The following topics will be addressed:

- Conducting a needs assessment
- Selecting a distribution
- Verifying system requirements and hardware compatibility
- Planning the file system
- Selecting software packages
- Identifying user accounts
- Gathering network information
- Selecting an installation source

The first step in any deployment plan is to conduct a needs assessment. Let's discuss this topic next.

Conducting a Needs Assessment

Conducting a needs assessment is one of the most important aspects of creating a Linux deployment plan. It's also the most frequently skipped step. Unfortunately, even when it is done, it's usually done poorly.

So, what exactly is a needs assessment? It's the process of determining *why* the Linux deployment is being undertaken, *what* outcomes are expected, and *when* it is expected to be complete. Completing a needs assessment will require you to remove your technician hat and put on your project manager hat.

In this role, you will need to meet with a variety of different individuals and gather data about the deployment. Yes, this means you will have to interface with carbon-based life forms. You can do it! I have faith in you! Your findings should be recorded in a word processing document that can be easily distributed and reviewed by others. When you're done, the needs assessment portion of your deployment plan should contain the following information (at a minimum):

- *What are the goals of the project?* You should find out why the implementation is being requested. What problem will this installation fix? What will be the final result of the implementation? What organizational objectives will be met by the implementation? When you list the goals of the project, be sure to use language that is clear and measurable.

Case Study

When determining goals, be sure to talk to everyone involved. If you don't, you won't be getting a clear picture of what is expected and will probably fail to meet a particular goal. Let me give you an example. Several years ago, I was contracted by a financial organization to deploy a Linux server in its new main office and implement all of the wiring necessary to provide network connectivity to each employee's office. I spent a considerable amount of time interviewing one of the owners when I conducted the needs assessment. When I was done, I felt that I had a pretty solid understanding of what they wanted.

To make a long story short, I wired the office and then implemented the Linux server. I was feeling very good about the smoothness of the deployment. As I was packing up to leave, the owner walked into the server room and handed me a CD containing a popular network-based financial accounting software application. He told me that his staff needed to use this software to complete their day-to-day jobs. I cringed when I looked at the system requirements and discovered that it required a Windows server.

Where did I go wrong? I didn't take the time to talk to the employees in the office who would be using the new server. Talking to just one person wasn't enough. The owner didn't know this particular software package was needed when I initially interviewed him during the needs assessment. If he had, I could have accounted for this software in our plan, and I could have gone home on time that night.

- *Who are the stakeholders in this project?* As a part of your needs assessment, you should identify all individuals who will be impacted by the project in any way. You should ask the following questions:

  - Who requested the new system?

  - Who will use the system after it's installed?

  - Who has the authority to approve funds for the project?

  - Who has the authority to allocate your time to the project?

  - Who must give final approval to this project before it can begin?

  - Who will maintain and support the system after it is implemented?

  - Is the new system a fit with the company's current technology environment and strategy direction?

  These are absolutely critical questions that must be answered before you begin any project. You'll be surprised at how many employees in your company will try to circumvent established policies and try to get you to do something for them without the proper approvals.

  Don't make the mistake of assuming that a project has been approved and funded simply because someone asks you to work on it for them. (Trust me, it happens all the time.) If you identify all the stakeholders in the project, you can be sure that the project has been approved and that the necessary funds have been allocated before you place your first order.

- *When is the system needed?* A key question you should ask is when the project should be completed. Before you can create a schedule for your project, you need to know when your stakeholders expect it to be complete.

By gathering this data in your needs assessment, you can define one of the most critical components in your installation plan: the project scope. The *project scope* defines exactly *what* to do, *when* to do it, and *who* will do it. If you've ever managed a project before, you know that every project is a three-way tug-of-war between the following elements:

- Schedule

- Resources

- Scale

This delicate balancing act is shown in Figure 5-1.

To successfully manage any project, you must keep these three elements in balance. If the schedule is excessively short, you will need to either increase the number of resources assigned to the project or decrease the scale of the project. For example, suppose your installation project involves rolling out 300 Linux desktops and you are the only resource assigned to the project. As long as the schedule allows enough time, you can complete this task. However, if the schedule specifies that the project be done in a week, you will probably need to add more resources to the project, decrease the number of desktops included in the project, or eliminate your biological need to eat and sleep.

Figure 5-1
The schedule,
resources, and
scale in the
project scope

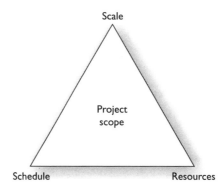

I call this relationship the "three-legged stool of project management." If all of the legs on a three-legged stool aren't the same length, the stool will be unbalanced. The same holds true with project management. If your schedule, scale, and resources aren't in balance, the project will probably fail in some way.

I've been responsible for managing projects for most of my career, and this analogy has come in very handy on many occasions. The issue here is that your project sponsor will probably want you to do way more than is feasible in an unrealistic amount of time and with too few resources.

Early in my career, I wanted to impress my managers and I frequently agreed to take on projects involving impossible parameters. This was not a wise thing to do. The relentless stress and long hours can take an awful toll on your health. As a result, I learned that you must push back to get these three parameters in balance. I've found that using a simple diagram such as that shown in Figure 5-1 or using the three-legged stool analogy can be a very effective tool to communicate the need for balance to project sponsors.

Using project management software can be extremely helpful in helping you calculate exactly how long a project will take. Using project management software, you can assign specific tasks to specific resources and assign durations. In addition, you can define *dependencies,* which are used to specify which tasks must be completed before other tasks can begin. A sample project with dependencies is shown in Figure 5-2.

ID	Description	Start	End
1	⊟Design Phase	6/05/06	6/15/06
2	Research Existing Content	6/05/06	6/06/06
3	Set Up Equipment and Software	6/07/06	6/07/06
4	Set Up Document Template	6/08/06	6/08/06
5	Create Design Document	6/09/06	6/15/06
6	⊟Alpha Development	6/16/06	8/16/06
7	Develop Alpha Draft of Administration Guide	6/16/06	7/27/06
8	SME Review of Alpha Draft	7/28/06	8/03/06
9	Input SME Review Changes	8/04/06	8/10/06
10	Edit Alpha Draft	8/11/06	8/16/06

Figure 5-2   Using project management software to plan a project and define dependencies

The great thing about project management software is that it can calculate your schedule for you. By entering tasks and durations and then associating them with specific resources, you can easily see how long a project is going to take. You can also adjust various parameters (remember the three-legged stool) to see what the effect will be. For example, you can add an additional resource to the project and see the effect it has on your overall schedule. You can also see the effect of specifying nine-hour days instead of eight-hour days.

However, be sure to use common sense when manipulating your project. I've worked with many project managers who get very excited when they see that they can pull their project's schedule in by a significant amount of time by manipulating various parameters. However, the adjustments they make aren't realistic. For example, you can really shorten a project schedule by specifying 18-hour working days for all resources involved. However, most people can't handle working that many hours for long stretches of time. Family life suffers, personal health suffers, burnout sets in, and productivity plummets. In short, do a reality check against your schedule. Remember that what looks good on paper may not work in real life.

With your project scope defined, you're ready to move on to the next component in your project plan. Let's next discuss selecting a distribution.

Selecting a Distribution

As we discussed earlier in this book, Linux is available in a wide variety of flavors called *distributions.* One of the key parts of your deployment plan is specifying which of these distributions you will use on your system. Which one is best? That depends on your preferences and what you want the system to do. Here are some guidelines you can use to select the right distribution.

Will the System Function as a Workstation or a Server?

One of the cool things about Linux is the fact that you can implement just about any distribution as either a workstation or a server. This is unique among operating systems. Most operating systems are designed to function either as a server or as a workstation, but not both. Most Linux distributions, on the other hand, can be used in either role.

However, be aware that there are Linux distributions available that are specifically designed and optimized to function as servers and others as workstations. For example, Red Hat provides the Red Hat Enterprise Linux distribution that is designed for providing network services for medium to very large organizations with heavy server utilization.

Red Hat also provides two distributions that are designed specifically for use in desktop systems:

- **Red Hat Enterprise Linux Desktop**   This distribution is designed for use by the average end user on desktop systems used to complete day-to-day work.

- **Red Hat Enterprise Linux Workstation**   This distribution is intended for use by high-end users, such as engineers and graphic designers, who need high-end desktop hardware to complete more advanced computing tasks.

- **Red Hat Enterprise Linux Developer**   This distribution is intended for use by software developers writing new applications. The operating system has been optimized to make software development as fast as possible.

Likewise, Novell sells two versions of SUSE Linux:

- **SUSE Linux Enterprise Server**   This distribution is designed for use in high-end server systems in very large organizations.
- **SUSE Linux Enterprise Desktop**   This distribution is designed for use by end users on their desktop workstations.

There are also purpose-specific distributions to create Linux-based appliances using standard PC hardware. For example, you can create a powerful network firewall using distributions such as Untangle.

Does the Distribution Offer Support?

Some vendors offer technical support for their Linux distributions, whereas others offer limited support or no support at all. If the system will be used in a corporate environment, you should implement a well-supported distribution. If a problem occurs at some point after the system has been installed, you need to be able to resolve the issue and get the system back into production as fast as possible. You're not going to have time to scour the Internet trying to find a solution. You need to be able to call someone and get an answer immediately.

Be aware that although the distribution itself may be free or nearly free, you will be required to pay for technical support. The price charged for support varies from vendor to vendor, so it pays to shop around.

There's a lot of confusion in the industry right now about the difference between Linux distributions from the same vendor. Usually one version is free; the other requires a fee. For example, you can purchase a copy of Red Hat Enterprise Linux Desktop or you can download a copy of Fedora for free. One of the key differences is support. If you purchase a copy of Red Hat Enterprise Linux Desktop, you are entitled to tech support from Red Hat. The more you pay, the better the level of support you receive. If you download a free copy, you must support yourself using websites, forums, and newsgroups.

To save your hard-earned cash, we're going to be using Fedora, openSUSE, and Ubuntu in this book. However, I strongly recommend that you consider a supported version of Linux if you're going to deploy it in a production environment.

Will the Applications You Need Run on the Distribution?

Before selecting a specific distribution, you should evaluate the software you want to run and verify that it is supported by the operating system.

In addition to these considerations, you should also verify that the distribution you want to use runs on your system hardware. Let's discuss this factor next.

Verifying System Requirements and Hardware Compatibility

As a techie, you probably love ordering hardware. It's even more fun if your employer is footing the bill! Because of this, you may be strongly tempted to start browsing vendor websites to order your new systems before your Linux deployment plan is complete.

Resist this urge at all costs! Before you download or purchase your Linux distribution, you need to make sure it will actually run on your hardware. Many system administrators I work with ignore this process. In fact, I'll admit to having done this myself. It's a poor practice, and you're pretty much guaranteed to have a "duh" moment at some point. This is because you may end up with hardware that isn't compatible with your operating system. When this happens, your project schedule will be put at risk and lots of people will not be happy with you. It can take a considerable amount of time to return and reorder hardware. If this happens, you'll get to spend quality time in your supervisor's office explaining why the project is behind schedule.

In this topic, we're going to discuss two things you can do to keep this from happening:

- Checking hardware compatibility
- Verifying system requirements

Let's begin by discussing hardware compatibility.

Checking Hardware Compatibility

Back in the early days of Linux, hardware compatibility was problematic, especially if you were trying to install Linux on a notebook or other system with a lot of proprietary hardware. There just weren't enough developers writing Linux drivers. If you were installing Linux on a generic system using common hardware components, you usually could get Linux installed and working correctly. However, if your system used atypical or proprietary hardware, such as a high-end video board, then you may or may not have been able to get Linux running correctly.

Back then, most hardware vendors didn't provide Linux device drivers for their devices. They didn't perceive Linux as a widely used operating system and didn't want to devote time and money to developing device drivers for it. Instead, you had to rely on the good will of a developer somewhere in the world to write a driver for your particular piece of hardware. If a driver didn't exist for your device, you were out of luck.

Today, this is less of an issue. Most vendors now offer a Linux version of the drivers for their hardware. In addition, most of the drivers for common PC hardware are now included with the various Linux distributions.

To be safe, however, it is still a very good idea to check your distribution's website and verify that your system hardware is listed on the distribution's hardware compatibility list (HCL). Even though hardware support for Linux has become much better in the last decade, there are still some devices that aren't supported. A good example is the integrated wireless network interfaces used in many notebook systems. Support for this type of hardware under Linux is hit and miss. You can use your distribution's HCL to verify that your system's devices are supported.

HCLs are usually available in two locations. First, most distributions include a list of supported hardware in a text file on the installation DVD. However, I rarely use this version of the HCL. Because it's a static document, it hasn't been updated since the disc image was created. If a device in your computer was released at some point after the disc image was created, you have no idea whether it's supported or not.

Instead, I prefer using the HCL maintained on most distribution websites. This version of the HCL usually contains the most current data on supported hardware. For example, if you choose to install the openSUSE distribution on your system, you can use a web browser to access its HCL at http://en.opensuse.org/Hardware. Once there, you can search for your particular system hardware and see if it is supported. In Figure 5-3, the openSUSE HCL for video boards is displayed.

Figure 5-3 Using the openSUSE HCL

If you choose to use a Red Hat distribution, you can likewise check the HCL on Red Hat's website (https://access.redhat.com/search/browse/certified-hardware#?) to verify that your system hardware is supported.

Most distributions include some kind of HCL on their website, but not all. Some distribution vendors simply don't have the time or resources to conduct extensive hardware testing to verify the myriad of PC devices available on the market.

NOTE Driver availability is one of the reasons I prefer to stick with big-name, well-supported Linux distributions when deploying in a production environment. Sure, I'll experiment with a poorly supported distribution at home or in a lab environment at work. If something goes wrong, nothing is lost in this situation. However, one of my key roles as a Linux system administrator in a production environment is to protect data and to ensure systems run at maximum efficiency. In this situation I need to know that my hardware is supported. I can't afford to mess around scouring the Internet trying to find a driver, nor do I want to waste time troubleshooting a system that functions erratically.

In addition to checking the HCL, you also need to check your distribution's system requirements. Let's discuss this issue next.

Verifying System Requirements

Back in the early days of Linux, we didn't worry much about system requirements for the various distributions. That was because the early versions of Linux would run on ridiculously minimal hardware. They didn't require much memory, disk space, or processing power.

However, as Linux has matured over the years, most distributions are now beginning to require much more robust system hardware to provide an acceptable degree of performance. How do you know what the system requirements are? Once again, check your distribution vendor's website.

When formulating your deployment plan, be sure to specify the hardware needed by the distribution you've selected.

A key aspect of your system requirements is your PC's CPU architecture. When downloading your Linux distribution, be sure you select the correct architecture for your system's CPU. For years, we didn't worry much about this issue because we really only worked with a single architecture: Intel's 32-bit x86 architecture. Although most early distributions were available for the x86 and the Alpha CPU architectures, the average system administrator didn't have many Alpha machines. Nearly every system we worked with ran on some variation of the x86 architecture.

Today, however, there are many more hardware options available to us as system administrators. We still have the venerable x86 and Alpha architectures, but we also have the newer 64-bit x86 architecture. In addition, Intel produces the IA-64 architecture used by their Itanium CPUs. Each of these architectures requires a different version of Linux. In fact, many Linux distributions have even been ported to run on the Power PC (PPC) architecture from Apple Computer. Other distributions are available for the iSeries, pSeries, and RS/6000 servers from IBM. There are now even versions of Linux that have been ported to run on the ARM architecture used by tablet devices.

The important point is to be sure that you select the appropriate architecture for your distribution. For example, if you selected Ubuntu as your distribution and accessed the distribution's download page on the Internet, you would see the options displayed in Figure 5-4.

Regardless of which distribution you choose, make sure you download the correct version for your system's architecture. For example, if you are going to install Linux on a system with a 32-bit CPU, you need the x86 (32-bit) version of your distribution. If your hardware uses an a 64-bit CPU, you need the x86-64 (64-bit) version of the distribution. If you pick the wrong one, most Linux installers will generate an error and you won't be able to complete the installation.

With hardware issues out of the way, you can now move on to the next component of your plan, where you will specify how the Linux file system will be configured. Let's discuss this topic next.

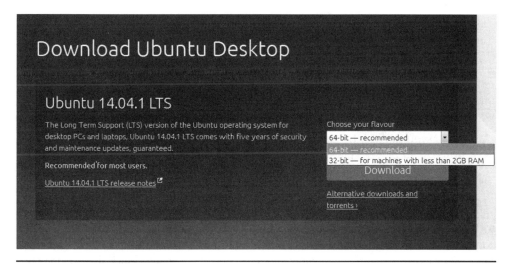

Figure 5-4 Ubuntu architectures

Planning the File System

When planning a Linux implementation, you need to include specifications for how the file system will be created and maintained on the system's hard disk drive. This is yet another unique aspect of the Linux operating system. When implementing other operating systems, such as Microsoft Windows, you usually create only a single disk partition and format it using the NTFS file system.

With Linux, however, you have many more choices to make. You can customize how your disk will be partitioned and what file system will be used. In this part of the chapter, we'll discuss the following:

- Choosing a file system
- Planning your partitions

Let's begin by discussing file systems.

Choosing a File System

Because you're a techie, you already know how a hard disk drive works. The drive is made up of multiple aluminum platters, each with two read-write heads that are used to read and write data. When conducting disk I/O operations, the operating system needs to know where data is stored, how to access it, and where it is safe to write new information.

This is the job of the *file system,* which reliably stores data on the hard drive and organizes it in such a way that it is easily accessible. When you use a file browser to navigate through the directories on a hard disk drive and open a file, it's the file system that makes the entire process possible.

Most Linux distributions offer a wide variety of file systems that you can choose from. In this topic, we'll review some of the most widely used types:

- ext2
- ext3
- Reiser
- ext4
- btrfs

 NOTE You can also use many other file systems with Linux. For example, you can use the XFS file system from Silicon Graphics. You can even use the VFAT or NTFS file system, although NTFS support isn't fully baked yet. We'll discuss creating VFAT and XFS file systems in Chapter 10.

Let's begin by discussing the ext2 file system.

ext2 The ext2 file system is one of the oldest Linux file systems still available. The acronym *ext2* stands for "Second Extended File System." Originally introduced back in 1993, ext2 stores data in the standard hierarchical fashion used by most other file systems. Data is stored in files; files are stored in directories. A directory can contain either files or other directories (subdirectories).

The maximum file size supported in the ext2 file system is 2TB (terabytes). An ext2 volume can be up to 4TB. File names can be up to 255 characters long. The ext2 file system supports Linux file system users, groups, and permissions (called POSIX permissions). It also supports file compression.

The ext2 file system is a fantastic file system. It has been around long enough for most of its bugs to be worked out. In fact, it's probably the most widely used Linux file system ever implemented. It's also reputed to be the fastest Linux file system available.

However, ext2 has one key weakness that has led to the development of other file systems. This is the fact that ext2 takes a long time to recover if the system shuts down abruptly. When shutting down the Linux system, the operating system first cleanly dismounts the file system, ensuring all pending file system transactions are written to disk before the system shuts off.

The problem arises when the system halts without completing this clean dismount procedure. For example, suppose a power outage occurs and the Linux system shuts off suddenly without going through the proper shutdown procedure. When this happens, it is possible that pending disk transactions weren't completed.

 TIP You're using an uninterruptible power supply to keep this from happening, right? If not, do so! I lost data once on an ext2 file system due to a power outage, and I've sworn to never let it happen again.

To clean up the file system, the ext2 file system will automatically run a program called e2fsck the next time the system is booted. This utility tries to fix any problems that were created when the system went down without properly dismounting the disk. If it finds unallocated files or unclaimed blocks of data, it will write this information in a directory called lost+found. By doing this, ext2 tries to ensure that data integrity is maintained in spite of the improper shutdown.

The issue here is that e2fsck will analyze the entire file system when this happens, not just the last few files that were in the process of being modified. On a basic Linux system, this can take from 10 to 15 minutes. On an extensive system that has a lot of file system data (such as a network file server), this process can take several hours. It's bad enough that the system went down unexpectedly in the first place; now you have to wait hours for it to start back up again!

Because of this issue, other Linux file systems have started replacing ext2. The first of these is ext3. Let's discuss this file system next.

ext3 The ext3 file system is an updated version of ext2. In fact, *ext3* stands for "Third Extended File System." The two are so similar that most of the file system utilities used by ext2 are also used by ext3. You can easily upgrade ext2 file systems to ext3. You can even downgrade an ext3 file system to ext2.

However, the ext3 file system offers one key advantage that makes it highly preferable over ext2: *journaling*. Remember that the key disadvantage of ext2 is the fact that it must check the entire file system if the system goes down uncleanly. Journaling eliminates this problem.

Before committing a transaction to the hard disk drive, the ext3 file system records the transaction to a journal and marks it as *incomplete*. After the disk transaction is complete, the ext3 file system marks the transaction as *complete* in the journal. By doing this, the ext3 file system can keep a log (a *journal*) of the most recent file transactions and whether or not they were actually completed.

If an event such as a power outage occurs that causes the system to shut down without properly dismounting the disk, the ext3 file system will replay the journal when the system comes back up. This allows the file system to verify the data on the disk and bring it back to a consistent state (if possible) using the information stored in the journal. Unlike ext2, the ext3 file system doesn't need to check the entire file system. Because it has a log of the most recent transactions in the journal, the ext3 file system simply checks the transactions that are listed as incomplete.

Using journaling, disk recovery time after an improper shutdown takes dramatically less time than that experienced using ext2. Instead of taking hours, the ext3 file system can replay the journal in only a few seconds or minutes, even if the file system is very large.

The disadvantage of ext3 is the fact that the journaling process uses up more system memory and slows down disk I/O operations slightly. However, because it does a better job of ensuring data integrity and does it faster, most system administrators prefer ext3 over ext2 in spite of the slightly decreased performance.

Reiser   The Reiser file system is an alternative to the ext3 file system. Like ext3, Reiser utilizes journaling to make crash recovery very fast. However, Reiser is a completely different file system from ext2 and ext3, using a dramatically different internal structure. This allows the Reiser file system to support a larger maximum file size of 8TB and maximum volume size of 16TB. In addition, the structure of Reiser allows it to perform much faster than ext2 or ext3.

ext4   The ext4 file system was released in late 2008. As you might guess, ext4 (Fourth Extended File System) is an updated version of ext3. Just as ext3 is backward compatible with ext2, ext4 is backward compatible with ext3 (and ext2, for that matter). The ext4 file system supports volumes up to 1 exabyte in size and files up to 16 terabytes in size. You can have a maximum of four billion files in an ext4 file system. As with ext2 and ext3, the maximum length of a file or directory name is 255 characters. Ext4 also uses checksums to verify the journal file itself. This helps improve the overall reliability of the system because the journal file is one of the most heavily used files of the disk. As you can see, ext4 represents a dramatic leap forward over ext3 and Reiser.

btrfs   The btrfs (pronounced "butter-fs") file system is a newer Linux file system that represents an evolutionary leap in the way file systems organize and protect data. Btrfs is a type of "copy-on-write" file system that is very similar to the NSS file system found in Novell products as well as the Storage Space technology found in the latest versions of Windows.

Using copy-on-write technology, btrfs provides several key new features not found in earlier file systems:

- Storage pools
- Snapshots

The btrfs file system provides an alternative to the traditional process of creating disk partitions. Instead, you create storage pools from storage devices in your system. From the storage pool, you can allocate space to specific storage volumes. Instead of mounting partitions, you mount storage volumes at mount points in your file system. This provides you with a great deal of flexibility when allocating space on the system. For example, suppose you are out of space on the /home volume. To add capacity, all you have to do is install a new hard drive in the system and then allocate its space to the pool where the /home volume lives. When you do, the size of the volume is automatically increased. You didn't have to back up the data and restore it as you would with traditional partitions.

The snapshot functionality provided by btrfs protects your data. Essentially, it can be configured to take snapshots of your data at specified intervals and save it on separate media. If a file ever gets lost or corrupted, you can grab a previous version of the file from a saved snapshot and restore it in a matter of seconds.

Most distributions will allow you to choose which file system you want to implement when you partition your system's hard disk drives during the installation process. You should already know what file system you want to use before you reach that point. Therefore, when planning your Linux implementation, you should specify which of these file systems you want to use in your deployment plan.

So which file system should you use? It depends on your personal preferences and the needs of your deployment. My choice for many years was the Reiser file system. However, lately ext4 has been my file system of choice.

In addition to specifying which file system you will use, you also need to specify how your system's hard disk will be partitioned in your deployment plan. Let's talk about how this is done next.

Planning Your Partitions

A *partition* is a logical division of your hard disk drive. Using the read-write heads inside the hard disk drive, a partitioning utility can create magnetic divisions on the drive platters to divide it into separate sections. A hard drive can have a single partition that encompasses the entire hard drive or it can have many partitions.

With a Linux system, you will use at least two partitions, but you can create many more. These partitions need to be defined during the initial installation of the system. Changing your disk partitioning after the system is installed can be done, but it is somewhat challenging and time consuming. Therefore, it's a best practice to plan out how you will partition your system hard drive before you start the installation process.

By default, most Linux distributions propose two partitions during the installation process, as shown in Figure 5-5:

- **swap** This partition is used for virtual memory by the Linux operating system. Essentially, Linux will use the hard disk space contained in the swap partition as though it were system RAM. When the system RAM is under heavy load, the operating system can move information loaded into RAM but not currently in use into the swap partition. This is called *swapping,* which is the process of moving a page of memory to the preconfigured swap partition on the hard disk.

  When the data is needed again, it is moved from the swap partition back into RAM. Essentially this allows the system to simultaneously run more programs than it has enough physical RAM to support.

  The appropriate size for your swap partition depends on how the system is used. For desktop systems, the general rule of thumb is to use a swap partition that is about twice the size of your system RAM. This is because desktop systems usually run a large number of applications that can be easily swapped to disk. For example, if your desktop has 2GB

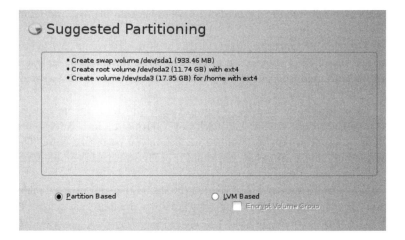

Figure 5-5
Default Linux partitioning

of RAM installed, you should have a swap partition that is about 4GB in size. For server systems, you typically don't need as much swap space. Usually, a swap partition that is about the same size as your installed RAM is sufficient.

 TIP You can also use a swap *file* instead of a swap partition with Linux. We'll talk about how this is done in Chapter 10.

- / This partition is mounted at the root directory (/) of the Linux file system. All user data, programs, log files, and configuration files are contained in this single disk partition.

Even though this is the default partitioning proposal made by most Linux distributions during installation, you should consider creating more partitions than the two or three that are created by default. To understand why we do this, you need to first understand that Linux uses a single file system structure to represent all of the storage space available to the Linux system. This is shown in Figure 5-6.

Different partitions can be mounted at different points in this hierarchy. For example, in Figure 5-7, an extra partition (/dev/sda3) has been created on the first SATA hard disk drive in the system (/dev/sda), which is mounted at the /home directory.

When you navigate through the Linux file system hierarchy and double-click the /home directory, you are actually redirected to a different partition on the hard drive. If you had multiple hard drives in the system, you could even put the partition mounted in /home on a completely different hard drive. The partitioning is completely transparent to the end user.

I encourage you, when planning your Linux partitions, to create many partitions on your hard drives. Doing this can add a degree of fault tolerance to your Linux system. Problems encountered in one partition are isolated from the other partitions in the system. For example, suppose you used the default partitioning proposal when installing Linux and had your entire file system mounted at the root directory (/). If a user were to consume all of the available space on the partition by copying huge files to his home directory in /home, it could cause the entire system to crash because the operating system would no longer be able to write critical system files to disk.

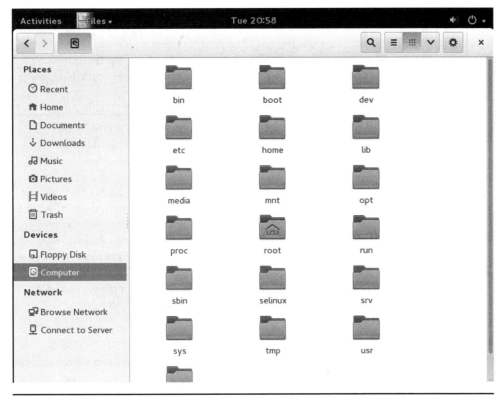

Figure 5-6   The Linux file system hierarchy

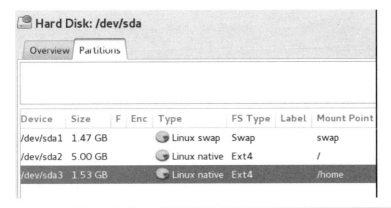

Figure 5-7   Mounting /dev/sda3 in /home

If, on the other hand, you were to create a separate partition for /home and the user were to again consume all the available disk space on the /home partition by copying very large files to his home directory, the system will remain running. The partitions containing your system files, log files, and application files are not affected because the issue is isolated to a single partition.

When planning your Linux partitions, you should consider creating separate partitions for the directories listed in Table 5-1.

 CAUTION   The /boot partition must be created within the first 1,024 cylinders of the hard disk. To be safe, I always create this partition such that it begins with cylinder 0.

Using these recommended partitions will add a degree of stability to your system. Unfortunately, this partitioning scheme doesn't use disk space efficiently. For example, your /home partition may run out of space and users won't be able to save additional data, even though there may be plenty of extra space available in other partitions on the disk. However, the added stability is worth the inefficiency. I've often heard it said that hard disks are cheap whereas data is priceless, and I believe this is true.

Once you've planned out your partitions, the next task you need to complete is to specify the software you want to install on your Linux system. Let's discuss how this is done next.

Selecting Software Packages

One of the things that I absolutely love about Linux is the wide array of open source software available. Your Linux distribution probably includes a fairly extensive sampling of packages that you can specify to be installed along with the operating system. In fact, it's the inclusion of this extra software that makes your installation set so big. Most distributions require a full DVD to store all the packages you can install.

Case Study

Several years ago, I received a call from a client indicating their Linux server wasn't functioning properly and nobody in the office could get to their files. Needless to say, he was in a panic. Upon investigation, I found that the configuration file that controls the rotation of system logs had several mistakes in it. The result was that none of the system log files had been rotated in years! The system log files had grown so big that they consumed all of the remaining space on the hard drive.

The problem in this situation was twofold. First, whoever customized the log rotation configuration should have verified it was actually working before walking away and letting it run. Second, the server used the default disk partitioning scheme of one swap partition and a second partition mounted at /. If the original implementer had created a separate partition for the /var directory (where most of the system log files are stored), the fault would have been isolated to that partition and the users would have still been able to do their work.

Mount Point	Recommendation
/	Create a partition for the root directory. This partition should be at least 4GB in size. I recommend that it be much larger, however, to accommodate software updates that will be installed later on during the life cycle of the system.
/boot	Create a partition for the /boot directory, which contains your Linux system files. This partition doesn't require much space. Usually 100MB to 200MB is plenty.
/home	Create a partition for users' files. You should allocate as much space as necessary to accommodate your users' data. Of course, no matter how much space you allocate to this partition, it seems like it's never enough.
/opt	Create a partition for application files installed into /opt. You should allocate as much space as necessary to accommodate applications that use this directory.
/tmp	Create a partition for your system's temporary files stored in /tmp. You should allocate at least 1GB or more for this partition.
/usr	Create a partition for the system utilities stored in /usr. You should allocate at least 5GB to this partition. You may need to allocate a lot more, depending on what packages you choose to install.
/var	Create a partition for the log files stored in /var. Because log files can become quite large, it's a good idea to isolate them in their own partition. You should allocate at least 3GB of space for this partition. Personally, I would allocate much more.

Table 5-1   Recommended Linux Partitions

You'll be mesmerized the first time you see the list of available software. For example, openSUSE offers many different games alone that you can install, as shown in Figure 5-8.

As a techie, you may be tempted to install just about everything. Free software! However, you should not do this. You will install really powerful software that you probably don't want your end users to have access to. For example, you probably don't want your end users hosting their own website from their desktop because you installed the Apache web server on their system. More importantly, installing excess software on these systems could potentially open up hidden avenues of access, thus creating security issues.

A much better approach is to use your deployment plan to identify the role the system will play. (We discussed how to do this earlier in the chapter.) With this information in hand, review the packages available with your distribution and specify exactly which packages you need to include in the installation. The general rule of thumb is this: install only what is needed to do the job and nothing more.

For example, if the system is going to function as a network server providing domain authentication, file, and print services, you will need to install the Samba and CUPS (Common UNIX Printing System) packages. If it is a network server that will function as a web and e-mail server, you may need to install the Apache, Tomcat, Postfix, and IMAP packages. If the system is going to be used as a desktop system, you may want to install OpenOffice.org to provide end users with word processing, spreadsheet, and presentation software.

The point is this: make sure you install the packages that are needed and avoid installing software that isn't. If, after installing the system, you determine you need additional packages, you can easily install them after the fact. I'll show you how to do this in Chapter 8.

Figure 5-8   Installing software packages in openSUSE Linux

One of the nice features of most graphical Linux installers is that they automatically calculate *dependencies* for you. A dependency is a particular software package that another software package needs in order to run. Most Linux packages that you install during the installation process will have many dependencies associated with them.

In the early days of Linux, you had to manually figure out which packages had what dependencies and be sure you included them in the installation. It could turn into quite a mess with layer upon layer of dependencies, as shown in Figure 5-9.

The good news is that the installers used by most distributions now automatically calculate package dependencies for you and will include the necessary dependent packages in the installation.

Once this part of your plan is complete, you next need to specify the users that will be created on the system.

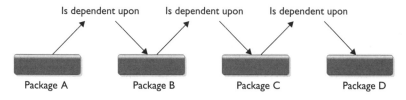

Figure 5-9   The never-ending chain of package dependencies

Identifying User Accounts

Linux is a true multiuser operating system. This means that a single system can include multiple user accounts. In fact, multiple users can use the same system at the same time using a network connection.

Therefore, when planning to install your Linux system, you should determine the user accounts that will be needed on the system. The installation utilities used by most Linux distributions provide you with the ability to create these accounts during the installation process. No matter what distribution you use, you will always create the root user account during the installation, along with one standard user account.

The root user account is the superuser account for a Linux system. The root account can do anything it wants on the Linux system. The root user account is very powerful and must be used judiciously. Put bluntly, you can really make a mess of your system if you do something wrong. Because you're logged in as root, the system assumes you know what you're doing and will let you do it. For safety and security reasons, you should not use the root account for day-to-day work. Instead, you should create a standard user account for these tasks. When you actually need superuser privileges to complete a task, you can switch to the root user account. When the task is complete, you should switch back to your standard user account.

When you install Linux, you'll be prompted to provide a password for the root user account. You'll also be given the opportunity to create additional user accounts on the system. In your deployment plan, specify which user accounts you plan on creating. As with software packages, it's not a problem if you need to add or remove user accounts later on after the installation is complete. Linux provides an extensive set of tools to manage user accounts and passwords. I'll show you how to do this in Chapter 9.

Once this information is in your plan, you're ready to move on to the next step: gathering network information. Let's review how this is done next.

Gathering Network Information

In today's networked world, most of the Linux systems you will be working with will probably be connected to some type of computer network. Therefore, you need to gather the network information necessary for your system to connect to the network before you start the installation and include it in your deployment plan. Here's a list of questions you need to answer:

- *Will the system have its networking configuration dynamically assigned, or will it need to be manually configured?* Most IP networks today use a Dynamic Host Configuration

Protocol (DHCP) server to dynamically assign IP addresses and various other networking parameters to a workstation when it is booted on the network. Most Linux systems that will function as a desktop workstation will probably use this option. If this is the case, you don't need to do much to configure your networking parameters. The information will be dynamically assigned to the system every time it boots up.

However, if the Linux system is going to function as a server in the network, you shouldn't use DHCP to dynamically assign network configuration information. Using DHCP, the system could receive a different IP address each time it's booted. Although this won't hurt a workstation, it can cause tons of problems with servers. Hence, network servers are usually assigned a static IP address that doesn't change.

If your system needs to have a static IP address assigned, you need to gather the following parameters:

- IP address
- Subnet mask
- Router address
- DNS server address(es)

- *What hostname will be assigned to the system?* Every Linux system needs to have a hostname assigned. This hostname should be unique on your network, meaning no other system on the network should have the same hostname assigned. During the installation process, you will be prompted to provide a hostname.

- *What is the name of the DNS domain the system will reside in?* More than likely, your organization has its own DNS domain, such as mycorp.com. You will be asked to provide your organization's domain name during the installation process.

- *Will the system need a host firewall configured?* Most Linux distributions include a host firewall that gets enabled by default during the installation process. A host firewall can be an invaluable asset to your organization's security. Essentially, the host-based firewall prevents other systems on the network from establishing connections to the system.

For workstation systems, you should enable this firewall and block all of your IP ports and services. You should also enable the host firewall on server systems. However, most server systems run applications that provide network-based services to other hosts on the network. Therefore, you will need to open up the necessary IP ports in the firewall to allow network hosts to connect to the associated services.

If you're installing a server system, you should list the network services it will provide in your deployment plan, along with their associated port numbers. This list will provide you with the information you need to make the necessary exceptions in your firewall configuration. For example, if you're installing a Linux system that will function as a web server, you will need to open ports 80 and 443 in the host firewall to allow clients to connect to the httpd service running on the system.

With your network configuration information specified, you're ready to move on to the last part of your deployment plan: selecting an installation source. Let's discuss how this is done next.

Selecting an Installation Source

Most Linux distributions provide you with many different options for installing the system. These options include the following:

- Installing locally from an optical disc
- Installing remotely from a network server
- Completing a remote installation using VNC

Let's first discuss how to complete an installation from a local optical disc.

Installing Locally from an Optical Disc

One of the more common methods for installing Linux is to install locally from a set of installation discs. Using this method, you simply insert the appropriate optical disc into the system's optical drive and boot the system from the disc.

For most distributions, you can simply download a copy of the installation disc image(s) from the vendor's website. For example, if you wanted to install Fedora, you could open a web browser and navigate to http://fedora.project.org and select the Download link. After selecting your system architecture, you are connected to a mirror site on the Internet that contains the distribution.

You'll notice that the downloaded file has an .iso extension. These are called *ISO images*. Once you've downloaded the appropriate .iso file, you can use your optical-disc-burning software to burn the ISO image to a physical disc. Check your documentation to see how it's done with your particular package.

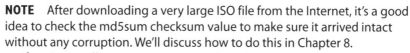

NOTE   After downloading a very large ISO file from the Internet, it's a good idea to check the md5sum checksum value to make sure it arrived intact without any corruption. We'll discuss how to do this in Chapter 8.

If you're installing Linux into a virtual machine, you don't have to burn the ISO image to disc. Instead, you can configure the virtual machine to connect directly to the ISO image itself. The virtual machine will think that the image is actually a real CD or DVD and install from it. Installing Linux using this method is much faster because the data is stored on a hard drive instead of an optical disc and the access speed is much quicker.

In addition to installing from an optical disc, you can also remotely install Linux over a network connection. Let's discuss how this is done next.

Installing Remotely from a Network Server

Another cool option for installing a Linux system is to install from a network server. You can install from a Linux server on the network that has been configured as an installation source using the SMB, NFS, HTTP, or FTP protocol. You can even install directly from an FTP or HTTP server on the Internet.

NOTE   Not all Linux distributions support a network-based installation.

The key advantage of performing a network installation of Linux is the fact that you can install a large number of systems at once without having to burn a DVD for each one. The disadvantage of this method is that the installation usually runs slower than a DVD install. An installation over the Internet can be quite slow.

To complete a network installation, you must first complete several preparatory steps. First, if you intend to install over the network from a local server, you need to copy the Linux installation files from the DVD to a directory on the server. Alternatively, you could also mount the DVD or ISO file in the file system where network clients can access it. Then you need to select the protocol that will be used to access it. For example, if you want to use the SMB protocol to access the installation files, you must install and configure the Samba service on the server. Once done, you must create a share for the directory where the installation files reside. You could also configure the HTTP, NFS, or FTP service on the server to accomplish the same task.

Once the installation source server is set up, you next need to download a basic installation CD image. For example, if you wanted to complete a network installation of SUSE Linux, you would use a browser to navigate to http://en.opensuse.org and select the Downloads link. In the page that is displayed, you can download a network boot image, as shown in Figure 5-10.

You will need to burn this image to disc and then boot the system from it. For our purposes here, we're going to look at how to do this with openSUSE. Most of the other distributions that also support network installs will use a similar process.

 TIP If you're installing a Fedora system, you can burn a network disc from the appropriate image file in the /images directory on the installation DVD and boot the system from it. You can then select your alternate installation source.

In the first installation screen, press F4 to specify the installation source, as shown in Figure 5-11.

If you select SMB/CIFS, you must specify the installation server address, the name of the share and directory where the installation files are located, the name of the domain, and the username and password of a user who has permissions to access the share. This is shown in Figure 5-12.

If you select FTP, you must specify the installation server's IP address or DNS name, the directory where the installation files reside, and a username and password authorized to access the FTP service on the remote server. The remote server could be a server on the local network or an FTP server on the Internet. Check your distribution's website for a list of FTP-based network installation repositories on the Internet. The FTP installation server configuration screen is shown in Figure 5-13.

If you select HTTP, you must specify the URL to the installation server and the directory on the remote server where the installation files reside. As with an FTP installation, the HTTP installation server can reside on the local network or somewhere on the Internet. Check your

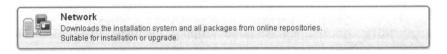

Figure 5-10   Downloading a network boot image

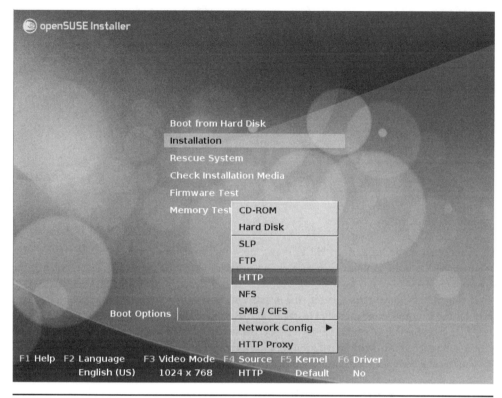

Figure 5-11   Selecting an installation source

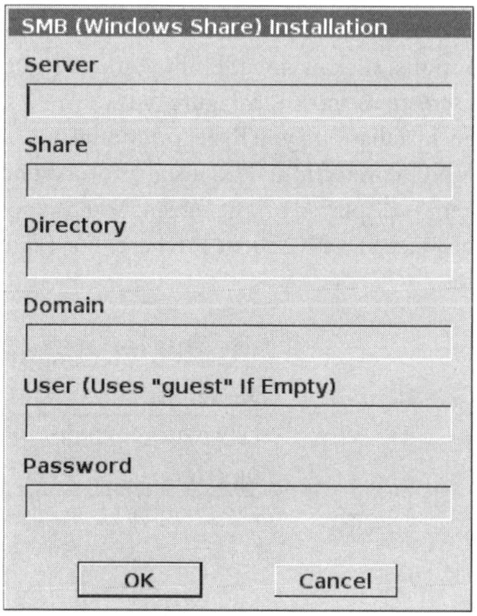

Figure 5-12
Configuring
a network
installation using
the SMB protocol

SMB (Windows Share) Installation

Server

Share

Directory

Domain

User (Uses "guest" If Empty)

Password

OK   Cancel

Figure 5-13
Configuring
a network
installation using
the FTP protocol

distribution's website for a list of HTTP-based network installation repositories. In Figure 5-14, the installer has been configured to perform an installation from a SUSE HTTP server over the Internet.

If you select NFS, you must specify the installation server's IP address or DNS name and directory on the remote server where the installation files reside. This is shown in Figure 5-15.

Once you select the installation source, select Installation from the main menu and the installation will proceed using the installation files from the remote server.

You can also complete an installation using a VNC connection. Let's review how this is done next.

Completing a Remote Installation Using VNC

VNC stands for *Virtual Network Computing*. Essentially, VNC allows you to redirect the video output from one system to another system. Using the VNC protocol, you can start the installation on your target system but then use a web browser or VNC client software on another system to view the installation screens.

On many distributions, such as openSUSE, you can enter **vnc=1** in the Boot Options field in the first installation screen, as shown in Figure 5-16.

After starting the installation, you'll be prompted to provide various network parameters needed to create a VNC connection. The installation system loads, and the IP address you can use to access the system is displayed on the screen. You can access the installation screens remotely using either a web browser or VNC client software. For example, you could open a web browser

Figure 5-14
Configuring
a network
installation
using the HTTP
protocol

Figure 5-15
Configuring
a network
installation using
the NFS protocol

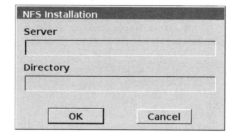

on another system and navigate to http://*IP_address_of_system*:5801. If I assigned my system an
IP address of 192.168.1.126 in the initial VNC configuration screens, I could access it by opening
http://192.168.1.126:5801 in a browser, as shown in Figure 5-17.

You could also access the installation using VNC client software. Most Linux distributions
include the vncviewer utility, which you can use to connect to a VNC server. Likewise, on
Windows systems, you can use VNC Viewer from RealVNC. When using VNC viewer utilities,
you need to specify the IP address of the system being installed along with the display number you
want to access—for example, 192.168.1.126:1.

Using this VNC connection, you can complete the installation process from the comfort of
your own office.

For your deployment plan, you need to determine which installation source you are going to
use and prepare the prerequisite systems if necessary.

Once you've completed this step, your Linux deployment plan is complete. You should now
have the data you need to complete the installation in an organized, efficient, measurable manner.
File your deployment plan in a safe place once your installation is complete. This information can
be an invaluable help for other system administrators who may need to work on your systems at
some point.

Figure 5-16
Configuring a
VNC installation

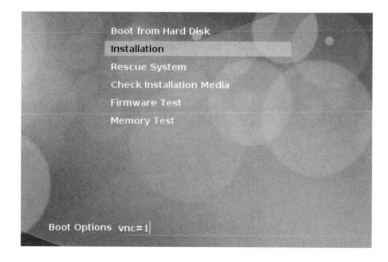

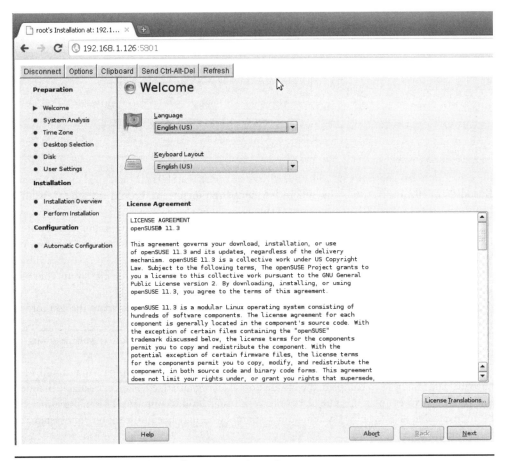

Figure 5-17 Completing the installation remotely in a browser

In my line of work, I work for a variety of different companies under contract. When they have a problem, they call me and I go onsite to fix their systems. Most of the time this works out very well for everyone involved. However, from time to time, I have to go onsite for a company that hasn't documented their network or their computer systems. It can be an extremely frustrating experience. As a consultant, I have no idea how the system has been set up, nor do I know why it was configured the way it has been. What may have been obvious to the original implementer is not obvious at all to someone else working on the system later on. A job that should take two or three hours to complete ends up taking two or three days instead. That costs my clients a lot of extra money and it dramatically increases my blood pressure.

At this point, you're ready to order your hardware, download your distribution, and actually start installing a Linux system. Let's review how this is done next.

Installing Linux

It's finally time to start installing a Linux system! After spending hours creating a Linux deployment plan, most techies breathe a sigh of relief when they finally get their hands on their new software and start installing. This is what we live for!

When installing new systems, I strongly recommend that you set up an isolated lab environment and install your systems there. This will give you a chance to observe the systems and ensure that everything is working properly before turning your users loose with them.

Once you're sure everything is working correctly, you can move them from the lab environment to your users' production environment.

As I mentioned at the beginning of this chapter, there are simply too many different Linux distributions available to include them all on the LPIC-1/Linux+ exam or in this chapter. In this chapter, we're going to review how to perform an installation of Ubuntu Desktop.

Exercise 5-1: Installing a Linux System

In this exercise, we're going to install an Ubuntu workstation. At the time this book was written, Ubuntu 14.04 was the most current version available. By the time you read this, a newer version may have been released, so you may need to adjust the steps presented here to accommodate the updated software.

 VIDEO Please watch the Exercise 5-1 video for a demonstration on how to perform this task.

Complete the following:

1. On a workstation with DVD burner, open a web browser and navigate to www.ubuntu .com and select Ubuntu Desktop.

2. Follow the instructions on the web page to download the latest Ubuntu release appropriate for your CPU architecture.

3. Launch Oracle VM VirtualBox on your workstation.

4. Click **New**.

5. Enter the following, then click **Next**:
   - Name: **Ubuntu**
   - Type: **Linux**
   - Version: (Select the appropriate version for the ISO file you downloaded.)

6. Set the memory size to **1024 MB**, then click **Next**.

7. Click **Create**.

8. Under hard drive type, mark **VDI** and select **Next**.

9. Select **Dynamically allocated** and then select **Next**.

10. Click **Create**.

11. In the list of virtual machines, click **Storage**.

12. Click the optical disc icon and then click the disc icon under Attributes and select **Choose a virtual CD/DVD disk file**.

13. Browse to and select the ISO file you just downloaded and then click **Open | OK**.

14. Click **Start** and wait for the virtual machine to boot.

15. In the Install screen, select your language and then click **Install Ubuntu**.

16. In the Preparing to Install Ubuntu screen, click **Continue**.

17. In the Installation Type screen, select **Erase disk and install Ubuntu** and then click **Install Now**.

18. In the Where Are You screen, select your location and then click **Continue**.

19. Select your keyboard layout and language and then click **Continue**.

20. In the Who Are You screen, enter the following and then click **Continue**:

    - Your name
    - Your computer's name
    - Your username
    - Your password

21. Wait while the system is installed.

22. When prompted that the system needs to restart to complete the installation, click **Restart Now**.

23. When prompted to remove the installation disc, press ENTER.

Congratulations! You now have a running Linux system. As we go through the rest of this book, you will learn how to configure and manage this system.

Configuring Locale Settings

When you install a Linux system, you typically configure the system's *locale* during the installation process. The system's locale determines the following:

- The language and encoding of text displayed on the screen
- Your character classes
- The default sort order
- The default number format
- The default currency format
- How the date and time are displayed

Your locale settings are determined by the values assigned to the following environment variables:

- **LC_CTYPE**   Configures the default character type and encoding
- **LC_MESSAGES**   Configures natural language messages
- **LC_COLLATE**   Configures your sorting rules
- **LC_NUMERIC**   Configures your number format
- **LC_MONETARY**   Configures your currency format
- **LC_TIME**   Configures the date and time display
- **LC_PAPER**   Configures your default paper size
- **LC_NAME**   Configures the default personal name format
- **LC_ADDRESS**   Configures the default address format
- **LC_TELEPHONE**   Configures the default telephone number format
- **LC_MEASUREMENT**   Configures the default measurement unit
- **LC_ALL**   Overrides all other LC_ environment variables
- **LANG**   Specifies the default locale value for all LC_ variables
- **LANGUAGE**   Overrides LC_MESSAGES

The LC_CTYPE locale variable can be assigned a locale value using the following syntax:

```
language_territory.codeset @modifier
```

This syntax uses these values:

- *language*   Specifies the ISO 639 language code to be used (specified in lowercase)
- *territory*   Specifies the ISO 3166 country code to be used (specified in uppercase)
- *codeset*   Specifies the character set to be used
- *modifier*   Specifies other locale attributes, such as dialect or currency

Consider the following examples:

- **en_US**   The language and territory for English in the United States
- **en_CA**   The language and territory for English in Canada
- **fr_CA**   The language and territory for French Canadian

You can also specify an encoding in the locale. For example, you could use en_US.UTF-8 to configure a default locale of U.S. English using UTF-8 character encoding (also known as *Unicode* encoding).

When you installed your Linux system, your locale settings were automatically defined for you based on your selections during the installation process. To view them at the shell prompt, you can use the echo command. Here is an example:

```
openSUSE:~ # echo $LC_CTYPE
en_US.UTF-8
openSUSE:~ #
```

As you can see in this example, the LC_CYTPE variable was populated on this system during installation. This variable defines the default character type and encoding used on the system. As you can see, this system uses a locale of U.S. English with Unicode text encoding.

Just as an aside, you can also use a locale named C. This locale is very useful if you create a lot of shell scripts at the shell prompt. It configures the following default locale settings:

- ASCII encoding
- POSIX character classes
- U.S. English time, date, number, and currency formats

If for some reason you need to localize a Linux system to a locale other than the default that was configured at installation, you simply change the value of the appropriate environment variable. Generally, all of these variables will be set to the same value (or the LC_ALL or LANG variable will be used to specify the default locale for all variables). However, if necessary, you can also set them independently to different values.

If you do this, however, be aware that not all of the LC_ variables have the same level of precedence. Linux uses the following rules to determine which locale setting to use:

1. If the LC_ALL variable is defined, its value is used and the values assigned to all other LC_ variables are not checked.

2. If LC_ALL is undefined, the specific LC_ variable in question is checked. If the specific LC_ variable has a value, it is used.

3. If the LC_ variable in question has a null value, the LANG environment variable is used.

If you want all of your LC_ variables to use the same value, you can set the LC_ALL variable, thus eliminating the need to set each individual variable. However, if you want to use different values for your LC_ variables, you must first set LC_ALL to a null value. In fact, many distributions leave LC_ALL undefined for this very reason. Instead, they set the value of LC_CTYPE to define the default encoding and the value of LANG to provide a default value to all of your other LC_ variables. However, because LANG is third in priority, you can manually set the value of an LC_ variable without impacting any other LC_ variables.

To view all of your current locale settings, enter the **/usr/bin/locale** command at the shell prompt. Here is an example:

```
openSUSE:~ # locale
LANG=POSIX
LC_CTYPE=en_US.UTF-8
LC_NUMERIC="POSIX"
```

```
LC_TIME="POSIX"
LC_COLLATE="POSIX"
LC_MONETARY="POSIX"
LC_MESSAGES="POSIX"
LC_PAPER="POSIX"
LC_NAME="POSIX"
LC_ADDRESS="POSIX"
LC_TELEPHONE="POSIX"
LC_MEASUREMENT="POSIX"
LC_IDENTIFICATION="POSIX"
LC_ALL=
```

In this example, only the LANG and the LC_CTYPE variables are actually defined. The other LC_ variables are automatically populated with the value assigned to LANG.

You can also enter **locale charmap** at the shell prompt to view the type of encoding used. Here's an example

```
openSUSE:~ # locale charmap
UTF-8
ws1:~ #
```

If you need to localize the system by changing the locale or the encoding, you first must determine what locales have been installed on your system. To do this, use the –a option with the locale command to generate a list of all available locales. You can also use the –m option with the locale command to view a list of available encodings. An example follows:

```
openSUSE:~ # locale -a
C
POSIX
aa_DJ
aa_DJ.utf8
aa_ER
aa_ER.utf8
....
ws1:~ # locale -m
ANSI_X3.110-1983
ANSI_X3.4-1968
ARMSCII-8
....
```

Be aware that if you change the encoding used by the system, you may have trouble viewing some files correctly if they were created using a different encoding. You can convert the encoding from one encoding to a new one using the iconv command at the shell prompt. The syntax is as follows:

```
iconv -f source_encoding -t destination_encoding -o output_filename input_
filename
```

In addition to configuring the locale of your Linux system, you may also need to configure your system's time zone settings. Let's look at how this is done next.

Configuring Time Zone Settings

If a Linux system is moved to a different physical location, you may need to configure your time zone settings as well as your local settings. This may seem simple on the surface. However, time on a Linux system is managed differently than on other operating systems you may be familiar with. In this part of the chapter, we're going to review the following topics:

- How time works on Linux
- Configuring the time zone

How Time Works on Linux

Before managing time zones on Linux, you need to understand how time works on Linux. The first thing you need to understand is that there are two main clocks in a Linux system:

- **Hardware clock**   This clock runs independently all the time, even when the system is powered off. The hardware clock is called by a variety of names, including the Real Time Clock (RTC) or the BIOS/CMOS clock.

 TIP   You can use the hwclock command at the shell prompt to set the time in the hardware clock.

- **System time**   This clock runs via software inside the Linux kernel itself. It is driven by an ISA timer interrupt. System time is measured as the number of seconds since 00:00:00 January 1, 1970 UTC.

The key thing to remember is that the hardware clock and the system time may not be the same. When managing a Linux system, we are more concerned with the system time than the time reported by the hardware clock. The role of the hardware clock is pretty basic. Its job is to keep time when the system is powered off. The system time is synchronized to the hardware clock time when the Linux operating system starts. After booting, Linux only uses system time. The hardware clock is ignored. When setting the time on your hardware clock, you should set it to one of the following:

- **Universal Time Coordinated (UTC)**   UTC is the standard by which the world regulates time. UTC is the current mean solar time at the Royal Observatory in Greenwich, London, in England. Thus, UTC is also referred to as *Greenwich Mean Time (GMT)*. Your local time is determined by adding or subtracting one hour to or from UTC for each time zone you are away from UTC. For example, I live seven time zones away from Greenwich, so my time is UTC –7. Therefore, at 10:58 A.M. my local time, it's 5:58 P.M. UTC. If your hardware clock is set to UTC instead of the local time, you need to set the HWCLOCK directive in the /etc/sysconfig/clock file to **–u**. Your Linux system will automatically calculate daylight savings time offsets according to your local time zone.

NOTE For Linux systems, it is actually preferred that you set your hardware clock to UTC instead of local time.

- **Local time** The hardware clock in most systems you will encounter will be set to local time by default. If this is the case, the HWCLOCK directive in the /etc/sysconfig/clock file will be set to --**localtime**.

Setting your hardware clock to UTC is the preferred option when working with Linux systems. Using UTC makes calculating time zone differences much easier. In fact, if you install certain groupware applications on your Linux system, you may be required to set your hardware clock to UTC because it makes it easier to coordinate time stamps among a large number of computers located in different time zones.

Configuring the Time Zone

During the initial installation of your Linux system, you are prompted to specify the time zone the system is located in. On some distributions (such as Ubuntu), the time zone you specify is saved in the /etc/timezone file. You can view your system's current time zone by displaying the contents of this file at the shell prompt using the cat command. Here's an example:

```
rtracy@ubuntu:~$ cat /etc/timezone
America/Denver
```

Other distributions (such as openSUSE) save this information in the /etc/sysconfig/clock file instead. The TIMEZONE= directive in this file configures the zone file to use, as you see here:

```
TIMEZONE="America/Boise"
```

You can also view the current time zone by entering **date** at the shell prompt, as shown next:

```
openSUSE:~ # date
Wed Feb  9 11:40:05 MST 2014
openSUSE:~ #
```

If you need to change time zones after installation, you can use the **tzselect** or **tzconfig** command at the shell prompt. Debian-based distributions use the tzconfig command whereas other distributions such as openSUSE and Fedora use the tzselect command. This command must be run as root. Here is an example:

```
openSUSE:~ # tzselect
Please identify a location so that time zone rules can be set correctly.
Please select a continent or ocean.
 1) Africa
 2) Americas
 3) Antarctica
 4) Arctic Ocean
 5) Asia
 6) Atlantic Ocean
 7) Australia
 8) Europe
 9) Indian Ocean
```

```
10) Pacific Ocean
11) none - I want to specify the time zone using the Posix TZ format.
```

The tzselect command first displays a list of continents and oceans. Enter the appropriate number for the region where the time zone you want to switch to is located. When you do, a list of countries in the region is displayed. Enter the number for the country where the system will be located; then enter the number for the appropriate time zone. You are prompted to confirm the time zone change, as shown in this example:

```
The following information has been given:

        United States
        Mountain Time

Therefore TZ='America/Denver' will be used.
Local time is now:     Wed Feb  9 11:50:10 MST 2011.
Universal Time is now: Wed Feb  9 18:50:10 UTC 2011.
Is the above information OK?
1) Yes
2) No
#?
```

If the change is correct, enter **1** to confirm. Notice in the preceding example that tzselect switches time zones by setting the value of the TZ environment variable. You can actually change time zones from the shell prompt without tzselect by setting the value of the TZ environment variable and then exporting it. This is useful in situations where you don't have the root password for the system or if you want to use a different time zone for your account without changing the time zone used by other users. The syntax is **export TZ=*time_zone***. A list of available time zones can be found in the /usr/share/zoneinfo/ directory, as shown here:

```
openSUSE:~ # ls /usr/share/zoneinfo/
Africa      Canada    Factory     Iceland    MST7MDT    Portugal    Zulu
America     Chile     GB          Indian     Mexico     ROK         iso3166.tab
Antarctica  Cuba      GB-Eire     Iran       Mideast    Singapore   posix
Arctic      EET       GMT         Israel     NZ         Turkey      posixrules
Asia        EST       GMT+0       Jamaica    NZ-CHAT    UCT         right
Atlantic    EST5EDT   GMT-0       Japan      Navajo     US          zone.tab
Australia   Egypt     GMT0        Kwajalein  PRC        UTC
Brazil      Eire      Greenwich   Libya      PST8PDT    Universal
CET         Etc       HST         MET        Pacific    W-SU
CST6CDT     Europe    Hongkong    MST        Poland     WET
ws1:~ #
```

Be aware that this change is not persistent. If you reboot your system, the time zone change will be lost. You can make the time zone change persistent for your user account by adding the following to the .profile file in your user's home directory:

```
export TZ='America/Denver'
```

You can also change time zones using the /etc/localtime file and the various zone files in /usr/share/zoneinfo that we looked at earlier. To do this, create a symbolic link to the appropriate time zone file in /usr/share/zoneinfo from /etc/localtime. For example, if you wanted to switch to the Mountain Standard Time zone in the United States, you would enter **ln –sf /usr/share/zoneinfo/ MST /etc/localtime** at the shell prompt.

> **NOTE** Commonly used text encodings include iso8859 (also called Latin-9 encoding), which is designed for Western European languages; ASCII, which uses an English-based character-encoding scheme; and Unicode, which is designed to handle character sets from languages around the world.

Chapter Review

In this chapter, we emphasized the importance of creating a deployment plan when implementing new Linux systems. The first component in this plan is to conduct a needs assessment. When conducting a needs assessment, you should first determine the goals of the project and identify who the stakeholders are. You should get approval from all concerned parties before actually starting the project. You should use the information gathered in the needs assessment to develop the project scope, which states exactly what will be done in the project. The project scope comprises the project schedule, the resources assigned to the project, and the range of tasks to be completed. I pointed out that any project involves a three-way balancing act between schedule, resources, and scale. Changes in any one of these factors necessitate changes in the other two.

The next component in your deployment plan is to select a Linux distribution to install. I emphasized that you must evaluate the role of the system to determine the best distribution. If the system is going to provide network services to client systems, then a Linux distribution optimized to function as a server would be the best choice. If the system is going to be used as a desktop system, then a distribution optimized to function as a workstation would be the best choice. I also emphasized the importance of technical support. An unsupported distribution may be a fine choice for an experimental lab system, but a supported distribution is a better choice for systems that will be used in a production environment.

The next component in your deployment plan is to verify that your hardware is compatible with your chosen Linux distribution. I pointed out that most distributions include some type of hardware compatibility list. You should check your hardware against this list. You should also verify that your hardware meets your distribution's minimum system requirements. I emphasized that you must download the correct version of the distribution for your CPU's architecture.

After verifying your hardware, you should next plan your file system. I emphasized that the Linux file system requires more forethought and planning than the file system in other operating systems. I pointed out that you could choose from the ext2, ext3, Reiser, and ext4 file systems when implementing a Linux system. We discussed the advantages and disadvantages of each file system. I also pointed out that the hard disk in a Linux system should have multiple partitions. We discussed guidelines for the size of your swap partition. I also emphasized that you should consider creating separate partitions for the /, /boot, /home, /opt, /tmp, /usr, and /var directories.

Next, you need to specify the software that will be installed on your Linux system. I emphasized that there are many packages that you can choose from when implementing a Linux system. However, you should only install the software that will be needed on the system. I also pointed out that most packages have dependencies that must be taken into account when you're installing your Linux system.

After specifying your software, your deployment plan should next specify which user accounts need to be created on the system. I pointed out that all Linux systems have the superuser account named root. I emphasized that root should only be used for administrative tasks. You should create an additional standard user account for completing day-to-day tasks. Any other users who will use the system will also need user accounts.

Next, you need to gather networking information for your system. You first need to specify whether the system will use static or dynamic IP addressing. If the system will use static addressing, you need to gather the appropriate IP address, subnet mask, router address, and DNS server address for your network. You also need to define the hostname that will be used by the system as well as the DNS domain in which the system will reside. I also pointed out that most distributions include a host-based firewall that is used to prevent other systems on the network from connecting to your system. If the system will function as a server, you need to identify which IP ports will need to be opened in the host firewall to allow network clients to connect to the services provided by the system.

Next, you need to identify your installation source in your deployment plan. I pointed out that most system administrators install Linux using a DVD. We discussed how you could download ISO images from your Linux vendor's website and burn them to optical discs. I also pointed out that the installation files can be copied to a network server, allowing you to complete an installation over the wire using the SMB, NFS, HTTP, or FTP protocol. This strategy also allows you to install a Linux system directly from an installation repository on the Internet. You can use VNC to remotely install Linux from a web browser running on a different computer.

With this information gathered, your deployment plan is complete. I emphasized that keeping this documentation on hand can be extremely valuable when the system needs maintenance later on. With the deployment plan in hand, you're ready to install a Linux system.

Finally, you practiced installing an openSUSE system. We then discussed how to localize an installed system by changing the local settings and the time zone.

Accelerated Review

- Installing Linux requires more planning than other operating systems.
- System administrators don't like to plan or document their work.
- Properly planning and documenting a Linux deployment will save time and money in the long run.
- The first component in a Linux deployment plan is a needs assessment.
- You should ask the following questions in your needs assessment:
  - What are the goals of the project?
  - Who are the stakeholders?
  - What is the scope of the project?
- The project scope is composed of three factors that must remain in balance:
  - Schedule
  - Resources
  - Scale
- Using project management software can help you plan and manage your deployment.

- Your deployment plan should specify which distribution you are going to use.
- You should determine the role of the system before selecting a distribution.
- Systems used in a production environment should provide technical support.
- You should verify that your software will run on your selected distribution before deploying it.
- You should check your distribution's HCL to determine if your hardware is compatible.
- You should verify that your hardware meets your distribution's minimum system requirements.
- You need to determine your CPU's architecture before downloading a distribution.
- You need to plan your file system in your deployment plan.
- You should select one of the following file systems:
  - ext2
  - ext3
  - Reiser
  - ext4
  - btrfs
- You should create separate partitions for different directories in your file system to ensure system stability.
- The optimal size of your swap partition depends on what the system will be used for.
- Your implementation plan should specify the software packages you intend to install on your system.
- You should install only the packages needed.
- You need to keep package dependencies in mind when installing software.
- Your deployment plan should specify which user accounts will be created on the system.
- The root user account is the superuser.
- You should use root only for administrative tasks.
- You should create a standard user account for day-to-day tasks.
- Your deployment plan should include networking parameters.
- Systems can have the IP addressing information dynamically or statically assigned.
- You need to determine how the host-based firewall will be configured in your deployment plan.
- Your deployment plan should specify what installation source will be used to install Linux.
- You can download ISO images from your Linux vendor's website and burn them to a DVD.
- You can copy the Linux installation files to a server on your network and install across the wire using the SMB, NFS, HTTP, or FTP protocol.

- You can install directly from the Internet using the HTTP or FTP protocol.
- You can configure VNC to complete an installation from a remote workstation using a web browser.
- To practice installing Linux, you should purchase a lab system or use virtualization software such as VirtualBox or VMware.
- Back up any important data from the hard drive before installing; otherwise, it will be erased when the disk is partitioned.
- The system's locale determines the following:
  - The language and encoding of text displayed on the screen
  - Your character classes
  - The default sort order
  - The default number format
  - The default currency format
  - How the date and time are displayed
- Your locale settings are determined by the values assigned to the following environment variables:
  - LC_CTYPE
  - LC_MESSAGES
  - LC_COLLATE
  - LC_NUMERIC
  - LC_MONETARY
  - LC_TIME
  - LC_PAPER
  - LC_NAME
  - LC_ADDRESS
  - LC_TELEPHONE
  - LC_MEASUREMENT
  - LC_ALL
  - LANG
  - LANGUAGE
- To view all of your current locale settings, enter the **locale** command at the shell prompt.
- You can convert a file from one encoding to another using the **iconv** command at the shell prompt.
- There are two main clocks in a Linux system: the hardware clock and the system clock.

- The hardware clock can be set to UTC time or local time.
- The time zone you specify during installation is saved in the /etc/timezone file or the /etc/sysconfig/clock file.
- You can view the current time zone by entering **date** at the shell prompt.
- If you need to change time zones after installation, you can enter the **tzselect** or **tzconfig** command at the shell prompt.
- You can also change time zones from the shell prompt by setting the value of the TZ environment variable and then exporting it.
- You can also change time zones using the /etc/localtime file and the various zone files in /usr/share/zoneinfo.

Questions

1. When conducting a needs assessment, what questions should you ask? (Choose two.)
   A. What problem will this installation fix?
   B. Which distribution should I use?
   C. Where can I get the best price on a new server?
   D. Who is requesting the new systems?

2. Which of the following is a properly stated goal in a needs assessment?
   A. Mike's boss wants a new server, so we're going to install it.
   B. We're going to install Linux on everyone's desktop.
   C. We need a new Linux server.
   D. The new Linux system will provide a network database to increase the documentation team's productivity by an anticipated 20 percent.

3. Suppose Karen from Customer Service approaches you and asks for a new Linux server for her team. Who else should you talk to as a part of your needs assessment? (Choose two.)
   A. Karen's boss
   B. Karen's coworkers
   C. The Technical Support supervisor
   D. Your hardware vendor

4. Which of the following are components of your project scope? (Choose two.)
   A. Customer demands
   B. Management decision-making
   C. Schedule
   D. Scale

5. You're responsible for implementing five new Linux servers in your organization's Technical Support department. The Technical Support supervisor has asked that four additional servers be added to the project. Due to time constraints, he won't allow you to adjust the original schedule. Which of the following is the most appropriate response?

    A. Ignore the request.

    B. Inform the supervisor that additional resources will have to be added to the project.

    C. Resign in protest.

    D. Cheerfully agree to the request and then miss the deadline.

6. You're installing new Linux systems that will be used by software engineers to develop advanced computer-aided design applications. Which distributions would be the best choice for this deployment? (Choose two.)

    A. Red Hat Enterprise Linux

    B. Red Hat Enterprise Desktop

    C. Red Hat Enterprise Linux Workstation

    D. SUSE Linux Enterprise Server

    E. SUSE Linux Enterprise Desktop

7. You're installing a new Linux system that will be used by an administrative assistant to type documents, create presentations, and manage e-mail. Which distribution would be the best choice for this deployment? (Choose two.)

    A. Red Hat Enterprise Linux

    B. Red Hat Enterprise Desktop

    C. Red Hat Enterprise Linux Workstation

    D. SUSE Linux Enterprise Server

    E. SUSE Linux Enterprise Desktop

8. You're installing a new Linux server that will be used to host mission-critical database applications. This server will be heavily utilized by a large number of users every day. Which distributions would be the best choice for this deployment? (Choose two.)

    A. Red Hat Enterprise Linux

    B. Red Hat Client

    C. Red Hat Enterprise Linux Workstation

    D. SUSE Linux Enterprise Server

    E. SUSE Linux Enterprise Desktop

9. You're planning to install Linux on a system that you've built out of spare parts. Several components in the system aren't listed on your distribution's HCL. This system will be used by your team's administrative assistant to manage employee schedules, send and receive e-mail, and track employee hours. What should you do?

    A. Install the distribution anyway and hope for the best.

    B. Install the distribution and then install the latest product updates.

    C. Replace the incompatible parts with supported hardware.

    D. Spend three days scouring the Internet looking for drivers.

10. You're planning to install Fedora on a system that uses a 32-bit CPU. Which distribution architecture should you download?

    A. IA-64

    B. x86-Celeron

    C. x86-64

    D. x86

    E. PPC

11. You're planning to install Fedora on a system that uses a 64-bit AMD multicore CPU. Which distribution architecture should you download?

    A. IA-64

    B. x86-AMD

    C. x86-64

    D. x86

    E. PPC

12. You're installing a new Linux system. This system will be used by a civil engineer to model the behavior of buildings and bridges during an earthquake. This system must run as fast as possible. It must protect the integrity of the data if the system goes down unexpectedly. If it does go down, the system needs to be back up and running as quickly as possible. Which file system would be the best choice?

    A. VFAT

    B. FAT32

    C. ext4

    D. ext3

    E. ext2

13. Which partition is used for virtual memory by a Linux system?

    A. pagefile

    B. swap

    C. /swap

    D. /boot

    E. /tmp

14. If your system has 1GB of RAM installed, how big should your swap partition be?

    A. 256MB

    B. 1GB

    C. 512GB

    D. Depends on what the system will be used for

15. Which of the following directories should have their own partition? (Choose three.)

    A. /bin

    B. /boot

    C. /etc

    D. /usr

    E. /home

    F. /root

    G. /dev

16. You're installing a new Linux server. This system will function as an e-mail server for your organization. What ports should you open on its host firewall? (Choose three.)

    A. 110

    B. 80

    C. 25

    D. 143

    E. 443

17. You need to install Linux on a workstation. The hard drive has been wiped and is ready for the new operating system. You insert your Linux installation DVD in the optical drive and boot the system. Instead of the installation routine starting, the screen displays an error message indicating that an operating system couldn't be found. What's the most likely cause of the problem?

    A. Your Linux DVD is damaged.

    B. The hard drive is failing and needs to be replaced.

    C. The DVD drive is malfunctioning.

    D. The boot device order is set incorrectly in the BIOS.

18. Your Linux system uses two SATA hard disk drives. Which of the following refers to the second SATA drive in the system?

    A. /dev/sda

    B. /dev/sdc

    C. /dev/sdb

    D. /dev/sdd

19. Your Linux system uses a single SATA hard disk drive. Which of the following refers to the first partition on the drive?

    A. /dev/sda1

    B. /dev/sdb1

    C. /dev/sda2

    D. /dev/pdb2

20. Your Linux system uses a single SATA hard disk drive. Which of the following refers to the second partition on the drive?

    A. /dev/sda1

    B. /dev/hdb1

    C. /dev/sda2

    D. /dev/hdb2

21. Your Linux system uses two SCSI hard disk drives. The first drive is assigned SCSI ID 0; the second drive is assigned SCSI ID 1. Which of the following refers to the first partition on the second SCSI drive in the system?

    A. /dev/sda1

    B. /dev/sdc1

    C. /dev/sdb1

    D. /dev/sdd1

22. Which locale environment variable configures your default character encoding?

    A. LC_NUMERIC

    B. LC_CTYPE

    C. LC_MEASUREMENT

    D. LC_CHAR

23. Which locale value specifies French Canadian using Unicode encoding?

    A. en_US.UTF-8

    B. fr_CA.UTF-8

    C. fr_CA.ASCII

    D. en_CA.ASCII

24. Which locale variable overrides all other locale variables?

    A. LC_ALL

    B. LANG

    C. LANGUAGE

    D. LC_CTYPE

25. If you are using standard time in the U.S. Central Time zone and UTC is 5:00 P.M., what is the local time?

   A. 10:00 A.M.

   B. 12:00 P.M.

   C. 11:00 A.M.

   D. 11:00 P.M.

26. Which directive in the /etc/sysconfig/clock file configures the time zone a Linux system will use?

   A. TIMEZONE

   B. ZONE

   C. UTC

   D. HWCLOCK

27. Which environment variable can be used to set the current time zone on a Linux system?

   A. TIMEZONE

   B. UTC

   C. TZ

   D. TIME

Answers

   1. **A, D.** You should determine why the new systems are needed and who will be using them.

   2. **D.** This response clearly states the goal of the project and is measurable.

   3. **A, B.** Karen's boss and her coworkers are key stakeholders in the project.

   4. **C, D.** The project scope is composed of schedule, scale, and resources.

   5. **B.** The best response to this situation is to have a frank discussion with the stakeholder and point out the consequences of the decision. Either the scale will have to be reduced or more resources must be added to the project to complete it in the same time frame.

   6. **C, E.** Technically, any Linux distribution could be used in this role. However, options **C** and **E** are specifically optimized for these kinds of tasks.

   7. **B, E.** Red Hat Enterprise Desktop and SLED are optimized for basic workstation tasks such as word processing.

   8. **A, D.** Red Hat Enterprise Linux and SUSE Linux Enterprise Server are designed for high-demand network servers.

   9. **C.** The best approach is to use supported hardware.

   10. **D.** A 32-bit CPU uses the x86 architecture.

   11. **C.** The 64-bit AMD CPU uses a 64-bit x86 architecture.

12. **C.** The ext4 file system is the fastest, and it uses enhanced journaling to speed crash recovery while maintaining the overall integrity of the system.

13. **B.** Linux systems use a dedicated swap partition by default for virtual memory.

14. **D.** The optimal size of the swap partition depends on what the system will be used for. A workstation running lots of applications at once will need a large swap partition. A server providing network services may not need one as large.

15. **B, D, E.** You should consider creating separate partitions for /boot, /usr, and /home.

16. **A, C, D.** Port 110 is used by the POP3 e-mail protocol. Port 25 is used by the SMTP e-mail protocol. Port 143 is used by the IMAP e-mail protocol.

17. **D.** The most likely cause of this problem is that the system is set to boot off the hard drive first. When it can't find the operating system on the hard drive, the error message is displayed.

18. **C.** /dev/sdb points to the second hard drive installed in a system.

19. **A.** /dev/sda1 points to the first partition on the first hard drive in the system.

20. **C.** /dev/sda2 points to the second partition on the first hard drive in the system.

21. **C.** /dev/sdb1 points to the first partition on the second hard drive in the system.

22. **B.** The LC_CTYPE environment variable configures the default character encoding.

23. **B.** The fr_CA.UTF-8 locale value specifies French Canadian using Unicode encoding.

24. **A.** The LC_ALL locale variable overrides all other locale variables.

25. **C.** When it is 5:00 p.m. UTC/GMT, it is 11:00 a.m. CST because CST is six time zones behind UTC.

26. **A.** The TIMEZONE directive in the /etc/sysconfig/clock file specifies which time zone a Linux system uses.

27. **C.** The TZ environment variable can be used to set the current time zone on a Linux system.

Managing the Linux Boot Process

In this chapter, you will learn about:

- The Linux boot process
- Configuring the bootloader
- Managing Linux runlevels with init
- Managing Linux boot targets
- Shutting down the system

In the preceding chapter, you learned about installing Linux. Now that you have a Linux system up and running, you need to learn how to manage the way it boots as well as how to start and stop services on the system. In this chapter, we're going to go into depth about the Linux boot process and how to manage runlevels.

EXAM TIP For your LPIC-1/Linux+ exam, you need to have a sound understanding of how the Linux boot process works for both init and systemd. If you can draw a diagram of each process, you should be in good shape for the exam. In addition, you need to be very familiar with the LILO, GRUB, and GRUB2 bootloaders. Given a particular Linux system, you need to be able to identify which bootloader it's using and know how to configure it. You also need to know how to manage Linux runlevels as well as how to change runlevels from the shell prompt. You should know how to use the inittab file to specify the default runlevel for the system, and you must also know how to specify which services run by default at each runlevel.

Let's begin this chapter by discussing how the Linux boot process works.

The Linux Boot Process

A key concept that you as a Linux administrator need to understand is how the operating system itself boots. The Linux boot process is a little more complicated than the boot process used by other operating systems that you may already be familiar with. Therefore, we're going to spend some time at the beginning of this chapter outlining how the process works. Understanding the boot process will be of great benefit to you when we discuss how to configure bootloaders, runlevels, and init scripts later in this chapter.

 NOTE The boot process we'll discuss in this chapter is generic in nature. Most Linux distributions will follow the same basic process, although the specific implementation of the process may vary between distributions. The process also varies between older and newer versions of the Linux kernel.

The first time I booted a Linux system back in the mid-1990s, a string of unintelligible messages (at least to me) was displayed on the screen as the system started up. I cut my computer teeth on DOS and NetWare; I had no idea what these messages were talking about. What's this vmlinuz thing anyway?

Today, most of the Linux operating system's boot messages are hidden by splash screens on most popular distributions, as shown in Figure 6-1.

These splash screens make things pretty and less intimidating to the novice user, but they also hide a lot of useful information. Fortunately, with most distributions, you can still view these messages if you press the ESC key when the splash screen is displayed. A sample is shown in Figure 6-2.

Figure 6-1   Linux splash screen

```
Invoking in-kernel resume from /dev/sda1
Waiting for device /dev/root to appear:  ok
fsck from util-linux 2.23.2
[/sbin/fsck.ext4 (1) -- /] fsck.ext4 -a /dev/sda2
/dev/sda2: clean, 169814/402400 files, 1394002/1606656 blocks
fsck succeeded. Mounting root device read-write.
Mounting root /dev/root
mount -o rw,acl,user_xattr -t ext4 /dev/root /root

Welcome to openSUSE 13.1 (Bottle) (i586)!

[  OK  ] Listening on Syslog Socket.
[  OK  ] Reached target System Time Synchronized.
[  OK  ] Reached target Remote File Systems (Pre).
[  OK  ] Reached target Remote File Systems.
[  OK  ] Listening on Delayed Shutdown Socket.
[  OK  ] Listening on /dev/initctl Compatibility Named Pipe.
[  OK  ] Listening on LVM2 metadata daemon socket.
[  OK  ] Set up automount Arbitrary Executable File Formats File System Automount Point.
[  OK  ] Reached target Encrypted Volumes.
[  OK  ] Listening on Journal Socket.
         Starting Setup Virtual Console...
         Mounting Debug File System...
         Mounting POSIX Message Queue File System...
         Starting Create dynamic rule for /dev/root link...
         Mounting Huge Pages File System...
         Starting LSB: Set default boot entry if called...
         Starting Journal Service...
[  OK  ] Started Journal Service.
[  OK  ] Listening on udev Kernel Socket.
[  OK  ] Listening on udev Control Socket.
         Starting Create list of required static device nodes for the current kernel...
         Starting Load Kernel Modules...
         Expecting device dev-sda1.device...
         Starting Remount Root and Kernel File Systems...
[  OK  ] Created slice Root Slice.
```

Figure 6-2   Linux boot messages

TIP   The boot messages often scroll by too quickly to read. You can enter **dmesg | more** at the shell prompt to review the messages displayed during the boot process.

I highly recommend that you do this very thing after reading this part of this chapter. It will help solidify the boot process concepts we're going to be reviewing. To make the Linux boot process more digestible, we're going to break it down into the following phases:

- The BIOS phase
- The bootloader phase
- The kernel phase

Let's start by discussing the BIOS phase.

The BIOS Phase

Regardless of what operating system you're using, when you first power on an x86 or x86-64 personal computer, the system BIOS is the first component to take charge of the boot process. The system BIOS is a ROM chip integrated in the motherboard that contains a series of very small programs and drivers that allow the CPU to communicate with basic system devices, such as the keyboard, I/O ports, the system speaker, system RAM, floppy disk drives, and hard drives. Variable information about your system, such as the amount of RAM installed and the geometry of your hard drives, is stored in the CMOS chip. The BIOS uses the data in the CMOS chip to address these devices.

The BIOS plays two key roles during the boot process. First, it tests the various system components and makes sure they are working properly. This is called the *power-on self-test,* otherwise affectionately known as *POST.* If the BIOS encounters any problems with system devices during POST, it will either display a cryptic error message on the screen or play a series of beeps in code. You can use your BIOS documentation—easily available on the Internet by searching on the motherboard model number or BIOS manufacturer, or sometimes included in the manual for your motherboard—to interpret these messages to determine what exactly is wrong with the system.

The second role played by the BIOS is that it selects a storage device to boot the operating system from. Most CMOS system setup programs allow you to configure the order in which the BIOS should look for bootable media. In Figure 6-3, the system has been configured to first look on any removable devices, then on the local hard disk drive, and then on the optical drive.

The BIOS will boot from the first bootable device it finds in the list. Recall in the preceding chapter that I told you to be sure your BIOS is set to boot off the optical drive first; otherwise, you probably won't be able to load the Linux installation program. If the BIOS finds a bootable device higher up in the list, it won't get to the optical disc that you want to boot from.

Figure 6-3
BIOS boot media options

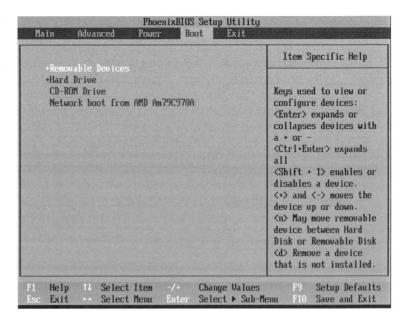

So how does the BIOS know if a device is bootable or not? It looks in the first sector of the device, which is called the *boot sector.* On a hard disk drive, the boot sector contains the master boot record (MBR). Let's discuss the role of the MBR next in the bootloader phase.

The Bootloader Phase

After running POST, the BIOS really doesn't have much more to do. It has done its job and is ready to turn control of the system over to someone else. To do this, it needs to know where programming resides that can take over the system. To learn this, it looks for the MBR on your system's hard drive.

The MBR resides in the boot sector of your system's hard disk drive. It plays a key role in the process of booting your Linux system. The MBR tells the system where a bootloader resides. The bootloader has a very important job. The issue here is that your computer needs an operating system of some type to access the hard disk drive and load data into RAM from it. At this point in the boot process, we need to load the operating system itself from the hard drive into memory. How do you load an operating system into memory from the hard drive if you need to have an operating system to load data from the hard drive?

This is the job of the bootloader. The *bootloader* is software that the BIOS can load from the MBR of the hard drive that will allow the CPU to access the disk and load the operating system into RAM. To do this, the bootloader is configured with the location of the operating system files on the hard disk drive.

The bootloader software itself may or may not actually be in the MBR. As you'll see later in this chapter, you can install some bootloaders within the MBR or you can install them within a partition somewhere else on the hard drive and place a pointer in the MBR. Other bootloaders actually reside in both places.

After loading the bootloader software into memory, the BIOS turns control of the system over to the bootloader. The bootloader may be configured to automatically load an operating system from the hard drive, or it may be configured to provide end users with a menu that allows them to select which operating system to load.

With later Linux kernels, the bootloader may also create a temporary, virtual file system in your system RAM called a *ramdisk.* Depending on your distribution, this file system is called either the *initrd image* or the *initramfs image.*

 NOTE   The term *initrd* stands for "initial ramdisk" whereas *initramfs* stands for "initial ram file system." Both image types perform the same function, which is to provide the *linuxrc* that sets up the system.

The image contains a basic file system that can be used to complete a variety of startup tasks. The reason a RAM image is used is because Linux systems can use a wide variety of devices for the root (/) file system. Some devices may be created from external USB storage devices or from a software RAID array; some devices may even reside on a different computer and are accessed through the NFS, Samba, or iSCSI services. These types of file systems can't be mounted by the kernel until special software is loaded, which, of course, resides on those file systems. It can't be done!

To make the system boot correctly in these situations, the bootloader creates a small, virtual hard drive in memory called a *ramdisk* and transfers a temporary root file system from the initrd or initramfs image to it. The Linux kernel can then use this temporary file system to load the software and complete the tasks required for it to mount the real file systems on these other types of devices.

The Kernel Phase

After selecting the operating system to run, the bootloader loads the operating system kernel into RAM from the hard drive. For our purposes, the bootloader loads the Linux kernel into RAM. The Linux kernel is located in the /boot directory of the file system, as shown here:

```
openSUSE:/boot # ls -l
total 71624
-rw-r--r-- 1 root root  2121532 Jul 22 10:03 System.map-3.11.10-21-desktop
-rw-r--r-- 1 root root  2133585 Nov  1  2013 System.map-3.11.6-4-desktop
-rw-r--r-- 1 root root      512 Nov 12 09:06 backup_mbr
lrwxrwxrwx 1 root root        1 Nov 12 08:53 boot -> .
-rw-r--r-- 1 root root     1484 Oct 18  2013 boot.readme
-rw-r--r-- 1 root root   142128 Jul 22 09:19 config-3.11.10-21-desktop
-rw-r--r-- 1 root root   141289 Nov  1  2013 config-3.11.6-4-desktop
drwxr-xr-x 2 root root     4096 Nov 12 08:53 grub
drwxr-xr-x 7 root root     4096 Nov 25 19:21 grub2
lrwxrwxrwx 1 root root       25 Nov 25 19:20 initrd -> initrd-3.11.10-21-desktop
-rw------- 1 root root 22073671 Nov 25 19:20 initrd-3.11.10-21-desktop
-rw------- 1 root root 22072513 Nov 25 19:21 initrd-3.11.6-4-desktop
-rw-r--r-- 1 root root   620544 Nov  6  2013 message
-rw-r--r-- 1 root root   259397 Jul 22 10:15 symvers-3.11.10-21-desktop.gz
-rw-r--r-- 1 root root   258310 Nov  1  2013 symvers-3.11.6-4-desktop.gz
-rw-r--r-- 1 root root      500 Jul 22 10:14 sysctl.conf-3.11.10-21-desktop
-rw-r--r-- 1 root root      500 Nov  1  2013 sysctl.conf-3.11.6-4-desktop
-rw-r--r-- 1 root root  6576950 Jul 22 10:14 vmlinux-3.11.10-21-desktop.gz
-rw-r--r-- 1 root root  6614802 Nov  1  2013 vmlinux-3.11.6-4-desktop.gz
lrwxrwxrwx 1 root root       26 Nov 12 11:12 vmlinuz -> vmlinuz-3.11.10-21-desktop
-rw-r--r-- 1 root root  5125904 Jul 22 10:03 vmlinuz-3.11.10-21-desktop
-rw-r--r-- 1 root root  5154672 Nov  1  2013 vmlinuz-3.11.6-4-desktop
```

Your kernel is the vmlinuz-*version*.gz file located in this directory. You may have noticed that the kernel is a .gz file. That's because the kernel resides as a compressed file on the hard drive. You may have noticed when you first boot a Linux system that a message stating something to the effect of "Uncompressing Linux" is sometimes displayed on the screen. Now you know why!

After the kernel loads, several key things happen, including the following:

- The kernel initializes the basic hardware in your system using the various settings in your BIOS and your CMOS chips.

- The kernel searches for and uses the initrd or initramfs file system to run the linuxrc program to set up the system.

- When linuxrc has finished executing, the initrd or initramfs file system is dismounted and the ramdisk is destroyed.

- The kernel probes for new hardware and loads the appropriate driver modules.

- The real root (/) file system is mounted.

- The kernel loads the init or systemd process.

Which process is used depends on your distribution. Older Linux distributions almost exclusively used the init daemon. However, most current distributions have switched to the systemd daemon instead. As such, the systemd process replaces the init process and its associated startup scripts (which we will review later in this chapter). The systemd process also controls many other Linux services that were not managed by the traditional init daemon, such as user login and hostname configuration. Another key difference is that systemd can run its startup processes in parallel, instead of sequentially as the older init process did.

Regardless of which daemon your distribution uses, the init or systemd processes are the key, critical processes required to run the rest of the system. At this point in the boot process, the configuration parameters found in the /etc/inittab file are used to load system processes and get the system up and running. Once this is done, you can then log in and use the system.

NOTE The changeover from init to systemd has been controversial in the Linux community. Many Linux software developers and administrators prefer init over systemd, whereas others prefer the opposite. Because of this, some distributions have refused to migrate to systemd and insist on using init. You should also be aware that there was short-lived third option used in the mid-2000s called the Upstart daemon. It performed the same function as init and systemd. At this point in time, only the Google Chrome OS distribution still uses Upstart. All other distributions that used Upstart have since switched to systemd.

An overview of the boot process is shown in Figure 6-4.

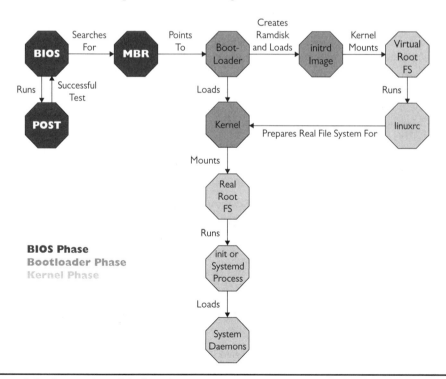

Figure 6-4 An overview of the Linux boot process

With this information in mind, you're ready to learn about configuring bootloaders. Let's discuss how this is done next.

Configuring the Bootloader

As you can see, the bootloader plays an extremely important role in the Linux boot process. Without a bootloader, the BIOS wouldn't be able to load an operating system off of the system's hard disk drive. Therefore, it's very important that you have a sound understanding of how to configure the bootloaders used by Linux.

As with so many aspects of Linux, you can choose from many different bootloaders to use with your Linux system. For your LPIC-1/Linux+ exam, however, you need to be familiar with only two bootloaders: GRUB Legacy and GRUB2. Therefore, in this part of this chapter we're going to spend some time looking at the following topics:

- Configuring GRUB Legacy
- Configuring GRUB2

Let's start by looking at GRUB Legacy.

Configuring GRUB Legacy

GRUB. What a name for a bootloader! The acronym *GRUB* doesn't sound very appealing, does it? However, as bootloaders go, GRUB is fantastic. GRUB stands for *GRand Unified Bootloader*. GRUB is a bootloader that can be used to boot a Linux kernel (or any other operating system kernel, for that matter) from your system's hard drive.

The GRUB Legacy bootloader was very popular and very widely used for a number of years. However, in the last couple of years, there has been a steady shift away from GRUB Legacy toward GRUB2 on the part of most distributions. However, you still need to have a solid understanding of how GRUB Legacy works and how to configure it.

In this part of this chapter, we're going to discuss the following GRUB topics:

- How GRUB Legacy works
- Installing GRUB Legacy
- Configuring GRUB Legacy

Let's begin by discussing how GRUB Legacy works.

How GRUB Legacy Works

The GRUB Legacy bootloader is divided into separate chunks called *stages*. These include the following:

- **Stage 1** This stage of GRUB is usually stored in the MBR. Its only real job is to point to the location of Stage 1.5 or Stage 2.
- **Stage 1.5** This stage of GRUB is located in the first 30KB of the hard drive immediately after the MBR, but before the first partition. Stage 1.5 contains any drivers needed to load Stage 2.

TIP Stage 1 can skip Stage 1.5 and load Stage 2 directly, but it's usually configured to load Stage 1.5 first.

- **Stage 2** This stage of GRUB is stored in a disk partition. When loaded by Stage 1 or Stage 1.5, Stage 2 presents a graphical menu on the screen that allows the user to select the kernel image that should be loaded. You can configure GRUB with a default image and a timeout value. If the user doesn't select an option within the timeout period, the system will automatically boot the default kernel image. A typical GRUB menu is shown in Figure 6-5.

NOTE GRUB also allows installing Stage 1 in the boot partition.

With this overview in mind, let's talk about installing GRUB.

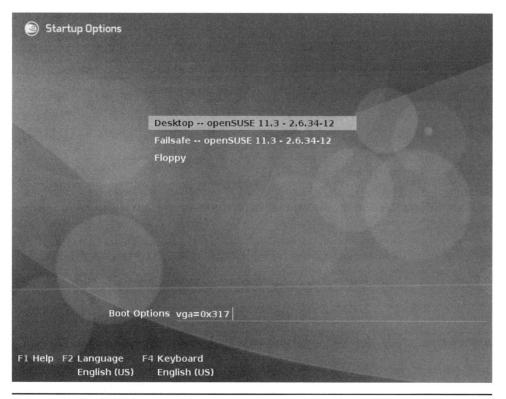

Figure 6-5 The GRUB boot menu

Installing GRUB Legacy

One of the things I really like about GRUB is the fact that you don't have to reinstall the bootloader every time you make a minor configuration change. After the bootloader is initially installed, you can modify your configuration files and the changes will be applied the next time GRUB is loaded because Stage 2 reads directly from the configuration file on disk.

To initially install GRUB, you need to first verify that the grub packages have been installed on the system. This can be done on rpm-based distributions by entering **rpm –q grub** at the shell prompt, as shown here:

```
fs2:~ # rpm -q grub
grub-0.97-171.1.x86_64
```

This output tells us that the GRUB package has been installed. If you see no output from the command, you know that GRUB has not been installed and must be installed before proceeding.

To install the GRUB bootloader itself, enter **grub-install** *device* at the shell prompt. The *device* option is the name of the device whose MBR you want to install Stage 1 into. For example, if you wanted to install GRUB Stage 1 in the MBR of the first hard drive in your system, you would enter **grub-install /dev/sda**, as shown in this example:

```
fs2:~ # grub-install /dev/sda
Installation finished. No error reported.
This is the contents of the device map /boot/grub/device.map.
Check if this is correct or not. If any of the lines is incorrect,
fix it and re-run the script 'grub-install'.

(fd0)  /dev/fd0
(hd0)  /dev/sda
```

With GRUB installed, you're ready to configure it. Let's discuss how this is done next.

Configuring GRUB

To configure GRUB, you need to edit a text-based configuration file. However, the name of the file you need to edit can vary from distribution to distribution. Table 6-1 lists some common implementations by distribution.

Some distributions, such as Fedora, symbolically link /boot/grub/menu.lst to the /boot/grub/grub.conf file, so no matter which file you edit, you'll be making the changes in the right place. Fedora also symbolically links the /etc/grub.conf file to /boot/grub/grub.conf, so you can load this file in an editor as well to make changes to your GRUB configuration. The easiest way to find out

Table 6-1 GRUB Configuration Files	GRUB Configuration File	Distribution
	/boot/grub/grub.conf	Fedora
	/boot/grub/menu.lst	SUSE Linux, Debian

which file you should use to configure GRUB is to simply switch to your /boot/grub directory and look for either a grub.conf or a menu.lst file, as shown here:

```
fs2:~ # ls /boot/grub/ -l
total 216
-rw------- 1 root root      30 Jan 19 10:37 device.map
-rw-r--r-- 1 root root      29 Jan 19 10:24 device.map.old
-rw-r--r-- 1 root root    8608 Jul  5  2010 e2fs_stage1_5
-rw-r--r-- 1 root root    7872 Jul  5  2010 fat_stage1_5
-rw-r--r-- 1 root root    7136 Jul  5  2010 ffs_stage1_5
-rw-r--r-- 1 root root    7136 Jul  5  2010 iso9660_stage1_5
-rw-r--r-- 1 root root    8576 Jul  5  2010 jfs_stage1_5
-rw------- 1 root root    1088 Jan 19 10:37 menu.lst
-rw-r--r-- 1 root root     983 Jan 19 10:24 menu.lst.old
-rw-r--r-- 1 root root    7296 Jul  5  2010 minix_stage1_5
-rw-r--r-- 1 root root    9632 Jul  5  2010 reiserfs_stage1_5
-rw-r--r-- 1 root root     512 Jul  5  2010 stage1
-rw-r--r-- 1 root root  102026 Feb 11 12:18 stage2
-rw-r--r-- 1 root root    7456 Jul  5  2010 ufs2_stage1_5
-rw-r--r-- 1 root root    6688 Jul  5  2010 vstafs_stage1_5
-rw-r--r-- 1 root root    9288 Jul  5  2010 xfs_stage1_5
```

Whichever file your GRUB configuration file uses, it will use a standard structure. The first part of your GRUB configuration file contains global options that apply to all menu items. Then it has one or more title sections that are used to launch a specific operating system. A typical GRUB configuration file is shown here:

```
fs2:~ # cat /boot/grub/menu.lst
# Modified by YaST2. Last modification on Wed Jan 19 10:37:45 MST 2011
# THIS FILE WILL BE PARTIALLY OVERWRITTEN by perl-Bootloader
# Configure custom boot parameters for updated kernels in
/etc/sysconfig/bootloader

default 0
timeout 8
##YaST - generic_mbr
gfxmenu (hd0,1)/boot/message
##YaST - activate

###Don't change this comment - YaST2 identifier: Original name: linux###
title Desktop -- openSUSE 11.3 - 2.6.34-12
    root (hd0,1)
    kernel /boot/vmlinuz-2.6.34-12-desktop root=/dev/sda2 resume=/dev/sda1
splash=silent quiet showopts vga=0x317
    initrd /boot/initrd-2.6.34-12-desktop

###Don't change this comment - YaST2 identifier: Original name: failsafe###
title Failsafe -- openSUSE 11.3 - 2.6.34-12
    root (hd0,1)
    kernel /boot/vmlinuz-2.6.34-12-desktop root=/dev/sda2 showopts apm=off
noresume edd=off powersaved=off nohz=off highres=off processor.max_cstate=1
nomodeset x11failsafe vga=0x317
    initrd /boot/initrd-2.6.34-12-desktop

###Don't change this comment - YaST2 identifier: Original name: floppy###
title Floppy
    rootnoverify (fd0)
    chainloader +1
```

Before we explore the entries in this sample GRUB configuration file, we need to review some GRUB nomenclature. First of all, GRUB references disks and partitions in your system in a manner that may be unfamiliar. Instead of using a /dev entry, GRUB uses the following syntax:

```
hddrive_number,partition_number
```

For example, the first partition on the first hard drive (/dev/sda1) is referenced by GRUB as hd0,0. It doesn't matter if the first disk is an IDE, SATA, or SCSI drive—GRUB refers to it as hd0.

Another thing that may throw you is the fact that GRUB creates its own "root" called the *GRUB root*. This isn't necessarily the root file system mounted at /. Instead, it's the partition where the /boot directory resides (where Stage 2 is installed). Here's the confusing part: if you haven't created a separate partition for /boot when you first partitioned your hard drive, GRUB will use the full path to refer to the GRUB root, which is usually /boot/grub. If, on the other hand, you have created a separate partition for /boot (a very good practice), this partition becomes the GRUB root. GRUB then refers to files in the GRUB root *without* including /boot in path. This will drive you crazy until you get used to it. You need to understand these two facts before proceeding; otherwise, many of the entries in the GRUB configuration file won't make sense.

Table 6-2 steps through the lines in the GRUB configuration file and describes what each does.

Section	Option	Description
Global	Color	Specifies the colors to be used in the GRUB menu.
	default	Specifies the menu item that will be booted automatically if the user doesn't make a manual selection. In the example shown in this chapter, the first menu option (0) will be booted automatically if the user doesn't specify otherwise.
	timeout	Specifies the number of seconds to wait until the default menu item is automatically booted. In the example shown in this chapter, the timeout period is set to 8 seconds.
	gfxmenu	Specifies the location of the image file that will be used to display the graphical GRUB boot menu. In the example shown in this chapter, the /boot/message file on the second partition (1) of the first hard drive (hd0) will be used for the GRUB boot menu.
Title	title	Specifies the title of the menu item in the GRUB boot menu.
	root	Specifies the location of the partition that is to be mounted as the GRUB root. In the example in this chapter, this is hd0,1, which specifies the second partition (1) of the first hard drive (hd0).
	kernel	Specifies the location of the Linux kernel. In the example shown in this chapter, the GRUB menu points to /boot/vmlinuz-2.6.34-12-desktop. Some distributions will just point to the /boot/vmlinuz file, which is actually a symbolic link to the real kernel file. The root= option specifies the partition that will be mounted as the root file system. The vga= option specifies the VGA mode the system should use during boot. The resume= option points to the system's swap partition.
	initrd	Specifies the initrd image that should be used by GRUB to create the initial ramdisk image during boot. In the example shown in this chapter, the /boot/initrd-2.6.34-12-desktop is specified. Some distributions will just point to the /boot/initrd image. Just remember that, like vmlinuz, the initrd file in /boot is actually a link to the real initrd image file.

Table 6-2 GRUB Configuration File Options

One of the cool things about GRUB is that you can manage the boot process interactively. Instead of being stuck with whatever is configured in the menu.lst or grub.conf file, you can customize your own boot process on the fly. To do this, complete the following steps:

1. In the GRUB menu, press the ESC key.

2. When prompted that you are leaving the graphical boot menu, select OK. When you do, the text-based GRUB menu is displayed, as shown in Figure 6-6.

3. If you want to edit the menu item, press E. When you do, the screen in Figure 6-7 is displayed.

    In this screen, you can arrow up or down to select the appropriate line and then press E again to edit. If you want to add a new line, press O. Press D to delete a line. Press B when you're ready to start the boot process. You can also press ESC to go back to the GRUB menu.

4. You can also access a GRUB prompt by pressing C. When you do, the screen shown in Figure 6-8 is displayed.

You can enter **help** at the grub> prompt to display information about creating GRUB menu lines from the grub> prompt. You can also press TAB to see a list of commands that you can enter at the grub> prompt. In addition, you can press ESC to return to the GRUB menu.

NOTE   You can also access the grub> prompt from within a running Linux system. To do this, just enter **grub** at the shell prompt.

```
    GNU GRUB  version 0.97  (638K lower / 522112K upper memory)

   ┌────────────────────────────────────────────────────────────────┐
   │ Desktop -- openSUSE 11.3 - 2.6.34-12                             │
   │ Failsafe -- openSUSE 11.3 - 2.6.34-12                            │
   │ Floppy                                                           │
   │                                                                  │
   │                                                                  │
   │                                                                  │
   │                                                                  │
   │                                                                  │
   └────────────────────────────────────────────────────────────────┘

        Use the ↑ and ↓ keys to select which entry is highlighted.
        Press enter to boot the selected OS, 'e' to edit the
        commands before booting, or 'c' for a command-line.
```

Figure 6-6   The text-based GRUB menu

```
 GNU GRUB  version 0.97  (638K lower / 522112K upper memory)

┌─────────────────────────────────────────────────────────────────┐
│root (hd0,1)                                                       │
│kernel /boot/vmlinuz-2.6.34-12-desktop root=/dev/sda2 resume=/dev/sda→│
│initrd /boot/initrd-2.6.34-12-desktop                              │
│                                                                   │
│                                                                   │
│                                                                   │
│                                                                   │
│                                                                   │
│                                                                   │
└─────────────────────────────────────────────────────────────────┘
    Use the ↑ and ↓ keys to select which entry is highlighted.
    Press 'b' to boot, 'e' to edit the selected command in the
    boot sequence, 'c' for a command-line, 'o' to open a new line
    after ('O' for before) the selected line, 'd' to remove the
    selected line, or escape to go back to the main menu.
```

Figure 6-7   Editing a GRUB menu item

The GRUB menu can be extremely useful tool. On most distributions, the Boot Options field is displayed by default in the GRUB menu. An example is shown in Figure 6-9.

You can use this field to send boot options to the Linux kernel that are not contained in a GRUB menu item to customize the way the kernel will function. To do this, you first select the desired GRUB menu item and then enter the appropriate kernel options you want to use in the Boot Options field. For example, if you have a Linux system that no longer boots for some unknown reason, you can use the Boot Options field to tell the kernel not to load the init process at startup but to load a different program instead.

NOTE   We'll discuss the init process in more detail later in this chapter.

To do this, you enter **init=*program_name*** in the Boot Options field. For example, to skip loading the init process and load the bash shell instead, you would enter **init=/bin/bash** in the

```
 GNU GRUB  version 0.97  (638K lower / 522112K upper memory)

 [ Minimal BASH-like line editing is supported.  For the first word, TAB
   lists possible command completions.  Anywhere else TAB lists the possible
   completions of a device/filename.  ESC at any time exits. ]

grub> _
```

Figure 6-8   The GRUB prompt

Boot Options vga=0x317

Figure 6-9   Sending boot options to the Linux kernel

Boot Options field. When you boot the system, the bash shell is loaded and you have full root-level access to the system, allowing you to diagnose and repair whatever is keeping the system from booting normally. This is shown in Figure 6-10.

TIP   You won't be prompted to provide your root password. Because of this, you can use this technique to rescue a system if you've forgotten its root user's password.

However, be aware that the root (/) file system will be mounted in read-only mode on some distributions. If this is the case, you will need to remount it in read-write mode before you can make changes to a configuration file by entering **mount –o remount,rw,sync –t** *filesystem device_name mount_point* at the shell prompt. After making the necessary changes, you can tell the kernel to resume the normal boot process via init by entering **exec /sbin/init** at the shell prompt.

Although the ability to customize GRUB and its menu items can be very useful, it also can be a bit of a security risk. As noted, it can potentially provide anyone, who knows how, root-level access to your system without providing a password. This can be a very bad thing, especially on Linux systems that may contain sensitive or proprietary information.

```
doing fast boot
Creating device nodes with udev
[    3.737221] sd 0:0:0:0: [sda] Assuming drive cache: write through
[    3.739793] sd 0:0:0:0: [sda] Assuming drive cache: write through
[    3.777103] sd 0:0:0:0: [sda] Assuming drive cache: write through
Trying manual resume from /dev/sda1
Invoking userspace resume from /dev/sda1
resume: libgcrypt version: 1.4.4
Trying manual resume from /dev/sda1
Invoking in-kernel resume from /dev/sda1
Waiting for device /dev/sda2 to appear:  ok
fsck from util-linux-ng 2.17.2
[/sbin/fsck.ext4 (1) -- /] fsck.ext4 -a -C0 /dev/sda2
/dev/sda2: clean, 155384/407200 files, 1124950/1626624 blocks
fsck succeeded. Mounting root device read-write.
Mounting root /dev/sda2
mount -o rw,acl,user_xattr -t ext4 /dev/sda2 /root
bash: cannot set terminal process group (-1): Inappropriate ioctl for device
bash: no job control in this shell
(none):/ #
```

Figure 6-10   Replacing init with the bash shell

```
GNU GRUB  version 0.97  (638K lower / 522112K upper memory)

┌────────────────────────────────────────────────────────────────────┐
│Desktop -- openSUSE 11.3 - 2.6.34-12                                  │
│Failsafe -- openSUSE 11.3 - 2.6.34-12                                 │
│Floppy                                                                │
│                                                                      │
│                                                                      │
│                                                                      │
│                                                                      │
│                                                                      │
│                                                                      │
└────────────────────────────────────────────────────────────────────┘
      Use the ↑ and ↓ keys to select which entry is highlighted.
         WARNING: graphical menu doesn't work        in conjunction with the pas
sword feature
      Press enter to boot the selected OS or 'p' to enter a
      password to unlock the next set of features.
```

Figure 6-11   Using a password in the GRUB configuration file

To increase the security of the GRUB menu, you can add a GRUB password. Once the menu is configured this way, you can only modify your GRUB boot options after the correct password has been supplied. The simplest way to do this is to edit your GRUB configuration file (menu.lst or grub.conf) and enter the following:

```
password password
```

Here's an example:

```
password natasha01
```

Be aware that adding this parameter to your configuration file will cause GRUB to display its menu in text-only mode. An example is shown in Figure 6-11.

When GRUB is configured this way, users can still select any menu item they want without the password, but editing any GRUB menu item will require them to enter the password you specified. If you want to require users to enter the password before they can select a menu item too, you need to add the lock parameter within the appropriate title elements in the GRUB configuration file, as shown in this example:

```
fs2:~ # cat /boot/grub/menu.lst
# Modified by YaST2. Last modification on Wed Jan 19 10:37:45 MST 2011
# THIS FILE WILL BE PARTIALLY OVERWRITTEN by perl-Bootloader
# Configure custom boot parameters for updated kernels in
/etc/sysconfig/bootloader

default 0
timeout 8
```

```
##YaST - generic_mbr
gfxmenu (hd0,1)/boot/message
##YaST - activate
password natasha01

###Don't change this comment - YaST2 identifier: Original name: linux###
title Desktop -- openSUSE 11.3 - 2.6.34-12
    lock
    root (hd0,1)
    kernel /boot/vmlinuz-2.6.34-12-desktop root=/dev/sda2 resume=/dev/sda1
splash=silent quiet showopts vga=0x317
    initrd /boot/initrd-2.6.34-12-desktop

###Don't change this comment - YaST2 identifier: Original name: failsafe###
title Failsafe -- openSUSE 11.3 - 2.6.34-12
    lock
    root (hd0,1)
    kernel /boot/vmlinuz-2.6.34-12-desktop root=/dev/sda2 showopts apm=off
noresume edd=off powersaved=off nohz=off highres=off processor.max_cstate=1
nomodeset x11failsafe vga=0x317
    initrd /boot/initrd-2.6.34-12-desktop

###Don't change this comment - YaST2 identifier: Original name: floppy###
title Floppy
    lock
    rootnoverify (fd0)
    chainloader +1
```

In this configuration, users must enter the password you specify in order to select a GRUB menu item. This is done by pressing p and then entering the appropriate password. If they don't, the screen shown in Figure 6-12 is displayed.

Notice in the preceding example that the password directive is placed in the global section of the file. This defines the password for all of the title directives that come after it. In this configuration, all of the GRUB menu items use the same password. If you want to define different passwords for each GRUB menu item, you can place **password** *password* directives within each title element.

Also notice in the preceding example that the password is stored as clear text in the GRUB configuration file. This is somewhat insecure. If users were to get read access to the GRUB configuration file (which they shouldn't by default, but accidents do happen), then they would have easy access to the GRUB password you set.

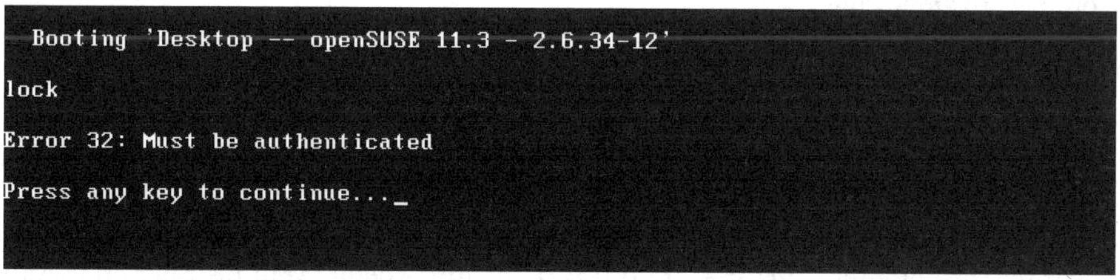

Figure 6-12   Denying access to a GRUB menu item

To make the configuration more secure, you can encrypt the GRUB password in the configuration file. This way, even if a user gets access to the GRUB configuration file, he won't be able to read the password you specify. To encrypt the password, do the following:

1. Open a terminal session and switch to root.

2. At the shell prompt, enter **grub-md5-crypt**.

3. When prompted, enter the password you want to assign to the GRUB menu.

   When complete, the hashed form of the password is displayed on the screen. An example follows:

   ```
   fs2:~ # grub-md5-crypt
   Password:
   Retype password:
   $1$WLZwz/$DP3wgbtInP1KJOL.Wg3t00
   ```

4. Open the GRUB configuration file in a text editor.

 TIP It's easier to copy and paste in gedit, but this can be done in vi as well.

---

5. In the GRUB configuration file, enter **password --md5** *hashed_password*. Here is an example:

   ```
   password --md5 $1$WLZwz/$DP3wgbtInP1KJOL.Wg3t00
   ```

6. Save your changes to the file and reboot the system.

Let's practice working with the GRUB bootloader in the following exercise.

Exercise 6-1: Working with GRUB

In this exercise, you will practice customizing your GRUB menu. This exercise assumes that you've installed a distribution that uses GRUB. You can perform this exercise using the virtual machine that comes with this book. Run snapshot 6-1 for the correctly configured environment.

 VIDEO Please watch the Exercise 6-1 video for a demonstration on how to perform this task.

Complete the following:

1. Boot your Linux system and log in as your student user with a password of **student**.

2. Open a terminal session.

3. Switch to your root user account by entering **su –** followed by your root user's password (**student**).

4. At the shell prompt, enter **ls –l /boot/grub**. Identify whether your distribution uses the grub.conf or the menu.lst file to configure grub.

5. Create an encrypted password for your GRUB menu by entering **grub-md5-crypt** at the shell prompt.

6. When prompted, enter a password for your GRUB menu.

7. Record the hashed password displayed on the screen.

8. At the shell prompt, enter **vi /boot/grub/menu.lst** or **vi /boot/grub/grub.conf**, depending on which file your system uses.

9. Press INSERT.

10. Scroll down to the timeout line and put a # in front of it to disable this functionality. Because we are going to require a password to boot, we don't want GRUB to try to boot the system automatically.

11. Beneath the gfxmenu line, add a global password to the GRUB menu by entering **password --md5** *hashed_password*.

12. Add the **lock** directive to each title element in your GRUB configuration file. This will cause GRUB to require a password to select a menu item.

13. Press ESC.

14. Save your changes to the file and exit vi by entering **:exit**.

15. At the shell prompt, enter **reboot**. Wait while the system restarts.

16. Notice in the GRUB menu that you now have to enter a password to boot the system.

17. Press P and then enter your password.

18. Select the appropriate GRUB menu item to boot the system.

Now let's move on and look at GRUB2.

Configuring GRUB2

As you might guess, GRUB2 is a newer version of the original GRUB bootloader. GRUB2 works in a completely different manner than the original GRUB Legacy bootloader. Be aware that GRUB version 1.98 or later is actually considered "GRUB2." Any version of GRUB earlier than 1.98 is considered "GRUB Legacy." You can run one of two commands at the shell prompt (as root) to see which version of GRUB your particular Linux system is using:

- grub-install –v
- grub2-install -v

An example is shown here:

```
openSUSE:/boot # grub2-install -v
grub2-install (GRUB2) 2.00
```

It's very important that you become familiar with GRUB2 for two reasons:

- It's the default bootloader used by most current Linux distributions.
- It works in a completely different manner than the original GRUB Legacy bootloader.

GRUB2 uses a completely different set of configuration files as compared to the GRUB Legacy bootloader. Here are the configuration files used by GRUB2:

- The /boot/grub/grub.cfg file
- The files within the /etc/grub.d directory
- The /etc/default/grub file

When you're working with the GRUB Legacy bootloader, you make all your configuration changes within the menu.lst file. With GRUB2, there is no menu.lst file. It has been replaced by the /boot/grub2/grub.cfg file.

TIP   On some distributions, the grub.cfg file is located in /boot/grub instead of /boot/grub2.

However, unlike the menu.lst file, grub.cfg is automatically updated every time you make a configuration change and then run one of the following commands:

- Some distributions (such as Ubuntu) use the **update-grub** command.
- Other distributions (such as openSUSE) use the **grub2-mkconfig -o /boot/grub2/grub .cfg** command.

You should not directly edit grub.cfg. Instead, you should edit the appropriate configuration file when you need to make a change to the GRUB2 bootloader, and then run the update-grub or grub2-mkconfig command.

TIP   You have to run update-grub or grub2-mkconfig after making any configuration changes to the GRUB2 bootloader. They will not take effect until this has been done.

Even though grub.cfg is somewhat analogous to menu.lst, it doesn't actually contain the GRUB2 menu information. Instead, it is stored in several configuration files within the /etc/grub.d directory. All the files within /etc/grub.d are executable script files. If you make changes to one of these files and then run the update-grub or grub2-mkconfig command, the grub.cfg file is automatically updated with the new GRUB settings. So, in summary, the /etc/default/grub file contains the GRUB menu configuration settings, but the script files in /etc/grub.d are the ones you actually edit to make any changes. An example of creating the configuration file used by GRUB2 using the grub2-mkconfig command is shown here:

```
openSUSE:~ # grub2-mkconfig -o /boot/grub2/grub.cfg
Generating grub.cfg ...
Found theme: /boot/grub2/themes/openSUSE/theme.txt
Found linux image: /boot/vmlinuz-3.11.10-21-desktop
Found initrd image: /boot/initrd-3.11.10-21-desktop
Found linux image: /boot/vmlinuz-3.11.6-4-desktop
Found initrd image: /boot/initrd-3.11.6-4-desktop
done
```

NOTE Another aspect of GRUB2 to be aware of is the fact that the partition numbering syntax is slightly different. With GRUB Legacy, the first hard disk in the system is **hd0** and the first partition on that disk is **hd0,0**. This is no longer the case with GRUB2. With GRUB2, the first hard drive is still **hd0**. However, the first partition on the drive is assigned the number one instead of zero. Therefore, the first partition on the first hard drive will be referenced as **hd0,1** instead of **hd0,0** when working with GRUB2.

If you were to view the contents of the grub.cfg file, you would see that it's divided up into many sections. Each section begins with the text **###BEGIN**, as shown here:

```
### BEGIN /etc/grub.d/10_linux ###
menuentry 'openSUSE 13.1' --class 'opensuse-13-1' --class gnu-linux
--class gnu --class os $menuentry_id_option
'gnulinux-simple-7a115a99-8e42-49b3-a1db-db5a79437b95' {
        load_video
        set gfxpayload=keep
        insmod gzio
        insmod part_msdos
        insmod ext2
        set root='hd0,msdos2'
...
```

Each of the sections references a particular script in the /etc/grub.d directory from which it was generated by the update-grub or the grub2-mkconfig command. When you look at the files within /etc/grub.d, you'll see that they typically begin with a numeral, as shown here:

```
openSUSE:/etc/grub.d # ls
00_header  20_linux_xen   20_ppc_terminfo  40_custom  90_persistent
10_linux   20_memtest86+  30_os-prober     41_custom  README
```

This naming convention is important because the placement of the menu items within the grub.cfg file is determined by the numeric order of the script file names within /etc/grub.d. The lowest-numbered files are executed first by the update-grub or grub2-mkconfig command. So in this example, 00_header would be run first, 10_linux would be run second, and so on. Any script files using nonnumeric files names will not be run until after all the numerically named files are run first. This then influences the order in which the information from these script files appears within /boot/grub2/grub.cfg.

Let's take a look at some of the commonly used script files within grub.d. Be aware that the script files you see will vary from distribution to distribution. Likewise, you can add your own script files to this directory as well, but we're not going to delve into scripting yet. That will come later in the book.

The first file you should be familiar with is **00_header**. This file configures various parameters for the GRUB2 boot menu, such as the initial appearance, the graphics mode, the default selection, timeout values, and so on.

The next file is **10_linux**. This file identifies each of the Linux kernels that have been installed on the system. If you have multiple kernels installed, the 10_linux script will search within your boot folder and locate any installed Linux kernels. For each one it finds, it will create a separate GRUB menu entry.

The next file we need to look at is **30_os-prober**. This script searches for any other operating systems that may be installed on your system. If you just have Linux installed, this script will locate your Linux kernel and create a menu entry for it. However, if you have Linux and Windows installed on the same system, 30_os-prober will identify Linux as well as the Windows operating system that has been installed and automatically create a GRUB menu entry for each.

The last script file you need to be concerned with is **40_custom**. This file is designed for you to use to customize the behavior of the GRUB menu. Basically, it's a template for adding custom menu entries that will be inserted into the grub.cfg file.

Finally, we need to look at the /etc/default/grub configuration file. This file contains information that used to be contained in the upper section of the original GRUB Legacy menu. lst file, as shown here:

```
openSUSE:/etc/grub.d # cat /etc/default/grub
GRUB_DISTRIBUTOR="openSUSE 13.1"
GRUB_DEFAULT=saved
GRUB_HIDDEN_TIMEOUT=0
GRUB_HIDDEN_TIMEOUT_QUIET=true
GRUB_TIMEOUT=8
...
```

You can go ahead and edit this file and make whatever changes you need to and have those changes incorporated into grub.cfg when you run the update-grub or grub2-mkconfig command. Within this file are several different parameters you can use to change the way GRUB behaves and looks:

- **GRUB_DEFAULT**   This parameter sets the default menu entry. For example, if you were to configure **grub_default=0**, the first menu entry becomes the default menu entry. If you have a timer set and no selection is made by the user, the first menu entry will be automatically selected. You can specify either an entry number or an entry title.

- **GRUB_SAVED DEFAULT**   If you set this parameter to **true**, GRUB will automatically select the last selected operating system from the menu as the default operating system to be used on the next boot. As you can see, this parameter could potentially conflict with the grub_default parameter. Therefore, you can use either one, but not both.

- **GRUB_HIDDEN_TIMEOUT**   The grub_hidden_timeout parameter can be used to cause the boot process to pause and display a blank screen (or a splash image if you configure it to do so) for a specified number of seconds. After the end of the timeout period, the system will boot. The grub_hidden_timeout parameter determines how long (in seconds) the blank screen will be displayed. While the screen is blank, the user can press the SHIFT key to display the menu. If you don't want them to have that option, set this parameter to a value of zero. If you set this to a null value, the menu will be displayed for the number of seconds configured by the grub_timeout parameter.

NOTE   The default behavior of GRUB2 is to actually hide the menu if only one operating system has been installed on the system. If you have two operating systems installed, the default behavior is to show the menu with entries for both operating systems.

- **GRUB_HIDDEN_TIMEOUT_QUIET**   This parameter works in conjunction with the grub_hidden_timeout parameter. If it is set to **true**, no countdown is displayed. If it is set to **false**, a counter will be displayed on the blank screen for the duration of the value specified for grub_hidden_timeout.

- **GRUB_TIMEOUT**   This parameter specifies how long (in seconds) the user has to make a menu selection from the GRUB menu before the default operating system is booted. If you set this to a value of **–1**, the timer is disabled and GRUB will wait until the user makes a selection.

- **GRUB_CMDLINE_LINUX**   This parameter is used to pass options to the kernel. With the GRUB Legacy bootloader, this was done by adding options to the end of the kernel line. You can do the same thing in GRUB2 using the grub_command line_Linux parameter.

- **GRUB_GFX MODE**   This parameter sets the resolution of the graphical menu displayed by GRUB2. You can also append a color depth, if needed. For example, if you wanted the grub menu to use a screen resolution of 1440×900 and to use 24-bit color depth, you would set this parameter to a value of 1440×900×24. You can actually specify multiple resolutions with this parameter. List your preferred screen resolution first, then a comma, then the second one, and then a comma, and so on. GRUB2 will try to use the first resolution first. If the resolution is supported by the video display, it will be used and the others will be ignored. If it is not supported, GRUB will move on to the second resolution, and it will keep working its way down the list until it finds one that it can use. If this parameter is commented out, or if the resolution specified isn't supported, GRUB2 will use the default graphic mode setting specified in the /etc/grub.d/00_header file.

- **GRUB_INIT_TUNE**   You can use this parameter to play a single beep just prior to the GRUB2 menu being displayed. The syntax is to put an equal sign and then a quotation mark and then three numbers. The first number is the tempo to be used. The second number is the pitch of the tune. The third number is the duration of the tune. End the parameter with a closing quotation mark.

- **GRUB_BACKGROUND**   This parameter sets the background image used by the GRUB2 menu.

- **GRUB_DISABLE_OSPROBER**   Setting this parameter to a value of **true** will then disable the osprober check. This functionality looks for partitions on the hard drive that have other operating systems, such as Windows or other Linux distributions.

Exercise 6-2: Working with GRUB2

In this exercise, you will practice customizing your GRUB2 menu. You can perform this exercise using the virtual machine that comes with this book. Run snapshot 6-2 for the correctly configured environment.

   VIDEO   Please watch the Exercise 6-2 video for a demonstration on how to perform this task.

Complete the following:

1. Boot your Linux system and log in as your student user with a password of **student**.

2. Open a terminal session.

3. Switch to your root user account by entering **su –** followed by your root user's password (**student**).

4. At the shell prompt, enter **vi /etc/default/grub**.

5. Change the GRUB_TIMEOUT value to 15 seconds.

6. Change the GRUB_DEFAULT parameter to automatically load the first menu entry if the user makes no selection within the timeout period.

7. Save your changes and exit the vi editor.

8. Apply your changes by entering **grub2-mkconfig -o /boot/grub2/grub.cfg** at the shell prompt.

9. Reboot your system and verify the changes have been applied to the bootloader.

Managing Linux Runlevels with init

If you've worked with Linux before, you may have heard the term *runlevel* used. I've noticed that the concept of a runlevel is difficult for many new Linux users to understand. In this part of this chapter, we'll review what a runlevel is and how you can manage runlevels on your system. The following topics will be covered:

- How runlevels work
- Managing runlevels and init scripts

 NOTE Runlevels primarily apply to Linux distributions that use init. Distributions that use systemd use boot targets instead of runlevels. We'll discuss systemd later in this chapter.

Let's begin by discussing how runlevels work.

How Runlevels Work

To manage a Linux system, you need to have a sound understanding of how runlevels work. In this part of this chapter, we'll discuss the following:

- What is a runlevel?
- Defining runlevels in /etc/inittab

Let's begin by discussing what a runlevel is.

Runlevel	Description
0	Halts the system.
I	Runs Linux in single-user mode. The command-line interface is used.
2	Runs Linux in multiuser mode with networking disabled. The command-line interface is used.
3	Runs Linux in multiuser mode with networking enabled. The command-line interface is used.
4	Undefined by default. You can actually edit the /etc/inittab file and define your own custom runlevel using runlevel 4.
5	Runs Linux in multiuser mode with networking enabled. The graphical user interface is used.
6	Reboots the system.

Table 6-3 Linux Runlevels

What Is a Runlevel?

So what exactly is a runlevel? It sounds complicated, but when you get right down to it, it really isn't. A *runlevel* represents one of several different modes that your Linux system can run in. A runlevel on a Linux system is similar, in many ways, to a startup mode on a Windows system. If you've used Windows, you know that you can press the F8 key during system boot and select one of several startup modes. For example, if you're having trouble with a particular device or driver in your Windows system, you can boot it in Safe Mode, which will load the operating system with only a minimal set of drivers so that you can troubleshoot the problem.

Linux runlevels are similar. Like Windows startup modes, Linux runlevels allow you to specify the mode in which you want your system to run. Linux uses seven default runlevels that you can choose from, as shown in Table 6-3.

As you can see in Table 6-3, there are many differences between Linux runlevels and Windows startup modes. First of all, switching to runlevel 0 actually halts the system whereas switching to runlevel 6 reboots the system. In addition, you can specify a default runlevel that your system will boot into each time it's turned on. You can even dynamically switch between runlevels while the system is running. You can't do that with Windows!

These runlevels are defined through the /etc/inittab file. Let's review how this file works.

Defining Runlevels with /etc/inittab

For distributions that use init, the *init* process is the grandparent of all other processes on your Linux system. It is the first process run by the kernel at boot and is responsible for loading all other system processes that make Linux work. The init process is configured in the /etc/inittab file. An excerpt from a typical inittab file for an openSUSE system follows:

```
fs2:~ # cat /etc/inittab
# /etc/inittab
id:5:initdefault:
# First script to be executed, if not booting in emergency (-b) mode
si::bootwait:/etc/init.d/boot
l0:0:wait:/etc/init.d/rc 0
l1:1:wait:/etc/init.d/rc 1
```

```
l2:2:wait:/etc/init.d/rc 2
l3:3:wait:/etc/init.d/rc 3
#l4:4:wait:/etc/init.d/rc 4
l5:5:wait:/etc/init.d/rc 5
l6:6:wait:/etc/init.d/rc 6
# what to do in single-user mode
ls:S:wait:/etc/init.d/rc S
~~:S:respawn:/sbin/sulogin
# what to do when CTRL-ALT-DEL is pressed
ca::ctrlaltdel:/sbin/shutdown -r -t 4 now
# special keyboard request (Alt-UpArrow)
# look into the kbd-0.90 docs for this
kb::kbrequest:/bin/echo "Keyboard Request -- edit /etc/inittab to let this work."
# what to do when power fails/returns
pf::powerwait:/etc/init.d/powerfail start
pn::powerfailnow:/etc/init.d/powerfail now
#pn::powerfail:/etc/init.d/powerfail now
po::powerokwait:/etc/init.d/powerfail stop
...
# end of /etc/inittab
```

The first parameter defined in inittab specifies the default runlevel of the system. This parameter takes the form of id:5:initdefault. This command tells the init process to boot into runlevel 5 by default. Remember that runlevel 5 runs Linux in multiuser mode with networking, and the GUI desktop enabled.

Next, the inittab file tells the init process to run the /etc/init.d/boot script:

```
si::bootwait:/etc/init.d/boot
```

The bootwait parameter tells init to run this script and to wait for it to complete before proceeding with the boot process.

In addition, the inittab file also defines what *init scripts* are run in each runlevel. This is done using the following lines:

```
l0:0:wait:/etc/init.d/rc 0
l1:1:wait:/etc/init.d/rc 1
l2:2:wait:/etc/init.d/rc 2
l3:3:wait:/etc/init.d/rc 3
#l4:4:wait:/etc/init.d/rc 4
l5:5:wait:/etc/init.d/rc 5
l6:6:wait:/etc/init.d/rc 6
```

The syntax for commands within the inittab file is ***identifier:runlevel:action:command***. The *wait* action specified in these commands tells the init process to wait until the scripts for the specified runlevel have finished running before moving on. Also, notice that the definition for runlevel 4 is commented out. Runlevel 4 is left undefined by default in every Linux distribution I've ever used.

The /etc/inittab file also defines what should happen when the CTRL-ALT-DEL key combination is pressed. By default, the inittab file causes the system to restart when these keys are pressed, as shown here:

```
ca::ctrlaltdel:/sbin/shutdown -r -t 4 now
```

If you want to change the behavior of the system when these keys are pressed, just use a text editor to edit /etc/inittab and modify this line to specify the command that should be run.

CAUTION   Be very careful when editing the inittab file. If you make a mistake, it's very possible that your system may not boot.

Notice in the inittab example that a single-user mode is also defined (S):

```
# what to do in single-user mode
ls:S:wait:/etc/init.d/rc S
~~:S:respawn:/sbin/sulogin
```

The single-user mode is very useful when troubleshooting system problems. When you enter single-user mode, the /sbin/sulogin command is run, allowing you to log in as root and fix whatever problem is keeping the system from running correctly. To enter single-user mode while the system is running, enter **init S** at the shell prompt. When you do, you're prompted to provide your root user password. Once this is entered, you are granted root access to the system in single-user mode. This is shown in Figure 6-13.

You can also enter single-user mode at system startup by entering **S** in the Boot Options field of the GRUB menu.

The next block of the inittab file tells the init process what to do if a power failure has occurred. Depending on the nature of the failure, a different script file in /etc/init.d is run:

```
# what to do when power fails/returns
pf::powerwait:/etc/init.d/powerfail start
pn::powerfailnow:/etc/init.d/powerfail now
#pn::powerfail:/etc/init.d/powerfail now
po::powerokwait:/etc/init.d/powerfail stop
```

There's also a block in the inittab file that tells init which runlevel login processes (called *Get TTY* or *getty* processes) are started at login to prompt the user to enter a username and password. This is shown next:

```
1:2345:respawn:/sbin/mingetty --noclear tty1
2:2345:respawn:/sbin/mingetty tty2
3:2345:respawn:/sbin/mingetty tty3
4:2345:respawn:/sbin/mingetty tty4
5:2345:respawn:/sbin/mingetty tty5
6:2345:respawn:/sbin/mingetty tty6
```

```
Shutting down D-Bus daemon                                                        done
Saving random seed                                                                done
Shutting down xinetd: (waiting for all children to terminate)                     done
Shutting down (remotefs) network interfaces:
Shutting down sound driver                                                        done
Umount CIFS File Systems                                                          done
Shutting down NFS client services:/etc/init.d/nfs: line 262: test: S: integer expression expected
                                                                                  done
Shutting down rpcbind                                                             done
Shutting down syslog services                                                     done
Shutting down (localfs) network interfaces:
    eth1      device: Intel Corporation 82545EM Gigabit Ethernet Controller (Copper) (rev 01)
    eth1                                                                          done
Shutting down service (localfs) network                                           done
The System Time is in sync with Hardware Clock                                    good
Sending all processes the TERM signal...                                          done
Sending all processes the KILL signal...                                          done
Master Resource Control: runlevel S has been                                      reached
Skipped services in runlevel S:                                  SuSEfirewall2_setup
Give root password for login:
fs2:~ #
```

Figure 6-13   Entering single-user mode

As you can see in this example, login processes are created in runlevels 2, 3, 4 (if it was defined), and 5.

If you make any changes to your inittab file, you will need to tell init that changes have been made and that it needs to reread its configuration. To do this, enter the **init q** command at the shell prompt.

With this background in mind, you're ready to learn how to manage runlevels on your system. Let's do that next.

Managing Runlevels and init Scripts

Managing runlevels is an important aspect of administering a Linux system. You need to know how to configure the default runlevel as well as specify which system processes and services (daemons) are automatically started at a particular runlevel.

Recall in the preceding chapter that I mentioned that one of the first things I do after installing a new Linux system is to go through and turn off all the unneeded services that run automatically. This saves memory and CPU utilization and also plugs security holes in the system. In this part of the chapter, we're going to discuss how this is done. We'll cover the following topics:

- About init scripts
- Configuring the default system runlevel
- Changing runlevels from the shell prompt
- Configuring services to run by default at a specified runlevel

Let's begin by learning about init scripts.

About init Scripts

The system processes on your Linux system are started and stopped using an *init script*. An init script is used by the init process to start processes on system boot and whenever the current runlevel is changed. These scripts are stored in a specific directory on your Linux system. Which directory they are stored in depends on your Linux distribution. Most Linux distributions use one of two types of init scripts:

- **System V** Linux distributions that use System V init scripts store them in the /etc/rc.d directory. Within /etc/rc.d are a series of subdirectories named rc0.d through rc6.d. Each of these directories is associated with a particular runlevel. Within each of these subdirectories are symbolic links that point to the init scripts for your system daemons, which reside in /etc/rc.d/init.d.
- **BSD** Linux distributions that use BSD-style init scripts store them in the /etc/init.d directory. Within /etc/init.d are a series of directories named rc0.d through rc6.d. As with System V init scripts, these directories are associated with a specific runlevel. These directories contain links that point to the init scripts in /etc/init.d.

In addition to using the init process to run these scripts, you can run these scripts from the command prompt. Simply enter **/etc/init.d/**/*script_name* at the shell prompt (on a BSD-style system) or **/etc/rc.d/init.d/***script_name* (on a System V–style system). If you're not sure of which script name you should use, you can use the ls command to generate a listing of scripts in the init script directory, as shown here:

```
fs2:/etc/init.d # ls
...
aaeventd              boot.lvm              lm_sensors            rpmconfigcheck
acpid                 boot.md               mcelog                rsyncd
alsasound             boot.multipath        mdadmd                setserial
atd                   boot.proc             multipathd            single
auditd                boot.rootfsck         network               skeleton
autofs                boot.startpreload     network-remotefs      skeleton.compat
autoyast              boot.swap             nfs                   smartd
avahi-daemon          boot.sysctl           nmb                   smb
avahi-dnsconfd        boot.udev             nscd                  smolt
bluez-coldplug        boot.udev_retry       ntp                   splash
boot                  cifs                  openvpn               splash_early
boot.apparmor         cron                  pm-profiler           sshd
boot.cleanup          cups                  postfix               stoppreload
boot.clock            dbus                  powerd                svnserve
boot.crypto           dnsmasq               powerfail             syslog
boot.crypto-early     earlysyslog           random                vmtoolsd
boot.cycle            earlyxdm              raw                   xdm
boot.d                fbset                 rc                    xfs
boot.device-mapper    gpm                   rc0.d                 xinetd
boot.dmraid           haldaemon             rc1.d                 ypbind
boot.fuse             halt                  rc2.d
boot.ipconfig         halt.local            rc3.d
```

The actual scripts in your init directory depend on which services you've installed on your particular system. Whenever you use the rpm utility to install a service on your system, a corresponding init script is automatically installed in your init script directory. Once there, you can execute any script by simply running it from the command prompt. The syntax on a BSD-style system is as follows:

```
/etc/init.d/script_name start | stop | restart
```

You can use the following parameters when running init scripts:

- **start**   Use this parameter to start the associated service.
- **stop**   Use this parameter to stop the associated service.
- **status**   Use this parameter to view the status of the service, such as whether it is currently running.
- **restart**   Use this parameter to stop and then start the associated service. This is a very useful option if you've made extensive configuration changes to the service and it needs to be restarted to apply the changes.
- **reload**   Use this parameter to reread the service's configuration file without restarting the service itself. Not all daemons support this option.

For example, to run the smb service, you would enter **/etc/init.d/smb start** at the shell prompt. To stop it, you would enter **/etc/init.d/smb stop**. To restart it, you would enter **/etc/init.d/smb restart**.

On some distributions, such as SUSE Linux, you can also use the rc script to start, stop, or restart a service process without having to specify the full path to the script file. The syntax is **rc***script_name* **start | stop | restart**. For example, to start the smb service, you could enter **rcsmb start** at the shell prompt. To stop it, you could enter **rcsmb stop**. You could also use the restart option to restart it.

When the system boots up, init runs the scripts defined in /etc/inittab for the particular runlevel it's booting into. For example, if your system is configured to boot into runlevel 5, then init runs the scripts that are contained in /etc/rc.d/rc5.d or /etc/init.d/rc5.d, depending on your particular distribution. The runlevel 5 scripts for a typical openSUSE system are shown in Figure 6-14.

As you can see in Figure 6-14, the real scripts that actually start and stop services aren't located in the rc5.d subdirectory. Instead, the files in rc5.d are symbolic links that point to the real script files contained in the init directory (in this case, /etc/init.d).

In addition to init scripts, several other important script files are contained in /etc/init.d or /etc/rc.d/init.d that you need to be aware of. These are listed in Table 6-4.

In summary, the init process completes the following tasks as it initializes a BSD-type system:

- Runs the /etc/init.d/boot script to prepare the system

- Processes /etc/inittab to determine the appropriate runlevel and scripts

- Runs the scripts in the appropriate runlevel directory in /etc/init.d

- Runs the /etc/init.d/boot.local script

```
fs2:/etc/init.d/rc5.d # ls -l
total 0
lrwxrwxrwx 1 root root 22 Jan 19 10:37 K01SuSEfirewall2_setup -> ../SuSEfirewall
2_setup
lrwxrwxrwx 1 root root  9 Jan 19 10:24 K01auditd -> ../auditd
lrwxrwxrwx 1 root root 17 Jan 19 10:24 K01bluez-coldplug -> ../bluez-coldplug
lrwxrwxrwx 1 root root  7 Jan 19 10:24 K01cron -> ../cron
lrwxrwxrwx 1 root root 12 Jan 19 10:29 K01haldaemon -> ../haldaemon
lrwxrwxrwx 1 root root 15 Jan 19 10:24 K01irq_balancer -> ../irq_balancer
lrwxrwxrwx 1 root root  9 Jan 19 10:25 K01mcelog -> ../mcelog
lrwxrwxrwx 1 root root  7 Jan 19 10:24 K01nscd -> ../nscd
lrwxrwxrwx 1 root root  9 Jan 19 10:24 K01random -> ../random
lrwxrwxrwx 1 root root  9 Jan 19 10:25 K01smartd -> ../smartd
lrwxrwxrwx 1 root root  9 Jan 19 10:24 K01splash -> ../splash
lrwxrwxrwx 1 root root 15 Jan 19 10:24 K01splash_early -> ../splash_early
lrwxrwxrwx 1 root root  7 Jan 19 10:37 K01sshd -> ../sshd
lrwxrwxrwx 1 root root 14 Jan 19 10:24 K01stoppreload -> ../stoppreload
lrwxrwxrwx 1 root root 11 Jan 19 10:31 K01vmtoolsd -> ../vmtoolsd
lrwxrwxrwx 1 root root  6 Jan 19 10:24 K01xdm -> ../xdm
lrwxrwxrwx 1 root root  9 Feb  1 13:47 K01xinetd -> ../xinetd
lrwxrwxrwx 1 root root  8 Jan 19 10:24 K02acpid -> ../acpid
lrwxrwxrwx 1 root root 12 Jan 19 10:40 K02alsasound -> ../alsasound
lrwxrwxrwx 1 root root 15 Jan 19 10:24 K02avahi-daemon -> ../avahi-daemon
lrwxrwxrwx 1 root root  7 Jan 19 10:36 K02cups -> ../cups
```

Figure 6-14   The init scripts in /etc/init.d/rc5.d

File	Init Style	Function
rc	BSD and System V	This script is used to switch between runlevels while the system is running.
halt	BSD	This script can stop or reboot your system. It is run if the current runlevel is changed to 0 or 6.
boot	BSD	This script is run by init when the system first starts. It runs the scripts contained in /etc/init.d/boot.d. These scripts accomplish a variety of startup tasks, such as loading kernel modules, verifying the file systems, and setting the system clock.
boot.local	BSD	This script is also run by init at startup. It contains additional startup commands. This script is extremely useful. If you want to run a particular command automatically at startup, you can insert the command into this file with a text editor.
rc.sysinit	System V	This script's function is similar to the boot script on a BSD-type system. It's used to set the path, check the file system for errors, set the system clock, and so on.
rc.local	System V	This script's function is similar to that of the boot.local script on a BSD-type system. You can add your own commands to this script to ensure they are run every time the system boots.

Table 6-4   Important Files in /etc/init.d

On a System V–type system, the init process does the following as it gets the system up and running:

- Runs the /etc/rc.d/sysinit script to prepare the system
- Processes /etc/inittab to determine the appropriate runlevel and scripts
- Runs the scripts in the appropriate runlevel directory in /etc/rc.d/
- Runs the /etc/rc.d/rc.local script

Configuring the Default System Runlevel

As you saw earlier in this chapter, the system's default runlevel is specified in the /etc/inittab file. You can change the default runlevel by simply changing the second value in the command to the runlevel you want to use. For example, suppose I wanted to change my system from the default runlevel of 5 to 3. I would simply open /etc/inittab in a text editor and change the value 5 to **3**. After I save the file and reboot, the system would boot into runlevel 3.

In addition to changing runlevels at boot time, you can also change them on the fly as you're using the system. Let's discuss how this is done next.

Changing Runlevels from the Shell Prompt

If you think changing the default runlevel is easy, changing runlevels on the fly is even easier. This is done with the **init** command. The syntax for using init is **init** *runlevel*. For example, if my system is running in runlevel 5 and I want to switch to runlevel 3, I can simply enter **init 3**

```
Starting mail service (Postfix)                                                         done
Starting CRON daemon                                                                    done
Starting smartd                                                                       unused
                                                                                        done
Starting Firewall Initialization (phase 2 of 2) SuSEfirewall2: Warning: no default firewall zone defined, assuming 'ext'
                                                                                        done
Master Resource Control: runlevel 5 has been                                         reached
Failed services in runlevel 5:                                                          nscd
Skipped services in runlevel 5:                                            cifs nfs smartd

Welcome to openSUSE 11.3 "Teal" - Kernel 2.6.34-12-desktop (tty1).

fs2 login: WARNING: Number of errors: 0, skipped probes: 18

Welcome to openSUSE 11.3 "Teal" - Kernel 2.6.34-12-desktop (tty1).

fs2 login: _
```

Figure 6-15   Changing to runlevel 3 on the fly

at the shell prompt. After I enter the command, the system switches to runlevel 3, as shown in Figure 6-15.

 TIP   You have to switch to your root user account before you can run the init command.

When you change runlevels with the init command, the init process runs the rc script and tells it to switch to the appropriate level. The rc script reads /etc/inittab for the current runlevel and stops all the services associated with that runlevel using the scripts in the appropriate runlevel directory in your init directory. The rc script then reads /etc/inittab and runs the appropriate start scripts in the new runlevel's directory in the init directory.

If you look inside an rcx.d directory within your distribution's init directory, you will see two scripts for each system process. One starts with an *S,* and one starts with a *K.* The scripts that start with *S* are used to start a process, whereas the scripts that start with *K* are used to stop (kill) a process. When the init process calls rc and sends it a runlevel to change to, the rc process runs all the scripts in the corresponding rcx.d directory to start and stop services as appropriate for the runlevel being entered. These are the scripts employed when switching between runlevels on the fly as just described.

Even though we call these files "scripts," they aren't. They are actually symbolic links that point to the real script files in your init script directory. This makes updating your Linux system much easier. If individual init scripts were maintained in each rcx.d directory and an update needed to be applied to a particular service, each init script in each rcx.d directory would have to be individually updated. What a lot of work! The chance of errors and inconsistency would be huge!

Instead, because all the files in the various rcx.d directories are just symbolic links to the one copy of the service's init script in the init directory, any updates that need to be applied can be made to only the one file.

A sampling of the scripts in the rc5.d directory is shown in Figure 6-14. The *S* files call their associated init script with the **start** parameter, whereas the *K* files call their associated init script with the **stop** parameter.

Also notice in Figure 6-14 that the letter *K* or *S* is followed by a number and then the name of the init script. The number in the filename is very important. When init calls the rc script to switch runlevels, the rc script first looks at the rcx.d directory for the current runlevel and compares it with the rc*x*.d directory for the runlevel it is going to switch the system to. If there is a kill script for the service in the rc*x*.d directory for the current runlevel and a start script for the same service in the rc*x*.d directory for the new runlevel, the rc script leaves the service running because it should be running in both runlevels.

If, on the other hand, there is a kill script for the service in the rc*x*.d directory for the current runlevel but there is no start script for the same service in the rc*x*.d directory for the new runlevel, the rc script runs the kill script to stop the service. Conversely, if there is a start script for the service in the rc*x*.d directory for the new runlevel and there is no start script for the same service in the rc*x*.d directory for the current runlevel, the rc script runs the start script to start the service.

The number in the kill or start script filename comes into play at this point. This number determines the sequence in which the scripts are run. This ensures that services that other services are dependent on are started first. For example, a script assigned a number of 01 will be run before a script assigned a number of 02. This means a file in rc5.d named S02network is run after S01dbus but before S03syslog.

To make this clear, let's run through an example. Suppose you need to switch your system from runlevel 3 to runlevel 5. Here's what happens:

1. You enter **init 3** at the shell prompt (as your root user).

2. The init process checks the /etc/inittab configuration file, which usually specifies that it run the /etc/init.d/rc script, and tells it to switch the system to runlevel 5.

3. The rc process runs the kill scripts in the current runlevel directory for any running services that should be disabled in the new runlevel.

4. The rc process runs the start scripts in the new runlevel directory for any services that are not currently running but should be in the new runlevel.

NOTE If you enter **init 0** or **init 6** at the shell prompt, the system will halt (init 0) or reboot (init 6). You can also use the **telinit** command instead of init to change runlevels. The functionality and syntax are the same.

You can also change runlevels at system boot time by having your bootloader send the desired runlevel to the Linux kernel as a kernel option. For example, on some distributions you can simply add the runlevel you want to boot into as the last parameter in the Boot Options field in the GRUB boot menu. For example, in Figure 6-16, the number 3 has been added as the last boot option. This number is passed to the init process and tells init what runlevel to boot into.

Next, let's review the process for configuring services to run at specific runlevels.

Configuring Services to Run by Default at a Specified Runlevel

If you want to configure a system service to run automatically at boot, you must associate it with a system runlevel and specify whether the service will be turned off or on.

Figure 6-16
Configuring the system runlevel at boot

Boot Options vga=0x317 3

Whenever you install a daemon, whether during system installation or by using the rpm utility, an init script is copied to your init directory (/etc/init.d or /etc/rc.d/init.d). You can use either the insserv or chkconfig command to configure which runlevels each of your init scripts are associated with.

The insserv command reads the information in the INIT INFO block of an init script to determine which runlevels the associated service should run in by default. The INIT INFO block of the ntp init script on an openSUSE system is shown in this example:

```
### BEGIN INIT INFO
# Provides:       ntp ntpd xntpd
# Required-Start: $remote_fs $syslog $named
# Required-Stop:  $remote_fs $syslog
# Should-Start: network-remotefs
# Should-Stop: network-remotefs
# Default-Start:  3 5
# Default-Stop:   0 1 2 6
# Short-Description: Network time protocol daemon (ntpd)
# Description:    Start network time protocol daemon (NTPD).
### END INIT INFO
```

As you can see in this example, the INIT INFO block provides several key pieces of information for a given Linux daemon:

- The service the init script manages (Provides)
- The services that must be started before this service can start (Required-Start)
- The default runlevels that the daemon should run in (Default-Start)
- The default runlevels that the daemon should not run in (Default-Stop)

The Default-Start and Default-Stop parameters are used by the insserv command to determine which runlevel directories the appropriate start and kill scripts should be created in. Using the INIT INFO block shown in the preceding example, the insserv command will create start script links in the rc3.d and rc5.d directories while also creating kill script links in the rc1.d and rc2.d directories.

The syntax for using insserv is **insserv** *service_name*. This command enables the daemon specified at the runlevels listed in the Default-Start directive of the INIT INFO block of the service's init script. It also disables the daemon at the runlevels listed in the Default-Stop directive of the INIT INFO block.

The insserv utility can also be used to disable the service (thus removing all links for the service in the various rcx.d directories) and stop the service if it is currently running. The syntax to do this is **insserv –r** *service_name*.

If a service has already been enabled and you want to change its default runlevels, you can use insserv to implement the change. Do the following:

1. Open the appropriate init script in your init script directory and edit the Default-Start and Default-Stop parameters in the INIT INFO block.

2. Save your changes to the file.

3. Enter **insserv –d** *service_name* at the shell prompt.

When you do, the insserv command re-creates the appropriate start and kill script links in the various rc*.d directories.

You can also enable a daemon using insserv but completely ignore the Default-Start and Default-Stop parameters in its init script. To do so, take these steps:

1. If the daemon has already been enabled at its default runlevels, remove all start and kill script links by entering **insserv –r** *service_name* at the shell prompt.

2. Create new customized start and kill script links by entering **insserv** *service_name*,**start=***comma-separated_list_of_runlevels*. For example, enter **insserv ntp,start=3,5**.

In addition to insserv, you can also use the chkconfig command to manage a daemon's runlevels. If you want to view a service's current runlevel configuration, enter **chkconfig –l** *daemon_name* at the shell prompt. You can also enter **chkconfig –l** to see the status of all daemons installed on your system. In the example that follows, the chkconfig command is used to view the runlevel configuration of the ntp daemon:

```
ws1:/etc/init.d # chkconfig -l ntp
ntp                       0:off  1:off  2:off  3:off  4:off  5:off  6:off
```

As you can see here, the ntp service has not been configured to start at any runlevel. If you want to configure a daemon to start at its default runlevels, you can enter **chkconfig** *daemon_name* **on**. You can also specify exactly what levels you want a daemon to start on using the chkconfig command. For example, suppose we wanted the ntp daemon to run in runlevels 3 and 5. We could make this happen by entering **chkconfig –s ntp 35**. This specifies that the ntp service (specified by the –s option) be enabled at runlevels 3 and 5. This is shown here:

```
ws1:/etc/init.d # chkconfig -s ntp 35
ws1:/etc/init.d # chkconfig -l ntp
ntp                       0:off  1:off  2:off  3:on   4:off  5:on   6:off
```

To disable a service, enter **chkconfig** *service_name* **off**. For example, to disable the ntp service enabled previously, you would enter **chkconfig ntp off**:

```
ws1:/etc/init.d # chkconfig ntp off
ws1:/etc/init.d # chkconfig -l ntp
ntp                       0:off  1:off  2:off  3:off  4:off  5:off  6:off
```

You can also use chkconfig to view the runlevel configuration of all the services installed on your system by simply entering **chkconfig –l**, as shown here:

```
ws1:/etc/init.d # chkconfig -l
SuSEfirewall2_init        0:off  1:off  2:off  3:on   4:on   5:on   6:off
SuSEfirewall2_setup       0:off  1:off  2:off  3:on   4:on   5:on   6:off
aaeventd                  0:off  1:off  2:off  3:off  4:off  5:off  6:off
acpid                     0:off  1:off  2:on   3:on   4:off  5:on   6:off
alsasound                 0:off  1:off  2:on   3:on   4:off  5:on   6:off
atd                       0:off  1:off  2:off  3:off  4:off  5:off  6:off
auditd                    0:off  1:off  2:off  3:on   4:off  5:on   6:off
autofs                    0:off  1:off  2:off  3:off  4:off  5:off  6:off
...
```

Let's practice working with Linux runlevels in the following exercise.

Exercise 6-3: Working with Linux Runlevels

In this exercise, you practice manipulating runlevels on your Linux system.

 NOTE This exercise cannot be done using the virtual machines that come with this book. You must use an older distribution that uses init instead of systemd to complete this exercise.

 VIDEO Please watch the Exercise 6-3 video for a demonstration on how to perform this task.

Complete the following:

1. Boot your Linux system and log in as a standard user.

2. Open a terminal session.

3. Switch to your root user account by entering **su –** followed by your root user's password.

4. Practice changing your current runlevel from the shell prompt by doing the following:

    a. View your current runlevel by entering **runlevel** at the shell prompt. The first number displayed indicates your system's previous runlevel; the second number indicates your system's current runlevel.

    If you installed a graphical system, your current runlevel should be 5. If you installed a text-based system, your current runlevel should be 3. If you see *N* for your first runlevel parameter, it means the system has never been in any other runlevel than the current one.

    b. Switch to runlevel 3 by entering **init 3** at the shell prompt.

    c. When prompted, log in as your root user.

    d. Switch back to runlevel 5 by entering **init 5** at the shell prompt.

    e. Log back in to the system.

5. Change your default runlevel to 3 by doing the following:

    a. Open a terminal session.

    b. At the shell prompt, change to your root user account using the **su –** command.

    c. At the shell prompt, enter **vi /etc/inittab**.

    d. Scroll down to the line that reads id:5:initdefault:.

    e. Press INSERT.

    f. Change the number 5 in this line to **3**.

    g. Press ESC and then enter **:exit**.

h. Reboot your system by entering **init 6** at the shell prompt.

Your system should boot into a text-based login shell.

i. Log in as your root user.

j. At the shell prompt, use vi to edit /etc/inittab to change the default runlevel back to 5.

k. Power off the system by entering **init 0** at the shell prompt.

l. Power the system back on and log back in to your system as a normal user.

6. Practice enabling the ntp daemon at runlevels 3 and 5 on your system. The ntp daemon is used to synchronize your local Linux system's clock with the clock on other computer systems. Complete the following steps:

a. Open a terminal session and change to your root user account.

b. At the shell prompt, use the rpm utility to verify that the ntp package has been installed on your system by entering **rpm –q ntp**. If the rpm command returns a package name and version number, ntp has been installed. If it returns nothing, the ntp package hasn't been installed.

NOTE If the ntp package hasn't been installed, use the steps presented in Chapter 8 to install the package from your distribution DVD.

c. At the shell prompt, enter vi /etc/ntp.conf.

d. Scroll down to the lines that read

```
server      127.127.1.0 #local clock (LCL)
fudge       127.127.1.0 stratum 10 #LCL is unsynchronized
```

e. Press INSERT.

f. Add a new line below the fudge line.

g. Add the following directive on the new line:

```
server bigben.cac.washington.edu
```

This directive configures the ntp service to synchronize your local computer time with the time on the bigben.cac.washington.edu public ntp server on the Internet.

h. Press ESC; then enter **:exit**.

i. Start the ntp service by entering **/etc/init.d/ntp restart** or **/etc/rc.d/init.d/ntp restart** at the shell prompt. You should see messages that the daemon is starting and that it's getting its time from bigben.cac.washington.edu, as shown here:

```
ws1:~ # /etc/init.d/ntp restart
Shutting down network time protocol daemon (NTPD)
done
Time synchronized with bigben.cac.washington.edu
Starting network time protocol daemon (NTPD)
done
ws1:~ #
```

j. Configure the ntp daemon to automatically start at runlevels 3 and 5 by entering **chkconfig –s ntp 35** at the shell prompt.

k. Check the status of the ntp daemon by entering **chkconfig –l ntp** at the shell prompt. You should see runlevels 3 and 5 set to **on**, as shown here:

```
ws1:~ # chkconfig -l ntp
ntp                          0:off  1:off  2:off  3:on   4:off  5:on
6:off
ws1:~ #
```

With this in mind, we now need to look at Linux distributions that use systemd instead of init.

Managing Linux Boot Targets

In addition to the traditional init daemon, which manages just about everything on your Linux system, you can use two alternative daemons instead of init to manage the starting of tasks and managing of runlevels on Linux:

- Upstart
- systemd

Upstart was introduced in the mid-2000s and received a lukewarm reception. The key problem was the fact that it was very different from init and required a steep learning curve to master. As a result, only a very limited number of Linux distributions still use it.

However, systemd was introduced only a few years ago and it has pretty much taken over. Most Linux distributions today have started the migration away from init to systemd. Like Upstart, systemd is also a replacement for the traditional init daemon. Unlike Upstart, however, systemd can function as a drop-in replacement for init. If you're familiar with init, moving to systemd is much less painful.

One of the benefits of systemd is the fact that it can load services in parallel at system startup. The traditional init process starts services one at a time in sequential fashion. Starting services in parallel can dramatically decreases the amount of time needed to get the system up and running. The systemd daemon also supports snapshots, which provide options for restoring the system state, if necessary.

Because of its popularity, we will focus on systemd in this chapter. We need to discuss the following topics:

- Managing boot targets
- Managing services

With this in mind, let's begin by looking at how runlevels are managed on a Linux system that uses systemd.

Managing Boot Targets

If you're familiar with runlevels under init, then working with runlevels under systemd is fairly easy to understand. The commands you use to manage runlevels are different under systemd, but the concepts are similar. One of the key things to remember is the fact that systemd uses the concept of *boot targets,* which function in a similar way as runlevels. Each boot target is represented by a file in /usr/lib/systemd/system with an extension of **.target**. In the following list, traditional init runlevels are shown with their equivalent systemd boot target files:

- runlevel 3 = multi-user.target or runlevel3.target
- runlevel 5 = graphical.target or runlevel5.target

Notice that there are two target files for each runlevel. Be aware that runlevel3.target is actually just a symbolic link that points to the multi-user.target file. Likewise, the runlevel5.target file is a symbolic link that points to the graphical.target file.

On a system uses systemd, you use the **systemctl** command to manage services and runlevels. Instead of using init, chkconfig, or service, you use systemctl to manage most aspects of a systemd system. For example, to change runlevels you run systemctl and point to a particular boot target. The syntax is **systemctl isolate *boot_target*.**

For example, if I wanted to switch to the systemd equivalent of runlevel 5, I could enter either of the following commands:

- **systemctl isolate runlevel 5.target**
- **systemctl isolate graphical.target**

And just as with the traditional init process, changing boot targets on the fly with systemd only changes the current runlevel. If you reboot the system, it will boot back into the default runlevel. With systemd, you no longer use the inittab file to set the default runlevel. Instead, the etc/systemd/system/default.target file controls the default boot target. As you can see in the following example, this file is actually a symbolic link that points back to the boot target file that should be used by default:

```
openSUSE:/etc/systemd/system # ls -l default.target
lrwxrwxrwx 1 root root 40 Nov 12 09:05 default.target ->
/usr/lib/systemd/system/runlevel5.target
```

NOTE Some distributions that use systemd still retain the inittab file for backward compatibility.

To modify the default boot target, you need to modify the boot file that this symbolic link points to. This is done using the **systemctl set-default *boot_target*** command. For example, to set the default boot target to graphical mode, you would enter **systemctl set-default graphical .target** or **systemctl set-default runlevel 5.target**.

If you want to view the current runlevel, enter **systemctl get-default**. An example is shown here:

```
openSUSE:/etc/systemd/system # systemctl get-default
runlevel5.target
```

Let's now look at how you manage services on a Linux system that uses systemd.

Managing Services

You manage system daemons on a system using systemd in much the same manner that you do on a system that uses init. However, the command used is different. If you need to stop, start, restart, or view the status of a particular service on the system, you enter **systemctl** followed by the action you want performed, followed by the service name. Use the following syntax:

- To start a service, enter **systemctl start** *service***.service**. For example, to start the ntp daemon, you would enter **systemctl start ntp.service**.
- To stop a service, enter **systemctl stop** *service***.service**. For example, to stop the ntp daemon, you would enter **systemctl stop ntp.service**.
- To restart a service, enter **systemctl restart** *service***.service**. For example, to restart the ntp daemon, you would enter **systemctl restart ntp.service**.
- To check the status of a service, enter **systemctl status** *service***.service**. For example, to check the status of the ntp daemon, you would enter **systemctl status ntp.service**.

You can also use the systemctl command to enable or disable a particular service on system boot. You can also check to see whether or not it has been enabled. To do this, you use the following commands:

- To enable a service on system start, enter **systemctl enable** *service***.service**. For example, to enable the ntp daemon on system boot, you would enter **systemctl enable ntp.service**.
- To disable a service on system start, enter **systemctl disable** *service***.service**. For example, to disable the ntp daemon on system boot, you would enter **systemctl disable ntp .service**.
- To check and see whether a service is enabled or not on system startup, enter **systemctl is-enabled** *service***.service**. For example, to check the status of the ntp daemon, you would enter **systemctl is-enabled ntp.service**.

Exercise 6-4: Working with Linux Runlevels

In this exercise, you practice manipulating boot targets on your Linux system. You can perform this exercise using the virtual machine that comes with this book. Run snapshot 6-2 for the correctly configured environment.

 VIDEO   Please watch the Exercise 6-4 video for a demonstration on how to perform this task.

Complete the following:

1. Boot your Linux system and log in as your student user using a password of **student**.
2. Open a terminal session.
3. Switch to your root user account by entering **su** – followed by your root user's password (**student**).

4. Change your default boot target to the equivalent of runlevel 3 by doing the following:

    a. Open a terminal session.

    b. At the shell prompt, change to your root user account using the **su –** command.

    c. At the shell prompt, enter **systemctl set-default multi-user.target**.

    d. Reboot your system by entering **init 6** at the shell prompt.

        Notice that this command still works even though the system doesn't use the init daemon. Your system should boot into a text-based login shell.

    e. Log in as your root user.

    f. At the shell prompt, use the systemctl command to change the default boot target back to graphical.

    g. Power off the system by entering **init 0** at the shell prompt. Again, notice that the command works even though the system doesn't use the init daemon.

    h. Power the system back on and log back in to your system as a normal user.

5. Practice enabling the ntp daemon at system boot. Complete the following:

    a. Open a terminal session and change to your root user account.

    b. At the shell prompt, enter **vi /etc/ntp.conf**.

    c. Scroll down to the lines that read

```
server      127.127.1.0 #local clock (LCL)
fudge       127.127.1.0 stratum 10 #LCL is unsynchronized
```

    d. Press INSERT.

    e. Add a new line below the fudge line.

    f. Add the following directive on the new line:

```
server bigben.cac.washington.edu
```

        This directive configures the ntp service to synchronize your local computer time with the time on the bigben.cac.washington.edu public ntp server on the Internet.

    g. Press ESC; then enter **:exit**.

    h. Start the ntp service by entering **systemctl start ntp.service** at the shell prompt.

    i. Check the status of the ntp daemon by entering **systemctl status ntp.service** at the shell prompt.

        Let's end this chapter by discussing how to shut a Linux system down.

Shutting Down the System

As with any other operating system, you need to shut down a Linux system properly. This ensures any pending disk write operations are actually committed to disk before the system is powered off.

CAUTION If you power off a Linux system unexpectedly, you may introduce corruption and inconsistencies into your file system. Always use the proper shutdown procedure. In addition, I strongly recommend that you implement an uninterruptible power supply (UPS) with your systems. They are inexpensive and will save your bacon if the power goes off. Trust me, I know. I lost an unprotected server once due to a power outage, and I had to stay up all night restoring it from backup tapes. Never again!

You can use several commands to properly shut down a Linux system, including the following:

- **init 0**   Switches the system to runlevel 0, which halts the system
- **init 6**   Switches the system to runlevel 6, which reboots the system
- **halt**   Shuts down the system
- **reboot**   Reboots the system

In addition to these commands, you can also use the **shutdown** command to either shut down or reboot the system. It has several key advantages over the preceding commands:

- You can specify that the system go down after a specified period of time. This gives your users time to save their work and log out before the system goes down. It also allows you to shut down the system at a specified time even if you're not there to do it.
- It allows you to send a message to all logged-in users warning them that a shutdown is pending.
- It does not allow other users to log in before the pending shutdown.

The syntax for using shutdown is **shutdown +m –h|–r *message.*** The *+m* option specifies the amount of time (in minutes) before shutting down the system. You can also use the **now** option instead of *+m* to specify that the system go down immediately. If you need the system to go down at a specific time, you can replace *+m* with the time (entered as ***hh:mm***) when the shutdown should occur. The –h option specifies that the system be halted, whereas the –r option specifies that the system be rebooted. Some examples of using shutdown are shown here:

```
shutdown +10 -h Please save your work and log out.
```

When you enter this command, all other logged-in users see the following message:

```
tux@ws1:~/Desktop>
Broadcast message from root@ws1 (pts/3) (Thu Feb 17 10:29:59 2011):

Please save your work and log out.
The system is going DOWN for system halt in 10 minutes!
```

If you've scheduled a shutdown using the shutdown command and later need to cancel that shutdown, enter **shutdown –c** at the shell prompt.

You can also use the wall command to send messages to users to inform them of system events, such as a system reboot or a runlevel change. To use wall, you must send the message to the stdin of the wall command. An example is shown here:

```
openSUSE:~ # echo "The system is going down for a reboot." | wall

Broadcast Message from rtracy@openSUSE
        (/dev/pts/1) at 16:26 ...

The system is going down for a reboot.
```

Excellent work! You're on your way to LPIC-1/Linux+ certification! Let's review what you learned in this chapter.

Chapter Review

In this chapter, you learned how to manage the Linux boot process. I began this chapter by reviewing how the Linux boot process works. I broke the boot process down into three phases:

- The BIOS phase
- The bootloader phase
- The kernel phase

In the BIOS phase, the computer's BIOS chip has control of the system. Its main jobs are to set up the basic hardware in the system, test the hardware using the power-on self-test (POST) routine, and then locate a device with boot files on it.

In the bootloader phase, the BIOS turns control of the system over to a bootloader. The key job of the bootloader is to point to and load your operating system's kernel. The bootloader can reside in the master boot record (MBR) of the boot device or in the boot partition on the drive. Linux bootloaders can be configured with a menu that provides the end user with several options for booting the operating system. They can even be configured to load non-Linux operating systems, such as Windows.

The Linux bootloader creates a virtual hard drive in your system's RAM (called a *ramdisk)* and copies a basic root file system to it. This virtual file system can be used by your Linux kernel to load the software it needs to access your real storage devices, check them, and mount them. This virtual file system is called the *initrd image* or the *initramfs image,* depending on your distribution.

In the kernel phase, the bootloader loads the operating system into your system RAM from the hard drive or other boot device. Your Linux kernel is located in /boot in the file system and is named vmlinuz-*version*.gz. After the kernel has been loaded, the following occurs in the kernel phase:

- The kernel initializes the basic hardware in your system using the various settings in your BIOS and your CMOS chips.
- The kernel searches for and uses the initrd or initramfs file system to run the linuxrc program to set up the system.
- When linuxrc has finished executing, the initrd or initramfs file system is dismounted and the ramdisk is destroyed.

- The kernel probes for new hardware and loads the appropriate driver modules.
- The real root (/) file system is mounted.
- The kernel loads the init or the systemd process.

We then turned our attention to configuring Linux bootloaders. The first Linux bootloader we looked at was the GRUB Legacy bootloader. I pointed out that the GRUB Legacy bootloader was used by many current Linux distributions for a number of years. I pointed out that GRUB is divided into several stages:

- **Stage 1**   Usually stored in the MBR. It points to the location of Stage 1.5 or Stage 2.
- **Stage 1.5**   Stored in the first 30KB after the MBR. It points to the location of Stage 2.
- **Stage 2**   Stored within a disk partition. Presents the end user with a menu to select the operating system to boot.

I next pointed out that the file used to configure GRUB depends on your distribution. Some distributions use /boot/grub/grub.conf; others use /boot/grub/menu.lst. GRUB refers to hard disks in the system as hd*x,* where *x* is the number of the drive in the system. SCSI, SATA, and IDE (PATA) drives are referred to in this manner. Partitions on the drive are referred to as hd*x,y,* where *y* is the number of the partition on the drive.

If you've created a separate partition for your /boot directory in the file system, GRUB will use this as the GRUB root and will refer to files within /boot/grub without including /boot in the path. If your /boot directory doesn't have its own partition, GRUB will use the full path to refer to the /boot/grub/ files.

One of the cool features of GRUB is that it provides you with the ability to interactively manage the boot process. You can modify boot menu items at system startup to customize how the system boots. You can also create new boot menu items interactively by accessing the grub> prompt. We also discussed how to add an encrypted password to the items in your GRUB boot menu.

We then looked at the latest version of the GRUB bootloader, called GRUB2. GRUB2 works in a completely different manner than the original GRUB Legacy bootloader. Version 1.98 or later of GRUB is considered "GRUB2." GRUB2 uses a completely different set of configuration files as compared to the GRUB Legacy bootloader. The configuration files used by GRUB2 are

- The /boot/grub/grub.cfg file
- The files within the /etc/grub.d directory
- The /etc/default/grub file

With GRUB2, there is no menu.lst file. It has been replaced by the /boot/grub2/grub.cfg file. The grub.cfg file is automatically updated every time you make a configuration change and then run one of the following commands:

- Some distributions use the **update-grub** command.
- Other distributions use the **grub2-mkconfig -o /boot/grub2/grub.cfg** command.

The GRUB2 configuration is stored in several script files within the /etc/grub.d directory. If you make changes to one of these files and then run the update-grub or grub2-mkconfig command, the grub.cfg file is automatically updated with the new GRUB settings.

After discussing GRUB, we then turned our attention to managing runlevels on Linux. I first discussed how runlevels work. Linux defines seven runlevels (0–6) that do the following:

- **0**   Halts the system.

- **1**   Runs Linux in single-user mode.

- **2**   Runs Linux in multiuser mode with networking disabled.

- **3**   Runs Linux in multiuser mode with networking enabled.

- **4**   Unused.

- **5**   Runs Linux in multiuser mode with networking enabled. The graphical user interface is used.

- **6**   Reboots the system.

The /etc/inittab file is used to configure what happens in each runlevel. This file also defines the default runlevel that your system will boot into. Your system's init directory contains a series of subdirectories named rc.0 to rc.6, each of which contains symbolic links to init scripts that should be run for the respective runlevel.

On a BSD-type system, the init process completes the following tasks as it initializes the system:

- Runs the /etc/init.d/boot script to prepare the system

- Processes /etc/inittab to determine the appropriate runlevel and scripts

- Runs the scripts in the appropriate runlevel directory in /etc/init.d

- Runs the /etc/init.d/boot.local script

On a System V–type system, the init process does the following as it gets the system up and running:

- Runs the /etc/rc.d/sysinit script to prepare the system

- Processes /etc/inittab to determine the appropriate runlevel and scripts

- Runs the scripts in the appropriate runlevel directory in /etc/rc.d/

- Runs the /etc/rc.d/rc.local script

We then spent some time working with the init scripts in your init directory. The syntax for managing services with init scripts is **/etc/init.d/**_script_name_ **start | stop | restart**.

I then shifted gears and discussed how to manage runlevels. I first discussed how to configure the default system runlevel in /etc/inittab. I then discussed how to change runlevels on the fly. This is done using the init command. You simply enter **init _runlevel_** from the shell prompt. When you do this, the init process runs the rc script, which shuts down services associated with the current runlevel and starts scripts associated with the runlevel you're switching to.

We then turned our attention to systemd. Most Linux distributions today have migrated away from init to systemd. The systemd daemon is a replacement for the traditional init daemon. One of the benefits of systemd is the fact that it can load services in parallel at system startup. The systemd daemon uses the concept of *boot targets,* which function in a similar way as runlevels. The traditional init runlevels are shown next, with their equivalent systemd boot target files:

- runlevel 3 = multi-user.target or runlevel3.target
- runlevel 5 = graphical.target or runlevel5.target

On a system that uses systemd, you use the **systemctl** command to manage services and boot targets. To change runlevels, you run systemctl and point to a particular boot target. The syntax is **systemctl isolate** *boot_target*. The etc/systemd/system/default.target file controls the default boot target. To modify the default boot target, you need to modify the boot file that this symbolic link points to. This is done using the **systemctl set-default** *boot_target* command. If you want to view the current runlevel, enter **systemctl get-default**.

You manage system daemons on a system using systemd in much the same manner that you do on a system that uses init. However, the command used is different. If you need to stop, start, restart, or view the status of a particular service on the system, you enter **systemctl** followed by the action you want performed, followed by the service name. You can also use the systemctl command to enable or disable a particular service on system boot.

I ended the chapter by discussing how to specify which services run at each runlevel. This is done using the insserv and chkconfig commands. The insserv command reads the information in the INIT INFO block of an init script to determine which runlevels the associated service should run in by default. The syntax for using insserv is **insserv** *service_name*.

In addition to insserv, you can also use the chkconfig command to manage a daemon's runlevels. Entering **chkconfig –l** will list all services and the runlevels at which they are configured to run. To configure a service to start at a particular runlevel, enter **chkconfig –s** *service_name runlevels*. To turn off a service, enter **chkconfig** *service_name* **off**.

Accelerated Review

- In the BIOS phase, the computer's BIOS chip has control of the system.
- The BIOS tests the system hardware using the power-on self-test (POST) routine and then locates a storage device with boot files on it.
- In the bootloader phase, the BIOS turns control of the system over to a bootloader.
- The bootloader points to and loads your operating system's kernel.
- The bootloader can reside in the master boot record (MBR) of the boot device or in the boot partition on the drive.
- The Linux bootloader may also create a virtual hard drive in your system's RAM, called a *ramdisk,* and copy a basic root file system to it.
- This virtual file system (called the *initrd* or *initramfs image,* depending on your distribution) is used by the Linux kernel to load the software it needs to access your real storage devices, check them, and mount them.

- In the kernel phase, the bootloader loads the operating system into your system RAM from the hard drive or other boot device.

- The Linux kernel is located in /boot and is named vmlinuz-*version*.gz.

- The GRUB Legacy bootloader was widely used by many Linux distributions.

- GRUB Legacy is divided into several stages: Stage 1, Stage 1.5, and Stage 2.

- Some distributions use /boot/grub/grub.conf; others use /boot/grub/menu.lst to configure GRUB Legacy.

- GRUB Legacy refers to hard disks in the system as hd$x$, where x is the number of the drive in the system.

- Partitions on the drive are referred to as hdx,y, where y is the number of the partition on the drive.

- If you've created a separate partition for your /boot directory, GRUB Legacy will use this as the GRUB root and will refer to files within /boot/grub without including /boot in the path.

- If your /boot directory doesn't have its own partition, GRUB Legacy will use the full path to refer to the /boot/grub/ files.

- GRUB Legacy allows you to modify boot menu items at system startup to customize how the system boots.

- GRUB Legacy allows you to create new boot menu items interactively by accessing the grub> prompt.

- You can replace the init process with a different program (such as the bash shell) from the GRUB menu to troubleshoot a system that won't boot.

- You can add an encrypted password to your GRUB menu to restrict access.

- Version 1.98 or later of GRUB is considered "GRUB2."

  The configuration files used by GRUB2 are

  - The /boot/grub/grub.cfg file

  - The files within the /etc/grub.d directory

  - The /etc/default/grub file

- With GRUB2, the menu.lst file has been replaced by the /boot/grub2/grub.cfg file.

- The GRUB2 configuration is stored in several script files within the /etc/grub.d directory.

- After making a change to the GRUB2 configuration, you must run either the **update-grub** command or the **grub2-mkconfig -o /boot/grub2/grub.cfg** command.

- Linux defines seven runlevels (0–6):

  0   Halts the system.
  1   Runs Linux in single-user mode.
  2   Runs Linux in multiuser mode with networking disabled.
  3   Runs Linux in multiuser mode with networking enabled.

4 Unused.

5 Runs Linux in multiuser mode with networking enabled. The graphical user interface is used.

6 Reboots the system.

- The /etc/inittab file is used to configure what happens in each runlevel.

- /etc/inittab also defines the default runlevel that your system will boot into.

- The system processes on your Linux system are started and stopped using an init script.

- An init script is used by the init process to start processes on system boot and whenever the current runlevel is changed.

- Most Linux distributions use one of two types of init scripts:

  - System V

  - BSD

- The syntax for running init scripts is **/etc/init.d/***script_name* **start | stop | restart**.

- Your system's init directory contains a series of subdirectories named rc.0 to rc.6, each of which contains symbolic links to init scripts that should be run for the respective runlevel.

- You can change runlevels on the fly using the init command by entering **init** *runlevel* from the shell prompt.

- When you change runlevels, the init process runs the rc script, which shuts down services associated with the current runlevel and starts scripts associated with the runlevel you're switching to.

- You can configure services to run a specific runlevel using the insserv and chkconfig commands.

- The insserv command reads the information in the INIT INFO block of an init script to determine which runlevels the associated service should run in by default.

- The syntax for using insserv is **insserv** *service_name*.

- Entering **chkconfig –l** will list each service and the runlevels at which they are configured to run.

- To configure a service to start at a particular runlevel, enter **chkconfig –s** *service_name* *runlevels*.

- To turn off a service, enter **chkconfig** *service_name* **off**.

- Most Linux distributions today have migrated away from init to systemd.

- The systemd daemon uses the concept of *boot targets,* which function in a similar way as runlevels.

- The traditional init runlevels are shown here with their equivalent systemd boot target files:

  - runlevel 3 = multi-user.target or runlevel3.target

  - runlevel 5 = graphical.target or runlevel5.target

- On a system that uses systemd, you use the **systemctl** command to manage services and boot targets.

Questions

1. What is the role of the BIOS during system boot? (Choose two.)

   A. It tests system hardware.

   B. It creates an initrd image in a ramdisk.

   C. It locates a bootable storage device.

   D. It provides a menu that lets you choose which operating system to boot.

   E. It points to your operating system kernel.

2. Where can your Linux bootloader reside? (Choose two.)

   A. In the BIOS

   B. In an initrd image

   C. In the MBR of a storage device

   D. In the bootable partition

   E. In the system chipset

3. Where does the Linux kernel reside?

   A. In /boot

   B. In the MBR

   C. In /proc

   D. In /kernel

4. You want to install GRUB into the first partition on the first SATA hard disk drive of your system. Which shell command will do this?

   A. grub /dev/sda1

   B. grub-install /dev/sda1

   C. grub-install /dev/sda

   D. grub /dev/hda1

5. Which file is used to configure the GRUB bootloader?

   A. /etc/menu.lst

   B. /etc/grub.conf

   C. /boot/grub/grub.conf

   D. /boot/grub/menu.lst

6. Which of the following GRUB configuration file directives points to the partition on the hard drive where /boot resides?

   A. root

   B. boot

   C. kernel

   D. partition

7. When you're configuring your GRUB configuration file, which of the following points to /dev/sda2 on a SATA hard drive?

   A. hd1,2

   B. hd0,2

   C. sd0,2

   D. hd0,1

8. Which of the following configuration files is *not* used by the GRUB2 bootloader?

   A. /boot/grub/grub.cfg

   B. /etc/grub.d

   C. /etc/default/grub

   D. /boot/grub/menu.lst

9. Which GRUB2 configuration script file can detect a Windows installation on the same hard disk as Linux?

   A. 00_header

   B. 10_linux

   C. 30_os-prober

   D. 40_custom

10. Which configuration parameter in /etc/default/grub specifies how long the user has to make a menu selection from the GRUB menu before the default operating system is booted?

    A. GRUB_TIMEOUT

    B. GRUB_DEFAULT

    C. GRUB_SAVED DEFAULT

    D. GRUB_HIDDEN_TIMEOUT

11. Which runlevel uses a graphical user interface by default?

    A. 2

    B. 3

    C. 4

    D. 5

12. Which runlevels use a command-line user interface by default? (Choose two.)

    A. 0

    B. 2

    C. 3

    D. 5

    E. 4

13. To which file can you add commands that you want executed each time the system boots? (Choose two.)

    A. rc

    B. boot.local

    C. rc.local

    D. rc.systinit

    E. boot

14. Where are the init scripts stored on an older Fedora Linux system?

    A. /etc/rc.d/init.d

    B. /etc/init.d

    C. /etc/init

    D. /etc/rc.d/init.d/rcx.d

15. Which command can be used on an older openSUSE Linux system to start the Secure Shell server (sshd) daemon? (Choose two.)

    A. /etc/rc.d/init.d/sshd start

    B. /etc/init.d/sshd restart

    C. /etc/rc.d/init.d/sshd reload

    D. /etc/init.d/sshd start

    E. /etc/init.d/sshd reload

    F. /etc/rc.d/init.d/sshd restart

16. Which file is used to set the default runlevel of a Linux system that uses the init daemon?

    A. /etc/inittab

    B. /etc/runlevel.conf

    C. /etc/init.conf

    D. /etc/sysconfig/init

17. Which command can be used to switch runlevels while the system is running?

    A. runlevel

    B. chrun

    C. mode

    D. init

18. The following link files are located in the /etc/init.d/rc3.d directory. If the system is configured to boot into runlevel 3 by default, which file is run by init before any of the others?

    A. S09cups

    B. S05cifs

   C. S06kbd

   D. S10cron

19. Your older openSUSE Linux system is currently in runlevel 5. You enter the **init 3** command at the shell prompt as root to switch to runlevel 3. There is a kill script for the cups service in the /etc/init.d/rc3.d directory and a start script for the same service in the rc5.d directory. What happens to the cups service as the runlevel is changed?

   A. The rc script leaves the service running because it is configured to run in both runlevels.

   B. The rc script runs the kill script to stop the service but does not run the start script to run it.

   C. The rc script runs the start script to start the service but does not run the kill script to stop it.

   D. The rc script runs the kill script to stop the service and then runs the start script to restart the service.

20. The ntp daemon on your Linux system is currently configured to run in runlevels 3 and 5. You want to remove all kill and start scripts for the ntp daemon in the various rc*x*.d directories. Which command will do this?

   A. insserv ntp

   B. insserv –r ntp

   C. /etc/init.d/ntp stop

   D. chkconfig –l ntp

   E. chkconfig –s ntp 35

21. Your Linux system uses systemd instead of init. You need to switch the system into runlevel 3. Which command should you use?

   A. systemctl isolate graphical.target

   B. systemctl isolate multi-user.target

   C. systemctl isolate runlevel5.target

   D. systemctl isolate nongraphical.target

Answers

1. **A, C.** The BIOS tests your system hardware during the POST routine and then locates a bootable storage device.

2. **C, D.** The Linux bootloader can be stored in the MBR of the storage device and in the bootable partition on the disk.

3. **A.** The Linux kernel resides in /boot in the file system.

4. **B.** The **grub-install /dev/sda1** command will install GRUB into the first partition on the first hard disk drive.

5. **D.** The /boot/grub/menu.lst file is used to configure GRUB on an openSUSE system.

6. **A.** The root directive in the GRUB configuration file specifies the partition on the hard drive where /boot resides.

7. **D.** The term **hd0,1** in a GRUB configuration file points to the second partition on the first hard drive in the system.

8. **D.** The /boot/grub/menu.lst is used by GRUB Legacy. It's not used by GRUB2.

9. **C.** The 30_os-prober GRUB2 script can detect other operating systems, such as Windows, installed on the same system as Linux. It can use the information it finds to add menu items to the GRUB menu that will launch those operating systems.

10. **A.** The GRUB_TIMEOUT is used by GRUB2 to specify how long the user has to make a menu selection from the GRUB menu before the default operating system is booted.

11. **D.** Runlevel 5 uses a graphical user interface by default.

12. **B, C.** Runlevels 2 and 3 use a command-line interface by default.

13. **B, C.** You can enter commands in boot.local on BSD-type systems or rc.local on System V–type systems to have them automatically run each time the system boots.

14. **A.** The init scripts on a Fedora system are stored in /etc/rc.d/init.d.

15. **B, D.** Either the **/etc/init.d/sshd** restart or the **/etc/init.d/sshd start** command can be used on an openSUSE Linux system to start the Secure Shell server (sshd) daemon.

16. **A.** The /etc/inittab file is used to set the default runlevel of a Linux system.

17. **D.** The **init** command can be used to switch runlevels while the system is running.

18. **B.** The S05cifs link file (which starts the cifs daemon) is run before any of the other files due to the number assigned to the file.

19. **A.** Because cups is configured to run in both runlevels (and is therefore assumed to be running currently), the rc script does nothing. It just leaves the daemon running.

20. **B.** The **insserv –r ntp** command will disable the ntp service by removing all links for the ntp daemon in all the rcx.d subdirectories within your init script directory.

21. **B.** The **systemctl isolate multi-user.target** command will switch the system into the systemd equivalent of init runlevel 3.

Managing the Graphical Environment

In this chapter, you will learn about:
- How the X environment works
- Configuring the X environment
- Configuring a display manager
- Configuring accessibility

In previous chapters, you learned primarily about using Linux from the bash shell prompt. However, you can also implement a powerful graphical user interface (GUI) on your Linux system. Most system and network administrators are at ease with the Linux CLI. We're not intimidated by long shell commands that use a variety of options. However, I can promise you that your end users are not thrilled at all with the command-line interface. Frankly, most of them hate it and will probably refuse to use it. Instead, most end users are much more comfortable with a GUI.

Because of the dominance of Microsoft Windows in the home computer market, most end users have never even used a command-line interface. To make life easier, you can implement X along with a window manager and a desktop environment (such as GNOME or KDE) on your Linux systems. With a GUI in place, your users can interact with the Linux kernel using a mouse instead of just the keyboard. The GNOME desktop environment is shown in Figure 7-1.

EXAM TIP Be very familiar with the X Window System for your LPIC-1/Linux+ exam. Be sure you can identify which version of the X server a particular system is using. You should know how to use Linux tools to configure X to work with your video hardware. You should be familiar with video-related terms such as *synchronization rate*, *resolution*, and *color depth*. You also need to know how to specify which window manager your system should use.

In this chapter, we're going to part company with the shell prompt for a while and learn how to work with the Linux GUI. Let's begin this chapter by discussing how the X environment works.

Figure 7-1 The GNOME desktop environment

How the X Environment Works

As mentioned earlier, the GUI on a Linux system is created using the X Window System software.

NOTE Many times you will hear the X Window System referred to as "X Windows," "X11," or just "X."

The X Window System provides the base system for the graphical interface on Linux. It allows programmers to run applications in windows. It also allows users to move windows around on the screen as well as click items with the mouse. Essentially, you can implement a graphical user interface on your Linux system that works in a manner very similar to Microsoft Windows. You will find many of the desktop components you may be familiar with on Windows in the Linux GUI. For example, in the GNOME file browser, you can find Computer, Home, and Trash icons, as shown in Figure 7-2.

Whenever you delete a file from within the graphical environment, it is moved to the Trash. You can empty the Trash by right-clicking it and selecting **Empty Trash**. You can also restore deleted files by doing the following:

1. Select the Trash icon in the file browser.

2. Right-click the *file* or *directory* you want to restore.

3. Select **Restore** in the pop-up menu shown in Figure 7-3.

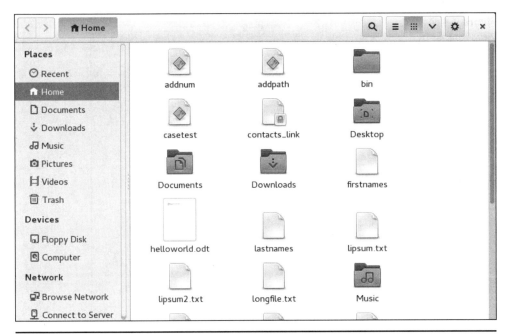

Figure 7-2 Computer, Home, and Trash icons in GNOME

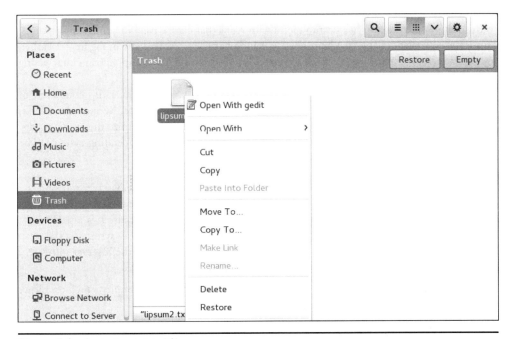

Figure 7-3 Restoring deleted files

Figure 7-4
Viewing network
hosts

You can browse other computers on the network by selecting **Browse Network**. A screen similar to that shown in Figure 7-4 is displayed.

In addition, the desktop has startup menu with icons that can be used to launch applications. This is the equivalent of the Start button on a Windows system. As you saw in Figure 7-1 earlier, you can launch the Firefox web browser or run a LibreOffice productivity application by selecting the appropriate icon.

One of the great things about the Linux GUI is that it is very modular. It's composed of several different pieces that work together to create the graphical interface. Because the GUI is modular, you can mix and match different components together to customize the way it works. This provides a degree of flexibility that just isn't available with other operating systems. The Linux GUI is composed of the following components:

- **X server** The heart of the Linux GUI is the X server software. The X server software is the component that draws windows graphically on the display screen. It's also responsible for managing your mouse and your keyboard. We call it a *server* because it is capable of displaying output not only on the local monitor but also on any other system on the network that is also running X server software. The location where the X server software sends its output is controlled by the DISPLAY environment variable.

  Over the years, two different X server software packages have been implemented on Linux systems:

  - **X.org-X11** X.org is the most commonly implemented X server system and is the default X server used by most modern Linux distributions.

- **XFree86** Until about 2004, XFree86 was the default version of X server used by most Linux distributions. It works in pretty much the same manner as X.org. In fact, the development of X.org was based on XFree86. Unfortunately, there were licensing issues associated with XFree86 that drove the Linux community to X.org as an alternative X server.

- **Window manager** Whereas X server creates windows within the GUI environment, the window manager's job is to customize how the windows look and behave. A wide variety of window managers is currently available for Linux. Each one offers a different look and feel for your GUI environment. Here are some of the more popular window managers:

  - enlightenment

  - fvwm

  - kwin

  - sawfish

  - twm

  - wmaker

  Which is best? None is best, really. It all depends on what you like. Some window managers are complex and full featured, such as enlightenment, kwin, and sawfish. In fact, the enlightenment and sawfish window managers are commonly used with the GNOME desktop environment, whereas the kwin window manager is commonly used with the KDE desktop environment. Other window managers are very basic. These include the feeble virtual window manager (fvwm), the tab window manager (twm), and the window maker (wmaker) window manager. Depending on your users' preferences, I would suggest that you deploy a more full-featured window manager on your system, such as enlightenment, sawfish, or kwin. These window managers create a look and feel that is very similar to Microsoft Windows, making it easy for your users to transition over.

- **Desktop environment** The desktop environment leverages the look and feel created by the window manager and adds a series of tools and utilities that make the GUI truly useful. Basically, it ties all your GUI components together into a cohesive environment. The desktop environment is optional but highly recommended. As with X server and window managers, the desktop environment is modular. You can try out the available environments and choose the one you like best. Two desktop environments are predominantly used with Linux systems today:

  - **KDE** KDE is an excellent desktop environment. It provides functionality that is very similar to Microsoft Windows. It's the default environment on many distributions. An example of the KDE desktop running on a Fedora system is shown in Figure 7-5.

  - **GNOME** The GNOME desktop environment is also excellent. GNOME is the default environment used on distributions such as Red Hat Fedora and openSUSE. An example of the GNOME desktop running on a openSUSE system was shown earlier in the chapter in Figure 7-1.

Figure 7-5 The KDE desktop environment

These three components—the X server software, the window manager, and the desktop environment—all work hand in hand to create the GUI environment on a Windows system. You can mix and match among these three different components to customize the system to match your particular tastes and preferences.

Let's now discuss how you go about configuring your graphical environment.

Configuring the X Environment

Because your graphical environment is composed of several modular components, you need to complete a variety of tasks to configure the GUI on a Linux system. In this part of the chapter, we're going to cover the following:

- Configuring the X server
- Configuring an X font server

Let's begin by discussing how to configure the X server.

Configuring the X Server

Because the X server works directly with your video board and monitor, configuring it is the most critical of all your GUI management tasks. It's imperative that you use the correct settings in your configuration. If you proceed incorrectly, you could potentially damage your monitor.

I know this because I had it happen to me once. I configured my system to use a sync rate that was too fast for an older CRT monitor I was using. It worked OK for a couple of weeks. However, one evening my monitor started hissing, sparking, and smoking. I pushed it too fast for too long and burned it up. Always check your video board and monitor documentation to obtain the correct specs!

Before you begin, you should pull out your video board and monitor documentation and identify the following information:

- Who's the manufacturer of the video board?
- What model number is the video board?
- How much memory is installed on the video board?
- What's the board's maximum resolution?
- What's the board's maximum color depth?
- What chipset is installed on the board?
- What's the maximum horizontal and vertical sync rate supported by your monitor?

With this information in hand, you need to check the HCL for your distribution and make sure your video board and monitor are supported. Trust me, having this information in hand before you begin will save you a lot of trouble. Be warned, however, that you will many times find that newer video boards are not listed in the HCL. Does this mean the board is not supported and won't work? Maybe, maybe not. Here's what you can do:

- See if an older driver will support your newer video board until a newer driver is released. Most X server implementations will include a set of generic drivers that will support most video boards at some level. It won't look great, but you can at least get your system up and running.
- Check the video board manufacturer's website and see if they have released a driver for their board that isn't included with your X server implementation.

Once you have this information gathered, you're ready to start configuring your X server. This can be done in two ways:

- Editing the X configuration file
- Using an X configuration utility

Let's look at the X configuration file first.

Editing the X Configuration File

Just like everything else in Linux, your X configuration is stored in a text file in the /etc directory.

 NOTE A good friend of mine coined an appropriate axiom: "Everything in Linux is a file." All of your system and service configurations are stored in files. You even access hardware devices through a file.

If you're using X.org on a Linux distribution that uses the init daemon, your configuration settings are saved in /etc/X11/xorg.conf. If you're using XFree86, your configuration settings are saved in /etc/X11/XF86Config. Here is a portion of a sample xorg.conf file:

```
Section "InputDevice"
  Driver       "vmmouse"
  Identifier   "VMware Mouse"
  Option       "Buttons" "5"
  Option       "Device" "/dev/input/mice"
  Option       "Name" "ImPS/2 Generic Wheel Mouse"
  Option       "Protocol" "IMPS/2"
  Option       "Vendor" "Sysp"
  Option       "ZAxisMapping" "4 5"
  Option          "Emulate3Buttons"        "true"
EndSection

Section "Modes"
  Identifier   "Modes[0]"
  Modeline      "1024x768" 65.0 1024 1048 1184 1344 768 771 777 806 -hsync -vsync
  Modeline      "1024x768" 61.89 1024 1080 1184 1344 768 769 772 794
EndSection
```

 NOTE Linux distributions that are based on systemd do not use the xorg.conf configuration file. Instead, the X11 configuration is stored in a series of configuration files located in /etc/X11/xorg.conf.d. However, the configuration principles are pretty much the same. Instead of a single file divided into multiple sections, these systems break up the one single file into separate files, such as 10-evdev.conf, 50-device.conf, 50-monitor.conf, and 50-screen.conf. The syntax within these files is the same as that used in the xorg.conf file.

Notice in this example that the xorg.conf file is broken into sections that begin with the **Section "*name*"** directive and end with **EndSection**.

 NOTE The XF86Config file version 4 and later use a similar structure. Older versions of XFree86 use a slightly different configuration file format.

Let's look at the most commonly used sections in a typical xorg.conf file. First is the Files section. This section tells the X server where to find the files it needs to do its job, such as font files and input device files. Here is an abbreviated example of a Files section:

```
Section "Files"
  FontPath     "/usr/X11R6/lib/X11/fonts/misc:unscaled"
  FontPath     "/usr/X11R6/lib/X11/fonts/local"
```

```
   FontPath        "/usr/X11R6/lib/X11/fonts/75dpi:unscaled"
   FontPath        "/usr/X11R6/lib/X11/fonts/100dpi:unscaled"
   ...
   FontPath        "/usr/X11R6/lib/X11/fonts/xtest"
   FontPath        "/opt/kde3/share/fonts"
   InputDevices "/dev/gpmdata"
   InputDevices "/dev/input/mice"
EndSection
```

Next is the ServerFlags section. This section specifies global X server options. This section is optional, and any options specified in it may be overridden by corresponding options with the same name listed in the ServerLayout section. Here is an example of a ServerFlags section in an xorg.conf file:

```
Section "ServerFlags"
   Option       "AllowMouseOpenFail" "on"
EndSection
```

In this example, the AllowMouseOpenFail option is set to a value of **on**. This allows the X server to start up even if a mouse isn't connected or can't be initialized.

Next is the Module section. This section tells the X server to load certain server extension and font rasterizer modules at startup. Here is an example:

```
Section "Module"
   Load         "dbe"
   Load         "type1"
   Load         "freetype"
   Load         "extmod"
   Load         "glx"
   Load         "v4l"
EndSection
```

The **Load *modulename*** directive tells the X server to load the specified module. Notice that the module name, not the module filename, is specified.

Next is the InputDevice section. This section configures the X server with the input devices it should use. You can use multiple InputDevice sections, one for each input device. For example, you will usually see an InputDevice section for the keyboard and another one for your mouse. Examples follow:

```
Section "InputDevice"
   Driver       "kbd"
   Identifier   "VMware Keyboard"
   Option       "Protocol" "Standard"
   Option       "XkbLayout" "us"
   Option       "XkbModel" "pc104"
   Option       "XkbRules" "xfree86"
EndSection

Section "InputDevice"
   Driver       "vmmouse"
   Identifier   "VMware Mouse"
   Option       "Buttons" "5"
   Option       "Device" "/dev/input/mice"
   Option       "Name" "ImPS/2 Generic Wheel Mouse"
   Option       "Protocol" "IMPS/2"
   Option       "Vendor" "Sysp"
```

```
    Option        "ZAxisMapping" "4 5"
    Option        "Emulate3Buttons"        "true"
EndSection
```

NOTE These sections are from a Linux system running as a VMware virtual machine. Therefore, generic VMware devices are specified. On a physical system, you would see manufacturer-specific devices.

As you can see in the preceding examples, the syntax used in an InputDevice section is as follows:

```
Section "InputDevice"
    Identifier "name"
    Driver     "driver_name"
    Option "options"
EndSection
```

The next section is the Modes section. The configuration file may have one or more of these sections. They define video modes the X server may use. Here is a sample:

```
Section "Modes"
  Identifier   "Modes[0]"
  Modeline     "1024x768" 65.0 1024 1048 1184 1344 768 771 777 806 -hsync –vsync
  Modeline     "1024x768" 61.89 1024 1080 1184 1344 768 769 772 794
EndSection
```

The syntax for the Modes section is as follows:

```
Section "Modes"
    Identifier "name"
    Modeline parameters
EndSection
```

The Modeline directive is used to define video modes for the monitor. It is composed of four components:

- **Pixel clock** This first component specifies the pixel clock rate in MHz. In the first Modeline in the preceding example, this is 65.0.

- **Horizontal timing** This second component is a list of four numbers that specify the horizontal timing: hdisp, hsyncstart, hsyncend, and htotal. In the first Modeline in the example, these values are 1024, 1048, 1184, and 1344, respectively.

- **Vertical timing** The third component is a list of four numbers that specify the vertical timing: vdisp, vsyncstart, vsyncend, and vtotal. In the first Modeline in the example, these values are 768, 771, 777, and 806, respectively.

- **Flags** The fourth component is a list of flags that configure the video mode. In the first Modeline in the example, the –hsync and –vsync flags are listed. These are used to set the polarity of the hsync and vsync signals.

The next section is the Screen section, which binds your video board to your monitor. Here is an example:

```
Section "Screen"
  Identifier    "Screen[0]"
    Device       "VMware SVGA"
    Monitor      "vmware"
    # Don't specify DefaultColorDepth unless you know what you're
    # doing. It will override the driver's preferences which can
    # cause the X server not to run if the host doesn't support the
    # depth.
    Subsection "Display"
        # VGA mode: better left untouched
        Depth        4
        Modes        "640x480"
        ViewPort     0 0
    EndSubsection
    Subsection "Display"
        Depth        8
        Modes        "1024x768"
        ViewPort     0 0
    EndSubsection
    Subsection "Display"
        Depth        15
        Modes        "1024x768"
        ViewPort     0 0
    EndSubsection
    Subsection "Display"
        Depth        16
        Modes        "1024x768"
        ViewPort     0 0
    EndSubsection
    Subsection "Display"
        Depth        24
        Modes        "1024x768"
        ViewPort     0 0
    EndSubsection
EndSection
```

The video board is specified by the Device directive, whereas your monitor is specified by the Monitor directive. The *device-id* used in the Device directive in the Screen section must match the Identifier directive within the Device section of the file (which will be discussed next). The syntax is as follows:

```
    Section "Screen"
        Identifier "name"
        Device     "device_id"
        Monitor    "monitor_id"
        SubSection "Display"
          ...
        EndSubSection
        ...
    EndSection
```

As you can see in the preceding examples, each Screen section can have multiple Display subsections. You can use the following directives within each Display subsection:

- **Depth** *depth*   Specifies the color depth as the number of bits per pixel. Most video drivers support color depths of 8, 15, 16, and 24.
- **Modes** *mode_name*   Specifies the list of video modes to use (contained in quotes). Each mode must match the appropriate entry in the Monitor section.
- **ViewPort** *x y*   Sets the upper-left corner of the display.

The next section you need to be familiar with is the Device section. There must be one Device section for each video adapter installed in your system. Here is a sample Device section:

```
Section "Device"
    Identifier   "VMware SVGA"
    Driver       "vmware"
EndSection
```

The Identifier directive defines a unique name for the video adapter. The Driver directive specifies which driver should be used for this video adapter.

The next section you need to be familiar with is the Monitor section, which defines parameters for the monitor connected to your display adapter. A sample Monitor section is shown next:

```
Section "Monitor"
    Identifier       "vmware"
    VendorName       "VMware, Inc"
    HorizSync        1-10000
    VertRefresh      1-10000
EndSection
```

You can use the following directives within the Monitor section:

- **Identifier "***name***"**   Defines a unique name for the monitor
- **VendorName "***vendor***"**   Specifies the monitor manufacturer
- **ModelName "***model***"**   Specifies the monitor model
- **HorizSync sync_range**   Defines the horizontal sync frequency range supported by the monitor, specified in KHz
- **VertRefresh *refresh_rate***   Defines the vertical sync frequency range supported by the monitor, specified in KHz

The last section we're going to look at here is the ServerLayout section. This is a key section. It "glues" all the preceding sections together into a complete configuration. The ServerLayout section uses the following syntax:

```
Section "ServerLayout"
    Identifier   "name"
    Screen       "screen_id"
    InputDevice  "input_dev_id"
    options
    ...
EndSection
```

The ServerLayout section binds together one or more Screen section(s) and one or more InputDevice section(s), as shown in the following example:

```
Section "ServerLayout"
  Identifier    "Layout[all]"
  Option        "Clone" "off"
  Option        "Xinerama" "off"
  Screen        "Screen[0]"
  InputDevice     "VMware Keyboard"      "CoreKeyboard"
  InputDevice "VMware Mouse"      "CorePointer"
EndSection
```

You can use the following directives within the ServerLayout section:

- **Identifier "*name*"**   Defines a unique name for the server layout.

- **Screen "*screen_id*"**   Specifies which screen parameters to use for the server layout.

- **InputDevice "*input_device_id*"**   Specifies which input devices are to be used for the server layout. You need one directive for each input device (usually one for the mouse and one for the keyboard).

- **Option "*option_name*"**   Any option that can be used in the ServerFlags section can also be specified here. If the same option is specified in both places, the option specified in the ServerLayout section overrides the option listed in the ServerFlags section.

Now that you understand how the X server configuration file is structured, you next need to learn how to configure it using an X configuration utility.

Using an X Configuration Utility

As with most Linux services, the X server configuration file is a text-based file that can be modified with a simple text editor such as vi. However, I strongly suggest that you *do not* do this unless absolutely necessary. This configuration file is complex, and a simple mistake can damage your hardware. You should instead use the configuration utility that came with your distribution to configure your X server settings. For example, on openSUSE systems, you can use the Displays applet, shown in Figure 7-6.

This applet allows you to configure your screen resolution. On older distributions, you can also run the sax2 command from the shell prompt. This provides you with a very handy interface that you can use to configure just about every aspect of your video subsystem. If you run SaX2 from within a graphical environment, the interface shown in Figure 7-7 is displayed.

You can use the SaX2 utility to configure your system's video adapter, monitor, resolution, and color depth. One of the things I like about SaX2 is the fact that you can run it from a text-only environment (such as when your video settings are so messed up that you have to boot into runlevel 3 to get the system running). If SaX2 can't get your graphical environment running due to a misconfiguration, it will load its own generic X server, probe your video subsystem, and automatically generate a proposed set of settings.

 NOTE   SaX2 was used on many distributions for some time. However, most modern distributions no longer use SaX2 to configure the video system.

Figure 7-6
The Displays
applet

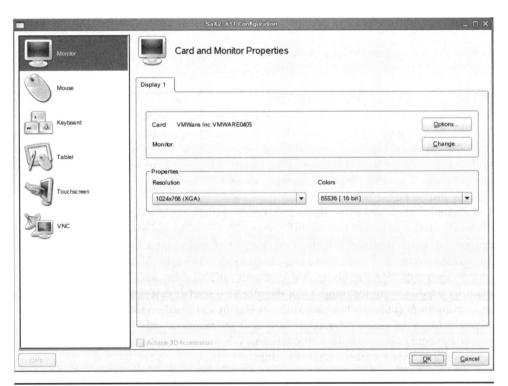

Figure 7-7   Using SaX2 to configure the video subsystem

Many other utilities and commands are used on various distributions to configure the X server system. Be aware that these tools tend to be distribution specific. They may be available on one distribution, but not another. To provide cross-distribution functionality, X.org (and XFree86) provides several generic configuration utilities that you can use to configure your X server settings. On X.org, you can use the xorgconfig utility in a text-based environment to configure your video board, monitor, resolution, color depth, and so on. This utility is shown in Figure 7-8.

The great thing about xorgconfig is that it tries to automatically detect your hardware for you (just as the SaX2 utility does). If you're a little hazy about what exactly is installed in the system, this can be a real lifesaver. In fact, if you enter **Xorg –configure** at the shell prompt, this utility will automatically detect all your hardware and create a configuration file named /root/xorg.conf. new for you. You can then test the configuration before committing it by entering **X –config /root/xorg.conf.new** at the shell prompt. If everything looks to be correct, rename the file to /etc/X11/xorg.conf to start using the new configuration.

X.org also provides a graphical version of the xorgconfig utility that is launched by entering **xorgcfg** from the shell prompt. This utility diagrams your monitor, video board, keyboard, and mouse, as shown in Figure 7-9. To modify a component, right-click the appropriate icon and select **Configure**.

If your distribution still uses the XFree86 X server, you can use the following utilities to accomplish the same tasks:

- **XFree-86 –configure**   Detects your hardware and creates a file named /etc/X11/ XF86Config.new that you can rename to XF86Config

- **xf86config**   A text-based X server configuration utility

- **xf86cfg**   A graphical X server configuration utility

```
First specify a mouse protocol type. Choose one from the following list:

1.   Auto [Auto detect]
2.   SysMouse [SysMouse]
3.   MouseSystems [Mouse Systems (3-button protocol)]
4.   PS/2 [PS/2 Mouse]
5.   Microsoft [Microsoft compatible (2-button protocol)]
6.   Busmouse [Bus Mouse]
7.   IMPS/2 [IntelliMouse PS/2]
8.   ExplorerPS/2 [Explorer PS/2]
9.   GlidePointPS/2 [GlidePoint PS/2]
10.  MouseManPlusPS/2 [MouseManPlus PS/2]
11.  NetMousePS/2 [NetMouse PS/2]
12.  NetScrollPS/2 [NetScroll PS/2]
13.  ThinkingMousePS/2 [ThinkingMouse PS/2]
14.  AceCad [AceCad]

The recommended protocol is Auto. If you have a very old mouse
or don't want OS support or auto detection, and you have a two-button
or three-button serial mouse, it is most likely of type Microsoft.

Enter a protocol number:
```

Figure 7-8   Using the xorgconfig utility

Figure 7-9

Using xorgcfg

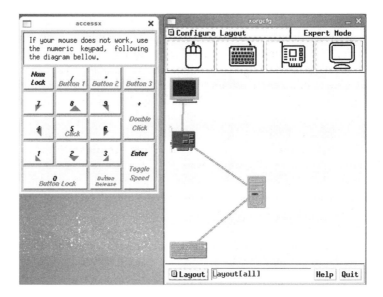

After making any changes to your X server configuration, keep the following in mind:

- The configuration utility will prompt you to test the new settings to make sure they work. You should always do this. It will save a ton of time if you've made a mistake somewhere in the configuration.

- After testing the configuration, you must restart your X server to apply the changes. The easiest way to do this is to simply log out and then log back in. Rebooting the system will also accomplish the same task. You can also restart the desktop environment by switching to your init directory and restart the desktop manager using its init script (such as xdm).

- If something is misconfigured and your X server software gets hung, you can kill it by pressing CTRL-ALT-BACKSPACE.

- If you want to fine-tune your X server configuration, run the xvidtune utility from the shell prompt. This utility allows you to customize your monitor's horizontal and vertical synchronization. However, do so with extreme caution. Remember that using sync parameters that are beyond the monitor's capabilities will eventually damage it.

- If you're in runlevel 3 and want to start the Linux GUI, simply enter **startx** (which is a simple shell script wrapper for xinit) or just **X** at the shell prompt.

 EXAM TIP The xwininfo command can be used to display information about open windows on your graphical desktop. You can run the command and then click the window you want to get information about. You can also just specify the ID of the window you want to get information about using the –id option with the command. The xdpyinfo command can be used to display the capabilities of a server, the various parameters used when communicating between clients and the server, and the different screen modes available.

Next, let's look at configuring an X font server.

Configuring an X Font Server

An X font server allows you to configure X server fonts on one Linux system in your network and then have the X servers on other Linux systems connect to it. Setting up your fonts in this way allows you to configure fonts for an entire organization from a single central location.

 NOTE To be candid, I suspect that you may never actually set up an X font server. I haven't found the need to set up one for over a decade. However, it's a task you need to be able to do for your LPIC-1/Linux+ exam, so we're going to discuss how to do it here.

To do this, you need to complete the following tasks:

- Configure fonts on the X font server.
- Configure remote X servers to access the font server.

Let's begin by discussing how to configure fonts on the X font server.

Configure Fonts on the X Font Server

If you want to install fonts in addition to the default fonts installed with the X server on your X font server, the first thing you need to do when configuring an X font server is to actually install the fonts you want to distribute on it. If your Linux distribution is running X.org, your fonts need to be installed to the /usr/share/X11/fonts directory or the /usr/share/fonts directory. Here is an example:

```
fs2:/usr/share/fonts # ls
100dpi  75dpi  Speedo  Type1  URW  cyrillic  encodings  misc  truetype
```

Linux fonts come in two varieties:

- **Bitmap fonts** Bitmap fonts are the oldest type of Linux fonts. As the name implies, bitmap fonts use a series of pixels to represent characters on the screen. They are easy to use and don't require much computing horsepower to display on the screen. However, they do have one glaring weakness: they scale poorly. Basically, you need a different version of the same font for each screen resolution and each font point size. In other words, installing one bitmap font on your Linux system will probably require you to install multiple font files. In the preceding example, you can see that there is one directory in the fonts directory named 100dpi and another directory named 75dpi. Most X servers install a limited number of bitmap fonts by default.

- **Scalable fonts** Scalable fonts, as their name implies, are scalable. Instead of using pixels to represent characters, they use vector lines that are dynamically sized as needed. As a result, you only need a single font file for each font. There are two commonly used formats for scalable fonts:

  - **PostScript Type 1** In the preceding example, these fonts are stored in the Type1 subdirectory.

  - **TrueType** In the preceding example, these fonts are stored in the truetype subdirectory.

To install a font, copy the font files to the appropriate subdirectory of your system's fonts directory. For Type1 fonts, you need to copy the .pfa or .pfb file for the font. For TrueType fonts, you need to copy the .ttf file for the font. Bitmap font files need to go into the 100dpi and/or 75dpi directories.

Then you need to create a font description file for the font and register it with the system. To do this, open a terminal session and (as root) switch to the font directory and enter the **mkfontscale** command followed by the **mkfontdir** command. These commands make an index of scalable (as well as bitmap) font files for the X server.

Next, you need to open port **7100** in the firewall of the X font server.

 TIP   If you installed the font in a directory other than one of the default directories (Type1 or truetype) in the fonts directory, you must manually edit your X configuration file (such as xorg.conf) and add a FontPath directive to your Files section for the new directory.

The next thing you need to do is tell the X font service (xfs) that the fonts are there and should be made available to remote X server clients. This is done by editing the /etc/X11/fs/config file, a sample of which follows:

```
fs2:/etc/X11/fs # cat ./config
no-listen = tcp
port = 7100
client-limit = 10
clone-self = on
use-syslog = on
deferglyphs = 16
catalogue = /usr/share/fonts/misc:unscaled,
        /usr/share/fonts/75dpi:unscaled,
        /usr/share/fonts/100dpi:unscaled,
        /usr/share/fonts/japanese:unscaled,
        /usr/share/fonts/baekmuk:unscaled,
        /usr/share/fonts/Type1,
        /usr/share/fonts/URW,
        /usr/share/fonts/Speedo,
        /usr/share/fonts/CID,
        /usr/share/fonts/PEX,
        /usr/share/fonts/cyrillic,
        /usr/share/fonts/latin2/misc,
        /usr/share/fonts/latin2/75dpi,
        /usr/share/fonts/latin2/100dpi,
        /usr/share/fonts/latin2/Type1,
        /usr/share/fonts/latin7/75dpi,
        /usr/share/fonts/kwintv,
        /usr/share/fonts/truetype,
        /usr/share/fonts/uni,
        /usr/share/fonts/ucs/misc,
        /usr/share/fonts/ucs/75dpi,
        /usr/share/fonts/ucs/100dpi,
        /usr/share/fonts/hellas/misc,
        /usr/share/fonts/hellas/75dpi,
        /usr/share/fonts/hellas/100dpi,
        /usr/share/fonts/hellas/Type1
# in decipoints
default-point-size = 120
default-resolutions = 75,75,100,100
# font cache control, specified in KB
cache-hi-mark = 2048
cache-low-mark = 1433
cache-balance = 70
```

Locate the **no-listen = tcp** line and remark it out with a **#** sign. Then review the **catalogue =** section and verify that your fonts directory is listed. When finished, save your changes to the file and exit your text editor.

At this point, you need to start the X font server. This is done by switching to your init script directory and entering **./xfs start** at the shell prompt (as root). If desired, use the insserv or chkconfig command to configure the xfs daemon to start every time the system boots. Then restart your X server.

Configure Remote X Servers to Access the Font Server

Once you have configured the X font server, you can then configure the X servers on the various client systems to use it. Open each X server configuration file (usually xorg.conf) and locate the Files section. In this section, add a new **FontPath** directive for the X font server. This is done using the following syntax:

```
Section "Files"
    ...
    FontPath    "tcp/server_address:7100"
    ...
EndSection
```

As with the X font server, you must open port 7100 in your host firewall and then restart the X server.

With this in mind, let's next discuss how to specify a particular window manager or desktop environment.

Configuring a Display Manager

For your LPIC-1/Linux+ exam, you also need to be familiar with how to configure your display manager and desktop environment. In this part of this chapter, you will learn how to do this. The following topics are addressed:

- Trying out desktop environments
- Managing a display manager

Let's begin by discussing how to try out different desktop environments on Linux.

Trying Out Desktop Environments

As stated earlier, the window manager and desktop environment components used by your Linux system are modular. You can try out the various window managers and desktop environments to see which one suits you. To do this, do the following:

1. Use the rpm utility (or other package installation utility) to install the window managers or desktop environments you want to try.

2. When this is complete, log out. In your login screen, you should see an option called Session Type. When you select this option, a list of window managers and desktop environments installed on the system is displayed, as shown in Figure 7-10. Select the window manager or desktop environment you want to use.

Figure 7-10

Selecting a
desktop manager

At this point, your system will load with the window manager or desktop environment you specified. If you like what you see, you can make it permanent. If your system boots to runlevel 3 by default and you use the startx command to load the Linux GUI, you need to locate a hidden script file named .xinitrc in your user's home directory (using ls –a). Open this file in a text editor and locate the line that reads **exec $WINDOWMANAGER**, shown next:

```
# finally start the window manager
#
unset WINDOW_MANAGER STARTUP
exec $WINDOWMANAGER
# call failsafe
exit 0
```

Replace $WINDOWMANAGER with the name of the window manager or desktop environment you want to use. Use the following:

- **KDE**   /usr/bin/startkde
- **GNOME**   /usr/bin/gnome

TIP   Notice that $WINDOWMANAGER references the WINDOWMANAGER environment variable. Instead of editing your .xinitrc file, you could just set the value of the WINDOWMANAGER variable to the path and executable for the window manager you want to use.

Save the file and run startx.

If your system boots into runlevel 5 by default, you make the same changes to the .Xsession, .Xdefaults, or .Xclients file in your home directory, whichever one is used by your particular distribution.

Let's next look at how you configure your display manager.

Managing a Display Manager

As we discussed earlier in this chapter, a Linux display manager is a specialized client application that works with the X server to provide window control elements, manage virtual desktops, and provide window frames functionality (for example, changing the size of a window or moving it around on the screen). The X server is not linked to any specific window manager and therefore is not linked to any particular look and feel.

For your LPIC-1/Linux+ exam, you need to know how to do the following with the display manager:

- Enabling or disabling the display manager
- Configuring the display manager
- Configuring remote access to the display manager

Enabling or Disabling the Display Manager

You can enable or disable the display manager using an init script. Which one depends on the Linux distribution you're using. On many Linux distributions, such as openSUSE, the display manager is managed by the xdm init script located in the /etc/init.d directory. Other distributions may use the GNOME display manager (gdm) or the KDE display manager (kdm). To manually manage the display manager, enter **/etc/init.d/**_init_script_ **stop** or **start** at the shell prompt.

TIP   You can also use **rcxdm stop** or **start** to accomplish the same thing.

Because the display manager is managed using an init script, you can control whether or not the display manager is loaded when the system boots using the chkconfig command. For example, to configure the xdm display manager to not load at boot, enter **chkconfig xdm off**. You can verify that it is disabled by entering **chkconfig xdm –l** at the shell prompt. Here is an example:

```
ws1:/ # chkconfig xdm off
ws1:/ # chkconfig xdm -l
xdm                         0:off  1:off  2:off  3:off  4:off  5:off  6:off
```

Alternatively, to configure the display to automatically load at system start, you would enter **chkconfig xdm on**. Again, enter **chkconfig xdm –l** to verify that the display manager is configured to start automatically at runlevel 5, as shown here:

```
ws1:/ # chkconfig xdm on
ws1:/ # chkconfig xdm -l
xdm                         0:off  1:off  2:off  3:off  4:off  5:on   6:off
```

Configuring the Display Manager

You can configure your display manager by editing the appropriate configuration file:

- **xdm**   /etc/X11/xdm/xdm-config
- **LightDM**   The LightDM display manager is configured using several different files:
  - /usr/share/lightdm/lightdm.conf.d
  - /etc/lightdm/lightdm.conf.d
  - /etc/lightdm/lightdm.conf

NOTE   We are going to focus on configuring the LightDM display manager in this chapter.

- **kdm**   The KDE display manager is actually based on xdm and usually uses the xdm configuration files. However, some distributions store your kdm settings in /etc/kde/kdm or /etc/X11/ kdm instead. In this situation, you will use the kdmrc file in either of these directories to make most configuration changes.
- **gdm**   /etc/X11/gdm

When working with the LightDM display manager, it's important to remember that all of its configuration files are combined together to configure LightDM. The key is the fact the files are applied in the order shown previously.

The default LightDM configuration is stored in the configuration files in /usr/share/lightdm /lightdm.conf.d/. These files are generated by the system and should not be edited directly. Instead, you should create override files containing the changes you want to make in /etc/lightdm /lightdm.conf.d/. (Alternatively, you can also enter them into the /etc/lightdm/lightdm.conf file.) If there are identical settings in more than one file, the setting in the last file processed is applied and the others are overridden. For example, suppose you wanted to override the default session type (configured in /usr/share/lightdm/lightdm.conf.d/50-ubuntu.conf); you could make a file named /etc/lightdm/lightdm.conf.d/50-myconfig.conf and enter the appropriate configuration settings.

LightDM uses the concept of a *greeter,* which is basically a user interface for interacting with LightDM. For example, the Ubuntu distribution uses the Unity greeter by default. You can customize the way LightDM works and which greeter it uses using the LightDM configuration files, including the following:

- You can change which greeter LightDM uses. To do this, create the appropriate file in /etc/lightdm/lightdm.conf.d/ and specify the name of a greeter file (which has a .desktop extension) that you want to use in /usr/share/xgreeters. Use the following syntax:

```
[SeatDefaults]
greeter-session=file_name
```

- You can disable guest logins. By default, LightDM allows you to log in to the system as a guest user. For security reasons, you may want to disable this functionality. To do this, create the appropriate file in /etc/lightdm/lightdm.conf.d/ and enter the following lines:

```
[SeatDefaults]
allow-guest=false
```

- You can hide the user list. Many LightDM greeters display a list of possible user accounts by default. Again, for security reasons, you may want to disable this functionality. Create the appropriate file in /etc/lightdm/lightdm.conf.d/ and enter the following lines:

```
[SeatDefaults]
greeter-hide-users=true
```

- You can configure LightDM to allow manual logins. By default, the Unity greeter doesn't allow you to manually enter a username when logging in to the system. You can reconfigure Unity to allow this by creating the appropriate file in /etc/lightdm/lightdm.conf.d/ and enter the following lines:

```
[SeatDefaults]
greeter-show-manual-login=true
```

- You can change the default session type used by LightDM by manually specifying a session file. These files have a .desktop extension and are located in /usr/share/xsessions. Again, create the appropriate file in /etc/lightdm/lightdm.conf.d/ and enter the following lines:

```
[SeatDefaults]
user-session=file_name
```

Next, let's discuss how you configure the display manager to support remote X terminals.

Configuring Remote Access to the Display Manager

Many organizations use thin client systems for their end users. A thin client is a minimal computer system that uses X server software to connect to and run a display manager from a remote X server over a network connection. This allows the remote X server output presented by the display manager to be displayed on the thin client's local monitor. This implementation allows these organizations to provide a full graphical desktop to all its users using only a small number of high-end xdm systems and a larger number of inexpensive thin clients.

 NOTE   Some thin client systems are extremely Spartan. They may not even have a hard disk drive. The minimal Linux operating system and X server software needed to connect to the xdm host are embedded in the firmware of the thin client system.

To configure remote access to the display manager on your xdm host, you need to configure it to listen on the network for inbound connection requests from the X server software on the thin clients. These requests use the xdm Control Protocol (XDMCP) on port 177. Do the following:

1. If your host is running xdm or kdm, edit the /etc/X11/xdm/Xservers file and find the line that begins with :0, shown here:

    ```
    :0 local /usr/X11R6/bin/X -nolisten tcp -br vt7
    ```

    Remove the –nolisten tcp option; then save your changes to the file and restart the system.

2. If your system is running gdm, edit the /etc/X11/gdm/gdm.conf file and set DisallowTCP= to **false**.

3. If you are running openSUSE, you need to edit the /etc/sysconfig/displaymanager file and make the following changes:

    ```
    DISPLAYMANAGER_REMOTE_ACCESS="yes"
    DISPLAYMANAGER_XSERVER_TCP_PORT_6000_OPEN="yes"
    ```

4. Open port 177 in the xdm host's firewall.

5. Open the /etc/X11/xdm/Xaccess file on the xdm host in a text editor. This file is used to configure access controls for XDMCP connections.

    To enable remote access, add an entry for each remote thin client system that will access the xdm service on the host. You can add each system's hostname individually, or you can allow access for an entire domain.

    For example, to allow access to the xdm service for all systems from the mydomain.com domain, you would add ***.mydomain.com** to the file.

    To restrict specific thin clients from accessing the xdm service on the host, add their hostnames to the file with an exclamation point. For example, to prevent the ws1.mydomain.com host from accessing the xdm service, you would enter **!ws1.mydomain.com** in the file.

The last topic we need to discuss in this chapter is configuring accessibility settings. Let's look at how to do this next.

Configuring Accessibility

To support a diverse workforce, you need to be familiar with how to configure accessibility settings on the Linux systems you manage. In this part of the chapter, you will learn how to configure accessibility settings for physically and visually impaired users using the following tools:

- Keyboard accessibility
- Mouse accessibility
- Screen readers
- Screen magnifiers
- Braille devices
- Desktop themes

Before you can use many of these tools, however, you need to enable Assistive Technologies. To do this, you need to access your Assistive Technologies Preferences application. On a Fedora system, this is done by searching for and selecting **Universal Access**. The screen in Figure 7-11 is displayed.

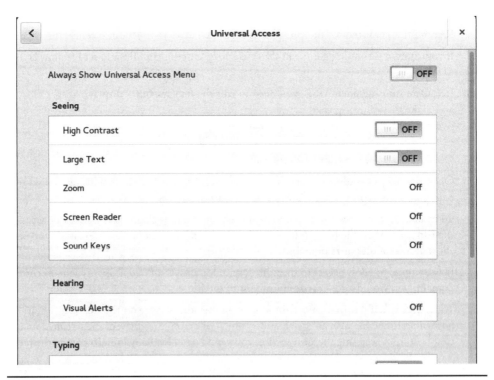

Figure 7-11   Enabling Assistive Technologies

At this point, you can configure a variety of accessibility tools on your Linux system. Let's begin by looking at using AccessX to provide keyboard accessibility.

Keyboard Accessibility

Most Linux distributions include a variety of accessibility tools to assist users who have physical impairments that make it difficult for them to use a traditional mouse or keyboard. One of the tools you can use is called *AccessX*, which is an application included with most Linux desktop managers that allows you to configure a wide variety of keyboard accessibility settings. These settings are designed to enable physically impaired users to use a traditional keyboard. You can configure the following:

- **StickyKeys** Allows users to lock modifier keys such as CTRL and SHIFT. This enables them to complete keyboard tasks with just one finger that would normally require two or more fingers.

- **MouseKeys** Enables key sequences to be used to move the mouse cursor on the screen and to send mouse clicks.

- **SlowKeys** Configures the keyboard such that the user must hold a key down for a specified period of time before the keystroke is actually sent. This helps the user avoid sending accidental keystrokes.

- **ToggleKeys** Sounds an audible alert if either the CAPS LOCK key or the NUM LOCK key is on.

- **RepeatKeys** Configures the keyboard to allow the user extra time to release a pressed key before sending multiple keystrokes.

- **BounceKeys and DelayKeys** Inserts a slight delay between keystrokes to prevent the keyboard from sending unintentional keystrokes.

To configure AccessX settings, access Universal Access and select the option to configure keyboard preferences. For example, on a Fedora system, you would select **Typing Assist (AccessX)** under Typing. When you do, the screen shown in Figure 7-12 is displayed.

For physically impaired users who aren't able to use a traditional keyboard, Linux provides the option of using an *onscreen keyboard,* which allows users to use any pointing device (such as a mouse) to select keys on a virtual keyboard. Commonly used onscreen keyboard applications include GOK (GNOME Onscreen Keyboard) and GTkeyboard.

You use the Universal Access panel to configure onscreen keyboards. On a Fedora system, you would set the Screen Keyboard setting to **On** under Typing.

Mouse Accessibility

In addition to keyboard accessibility, Assistive Technologies also provides mouse accessibility options for physically impaired users. For example, on a Fedora system, you can configure mouse options under Pointing and Clicking in the Universal Access panel.

Figure 7-12
Configuring
keyboard
accessibility
settings

Depending on the distribution, you can configure the following:

- **Simulated secondary click**   This option allows you to send a double-click by simply holding down the primary mouse button for a specified amount of time.

- **Dwell click**   This option sends a mouse click whenever the mouse pointer stops moving for a specified amount of time.

- **Mouse gestures**   Mouse gestures are the equivalent of keyboard shortcuts. Mouse gestures allow you to complete a certain task when you move the mouse in a specific way. You can configure your desired actions for each of the following mouse gestures:

  - Single Click
  - Double Click
  - Drag Click
  - Secondary Click

  For each gesture, you can configure one of the following actions:

  - Move Left
  - Move Right
  - Move Up
  - Move Down

With this in mind, let's now look at several accessibility options available for visually impaired users.

Screen Readers

One option available to visually impaired users is a *screen reader,* which "reads" the text displayed on the screen audibly for the user. Some screen readers can use your computer's sound interface, whereas others require special speech synthesizer hardware. The Orca application is probably the most commonly used screen reader. Unlike many other screen readers, Orca can read text from the GNOME desktop. Many other screen readers, such as emacspeak, only work with text-based terminal screens.

To configure a screen reader, open Universal Access and then click **Screen Reader**. You can use the option shown in Figure 7-13 to turn the screen reader on.

You can also enable screen magnification options. Let's discuss how this technology works next.

Screen Magnifiers

A *screen magnifier* allows visually impaired users to magnify areas of the screen as if they were using a real magnifying glass. You can choose from a wide variety of screen magnifiers, including Orca, GNOME Magnifier, and KDE Magnifier. Of these, Orca is probably the most popular, primarily because it can function as both a screen reader and a screen magnifier.

 NOTE   You can start Orca from the shell prompt by entering **orca –e magnifier**.

To configure a screen magnifier, do the following:

1. Access the Universal Access panel and select **Zoom**. The screen in Figure 7-14 is displayed.

2. Configure the following magnification options:
   - **Magnification**   The level of magnification to be used
   - **Magnifier position**   The size and color of the magnifier's cursor

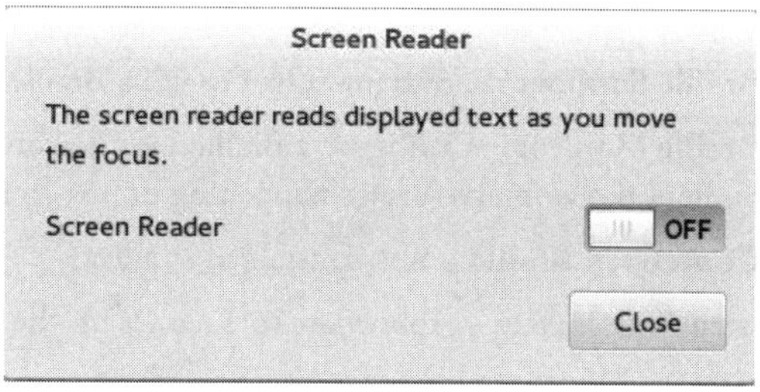

Figure 7-13
Enabling a screen reader

Screen Reader

The screen reader reads displayed text as you move the focus.

Screen Reader   OFF

Close

Figure 7-14

Configuring a screen magnifier

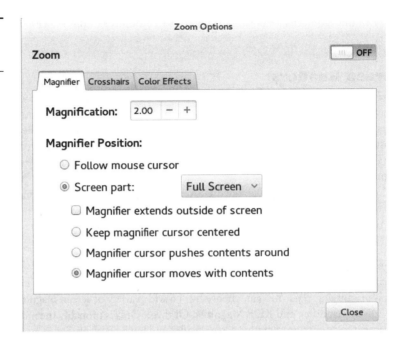

- **Crosshairs Settings**   The magnifier's area-targeting cursor
- **Color Effects Settings**   The color of the magnified region

3. When you're done, select **Close**.

Braille Devices

Visually impaired Linux users can also use Braille hardware devices. Several types of Braille displays and embossers are supported. To interface with these types of devices, the Linux system must be running the brltty daemon.

The Orca utility mentioned earlier can be used to support Braille devices. Start Orca by searching for **Orca** and selecting its icon. Then select the **Braille** tab in the Orca preferences. The screen shown in Figure 7-15 is displayed.

Configure the following Braille options, as appropriate for your preferences and for your Braille devices:

- **Enable Braille Support**   Configure Orca to use a Braille display.
- **Enable Braille Monitor**   Configure a Braille monitor on the regular display, which allows you to visually observe what's happening on the Braille display device.
- **Enable Contracted Braille**   Use contracted Braille.
- **Abbreviated Role Names**   Abbreviate role names on the Braille display.

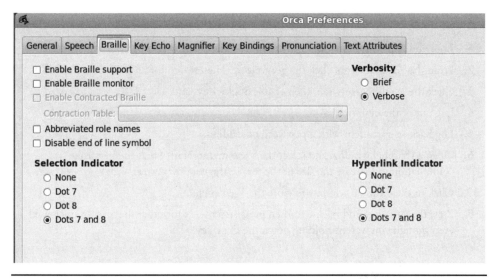

Figure 7-15 Configuring Braille support in Orca

- **Disable End of Line Symbol**   Do not send the $l end-of-line characters to the Braille display.
- **Verbosity**   Controls the level of information to be sent to the Braille display.
- **Selection Indicator**   How selected text on the screen will be underlined on the Braille display.
- **Hyperlink Indicator**   How hypertext on the screen will be underlined on the Braille display.

Select **OK** to save your changes to the Orca Braille configuration.

High-Contrast, Large-Text Desktop Themes

The last visibility accessibility option we're going to look at here involves high-contrast, large-text desktop themes. In the Universal Access panel, enable the High Contrast and Large Text options under Seeing. These options were shown earlier in Figure 7-11.

Let's practice working with Accessibility Settings in the following exercise.

Exercise 7-1: Working with Accessibility Settings

In this exercise, you practice enabling Accessibility Settings on your Linux system. You can perform this exercise using the virtual machine that comes with this book. Run snapshot 7-1 for the correctly configured environment.

VIDEO   Please watch the Exercise 7-1 video for a demonstration on how to perform this task.

Do the following:

1. Boot your Linux system and log in as your student user with a password of **student**.

2. From the KDE desktop, click the gecko icon. Then search for and select **Accessibility**.

3. Click the Modifier Keys tab; then enable Sticky Keys and select **OK**.

4. Log out of the desktop.

5. Log back in as student with a password of **student**.

6. Open a terminal window and select the View menu. Notice that the keystroke combination to increase the size of the text in the window is CTRL-+.

7. Click in the terminal window to close the View menu.

8. Press the CTRL key and release it; then press SHIFT-+. Notice that the text size increased even though you weren't holding down the CTRL key.

Chapter Review

In this chapter, I discussed how to configure the graphical X environment on your Linux system. I pointed out that the Linux graphical environment is composed of the following components:

- X server
- Window manager
- Desktop environment

Each of these components is modular. You can choose from a variety of packages to customize your graphical environment to suit your tastes.

We next looked at the process of configuring your X environment. I noted that it's imperative that you use the correct settings in your configuration. If done incorrectly, you could potentially damage your monitor. Before you begin, you should pull out your video board and monitor documentation and identify the following information:

- Who's the manufacturer of the video board?
- What model number is the video board?
- How much memory is installed on the video board?
- What's the board's maximum resolution?
- What's the board's maximum color depth?
- What chipset is installed on the board?
- What are the maximum horizontal and vertical sync rates supported by your monitor?

Just like everything else Linux, your X configuration is stored in a text file in the /etc directory. If you're using X.org, your configuration settings are saved in /etc/X11/xorg.conf. If you're using XFree86, your configuration settings are saved in /etc/X11/XF86Config. The xorg.conf file is divided into sections that begin with the **Section** "*name*" directive and end with **EndSection**. This file is composed of the following sections:

- **Files** This section tells the X server where to find the files it needs to do its job, such as font files and input device files.
- **ServerFlags** This section specifies global X server options.
- **Module** This section tells the X server to load certain server extension and font rasterizer modules at startup.
- **InputDevice** This section configures the X server with the input devices it should use.
- **Modes** This section defines video modes the X server may use.
- **Screen** This section binds your video board to your monitor.
- **Monitor** This section defines parameters for the monitor connected to your display adapter.
- **ServerLayout** This section glues all the preceding sections together into a complete configuration.

Linux distributions that are based on systemd do not use the xorg.conf configuration file. Instead, the X11 configuration is stored in a series of configuration files located in /etc/X11/xorg .conf.d. However, the configuration principles are pretty much the same. Instead of a single file divided into multiple sections, these systems break up the one single file into separate files, such as 10-evdev.conf, 50-device.conf, 50-monitor.conf, and 50-screen.conf. The syntax within these files is the same as that used in the xorg.conf file.

I pointed out that you should avoid directly editing your X server configuration file. Instead, you should use a configuration utility to avoid mistakes that could potentially damage your hardware. Depending on your distribution, you can use one of the following utilities:

- YaST
- SaX2
- xorgconfig or xorgcfg
- Xorg –configure
- XFree-86 –configure
- xf86config or xf86cfg
- xvidtune

To specify your default window manager, you need to edit a hidden configuration file in your user's home directory. The name of the file depends on your distribution and your default runlevel:

- .xinitrc (runlevel 3)
- .Xsession (runlevel 5)
- .Xdefaults (runlevel 5)
- .Xclients (runlevel 5)

You can also set the value of the WINDOWMANAGER environment variable to the desktop environment you want to use.

The xwininfo command can be used to display information about open windows on your graphical desktop. You can run the command and then click the window you want to get information about. You can also just specify the ID of the window you want to get information about using the –id option with the command. The xdpyinfo command can be used to display the capabilities of a server, the various parameters used when communicating between clients and the server, and the different screens modes available.

I next discussed how to configure an X font server. An X font server allows you to configure fonts for an entire organization from a single central location. The first thing you need to do is install the fonts you want to share on the X font server. I discussed the difference between bitmap fonts and scalable fonts. I then discussed where to install the fonts:

- **Type 1**   /usr/share/fonts/Type1
- **TrueType**   /usr/share/fonts/truetype

After copying the font files to the appropriate directory, you next need to run the mkfontscale and mkfontdir commands to create a font description file and index the font. Then you need to open port 7100 in the X server host's firewall. The next thing you need to do is tell the X font service (xfs) that the fonts are there and should be made available to remote X server clients by editing the /etc/X11/fs/config file. In this file, you need to remark out the no-listen = tcp line and then verify that the appropriate font path is listed under catalogue =.

Once this is done, you need to start the xfs daemon and configure it to start each time the system boots. Then restart your X server.

At this point, I discussed how to configure the remote X servers to consume the fonts provided by the X font server. This is done by adding a new FontPath directive to the Files section of the xorg.conf file that points to the X font server using the following syntax:

```
FontPath     "tcp/server_address:7100"
```

I then discussed how you go about configuring your display manager. You can enable or disable the display manager using the xdm init script in the init script directory. You can use the chkconfig command to enable or disable the init script at system boot.

You can configure your display manager by editing the appropriate configuration file:

- **xdm**   /etc/X11/xdm/xdm-config
- **kdm**   The KDE display manager is actually based on xdm and usually uses the xdm configuration files. However, some distributions store kdm settings in /etc/kde/kdm or /etc/X11/ kdm instead.
- **gdm**   /etc/X11/gdm
- **LightDM**   The LightDM display manager is configured using several different files:
  - /usr/share/lightdm/lightdm.conf.d
  - /etc/lightdm/lightdm.conf.d
  - /etc/lightdm/lightdm.conf

I ended this chapter by discussing how to configure accessibility settings on a Linux system. To do this, you need to enable Assistive Technologies. One of the tools you can use is called AccessX, which allows you to configure a wide variety of keyboard accessibility settings that enable physically impaired users to use a traditional keyboard:

- StickyKeys
- MouseKeys
- SlowKeys
- ToggleKeys
- RepeatKeys
- BounceKeys
- DelayKeys

For physically impaired users who aren't able to use a traditional keyboard, Linux provides the option of using an onscreen keyboard, which allows users to use any pointing device (such as a mouse) to select keys on a virtual keyboard.

In addition to keyboard accessibility, Assistive Technologies also provides mouse accessibility options for physically impaired users. You can configure the following:

- Simulated secondary click
- Dwell click
- Mouse gestures

We next looked at using screen readers to help visually impaired users. Screen readers "read" the text displayed on the screen audibly for the user. A screen magnifier allows visually impaired users to magnify areas of the screen as if they were using a real magnifying glass.

We then looked at using Braille devices with Linux to support visually impaired users. Several types of Braille displays and embossers are supported. To interface with these types of devices, the Linux system must be running the brltty daemon. The Orca application can also be used to interface with Braille devices.

To assist visually impaired users, you can also implement high-contrast, large-text desktop themes.

Accelerated Review

- The Linux graphical environment is composed of the following components:
  - X server
  - Window manager
  - Desktop environment
- Two different X server software packages have been implemented on Linux systems:
  - X.org-X11
  - XFree86

- Some of the more popular window managers include the following:
  - enlightenment
  - fvwm
  - kwin
  - sawfish
  - twm
  - wmaker
- Two desktop environments are predominantly used with Linux systems today:
  - KDE
  - GNOME
- Before implementing a video board/monitor combination with Linux, you need to check the HCL for your distribution and make sure your video board and monitor are supported.
- Your X configuration is stored in a text file in the /etc directory:
  - **XFree86**   /etc/X11/XF86Config
  - **X.org**   /etc/X11/xorg.conf
- The xorg.conf file is broken into sections that begin with the Section directive and end with EndSection.
- The most commonly used sections in a typical xorg.conf include the following:
  - **Files**   Tells the X server where to find the files it needs to do its job
  - **ServerFlags**   Specifies global X server options
  - **Module**   Tells the X server to load certain server extension and font rasterizer modules at startup
  - **InputDevice**   Configures the X server with the input devices it should use
  - **Modes**   Defines video modes the X server may use
  - **Screen**   Binds your video board to your monitor
  - **Monitor**   Defines parameters for the monitor connected to your display adapter
  - **ServerLayout**   Glues all the preceding sections together into a complete configuration
- You should use a configuration utility to configure your X server software to avoid mistakes that could potentially damage your hardware.
- You can use one of the following utilities to configure your X server software:
  - YaST
  - SaX2
  - xorgconfig or xorgcfg
  - Xorg –configure

- XFree-86 –configure
- xf86config or xf86cfg
- xvidtune
- An X font server allows you to configure fonts for an entire organization from a single central location.
- You need to install the fonts you want to share on the X font server.
- Fonts are installed in the following directories:
  - **Type 1**   /usr/share/fonts/Type1
  - **TrueType**   /usr/share/fonts/truetype
- You need to run the mkfontscale and mkfontdir commands to create a font description file and index the font.
- For remote X terminals to connect, you need to open port 7100 in the X server host's firewall.
- You need to tell the X font service (xfs) that the fonts should be made available to remote X server clients by editing the /etc/X11/fs/config file.
- Remark out the no-listen = tcp line and verify that the appropriate font path is listed under catalogue =.
- Start the xfs daemon and configure it to start each time the system boots.
- To configure the remote X servers to consume the fonts provided by the X font server, you must add a new FontPath directive to the Files section of the xorg.conf file that points to the X font server.
- You can choose from a variety of packages to customize your graphical environment.
- You can edit a hidden configuration file in your user's home directory to specify your default window manager:
  - .xinitrc (runlevel 3)
  - .Xsession (runlevel 5)
  - .Xdefaults (runlevel 5)
  - .Xclients (runlevel 5)
- You can set the value of the WINDOWMANAGER environment variable to the desktop environment you want to use.
- You can enable or disable the display manager using the xdm init script in the init script directory.
- You can use the chkconfig command to enable or disable the init script at system boot.
- You can configure your display manager by editing the appropriate configuration file:
  - **xdm**   /etc/X11/xdm/xdm-config
  - **kdm**   The KDE display manager is actually based on xdm and usually uses the xdm configuration files. However, some distributions store kdm settings in /etc/kde/kdm or /etc/X11/ kdm instead.

- **gdm**   /etc/X11/gdm
- **LightDM**   The LightDM display manager is configured using several different files:
  - /usr/share/lightdm/lightdm.conf.d
  - /etc/lightdm/lightdm.conf.d
  - /etc/lightdm/lightdm.conf
- You can configure accessibility settings on a Linux system by enabling Assistive Technologies.
- AccessX allows you to configure a wide variety of keyboard accessibility settings that enable physically impaired users to use a traditional keyboard:
  - StickyKeys
  - MouseKeys
  - SlowKeys
  - ToggleKeys
  - RepeatKeys
  - BounceKeys
  - DelayKeys
- Linux provides the option of using an onscreen keyboard, which allows users of any pointing device (such as a mouse) to select keys on a virtual keyboard.
- Assistive Technologies also provides mouse accessibility options for physically impaired users. You can configure the following:
  - Simulated secondary click
  - Dwell click
  - Mouse gestures
- You can configure screen readers to help visually impaired users.
- Screen readers "read" the text displayed on the screen audibly for the user.
- Screen magnifiers allow visually impaired users to magnify areas of the screen as if they were using a real magnifying glass.
- You can use Braille devices with Linux to support visually impaired users.
- Several types of Braille displays and embossers are supported.
- The Linux system must be running the brltty daemon.
- The Orca application can also be used to interface with Braille devices.
- To assist visually impaired users, you can also implement high-contrast, large-text desktop themes.

Questions

1. Which of the following draws graphical windows on the display?

   A. KDE

   B. fvwm

   C. sawfish

   D. X.org

2. Your Linux system uses X.org as its X server. Which configuration file is used to configure this service?

   A. /etc/X11/XF86Config

   B. /etc/X11/x11.conf

   C. /etc/X11/XFree86.conf

   D. /etc/X11/xorg.conf

3. Which utility could you use on a Fedora Linux system to configure the X server?

   A. xf86config

   B. YaST

   C. xorgcfg

   D. xf86cfg

4. Your system is configured to boot to runlevel 3 by default. You use the startx command to start your graphical environment. What file can you edit in your home directory to specify your default window manager?

   A. .xinitrc

   B. .Xsession

   C. .Xdefaults

   D. .Xclients

5. Which section of the xorg.conf file tells the X server where to find font files?

   A. Files

   B. Fonts

   C. InputDevice

   D. Modes

6. Which section of the xorg.conf file defines video modes for the X server?

   A. Files

   B. Screen

   C. Monitor

   D. Modes

7. Which section of the xorg.conf file is used to define a keyboard and a mouse for the X server to use?

   A. Modes

   B. InputDevice

   C. Module

   D. Monitor

8. Which section of the xorg.conf file glues all the various sections into a complete configuration for the X server?

   A. ServerLayout

   B. Module

   C. Files

   D. Modes

9. Which command will automatically detect all your video subsystem hardware and create a configuration file named /root/xorg.conf.new for you?

   A. Xorg –configure

   B. XFree-86 –configure

   C. Xorgcfg

   D. system-config-display

10. You want to install a font file on your Linux X font server. The font file name has a .pfa extension. Where should it be copied to?

    A. /usr/share/fonts/100dpi

    B. /usr/share/fonts/truetype

    C. /usr/share/fonts/Type1

    D. /usr/share/fonts/75dpi

11. Which LightDM configuration parameter specifies which greeter the display manager should use?

    A. greeter-session

    B. allow-guest

    C. greeter-hide-users

    D. user-session

12. Which environment variable can be used on most Linux distributions to configure the display manager you want to use?

    A. WINDOWMANAGER

    B. DISPLAYMANAGER

    C. X11

    D. XORG

13. Which configuration file is used by the xdm display manager?

    A. /etc/kde/kdm

    B. /etc/X11/kdm

    C. /etc/X11/xdm/xdm-config

    D. /etc/X11/gdm

14. Which keyboard accessibility option allows users to lock modifier keys, enabling them to complete keyboard tasks with just one finger that would normally require two or more fingers?

    A. MouseKeys

    B. SlowKeys

    C. StickyKeys

    D. ToggleKeys

15. Which mouse accessibility option allows you to complete a certain task when you move the mouse in a specific way?

    A. MouseKeys

    B. Mouse Gestures

    C. Dwell Click

    D. Simulated Secondary Click

16. Which Linux daemon must be loaded to allow Orca to communicate with Braille devices?

    A. brailled

    B. brltty

    C. orcad

    D. braillettyd

Answers

1. **D.** The X.org X server graphically draws windows on the display.

2. **D.** X.org uses the /etc/X11/xorg.conf configuration file.

3. **C.** The xorgcfg utility can be used to configure X on a Fedora system.

4. **A.** The .xinitrc file in your home directory is used to specify your default window manager when the startx command is used.

5. **A.** The Files section of the xorg.conf file tells the X server where to find font files.

6. **D.** The Modes section of the xorg.conf file defines video modes for the X server.

7. **B.** The InputDevice section of the xorg.conf file is used to define a keyboard and a mouse for the X server to use.

8. **A.** The ServerLayout section of the xorg.conf file glues all the various sections into a complete configuration for the X server.

9. **A.** The Xorg –configure command will automatically detect all your video subsystem hardware and create a configuration file named /root/xorg.conf.new.

10. **C.** Font files whose names have a .pfa or .pfb extension are PostScript Type 1 fonts and should be copied to /usr/share/fonts/Type1.

11. **A.** The greeter-session configuration specifies which greeter the LightDM display manager should use.

12. **A.** The WINDOWMANAGER environment variable can be used on most Linux distributions to configure the display manager you want to use.

13. **C.** The /etc/X11/xdm/xdm-config configuration file is used by the xdm display manager.

14. **C.** StickyKeys allows users to lock modifier keys, enabling them to complete keyboard tasks with just one finger that would normally require two or more fingers.

15. **B.** Mouse Gestures allow you to complete a certain task when you move the mouse in a specific way.

16. **B.** The brltty daemon must be loaded to allow Orca to communicate with Braille devices.

Managing Linux Software

In this chapter, you will learn about:
- Managing software with RPM
- Installing software from source code
- Managing Debian software packages
- Managing shared libraries

As a Linux system administrator, you need to know how to install and manage software on a Linux system. "Ha!" you may be thinking. "How hard can it be to install software? I can install software on Windows with my eyes closed!" Actually, installing software on Linux can be somewhat challenging to those new to this operating system. It's not that installing software on Linux is any more difficult than on other operating systems. It's just that it's different.

If you have experience installing Windows applications, you need to momentarily shelve what you already know about installing software and be prepared to approach the process from a new perspective. My past experience has been that if students new to Linux hang on too tightly to their "Windows way" of doing things, they really struggle when working with Linux software. There just aren't enough similarities. If, on the other hand, you let Windows go and learn how to do things in a new way, you're going to be just fine.

 EXAM TIP Be prepared to answer a moderate number of installation-related items when you take your LPIC-1/Linux+ exam. Be sure you know the shell commands that are used to manage RPM and Debian packages, including how to install packages, uninstall packages, and query the package database for information about installed packages.

Let's begin by discussing how to use RPM to manage software on a Linux system.

Managing Software with RPM

When installing software on a Linux system, you essentially have two choices:

- Install a precompiled application or service from a software *package*. Packages contain executables (and other files) that have been precompiled and configured for a specific hardware architecture and/or Linux distribution.

- Install from *source.* When you install from source, you use a compiler on your system to compile the application's source code into executables that can run on your hardware and distribution.

To install software from source, you must have a compiler (such as gcc) already installed on your Linux system. To install software from packages, you must have a package manager installed. Many distributions, including openSUSE and Fedora, use the Red Hat Package Manager (RPM) to install and manage RPM packages on the system. Other distributions, such as Ubuntu, use the Debian package management system.

Regardless of which package manager your distribution uses, they all perform similar tasks, including the following:

- Install software
- Update software that's already been installed
- Uninstall software
- Query installed software
- Verify the integrity of installed software

To keep track of all this information, RPM stores information about installed packages in the RPM database file (/var/lib/rpm). Whenever you install, update, or uninstall a package, a corresponding entry is made in the RPM database.

 TIP I've seen this database file get corrupted on occasion. What a headache! If this happens to you, try rebuilding the RPM database using the rpm --rebuilddb command at the shell prompt (as root).

In this part of the chapter, we'll look at the following:

- Installing software with RPM
- Managing installed software with RPM
- Using yum to install RPM packages

Installing Software with RPM

As with many of the other tasks we've discussed in this book, you can use a variety of tools to install and manage software on a Linux system. Some of these tools are run from the shell prompt; others are graphical utilities that can be used from within the KDE or GNOME desktop environment. For example, the openSUSE distribution includes the Software Management module within the YaST configuration utility. This is shown in Figure 8-1.

The Software Management module allows you to perform a variety of software administrative tasks, such as installing, updating, and removing packages. Other distributions provide similar graphical utilities.

Figure 8-1 Using the YaST Software Management module

These graphical utilities have many advantages. In addition to the easy-to-use interface, most will also automatically detect and resolve package *dependencies* for you. We'll discuss how dependencies work later in this chapter.

We're not going to spend much time working with these utilities in this chapter. This is done for a variety of reasons. First of all, as with most of the other tasks we've discussed in this book, a good Linux admin needs to know how to manage software from the command line. You really need to understand what's going on "under the hood" of the graphical utility (which are usually just graphical front ends for a command-line utility).

In addition, most graphical management utilities can only manage software *packages*. Many of the programs you will install on a Linux system will need to be installed from a source code package. These types of programs must be uncompressed and compiled. The only way to do this is from the shell prompt. Finally, the LPIC-1/Linux+ exam requires you to know how to manage software from the shell prompt.

In accordance, in this part of the chapter we're going to look at the RPM utility to install software. Let's look at the following topics:

- Obtaining Linux software
- Installing software packages

We'll begin by reviewing where you can get Linux software for your system.

Obtaining Linux Software

One of the things I love most about Linux is the fact that a wealth of software is available for your system from a variety of sources, most at little or no cost. Back in the early days of Linux, this wasn't the case. In fact, one of the great impediments that prevented the widespread adoption of Linux in the early days was the lack of applications, particularly office productivity applications.

Today, however, that has all changed. You name a particular task you need to complete with a Linux system, and you can probably find an application or service somewhere that can handle the job.

So where can you get Linux software? As we discussed earlier in this book, the Linux development model violates most of the accepted norms. With other operating systems, you obtain software by visiting your local computer store and purchasing a box copy of your desired application. Many vendors also allow you to purchase an application license online and download a copy.

With Linux, however, this usually isn't the case. Most of your Linux software is obtained from alternative sources. Let's take a look at a few here.

Sources for Linux Software   You can obtain software for your Linux system from a variety of sources other than the computer section of your local big-box store. The first source you should be aware of (and a source that many Linux users overlook) is your distribution discs. Many distributions include a cornucopia of applications and services that you can install. For example, the openSUSE installation DVD includes hundreds of application and service RPMs in the subdirectories of the suse directory, as shown in Figure 8-2.

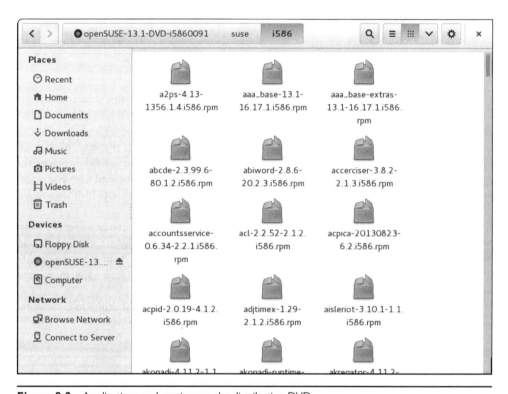

Figure 8-2   Applications and services on the distribution DVD

In addition to your distribution disc, you can also download software for your Linux system from a host of websites on the Internet. Most open source applications have their own websites where you can learn about the software and download the latest version. For example, you can visit www.pureftpd.org to learn about and download the pure-ftpd service, which is used to configure an FTP service on your Linux system. This website is shown in Figure 8-3.

In addition to individual project websites, you can also use several other websites that provide you with links to many different programs from a single location. One of my favorites is www .rpmfind.net. This website provides an RPM repository you can search to locate and download an RPM package for your Linux system.

Another great source for Linux software is SourceForge (http://sourceforge.net). The Source-Forge website is a central repository for open source software. As of the date this was written, there were thousands of different programs available on this site. As with the rpmfind website, you can search SourceForge to locate and download a particular package. The results are displayed with links that will allow you to download the appropriate programs.

As you can see, you can download just about anything you need from these websites.

With some distributions, you can also go directly to the distribution's website and download packages from there. For example, you can go to http://software.opensuse.org and download packages for your specific version of openSUSE. This is shown in Figure 8-4.

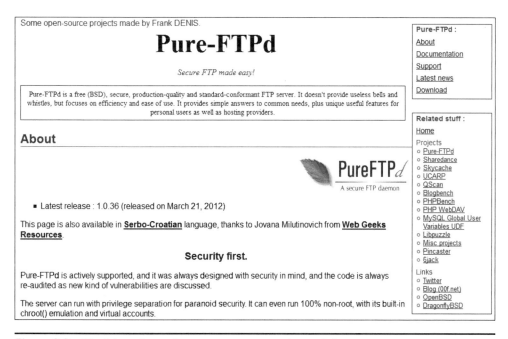

Figure 8-3   Obtaining software from an open source project website

Figure 8-4 Searching for software on the openSUSE website

So in summary, many resources are available to you for obtaining Linux software, including the following:

- Your installation CD or DVD
- Open source project websites
- www.rpmfind.net
- www.sourceforge.net
- linux.tucows.com
- www.freshmeat.net
- www.linux.org

The point is that software is readily available for you to use on your system. Spend some time reviewing what's available on these sites. You'll be glad you did!

When you download a program from one of these sites, you should check your download and verify that it didn't get corrupted along the way. Let's talk about how this is done next.

Verifying Your Downloads For the most part, files downloaded from the Internet arrive at your local system intact. However, it is possible for corruption to occur. There are few things more frustrating than downloading a file, especially a distribution ISO image, only to find that the file got corrupted somewhere along the way. You also need to be sure the file is authentic and hasn't been tampered with by some nefarious individual who is trying to insert malware into your system.

The good news is that you can check your files after they are downloaded to verify that the copy on your local system is the same as the copy on the server you downloaded from. This can be done by creating and comparing the file's checksum value against the source file. A *checksum* is a value generated by calculating the contents of a file using a Message Digest 5 (MD5) algorithm. For example, if you were downloading a DVD ISO image from www.opensuse.org, you could view the checksum for the file using the link provided in the download page. This would display the checksum values for the source file, as shown in Figure 8-5.

Verify your download (optional, for experts)

Many applications can verify the checksum of a download. To verify your download can be important as it verifies you really have got the ISO file you wanted to download and not some broken version. You could verify the file in the process of downloading. For example a checksum (SHA256) will be used automatically if you choose Metalink in the field above and use the add-on DownThemAll! in Firefox. We offer three different checksums:

- gpg signature offers the most security as you can verify who signed it. It should be 79C1 79B2 E1C8 20C1 890F 9994 A84E DAE8 9C80 0ACA.
- md5 checksum is still the most commonly used checksum. Many ISO burners display it right before burning.
- sha1 checksum is the less known but more secure checksum than md5.

Figure 8-5 Viewing source file checksum values

After downloading the file, you could then use the sum command from the shell prompt to calculate a checksum for the local copy of the file. To do this, you simply enter **sum** *path/ filename*. For example, if you downloaded the pure-ftpd-1.0.29-1.1 .t.x86_ 64.rpm file to the ~/Downloads directory, you would enter **sum ~/Downloads/pure-ftpd-1.0.29-1.1.x86_64.rpm**. The sum utility reads the file, generates a checksum value for the file, and displays it onscreen. Here is an example:

```
rtracy@openSUSE:~> sum ~/Downloads/pure-ftpd-1.0.29-1.4.x86_64.rpm
56738    205
```

You can then compare the checksum for the original file on the website against the checksum for the local file. If the checksums are the same, you're in good shape. That means the files are identical. No corruption occurred during transit.

However, if the checksums are different, that indicates somehow the two copies of the file are different in some way. More than likely, something happened during the download process that corrupted the copy. In this situation, don't try to salvage the local copy. Delete it, download a new copy, and verify the checksum values again.

Let's practice using web resources to obtain Linux software in the following exercise.

Exercise 8-1: Using Web Resources to Obtain Linux Software

In this exercise, you will practice using web resources to download Linux software. The following steps were accurate as of the time this book was written. Because of the ever-changing nature of the Web, you may need to modify these steps as new versions of software are released and websites are updated. You can perform this exercise using the virtual machine that comes with this book. Run snapshot 8-1 for the correctly configured environment.

VIDEO   Please watch the Exercise 8-1 video for a demonstration on how to perform this task.

With this in mind, complete the following:

1. Boot your Linux system and log in as the **student** user with a password of **student**.

2. Open a web browser and navigate to **http://www.sourceforge.net**.

 NOTE These steps were written using Firefox. If you find that you are unable to connect to the Internet after restoring snapshot 8-1, open a terminal window, use **su** - to switch to root, and then enter **systemctl restart network** at the shell prompt.

---

3. In the Search field on the SourceForge home page, enter **filezilla** and then select **Search**.

4. Locate the Filezilla **Download Now** link in the list of search results and select it.

5. Download the latest version of Filezilla for your distribution and architecture in tar.bz2 format to the Downloads directory in your home directory (~). (Your browser may prompt you to open the file with a graphical archive utility. Don't select this option.)

6. In your browser, navigate to **http://www.rpmfind.net/**.

7. In the Search field, enter **gftp** and then select **Search**.

8. In the list of search results, identify the appropriate RPM package for your distribution and architecture.

 TIP You can press CTRL-F and search the page for your distribution and architecture.

---

9. Select the appropriate link to download the correct RPM for your system and save the file to ~/Downloads.

10. Close your browser window.

Now you're ready to start installing files. Let's review how this is done next.

Installing Software Packages

You can also install precompiled, preconfigured applications and services on your Linux system using *packaged software*. With packaged software, the source code is prebuilt and configured for a particular system architecture—and in some cases, a specific Linux distribution.

The great thing about RPM is the fact that it makes it easy to install and manage software (more so than the source code option we will discuss later in this chapter), especially for new or novice Linux users. Frankly, you have to know your stuff with Linux to install and compile source code. You're likely to find that the skills and knowledge required are way beyond that of most of your end users.

RPM packages are quite easy to install. Most RPM packages are downloaded in a single file that you process directly. You simply use the rpm utility at the shell prompt to install a package file.

Before I show you how to do this, I first need to discuss the naming conventions used by RPM packages. This is very important because RPM packages are built for a specific CPU architecture and sometimes even for a specific Linux distribution. Unlike source code installs, which customize the program for the particular architecture during the installation process, RPM packages come precompiled for a specific architecture. That means multiple versions of a particular RPM may be available to accommodate different platforms.

The important point is to make sure you're downloading and installing the correct version of a given RPM for your particular system. You can check this by looking at the name of the RPM package. Consider the following example:

```
gftp-2.0.19-7.1.x86_64.rpm
```

This RPM is used to install the gFTP software. It provides a graphical FTP client application that users can run to access files on an FTP server. Different parts of the filename are used to indicate different information about the package, including the following:

- **Package Name** This part of the filename simply identifies the name of the package. In this example, the name of the package is gftp.

- **Version Number** This part of the filename specifies the version of the software in the package. In this case, the software version is 2.0.19.

- **Release Number** This part of the filename indicates the current release of the software version. On occasion, errors are encountered in the process of creating an RPM package. When a new package release is made available for the same version of the software that fixes an error, the release number is incremented. In the example just shown, the release number is 7.1. This field may also include an optional distribution designator that indicates that the package has been compiled for a specific Linux distribution. The designators include the following:

  - **fc*x*** Specifies that the package is intended for Fedora Core version *x*. For example, fc4 indicates the package is for Fedora Core 4.

  - **rhl*x*** Specifies that the package is intended for Red Hat Linux version *x*.

  - **suse*xxx*** Specifies that the package is intended for SUSE Linux version *xxx*. For example, suse101 indicates that the package is intended for SUSE Linux 10.1.

- **Architecture Type** This part of the filename specifies the CPU architecture that the software inside the package will run on. In the preceding example, the architecture is specified as x86_64. That means the software will run on 64-bit x86 CPUs. You may also see the following architectures specified in a package's filename:

  - **i386** Specifies that the software will run on an Intel 80386 or later CPU

  - **i586** Specifies that the software will run on an Intel Pentium or later CPU

  - **i686** Specifies that the software will run on Intel Pentium 4 or later CPUs

  - **x86_64** Specifies that the software will run on 64-bit x86 CPUs

  - **athlon** Specifies that the software is intended to run on an AMD Athlon CPU

  - **ppc** Specifies that the software is intended to run on the PowerPC CPU

  - **noarch** Specifies that the package is not architecture dependent

RPM packages can be located on your distribution installation CD or DVD as well as a variety of locations on the Internet. After downloading an RPM package, you should use the sum command to generate a checksum and compare it to the checksum of the original file, as we discussed earlier.

In addition, you can also use the rpm command to check the authenticity of the package. Doing so lets you know whether the package you downloaded came directly from the organization responsible for maintaining the software or whether it has been altered in some way by a third party. This is done by entering **rpm --checksig** *package_filename*. This command will query the package for its digital signing key. If anyone altered the package at some point, the key will become invalid.

In the next example, the pure-ftpd package has been downloaded from the Internet. To verify the integrity of the package, you first switch to the directory where the package file is stored. You then enter **rpm --checksig pure-ftpd-1.0.29-1.4.x86_64.rpm** to check the digital signature applied:

```
rtracy@openSUSE:~/Downloads> rpm --checksig pure-ftpd-1.0.29-1.4.x86_64.rpm
pure-ftpd-1.0.29-1.4.x86_64.rpm: rsa sha1 (md5) pgp md5 OK
```

Notice that the output of the command says that the signature is OK, indicating that the package hasn't been altered by anyone since it was created.

Once you're confident that the package has arrived to your local system intact, you can install it using the rpm command again. This is done by entering **rpm –i** *package_filename*. The –i option tells the rpm utility to install the package specified. For example, you could install the gFTP package downloaded earlier by first switching to the directory where the package file is located and then entering (as root) **rpm –i gftp-2.0.19-7.1.x86_64.rpm**. This is shown here:

```
rtracy@openSUSE:~> su -
Password:
openSUSE:~ # cd /home/rtracy/Downloads/
openSUSE:/home/rtracy/Downloads # rpm -i gftp-2.0.19-7.1.x86_64.rpm
```

The software is now installed on the system and ready for you to use. That was easy!

 TIP If you know the full URL to the package you want to install, you can install it directly from the Internet. Just enter **rpm –i** *url/filename*.**rpm**.

You'll notice in the preceding example that the rpm utility didn't provide much in the way of feedback as it was installing the package. Some Linux administrators prefer it this way; others prefer to see some visual queues that indicate the progress of the installation. This can be done using the –ihv option with rpm, as shown in this example:

```
openSUSE:/home/rtracy/Downloads # rpm -ihv gftp-2.0.19-7.1.x86_64.rpm
Preparing...                      ######################################## [100%]
   1:gftp                         ######################################## [100%]
```

The –h option tells rpm to print hash marks on the screen as a progress indicator. The –v option tells rpm to operate verbosely, printing output to the screen.

Personally, I prefer the –ihv option when I use rpm. It's not much of an issue when installing small packages. However, installing a large RPM package can take several minutes. If you don't use the –ihv option, the session will just sit there while the installation process runs. This makes me uneasy because I don't know whether or not everything is processing correctly. If it takes too long, I start to wonder if something caused rpm to hang. I much prefer seeing a visual progress indicator, even if it is only a bunch of hash marks, to let me know that everything is progressing normally. If you're the type of person who is obsessed with details, you can get even more information about the installation by using the –vv option with the rpm utility.

One of the fantastic features of the rpm utility is that it automatically calculates dependencies for you. You need to understand that a given Linux software package may be dependent upon another package being installed on the system first before it can work properly. If this is the case, the dependent package is called a *dependency*. When you run the rpm utility, it queries the package you want to install and automatically checks to see if you have the dependent packages installed. If not, it will generate an error and prompt you to install the necessary packages required for the software to work.

If you want to check for dependencies without actually installing the software, you can use the --test option with the rpm utility. If there are any failed dependency tests, they will be printed on the screen, allowing you to install the necessary software. You can skip the dependency tests completely and install the package even if dependent software isn't present (not a good idea, by the way) by using the --nodeps option with rpm.

NOTE One of the things I love about the graphical software management utilities, such as YaST, is the fact that they not only calculate dependencies for you, but they also install them for you as well. With the command-line rpm utility, you must use it to manually install all dependent packages.

After running rpm, you can then use the installed software. Some packages will create a menu item or icon in your KDE or GNOME desktop environment that you can use to launch the application.

Other packages—particularly those that install system services—will have to be started from the shell prompt using a startup script or by running the executable filename. For example, you can also start the gFTP client we installed by entering **gftp** at the shell prompt.

Let's practice installing software from an RPM package in the following exercise.

Exercise 8-2: Installing RPM Packages

In this exercise, you will practice installing the gFTP client. You can perform this exercise using the virtual machine that comes with this book. Run snapshot 8-2 for the correctly configured environment.

VIDEO Please watch the Exercise 8-2 video for a demonstration on how to perform this task.

Complete the following:

1. With your system running, open a terminal session.

2. If necessary, change to your root user account by entering **su –** followed by a password of **student**.

3. Change to your home directory by entering **cd ~**. Use the **ls** command to view the gftp package's filename.

4. At the shell prompt, enter **rpm –ihv gftp-*version.architecture*.rpm**. Replace *version* and *architecture,* respectively, with the current version number and architecture of the RPM package.

5. Run the gFTP client by entering **gftp &** at the shell prompt.

6. If your network is connected to the Internet, enter **ftp.openssl.org** in the Host field and **Anonymous** in the User field; then connect. You should see that you are connected to the OpenSSL FTP server, as shown in Figure 8-6.

7. Close your gftp window.

Now that you know how to install software from an RPM package, let's shift gears and discuss how to manage installed software on your system with rpm.

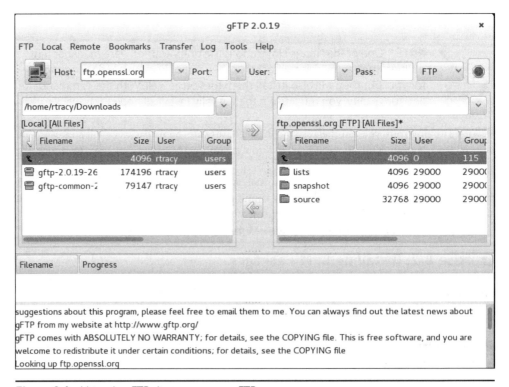

Figure 8-6 Using the gFTP client to access an FTP server

Managing Installed Software with RPM

If you've worked with computers for very long, you know that occasionally you'll need to repair or even uninstall software from a system. The same holds true with Linux. In this part of this chapter, we're going to spend a few pages covering how to manage software that is currently installed on the system. We're going to discuss the following topics:

- Uninstalling software
- Updating software
- Querying packages
- Verifying packages
- Extracting files from packages

Let's begin by discussing how you uninstall software on Linux.

Uninstalling Software

Believe it or not, you will probably need to uninstall a lot of software as a Linux system administrator. It's not because there's anything wrong with the software itself; it's because most Linux distributions install a host of packages on a given system as a part of the base installation proposal. Unless you take the time during the install process to manually specify exactly which software is to be installed, it's very likely that many software packages will be installed on your systems that aren't needed. At best, these unnecessary packages use up disk space; at worst, they could potentially open up security holes in the system.

After installing any Linux system, I strongly recommend that you spend a few minutes reviewing the software that was included in the installation. If you have unnecessary software on the system, uninstall it!

As with installing RPM packages, the process for uninstalling them is relatively easy and straightforward. To do this, enter **rpm –e *package_name*** at the shell prompt. The –e option tells the rpm utility to erase the specified package. For example, earlier we installed the gFTP package using rpm. You could uninstall this same package by entering **rpm –e gftp** at the shell prompt, as is shown in this example:

```
openSUSE:/home/rtracy/Downloads # rpm -e gftp
```

Be warned that the rpm utility checks dependencies during uninstall as well as install operations. If other software is installed on the system that is dependent on the package you are trying to uninstall, an error message will be displayed listing the dependent packages. You must first uninstall those packages before you can continue.

Let's practice uninstalling an RPM package in the following exercise.

Exercise 8-3: Uninstalling RPM Packages

In this exercise, you will practice uninstalling the gftp client you installed in the previous exercise. You can perform this exercise using the virtual machine that comes with this book. Run snapshot 8-3 for the correctly configured environment.

VIDEO Please watch the Exercise 8-3 video for a demonstration on how to perform this task.

Complete the following:

1. With your system running, open a terminal session.

2. If necessary, change to your root user account by entering **su –** followed by password of **student**.

3. At the shell prompt, enter **rpm –e gftp**. You should see a message indicating that gftp has been erased.

Let's next discuss how you can update RPM packages.

Updating Software

The ability of the rpm utility to manage dependencies is a real time saver. However, it brings up the issue of updates. What if you have a package installed that needs to be updated, but it has many other packages that are dependent on it? Do you have to uninstall all of them before you can update the package? That would be a real pain!

Fortunately, this isn't the case. You can use the rpm utility to update an existing package without having to uninstall all of its dependent packages. This is done using the –U option with rpm. With this option, the rpm utility will remove any existing older packages and then install a newer version of the package. For example, suppose you had an older version of gftp installed on your system and wanted to upgrade to version 2.0.19. To do this, you would enter **rpm –U gftp-2.0.19-7.1.x86_64.rpm** at the shell prompt. Here is an example:

```
openSUSE:/home/rtracy/Downloads # rpm -Uhv gftp-2.0.19-7.1.x86_64.rpm
Preparing...                    ######################################### [100%]
   1:gftp                       ######################################### [100%]
```

TIP If you try to use the –U option to update a package that hasn't actually been installed yet, rpm will just install it. In fact, I actually just use –U all the time, regardless of whether I'm installing or updating a package. You can also use the –h and –v options with –U to display a progress indicator.

Let's next discuss how you can query packages installed on your system.

Querying Packages

In addition to installing and upgrading packages on your system, you can also use the rpm command to query packages for information. This can be done using the –q (for *query)* option with rpm. Using the –q option, you can list all the packages installed on the system, view the version and release number of a specific package installed on the system, or view details about a package.

The –q option requires that you specify exactly what you want to query. For example, if you want to generate a list of all packages installed on the system, you would enter **rpm –qa**. A list of installed packages will then be displayed on the screen, as is shown in this example:

```
openSUSE:~ # rpm -qa
xorg-x11-libXau-7.5-1.9.x86_64
libsqlite3-0-3.6.23-4.1.x86_64
libnuma1-2.0.4.rc2-1.2.x86_64
libgssglue1-0.1-13.1.x86_64
libdaemon0-0.13-8.2.x86_64
libaio-0.3.107-4.1.x86_64
pptp-1.7.2-28.1.x86_64
...
```

Be warned that the list will be very long! If you need information about a specific package, you can use the following options with –q:

- **–i** This option displays summary information about a specific package. For example, you can enter **rpm –qi postfix** to display information about the postfix package installed on the system, as shown here:

```
openSUSE:~ # rpm -qi postfix
Name         : postfix                    Relocations: (not
relocatable)
Version      : 2.7.1                           Vendor: openSUSE
Release      : 2.2.1                       Build Date: Tue Sep 14
08:07:39 2010
Install Date: Wed Mar  9 11:36:14 2011      Build Host: e133
Group        : Productivity/Networking/Email/Servers   Source RPM:
postfix-2.7.1-2.2.1.src.rpm
Size         : 2670578                        License: IBM Public
License ..
Signature    : RSA/8, Tue Sep 14 08:08:16 2010, Key ID b88b2fd43dbdc284
Packager     : http://bugs.opensuse.org
URL          : http://www.postfix.org/
Summary      : A fast, secure, and flexible mailer
Description  :
Postfix aims to be an alternative to the widely-used sendmail program.

Authors:
--------
    Wietse Venema wietse@porcupine.org
Distribution: openSUSE 11.3
```

- **--whatrequires** This option displays a list of packages that require the specified packages. For example, entering **rpm –q --whatrequires postfix** will display a list of packages that require the postfix package, as shown in this example:

```
openSUSE:~ # rpm -q --whatrequires postfix
no package requires postfix
```

- **–l** This option displays a list of files that are included in an RPM package.
- **--provides** This option displays the functionality the specified package supplies.

- **--requires** This useful option displays the functionality required by the specified package. In the next example, the **rpm –q --requires postfix** command has been entered at the shell prompt:

```
openSUSE:~ # rpm -q --requires postfix
insserv
sed
fillup
coreutils
grep
diffutils
/usr/bin/getent
...
```

Notice that a list of system requirements is displayed on the screen. If you want to find out what package provides a particular requirement, you can enter **rpm –q --whatprovides** *utility _name* at the shell prompt. The rpm utility will then determine the name of the package that provides this program. In the following example, you can see that the sed-4.1.5-134.1.x86_64 package provides the sed utility:

```
openSUSE:~ # rpm -q --whatprovides sed
sed-4.1.5-134.1.x86_64
```

Let's next discuss how you can use the rpm utility to verify packages.

Verifying Packages

In addition to querying packages, the rpm utility can also be used to verify packages on your system. As you are probably (painfully) aware, software can get corrupted, deleted, or otherwise messed up on any given computer system, regardless of the operating system. You can use the rpm utility to verify your installed packages and make sure everything is working the way it is supposed to. This is done using the –V option.

You can use –V to verify a single package by specifying its package name, such as **rpm –V gftp**. You can also verify all packages on the system by entering **rpm –Va**. Regardless of which option you choose, rpm will return no output if no errors are found. In the next example, the **rpm –V gftp** command was issued at the command prompt. Because the package had no errors, nothing was written to the screen and the rpm utility exited.

```
openSUSE:~ # rpm -V gftp
```

If an error does occur, rpm prints out the error message and the associated filename, as shown here:

```
openSUSE:~ # rpm -Va
S.5....T.  c /etc/xinetd.d/vnc
S.5....T.  c /etc/sane.d/dll.conf
S.5....T.  c /etc/maven/maven2-depmap.xml
.M......    /etc/cups
S.5....T.  c /etc/environment
....L....  c /etc/pam.d/common-account
....L....  c /etc/pam.d/common-auth
....L....  c /etc/pam.d/common-password
....L....  c /etc/pam.d/common-session
```

The error messages generated during the verification process follow the syntax of

```
SM5DLUGT c filename
```

The parameters in the error message stand for the following:

- **S**   Indicates a problem in the size of a file
- **M**   Indicates a problem with a file's mode
- **5**   Indicates a problem with the MD5 checksum of a file
- **D**   Indicates a problem with a file's revision numbers
- **L**   Indicates a problem with a file's symbolic link
- **U**   Indicates a problem with a file's ownership
- **G**   Indicates a problem with a file's group
- **T**   Indicates a problem with the modification time of a file
- **c**   Indicates the specified file is a configuration file
- *filename*   Specifies the name of the file that failed verification

In the example we looked at earlier, any time one of the preceding letters is represented by a period (.) in the output, it indicates that no problem was found with this parameter for the specified file. A letter displayed indicates a problem was found for this particular parameter for the specified file. For example, the /etc/xinetd.d/vnc file had errors S, 5, and T, indicating there was a problem with the size, checksum, and modification time of the file. We also know that it is a configuration file because there's a *c* on the line as well.

In the example, notice that most of the errors encountered by rpm were associated with configuration files. This actually isn't a problem. Configuration files, naturally, get modified all the time and, hence, may fail to verify.

However, if other files, such as executables, fail to verify, then you should be more concerned. Based on the output from rpm –V, you may determine that you need to repair an installed package. You can use rpm to do this as well, using the –U --replacepkgs option. For example, if I determined that I needed to reinstall the gFTP package, I could enter **rpm –U --replacepkgs gftp-2.0.19-7.1.x86_64.rpm** at the shell prompt to force rpm to install the gFTP package from the original rpm, even though it is already installed.

Extracting Files from Packages

From time to time, you may need to extract one or more individual files from a package file. One option for doing this is the rpm2cpio utility. This command takes an RPM package file and converts it to a cpio archive.

 NOTE   We'll discuss how to work with cpio archives in Chapter 10. For now, just think of a cpio archive as the equivalent of a tar archive or a zip file.

The syntax for using rpm2cpio is as follows:

```
rpm2cpio package_name > archive_filename
```

For example, if you needed to get a file out of the gFTP rpm package, you could convert it to a cpio archive using the following command:

```
rpm2cpio gftp-2.0.19-7.1.x86_64.rpm > gftp.cpio
```

You could then extract the file you need from the cpio archive created using the cpio utility. Let's practice managing RPM packages in the following exercise.

Exercise 8-4: Managing RPM Packages

In this exercise, you will practice managing RPM packages installed on your system. You can perform this exercise using the virtual machine that comes with this book. Run snapshot 8-3 for the correctly configured environment.

 VIDEO Please watch the Exercise 8-4 video for a demonstration on how to perform this task.

Complete the following:

1. With your system running, open a terminal session.

2. If necessary, change to your root user account by entering **su –** followed by a password of **student**.

3. List all of the RPM packages installed on your system by entering **rpm –qa** at the shell prompt.

4. View information about the rpm utility itself by entering **rpm –qi rpm**.

5. Identify packages that require the rpm package by entering **rpm –q-- whatrequires rpm**. What packages require rpm?

6. Identify components required by the rpm utility by entering **rpm –q --requires rpm**. What is required by rpm?

7. One of the components required by rpm is libz.so.1. Determine what package provides this component by entering **rpm –q --whatprovides libz.so.1**. What package provides this component?

Using yum to Install RPM Packages

In addition to rpm, you can also use the yum command at the shell prompt to install RPM packages. The yum (Yellowdog Updater Modified) command is just a front end to rpm, but it has several key advantages over using rpm alone:

- It allows you to install a package *and* all of its dependencies with a single command. This is huge! Managing dependencies can be a real problem when installing packages with rpm. It's called "dependency hell." Here's what happens: You decide you want to install package X with rpm at the shell prompt. However, when you run the command, you're informed that package X is dependent on packages Y and Z; you must install these packages first. So, you download and then try to install packages Y and Z with rpm. Again when you do, you discover that Y is dependent upon packages A, B, and C while package Z is dependent upon packages E, F, and G. Of course, you then discover packages A, B, C, E, F, and G all have dependencies of their own. Before you know it, you're installing 20 or more separate packages just to get package X installed on your system. What a nightmare! This is where yum really shines! The yum command busts you out of your dependency hell by automatically calculating and installing all of the dependent packages for you.

- It locates packages for you by searching one or more repositories on the Internet. Again, this is a key strength of yum. I can't tell you how many hours I've wasted (before I learned about yum) trying to find version 3.5 of a particular package to meet a dependency requirement and only being able to find version 3.3. With yum, there's no more digging around the Web trying to find the right package to resolve a dependency issue. It takes care of everything for you.

Once you start using yum, you may never use rpm again! When run from the command prompt, yum finds the latest version of the requested package, downloads it, installs its dependencies, and then installs the requested package itself.

 CAUTION The yum utility is not supported by all distributions. It was originally developed for Red Hat systems, so it's supported well by Red Hat and Fedora. It's not installed by default on openSUSE but can be installed manually.

The basic syntax for using yum is as follows:

```
yum option command package_name
```

Common yum commands are shown in Table 8-1.

For example, in Figure 8-7 the **yum install gcc** command has been entered at the shell prompt to install the GNU C Compiler package on a Fedora system. The yum utility searches the repositories it has been configured to use, locates the latest gcc package, calculates dependencies, installs dependencies, and then installs the gcc package.

If you only want to download the file but not install it, you can use the yumdownloader command instead of yum. The syntax is **yumdownloader** *package_name*. The yumdownloader utility locates the latest version of the package from its configured list of repositories and downloads it to your system. You can then install it manually at your pleasure.

Of course, yum and yumdownloader don't magically know where to find the RPM packages you want to install. You have to tell it where to look using two configuration files:

- **/etc/yum.conf** The yum.conf file is the configuration file for yum. This file defines such things as the software repository URLs and their names where yum will search for packages,

Command	Description
yum install *package_name*	This command installs the specified package.
yum remove *package_name*	This command uninstalls the specified package.
yum list all	This command lists all packages in a repository and packages installed on your system.
yum list installed	This command lists all packages installed on your system.
yum list installed *package_name*	This command checks to see if the specified package is installed on your system.
yum list *package_name*	This command searches the configured repositories for the specified package.
yum list available	This command displays a list of all packages available for installation in the configured repositories.
yum list updates	This command generates a list of updates for all installed packages.
yum list update *package_name*	This command checks for updates for the specified package.
yum info *package_name*	This command displays information about the specified package, including its version and dependencies.
yum whatprovides *path/filename*	This command identifies the RPM package that provides the specified file.
createrepo */path*	This command defines the path to a package repository.

Table 8-1 yum Commands

```
glibc-headers          x86_64     2.13-1                   updates      599 k
kernel-headers         x86_64     2.6.35.11-83.fc14        updates      742 k
libmpc                 x86_64     0.8.1-1.fc13             fedora        44 k
ppl                    x86_64     0.10.2-10.fc12          fedora       1.1 M
Updating for dependencies:
 glibc                 x86_64     2.13-1                   updates      3.8 M
 glibc-common          x86_64     2.13-1                   updates       14 M

Transaction Summary
================================================================================
Install      9 Package(s)
Upgrade      2 Package(s)

Total download size: 43 M
Is this ok [y/N]: y
Downloading Packages:
Setting up and reading Presto delta metadata
fedora/prestodelta                                    | 114 kB    00:00
updates/prestodelta                                   | 852 kB    00:02
Processing delta metadata
Download delta size: 12 M
(1/2): glibc-2.12.90-17_2.13-1.x86_64.drpm            | 1.1 MB    00:04
(2/2): glibc-common-2. (43%) 37% [====      ] 292 kB/s | 4.0 MB    00:23 ETA
```

Figure 8-7 Installing the gcc package with yum

the directory (cachedir) where downloaded packages will be saved, and where the yum log file (logfile) will be saved. This is a sample yum.conf file from a Fedora system:

```
[root@fs3 ~]# cat /etc/yum.conf
[main]
cachedir=/var/cache/yum/$basearch/$releasever
keepcache=0
debuglevel=2
logfile=/var/log/yum.log
exactarch=1
obsoletes=1
gpgcheck=1
plugins=1
installonly_limit=3
color=never
# metadata_expire=90m

# PUT YOUR REPOS HERE OR IN separate files named file.repo
# in /etc/yum.repos.d
```

- **/etc/yum.repos.d/**   Notice in the preceding example that the repository information can be stored in this file or in separate files named *filename*.repo in the /etc/yum.repos.d directory. Even though you're allowed to, you generally won't put your repository configuration information in the yum.conf file. Instead, you will create a separate file for each repository, name it appropriately, and save it in this directory. Here is a listing of repositories for our sample Fedora system:

```
[root@fs3 yum.repos.d]# ls
fedora.repo             fedora-updates-testing.repo
fedora-updates.repo  packagekit-media.repo
```

As you can see in this example, this Fedora system has four yum repositories configured where it will search for packages. An example of a repository configuration file used to store Fedora updates is shown next:

```
 [root@fs3 yum.repos.d]# cat fedora-updates.repo
[updates]
name=Fedora $releasever - $basearch - Updates
failovermethod=priority
#baseurl=http://download.fedoraproject.org/pub/fedora/linux/updates/
$releasever/$basearch/
mirrorlist=https://mirrors.fedoraproject.org/metalink?repo=updates-released-
f$releasever&arch=$basearch
enabled=1
gpgcheck=1
gpgkey=file:///etc/pki/rpm-gpg/RPM-GPG-KEY-fedora-$basearch

[updates-debuginfo]
name=Fedora $releasever - $basearch - Updates – Debug
failovermethod=priority
#baseurl=http://download.fedoraproject.org/pub/fedora/linux/updates/
$releasever/$basearch/debug/
mirrorlist=https://mirrors.fedoraproject.org/metalink?repo=updates-released-
debug-f$releasever&arch=$basearch
enabled=0
gpgcheck=1
```

Element	Description
[repo_name]	Defines a repository.
name=	Defines a name for the repository.
baseurl=	Defines a URL where the file is located. In the examples given in the text, the repositories are located on the Internet. However, you can also define a local repository either on a repo server on your network or even in your local file system. The syntax for baseurl= in these situations is *protocol:///path_to_repo*. For example, if the repository is located on the local hard drive in the /var/repos directory, you would use a baseurl of **file:///var/repos**.
enabled=	Enables (1) or disables (0) the repository.
gpgcheck=	Enables (1) or disables (0) GPG security key checking to validate repository files.
gpgkey=	Specifies the location of the GPG security key.

Table 8-2   yum Repository Configuration File Information

```
gpgkey=file:///etc/pki/rpm-gpg/RPM-GPG-KEY-fedora-$basearch

[updates-source]
name=Fedora $releasever - Updates Source
failovermethod=priority
#baseurl=http://download.fedoraproject.org/pub/fedora/linux/updates/
$releasever/SRPMS/
mirrorlist=https://mirrors.fedoraproject.org/metalink?repo=updates-released-
source-f$releasever&arch=$basearch
enabled=0
gpgcheck=1
gpgkey=file:///etc/pki/rpm-gpg/RPM-GPG-KEY-fedora-$basearch
```

This repository configuration file contains several key elements, as described in Table 8-2.

Installing Software from Source Code

In addition to installing software using a package manager, you can also install software on Linux from source code. In fact, many of the applications and services you will install on a Linux system will be delivered as source code, not as a binary executable. When you install the software on your local system, you actually compile the source code from the installation files into a binary executable that can be run.

For example, let's suppose you wanted to install and configure an FTP service on your local Linux system. You've done some research and determined that the Pure-FTPd service is the one you want to use to set up your FTP server. When you download and extract the installation files, you notice that a directory named src is created. Within this directory are a number of text files that contain the source code for the Pure-FTPd service. An example of one of the source code files for this service is shown here:

```
openSUSE:/home/rtracy/Downloads/pure-ftpd-1.0.29/src # cat main.c
#include <config.h>
#include "ftpd.h"
```

```
int main(int argc, char *argv[])
{
    return pureftpd_start(argc, argv, NULL);
}
```

Distributing software in this manner has many advantages. Key among these is the fact that you don't have to create a separate executable and installation package for each delivery architecture and platform. You can have the installation process detect the type of system the software is being installed on and compile the software appropriately. The key disadvantage to this approach is the fact that it makes the installation process much more complex. Users must have a compiler installed on their system; otherwise, they won't be able to compile the source code into a binary executable. In addition, the user must know the proper procedure for compiling the source code and installing the resulting executable.

Fortunately, a standard process for completing this task has been adopted by most developers. This process is composed of the following elements:

- Preparing the installation files
- Compiling the executable
- Installing the executable
- Uninstalling software compiled from source code

Let's begin by discussing how to prepare the installation files.

Preparing the Installation Files

The first step in installing an application from source code is to download the appropriate installation files from the Internet. For example, if you wanted to install the pure-ftpd service we've used in the preceding examples, you would navigate to the appropriate website and download the installation files.

One thing you'll notice about installation files used to install from source code is that they are usually distributed as a tarball file (tarred and gzipped). Tarball files usually have a .tar.gz extension. Because these applications are distributed as tarballs, you must first unzip and untar them after downloading them from the Internet before you can do anything else. This is done using the tar command. The tar command is used to create archive files. It can also be used to extract files from archives such as tarballs.

To do this on your system, switch to the directory where you downloaded the tarball using the cd command from the shell prompt. Then enter **tar –zxvf** *filename*. The –z option tells tar to use gzip to decompress the tarball first. The –x option tells tar to extract the files from the decompressed archive file. The –v option tells tar to operate verbosely, displaying each file onscreen as it is processed. The –f option tells tar the name of the file to extract.

For example, suppose you downloaded the pure-ftpd-1.0.29.tar.gz file. To extract this file, you would enter **tar –zxvf pure-ftpd-1.0.29.tar.gz** at the shell prompt. The files are extracted to a directory named pure-ftpd-1.0.29 in the current directory. This directory contains the source code files that will be used to create the executable program. It also contains a variety of utilities needed to help create the executable. These are shown here:

```
openSUSE:/home/rtracy/Downloads/pure-ftpd-1.0.29 # ls
AUTHORS                         README.Donations        depcomp
CONTACT                         README.LDAP             gui
COPYING                         README.MacOS-X          install-sh
ChangeLog                       README.MySQL            m4
FAQ                             README.PGSQL            man
HISTORY                         README.TLS              missing
INSTALL                         README.Virtual-Users    pam
Makefile.am                     README.Windows          pure-ftpd.png
Makefile.gui                    THANKS                  pure-ftpd.spec
Makefile.in                     aclocal.m4              pure-ftpd.spec.in
NEWS                            compile                 puredb
README                          config.h.in             pureftpd-ldap.conf
README.Authentication-Modules   configuration-file      pureftpd-mysql.conf
README.Configuration-File       configure               pureftpd-pgsql.conf
README.Contrib                  configure.ac            pureftpd.schema
README.Debian                   contrib                 src
```

With the files extracted, you next need to prepare the installation files to be compiled. This is done using the configure command shown in the preceding example. To run this command, first verify that you're in the directory created when the tarball was extracted; then enter **./configure** at the shell prompt, as shown here:

```
openSUSE:/home/rtracy/Downloads/pure-ftpd-1.0.29 # ./configure
checking for a BSD-compatible install... /usr/bin/install -c
checking whether build environment is sane... yes
checking for a thread-safe mkdir -p... /bin/mkdir -p
checking for gawk... gawk
checking whether make sets $(MAKE)... yes
checking for ranlib... ranlib
checking for gcc... gcc
checking whether the C compiler works... yes
checking for C compiler default output file name... a.out
...
```

The configure file is a script that does two things when it is run. First, it checks your system to make sure all the necessary components required to compile the program are available. One of the most important things it checks for is the existence of a compiler compatible with the C programming language. If you don't have a C compiler, such as the GNU C Compiler (gcc) or the GNU C++ Compiler (gcc-c++), the configure command will display an error on the screen instructing you to install a compiler and then run configure again. It also verifies that your overall system environment is compatible with the program you're going to install.

Second, it also creates a very important file called Makefile. Because most source code applications are designed to be deployed on a variety of distributions and architectures, the installation program needs to know how to customize the source code files such that the resulting executable will run on your particular system. One of the last things the configure script does is create a series of Makefile files. The Makefile file contains specific instructions for how the executable should be compiled to run on your platform.

Although not required, it's usually a good idea to check the Makefile file after running configure to verify that the program is going to be installed in the manner you want. If you see something you want to change, you can use a text editor to make the appropriate changes and save the file.

Once configure has been run and the Makefile file is ready, the next step in the process is to actually compile the executable. Let's discuss how this is done next.

Compiling the Executable

At this point in the process, the program you want to install still exists only as source code in your file system. Before you can run it, you must convert the text-based source code into a binary executable file. This is done using the make command. The make command calls your system's C compiler (such as gcc) and directs it to read the source code files, using the specifications and options listed in the Makefile file, and generate a compiled executable file. This is done by entering **make** at the shell prompt without any options while you are still in the directory created when you untarred the tarball file. Here is an example:

```
openSUSE:/home/rtracy/Downloads/pure-ftpd-1.0.29 # make
make  all-recursive
make[1]: Entering directory '/home/tux/Downloads/pure-ftpd-1.0.29'
Making all in puredb
make[2]: Entering directory '/home/tux/Downloads/pure-ftpd-1.0.29/puredb'
Making all in src
make[3]: Entering directory '/home/tux/Downloads/pure-ftpd-1.0.29/puredb/src'
gcc -DHAVE_CONFIG_H -I. -I../..   -I/usr/local/include -DCONFDIR=\"/etc\" -
DSTATEDIR=\"/var\"  -g -O2 -MT puredb_read.o -MD -MP -MF .deps/puredb_read.
Tpo -c
-o puredb_read.o puredb_read.c
mv -f .deps/puredb_read.Tpo .deps/puredb_read.Po
rm -f libpuredb_read.a
ar cru libpuredb_read.a puredb_read.o
...
```

Be aware, however, that make only creates the executable. Before you can use it, it needs to be actually installed on the system; doing this will copy the executable, startup scripts, and documentation files to the appropriate directories in your file system. Let's discuss how this is done next.

Installing the Executable

To actually install the program on your system, you use the make command a second time. However, this time you specify a target with make install. This tells make to install the program using the information specified in the INSTALL portion of the Makefile file.

To do this, make sure you're still in the directory created when you untarred the tarball file. Then enter **make install** at the shell prompt. The make utility will then follow the instructions in the Makefile file to install the application, as shown here:

```
openSUSE:/home/rtracy/Downloads/pure-ftpd-1.0.29 # make install
Making install in puredb
make[1]: Entering directory '/home/tux/Downloads/pure-ftpd-1.0.29/puredb'
Making install in src
make[2]: Entering directory '/home/tux/Downloads/pure-ftpd-1.0.29/puredb/src'
```

```
make[3]: Entering directory '/home/tux/Downloads/pure-ftpd-1.0.29/puredb/src'
make[3]: Nothing to be done for 'install-exec-am'.
make[3]: Nothing to be done for 'install-data-am'.
...
```

At this point, the application or service is ready to run. Simply enter the appropriate commands at the shell prompt.

Let's practice installing software from source code in the following exercise.

Exercise 8-5: Building Software from Source Code

In this exercise, you will practice installing the Pure-FTPd software from a tarball. You can perform this exercise using the virtual machine that comes with this book. Run snapshot 8-3 for the correctly configured environment.

 VIDEO   Please watch the Exercise 8-5 video for a demonstration on how to perform this task.

Complete the following:

1. With your system running, open a terminal session.

2. Change to your root user account by entering **su –** followed by a password of **student**.

3. Use the **cd** command to change to your home directory. This is where the Pure-FTPd tarball file is saved. Use the **ls** command to view the file's name.

4. At the shell prompt, enter **tar –zxvf ./pure-ftpd-*version*.tar.gz**. Replace *version* with the current version number of the tarball you downloaded.

 TIP   You can use the tab complete feature of Linux to make entering these commands easier. To use tab complete, enter **tar –zxvf ./pure-** and then press TAB. The rest of the filename will be automatically filled in for you!

5. Use the **cd** command to change to the directory created by tar. This should be pure-ftpd-*version*.

6. Enter **ls** to view the files extracted from the tarball.

7. At the shell prompt, enter **./configure**. The configure script will check your system and verify that the software can be installed. You must have a C compiler installed on your system. If configure reports that you're missing a compiler, locate the gcc RPM package on your distribution CD and install it by entering **rpm –i** at the shell prompt. Be warned, however, that gcc has many dependencies, so you may want to use yum or a graphical software installation utility to expedite the install!

8. When the configure script is done, compile the executable by entering **make** at the shell prompt.

9. When the compilation is complete, install the executable by entering **make install** at the shell prompt.

10. Start the service by entering **/usr/local/sbin/pure-ftpd &** at the shell prompt.

11. Test the system by entering **ftp localhost** at the shell prompt.

12. When prompted, enter a username of **anonymous**. You should be logged in to the FTP server at this point.

13. Close the connection by entering **quit**.

At this point, you have a functioning FTP server running on your Linux system!

 NOTE It won't be accessible by other workstations yet because your system's host firewall is probably blocking traffic on the IP ports used by the FTP protocol.

In addition to installing software from source code, you can also uninstall it. Let's discuss how this is done next.

Uninstalling Software Compiled from Source Code

The process for uninstalling software of this variety is very similar to the installation process.

For most applications or services that are installed using the standard build process we discussed earlier, you must (in most cases) have access to your installation files to uninstall the associated software. The issue here is that many Linux administrators delete the installation source files once the installation process is complete to save disk space. If you do this, you've just deleted the files you'll need if you ever decide to uninstall the software. I recommend that you create a protected directory in your file system somewhere that only root can access and keep your source installation files in it. Yes, it does take up a little bit of disk space, but you'll have the files you need if uninstalling ever becomes necessary.

The uninstall process can vary slightly from product to product. Some applications or services may include an uninstall script in the files you extract from the tarball. If this is the case, you can execute this script to uninstall the application from your system.

Other products may include an UNINSTALL target in their Makefile file. If this is the case, you must first run configure from the directory created when you originally extracted the downloaded tarball file, just as you did when you first installed the software. Then, instead of running **make install**, you run **make uninstall**. This will cause the make utility to follow the instructions in the uninstall portion of the Makefile file to remove the software from your system. For example, you can use the make uninstall command to remove the Pure-FTPd service from the system.

How do you know what method to use? The tarball you downloaded should include a README file of some sort that documents both the install and uninstall processes for the particular software you are working with. Check this file first. If the information isn't available, then check the FAQ or knowledge base on the website of the organization that produced the software. One of these resources should provide you with the steps you need to follow to uninstall the software.

It's time to shift gears and look at managing Debian software packages.

Managing Debian Software Packages

Not all distributions use RPM to manage software packages. Distributions based on the Debian distribution use the Debian Package Manager (dpkg) instead. Ubuntu is probably one of the most popular Debian-based distributions that uses dpkg to manage software, instead of RPM. Debian packages are similar to RPMs in functionality but are totally different in the way they are implemented.

 NOTE Occasionally, I encounter folks who mistakenly think RPM and Debian packages are cross-platform compatible. They are not. You can only install RPM packages on RPM-based systems and Debian packages on Debian-based systems. However, you can use a utility called **alien** to convert packages between formats.

In this part of the chapter, we'll discuss how to manage Debian software packages. The following topics will be addressed:

- Debian package naming
- Installing packages with dpkg
- Viewing package information with apt-cache
- Installing packages with apt-get
- Using aptitude

Let's begin by looking at the naming convention used by Debian packages.

Debian Package Naming

Debian packages use a naming convention that is similar to that used by RPM packages. The syntax is *packagename_version_architecture*.deb (for example, 3dchess_0.8.1-16_i386.deb).

Here's a breakdown of how to interpret Debian package filenames:

- *packagename* Like an RPM package name, this simply provides the name of the package. In the example here, the name of the application in the package is **3dchess**.
- *version* Specifies the version number of the package. In this example, it is **0.8.1-16**.
- *architecture* Specifies the hardware architecture the package will run on. In the example here, **i386** indicates the package will run on Intel 80386 or later CPUs.

Like RPM packages, Debian packages include dependency information. Before a given package can be installed, all of the other packages it is dependent upon must be installed first.

 TIP You can download a wealth of Debian packages from http://packages .debian.org.

With this in mind, let's discuss how you go about installing Debian packages.

Installing Packages with dpkg

As with RPM packages, you have two options on most distributions for installing Debian packages. The first is to use a nice graphical utility. For example, on Ubuntu you can use the Ubuntu Software Center by selecting Applications | Ubuntu Software Center. This utility allows you to use a GUI menu system to manage your Debian packages, as shown in Figure 8-8.

Just like the RPM graphical utilities we looked at earlier, the Ubuntu Software Center allows you to install new packages, remove installed packages, and update installed packages. It downloads packages from its configured repositories. It also automatically calculates package dependencies and installs them for you.

However, as nice as these graphical package management utilities may be, they aren't covered on the LPCI-1/Linux+ exam. To pass this exam, you have to know how to manage packages using command-line tools.

The key command-line utility used to manage Debian packages is dpkg. The syntax for using dpkg is

```
dpkg options action package_name or package_filename
```

You can use the actions and options listed in Tables 8-3 and 8-4 with the dpkg command.

For example, if you download a package named 3dchess_0.8.1-16_i386.deb and want to install it, you would first use the cd command at the shell prompt to change to the directory

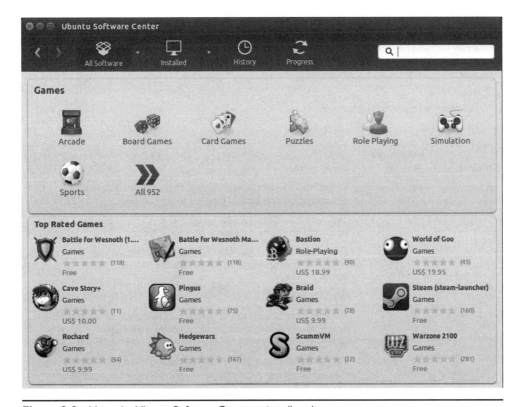

Figure 8-8   Using the Ubuntu Software Center to install packages

Action	Description
–i	Installs the specified package.
–r	Uninstalls the specified package but does not delete its configuration files.
–P	Uninstalls the specified package and deletes all of its configuration files.
--configure	Reconfigures the specified package (can also be done with dpkg-reconfigure).
–p	Displays information about the specified package. The package must already be installed.
–I	Displays information about a package that isn't currently installed on the system.
–l	Lists all installed packages on the system.
–L	Lists all files that were installed by the specified package on the system.
–S *filename*	Identifies the package that installed the specified file.

Table 8-3   dpkg Command Actions

where the file resides. Then, as root, you would enter **dpkg –i 3dchess_0.8.1-16_i386.deb** at the shell prompt, as shown in this example:

```
rtracy@Ubuntu-Desktop:~$ su -
Password:
root@Ubuntu-Desktop:~# cd /home/rtracy/Downloads
root@Ubuntu-Desktop:/home/rtracy/Downloads# ls
3dchess_0.8.1-16_i386.deb
root@Ubuntu-Desktop:/home/rtracy/Downloads# dpkg -i 3dchess_0.8.1-16_i386.deb
(Reading database ... 138218 files and directories currently installed.)
Unpacking 3dchess (from 3dchess_0.8.1-16_i386.deb) ...
Setting up 3dchess (0.8.1-16) ...

Processing triggers for desktop-file-utils ...
Processing triggers for man-db ...
```

Option	Associated Action	Description
–B	–r	When you're uninstalling a package that other packages are dependent on, this option disables those packages.
–G	–i	This option tells dpkg to not install the specified package if a newer version of the same package is already installed.
–E	–i	This option tells dpkg to not install the specified package if the same version of that package is already installed.
--ignore	–i or –r	This option causes dpkg to ignore dependency information when installing or removing a package.
--no-act	–i or –r	This option tells dpkg to check for problems, such as unresolved dependencies, when installing or removing a package.
--recursive	–i	This option allows you to install multiple packages at once using * in the package filename part of the command. All matching packages in the current directory as well as subdirectories will be installed.

Table 8-4   dpkg Command Options

Notice in this command that I had to enter the full filename of the package because it wasn't installed yet. After the package has been installed, you can refer to it by just the package name. For example, to view information about the 3dchess package we just installed, you would enter **dpkg –p 3dchess**, as shown in this example:

```
root@Ubuntu-Desktop:/home/rtracy/Downloads# dpkg -p 3dchess
Package: 3dchess
Priority: optional
Section: games
Installed-Size: 144
Maintainer: Debian Games Team pkg-games-devel@lists.alioth.debian.org
Architecture: i386
Version: 0.8.1-16
Depends: libc6 (>= 2.7-1), libx11-6, libxext6, libxmu6, libxpm4, libxt6,
xaw3dg
(>= 1.5+E-1)
Size: 34932
Description: 3D chess for X11
 3 dimensional Chess game for X11R6.  There are three boards, stacked
 vertically; 96 pieces of which most are the traditional chess pieces with
 just a couple of additions; 26 possible directions in which to move.  The
 AI isn't wonderful, but provides a challenging enough game to all but the
 most highly skilled players.
```

Likewise, you could uninstall the 3dchess package using the **dpkg –r 3dchess** command, as shown here:

```
root@Ubuntu-Desktop:/home/rtracy/Downloads# dpkg -r 3dchess
(Reading database ... 138218 files and directories currently installed.)
Removing 3dchess ...
Processing triggers for man-db ...
Processing triggers for desktop-file-utils ...
```

Now that you know how to manage packages with dpkg, let's next look at the apt-cache command.

Viewing Package Information with apt-cache

In addition to dpkg, you can also use several apt (Advanced Package Tool) tools to manage packages on a Debian-based system. The first apt tool you need to be familiar with is apt-cache. This command is comparable to the rpm –q command in that it is used to query package information from the Debian package database (called the *package cache*). Common apt-cache commands are shown in Table 8-5.

For example, to see if the 3dchess package we were working with previously is installed on the system, you could enter **apt-cache pkgnames 3dchess** at the shell prompt, as shown in this example:

```
root@Ubuntu-Desktop:~# apt-cache pkgnames 3dchess
3dchess
```

Common apt-cache Command	Description
apt-cache showpkg *package_name* or apt-cache show *package_name*	Displays information about the package.
apt-cache stats	Displays the number of packages installed, dependency information, and other package cache statistics.
apt-cache unmet	Reports any missing dependencies in the package cache.
apt-cache depends *package_name*	Displays all of the package's dependencies.
apt-cache pkgnames *package_name*	Checks to see whether or not a package is installed on the system. Leaving out the package name displays a list of all the packages installed on the system.
apt-cache search *keyword*	Searches package descriptions for the specified keyword.

Table 8-5   Common apt-cache Commands

To view information about the 3dchess package, you could enter **apt-cache showpkg 3dchess** at the shell prompt, as shown next:

```
root@Ubuntu-Desktop:~# apt-cache showpkg 3dchess
Package: 3dchess
Versions:
0.8.1-16 (/var/lib/apt/lists/us.archive.ubuntu.com_ubuntu_dists_karmic_
universe_binary-
i386_Packages)
 Description Language:
               File: /var/lib/apt/lists/us.archive.ubuntu.com_ubuntu_dists_
karmic_universe_binary-
i386_Packages
               MD5: c8da6105051b2cae45e59fac61bb2a2a
0.8.1-16 (/var/lib/dpkg/status)
 Description Language:
               File: /var/lib/dpkg/status
               MD5: c8da6105051b2cae45e59fac61bb2a2a
Reverse Depends:
Dependencies:
0.8.1-16 - libc6 (2 2.4) libx11-6 (0 (null)) libxext6 (0 (null)) libxmu6
(0 (null)) libxpm4 (0 (null)) libxt6 (0 (null)) xaw3dg (2 1.5+E-1)
0.8.1-16 - libc6 (2 2.7-1) libx11-6 (0 (null)) libxext6 (0 (null)) libxmu6
(0 (null)) libxpm4 (0 (null)) libxt6 (0 (null)) xaw3dg (2 1.5+E-1)
Provides:
0.8.1-16 -
0.8.1-16 -
Reverse Provides:
```

To view the 3dchess package's dependency information, you enter **apt-cache depends 3dchess** at the shell prompt, as shown here:

```
root@Ubuntu-Desktop:~# apt-cache depends 3dchess
3dchess
  Depends: libc6
  Depends: libx11-6
  Depends: libxext6
```

```
Depends: libxmu6
Depends: libxpm4
Depends: libxt6
Depends: xaw3dg
```

Now that you understand how to use apt-cache, you next need to learn about apt-get.

Installing Packages with apt-get

In addition to apt-cache, the apt suite of tools also includes the apt-get utility, which is the equivalent of the yum utility on an RPM system. It automatically downloads and installs packages (along with all dependent packages) for you.

The /etc/apt/sources.list file defines the repositories from where apt-get can install packages. As with yum, these repositories can reside on a local optical disc (such as your installation disc), a local hard drive, or a server on the Internet (via the HTTP or FTP protocol). A sample sources .list file is shown here:

```
root@Ubuntu-Desktop:/etc/apt# cat sources.list
#deb cdrom:[Ubuntu 9.10 _Karmic Koala_ - Release i386 (20091028.5)]/
karmic main restricted
deb http://us.archive.ubuntu.com/ubuntu/ karmic main restricted
deb-src http://us.archive.ubuntu.com/ubuntu/ karmic main restricted
deb http://us.archive.ubuntu.com/ubuntu/ karmic universe
deb-src http://us.archive.ubuntu.com/ubuntu/ karmic universe
deb http://us.archive.ubuntu.com/ubuntu/ karmic-updates universe
deb-src http://us.archive.ubuntu.com/ubuntu/ karmic-updates universe
deb http://us.archive.ubuntu.com/ubuntu/ karmic multiverse
deb-src http://us.archive.ubuntu.com/ubuntu/ karmic multiverse
deb http://us.archive.ubuntu.com/ubuntu/ karmic-updates multiverse
deb-src http://us.archive.ubuntu.com/ubuntu/ karmic-updates multiverse
deb http://security.ubuntu.com/ubuntu karmic-security main restricted
deb-src http://security.ubuntu.com/ubuntu karmic-security main restricted
deb http://security.ubuntu.com/ubuntu karmic-security universe
deb-src http://security.ubuntu.com/ubuntu karmic-security universe
deb http://security.ubuntu.com/ubuntu karmic-security multiverse
deb-src http://security.ubuntu.com/ubuntu karmic-security multiverse
```

Package repositories are identified in this file with the prefix *deb,* whereas source file repositories are identified with *deb-src.* After the prefix, the URL to the repository is specified.

The syntax for using apt-get is pretty straightforward:

```
apt-get options command package_name
```

Commonly used apt-get commands and options are listed in Tables 8-6 and 8-7, respectively.

For example, if you wanted to install a new package with apt-get, you would enter (as root) **apt-get install** *package_name*. If you wanted to install the Blender 3-D modeling software, you would enter **apt-get install blender** at the shell prompt of the system. Here is an example:

```
root@Ubuntu-Desktop:~# apt-get install blender
Reading package lists... Done
Building dependency tree
Reading state information... Done
The following packages were automatically installed and are no longer
required:
```

apt-get Command	Description
install	Installs the latest version of a specified package
remove	Removes the specified package
update	Displays updated information about all packages available in your configured package repositories
upgrade	Upgrades all installed packages to the newest version
dist-upgrade	Upgrades all installed packages to the newest version, but avoids upgrading packages if the upgrade would break a dependency
check	Verifies the integrity of installed packages as well as the package database
clean	Removes outdated information from the package database

Table 8-6 Common apt-get Commands

```
    linux-headers-2.6.31-14 xaw3dg linux-headers-2.6.31-14-generic
Use 'apt-get autoremove' to remove them.
The following extra packages will be installed:
  cvs gettext libalut0 libavcodec52 libavdevice52 libavformat52 libavutil49
  libdc1394-22 libftgl2 libgsm1 libopenal1 libopenjpeg2 libschroedinger-1.0-0
  libswscale0 ttf-dejavu ttf-dejavu-extra
Suggested packages:
  yafray gettext-doc
The following NEW packages will be installed:
  blender cvs gettext libalut0 libavcodec52 libavdevice52 libavformat52
  libavutil49 libdc1394-22 libftgl2 libgsm1 libopenal1 libopenjpeg2
  libschroedinger-1.0-0 libswscale0 ttf-dejavu ttf-dejavu-extra
0 upgraded, 17 newly installed, 0 to remove and 276 not upgraded.
Need to get 23.2MB of archives.
After this operation, 61.0MB of additional disk space will be used.
Do you want to continue [Y/n]? Y
```

apt–get Option	Associated Command	Description
–d	upgrade install	Downloads the specified package but doesn't install it
–s	All commands	Simulates the actions associated with the specified command but doesn't actually perform them
–f	install remove	Checks for unmet dependencies and fixes them, if possible
–q	All commands	Suppresses progress information
–y	All commands	Sends a default **yes** answer to any prompts displayed in the action
--no-upgrade		Tells apt-get not to upgrade a package if an older version of the package has already been installed

Table 8-7 Common apt-get Options

As you can see in this example, apt-get located the Blender package in one of its configured repositories, calculated dependencies, and then prompted the user to begin the download of the required packages prior to installing them. How easy is that? Here are some more sample apt-get commands:

- **apt-get upgrade** *package_name*   Upgrades the package to the newest version
- **apt-get remove** *package_name*   Uninstalls the specified package
- **apt-get dist-upgrade**   Upgrades all packages installed on the system

Next, let's look at using the aptitude utility.

Using aptitude

All the apt tools we have looked at thus far in this chapter have been command-line utilities. However, this tool suite also provides a text-based, menu-driven package management utility that is really handy, called aptitude. You run aptitude by simply entering **aptitude** at the shell prompt. When you do, the interface shown in Figure 8-9 is displayed.

You can use aptitude to do just about anything you can do with dpkg or apt-get. You can install packages, uninstall packages, and update packages. For example, to install a new package, you would arrow down to and select Not Installed Packages; then you would browse to the package

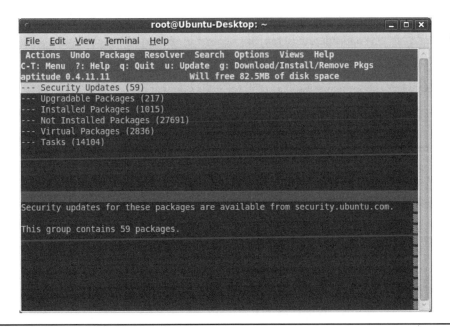

Figure 8-9   Using aptitude to manage packages

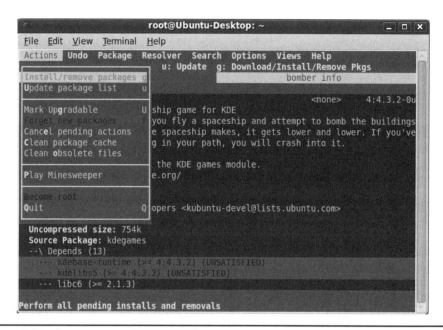

Figure 8-10   Accessing aptitude menus

you want to install and press G. You can also press CTRL-T to access the aptitude menus, as shown in Figure 8-10. The aptitude utility can also be used in command-line mode using the syntax shown in Table 8-8.

Now that you understand how to manage both RPM and Debian packages on a Linux system, you need to learn about managing shared libraries. Let's do that next.

aptitude Command	Description
aptitude install *package_name*	Downloads and installs the specified package
aptitude remove *package_name*	Uninstalls the specified package
aptitude purge *package_name*	Uninstalls the specified package and also deletes its associated configuration files and data files
aptitude update	Updates the list of available packages
aptitude full-upgrade	Upgrades all the installed packages on your system to the latest version
aptitude search *search_term*	Searches for patterns that contain the specified search term

Table 8-8   Command-Line aptitude Commands

Managing Shared Libraries

In addition to checking for software package dependencies, you may also need to verify that your system is configured properly to access the libraries an application needs to run. In this part of the chapter, you will learn how to do this. The following topics are addressed:

- How shared libraries work
- Managing shared library dependencies

Let's begin by discussing how shared libraries work.

How Shared Libraries Work

On Linux, applications running on the system can share code elements called *shared libraries*. This is very useful. Shared libraries make it such that software developers don't have to reinvent the wheel each time they write a new program.

If you think about it, many functions are commonly used across many programs. For example, the process for opening a file, saving a file, and closing an open file are the same no matter what application is being used. Without shared libraries, programmers would have to include the code for completing these basic tasks in each application they write. What a waste of time and resources!

Instead, with shared libraries, software developers can focus on the code elements that are unique to the individual application. For common elements that are shared across applications, they can simply link to the prewritten code in a shared library and not worry about rewriting the code.

 TIP Shared libraries in Linux work in much the same manner as dynamic link libraries (DLLs) on Windows systems.

Using shared libraries has many benefits. Obviously, it dramatically speeds up development time. It also makes the programs being written smaller and leaner.

There are two types of shared libraries on Linux:

- **Dynamic**   Dynamic shared libraries exist as files in the Linux file system. Programmers simply insert links to the functions in these shared libraries in their program code. The functions are called from the dynamic shared libraries when the program is run, not integrated into the program itself. A configuration file on the system contains a list of installed dynamic shared libraries and where they are located in the file system. Using dynamic shared libraries decreases the overall size of the executable after it's compiled. However, they do create a dependency issue. If the program calls a function from a dynamic shared library that isn't installed on the system (or has become unavailable for some reason), the application will malfunction.

- **Static**   In contrast to dynamic shared libraries, static shared libraries are linked statically into the program when it's compiled. In essence, with static libraries, the actual code elements for the functions called are integrated directly into the application itself. Obviously, this results in larger applications. However, it has the advantage of making the application independent of having the shared libraries installed on the system where it is running, as is the case with dynamic libraries.

Which type is best? It depends on the application. Most applications you will use on a day-to-day basis use dynamic shared libraries. This allows them to provide a lot of functionality with a relatively small footprint on the hard drive. However, there are many applications that use static libraries, especially applications that are designed to help you rescue a malfunctioning system. Instead of linking to dynamic shared libraries (which may not be available in a system rescue scenario), these applications are completely self-contained and can run in a minimal Linux environment.

 NOTE A good example of an application that uses static shared libraries is the Stand-Alone Shell (sash). It's designed to help you rescue a kaput Linux system and has many functions built in to the shell itself. That way, if the partition where the shared libraries reside is toast, the program can still run and allow you to perform useful tasks to rescue the system.

Shared library files use a special naming format to help you identify the type of shared library it is. This syntax is as follows:

```
libname.type.version
```

Notice that the filename of all shared libraries starts with *lib*. It is followed by the name of the shared library. The *type* part of the filename identifies the type of shared library. The characters "so" here indicate the file is a dynamic shared library, whereas "a" indicates the file is a static library. The *version* part of the filename specifies the version number of the library. For example, libfreetype.so.6.4.0 is a dynamic shared library.

With this in mind, let's discuss how you manage shared library dependencies.

Managing Shared Library Dependencies

As noted earlier, Linux uses a configuration file to tell applications running on the system where they can find the dynamic shared library files on the system. Using this type of configuration provides application developers with a degree of independence. They don't have to worry about where the shared libraries will reside when their programs are run. They let the configuration file tell the program where they are, wherever that happens to be on a particular Linux system.

The dynamic shared library configuration file is /etc/ld.so.conf. Here is a sample file:

```
openSUSE:/etc # cat ld.so.conf
/usr/X11R6/lib64/Xaw3d
/usr/X11R6/lib64
/usr/lib64/Xaw3d
/usr/X11R6/lib/Xaw3d
/usr/X11R6/lib
/usr/lib/Xaw3d
/usr/x86_64-suse-linux/lib
/usr/local/lib
/opt/kde3/lib
/lib64
/lib
/usr/lib64
/usr/lib
/usr/local/lib64
/opt/kde3/lib64
include /etc/ld.so.conf.d/*.conf
```

As you can see in this example, the file simply contains a list of paths in the file system where shared library files are stored. Applications that are linked to functions in these files can search through these paths to locate the appropriate libraries.

 TIP The /lib/ and /usr/lib/ directories are always assumed to contain shared libraries, so they aren't listed in the /etc/ld.so.conf file.

To view a list of all shared libraries available on your Linux system, enter **ldconfig –p** at the shell prompt. Here is an example:

```
openSUSE:~ # ldconfig -p
1423 libs found in cache '/etc/ld.so.cache'
    libzypp.so.706 (libc6,x86-64) => /usr/lib64/libzypp.so.706
    libzio.so.0 (libc6,x86-64) => /usr/lib64/libzio.so.0
    libz.so.1 (libc6,x86-64) => /lib64/libz.so.1
    libz.so.1 (libc6) => /lib/libz.so.1
    libz.so (libc6,x86-64) => /usr/lib64/libz.so
    liby2util.so.4 (libc6,x86-64) => /usr/lib64/liby2util.so.4
    liby2.so.2 (libc6,x86-64) => /usr/lib64/liby2.so.2
    libyui.so.3 (libc6,x86-64) => /usr/lib64/libyui.so.3
    libycpvalues.so.3 (libc6,x86-64) => /usr/lib64/libycpvalues.so.3
...
```

 NOTE If you're not logged in as root, you must specify the full path to ldconfig in the command (/sbin/ldconfig).

You can also view the shared libraries required by a specific application using the ldd command. The syntax is **ldd –v** *executable_filename*. For example, if you wanted to see what shared libraries are required by the ip command (which is used to manage network connections), you would enter **ldd –v /sbin/ip** at the shell prompt.

 NOTE You need to specify the full path to the executable along with the executable's filename with the ldd command.

An example is shown next:

```
openSUSE:~ # ldd -v /sbin/ip
    linux-vdso.so.1 =>  (0x00007fffe4ab2000)
    libdl.so.2 => /lib64/libdl.so.2 (0x00007f7c07e7d000)
    libc.so.6 => /lib64/libc.so.6 (0x00007f7c07b1d000)
    /lib64/ld-linux-x86-64.so.2 (0x00007f7c08081000)

    Version information:
    /sbin/ip:
        libdl.so.2 (GLIBC_2.2.5) => /lib64/libdl.so.2
        libc.so.6 (GLIBC_2.7) => /lib64/libc.so.6
        libc.so.6 (GLIBC_2.4) => /lib64/libc.so.6
```

```
        libc.so.6 (GLIBC_2.3.4) => /lib64/libc.so.6
        libc.so.6 (GLIBC_2.2.5) => /lib64/libc.so.6
  /lib64/libdl.so.2:
        ld-linux-x86-64.so.2 (GLIBC_PRIVATE) => /lib64/ld-linux-x86-64.so.2
        libc.so.6 (GLIBC_PRIVATE) => /lib64/libc.so.6
        libc.so.6 (GLIBC_2.2.5) => /lib64/libc.so.6
  /lib64/libc.so.6:
        ld-linux-x86-64.so.2 (GLIBC_PRIVATE) => /lib64/ld-linux-x86-64.so.2
        ld-linux-x86-64.so.2 (GLIBC_2.3) => /lib64/ld-linux-x86-64.so.2
```

One of the key uses for the ldd command is to check for shared library dependencies. It determines whether all of the libraries required by the application in question have been installed. If they have, you won't see any error messages, as shown in the preceding example. If a library file is missing, an error message will be displayed. You can then locate and install the missing library and all will be well with the world.

So, how does an application know which directories to look in when trying to locate a shared library? The applications don't actually check the /etc/ld.so.conf conf file. Instead, they check the library cache and the LD_LIBRARY_PATH environment variable. The library cache is /etc/ld.so.cache. This file contains a list of all the system libraries and is refreshed when the system is initially booted.

This is key. If you add a new dynamic library directory to the /etc/ld.so.conf file, you'll be very frustrated when you try to run the applications that are linked to the libraries in this directory. That's because the library cache hasn't been updated with the new information. To fix this, you have two options:

- *Use ldconfig*. The ldconfig command is used to rebuild the library cache manually.

- *Set LD_LIBRARY_PATH*. You can also add the path to the LD_LIBRARY_PATH environment variable. You probably want to add the new path to the end of the list of directories that may already exist in the variable, so you should use the following commands:

```
set LD_LIBRARY_PATH=$LD_LIBRARY_PATH;new_path
export LD_LIBRARY_PATH
```

Generally speaking, the first option is the preferred one. This ensures the shared libraries are always available to the applications that need them, even if the system is rebooted. I usually set the value of LD_LIBRARY_PATH only in situations where I have two versions of the same shared library installed in different directories and I want to use one version over the other.

Exercise 8-6: Working with Shared Libraries

In this exercise, you will practice managing shared libraries. You can perform this exercise using the virtual machine that comes with this book. Run snapshot 8-3 for the correctly configured environment.

 VIDEO   Please watch the Exercise 8-6 video for a demonstration on how to perform this task.

Complete the following:

1. With your system running, open a terminal session.

2. If necessary, change to your root user account by entering **su –** followed by your root user's password.

3. View the shared libraries used by the ping executable on your system by entering **ldd –v /bin/ping** at the shell prompt. You should see that ping requires the libc.so.6 shared library.

4. Find the location of the lib64/libc.so.6 library file on your system by entering **find / –name libc.so.6** at the shell prompt. On a 32-bit system, you should see that the file resides in /lib. On a 64-bit system, it probably resides in /lib64.

5. View your system's library cache by entering **ldconfig –p** at the shell prompt.

6. Rebuild your library cache by entering **ldconfig –v** at the shell prompt.

That's it for this chapter! Terms such as *apt, tarball,* and *rpm* should no longer frighten you because you know how to effectively manage software on a Linux system!

Chapter Review

In this chapter, we discussed how you go about managing software on a Linux system. I first pointed out that you can use either graphical or command-line tools to manage software on a Linux system. I emphasized that a good Linux admin shouldn't be dependent on the graphical tools to manage software. He or she should also know how to use command-line software management tools. I also pointed out that not all software can be managed using graphical utilities. In fact, the LPIC-1/Linux+ exam focuses strictly on command-line utilities.

We first looked at managing RPM packages. I pointed out that RPM stores information about installed packages in the RPM database file (/var/lib/rpm). I spent time reviewing the various resources available to you for obtaining Linux software. These include the following:

- Your installation CD or DVD
- Open source project websites
- www.rpmfind.net
- www.sourceforge.net
- linux.tucows.com
- www.freshmeat.net
- www.linux.org

I pointed out that you should verify your downloads using checksums whenever possible. You can generate a checksum using the sum command on the file you downloaded and compare it to the checksum provided on the website where you obtained it.

You should be familiar with the process for installing software using RPM packages. I pointed out that you have to use a package manager to manage packaged software, such as the Red Hat Package Manager (RPM). RPM packages are precompiled software packages that the package manager can install on your system. Because they are precompiled, you need to verify that a given package is compatible with your system before installing it. To do this, you need to review the package filename. The package filename includes the following information:

- Package name
- Version number
- Release number
- Compatible distribution (optional)
- Architecture type

You can enter **rpm --checksig** to verify the digital signature of an RPM package before you install it. You can then enter **rpm –i** to actually install the package file on your system. I pointed out that many RPM packages are dependent on other packages being installed on the system for them to work properly. If these packages aren't present, the software won't run. The rpm utility automatically checks to see if dependent software is installed before it installs a new package. You can also run **rpm --test** to check for dependencies before installing.

You should also be familiar with the process you need to follow to uninstall software from your Linux system. To uninstall an RPM package, you enter **rpm –e**.

I also pointed out that you can use the rpm command to update an existing package to a newer version. This is done using the rpm –U command. The rpm command can also be used to query and verify RPM packages. To query a package, you use the –q option with rpm. To verify a package, you use the –V option. If you determine that a package has been damaged, you can reinstall an existing package by entering **rpm –U --replacepkgs**.

Next, we looked at using the yum command as an alternative to rpm. I pointed out that yum allows you to download and then install a package and all its dependencies with a single command. We looked at commonly used yum commands, such as yum install *packagename* and yum remove *packagename*. If you only want to download the file but not install it, you can use the yumdownloader command instead of yum. We looked at the yum.conf file, which is the configuration file for yum. It defines such things as the software repository URLs and their names where yum will search for packages as well as the directory (cachedir) where downloaded packages will be saved and where the yum log file (logfile) will be saved. I also pointed out that repository information can be stored in this file or in separate files named *filename*.repo in the /etc/yum .repos.d directory.

We then discussed the process you need to follow to install software from source code. I pointed out that most software installed in this manner is distributed in tarball format. After downloading the file, you need to use the **tar –zxvf** command to extract the files from the tarball file. Once they are extracted, you switch to the new directory created when the tarball was extracted and run **./configure**. This script checks your system and creates the Makefile file. You then run the make command to create the binary executable file from the source code text files using the instructions provided in the Makefile file. Once this is done, you use the make install command to install the executable on the system. Software installed from source code will use either an uninstall script in the original installation files or an uninstall target in the Makefile file that is called using the make uninstall command.

You should also be familiar with managing Debian software packages. Distributions based on the Debian distribution use the Debian Package Manager (dpkg). Debian packages use a naming convention that is similar to that used by RPM packages: *packagename_version_architecture*.deb. Like RPM packages, Debian packages include dependency information.

We then looked at using the dpkg command to install, uninstall, query, and verify Debian packages. We also looked at the apt-cache command, which is used to query package information from the Debian package database (called the package cache). I also reviewed how to use apt-get, which is the Debian equivalent of yum on an RPM-based system. It automatically downloads and installs packages (along with all dependent packages) for you. The /etc/apt/sources.list file defines the repositories where apt-get can install packages from. I ended the Debian section of this chapter by looking at the aptitude utility, which uses a text-based, menu-driven interface to manage Debian packages.

We ended this chapter by discussing how to manage shared libraries. I pointed out that applications running on the system can share code elements called *shared libraries*. Shared libraries make it such that software developers don't have to reinvent the wheel each time they write a new program. Linux applications can use either dynamic or static shared libraries. The dynamic shared library configuration file is /etc/ld.so.conf. It contains a list of paths in the file system where shared library files are stored. To view a list of all shared libraries available on your Linux system, enter **ldconfig –p** at the shell prompt.

You can also view the shared libraries required by a specific application using the ldd command. The syntax is **ldd –v *executable_filename***. The library cache is /etc/ld.so.cache. This file contains a list of all the system libraries and is refreshed when the system is initially booted. If you add library files to a directory not listed in the ld.so.conf file, you must add them and then use the ldconfig command to rebuild the library cache manually. You can also add the path to the LD_LIBRARY_PATH environment variable.

Accelerated Review

- You can use either graphical or command-line tools to manage Linux software.

- A good Linux administrator can use either type of utility.

- A great deal of software is freely available for Linux systems.

- Your distribution media (CDs or DVD) is a great resource for Linux software.

- A variety of websites are available for downloading Linux software.

- If possible, you should verify your downloads by comparing a checksum value you create with the sum command against the checksum value specified on the website where you obtained the file.

- RPM packages are installed using the Red Hat Package Manager (rpm).

- RPM packages are compiled for a specific architecture and sometimes a specific Linux distribution.

- You can tell what architecture a package file is intended for by looking at the filename, which contains the following information:
  - Package name
  - Version number
  - Release number
  - Compatible distribution (optional)
  - Architecture type
- You can enter **rpm --checksig** to verify the digital signature of an RPM package before you install it.
- You can enter **rpm –i** to install a package file on your system.
- To uninstall an RPM package, you use the **rpm –e** command.
- You can update an existing package to a newer version using the **rpm –U** command.
- To query a package, you use the –q option with rpm.
- To verify a package, you use the –V option with rpm.
- If you determine that a package has been damaged, you can reinstall an existing package by entering **rpm –U --replacepkgs**.
- The yum utility allows you to download and then install a package and all its dependencies with a single command.
- The yum install *packagename* command installs a package.
- The yum remove *packagename* command uninstalls a package.
- The yum.conf file is the configuration file for yum.
- The yum.conf file defines such things as the software repository URLs and their names where yum will search for packages as well as the directory (cachedir) where downloaded packages will be saved and where the yum log file (logfile) will be saved.
- Repository information can be stored in yum.conf or in separate files named *filename*.repo in the /etc/yum.repos.d directory.
- To install from source code, you first download and extract a tarball file.
- In the installation directory, you run configure, make, and make install.
- The configure command checks your system to verify compatibility and creates the Makefile file.
- The make command compiles a binary executable from the source code text using the specifications in the Makefile file.
- The make install command installs the compiled executable.
- The make uninstall command is typically used to uninstall an executable installed from source.
- Distributions based on the Debian distribution use the Debian Package Manager (dpkg).
- Debian packages use a naming convention that is similar to that used by RPM packages.

- Debian packages include dependency information.

- You use the dpkg command to install, uninstall, query, and verify Debian packages in much the same manner as the rpm command.

- The apt-cache command is used to query package information from the Debian package database (called the package cache).

- The apt-get command automatically downloads and installs packages (along with all dependent packages) for you.

- The aptitude utility uses a text-based, menu-driven interface to manage Debian packages.

- Applications running on a Linux system can share code elements called *shared libraries*.

- Linux applications can use either dynamic or static shared libraries.

- The dynamic shared library configuration file is /etc/ld.so.conf.

- The /etc/ld.so.conf file contains a list of paths in the file system where shared library files are stored.

- To view a list of all the shared libraries available on your Linux system, enter **ldconfig –p** at the shell prompt.

- You can view the shared libraries required by a specific application by entering **ldd –v** *executable_filename* at the shell prompt.

- The library cache is /etc/ld.so.cache.

- The ld.so.cache file contains a list of all the system libraries and is refreshed when the system is initially booted.

- If you add library files to a directory not listed in the ld.so.conf file, you must add them and then use the ldconfig command to rebuild the library cache manually.

- You can also add a new library file path to the LD_LIBRARY_PATH environment variable.

Questions

1. What type of software can be managed with a graphical software utility such as YaST? (Choose two.)

   A. RPM packages

   B. Text-based script files

   C. Software compiled from downloaded source code

   D. Debian packages

2. You've just downloaded a file named FC-6-i386-DVD.iso to the /home/tux directory on your Linux system. What command would you use to generate a checksum value?

   A. checksum /home/tux/FC-6-i386-DVD.iso

   B. sum /home/tux/FC-6-i386-DVD.iso

   C. verify /home/tux/FC-6-i386-DVD.iso

   D. rpm –V /home/tux/FC-6-i386-DVD.iso

3. You've just downloaded a file named FC-6-i386-DVD.iso and have generated a checksum value. The value generated is slightly different from that shown on the download website. What does this imply?

   A. The downloaded copy is different from the original, but the download is still usable as long as the differences are minor.

   B. The version number is incremented by 1 when the file was downloaded.

   C. The downloaded copy is different from the original copy and shouldn't be used.

   D. The downloaded copy is exactly the same as the original copy.

4. You've just downloaded a file named BitTorrent-5.0.1.tar.gz to your home directory. Assuming the current directory is ~, what command would you enter at the shell prompt to extract all the files from this archive?

   A. gzip –d ./BitTorrent-5.0.1.tar.gz

   B. tar –axvf ./BitTorrent-5.0.1.tar.gz

   C. tar –xvf ./BitTorrent-5.0.1.tar.gz

   D. tar –zxvf ./BitTorrent-5.0.1.tar.gz

5. Where does the RPM store its database of installed packages?

   A. /var/lib/rpm

   B. /etc/rpm

   C. /var/rpmdb

   D. /tmp/rpm

6. You've just downloaded an RPM package file named evolution-2.6.0-41.i586.rpm to your home directory. Assuming the current directory is ~, what command could you use to check the digital signature of the downloaded file to verify that it hasn't been tampered with?

   A. rpm --checksig evolution-2.6.0-41.i586.rpm

   B. rpm --verify evolution-2.6.0-41.i586.rpm

   C. rpm –tamperproof evolution-2.6.0-41.i586.rpm

   D. rpm --signature evolution-2.6.0-41.i586.rpm

7. You've just downloaded an RPM package file named evolution-2.6.0-41.i586.rpm to your home directory. Assuming the current directory is ~, what command could you use to install the package on your system, displaying a progress indicator as the installation is completed? (Choose two.)

   A. rpm –i evolution-2.6.0-41.i586.rpm

   B. rpm –ihv evolution-2.6.0-41.i586.rpm

   C. rpm –U evolution-2.6.0-41.i586.rpm

   D. rpm –install --progress evolution-2.6.0-41.i586.rpm

   E. rpm –Uhv evolution-2.6.0-41.i586.rpm

8. You've just downloaded an RPM package file named evolution-2.6.0-41.i586.rpm to your home directory. Assuming the current directory is ~, what command could you use to check the package for dependencies? (Choose two.)

   A. rpm –i evolution-2.6.0-41.i586.rpm

   B. rpm –i --test evolution-2.6.0-41.i586.rpm

   C. rpm –V evolution-2.6.0-41.i586.rpm

   D. rpm --deps evolution-2.6.0-41.i586.rpm

   E. rpm --checkdeps evolution-2.6.0-41.i586.rpm

9. You need to uninstall the Pure-FTPd service from your Linux system. You've switched to the directory where the original installation files are located. What's the first command you need to enter to uninstall this package?

   A. ./configure

   B. make

   C. make remove

   D. make uninstall

10. You've installed an RPM package file named evolution-2.6.0-41.i586.rpm on your Linux system. What command would you use to uninstall this package?

    A. rpm –U evolution

    B. rpm –U --remove evolution

    C. rpm –i --remove evolution

    D. rpm –e evolution

11. You currently have an RPM package file named evolution-2.2.0-2.i586.rpm installed on your Linux system. You've recently downloaded the evolution-2.6.0-41.i586.rpm package from http://www.sourceforge.net. What command would you use to install the newer version of this package?

    A. rpm –U evolution-2.6.0-41.i586.rpm

    B. rpm –i evolution-2.6.0-41.i586.rpm

    C. rpm –i --upgrade evolution-2.6.0-41.i586.rpm

    D. rpm –e evolution-2.2.0-2.i586.rpm

12. You currently have an RPM package file named evolution-2.6.0-41.i586.rpm installed on your Linux system. What command would you enter to display summary information about the package?

    A. rpm –s evolution

    B. rpm –qs evolution

    C. rpm –qi evolution

    D. rpm –V --summary evolution

13. You've used the rpm command with the –q --requires option to determine the components required by the rpm package. One of the required components is /usr/bin/perl. What command would you enter to find out which RPM package provides this component?

   A. rpm –q --whatprovides /usr/bin/perl

   B. rpm –qs --requires /usr/bin/perl

   C. rpm –qi --requires /usr/bin/perl

   D. rpm –q --provides perl

14. You've used the rpm command with the –V option to verify an rpm package installed on your system. The output from the command listed the following error code:

```
S.5....T    c    /opt/kde3/share/config/kdm/kdmrc
```

   What does this error code indicate? (Choose two.)

   A. There's a problem with the size of the file.

   B. There's a problem with the mode of the file.

   C. There's a problem with the timestamp of the file.

   D. There's a problem with a file's revision numbers.

   E. There's a problem with a file's ownership.

15. You need to extract a single file out of an RPM package. Which utility can be used to do this?

   A. tar

   B. rpm

   C. dpkg

   D. rpm2cpio

16. You need to install the GNU C Compiler (gcc) package on your system. Which yum command will do this?

   A. yum gcc

   B. yum install gcc

   C. yum update gcc

   D. yum installpkg gcc

17. Which yum command generates a list of available updates for all installed packages on a Linux system?

   A. yum list updates

   B. yum info

   C. yum list available

   D. yum list all

18. What does the configure script do in an application's installation directory? (Choose two.)

    A. It compiles the source code into a binary executable.

    B. It checks the local system to verify that the necessary components are available.

    C. It copies the binary executable and other files, such as documentation, to the appropriate directories in the file system.

    D. It creates the Makefile file.

    E. It verifies that the installation files haven't been corrupted or tampered with.

19. What does the make command do when installing an application from source code?

    A. It compiles the source code into a binary executable.

    B. It checks the local system to verify that the necessary components are available.

    C. It copies the binary executable and other files, such as documentation, to the appropriate directories in the file system.

    D. It creates the Makefile file.

    E. It verifies that the installation files haven't been corrupted or tampered with.

20. What does the make install command do when installing an application from source code?

    A. It compiles the source code into a binary executable.

    B. It checks the local system to verify that the necessary components are available.

    C. It copies the binary executable and other files, such as documentation, to the appropriate directories in the file system.

    D. It creates the Makefile file.

    E. It verifies that the installation files haven't been corrupted or tampered with.

21. Which action, when used with the dpkg command, uninstalls a specified package and deletes all of its configuration files?

    A. –r

    B. –p

    C. –P

    D. –U

22. You want to use apt-get to download and install the 3dchess package on your Linux system. Which command can you use to do this?

    A. apt-get install 3dchess

    B. apt-get –d install 3dchess

    C. apt-get upgrade 3dchess

    D. apt-get –s install 3dchess

23. Which type of shared library is integrated directly into an executable file when it is initially compiled?

  A. Dynamic

  B. Shared

  C. Static

  D. Linked

24. Which file is checked by applications on startup for the location of shared libraries on the Linux system?

  A. /etc/ld.so.conf

  B. /etc/ld.so.cache

  C. /lib/ld.so

  D. /usr/lib/ld.so

Answers

1. **A, D.** Most graphical software management utilities can manage RPM or Debian package files.

2. **B.** The sum /home/tux/ FC-6-i386-DVD.iso command will generate a checksum value for the file specified.

3. **C.** A variance in the checksum values indicates the two copies of the file are different in some way. You shouldn't use the file in this situation because it probably is corrupt or has been tampered with.

4. **D.** To extract the file, you would enter **tar –zxvf ./BitTorrent-5.0.1.tar.gz**.

5. **A.** The RPM database is stored in /var/lib/rpm.

6. **A.** The rpm --checksig evolution-2.6.0-41.i586.rpm command would be used to check the file's digital signature.

7. **B, E.** Either the rpm –ihv evolution-2.6.0-41.i586.rpm command or the rpm –Uhv evolution-2.6.0-41.i586.rpm command will install the file and display a progress indicator composed of hash marks on the screen as the installation progresses.

8. **A, B.** Both the rpm –i evolution-2.6.0-41.i586.rpm command and the rpm –i --test evolution-2.6.0-41.i586.rpm command will automatically check the package for required dependencies and prompt you if any are missing.

9. **A.** The ./configure command would be used first to generate the Makefile file. This file contains the UNINSTALL target that can then be used with the make utility to uninstall the software.

10. **D.** To erase rpm from the system, you would enter **rpm –e evolution**.

11. **A.** The rpm –U evolution-2.6.0-41.i586.rpm command will upgrade the existing rpm to the newer version.

12. **C.** The rpm –qi evolution-2.6.0-41.i586.rpm command will query the package and display summary information on the screen.

13. **A.** The rpm –q --whatprovides /usr/bin/perl command displays the name of the package that provides this component.

14. **A, C.** The S, 5, and T in the error code indicate that there is a problem with the file's size, MD5 checksum, and timestamp. The c indicates that the file is a configuration file, so these errors may or may not be significant.

15. **D.** The rpm2cpio utility can be used to create a cpio archive file from the RPM package. You can then extract individual files from the archive using the cpio utility.

16. **B.** The yum install gcc command can be used to download and install the gcc package on your Linux system, including all packages it is dependent on.

17. **A.** The yum list updates command can be used to generate a list of available updates for all installed packages on a Linux system.

18. **B, D.** The configure script is used to check the local system to make sure it has the components required to install and run the software. It also creates the Makefile file.

19. **A.** The make command compiles the text-based source code into a binary executable that can be run on the system.

20. **C.** The make install command actually installs the program and its associated support files (such as documentation and configuration files) into the appropriate directories in the file system.

21. **C.** The –P option, when used with the dpkg command, uninstalls a specified package and deletes all of its configuration files.

22. **A.** The apt-get install 3dchess command can be used to download and install the 3dchess package on your Linux system, along with all other packages it is dependent on.

23. **C.** Static shared libraries are integrated directly into an executable file when it is initially compiled.

24. **B.** The /etc/ld.so.cache file is checked by applications on startup for the location of shared libraries on the Linux system.

Managing Linux Users and Groups

In this chapter, you will learn about:

- Understanding Linux users and groups
- Managing Linux user accounts
- Managing Linux group accounts

One of the great things about Linux is the fact that it is a true multiuser operating system. A single Linux system can be configured with one, two, five, ten, or more user accounts. Each user on the system is provided with his or her own computing environment that is unique to the user. For example, in Figure 9-1, the current user is named ksanders.

Notice that ksanders has her own directory in /home named ksanders. Within her home directory, she has a variety of subdirectories, including the following:

- **Desktop** Contains the files and icons displayed on ksanders' desktop.
- **Documents** Contains ksanders' documents.
- **public_html** Contains ksanders' personal web pages.
- **bin** Contains executable files and scripts that ksanders may need to run. This directory is automatically added to the PATH environment variable for the ksanders user, so she doesn't need to specify the full path to any executable stored here.
- **Downloads** Contains files downloaded from the Internet by ksanders' web browser.
- **Music** Contains ksanders' music files.
- **Pictures** Contains ksanders' image files.
- **Videos** Contains ksanders' video files.

When ksanders logs in to the system, her own desktop preferences are loaded and she has access to her files stored in /home/ksanders. If a different user logs in, his or her desktop preferences are loaded and access is provided to that user's home directory. If the system has been configured to work on a computer network, then users can log in to the system remotely and access their desktop and home directory as if they were sitting in front of the computer. In this scenario, multiple users can be logged in and using the same computer at the same time.

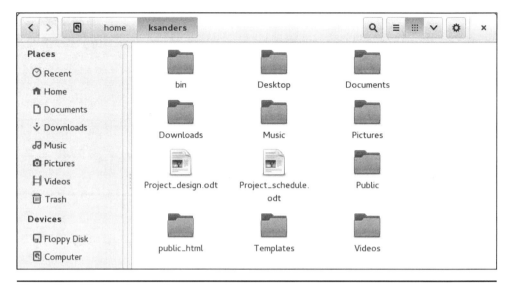

Figure 9-1   The ksanders user's system environment

Because Linux is a multiuser operating system, we need some way to control who has access to what in the system. For example, suppose you have a Linux system with five user accounts:

- ksanders
- jelison
- hsaez
- ebuchannan
- aebbert

You need some way to make sure each of these users can access what he or she needs in the file system and nothing more. For example, you need to ensure that hsaez can access her files but can't access jelison's files and directories. Imagine what a nightmare it would be if one user on the system could access and tinker with files owned by a different user.

I had an experience early in my career where this actually happened. My first job out of college was with a microchip manufacturer. This particular employer ran several shifts each day. To save money, the cubicles and computers used by day shift workers were shared with night shift workers. In the Navy, they call this "hot-bunking." Because of this, I shared my chair and computer system with a night shift employee. I started my shift at 8:00 A.M. and he ended his shift at 7:00 A.M. The computer system we shared was a blazing fast 486 DX2 66 system running Windows 3.1.

Now, early versions of Windows were not true multiuser operating systems. In fact, with Windows 3.1, you didn't even have to log in. That meant whoever was using the computer at any given point in time had full unfettered access to the *entire* file system. In my hot-bunking employment situation, my night shift compatriot had full and unfettered access to my files and I likewise had access to his files during the daytime.

At first, we managed to stay out of each other's way reasonably well. However, as time passed, this got to be a real issue. The problem was that, at this point in time, a 500MB hard drive was considered "cutting edge" and the first 1GB hard disk drives were just starting to come onto the market (although they were far too expensive for most of us to actually buy).

Because we were limited to a 500MB hard drive, we were constantly running out of disk space. You can probably guess what started to happen. During the day, I'd need more disk space on our shared system and I'd poke around the file system looking for files that could be deleted. My compatriot did the same thing at night. It didn't take long for us to start deleting each other's important files. As the wise philosopher George Carlin has noted, "Have you ever noticed that your junk is stuff and other people's stuff is junk?" OK, so I had to edit that quote a little bit. This is a family book after all. At any rate, my night shift compatriot would delete my "junk" so he could save his "stuff." I would do the same thing during the day.

The moral of this story is that you must implement some kind of file system access controls that prevent users from accessing "stuff" they shouldn't. Linux does just this using users, groups, ownership, and permissions.

Let's begin this chapter by introducing you to Linux users and groups.

 EXAM TIP   To pass your Linux+ exam, you must know Linux users, groups, ownership, and permissions inside and out! These concepts are central to the management of a Linux system. If you don't understand them, you are very likely to fail the exam. To be properly prepared, you should understand how users are implemented on Linux, the difference between system and regular users, and how to manage accounts from the command line. You should also know how groups are used on Linux and how to manage them from the command line as well. You should also understand the three Linux permissions and how they affect user access to files in the file system. You should know how to use command-line utilities to modify permissions assigned to a file or directory. You should also know how to use command-line utilities to manage file ownership.

Understanding Linux Users and Groups

To control access to a Linux system and the data it contains, we need to do two things:

- We need to require users to supply a set of credentials before they will be granted access to the system.

- We need access controls that specify what individual users can do with files and directories in the file system after they have logged in.

We're going to address the first condition in this chapter. To control overall access to the system itself, we need to implement users and groups. In this part of this chapter, we're going to discuss how to do this. Specifically, we're going to cover the following:

- Linux user accounts
- Linux groups

Let's begin by discussing how Linux user accounts work.

Linux User Accounts

One of the key problems in the employment situation I described at the beginning of this chapter is the fact that my Windows 3.1 system didn't implement individual user accounts. Whoever sat down in front of the computer and turned it on had full access to all the data on the hard drive *without a password.* It didn't matter if it was me, my coworker, my boss, the night custodian, or (of more concern) a corporate spy from a competitor. This was a great weakness of this particular operating system.

To remedy this problem, I needed a workstation operating system that used true user accounts. Fortunately, the days of the "userless" operating system are all but gone. Most modern operating systems include some type of user authentication system based on user accounts. Linux in particular performs this function very well. In this part of the chapter, we're going to discuss the following:

- How Linux user accounts work
- Where Linux user accounts are stored
- Creating and managing user accounts from the command line

Let's begin by discussing how Linux user accounts work.

How Linux User Accounts Work

You've probably noticed as we've worked through the various exercises in this book that you must log in before you can use your Linux system. This is called *authentication.* To authenticate, you must supply the following credentials:

- Username
- Password

NOTE   A variety of other authentication methods are available for Linux systems. Instead of manually entering usernames and passwords, you can configure Linux to use smart cards, proximity cards, biometric readers, and so on. This is made possible because Linux uses *Pluggable Authentication Modules (PAM)* to manage authentication to the system. PAM makes Linux authentication extremely flexible.

After logging in, your user's unique system environment is created. In Figure 9-2, the ksanders user has logged in to the local system. Her customized desktop preferences have been loaded and access has been granted to her home directory in /home/ksanders.

If another user were to log in to the same system, his preferences would be loaded instead of ksanders' preferences. That user would also be provided with access to his home directory. An important point to remember is that files saved in a given user's home directory are protected from all other users on the system. For example, if ksanders were to save files in /home/ksanders, the hsaez user on this system would not be able to access them.

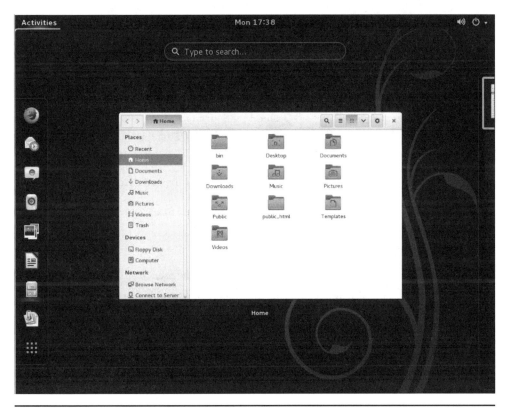

Figure 9-2   The ksanders desktop environment

By default, all user home directories are created and maintained in the /home directory. For example, in Figure 9-3 two user accounts have been created on the Linux system: hsaez and ksanders.

Both users have home directories created for them in /home. There is one exception to this rule, however. Remember that all Linux systems use a superuser account named *root*. Notice in Figure 9-3 that there is no home directory in /home for the root user account. Is root homeless? Actually, no. The root user account is given a home directory, too. However, it isn't maintained in /home. Instead, the root user's home directory is /root. This is root's home directory and, of course, only root can access it.

Figure 9-3   User accounts in /home

You can view information about any user account on your system using the **finger *username***
command from the shell prompt. For example, if I wanted to view information about the ksanders
account on my Linux system, I would enter **finger ksanders**. When I do, useful information about
the ksanders account is displayed, as shown here:

```
openSUSE:~/Desktop # finger ksanders
Login: ksanders                    Name: Kimberly Sanders
Directory: /home/ksanders          Shell: /bin/bash
Last login Thu Mar 10 16:44 (MST) on :0 from console
No Mail.
No Plan.
```

Notice that finger displays the following information about the ksanders account:

- **Login**   This is the username that is used to authenticate to the system.
- **Name**   This is the user's full name.
- **Directory**   This is the user's home directory.
- **Shell**   This is the default shell that will be started by the user.
- **Last Login**   This displays the last time the user logged in and where from.

In addition to having a home directory and default shell assigned, each user account is also
assigned a unique user ID (UID) number when it is created. No two user accounts on the system
will have the same UID. To view the UID for a given user account, you can use the **id *username***
command from the shell prompt. For example, to view information about our hsaez user account,
we can enter **id hsaez** at the shell prompt. Here is the output from this command:

```
openSUSE:~ # id hsaez
uid=1003(hsaez) gid=100(users) groups=100(users)
```

Notice that on this system, the hsaez user account has been assigned a UID of 1003. On a SUSE
Linux system, the first regular user account created on the system is always assigned a UID of
1000. The next user account will be assigned a UID of 1001, and so on.

Other distributions may use a different numbering scheme for the UID, however. For example, UIDs on a Fedora system start at 500 instead of 1000. Next, you can see that the rtracy user
on this Fedora system has a UID of 500 because it was the first standard user account created:

```
[root@fs3 ~]# id rtracy
uid=500(rtracy) gid=500(rtracy) groups=500(rtracy)
```

Notice that the preceding paragraphs refer to UIDs assigned to standard user accounts. What
about the root user? The root user account is always assigned a UID of 0 on most Linux distributions. This is shown next:

```
openSUSE:~ # id root
uid=0(root) gid=0(root) groups=0(root)
```

It's the UID that the operating system actually uses to control access to files and directories in
the file system. For now, however, we need to discuss where Linux user accounts are saved in the
system. Let's do that next.

Where Linux User Accounts Are Stored

Linux is a very flexible operating system. One of its flexible features is the location of user accounts on the system. When you originally installed the system, your distribution may have given you several options for where you wanted to store your user accounts. For example, most distributions allow you to choose from the following authentication methods:

- **Local** This option stores user accounts in the /etc/passwd file. This has been the default configuration used by Linux systems for many years.

- **LDAP** This is an option that many Linux administrators are starting to adopt more and more. Instead of storing user accounts in a file in the file system, user accounts are stored in a directory service and accessed via the Lightweight Directory Access Protocol (LDAP). Unlike local authentication, which stores accounts in a simple flat file, the directory service is hierarchical in nature, allowing you to sort and organize your user accounts by location, function, or department. The directory database can also be replicated among several different Linux systems, providing fault tolerance. The key benefit of this option is that it allows you to maintain a single set of user accounts that can be used to authenticate to many different Linux systems.

 NOTE Essentially, the LDAP option moves Linux in the direction of other server operating systems that use directory services, such as Microsoft's Active Directory.

- **NIS** This option stands for *Network Information Service.* NIS is also designed to provide centralized user account management when you have multiple systems that all need the same user accounts. To do this, NIS configures systems to all use a common passwd and shadow file.

- **Windows Domain** If you have a Windows domain controller in your network (or another Linux server running the Samba service), you can configure your Linux system to use the user accounts in the domain to authenticate to the local system.

 EXAM TIP For your LPIC-1/Linux+ exam, you need to be concerned with the Local option. All Linux distributions can use the /etc/passwd and /etc/shadow files for authentication.

Which of these options is best? It depends on what you need your system to do. If the system is a stand-alone workstation, the Local option is usually sufficient. You could also optionally use the LDAP option.

If your system is going to participate on a network where lots of different users will need access to your system, you may want to consider using LDAP, NIS, or Windows Domain authentication.

For our purposes here, we're going to focus on the Local option. This option stores user and group information in the following files in the file system:

- **/etc/passwd** This file contains the user account information for your system.

- **/etc/shadow** This file contains passwords for your user accounts.

- **/etc/group** This file contains your system's groups. (We'll discuss groups later in this chapter.)

Let's look at the /etc/passwd file first.

The /etc/passwd File If configured to use local authentication, your /etc/passwd file contains your system's user accounts. Each user account on your system is represented by a single line in the file, as shown in this example:

```
openSUSE:~ # cat /etc/passwd
...
root:x:0:0:root:/root:/bin/bash
wwwrun:x:30:8:WWW daemon apache:/var/lib/wwwrun:/bin/false
hsaez:x:1003:100:Heather Saez:/home/hsaez:/bin/bash
ksanders:x:1002:100:Kimberly Sanders:/home/ksanders:/bin/bash
rtracy:x:1001:100:Robb Tracy:/home/rtracy:/bin/bash
```

Each account record is composed of several different fields in the line, separated by a colon (:). These are organized as follows:

```
Username:Password:UID:GID:Full_Name:Home_Directory:Default_Shell
```

Here's an example:

```
ksanders:x:1002:100:Kimberly Sanders:/home/ksanders:/bin/bash
```

Here's what these fields contain:

- **Username** The Username field simply identifies the username the user will supply when logging in to the system. In this example, it is ksanders.

- **Password** This is a legacy field. At one time, the user's password was stored in encrypted form in this field in the passwd file. However, for security reasons, the password has been moved from /etc/passwd to /etc/shadow. (We'll look at this file in more detail later.) Therefore, only the character *x* is shown in this field.

- **UID** This is the user ID for the user account. We discussed the UID earlier in this chapter. In this example, the UID for the ksanders account is 1002.

- **GID** This field references the group ID number of the user's default group. In this example, the GID for the ksanders account is 100. As you'll see later in this chapter, this references the users group.

- **Full_Name** This field contains the user's full name. In this example, it's Kimberly Sanders.

- **Home_Directory** This field contains the path to the user's home directory. In this case, the home directory is /home/ksanders.

- **Default_Shell** This field specifies the shell that will be used by default. For ksanders, this is /bin/bash (the Bourne-Again SHell).

There are actually a lot of user accounts listed in the /etc/passwd file on any Linux system, even if you've only created one or two accounts. All of the other user accounts are *system* user accounts. Three sample system user accounts are shown here:

```
sshd:x:495:494:SSH daemon:/var/lib/sshd:/bin/false
uucp:x:10:14:Unix-to-Unix CoPy system:/etc/uucp:/bin/bash
wwwrun:x:30:8:WWW daemon apache:/var/lib/wwwrun:/bin/false
```

System user accounts aren't used for login. Instead, they are used by services running on the system. When one of these services needs to do something in the Linux file system, it does so as its associated user account from /etc/passwd. Notice that the system user accounts have a much lower UID number as compared to standard user accounts. UIDs between 0 and 499 are typically reserved for system accounts, depending on the distribution.

For example, suppose I've logged in to the ftp service on my Linux system as an anonymous user and uploaded a file. This file needs to be written to the ftp service's default directory in the file system. When it writes, it does so as the ftp user. By doing this, I can use permissions (discussed later in the chapter) to control what a given service can or can't do.

Let's next look at the /etc/shadow file.

The /etc/shadow File With most Linux distributions that use local authentication, your users' passwords will be stored in encrypted format in the /etc/shadow file. This file is linked to the /etc/passwd file we discussed previously. Each of the user accounts listed in /etc/passwd has a corresponding entry in /etc/shadow, as shown in this example:

```
openSUSE:~ # cat /etc/shadow
. . .
root:$2a$05$h03HfGFSi2i8GlotOYgreeBelUlHc.z/2KxyQQF7RSo./TdLOrDJa:15035::::::
sshd:*:14796:0:99999:7:::
uucp:*: 16015::::::
wwwrun:*: 16015::::::
hsaez:$6$JbgjOmU1SXu1$ON0iVUmsrzvVxd7D2AeYbriZ1gDRS/W/
xnoeXVzcBkZIeNSJMAKFWfMvl4RvWki0HIQLrfV6bkNIAk6vCEOyP0:16392:0:99999:7:::
ksanders:$2a$05$KL1DbTBqpSEMiL.2FoI3ue4bdyR.eL6GMKs7MU6.nZl5SCC7/
REUS:15043:0:99999:7:::
rtracy:$6$L58Cq/vWQJaM$u7.1.UmlGVquz6qQ0LaHXQzbTgc6kC6uc1sR/GgelNjbF/
FqJUkwmhVdxO3Qxs3HgXQJLIptYJ4HD7bvMoxbd0:16392:0:99999:7:::
```

As with /etc/passwd, each user account is represented by a single line in the /etc/shadow file. Each record is composed of the following fields, each separated by a colon:

```
Username:Password:Last_Modified:Min_Days:Max_Days:Days_Warn:Disabled_
Days:Expire
```

For example, the record for ksanders is as follows:

```
ksanders:$2a$05$KL1DbTBqpSEMiL.2FoI3ue4bdyR.eL6GMKs7MU6.nZl5SCC7/
REUS:15043:0:99999:7:::
```

Here's what each of these fields contains:

- **Username** This is the user's login name from /etc/passwd.

- **Password** This is the user's password in encrypted format. In the preceding example, the password for ksanders is M3linux273. However, to prevent someone from accessing the /etc/shadow file and grabbing the user passwords from it, it is stored in encrypted format. You may notice that all of the system user accounts have a simple asterisk in this field (*). This indicates that these accounts aren't allowed to log in to the system. For example, if I tried to log in to my system as ftp, I would be denied access even though the ftp user account exists.

- **Last_Modified** This field displays the number of days since January 1, 1970, that the password was last changed. In this example, it has been 15,043 days.

- **Min_Days** This field displays the minimum number of days required before a password can be changed. In this example, it is set to 0 days.

- **Max_Days** This field displays the maximum number of days before a password must be changed. In this example, it is set to 99,999 days. Effectively, this means a password change isn't required.

- **Days_Warn** This field displays the number of days prior to password expiration that the user will be warned of the pending expiration. In this case, it's set to 7 days.

- **Disabled_Days** This field displays the number of days to wait after a password has expired to disable the account. In this example, it's set to a null value.

- **Expire** This field displays the number of days since January 1, 1970, after which the account will be disabled. In this example, it is set to a null value, indicating the account never expires.

As you can see, it is very important that these two files stay synchronized with each other. If they get out of whack, then it's possible that a user may not be able to log in or a service may not be able to access the file system correctly.

The good news is that these files usually stay in sync as they are supposed to without any intervention on the part of the administrator. The only times I've seen these two files become unsynchronized is when the administrator decides to manually edit these files with a text editor. I strongly discourage this practice. Your Linux system includes a wide variety of utilities that are used to manage user accounts and passwords on your system. (We'll discuss how to use these utilities later in this chapter.) You should always use these utilities instead of a text editor to manage user accounts. Doing so will ensure that both files are edited appropriately and stay synchronized with each other.

To verify your /etc/passwd and /etc/shadow files, you can use the pwck command at the shell prompt. This utility will verify each line in the two files and make sure they are valid. Any errors are reported on the screen, as shown in this example:

```
openSUSE:/ # pwck
Checking '/etc/passwd'
User 'pulse': directory '/var/lib/pulseaudio' does not exist.
User 'usbmux': directory '/var/lib/usbmuxd'  does not exist.
Checking '/etc/shadow'.
```

As you can see, pwck found that the home directories specified for the pulse and usbmux system user accounts don't exist. Everything else checked out. If, for some reason, the /etc/passwd and the /etc/shadow files are out of synchronization, you can use the pwconv command at the shell prompt to fix the files. This utility will add any missing user accounts from /etc/passwd to /etc/shadow.

Next, we discuss how you manage user accounts.

Creating and Managing User Accounts from the Command Line

As we've encountered with many of the other tasks discussed in this book, you can manage user accounts on your Linux system either with graphical utilities or from the command line. For example, openSUSE includes the YaST User and Group Management module, shown in Figure 9-4, to manage user accounts.

As with everything else, these graphical utilities are just fine to use. I'll admit that I use them the majority of the time. However, you must know how to use the command-line user management utilities—both to be a truly effective Linux admin and to pass your LPIC-1/Linux+ exam. Therefore, we're going to focus on command-line tools in this chapter. Once you're comfortable with them, feel free to experiment with their graphical equivalents.

In this chapter, we're going to cover the following tools:

- useradd
- passwd
- usermod
- userdel

Let's begin by learning how to use useradd.

useradd As its name implies, the useradd utility is used to add users to the Linux system. The syntax for useradd is **useradd *options username***. For example, suppose I wanted to create a user account named lmorgan using default parameters. I would enter **useradd lmorgan** at the shell prompt, as shown here:

```
openSUSE:/ # useradd lmorgan
```

Figure 9-4 Using YaST to manage user accounts

The lmorgan account is created using the default parameters contained in the following configuration files:

- **/etc/default/useradd**   This file contains the defaults used by the useradd utility. Here is a sample:

```
openSUSE:/ # cat /etc/default/useradd
GROUP=100
HOME=/home
INACTIVE=-1
EXPIRE=
SHELL=/bin/bash
SKEL=/etc/skel
CREATE_MAIL_SPOOL=yes
```

Notice that this file specifies that the default group for new users is the group with a GID of 100 (that's the users group). It also specifies that a home directory for the user be created in /home. The inactive account parameter is set to –1, and the account is set to never expire. The default shell is set to /bin/bash. The skeleton directory is /etc/skel, and a mail spool directory is created for the user. As with any Linux configuration file, if you don't like these values, you can simply edit the useradd file with a text editor to customize it the way you like.

TIP   You can also view new user default values by entering **useradd –D** at the shell prompt.

- **/etc/login.defs**   This file contains values that can be used for the GID and UID parameters when creating an account with useradd. It also contains defaults for creating passwords in /etc/shadow. A portion of this file follows:

```
openSUSE:/ # cat /etc/login.defs
openSUSE:~ # cat /etc/login.defs
#
# /etc/login.defs - Configuration control definitions for the shadow
package.

...
UMASK                  022
PASS_MAX_DAYS       99999
PASS_MIN_DAYS        0
PASS_WARN_AGE        7
UID_MIN                    1000
UID_MAX                   60000
SYS_UID_MIN                100
SYS_UID_MAX                499

GID_MIN                    1000
GID_MAX                   60000
SYS_GID_MIN                100
SYS_GID_MAX                499
```

Notice that this file specifies default values for the fields we reviewed earlier in /etc/ shadow for each user account. It also specifies defaults used when useradd is assigning a UID to a new account. Earlier in this chapter, we noted that SUSE Linux starts UIDs at 1000 whereas Fedora starts UIDs at 500. This file is where this behavior comes from. It also defines the UID number range for system user accounts, as well as which executable to run when you run useradd or userdel from the shell prompt. If you don't like the defaults, you can always edit this file to match your preferences.

- **/etc/skel** The useradd command copies files from the skeleton directory (/etc/skel by default) into a newly created home directory when you create a new user. Typically, /etc/ skel also contains several user configuration flies, such as .bashrc and .profile. Here is an example:

```
openSUSE:~ # ls /etc/skel/
.bash_history  .config  .fonts   .local    .xim.template       bin
.bashrc        .emacs   .inputrc  profile  .xinitrc.template   public_
html
```

You can add any files and directories to this directory that you want each and every user to have by default when their account is created on the system.

You can override these defaults when running useradd by specifying a list of options in the command line. You can use the following:

- **–c** Includes the user's full name.

- **–e** Specifies the date when the user account will be disabled. Format the date as *yyyy-mm-dd*.

- **–f** Specifies the number of days after password expiration before the account is disabled. Use a value of **–1** to disable this functionality (for example, **useradd –f –1 jmcarthur**).

- **–g** Specifies the user's default group.

- **–G** Specifies additional groups that the user is to be made a member of.

- **–M** Specifies that the user account be created without a home directory.

- **–m** Specifies the user's home directory.

- **–n** Used only on Red Hat and Fedora systems. By default, these distributions create a new group with the same name as the user every time an account is created. Using this option will turn *off* this functionality.

- **–p** Specifies the user's encrypted password. You can encrypt the password you want to use with the **openssl passwd -crypt** command. Run this command and, when prompted, enter the password you want to assign to the user account. The command will output an encrypted version of the password on the screen. You can then use the encrypted password with the -p option of the useradd and usermod commands.

- **–r** Specifies that the user being created is a system user.

- **–s** Specifies the default shell for the user.

- **–u** Manually specifies a UID for the user.

For example, suppose I wanted to create a new user account for a user named Jackie McArthur on a Linux system. Further suppose that I want to specify a user name of jmcarthur, a full name of Jackie McArthur, a password of tux123, and that a home directory be created. To do this, I would first encrypt the tux123 password using the **openssl passwd -crypt** command, which returns 1k4LGDSCsTuQE as the encrypted version of the password. Then I would enter **useradd –c "Jackie McArthur" –m –p "1k4LGDSCsTuQE" –s "/bin/bash" jmcarthur** at the shell prompt. After I do so, the account will be created in /etc/passwd, as shown here:

```
openSUSE:~ # openssl passwd -crypt
Password:
Verifying - Password:
1k4LGDSCsTuQE
openSUSE:~ # useradd -c "Jackie McArthur" -m -p "1k4LGDSCsTuQE"
-s "/bin/bash" jmcarthur
openSUSE:~ # cat /etc/passwd
...
jmcarthur:x:1005:100:Jackie McArthur:/home/jmcarthur:/bin/bash
```

Notice that useradd used the parameters we specified in the command line. For parameters we didn't specify, such as the GID and UID, the defaults from /etc/default/useradd were used instead.

Let's next look at the passwd utility.

passwd The passwd utility is used to change an existing user's password. For example, earlier we created a new user named lmorgan with useradd. However, because we didn't use the –p option in the command line, the lmorgan account doesn't have a password and is locked. You can see this using the –S option with passwd. For example, we could enter **passwd –S lmorgan** at the shell prompt, as shown here:

```
openSUSE:/ # passwd -S lmorgan
lmorgan LK 03/14/2014 0 99999 7 -1
```

Notice that *LK* is displayed in the output. This indicates that the account is locked. The remaining parameters are various other password parameters, such as the date of the last password change, the minimum number of days required before a password can be changed, the maximum number of days before a password must be changed, the number of days prior to password expiration when the user will be warned of the pending expiration, and the number of days to wait after a password has expired to disable the account.

In short, this account is unusable. To enable this account, we need to add a password. We can do this using passwd. The syntax is **passwd *username*.** In this case, you would enter **passwd lmorgan** (as root). When you do, you are prompted to enter a password for the specified user, as shown here:

```
openSUSE:~ # passwd lmorgan
New password:
Retype new password:
passwd: password updated successfully
```

Enter the password you want to use at the prompts. After doing so, you can enter **passwd –S lmorgan** again to view the account status, as shown next:

```
ws1:/ # passwd -S lmorgan
lmorgan P 03/14/2014 0 99999 7 -1
```

Notice that the account status is set to P, indicating that the password has been set and is valid. When working with passwd, you can also use the following options:

- **−l**   Locks the user's account. This option invalidates the user's password.
- **−u**   Unlocks a user's account.
- **−d**   Removes a user's password.
- **−n**   Sets the minimum number of days required before a password can be changed.
- **−x**   Sets the maximum number of days before a password must be changed.
- **−w**   Sets the number of days prior to password expiration when the user will be warned of the pending expiration.
- **−i**   Sets the number of days to wait after a password has expired to disable the account.

Now that you know how to create a new user and how to set a user's password, let's next review how you go about modifying an existing user account.

usermod   From time to time, you will need to modify an existing user account. This can be done from the command line using the usermod utility. The syntax for usermod is very similar to that used by useradd. You enter **usermod** *options username* at the shell prompt. The options for usermod are likewise similar to those used by useradd. They include the following:

- **−c**   Edits the user's full name.
- **−e**   Sets the date when the user account will be disabled. Format the date as *yyyy-mm-dd*.
- **−f**   Sets the number of days after password expiration before the account is disabled. Use a value of **−1** to disable this functionality.
- **−g**   Sets the user's default group.
- **−G**   Specifies additional groups that the user is to be made a member of.
- **−l**   Changes the username.
- **−L**   Locks the user's account. This option invalidates the user's password.
- **−m**   Sets the user's home directory.
- **−p**   Sets the user's password. As with the useradd command, you must specify an encrypted password when using the –p option with usermod. You can use the **openssl passwd –crypt** command to generate an encrypted password that can be used with this option.
- **−s**   Specifies the default shell for the user.
- **−u**   Sets the UID for the user.
- **−U**   Unlocks a user's account that has been locked.

For example, suppose my jmcarthur user has recently married and changed her last name to Sanders. I could update her user account to reflect this change by entering **usermod –l jsanders**

–c **"Jackie Sanders" jmcarthur** at the shell prompt. When I do, the user's account information is updated in /etc/passwd, as shown here:

```
openSUSE:~ # usermod -l jsanders -c "Jackie Sanders" jmcarthur
openSUSE:~ # cat /etc/passwd...
jsanders:x:1005:100:Jackie Sanders:/home/jmcarthur:/bin/bash
```

 TIP If there's a space in the name, you will need to enclose it in quotes when using the usermod command. For example, we used the **jsanders –c "Jackie Sanders" jmcarthur** command to set the full name of the user.

The last user-related topic we need to cover here is that of deleting user accounts. Let's discuss how to do this next.

userdel From time to time, you will also need to remove a user account from your Linux system. This can be done from the shell prompt using the userdel utility. To delete a user, simply enter **userdel** *username*. For example, if we wanted to delete the lmorgan account we created earlier, we would enter **userdel lmorgan** at the shell prompt.

It's important to note that, by default, userdel will *not* remove the user's home directory from the file system. If you do want to remove the home directory when you delete the user, you need to use the –r option in the command line. For example, entering **userdel –r lmorgan** will remove the account and delete her home directory.

Let's practice managing users in the following exercise.

Exercise 9-1: Managing User Accounts from the Command Line

In this exercise, you will practice creating and modifying user accounts from the shell prompt of your Linux system. You can perform this exercise using the virtual machine that comes with this book. Run snapshot 9-1 for the correctly configured environment.

 VIDEO Please watch the Exercise 9-1 video for a demonstration on how to perform this task.

Complete the following:

1. Boot your Linux system and log in as the **student** user with a password of **student**.
2. Open a terminal session and change to your root user account by entering **su –** at the shell prompt and entering a password of **student**.
3. Create a user account for yourself by doing the following:
   a. Determine a *username* and *password* for yourself. A common convention is to use your first initial with your last name. Use the **openssl passwd –crypt** command to encrypt your password.
   b. At the shell prompt, enter **useradd –c** *"your_full_name"* **–m –p** *"your_ encrypted_password"* **–s** *"/bin/bash"* *your_username*.
   c. At the shell prompt, enter **tail /etc/passwd**. Verify that your new user account was created.

4. Create a user account using your system's default settings by entering **useradd dtracy** at the shell prompt.

5. At the shell prompt, enter **tail /etc/passwd**. Verify that your new user account was created. Notice that the new user is missing many parameters. Add these parameters by doing the following:

   a. Enter a full name for the dtracy user account by entering **usermod –c "Richard Tracy" dtracy** at the shell prompt.

   b. At the shell prompt, enter **tail /etc/passwd**. Verify that the full name was added to the dtracy account.

   c. Give dtracy a password by entering **passwd dtracy** at the shell prompt.

   d. When prompted, enter a new *password* for dtracy.

Now that you know how to manage users, we need to discuss how to manage groups. Let's do that next.

Linux Groups

Like other operating systems, Linux uses groups to make managing the system easier. In this part of this chapter, we're going to discuss the following:

- How Linux groups work
- Managing groups from the command line

Let's begin by discussing how Linux groups work.

How Linux Groups Work

Groups make our lives as system administrators easier! To understand why, let's take a look at a scenario. Suppose you have seven users on a Linux system. Of these users, five of them need almost the same level of access to files in the file system. Without groups, you would need to assign the necessary permissions separately to each of the five user accounts. That means you would be doing the same exact task five times over. That may not sound so bad, but just suppose you had 100 users that all needed the same level of access. What a waste of time!

Instead, you can implement groups on your Linux system. With groups, you assign permissions to the group and then make all the users that need that same level of access members of the group. That's much easier! You need to make only one set of assignments. If something changes in the level of access needed, you need to make the change only once to the group. All of the group members then automatically receive the change. Once again, this is much easier than the alternative!

If your Linux system has been configured to use local authentication, your groups are defined in the /etc/group file. A sample of this file follows:

```
openSUSE:~ # cat /etc/group
...
root:x:0:
rtkit:x:489:
scard:x:484:
```

```
shadow:x:15:
sshd:x:494:
svn:x:483:
sys:x:3:
systemd-journal:x:497:
tape:x:496:
tftp:x:492:dnsmasq,tftp
trusted:x:42:
tty:x:5:
utmp:x:22:
uucp:x:14:
video:x:33:gdm,hsaez,jsanders
wheel:x:10:
www:x:8:
xok:x:41:
users:x:100:
```

As with the /etc/passwd and the /etc/shadow files, each line in /etc/group is a single record that represents one group. Each record is composed of the following four fields:

Group:Password:GID:Users

For example, in the preceding example the record for the video group reads as follows:

video:x:33:gdm,hsaez,jsanders

- **Group**   Specifies the name of the group. In the example, the name of the group is "video."
- **Password**   Specifies the group password, if one is assigned.
- **GID**   Specifies the group ID (GID) number of the group. In this example, the GID of the video group is 33.
- **Users**   Lists the members of the group. In this case, the gdm, hsaez, and jsanders users are members of the video group.

Some distributions use an additional group file to store group passwords. Just as /etc/shadow is used to store encrypted passwords for users defined in /etc/passwd, the /etc/gshadow file is used to define group passwords for groups defined in /etc/group. Here is a sample /etc/gshadow file:

```
[root@fs3 ~]# cat /etc/gshadow
root:::root
bin:::root,bin,daemon
...
nobody:::
users:::
...
```

As with /etc/shadow, each line in /etc/gshadow represents a record for a single group. Each record is composed of the following fields:

Group_Name:Password:Group_Admins:Group_Members

With this in mind, let's review how you can manage your groups with command-line tools.

Managing Groups from the Command Line

As with users, you can also manage groups with either command-line or graphical tools. For example, both YaST and User Manager can be used to create, modify, and delete groups on your Linux system as well as user accounts.

However, for the reasons specified earlier, we're going to focus on managing groups from the shell prompt in this chapter. We will review the following tools:

- groupadd
- groupmod
- groupdel

Let's begin by looking at groupadd.

groupadd As you can probably guess from its name, the groupadd utility is used to add groups to your Linux system. The syntax for using groupadd at the shell prompt is relatively simple. Just enter **groupadd *options groupname***. For example, if I wanted to add a group named dbusers, I would enter **groupadd dbusers** at the shell prompt. When I do, a group is added to /etc/group using default parameters specified in /etc/login.defs.

When using groupadd, you can override the defaults in /etc/login.defs and customize the way the group is created using the following options:

- **–g** Specifies a GID for the new group.
- **–p** Specifies a password for the group. Just as with the useradd command, you must use the **openssl passwd –crypt** command to first encrypt the password you want to use with the –p option of groupadd.
- **–r** Specifies that the group being created is a system group.

Let's next look at groupmod.

groupmod You may have noticed that the groupadd command didn't add one key component to the new group: users! What good is a group if you don't have any users occupying it?

To modify a group, including adding users to the group membership, you use the groupmod utility. The syntax for using groupmod is similar to that used by usermod. Enter **groupmod *options group*** at the shell prompt. You can use the following options with the command:

- **–g** Changes the group's GID number.
- **–p** Changes the group's password. Just as with the usermod command, you must use the **openssl passwd –crypt** command to first encrypt the password you want to use with the –p option of groupmod.

In earlier versions of the groupmod command, you could use the –A and –R options to add and remove users to and from a group. However, these options are no longer available with groupmod. Instead, you must use the usermod command to add and remove users from a group. To add a user, you enter **usermod –aG group_name user_name** at the shell prompt. This command preserves all of the user's existing supplementary group memberships and adds the new group membership specified. The process for removing a user is a little more complex. You still use the usermod command with the –G option, but instead of including the –a (add) option, you use the –G option to explicitly specify all of the supplementary groups that the the user should be a member of, being sure to omit the group you want to remove the user from. For example, suppose the ksanders primary group is users current and she is also a member of the research and managers supplementary groups. If I wanted to remove her from the research group, I would enter usermod –G "managers" ksanders at the shell prompt. Because I only listed "managers" with the –G option, she is removed from membership in the research group while preserving her membership in the managers group.

Finally, let's look at deleting groups.

groupdel   If, for some reason, you need to delete an existing group from the system, you can do so using the groupdel command at the shell prompt. For example, to delete the dbusers group, you would enter **groupdel dbusers**.

Let's practice managing groups in the following exercise.

Exercise 9-2: Managing Groups from the Command Line

In this exercise, you will practice creating and modifying groups from the shell prompt of your Linux system. You can perform this exercise using the virtual machine that comes with this book. Run snapshot 9-2 for the correctly configured environment.

 VIDEO   Please watch the Exercise 9-2 video for a demonstration on how to perform this task.

Suppose your company is putting together a new research and development team that will be using your Linux system. You need to create a new group for users who will be members of this team. Complete the following:

1. Verify that you are logged in to your system.

2. If necessary, switch to your root user account with the **su –** command.

3. Create a new group named **research** by doing the following:

    a. At the shell prompt, enter **groupadd research**.

    b. Add the dtracy user account (created in the previous exercise) to the research group by entering **usermod –aG research dtracy** at the shell prompt. Repeat this process to add your user account to the research group.

    c. Verify that the users were added to the group by entering **tail /etc/group** at the shell prompt. You should see the following:

    ```
    research:!:1000:dtracy,rtracy
    ```

Chapter Review

We started this chapter discussing the need for a basic level of file system security on a Linux system. We reviewed a scenario where multiple users on the same system were able to access each other's files and the problems that were encountered as a result. The way to prevent these problems is to first control who can access the system and then control what they can access once they are in.

The first part is accomplished by using Linux user accounts. With user accounts, users must supply a valid username and password (called "credentials") before they are allowed to access the system. This is called "logging in" or "authentication." I pointed out that the Linux operating system will customize the system environment based on the username of the user who logged in. Users will have access to their own home directory and a customized desktop environment. I pointed out that, by default, user home directories are located in /home, except for the root user, whose home directory is located in /root. You can view specific information about a particular user using the **finger *username*** command at the shell prompt.

I also pointed out that each Linux user account has a unique ID number called the UID. No two users on the system have the same UID on the same system. Some distributions, such as openSUSE, start UIDs for standard users at 1000 by default. Other distributions, such as Fedora, start UIDs at 500. No matter what distribution you're using, the root user's UID is always set to 0. You can view a user's UID (as well as group membership) using the **id *username*** command.

We then discussed the various locations where user accounts can be saved on a Linux system. Using local authentication, user accounts are saved in /etc/passwd and /etc/shadow. Using LDAP authentication, user accounts are saved in an LDAP-compliant directory service. Using NIS authentication, user account files are distributed among several systems using the NIS service. Using Windows Domain authentication, user accounts are stored in a central database on a Windows (or Linux Samba) domain controller.

I pointed out that, for the LPIC-1/Linux+ exam, you only need to be familiar with the local authentication method. In this configuration, the /etc/passwd file contains your user account information while the /shadow file contains your users' encrypted passwords. The /etc/passwd file stores user accounts in the following format:

```
Username:Password:UID:GID:Full_Name:Home_Directory:Default_Shell
```

I also pointed out that the /etc/passwd file contains both standard and system user accounts. Standard user accounts are used for login. System user accounts can't be used for login. Instead, they are used by system services when they need to access the file system.

The /etc/shadow file stores user password information in the following format:

```
Username:Password:Last_Modified:Min_Days:Max_Days:Days_Warn:Disabled_
Days:Expire
```

The /etc/passwd and /etc/shadow files must stay synchronized. To do this, you should avoid editing these files directly with a text editor. Instead, you should use the various user and password management tools on your system. To check your files, you can use the pwck command. If you suspect the files are out of sync, you can use the pwconv command to add accounts from /etc/passwd to /etc/shadow.

We then discussed the different utilities you can use from the shell prompt to manage user accounts on your Linux system. To add a user, you use the useradd utility. If you don't supply any options when creating a user with useradd, the defaults contained in the /etc/default/useradd and /etc/login.defs files are used.

To set a user's password, you can use the passwd utility at the shell prompt. To view the status of a user's account, you can use the –S option with passwd. To modify an existing user account, you use the usermod utility. To remove a user account, you use the userdel utility. By default, userdel will not remove a user's home directory when deleting an account. If you want to remove the user's home directory, you can use the –r option with userdel.

We then shifted gears and discussed the role of Linux groups. Groups ease system administration by allowing you to group together users who need a common level of access to files and directories in the file system. Linux groups are stored in /etc/group. Group records in /etc/group are represented using the following syntax:

```
Group:Password:GID:Users
```

Some distributions store group passwords in /etc/group. Other distributions store them in a separate file (in encrypted format) in /etc/gshadow, much in the same manner as user accounts are stored in /etc/passwd and /etc/shadow. You create groups in your Linux system using the groupadd command. If you don't specify any options with the groupadd command, the group is created using default parameters found in /etc/login.defs.

To add users to a group, you must use the –aG options with the usermod command at the shell prompt. To remove users from a group, you use the –G option with the usermod command. You can also remove groups using the groupdel command.

Accelerated Review

- You need to control who can access a Linux system and what they can do with files and directories in the file system after they are in.
- To authenticate to a system, a user must supply a username and password (called "credentials").
- Linux restores user-specific information when a user logs in, such as a home directory and desktop environment.
- User home directories are created in /home by default.
- The root user's home directory is /root.
- You can use the finger command to view information about a user account.
- Every Linux user account has a unique user ID (UID) number assigned to it.
- The root user's UID is 0.
- The starting UID for standard users is 1000 on some distributions and 500 on others.
- You can use the id command to view a user's UID.
- You can use many different authentication methods with a Linux system.
- For your LPIC-1/Linux+ exam, you need to know how to use local authentication.
- Using local authentication, user accounts are stored in /etc/passwd and /etc/shadow.
- The /etc/passwd file stores user account information.
- The /etc/shadow file stores encrypted user passwords.
- You can use the pwck utility to verify that /etc/passwd and /etc/shadow are synchronized.

- You can use the pwconv utility to copy missing users from /etc/passwd to /etc/shadow.

- You can use the useradd utility to add users to a Linux system.

- When used without any options, useradd uses the system defaults contained in /etc/default/useradd and /etc/login.defs to create user accounts.

- You can use the passwd utility to set a user's password.

- The passwd utility can also be used to check the status of a user account.

- You can use the usermod utility to modify an existing user account.

- You can use the userdel utility to delete an existing user account.

- By default, userdel will not remove a user's home directory unless you specify the –r option with the command.

- Linux groups can be used to ease administration by grouping like user accounts together.

- User accounts are stored in /etc/group.

- Some distributions store group passwords in /etc/gshadow.

- You use the groupadd utility to add a new group to your system.

- You use the usermod utility to add or remove users to or from an existing group.

- You use the groupdel utility to delete an existing group.

Questions

1. Which of the following commands will display the UID of a user named dcoughanour when entered at the shell prompt?

    A. id dcoughanour

    B. finger dcoughanour

    C. UID dcoughanour

    D. info dcoughanour

2. Which of the following files is used to store user accounts on a Linux system that has been configured to use local authentication?

    A. /etc/shadow

    B. /etc/users

    C. /etc/passwd

    D. /etc/local/accounts

3. Which of the following files is used to store user passwords on a Linux system that has been configured to use local authentication?

    A. /etc/shadow

    B. /etc/users

    C. /etc/passwd

   D. /etc/local/accounts

4. Consider the following entry in /etc/passwd:

```
ksanders:x:1001:100:Kimberly Sanders:/home/ksanders:/bin/bash
```

What is the primary group for this user? (Choose two.)

   A. ksanders

   B. home

   C. 1001

   D. 100

   E. users

   F. video

5. Consider the following entry in /etc/shadow:

```
ksanders:$2a%05$fHzL5vsuk3ilLIuispxqKuCFEPg50ZhF8KshQyIZH7SDERJooEJTC:
13481:30:60:7:-1::
```

How often must this user change her password?

   A. Every 30 days.

   B. Every 60 days.

   C. Every 7 days.

   D. This feature is disabled. The user isn't required to change her password.

6. You need to create a new user account on a Linux system for Mike Huffman named mhuffman. Mike's password should be set (in encrypted form) to "3X.N3pL9U8HNM" and he needs a home directory created in /home/mhuffman. Which of the following commands will do this?

   A. useradd –c "Mike Huffman" –m –p "3X.N3pL9U8HNM" mhuffman

   B. usermod "Mike Huffman" –p "3X.N3pL9U8HNM" mhuffman

   C. useradd mhuffman

   D. useradd mhuffman –c "Mike Huffman" –m –p 3X.N3pL9U8HNM

7. A user named Diana Grow has recently married and changed her last name to Nelson. You need to change her username on her Linux system. Which command will do this?

   A. usermod –l "dgrow" –c "Diana Nelson" dnelson

   B. usermod –l "dnelson" –c "Diana Nelson" dgrow

   C. useradd dnelson

   D. usermod –c "dgrow" –l "dnelson" Diana Grow

8. You need to delete a user account named jcarr from your Linux system and remove his home directory contents. Which of the following commands will do this?

   A. userdel jcarr

   B. usermod --delete --rmhome jcarr

   C. userdel –r jcarr

   D. userdel --rmhome jcarr

9. Which file is used to store group information on a Linux system that has been configured to use local authentication?

   A. /etc/groups

   B. /etc/local/group

   C. /etc/groupinfo

   D. /etc/group

10. Which of the following commands can be used to add the users mhuffman, dnelson, and jcarr to a group named editors on a Linux system?

    A. groupadd –A "mhuffman,dnelson,jcarr" editors

    B. groupmod –A "mhuffman,dnelson,jcarr" editors

    C. groupmod editors –A "mhuffman,dnelson,jcarr"

    D. groupmod –R "mhuffman,dnelson,jcarr" editors

11. Which of the following commands will remove a user named dnelson from a group named editors?

    A. groupadd –R "dnelson" editors

    B. groupmod –A "dnelson" editors

    C. groupmod editors –R "dnelson"

    D. groupmod –R "dnelson" editors

Answers

1. **A.** Entering **id dcoughanour** will display the UID of that user account.

2. **C.** The /etc/passwd file stores user account information.

3. **A.** The /etc/shadow file stores user passwords.

4. **D, E.** The GID of ksanders' primary group is 100. On most distributions, this is the users group.

5. **B.** The user must change her password every 60 days. The value of 60 in the record shown specifies that the maximum age of a password is 60 days. After that, the user must change to a new password.

6. **A.** Entering **useradd –c "Mike Huffman" –m –p "3X.N3pL9U8HNM" mhuffman** will create the user mhuffman, set its full name to Mike Huffman, create a home directory (–m), and set the user's encrypted password to 3X.N3pL9U8HNM.

7. **B.** Entering **usermod –l "dnelson" –c "Diana Nelson" dgrow** at the shell prompt will rename the dgrow user account to dnelson.

8. **C.** Entering **userdel –r jcarr** will delete jcarr's account and remove his home directory.

9. **D.** The /etc/group file stores group information.

10. **B.** Entering **groupmod –A "mhuffman,dnelson,jcarr" editors** at the shell prompt will add the mhuffman, dnelson, and jcarr user accounts to the editors group.

11. **D.** Entering **groupmod –R "dnelson" editors** will remove the dnelson user account from the editors group.

Managing Linux File Systems

In this chapter, you will learn about:
- Managing disk partitions
- Mounting removable media
- Backing up data

It's time to dig in and really start working with Linux! All the chapters preceding this chapter have been designed to build a foundation of knowledge and skills that you will use throughout the rest of this book. In this chapter, we're going to take what you've learned thus far and apply it to learn how to manage partitions and file systems on a Linux system.

EXAM TIP Be prepared to be tested very heavily on this chapter in your LPIC-1/ Linux+ exam. Depending on which exam form you receive when you take your test, you may see 15–20 percent of your exam questions coming from this chapter alone.

Let's begin this chapter by discussing how to manage Linux disk partitions.

Managing Disk Partitions

When you initially install a Linux system, you define a series of partitions on your hard disk drives to host your file system. Depending on which distribution you installed, you probably used some kind of graphical or menu-driven partitioning utility to accomplish this.

After the system has been in use for a while, it's likely that you will need to add more storage space at some point. If you install a new hard disk in the system, you will need to partition it and create a file system on it. To do this, most distributions provide you with some type of graphical partitioning utility.

These utilities work great; however, for your LPIC-1/Linux+ certification exam, you have to know how to manage your partitions from the command line. In this part of the chapter, you will learn the following:

- Managing master boot record (MBR) disk partitions
- Managing globally unique identifier (GUID) partitions
- Building a file system
- Mounting a partition
- Understanding LVM
- Maintaining Linux file systems

Let's begin by learning how to use fdisk.

Managing Master Boot Record (MBR) Disk Partitions

The master boot record (MBR) partition format has been around since the early 1980s and is still used in many Linux systems. Therefore, you need to be familiar with managing these types of partitions.

The fdisk utility is used from the command line to view, create, or delete MBR partitions at the shell prompt. To use fdisk to create a new partition, first open a terminal session. Then, at the shell prompt, change to your root account by entering **su –** followed by your root user's password.

At the shell prompt, enter **fdisk *device***. For example, if you want to manage partitions on the first hard disk in your system, you would enter **fdisk /dev/sda**. At this point, you need to enter a command to tell fdisk what you want to do with the hard disk.

 TIP   You can enter **m** at the command prompt to display a list of all available commands.

For example, to view a list of partitions on the hard drive, you can enter **p**. This is shown in the following example:

```
openSUSE:~ # fdisk /dev/sda
Welcome to fdisk (util-linux 2.23.2).

Changes will remain in memory only, until you decide to write them.
Be careful before using the write command.

Command (m for help): p

Disk /dev/sda: 17.2 GB, 17179869184 bytes, 33554432 sectors
Units = sectors of 1 * 512 = 512 bytes
Sector size (logical/physical): 512 bytes / 512 bytes
I/O size (minimum/optimal): 512 bytes / 512 bytes
Disk label type: dos
Disk identifier: 0x0004eb7c

   Device Boot      Start         End      Blocks   Id  System
/dev/sda1            2048     4208639     2103296   82  Linux swap / Solaris
```

```
/dev/sda2    *     4208640    17061887    6426624  83  Linux
/dev/sda3          17061888   33554431    8246272  83  Linux

Command (m for help):
```

> **NOTE**   You can also display the partition table for a specified hard disk by entering **fdisk *device* –l** at the shell prompt. The output is similar to that shown here.

In the next example, a new hard disk (/dev/sdb) has been installed in the system and fdisk is being used to create a partition:

```
openSUSE:~ # fdisk /dev/sdb
Welcome to fdisk (util-linux 2.23.2).

Changes will remain in memory only, until you decide to write them.
Be careful before using the write command.

Device does not contain a recognized partition table
Building a new DOS disklabel with disk identifier 0x8239827b.

Command (m for help):
```

Notice that, because this is a new disk in the system, it has to be initialized with a disk label. The fdisk utility takes care of this for you when you load the program. However, the change won't be applied until you write your changes to the disk.

With fdisk running, you have a **Command:** prompt that you can use to enter fdisk commands. At this point, one of the best things you can do is to enter **m** to view the fdisk help. When you do, a list of commands is displayed that you can use to perform actions with fdisk, as shown in this example:

```
Command (m for help): m
Command action
   a   toggle a bootable flag
   b   edit bsd disklabel
   c   toggle the dos compatibility flag
   d   delete a partition
   g   create a new empty GPT partition table
   G   create an IRIX (SGI) partition table
   l   list known partition types
   m   print this menu
   n   add a new partition
   o   create a new empty DOS partition table
   p   print the partition table
   q   quit without saving changes
   s   create a new empty Sun disklabel
   t   change a partition's system id
   u   change display/entry units
   v   verify the partition table
   w   write table to disk and exit
   x   extra functionality (experts only)

Command (m for help):
```

CAUTION   You can enter **d** to delete an existing partition. Be very careful about using this action. Any data on that partition will be lost! Once the changes are committed to disk, they are not reversible. You can back off from changes made with fdisk without committing them to disk by entering **q**. With fdisk, **q** is your friend!

Before creating a partition, you should enter **p** to view any existing partitions on the disk. This will help you determine whether there is sufficient space and, if there is, what number must be assigned to a new partition created on the disk.

To create a new partition, you enter **n**. You can then specify whether you want to create a primary disk partition or an extended disk partition. Any hard disk in your system can have up to four partitions defined in its partition table. These can be either primary or extended partitions. If you intend to create four partitions or fewer, you can simply use primary partitions.

However, if you want to create more than four partitions on the disk, you must create at least one extended partition. Extended partitions are great. Within one extended partition, you can create many logical partitions. This allows you to get around the four-partition limitation. The general rule of thumb is to create your primary partitions first; then create your extended partition using the remaining space on the drive and create your logical partitions within it.

To create a primary partition, enter **p** when prompted. To create an extended partition, enter **e**. You are then prompted to specify a partition number, as shown in this example:

```
Command (m for help): n
Partition type:
   p   primary (0 primary, 0 extended, 4 free)
   e   extended
Select (default p): p
Partition number (1-4, default 1): 1
```

You need to specify the next available partition number for the partition being created. In other words, if your disk already has two partitions on it, you would enter **3**. In the preceding example, no partitions currently exist on the drive, so I've entered **1** to create the first primary partition. If you try to enter a partition number that has already being used by an existing partition, the fdisk utility will complain!

At this point, you must specify the size of the partition. This is done by specifying the beginning and ending cylinders. You first specify the cylinder on which you want to begin the partition. By default, fdisk displays the next available cylinder. If you don't have any partitions on the disk, this will be cylinder 1. If you already have partitions on the disk, the next unused cylinder will be listed. After specifying your start cylinder, you have several options for specifying the overall size of the partition, as shown here:

```
Partition number (1-4, default 1): 1
First sector (2048-2097151, default 2048): 2048
Last sector, +sectors or +size{K,M,G} (2048-2097151, default 2097151):
2097151
Partition 1 of type Linux and of size 1023 MiB is set
```

You can

- Enter the last cylinder to be used in the partition.
- Specify the size of the partition in gigabytes by entering *size*G. For example, you could create an 800GB partition by entering **800G**.

After specifying the size, you should verify your new partition by entering **p**. This will display all partitions for the disk, as shown in the next example:

```
Command (m for help): p

Disk /dev/sdb: 1073 MB, 1073741824 bytes, 2097152 sectors
Units = sectors of 1 * 512 = 512 bytes
Sector size (logical/physical): 512 bytes / 512 bytes
I/O size (minimum/optimal): 512 bytes / 512 bytes
Disk label type: dos
Disk identifier: 0xd489eb71

   Device Boot      Start         End      Blocks   Id  System
/dev/sdb1            2048     2097151     1047552   83  Linux

Command (m for help):
```

It's important to note that, at this point, the partition hasn't been written to disk. All changes are saved in memory before being committed to disk. This allows you to tweak your partitions before actually committing the changes.

Before committing the partition to disk, however, you may need to change the partition type. Notice in the preceding example that the partition being created is a standard Linux partition by default. Usually, this is sufficient. However, suppose you were creating a swap partition. You would need to use a different type of partition. This is done by entering **t** and then entering the ID of the partition type you want to change to. If you don't know the ID number of the partition type you want to use, you can enter **l** (lowercase *L*) to list all the valid partition types and their associated ID numbers, as shown here:

```
Command (m for help): l

 0  Empty           24  NEC DOS         81  Minix / old Lin bf  Solaris
 1  FAT12           27  Hidden NTFS Win 82  Linux swap / So c1  DRDOS/sec
 2  XENIX root      39  Plan 9          83  Linux           c4  DRDOS/sec
 3  XENIX usr       3c  PartitionMagic  84  OS/2 hidden C:  c6  DRDOS/sec
 4  FAT16 <32M      40  Venix 80286     85  Linux extended  c7  Syrinx
 5  Extended        41  PPC PReP Boot   86  NTFS volume set da  Non-FS data
 6  FAT16           42  SFS             87  NTFS volume set db  CP/M / CTOS
 7  HPFS/NTFS/exFAT 4d  QNX4.x          88  Linux plaintext de  Dell Utility
 8  AIX             4e  QNX4.x 2nd part 8e  Linux LVM       df  BootIt
 9  AIX bootable    4f  QNX4.x 3rd part 93  Amoeba          e1  DOS access
 a  OS/2 Boot Manag 50  OnTrack DM      94  Amoeba BBT      e3  DOS R/O
 b  W95 FAT32       51  OnTrack DM6 Aux 9f  BSD/OS          e4  SpeedStor
 c  W95 FAT32 (LBA) 52  CP/M            a0  IBM Thinkpad hi eb  BeOS fs
 e  W95 FAT16 (LBA) 53  OnTrack DM6 Aux a5  FreeBSD         ee  GPT
 f  W95 Ext'd (LBA) 54  OnTrackDM6      a6  OpenBSD         ef  EFI (FAT-12/16)
10  OPUS            55  EZ-Drive        a7  NeXTSTEP        f0  Linux/PA-RISC
11  Hidden FAT12    56  Golden Bow      a8  Darwin UFS      f1  SpeedStor
```

```
12   Compaq diagnost 5c   Priam Edisk       a9   NetBSD          f4   SpeedStor
14   Hidden FAT16 <3 61   SpeedStor         ab   Darwin boot     f2   DOS secondary
16   Hidden FAT16    63   GNU HURD or Sys   af   HFS / HFS+      fb   VMware VMFS
17   Hidden HPFS/NTF 64   Novell Netware    b7   BSDI fs         fc   VMware VMKCORE
18   AST SmartSleep  65   Novell Netware    b8   BSDI swap       fd   Linux raid auto
1b   Hidden W95 FAT3 70   DiskSecure Mult   bb   Boot Wizard hid fe   LANstep
1c   Hidden W95 FAT3 75   PC/IX             be   Solaris boot    ff   BBT
1e   Hidden W95 FAT1 80   Old Minix
```

For example, the ID for a Linux swap partition is 82. To change the type of the partition, you could enter **t** and specify a partition ID of **82** if you wanted to change the partition to a swap partition.

You can also delete partitions using fdisk. To do this, enter **d** at the command prompt and then specify the partition number you want to delete. Remember, any data that resides on this partition will be lost once you commit the change to disk!

At this point, you're ready to commit your partition to disk. If you're unhappy with the partitioning proposal, you can always enter **q** to quit without applying the changes. If you are happy, however, you can apply your changes by entering **w**. This will commit the partition to disk and exit fdisk, as shown in this example:

```
Command (m for help): w
The partition table has been altered!

Calling ioctl() to re-read partition table.
Syncing disks.
openSUSE:~ #
```

It's important to note here that you must reboot the system before the Linux kernel will recognize the partition changes you made with fdisk. However, you can also use the partprobe command at the shell prompt to force the kernel to recognize the new partition table without rebooting. The syntax is **partprobe –s**. The –s option causes the partprobe command to show a summary of devices and their partitions, as shown in this example:

```
openSUSE:~ # partprobe -s
/dev/sda: msdos partitions 1 2 3
/dev/sdb: msdos partitions 1
openSUSE:~ #
```

Now that you know how to manage partitions with fdisk, let's look at creating GUID partitions.

Managing Globally Unique Identifier (GUID) Partitions

As I mentioned previously, the MBR partitioning scheme has been in use for many years—since the early 1980s! As such, it has many limitations and shortcomings. Here are some examples:

- The MBR must be installed in the first 512 bytes of the hard disk.
- Only four primary partitions can be created on a storage device.
- The default block size of 512 bytes limits partitions to a maximum size of 2TB.

Many patches have been implemented over the years to get around these shortcomings:

- Using logical block addressing (LBA) to enable the use of larger hard disks

- Using 4,096-byte sectors to increase the maximum partition size on disk

- Defining one of your four available partitions as an extended partition, which can hold many logical partitions

These patches have served us well for a long time, but it's time for a new way to manage disk partitions. Recently, the globally unique identifier (GUID) partition table scheme was introduced for Linux as a replacement for MBR.

NOTE   We typically refer to this scheme as simply GPT (which stands for *GUID partition table*). We techies are famous for nesting acronyms within acronyms.

GPT is a part of the overall Unified Extensible Firmware Interface (UEFI) specification, which is designed to replace the BIOS on computer systems and provide a much most robust software-to-hardware interface. Think of UEFI as the BIOS on steroids. UEFI is only implemented on late-model computers. However, you can use GPT on older Linux systems that still use the BIOS. Using GPT has several key advantages over using MBR for your hard disk partitions:

- There are no such things as primary, extended, or logical partitions in GPT. All partitions are just plain old partitions.

- GPT supports gigantic disks and partitions. We're talking about sizes measured in *zebibytes* instead of terabytes.

- Most Linux distributions support up to 128 GPT partitions per disk. That's a lot more than the four we were stuck with using MBR.

- GPT provides partition fault tolerance by storing a copy of the partition table in the first and last sectors on the disk. This way, if one of the copies gets corrupted (it has happened to me), the redundant copy immediately takes over and the files on the disk remain accessible.

- GPT performs a cyclic redundancy check (CRC) to verify the integrity of the partition table.

- GPT assigns unique IDs to each disk and partition.

To manage GPT partitions, we can't use fdisk anymore. Instead, we use a utility named gdisk, which can be used to do a lot of things. For example, gdisk can be used to do the following:

- Convert an MBR partition table to a GPT partition table.

- Verify a hard disk.

- Create and delete GPT partitions.

- Display information about a partition.

- Change the name and type of a partition.

- Back up and restore a disk's partition table.

For example, suppose I added a second disk to my system and I wanted to create a GPT partition on it so I can use it to store information. To do this, I would first switch to my root user and then enter **gdisk /dev/sdb** at the shell prompt. If you're comfortable using fdisk, then the process of using gdisk will be a snap for you because many of the commands are the same. At the gdisk prompt, you can enter **?** to view a list of commands available. This is shown in the following example:

```
openSUSE:~ # gdisk /dev/sdb
GPT fdisk (gdisk) version 0.8.7

Partition table scan:
  MBR: not present
  BSD: not present
  APM: not present
  GPT: not present

Creating new GPT entries.

Command (? for help): ?
b       back up GPT data to a file
c       change a partition's name
d       delete a partition
i       show detailed information on a partition
l       list known partition types
n       add a new partition
o       create a new empty GUID partition table (GPT)
p       print the partition table
q       quit without saving changes
r       recovery and transformation options (experts only)
s       sort partitions
t       change a partition's type code
v       verify disk
w       write table to disk and exit
x       extra functionality (experts only)
?       print this menu

Command (? for help):
```

In this situation, I want to add a new partition to the disk, so I would enter **n** at the gdisk prompt. When I do, I'm prompted to specify the following:

- **The partition number**
- **The size of the partition**   This can be done by specifying the beginning and ending sectors of the partition. You can also specify where on the disk you want the partition to start and end (such as at the 10GB and 20GB points on the disk).
- **The type of partition**   The partition type numbers with gdisk are different from those used with MBR partitions. For example, to create a Linux partition, you use a partition type of **8300**. You can press **L** at the gdisk prompt to view a list of all possible partition types and their codes.

This process is shown in the following example:

```
Command (? for help): p
Disk /dev/sdb: 33554432 sectors, 16.0 GiB
```

```
Logical sector size: 512 bytes
Disk identifier (GUID): 1D3E9F48-D822-4DDF-AB94-C59B7A4E12C8
Partition table holds up to 128 entries
First usable sector is 34, last usable sector is 33554398
Partitions will be aligned on 2048-sector boundaries
Total free space is 12582845 sectors (6.0 GiB)

Number  Start (sector)    End (sector)  Size     Code  Name
   1           2048          20973567  10.0 GiB  8300  Linux filesystem

Command (? for help): w

Final checks complete. About to write GPT data. THIS WILL OVERWRITE EXISTING
PARTITIONS!!

Do you want to proceed? (Y/N): y
OK; writing new GUID partition table (GPT) to /dev/sdb.
The operation has completed successfully.
```

Once this is done, you can enter **p** at the gdisk prompt to view a list of the partitions on the disk. As with fdisk, the changes you make with gdisk are not actually committed to disk until you write them. If you like the changes you made to the disk partitioning, press **w** at the gdisk prompt. If you want to delete a partition, press **d**. If you want to change a partition's type, press **t** and then enter the partition type code you want to use. If you want to quit and start over without saving any changes, press **q** instead.

In addition to gdisk, you can also use the parted command at the shell prompt to manage GPT partitions. You can use it to add, delete, and edit the partitions on your disk.

 CAUTION   Unlike gdisk and fdisk, the parted command writes the partition changes you specify immediately to the disk. Be absolutely certain of the changes you want to make before using parted!

To use parted, enter **parted** at the shell prompt and then use the **select** command to specify which disk you want to manage. Be very careful, because if you don't manually specify a disk to manage, parted will automatically select your first hard disk for you—you know, the one with your system partitions and your home partition on it? Accidentally deleting a partition on this disk could be bad! If you intend to work on a disk other than /dev/sda, be sure you use the select command.

After selecting the appropriate hard disk, you can create a new partition using the mkpart command at the parted prompt. You need to specify the following:

- **The type of partition to be created**   For example, to create a standard Linux partition, you would specify a value of **linux**.

- **The starting point on the disk for the partition (in megabytes)**   For example, to create a partition that starts at the 1GB point on the disk, you would specify a value of **1024**.

- **The ending point on the disk for the partition (in megabytes)**   For example, to create a partition that ends at the 11GB point on the disk, you would specify a value of **11264**.

To view the partitions that have been created on the disk, you can use the **print** command at the parted prompt. In the following example, a 10GB partition is created on the second hard disk in the system (/dev/sdb):

```
openSUSE:~ # parted
GNU Parted 2.4
Using /dev/sda
Welcome to GNU Parted! Type 'help' to view a list of commands.
(parted) select /dev/sdb
Using /dev/sdb
(parted) mkpart linux 1024 11264
(parted) print
Model: VMware Virtual disk (scsi)
Disk /dev/sdb: 17.2GB
Sector size (logical/physical): 512B/512B
Partition Table: gpt

Number  Start   End     Size    File system  Name   Flags
 1      1024MB  11.3GB  10.2GB                linux

(parted)
```

You can also use the following commands at the parted prompt to manage disk partitions:

- To rename a partition, enter **name** *partition name*.
- To move a partition to a different location on the disk (which is a very handy thing to be able to do), enter **move** *partition start_point end_point*.
- To resize a partition on the disk (another very handy thing to be able to do), enter **resize** *partition start_point end_point*.
- To delete a partition from the disk, enter **rm** *partition*.

Now that you understand how to manage partitions, you need to learn how to make a file system on those partitions using mkfs.

Building a File System

Even though we've created a partition, we can't use it yet. That's because it hasn't been formatted with a file system yet. This is accomplished using one of the several commands. In this part of the chapter, we will look at the following topics:

- Using mkfs
- Using mkreiserfs
- Creating xfs and vfat file systems
- Using mkswap

Using mkfs

The mkfs utility is used to make an ext2, ext3, or ext4 file system on a partition. You can even use it to create an NTFS file system on the partition (which is used by Windows). This utility is actually just a front end for the real commands that make each specific type of file system:

- /sbin/mkfs.minix

- /sbin/mkfs.ntfs

- /sbin/mkfs.bfs

- /sbin/mkfs.ext4

- /sbin/mkfs.msdos

- /sbin/mkfs.cramfs

- /sbin/mkfs.ext3

- /sbin/mkfs.ext2

- /sbin/mkfs.vfat

- /sbin/mkfs.xfs

 NOTE If desired, you can run the mkfs.*x* utility in /sbin to create a specific file system. However, most Linux admins just use the mkfs front end. You can also use the mke2fs command at the shell prompt to create ext*x* file systems. If you need to get help creating a specific file system, enter **man mkfs.*x*** at the shell prompt.

Before you can create xfs file systems, xfs support must be added to the Linux kernel. Support for xfs is added by default during the installation of some distributions, such as Fedora. However, it is not included with other distributions, such as OpenSUSE and Ubuntu.

You specify which file system you want to use by entering the **–t** option and the type of file system. For example, if you want to create an ext4 file system on the first partition on the second hard disk drive in your system, you would enter **mkfs –t ext4 /dev/sdb1**. Here is an example:

```
openSUSE:~ # mkfs -t ext4 /dev/sdb1
mke2fs 1.42.8 (20-Jun-2013)
Filesystem label=
OS type: Linux
Block size=4096 (log=2)
Fragment size=4096 (log=2)
Stride=0 blocks, Stripe width=0 blocks
524288 inodes, 2096474 blocks
104823 blocks (5.00%) reserved for the super user
First data block=0
Maximum filesystem blocks=2147483648
64 block groups
32768 blocks per group, 32768 fragments per group
8192 inodes per group
Superblock backups stored on blocks:
     32768, 98304, 163840, 229376, 294912, 819200, 884736, 1605632
```

```
Allocating group tables: done
Writing inode tables: done
Creating journal (32768 blocks): done
Writing superblocks and filesystem accounting information: done
```

There are several options you can use with mkfs (in addition to –t) to customize the file system you create on the specified partition:

- **–b** *blocksize*   Specifies the size of the data blocks in the file system. Values of **1024**, **2048**, and **4096** are allowed.

- **–N** *inodes*   Specifies how many inodes are created on the file system.

 NOTE   Remember, an *inode* stores basic information about a file in the Linux file system, including its size, device, owner, and permissions. Each file has one inode (with the exception of hard links). Therefore, specifying an exact number of inodes effectively limits the total number of files that can be created on the file system.

- **–i** *bytes_per_inode*   Sets the size of the inode. For *bytes_per_inode*, you can use the same values available for the block size.

- **–j**   Creates a journal on the file system. This can be used to add a journal to an existing ext2 file system, effectively converting it to an ext3 file system.

If you do not include any options when running the mkfs command, an optimal data block size and the optional number of inodes will be calculated for you based on the size of the partition. In the preceding example, the following were calculated for us:

- **Block size=4096**   This specifies that the block size is 4KB. This value was determined to be optimal for the small 8GB partition that the file system was created on in this example. Smaller partitions will have small block sizes.

- **524288 inodes, 2096474 blocks**   The file system has a maximum of 524,288 inodes and 2,096,474 blocks. This means it can hold a maximum of 524,288 files on the partition, even if the sum of their sizes is less than the total space available. If you multiply the total number of blocks (2,086,474) by the block size (4,096), you can calculate the total size of the partition (in this case, about 8GB).

- **Superblock backups stored on blocks: 32768, 98304, 163840, 229376, 294912, 819200, 884736, 1605632**   The superblock is the block at the beginning of the partition (0) that contains information about the structure of the file system. In this file system, redundant copies of the superblock are stored in the specified blocks.

Using mkreiserfs

The mkreiserfs utility is used to make a Reiser file system on a partition. For example, if you want to create a Reiser file system on the first partition on the second hard drive in your system, you would enter **mkreiserfs /dev/sdb1**. When you do, a screen is displayed and a proposal is presented.

Figure 10-1

Checking for xfs

support

```
[root@fs3 ~]# find / -name mkfs.*
find: `/home/rtracy/.gvfs': Permission denied
/sbin/mkfs.ext4
/sbin/mkfs.msdos
/sbin/mkfs.ntfs
/sbin/mkfs.ext3
/sbin/mkfs.cramfs
/sbin/mkfs.ext4dev
/sbin/mkfs.ext2
/sbin/mkfs.vfat
/sbin/mkfs.xfs
```

TIP   You can also run **mkfs –t reiserfs** *device* at the shell prompt to create a Reiser file system.

Many of these parameters can be customized using mkreiserfs options. See the utility's man page for more information. Usually, however, the default parameters work just great. When prompted to continue, enter **y** to format the partition.

Creating xfs and vfat File Systems

In addition to creating ext2/3/4 and reiser partitions, you can also use mkfs to create xfs and vfat partitions. The Extents File System (xfs) file system was created by Silicon Graphics (SGI) for its IRIX operating system. It's a very fast, very flexible file system. It has been ported over to run on Linux as well, although in my opinion it doesn't function under Linux as well as it does under IRIX. An easy way to determine whether your Linux kernel has xfs support enabled is to open a shell prompt and (as root) enter **find / –name mkfs.***. If xfs support has been added to your kernel, you should see the mkfs.xfs utility installed on the system, as shown in Figure 10-1.

Creating an xfs file system is very easy. It is done in exactly the same manner as creating ext*x* file systems using the mkfs command. First, create a standard Linux partition (type 83) using fdisk. Then, at the shell prompt, enter **mkfs –t xfs** *device*. In Figure 10-2, the /dev/sdb1 partition is formatted with the xfs file system.

In addition, you can also create non-Linux file systems, such as FAT, on Linux partitions using the mkfs command. First, create a standard Linux partition (type 83) using fdisk. Then simply enter **mkfs –t vfat** *device* at the shell prompt. Here is an example:

```
openSUSE:~ # mkfs -t vfat /dev/sdb2
mkfs.vfat 3.0.22 (2013-07-19)
openSUSE:~ #
```

Figure 10-2

Creating an xfs

file system

```
[root@fs3 ~]# mkfs -t xfs /dev/sdb1
meta-data=/dev/sdb1              isize=256    agcount=4, agsize=524224 blks
         =                       sectsz=512   attr=2
data     =                       bsize=4096   blocks=2096896, imaxpct=25
         =                       sunit=0      swidth=0 blks
naming   =version 2             bsize=4096   ascii-ci=0
log      =internal log          bsize=4096   blocks=2560, version=2
         =                       sectsz=512   sunit=0 blks, lazy-count=1
realtime =none                   extsz=4096   blocks=0, rtextents=0
```

Using mkswap

So far so good, but what if you need to format the partition you just created as a swap partition instead of a data partition? Never fear, you can do this too using the mkswap command at the shell prompt. Just like a data partition, a partition used for swapping has to be prepared with the mkswap command.

 TIP A Linux system can have more than one swap partition. In fact, on a heavily used system, having multiple swap partitions spread across several hard disks can really increase performance.

The syntax for this command is **mkswap** *device*—for example, **mkswap /dev/sdb2**.

 CAUTION The type of the partition must be set to **82** using the fdisk utility first!

An example follows:

```
openSUSE:~ # mkswap /dev/sdb2
Setting up swapspace version 1, size = 1959924 KiB
no label, UUID=1f51a8d7-ac55-4572-b68a-7a3f179aac61
```

After configuring the partition as a swap partition, you use the swapon command at the shell prompt to enable it. The syntax is **swapon** *device*—for example, **swapon /dev/sdb2**.

You can disable an existing swap partition by entering **swapoff** *device* at the shell prompt—for example, **swapoff /dev/sdb2**.

 TIP If you want to activate all swap partitions at once, you can enter **swapon –a**. The swapon utility will search through your /etc/fstab file to identify all defined swap partitions and will mount them. To deactivate all currently enabled swap partitions, enter **swapoff –a** at the shell prompt.

Once your partition has been formatted with a file system, you must mount it before you can use it. Let's review how you do this next.

Mounting a Partition

One of the key differences between Linux and other operating systems (such as Windows) is the fact that you need to mount a file system before you can use it. This is another one of those "got-chas" that trip up new Linux administrators. You even have to mount hard disks, DVDs, and USB drives before you can use them! We'll talk about mounting removable media later in this chapter.

The good news is that the process of mounting a partition is relatively easy. This is done using the mount command. The mount utility mounts the partition into an existing directory in your file system. When you switch to that directory, you are actually switching to the partition.

New Linux admins sometimes struggle with this concept. Other operating systems, such as Windows, reference partitions on the disk using a drive letter such as C: or D: by default.

For example, if you have a hard disk in a Windows system that has two partitions on it, the first one would be accessed using drive letter C:, and the second partition would be accessed using drive letter D:. Each drive letter has its own separate hierarchy of directories and files.

Not so with Linux! Instead, Linux uses a virtual file system (VFS) that creates a single hierarchy that encompasses all partitions on all storage devices in the system. Switching to the directory where the partition is mounted switches you to that partition.

NOTE Newer versions of Windows also permit you to mount a partition in a directory as well. In my opinion, however, it isn't nearly as elegant as the way it's done under Linux.

To use the mount command to mount a partition, first switch to your root account using su. Then enter **mount –t** *file_system_type device mount_point* at the shell prompt. I know this looks complicated, but it really isn't. For example, suppose you created the ext4 file system on the first partition on the second hard disk in your system, and now you want to mount it in a directory named /mnt/extraspace. To do this, you would enter **mount –t ext4 /dev/sdb1 /mnt/ extraspace** at the shell prompt, as shown here:

```
openSUSE:~ # mount -t ext4 /dev/sdb1 /mnt/extraspace/
```

Now, whenever you switch to the /mnt/extraspace directory in the file system, you are switching to the new partition (/dev/sdb1). If you don't know what type of file system is used by the partition, you can use the –a option with the mount command instead of –t. This will cause mount to try to mount the partition using all supported file system types until one is successful.

On most distributions, the /mnt directory is the default directory for mounting local and remote file systems. You don't have to use it, of course. You can mount a partition into any directory you want. However, by convention, /mnt is used for this purpose. On some distributions, it's also the default location for mounting removable devices as well. However, some distributions, such as OpenSUSE and newer versions of Fedora, use /media as the default location for mounting removable media.

You can also use the –o option with the mount command to include a variety of mounting options with the command. For example, you could use **–o ro** to mount the partition as read-only. See the man page for mount for a complete listing of all the available options.

TIP One of the things I love about the mount command is the fact that it can be used to mount an ISO image in the file system, allowing you to access the files within it without burning it to an optical disc first. The syntax is **mount –o loop** *filename.iso mount_point*.

After mounting the partition, you can use the mount command with no switches to view all mounted file systems. You can look through the output to verify that the device is mounted.

For example, the following line from the output of the mount command indicates that /dev/ sdb1 is mounted on /mnt/extraspace and uses the ext4 file system:

```
/dev/sdb1 on /mnt/extraspace type ext4 (rw,relatime,data=ordered)
```

In addition, whenever you mount or unmount a partition, the /etc/mtab file is updated with a list of mounted file systems. You can view this file using the cat command to see a list of mounted file systems. For example, the following line from the mtab file also indicates that the /dev/sdb1 partition is mounted in /mnt/extraspace:

```
/dev/sdb1 /mnt/extraspace ext4 rw,relatime,data=ordered 0 0
```

You can also use the cat command to view the /proc/mounts file to see a list of mounted file systems. Another useful utility for viewing mounted partitions is df. This utility displays your partitions, where they're mounted, how much space has been used, and how much free space is still available.

If, for some reason, you need to unmount a partition, you can use the umount command. To unmount a partition, simply enter **umount** followed by the device or the mount directory for the partition. For example, to unmount the /dev/sdb1 partition shown in the last example, you would enter **umount /dev/sdb1** or **umount /mnt/extraspace**, like this:

```
openSUSE:~ # umount /dev/sdb1
```

TIP Notice that the command is "umount," *not* "unmount." This is yet another Linux gotcha!

This brings up yet another issue when working with Linux. Just because you mount a file system with mount does not mean it will stay mounted if you reboot the system. As long as the system stays running, the partition will stay mounted. However, if you reboot, the partition won't be remounted when the system starts back up.

You can remedy this using the /etc/fstab file. This file contains a list of file systems that the operating system mounts whenever it boots. A typical /etc/fstab file follows:

```
openSUSE:/ # cat /etc/fstab
/dev/sda1          swap                swap        defaults            0 0
/dev/sda2          /                   ext4        acl,user_xattr      1 1
/dev/sda3          /home               ext4        acl,user_xattr      1 2
```

I know this file looks a little confusing at first, but it really isn't too bad. Each line in the /etc/fstab file specifies a separate file system to be mounted on boot. Each line is composed of six fields, as listed in Table 10-1.

Notice that the /dev/sdb1 partition we created earlier isn't listed in the sample fstab file. That means it won't be mounted in /mnt/extraspace after a system reboot. We can fix this by adding the partition to the fstab file. Open /etc/fstab in an editor such as vi and then add the following line:

```
/dev/sdb1    /mnt/extraspace    ext3    acl,user_xattr    1    2
```

This specifies that the /dev/sdb1 partition be mounted in /mnt/extraspace using the ext4 file system. It also specifies that access control lists be enabled for the file system (a very good thing to

Field	Function
1	Specifies the device and partition to be mounted—for example, /dev/sda3.
2	The directory (mount point) where the partition is to be mounted.
3	The file system type of the partition.
4	Various mount options. You can use the following: • **rw** Mounts a file system in read/write mode. • **ro** Mounts a file system in read-only mode. • **sync** Enables synchronous I/O. Changes are written immediately. Generally used for removable devices such as floppy disks. • **async** Enables asynchronous I/O. Changes are cached and then written when the system isn't busy. Generally used for hard drives. • **atime** Specifies that the file access time is updated in the file's inode. • **noatime** Specifies that the file access time of files is not updated in the file's inode. This option usually provides better file system performance overall. • **nodev** Prevents interpretation of device files in /dev as block special devices. • **dev** Interprets device files in /dev as block special devices. • **noexec** Prevents binaries on the partition from being executed. • **exec** Allows binaries on the partition to be executed. • **nosuid** Blocks the use of suid and sgid bits. • **suid** Enables the use of suid and sgid bits. • **auto** The file system is mounted automatically on boot. • **noauto** The file system is not mounted automatically on boot. • **user** Allows users to mount the file system. • **nouser** Only root can mount the file system. • **defaults** Implements the default options of rw, suid, dev, exec, auto, nouser, and async.
5	Specifies whether the file system should be dumped: **0** means don't dump, whereas **1** means dump.
6	Specifies the order in which fsck should check the file system at reboot. The root partition should be set to a value of **1**. Other partitions should have a value of **2**.

Table 10-1   Fields in the /etc/fstab File

do!) and that extended user attributes be enabled for the file system as well. Now, whenever you reboot the system, the partition will be automatically mounted.

Next, we need to spend a few minutes discussing LVM.

Understanding LVM

Logical volume management (LVM) is an option you can use when partitioning Linux hard disk drives. It provides an alternative to the traditional process of creating disk partitions. Instead, you create volume groups from storage devices in your system. From the volume group, you allocate space to specific logical volumes, which are managed by the logical volume manager. Instead of mounting partitions, you mount logical volumes at mount points in your file system. This provides you with a great deal of flexibility when allocating space on the system. For example, if you mount a volume at /usr and a volume on /home and then the /home directory begins to run out of space, you can reallocate space from the volume mounted at /usr to the volume mounted at /home. That's very difficult to do with traditional disk partitions!

In addition, LVM allows you to dynamically add space to the system. For example, suppose you are out of space on the /home volume. To add capacity, all you have to do is install a new hard drive in the system and then allocate its space to the /home volume. Voilà! The size of the volume is increased. You didn't have to back up the data and restore it as you would with traditional partitions.

In this part of this chapter, we're going to look at the following LVM topics:

- LVM components
- LVM configuration

Let's begin by looking at the components that must be in place for LVM to work.

LVM Components

LVM creates a virtual pool of memory space (called a *volume group*) from which *logical volumes* can be created. Linux can use LVM logical volumes just like standard disk partitions you create with fdisk. However, the way logical volumes are defined is quite a bit more complex. The basic structure of LVM consists of the following components:

- **Physical volumes**   A physical volume can be either a partition or an entire hard disk.
- **Volume groups**   A volume group consists of one or more physical volumes grouped together. The key thing to remember is the fact that the physical volumes can come from different hard disks. This means you can add hard disks or partitions to the volume group whenever you need more storage space.
- **Logical volumes**   These are defined from a volume group. Logical volumes can be formatted with a Linux file system and mounted just like physical partitions.

The way these components work together to provide storage for the Linux system is shown in Figure 10-3.

Figure 10-3
LVM components

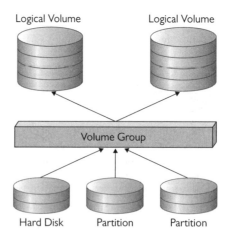

LVM Configuration

To create and mount logical volumes, you need to create physical volumes, volume groups, and then logical volumes (in that order).

Creating LVM Physical Volumes You can use disk partitions or even entire disks as physical LVM volumes. If you decide to use an existing partition, you should set the partition type to Linux LVM (8e). However, my experience has been that standard Linux partitions (type 83) work just as well. An example of setting the partition type with fdisk is shown here:

```
Command (m for help): t
Partition number (1,2, default 2): 1
Hex code (type L to list all codes): 8e
Changed type of partition 'Linux' to 'Linux LVM'
```

Be aware that if you want to use an entire hard disk as an LVM physical volume, it cannot contain a partition table. If the disk you want to use already has an existing partition table, you can use the dd command to obliterate it. In the example shown next, I overwrite the first 512KB block on the /dev/sdc hard disk (where the MBR partition resides) with junk null characters from the /dev/zero device file:

```
openSUSE:/media # dd if=/dev/zero of=/dev/sdc bs=512 count=1
1+0 records in
1+0 records out
512 bytes (512 B) copied, 0.2242 s, 2.3 kB/s
```

Once you have decided which disks/partitions you want to use, you run the pvcreate command at the shell prompt to define them as LVM physical volumes. The syntax is **pvcreate** *device*. In the following example, the first two partitions on /dev/sdb are defined as physical volumes as well as the entire /dev/sdc hard disk:

```
openSUSE:~ # pvcreate /dev/sdb1
openSUSE:~ # pvcreate /dev/sdb2
openSUSE:~ # pvcreate /dev/sdc
```

Once this is done, you can use the **pvscan -v** command to view all physical volumes on the system along with their size. This is shown in the following example:

```
openSUSE:~ # pvscan -v
    Volume Groups with the clustered attribute will be inaccessible.
    Wiping cache of LVM-capable devices
    Wiping internal VG cache
    Walking through all physical volumes
    PV /dev/sdc                     lvm2 [5.00 GiB]
    PV /dev/sdb1                    lvm2 [4.66 GiB]
    PV /dev/sdb2                    lvm2 [6.52 GiB]
    Total: 3 [16.18 GiB] / in use: 0 [0    ] / in no VG: 3 [16.18 GiB]
```

TIP If, at a later time, you need to remove a physical volume for some reason (such as a failing hard disk drive), you can use the pvmove utility to move the data from the physical volume to be removed to another physical volume you've defined in the system.

Once you have your physical volumes defined, you're ready to create your volume group. Let's review how to do that next.

Creating LVM Volume Groups   The vgcreate utility is used to create volume groups on your system. The syntax is **vgcreate** *volume_group_name physical_volume1 physical_volume2* .... In the following example, a volume group named DATA is created using the sdb1, sdb2, and sdc physical volumes:

```
openSUSE:~ # vgcreate DATA /dev/sdb1 /dev/sdb2 /dev/sdc
openSUSE:~ # pvscan -v
    Volume Groups with the clustered attribute will be inaccessible.
    Wiping cache of LVM-capable devices
    Wiping internal VG cache
    Walking through all physical volumes
    PV /dev/sdb1   VG DATA    lvm2 [4.65 GiB / 4.65 GiB free]
    PV /dev/sdb2   VG DATA    lvm2 [6.52 GiB / 6.52 GiB free]
    PV /dev/sdc    VG DATA    lvm2 [5.00 GiB / 5.00 GiB free]
    Total: 3 [16.16 GiB] / in use: 3 [16.16 GiB] / in no VG: 0 [0    ]
```

Notice in the output of the pvscan command that the three physical volumes are now members of the DATA volume group. After you initially create a volume group, you can use the following commands to manage it:

- Use **vgexpand** to add additional physical volumes to an existing volume group.

- Use **vgreduce** to remove a physical volume from an existing volume group. Before running vgreduce, you must use pvmove to shift the data in the physical volume to be removed to another physical volume on the system.

- Use **vgremove** to delete a volume group. Before you can use vgremove, you must first remove all logical volumes that have been defined in the volume group.

Once your volume group has been defined, you are ready to create logical volumes. Let's discuss how this is done next.

Creating LVM Logical Volumes   You use the lvcreate command to create logical volumes within a volume group. The syntax is **lvcreate –L** *volume_size* **–n** *volume_name volume_group_name*. In the following example, two 7GB volumes (named **research** and **development**) are defined in the DATA volume group:

```
openSUSE:~ # lvcreate -L 7G -n research DATA
openSUSE:~ # lvcreate -L 7G -n development DATA
openSUSE:~ # lvscan -v
    Volume Groups with the clustered attribute will be inaccessible.
    Finding all logical volumes
    ACTIVE              '/dev/DATA/research' [7.00 GiB] inherit
    ACTIVE              '/dev/DATA/development' [7.00 GiB] inherit
```

Notice that we used the lvscan command to view the logical volumes defined on the system. Also notice that we defined two logical volumes in the volume group, which itself is created by pooling together all the storage space from two disk partitions and one entire hard disk drive. Pretty cool!

To manage your logical volumes after they have been created, you use the following commands:

- Use **lvextend** to increase the size of a logical volume. You must first add additional physical volumes (disks or partitions) to the volume group to do this.

- Use **lvreduce** to reduce the size of a logical volume.

- Use **lvremove** to remove a logical volume from the system.

CAUTION   Use extreme caution when working with lvreduce and lvremove! If the file system is larger than the size you specify with lvreduce, you run risk of chopping off chunks of data. You should migrate any data you don't want to lose to a different logical volume if you decide to remove a logical volume with lvremove.

Once your logical volumes have been created, you need to create file systems on them and then mount them. You create a file system using mkfs, just as with traditional partitions. Use the following syntax:

```
mkfs -t file_system /dev/volume_group/logical_volume
```

You mount a logical volume using the mount command, just as you would to mount file systems on traditional partitions. Use the following syntax:

```
mount -t file_system /dev/volume_group/logical_volume /mount_point
```

Let's next talk about maintaining Linux file systems.

Maintaining Linux File Systems

Just as with any other operating system, you need to monitor and maintain your Linux file systems. In this part of the chapter, you learn how to do this as we cover the following topics:

- Checking partition and file usage
- Checking the file system integrity
- Checking for open files
- Identifying processes using files

Checking Partition and File Usage

One of the key problems you need to avoid when maintaining Linux file systems is running out of disk space. Linux provides the df and du utilities to help you keep track of how much space is used on a partition and which files are using that space.

The df utility shows you where your hard drive partitions, optical drives, and other storage devices (such as USB drives) are mounted in the file system. It also shows the total size of the device and how much of that space is used. Running df without any options shows information about all mounted file systems, as shown here:

```
openSUSE:/ # df
Filesystem     1K-blocks     Used Available Use% Mounted on
/dev/sda2       6194480 4528228   1328540  78% /
```

```
devtmpfs          760928       32    760896    1% /dev
tmpfs             772004       96    771908    1% /dev/shm
tmpfs             772004     3832    768172    1% /run
tmpfs             772004        0    772004    0% /sys/fs/cgroup
tmpfs             772004     3832    768172    1% /var/lock
tmpfs             772004     3832    768172    1% /var/run
/dev/sda3        7985600    21380   7535524    1% /home
/dev/sdb1        5029504    10232   4740744    1% /mnt/extraspace
```

You can also enter **df** *filename* at the shell prompt. This causes df to display information about the partition on which the specified file resides, as in this example:

```
openSUSE:/ # df /mnt/extraspace/myfile.txt
Filesystem     1K-blocks  Used Available Use% Mounted on
/dev/sdb1        5029504 10232   4740744    1% /mnt/extraspace
```

Notice in the preceding examples that, by default, df displays space statistics in blocks. This is fine if you are a bit-head and like to calculate available disk space from the number of blocks. I don't. Therefore, I always use the –h option with the df command. This causes df to display space statistics in human-readable format, such as KB, MB, and GB. An example of the same information in the preceding examples is shown next using the –h option:

```
openSUSE:/ # df -h
Filesystem      Size  Used Avail Use% Mounted on
/dev/sda2       6.0G  4.4G  1.3G  78% /
devtmpfs        744M   32K  744M   1% /dev
tmpfs           754M   96K  754M   1% /dev/shm
tmpfs           754M  3.8M  751M   1% /run
tmpfs           754M     0  754M   0% /sys/fs/cgroup
tmpfs           754M  3.8M  751M   1% /var/lock
tmpfs           754M  3.8M  751M   1% /var/run
/dev/sda3       7.7G   21M  7.2G   1% /home
/dev/sdb1       4.8G   10M  4.6G   1% /mnt/extraspace
```

Much better! If you want to view the type of file system used on each partition, you can add the –T option as well, as shown here:

```
openSUSE:/ # df -hT
Filesystem     Type      Size  Used Avail Use% Mounted on
/dev/sda2      ext4      6.0G  4.4G  1.3G  78% /
devtmpfs       devtmpfs  744M   32K  744M   1% /dev
tmpfs          tmpfs     754M   96K  754M   1% /dev/shm
tmpfs          tmpfs     754M  3.9M  751M   1% /run
tmpfs          tmpfs     754M     0  754M   0% /sys/fs/cgroup
tmpfs          tmpfs     754M  3.9M  751M   1% /var/lock
tmpfs          tmpfs     754M  3.9M  751M   1% /var/run
/dev/sda3      ext4      7.7G   43M  7.2G   1% /home
/dev/sdb1      ext4      4.8G   10M  4.6G   1% /mnt/extraspace
```

Another useful option you can use with df is –i, which lists inode usage information instead of disk space usage. Recall earlier in this chapter that when a file system is created on a partition, a fixed maximum number of inodes is assigned. If the file system stores a huge number of very small files, it's possible for it to run out of inodes even though plenty of disk space is still available. You can monitor inode usage using the **df –i** command, as shown here:

```
openSUSE:/ # df -i
Filesystem      Inodes  IUsed   IFree IUse% Mounted on
/dev/sda2       402400 168063 234337   42% /
devtmpfs        190232    376 189856    1% /dev
tmpfs           193001      9 192992    1% /dev/shm
tmpfs           193001    503 192498    1% /run
tmpfs           193001     13 192988    1% /sys/fs/cgroup
tmpfs           193001    503 192498    1% /var/lock
tmpfs           193001    503 192498    1% /var/run
/dev/sda3       516096    516 515580    1% /home
/dev/sdb1       327680     12 327668    1% /mnt/extraspace
```

Another utility you can use to monitor disk space usage is the du utility. Its function is to provide you with a summary of disk space usage of each file, recursively, for a specified directory. The syntax is **du** *directory*. Some useful options you can use with du include the following:

- **–c**   Used to calculate a grand total
- **–h**   Used to display output in human-readable format
- **--exclude** *filename_or_pattern*   Used to exclude all files that match the specified filename or pattern

The –h option is the most useful one, in my experience. Here is an example of viewing the space used by files in the /tmp directory in human-readable format:

```
openSUSE:/ # du -h /tmp
4.0K    /tmp/.esd-485
4.0K    /tmp/.X11-unix
4.0K    /tmp/.XIM-unix
4.0K    /tmp/.Test-unix
4.0K    /tmp/.esd-1000
4.0K    /tmp/.font-unix
4.0K    /tmp/systemd-private-otNWQw/tmp
8.0K    /tmp/systemd-private-otNWQw
4.0K    /tmp/VMwareDnD
4.0K    /tmp/.ICE-unix
4.0K    /tmp/vmware-root
4.0K    /tmp/systemd-private-OSAy3Q/tmp
8.0K    /tmp/systemd-private-OSAy3Q
4.0K    /tmp/orbit-student
64K     /tmp
```

Checking the File System Integrity

As with any other operating system, Linux partitions can sometimes encounter problems. These problems can be caused by a variety of conditions; however, my experience has been that the number-one source of partition corruption issues is a power outage that results in an unclean shutdown of the system. If your system goes down without properly unmounting a mounted partition, it's very likely that data corruption will occur.

NOTE This is a good argument for implementing an uninterruptible power supply (UPS) on your systems. Linux doesn't like unexpected shutdowns!

If something like this happens, you need to check your file systems for errors and make repairs, if necessary. This is done using the File System ChecK utility (fsck). To use this utility, you must first umount the file system you want to check. Then enter **fsck *device*** at the shell prompt. For example, if you want to check the file system on the first partition of the second hard drive in your system, you would enter **fsck /dev/sdb1**. The utility will then check the file system and report any errors encountered (or the lack thereof). Here is sample output from fsck:

```
openSUSE:~ # umount /dev/sdb1
openSUSE:~ # fsck /dev/sdb1fsck from util-linux 2.23.2
e2fsck 1.42.8 (20-Jun-2013)/dev/sdb1: clean, 12/402192 files, 61153/1605632 blocks
```

If errors are encountered, a code will be displayed that represents the sum of the errors encountered:

- **0**   No errors.
- **1**   File system errors corrected.
- **2**   System should be rebooted.
- **4**   File system errors left uncorrected.
- **8**   Operational error.
- **16**   Usage or syntax error.
- **32**   Fsck canceled by user request.
- **128**   Shared library error.

Notice in this example that e2fsck was run. That's because fsck is really just a front end to the following utilities:

- /sbin/fsck.msdos
- /sbin/fsck.cramfs
- /sbin/fsck.ext3
- /sbin/dosfsck
- /sbin/fsck.ext2
- /sbin/fsck
- /sbin/e2fsck
- /sbin/fsck.ext4
- /sbin/fsck.vfat
- /sbin/fsck.minix
- /sbin/fsck.reiserfs

If you run fsck without any options, it will query your /etc/fstab file to determine the file system type of the partition you want to check and then load the appropriate module for the file system. As you can see in the preceding list, versions of fsck exist for the Reiser, ext2, ext3, and ext4 file systems.

 NOTE The fsck.reiserfs utility can be run using the reiserfsck front end.

After the check is complete, you can remount the partition using the mount command.

One very useful feature of e2fsck is its ability to restore a damaged superblock on ext2/3/4 file systems. Remember from earlier in this chapter that the superblock is the block at the beginning of the partition that contains information about the structure of the file system. Also, most Linux file systems keep backup copies of the superblock at various locations in the partition. If the superblock gets corrupted, you can restore it using one of these backup copies. The syntax is **e2fsck –f –b** *backup_superblock device*. The –f option tells e2fsck to force a check, even if the file system seems to be clean. The –b option tells e2fsck which copy of the superblock it should use.

Here are some other useful file system management utilities:

- **tune2fs** This utility is used to adjust various file system parameters on ext2/3/4 file systems. These are some of the options you can use:

  - **–c** *n* Sets the number of mounts (*n*) after which the file system will automatically be checked by fsck.

  - **–i** *interval* **d|m|w** Sets the maximum time between file system checks in **d** (days), **m** (months), or **w** (weeks).

  - **–j** Adds a journal to an ext2 file system.

  - **–L** *volume_label* Sets the volume label of the file system.

  Here is an example:

  ```
  openSUSE:/ # tune2fs -L NewVol /dev/sdb1
  tune2fs 1.42.8 (20-Jun-2013)
  ```

- **reiserfstune** This is the Reiser equivalent of the tune2fs utility.

- **dumpe2fs** Displays lots of useful information about ext2/3/4 file systems. Use the –h option to make the output more readable. An example follows:

  ```
  openSUSE:/ # dumpe2fs -h /dev/sdb1
  dumpe2fs 1.42.8 (20-Jun-2013)
  Filesystem volume name:   NewVol
  Last mounted on:          /mnt/extraspace
  Filesystem UUID:          07ad1005-70c6-47f2-be9f-273ea6007878
  Filesystem magic number:  0xEF53
  Filesystem revision #:    1 (dynamic)
  Filesystem features:      has_journal ext_attr resize_inode dir_index
                            filetype needs_recovery extent flex_bg sparse_super
  ```

```
                                large_file huge_file uninit_bg dir_nlink extra_isize
Filesystem flags:               signed_directory_hash
Default mount options:          user_xattr acl
Filesystem state:               clean
Errors behavior:                Continue
Filesystem OS type:             Linux
Inode count:                    327680
Block count:                    1310720
Reserved block count:           65536
Free blocks:                    1254818
Free inodes:                    327668
First block:                    0
Block size:                     4096
Fragment size:                  4096
Reserved GDT blocks:            319
Blocks per group:               32768
Fragments per group:            32768
Inodes per group:               8192
Inode blocks per group:         512
Flex block group size:          16
Filesystem created:             Fri Jan 30 14:30:05 2015
Last mount time:                Fri Jan 30 15:05:16 2015
Last write time:                Fri Jan 30 15:05:28 2015
Mount count:                    2
Maximum mount count:            -1
Last checked:                   Fri Jan 30 14:30:05 2015
Check interval:                 0 (<none>)
Lifetime writes:                212 MB
Reserved blocks uid:            0 (user root)
Reserved blocks gid:            0 (group root)
First inode:                    11
Inode size:                     256
Required extra isize:           28
Desired extra isize:            28
Journal inode:                  8
Default directory hash:         half_md4
Directory Hash Seed:            feff3f13-c9f7-44b2-ba9b-d0290602f8f7
Journal backup:                 inode blocks
Journal features:               (none)
Journal size:                   128M
Journal length:                 32768
Journal sequence:               0x00000008
Journal start:                  0
```

- **debugfs** The debugfs program is an interactive file system debugger. It can be used to examine or even change the state of an ext2/3/4 file system. The syntax is **debugfs** *device*. When you run this command, the **debugfs:** prompt is displayed, as shown here:

```
openSUSE:/sbin # debugfs /dev/sdb1
debugfs 1.42.8 (20-Jun-2013)
debugfs:
```

By default, the file system is opened in read-only mode. If you need to make changes to the file system, you need to include the –w option to open it in read-write mode. Here are some of the commands you can enter at the **debugfs:** prompt:

- **show_super_stats** Displays information equivalent to that displayed by dumpe2fs.

- **write** *in_file out_file* Allows you to copy a file from the file system to another file system. This can be extremely useful in situations where you are trying to salvage an important file from a mangled file system.

- **stat** *file_or_directory_name*   Displays extended information about the file or directory specified. An example follows for a file named myfile2.txt:

```
Inode: 12   Type: regular    Mode:  0644   Flags: 0x80000
Generation: 556089601    Version: 0x00000000:00000001
User:     0   Group:     0   Size: 0
File ACL: 0    Directory ACL: 0
Links: 1   Blockcount: 0
Fragment:  Address: 0    Number: 0    Size: 0
 ctime: 0x4d812f93:d2d91b5c -- Wed Mar 16 15:45:55 2011
 atime: 0x4d812f93:d2d91b5c -- Wed Mar 16 15:45:55 2011
 mtime: 0x4d812f93:d2d91b5c -- Wed Mar 16 15:45:55 2011
crtime: 0x4d812f93:d2d91b5c -- Wed Mar 16 15:45:55 2011
Size of extra inode fields: 28
EXTENTS:
lines 1-12/12 (END)
```

- **list_deleted_inodes**   Displays a list of delete inodes in the file system.

You can do a lot with debugfs. We don't have the time or space to cover everything here. Have a look at the debugfs man page for more information.

- **xfs_admin**   The xfs equivalent of tune2fs. This utility actually uses the **xfs_db** executable to modify various parameters of an xfs file system. The file system must be unmounted before you can make any changes. Options you can use with this utility include the following:

  - **–j**   Enables version 2 log format, which is a journal format supporting larger log buffers.

  - **–l**   Displays the file system's label.

  - **–u**   Displays the file system's universally unique identifier (UUID).

  - **–L** *label*   Sets the file system's label.

  - **–U** *uuid*   Sets the UUID of the file system.

- **xfs_info**   Displays useful information about xfs file systems.

- **xfs_metadump**   Dumps xfs file system metadata (such as filenames and file sizes) to a file.

Let's next look at how you identify open files on a Linux file system.

Checking for Open Files

You can use the lsof command at the shell prompt to display a list of open files. Entering **lsof** at the shell prompt without any options lists all open files belonging to all active processes on the system. Useful options you can use with lsof include the following:

- **-s**   Displays file sizes.

- **-t**   Specifies that lsof should produce terse output with process identifiers only and no header. This is useful if you are piping the output of lsof to the kill command.

- **-u** *user_name*   Displays only open files associated with the specified user.

In the next example, a list of open files associated with the tux user on the system are displayed by lsof:

```
openSUSE:/sbin # lsof -u tux | more
lsof: WARNING: can't stat() fuse.gvfs-fuse-daemon file system /home/tux/.gvfs
      Output information may be incomplete.
COMMAND    PID USER   FD   TYPE             DEVICE SIZE/OFF     NODE NAME
gnome-key 3860  tux  cwd    DIR                8,3     4096        2 /
gnome-key 3860  tux  rtd    DIR                8,3     4096        2 /
gnome-key 3860  tux  txt    REG                8,3   878328   409704 /usr/
bin/gnome-keyring-daemon
gnome-key 3860  tux  mem    REG                8,3    19114   411496 /
lib64/libdl-2.11.2.so
gnome-key 3860  tux  mem    REG                8,3   122160   393375 /
lib64/libselinux.so.1
```

Let's next look at how you identify which processes are using a file.

Identifying Processes Using Files

In addition to listing open files, you may also need to identify processes running on your Linux system that are using a particular file in the file system. The fuser command displays the PIDs of processes using the specified files or file systems. By default, each filename is followed by a letter indicating the following:

- **c** Current directory
- **e** Executable being run
- **f** An open file
- **F** A file that is open for writing
- **r** The root directory
- **m** Memory mapped file or shared library

Options you can use with this command include the following:

- **–a** Show all files specified. By default, only files that are accessed by at least one process are shown.
- **–k** Kill processes accessing the file.
- **–i** Ask the user for confirmation before killing a process.
- **–u** Append the user name of the process owner to each process ID number (PID).

In the following example, you can see that the tux user is running the /usr/bin/top executable and that the process using the file has a PID of 9823:

```
openSUSE:/sbin # fuser -u /usr/bin/top
/usr/bin/top:        9823e(tux)
```

Now that you know how to manage partitions on a Linux system, let's practice in the following exercise.

Exercise 10-1: Managing Linux Partitions

In this exercise, you will practice working with Linux partitions. You can perform this exercise using the virtual machine that comes with this book. Run snapshot 10-1 for the correctly configured environment.

 VIDEO   Please watch the Exercise 10-1 video for a demonstration on how to perform this task.

Complete the following:

1. Power your system on and log in as your student user.

2. Change to your root user account by entering **su –** and entering a root password of **student**.

3. At the shell prompt, enter **fdisk /dev/sdb**.

4. View the existing partitions on the device by entering **p**.

5. Create a new partition by entering **n**.

6. Specify a primary partition by entering **p**.

7. Create the first partition on the disk by entering **1**.

8. Specify a first cylinder of **1**.

9. Use the default for the last cylinder by pressing ENTER.

10. Verify your new partition by entering **p**.

11. Write the partition to disk by entering **w**.

12. Format the new partition using the ext4 file system by entering **mkfs –t ext4 /dev/sdb1**.

13. Wait while the file system is created.

14. Create a new directory in /mnt named newdisk by entering **mkdir /mnt/newdisk**.

15. Mount the new file system in this directory by entering **mount –t auto /dev/sdb1 /mnt/newdisk**.

16. Verify that the disk was mounted by entering **mount**.

17. Configure the file system to be automatically mounted every time the system boots by entering **vi /etc/fstab** at the shell prompt.

18. Add the following line to the file:
    ```
    /dev/sdb1 /mnt/newdisk ext4 acl,user_xattr 1 2
    ```

19. Save your changes and exit vi.

20. Check your new file system by first unmounting it. Enter **umount /mnt/newdisk** at the shell prompt.

21. Enter **fsck /dev/sdb1** at the shell prompt. The fsck utility should report that the file system was clean.

22. Remount the device.

23. Return to your regular user account by entering **exit**.

Let's change our focus and talk about how to use removable media on a Linux system.

Mounting Removable Media

One of the more difficult aspects of working with a Linux system for those coming to Linux from Windows tends to be the subject of how to use removable media, including optical discs and USB drives. Using these types of storage on a Windows system is trivial. You just insert the disc and everything just works.

Using removable media with a Linux system, on the other hand, takes a little more effort. However, with a little bit of practice, it will become second nature to you. In this part of the chapter, you'll learn how to make it all work. Specifically, we're going to discuss the following tasks:

- Working with optical devices
- Working with USB and FireWire devices

Let's begin by discussing how to work with good ol' optical discs.

Working with Optical Devices

Just as you mount partitions, you must also mount optical drives, such as CDs, DVDs, or Blu-ray discs, before you can use them. The only real difference is the mount point used and the file system type. For most optical discs you can use the file system type of iso9660 with the mount command. For Blu-ray discs, you specify a file system type of udf. If you're unsure what file system type to use, just specify auto and let the mount command figure it out for you.

You can mount optical discs anywhere you want in the file system. However, by convention they are usually mounted in /media or /mnt, depending on your distribution.

NOTE Most modern Linux distributions implement a service called autofs to help you with mounting removable media. When configured and running, it will automatically detect when removable media has been inserted and mount it for you.

To mount a disc on a Linux system, insert it in your optical drive. Change to your root account and then enter **mount –t iso9660 *device mount_point***. For example, if you want to mount the disc into /media/dvd, you would enter **mount –t iso9660 /dev/sr0 /media/dvd**, as shown here:

```
openSUSE:/ # mount -t iso9660 /dev/sr0 /media/dvd/
mount: block device /dev/sr0 is write-protected, mounting read-only
```

NOTE   Most distributions also implement a symbolic link file named /dev/cdrom that points to /dev/sr0.

As with hard disk partitions, you can make the mounting process for optical devices easier by adding an entry to your /etc/fstab file. Consider the following:

```
/dev/sr0     /media/dvd     iso9660     noauto,user,sync     0     0
```

Adding this line makes it so you only need to enter **mount /dev/sr0** to mount an optical device. As with any mounted file system, you should use umount to unmount an optical disc before ejecting it.

Let's next discuss mounting external storage devices.

Working with USB and FireWire Devices

All Linux distributions support external storage devices using a USB or FireWire interface. Because Linux is plug-and-play compatible, it should automatically detect a new device when you connect external storage (such as a flash drive or an external hard drive).

Most Linux distributions will address these devices as a SCSI device. Your external devices are addressed through /dev/sdx. The value of x depends on how many hard drives you already have installed in the system. It will always be addressed as the last SCSI device in your system. For example, if you have a SATA hard drive and a SATA DVD drive, your external USB or FireWire device will be /dev/sdc.

To verify this, you can check your /var/log/messages file after connecting the device. You should see a kernel message indicating that a new SCSI disk was attached. If necessary, you can use the same procedure discussed previously to create a partition on the device and then create a file system. If a file system has already been created on the device, you only need to mount it.

You mount USB and FireWire devices in the same way you mount a typical hard disk partition. One issue that comes up here is that you may not be entirely sure what file system is being used on the external device, especially if the drive is being used among several different computers with different operating systems. Because of this, I recommend that you use the **–t auto** option with the mount command. This will cause mount to try to detect for you what file system has been used on the device.

Other than that, mounting a USB or FireWire device is relatively easy. Simply enter **mount –t auto *device mount_point***. For example, if I want to mount an external flash drive that is the fourth device in the system in the /media/THUMBDRIVE directory, I would enter **mount –t auto /dev/sdd /media/THUMBDRIVE**.

NOTE   If autofs is running on your system, it will automatically detect when USB or FireWire devices have been inserted and mount them for you.

As with any other device, you can add an entry to your /etc/fstab file to make the process easier. In addition, you must unmount the device before you remove it from the system using the umount command.

Now that you know how the Linux file system works and how to complete common file system tasks, let's talk about how you go about backing up the file system.

Backing Up Data

One of the key roles you must perform as a Linux system administrator is to ensure that the data on the systems you are responsible for is protected. One of the best ways you can do this is to back up the data. Having a backup creates a redundant copy of the data so that if a disaster occurs, the data can be restored.

It's important that you remember that data is stored, for the most part, on mechanical devices in your Linux system. Hard drives have motors and other moving parts that slowly wear out over time. In fact, hard drives usually have a mean time between failures (MTBF) value assigned to them by the manufacturer. This MTBF basically gives you an estimate of how long a drive will last before it fails. Basically, it's not a matter of *if* a hard drive will fail; it's a matter of *when*.

I relate this because I want you to take backing up seriously. Many system administrators, frankly, get very lazy about running backups. It's an easy task to blow off, thinking "I'll run a backup tomorrow...." Before you know it, it has been weeks since the last time a backup was run.

If you're employed by an organization to maintain their systems and you fail to run backups, I can just about guarantee you will lose your job if a disaster happens. Several years ago, I participated on a support call with a system administrator whose server had completely died. He had called us in a last-ditch effort hoping that we would have some kind of magic solution that would get his data back. When we told him that we couldn't and that he would have to reinstall and restore from his backups, there was silence on the other end of the phone for a long time. He got a little choked up and whispered, "I don't have any backups. I'm going to lose my job over this." Take my advice, develop a backup plan and stick to it religiously.

There are several components to a backup plan. In this part of the chapter, we're going to discuss the following:

- Selecting a backup medium
- Selecting a backup strategy
- Using Linux backup utilities

Let's begin by discussing how to select a backup medium.

Selecting a Backup Medium

Back in the "old days," we really only had two choices for backing up data: floppies and a tape drive. Floppies didn't hold much and were notoriously unreliable, so most system admins opted for tape drives.

Today, some admins still use tape drives to back up their data. Tape drives use magnetic tape, much like the tape used in an 8 mm video camera, to store data. Tape drives store a lot of data and are relatively inexpensive. They are an acceptable choice for backing up data on your Linux system.

However, tape drives have several limitations. First of all, they wear out. Tape drives have a lot of mechanical parts that wear out over time. The tape itself is run over the top of a read/write head in the tape drive, so it wears out over time as well due to friction. Second, tapes are relatively slow. Backing up large quantities of data can take hours.

As a result, many admins are exploring other media for backing up system data. For a while, read/write CDs and DVDs were in vogue for backups. However, modern hard drives are really big, making optical discs obsolete for running system-wide backups. Backing up a 3TB hard drive with DVDs today is similar to backing up a 100MB hard drive with floppy diskettes 20 years ago. Yes, it can be done, but it's a painful, time-consuming process. Unless the amount of data you're backing up is relatively small, I don't recommend this option.

Another option that many system administrators are exploring (and one that I really like personally) is the use of removable USB hard drives. Back in the old days, we used tape drives to back up our hard drives because hard disks were extremely expensive. The general rule of thumb back in the early 1990s was "$1 per megabyte" when buying a hard disk. It was just too expensive to use hard drives for backups. In addition, we didn't have a hot-swappable external interface for hard drives. Therefore, tape was one of the few viable options.

Today, however, the price of hard drives has dropped dramatically. You can buy a removable USB or FireWire hard drive for less than a $0.10 per gigabyte. Using external hard drives for backups has two distinct advantages. First, they are much, much faster than tapes. Backups that took hours on a tape drive take minutes on a hard disk. Second, hard drives tend to be more reliable than tape drives.

Of course, using hard drives for backups isn't a perfect solution. One of the key disadvantages is the fact that the disk partition must be mounted on the removable drive to run a backup. If something bad were to happen to the system that destroyed data on the main hard drive while the removable drive was connected, it could potentially destroy data on the removable drive as well.

As with any backup medium, you have to weigh the benefits and drawbacks when deciding to use external hard drives for backups.

 TIP Personally, I prefer a hot-backup solution over standard backups. I use the rsync utility on my mission-critical Linux systems to synchronize data to a second Linux system over the network, essentially creating a mirrored system. In my office, I synchronize every hour; but you could do this more or less frequently as needed. If my main system ever goes down, I can simply switch over to my backup system. I'm back up and running in only a few seconds!

 NOTE Many users today are opting to use cloud-based backups. After you subscribe to a cloud-based backup service, your system is automatically backed up over the Internet to a data farm somewhere else in the world. Cloud-based backups are reliable and very convenient. However, there are many security issues surrounding this option. How do I know my data is transmitted securely? How do I know the service provider's network and servers are secure?

At any rate, you first need to select the backup medium you will use, purchase the appropriate equipment, and connect it to your system. Once that's in place, you next need to select a backup strategy.

Selecting a Backup Strategy

When creating a backup plan, you have several different options for how you will conduct your backups. You need to consider the following:

- Selecting a backup type
- Selecting a backup schedule
- Determining what to back up

Let's start by choosing a backup type.

Selecting a Backup Type

Depending on the backup utility you choose, you will usually have at least three different types of backups that you can use (sometimes more). These include the following:

- **Full** In a full backup, all specified files are backed up, regardless of whether or not they've been modified since the last backup. After being backed up, each file is flagged as having been backed up.
- **Incremental** During an incremental backup, only the files that have been modified since the last backup (full or incremental) are backed up. After being backed up, each file is flagged as having been backed up.
- **Differential** During a differential backup, only the files that have been modified since the last full backup are backed up. Even though they have been backed up during a differential backup, the files involved are *not* flagged as having been backed up.

To determine your backup strategy, you need to select from the preceding backup types. For example, you could run a full backup every time. This strategy is thorough and exhaustive. It's also the fastest strategy when you need to restore data from a backup.

However, full backups can take a very long time to complete. This is because every single file is backed up regardless of whether or not it was changed since the last backup. Therefore, many administrators mix full backups with incremental or differential backups.

If you use a full/incremental strategy, you run a full backup once a week, usually when the system load is lightest, such as Friday night. Then you run incremental backups each of the other six days in the week. Using this strategy, you should end up with one full backup and six incremental backups for each week. The advantage of this strategy is primarily speed. Because incrementals only back up files that have changed since the last full *or* incremental backup, they usually run very fast. The drawback to this strategy is that you must restore six backups in exactly the correct order. The full backup is restored first, followed by the first incremental, then the second incremental, and so on. This can be a slow process.

Alternatively, you can also use full backups with differentials. In this strategy, you run a full backup on Friday night, usually. Then you run a differential each of the other nights of the week. Remember that a differential backup only backs up files that have changed since the last full backup, *not* since the last differential. Therefore, each day's backup gets progressively bigger. The main advantage to this strategy is that restores are really fast. Instead of seven backups to restore, you only have to restore two—the last full backup first, followed by the last differential backup (and no others!). The disadvantage to this method is that the differential backups start out very fast but can become almost as long as a full backup by the time you reach the last day in the cycle.

 CAUTION Whatever you do, don't mix incremental and differential backups together! Your backups will miss data because the files to be backed up will be flagged inconsistently.

Whichever strategy you choose, you should be sure to keep a rotation of backups. Many administrators will rotate their backup media so that they have three to four weeks' worth of past backups on hand. You never know when a file that was deleted two weeks ago will suddenly be needed again!

In addition, you should be sure to verify your backups. Most backup utilities provide you with the option of checking your backup after it's complete against the original files. If you don't, you may have errors in your backup.

Now that you've selected a backup type, you next need to set a backup schedule.

Selecting a Backup Schedule

You can use whatever backup schedule works best for you. However, most admins work on a weekly rotation, as discussed previously. Pick one day for your full backup and then the remaining days of the week for your incremental or differential backups.

You should also schedule your backups to occur when the load on the system is at its lightest. Late in the evening or in the early morning are usually best, depending on your organization's schedule.

Finally, you need to specify what will be backed up. Let's discuss this next.

Determining What to Back Up

Most Linux systems you're going to be working with will probably consume a fairly large amount of disk space, depending on the packages you've installed. You need to decide how much of this consumed disk space is going to be backed up.

One option is to back up the entire system. This is a safe, thorough option. However, it's also somewhat slow due to the sheer amount of data involved. Many administrators choose not to do this. Instead, they only back up critical data on the system, such as user data and configuration information. The theory behind this strategy is that you could, in the event of a disaster, simply reinstall a new system and then restore the critical data to it. If you choose this strategy, you should consider backing up the following directories in your Linux file system:

- /etc
- /home
- /opt
- /root
- /var
- /srv

Notice that this strategy doesn't back up your Linux system or its utilities. Instead, it only backs up your configuration files, your user data, your log files, and your web/ftp files.

Once you've determined what to back up, the next part of your plan is to determine what you'll back it up with.

Using Linux Backup Utilities

When working with Linux, you have a host of different utilities at your disposal to conduct a backup. Many come with the operating system; others can be obtained from third parties. For your LPIC-1/Linux+ exam, you need to be familiar with the tools that are common to most distributions and are run from the shell prompt. In this part of the chapter, we're going to look at the following:

- Using tar
- Using cpio
- Using dd to copy data

Let's begin by looking at the venerable tar utility.

Using tar

The tar utility has been around for a very long time and is a very commonly used Linux backup tool. The acronym "tar" stands for tape archive. The tar utility takes a list of specified files and copies them into a single archive file (.tar). The .tar file can then be compressed with the gzip utility on your Linux system, resulting in a file with a .tar.gz extension. This is called a *tarball*.

The tar utility can be used to send backup jobs to a variety of backup media, including tape drives and removable hard disk drives. The syntax for using tar to create backups is **tar –cvf** *filename directory*. The –c option tells tar to create a new archive. The –v option tells tar to work in verbose mode, displaying each file being backed up onscreen. The –f option specifies the name of the tar archive to be created.

For example, if you wanted to create a backup of the /home directory named backup.tar on an external USB hard drive mounted in /media/usb, you would enter **tar –cvf /media/usb/backup .tar /home**, as shown in this example:

```
openSUSE:/ # tar -cvf /media/usb/backup.tar /home
tar: Removing leading '/' from member names
/home/
/home/tux/
/home/tux/.gftp/
/home/tux/.gftp/gftp.log
/home/tux/.gftp/bookmarks
/home/tux/.gftp/gftprc
/home/tux/.nautilus/
/home/tux/.local/
/home/tux/.local/share/
...
```

Notice in this example that a message stating **tar: Removing leading '/' from member names** is displayed. When a tar archive is created, absolute paths are converted to relative paths by default. As a result, the leading / is removed.

Option	Function
–A --concatenate	Appends tar files to an existing archive.
–c --create	Creates a new archive file.
–d --compare	Identifies differences between an archive file and files in the file system.
–J --xz	Does one of two things. During archive creation, it compresses the new tar archive by running it through the xz utility. During extraction, it first decompresses the tar archive using the xz utility.
–P --absolute-names	Causes tar to *not* strip leading / from filenames.
–r --append	Adds files to the end of a tar archive.
–t --list	Lists the contents of an archive file.
–u --update	Appends files only if they are newer than the existing files in an archive.
–x --extract	Extracts files from an archive.
–z --gzip --gunzip	Does one of two things. During archive creation, it compresses the new tar archive by running it through the gzip utility. During extraction, it first decompresses the tar archive using the gunzip utility.
–j --bzip2 --bunzip	Does one of two things. During archive creation, it compresses the new tar archive by running it through the bzip2 utility. During extraction, it first decompresses the tar archive using the bunzip2 utility.
–X *filename* --exclude-from	Causes tar to exclude files listed in the text file specified.

Table 10-2   The tar Command Options

You can use the options shown in Table 10-2 with tar.

 NOTE   You can also compress/decompress tar archives (or any other files, for that matter) directly from the shell prompt using the gzip and gunzip utilities, the bzip2 and bunzip2 utilities, or the xz utility. Archive files compressed with bzip2 instead of gzip will usually have an extension of .bz2 instead of .gz. Archive files compressed with xz will usually have an extension of .xz or .lzma.

If you want to back up to a tape drive instead of a USB drive, you could do this by replacing the filename parameter in the tar command to the device name for your tape drive. On most distributions, the first SCSI tape drive in the system is referenced through /dev/st0. Therefore, you could enter **tar –cvf /dev/st0 /home** if you wanted to run the same backup as in the previous example, but send it to a SCSI tape drive instead.

To restore a tar archive, simply enter **tar –xvf** *filename*. For example, to extract the archive we just created, you would enter **tar –xvf /media/usb/backup.tar**. This will extract the archive into the current working directory. If the archive has been zipped, you can also use the –z option to unzip the archive before extracting it.

In addition to tar, you can also use cpio to create backups. Let's discuss how it is used next.

Using cpio

The cpio utility can also be used to make archive files just like tar. A key difference between tar and cpio is the fact that you must provide cpio with a list of files and directories to back up from the standard input. This can be done using cat to display the contents of a file or by generating a listing using find or ls.

For example, let's suppose you want to back up the contents of the /home/tux/myproject directory on your Linux system. To use cpio to do this, you must somehow generate a listing of files and directories in this directory and send it to cpio. Then you must redirect the output from cpio to a file. This can be done using the find utility, discussed earlier. You could switch to /home/tux/myproject and then enter **find . –print –depth | cpio –ov > /media/usb/backup.cpio**. The find utility will generate a listing of all files in the current directory. Because the –print option was used, find will print the full name of each file to the screen (the standard output). Because the –depth option was also used, find checks the contents of each directory before processing the directory itself.

 TIP If there are no subdirectories in the MyProjects directory, an easier way to do this would be to enter **ls | cpio –ov > /media/usb/backup.cpio**.

The key here is the fact that we've piped the standard output from find to the standard input of cpio. The cpio utility uses this as a list of files and directories to archive. The –o option tells cpio to create a new archive. The –v option simply tells cpio to run verbosely, displaying the name of each file and directory as it's processed. Finally, we have to redirect the standard output from cpio (the archive) to a file in the file system. This is done by entering > followed by the name of the archive file.

You can also compress a cpio archive by adding the gzip utility to the pipe[md]for example, **ls | cpio –ov | gzip > /media/usb/backup.cpio.gz**.

To restore files from a cpio archive, you run cpio from the shell prompt using the –i option and specifying the name of the archive to process. When you do, the archive files will be extracted into the current working directory. For example, we could extract the archive we just created by entering **cpio –iv < /media/usb/backup.cpio**, like this:

```
openSUSE:/tmp # cpio -iv < /media/usb/backup.cpio
acpidump
accessdb
acpisrc
.
341 blocks
```

If the cpio archive was compressed with gzip, you will have to run it through the gunzip command to decompress the archive before you can extract files from it with cpio. This is shown here:

```
openSUSE:/media/usb # ls
backup.cpio.gz  backup.tar
openSUSE:/media/usb # gunzip backup.cpio.gz
openSUSE:/media/usb # ls
backup.cpio  backup.tar
```

As you can see, the backup.cpio.gz file is decompressed by the gunzip command into the backup.cpio file, which can now be manipulated with the cpio command. Another way to do this is to add the –c option to the gunzip command and then pipe the results to cpio –i. The –c option tells gunzip to write the output of the command to the standard output, leaving the original file intact. Essentially, this just writes the uncompressed filename to the standard out, which is then sent to cpio for processing. Here is an example:

```
openSUSE:/media/usb # ls
backup.cpio.gz  backup.tar
openSUSE:/media/usb # gunzip -c backup.cpio.gz | cpio -i
341 blocks
openSUSE:/media/usb # ls
accessdb  acpidump  acpisrc  backup.cpio.gz  backup.tar
```

As you can see, the gunzip command extracted the name of the file compressed in the gzip archive and sent it to the cpio –i command, which then extracted the three files out of the archive to the local directory.

Before we end this chapter, we need to look at the dd utility. Let's do that next.

Using dd to Copy Data

You can use the dd command to convert and copy files. You can copy all kinds of Linux data with this command, including entire partitions. You may be thinking, "Big deal, I already know how to use cp and mv." Actually, the dd utility is quite useful. The key difference between dd and other file copy utilities is the fact that it copies data using *records*. The default size for a record is 512 bytes.

Let's first look at how you copy a file with dd. The syntax is **dd if=*input_file* of=*output_file***. Use the if= (input file) option to specify the file to be copied. Use the of= (output file) option to specify the name of the new file. Here is an example:

```
openSUSE:/ # dd if=/home/tux/MyProject/acpidump of=/home/tux/acpidump.copy
29+1 records in
29+1 records out
15112 bytes (15 kB) copied, 0.000263331 s, 57.4 MB/s
```

 NOTE You can modify the default record size using the **bs=*block_size*** option.

One of the cool things about dd is the fact that, because it uses records, it can copy an entire partition to a single file. This is powerful. Essentially, dd is a simple command-line tool that you can use to implement a form of drive imaging. I have a friend (who is Mr. Uber Linux Admin) and he uses dd in scripts to create his own imaging applications. Cool stuff!

To copy an entire partition, you enter **dd if=*device_file* of=*output_file*** at the shell prompt. The device file of the partition is used as the input file. All the contents of the partition are written to the output file specified. In the example that follows, the dd command is used to copy the /dev/sdb1 partition to a file named partitionbackup in the root user's home directory:

```
openSUSE:/ # dd if=/dev/sdb1 of=/root/partitionbackup
dd: writing to '/root/partitionbackup':
7500249+0 records in
7500248+0 records out
3840126976 bytes (3.8 GB) copied, 108.441 s, 35.4 MB/s
```

The dd command can even create an image file of an entire hard disk. The syntax again is **dd if=*device_file* of=*output_file***. The difference is that you simply specify the device file of the hard disk itself instead of a partition. In the next example, the entire /dev/sdb hard drive is archived into the drivebackup file:

```
openSUSE:~ # dd if=/dev/sdb of=/mnt/bigdrive/drivebackup
16777216+0 records in
16777216+0 records out
8589934592 bytes (8.6 GB) copied, 157.931 s, 54.4 MB/s
```

Another useful feature of dd is the fact that it can create a backup copy of your hard drive's master boot record (MBR) and partition table. Again, this is possible because it looks at data as records. The syntax is **dd if=*device_file* of=*output_file* bs=512 count=1**. This tells dd to grab just the first 512K block of the hard drive, which is where your MBR and partition table reside. This is shown in the following example:

```
openSUSE:/tmp # dd if=/dev/sda of=/root/mbrbackup bs=512 count=1
1+0 records in
1+0 records out
512 bytes (512 B) copied, 0.0123686 s, 41.4 kB/s
```

Let's practice backing up in the following exercise.

Exercise 10-2: Backing Up Data

In this exercise, you will practice backing up data. You can perform this exercise using the virtual machine that comes with this book. Run snapshot 10-2 for the correctly configured environment.

 VIDEO Please watch the Exercise 10-2 video for a demonstration on how to perform this task.

Complete the following:

1. With your system up and running, open a terminal session.

2. Change to your root user account.

3. At the shell prompt, enter **tar –cvf /mnt/newdisk/backup.tar /home**.

4. Enter **ls /mnt/newdisk**. Verify that the backup file exists.

5. Change to the /tmp directory by entering **cd /tmp** at the shell prompt.

6. Extract the tar file to the current directory by entering **tar –xvf /mnt/newdisk/backup.tar**.

7. Use the **ls** command to verify that the files from the tar archive were extracted to the current directory.

8. Switch back to your regular user account by entering **exit**.

You are becoming quite the Linux expert!

Chapter Review

In this chapter, I reviewed a variety of topics related to managing the Linux file system. The first topic I discussed was how to manage disk partitions. I pointed out that you must partition a disk before you can use it in a Linux system. One option for doing this is to create MBR partitions using the fdisk utility. I reviewed the steps for creating a new partition using this command. I emphasized that you must commit your changes to disk before fdisk actually writes the new partitions you created.

Newer Linux distributions can also support GPT partitions. GPT is a part of the overall Unified Extensible Firmware Interface (UEFI) specification and is designed to address many of the shortcomings of the venerable MBR partitioning scheme:

- There are no primary, extended, or logical partitions in GPT.
- GPT supports gigantic disks and partitions.
- Most Linux distributions support up to 128 GPT partitions per disk.
- GPT provides partition fault tolerance by storing a copy of the partition table in the first and last sectors on the disk.
- GPT performs a cyclic redundancy check (CRC) to verify the integrity of the partition table.

To manage GPT partitions, you use the gdisk utility, which can be used to perform the following tasks:

- Convert an MBR partition table to a GPT partition table.
- Verify a hard disk.
- Create and delete GPT partitions.
- Display information about a partition.
- Change the name and type of a partition.
- Back up and restore a disk's partition table.

In addition to gdisk, you can also use the parted command at the shell prompt to manage GPT partitions. You can use it to add, delete, and edit the partitions on your disk.

I then discussed how to format a partition with a file system. This is done using the mkfs utility. I related that you use mkfs to create file systems. This utility is actually a front end for the real commands that make each specific type of file system (ext2, ext3, ext4, msdos, vfat, and so on). The mkreiserfs utility is used to create Reiser file systems. You can also use the mke2fs command at the shell prompt to create ext*x* file systems.

You specify which file system you want to use by entering the –t option and the type of file system. I pointed out that xfs support must be added to the Linux kernel before you can create an xfs file system.

If you need to format a swap partition, you use the mkswap command at the shell prompt. The partition type must be switched to 82 first using fdisk. Next, you enter **mkswap *device*** at the shell prompt and then you use the swapon command to enable the new swap partition. You can disable an existing swap partition using the swapoff command.

After a partition has been formatted, you can then mount it using the mount command. I pointed out that Linux mounts all partitions in directories within the same file system. It doesn't use drive letters as Windows does. Switching to a directory in the file system where a partition is mounted switches you to that device. I discussed the syntax for mounting a partition with mount. I pointed out that mount can also be used to display mounted partitions. To unmount a partition, you use the umount command.

I discussed the role of the /etc/fstab file. I pointed out that a mounted file system won't stay mounted after the system is rebooted if it doesn't have an entry in the /etc/fstab file. I reviewed the six fields used for each fstab entry. I also discussed how you can add a new entry to ensure a file system is mounted at system boot.

We then transitioned to a discussion of LVM, which provides an alternative to the traditional process of creating disk partitions. Using LVM, you create volume groups from storage devices in your system. From the volume group, you allocate space to specific logical volumes, which are managed by the logical volume manager. Instead of mounting partitions, you mount logical volumes at mount points in your file system.

LVM allows you to dynamically add space to the system. To add capacity, all you have to do is install a new hard drive in the system and then allocate its space. You don't have to back up the data and restore it as you would with traditional partitions. To create LVM storage on your system, you use the following process:

1. Create physical volumes with the pvcreate command.

2. Create a volume group using the vgcreate command.

3. Create logical volumes using the lvcreate command.

I then shifted gears and discussed how to maintain the Linux file system. I first looked at checking space used by partitions, directories, and files by using the df and du utilities.

I then related that partitions can, occasionally, become damaged. If this happens, you can use the fsck utility to check and repair the partition. I pointed out that fsck is really a front end to various file system–specific repair utilities. I discussed how you can use the e2fsck utility to restore a damaged superblock.

I then looked at the following file system maintenance utilities:

- tune2fs
- reiserfstune
- dumpe2fs
- debugfs
- xfs_admin
- xfs_info
- xfs_metadump

I also looked at using the lsof command to check for open files in the file system. In addition, I related that you can use the fuser command to display the PIDs of processes using specified files or file systems.

I then reviewed how mount can also be used to mount removable media in the file system. Just as partitions are mounted in a directory, removable devices are also mounted in a directory in the file system. You access these devices through the directory where they are mounted (called a *mount point*). I reviewed the procedure for mounting floppy diskettes, optical discs, USB devices, and FireWire devices. I pointed out that if you don't know what kind of file system is used by a removable device, you can use the –t auto option to allow the mount utility to automatically determine the correct parameter to use.

I ended this chapter by discussing how to back up your Linux file system. I emphasized the importance of conducting backups on a regular schedule. I then discussed the elements required to create a backup plan for your systems. The first step is to select a backup medium. I discussed the advantages and disadvantages of tape drives, recordable optical drives, and removable hard drives.

The next step is to select a backup strategy. I discussed how full, incremental, and differential backups work and how to combine them to design your own backup strategy. I also emphasized the importance of rotating your backup media as well as verifying your backup.

The next step is to determine your backup schedule and then to decide what to back up. I reviewed the directories in the file system that are commonly backed up, including /etc, /home, /opt, /root, /var, and /srv.

I ended the chapter by reviewing some of the Linux backup utilities you can use to back up your system. I first reviewed the syntax for using tar, both with hard disks and with tape drives. I then reviewed the syntax for using cpio to create file archives. I discussed how to use gzip and bzip2 to compress/decompress tar and cpio archives. I also discussed how you can use dd to copy files and even create image files from entire disk partitions.

Accelerated Review

- You must partition and format a disk before you can mount it in the Linux file system.
- The fdisk utility is used to create an MBR partition on hard disks.
- You have to set the partition type when partitioning disks.
- Partition changes are only saved in memory until you commit them to disk.

- Newer Linux distributions support GPT partitions, which are designed to address many of the shortcomings of the older MBR-type partitions.

- To manage GPT partitions, you use the gdisk utility or the parted utility.

- After partitioning a disk, you need to format it with mkfs or mkreiserfs.

- After formatting a disk, you can mount it using the mount command.

- The /etc/mtab file can be used to view mounted file systems.

- You can also use /proc/mounts to view mounted file systems.

- You can unmount a mounted file system using the umount command.

- All file systems must be unmounted before Linux is shut down.

- Mounted file systems won't be remounted on reboot unless they have an entry in the /etc/fstab file.

- The /etc/fstab file specifies mount points and other options for specific devices.

- LVM provides an alternative to the traditional process of creating disk partitions.

- Using LVM, you create volume groups from storage devices in your system.

- From the volume group, you allocate space to specific logical volumes.

- Instead of mounting partitions, you mount logical volumes at mount points in your file system.

- LVM allows you to dynamically add space to the system.

- To create LVM storage on your system, you use the following process:

  - Create physical volumes with the pvcreate command.

  - Create a volume group using the vgcreate command.

  - Create logical volumes using the lvcreate command.

- You can monitor disk space and inode usage using the df and du utilities.

- The fsck utility is used to check and repair file systems.

- The e2fsck utility can be used to restore a damaged superblock on ext2/3/4 file systems.

- The tune2fs utility is used to adjust various file system parameters on ext2/3/4 file systems.

- The reiserfstune utility is the Reiser equivalent of the tune2fs utility.

- The dumpe2fs utility can display lots of useful information about ext2/3/4 file systems.

- The debugfs utility is an interactive file system debugger.

- The xfs_admin utility is the xfs equivalent of tune2fs.

- The xfs_info utility displays useful information about xfs file systems.

- The xfs_metadump utility dumps xfs file system metadata (such as filenames and sizes) to a file.

- You can use the lsof command at the shell prompt to display a list of open files.

- The fuser command displays the PIDs of processes using the specified files or file systems.

- Removable devices must be mounted in the Linux file system before they can be accessed.

- The mount command can be used to mount floppy diskettes.

- Floppies generally use the vfat file system type.

- The first floppy diskette in your system is /dev/fd0.

- You can use /etc/fstab to automate the process of mounting a floppy.

- You must use umount to unmount a floppy before you can remove it from the system.

- Optical discs must be mounted in the file system before they can be accessed.

- Optical discs are mounted using the iso9660 file system type.

- Optical discs are usually mounted in /media/cdrom, /media/cdrecorder, /media/dvd, or /mnt/cdrom.

- Linux sees USB and FireWire devices as SCSI devices.

- USB and FireWire devices are mounted using mount.

- If you don't know what type of file system is used on a USB or FireWire device, you can use –t auto to let mount try to determine the correct file system type.

- It is absolutely critical that you regularly back up your system.

- Tape drives are commonly used to back up data.

- Tape drives hold a large amount of data and are relatively inexpensive.

- Tape drives are also slow and tend to wear out.

- Rewritable CDs and DVDs can be used for backups, but they really don't hold enough information.

- Removable hard drives are becoming a popular solution for running backups.

- Removable hard drives are very fast and hold a lot of data; however, they are also susceptible to the same corruption issues as the hard disk being backed up.

- Full backups back up everything and flag the files as having been backed up.

- Incremental backups back up everything that has been modified since the last full or incremental backup and flag the files as having been backed up.

- Differential backups back up everything that has been backed up since the last full backup. However, they don't flag the files as having been backed up.

- You can mix full backups with incremental or differential backups, but you can't mix incremental and differential backups.

- You should keep a three- to four-week rotation of backups.

- You should verify your backups.

- You should set a schedule for your backups.

- You should carefully determine which directories to back up.

- You should consider backing up /etc, /home, /opt, /root, /var, and /srv.
- You can use tar to create backup files.
- The tar utility works with most backup media.
- You can also use cpio to archive data.
- You can use the dd command to convert and copy files.
- The dd utility can copy an entire partition or even an entire hard drive to a single file.

Questions

1. You need to use fdisk to create an MBR partition for the fourth SATA hard drive in your system. Which is the correct command to do this?

    A. fdisk /dev/hdd

    B. fdisk /dev/sdd

    C. fdisk /dev/sda4

    D. fdisk /dev/sdb2

2. You've used fdisk to create a new MBR partition on the second hard drive in your Linux system. You want to use the partition as a second swap partition for your system. Which partition type do you need to change it to?

    A. 83

    B. 82

    C. 85

    D. 1

    E. You can't use two swap partitions on the same system.

3. You need to format the first partition on the fourth SATA hard disk using the ext3 file system. Which is the correct command to do this?

    A. mkext3fs /dev/sdd1

    B. mkfs –t ext3 /dev/sdd1

    C. mkfs –t ext3 /dev/sda4

    D. mkreiserfs –t ext3 /dev/sdd1

4. On which block is the first redundant copy of a partition's superblock stored by default on an ext4 file system?

    A. 0

    B. 32768

    C. 98304

    D. 163840

5. You've created a new swap partition (/dev/sdb1) using the fdisk utility. You need to format and enable this partition. Which commands should you use to do this? (Choose two.)

   A. mkswap /dev/sdb1

   B. mkfs –t swap /dev/sdb1

   C. swapon /dev/sdb1

   D. swapon –a

   E. mkfs –t vfat /dev/sdb1

   F. swapon --enable /dev/sdb1

6. You created an ext4 file system on the first partition on the second hard disk in your system and now need to mount it in /mnt/extraspace in read-write mode. Which commands will do this? (Choose two.)

   A. mount –t ext4 /dev/sda1 /mnt/extraspace/

   B. mount –t ext4 /dev/sdb1 /mnt/extraspace/

   C. mount –a /dev/sdb1 /mnt/extraspace/

   D. mount –t ext /dev/sdb1 /mnt/extraspace/

   E. mount –t ext4 –o ro /dev/sdb1 /mnt/extraspace/

7. You have an ISO image file named discimage.iso in your home directory, and you want to mount it in the /mnt directory in your Linux file system so that you can extract several files from it. Which command will do this?

   A. mount ~/discimage.iso /mnt

   B. mount –a ~/discimage.iso /mnt

   C. mount –t iso9660 ~/discimage.iso /mnt

   D. mount –o loop ~/discimage.iso /mnt

8. You have mounted the /dev/sdb1 partition in the /mnt directory and now need to unmount it. Which commands will do this? (Choose two.)

   A. umount /mnt

   B. unmount /mnt

   C. umount /dev/sdb1

   D. mount --unmount /dev/sdb1

   E. unmount /dev/sdb1

9. Which file is used to automatically mount file systems when the system initially boots?

   A. /etc/mtab

   B. /proc/mounts

   C. /etc/inittab

   D. /etc/fstab

10. Which fstab mount option causes pending disk writes to be committed immediately?

   A. async

   B. sync

   C. rw

   D. auto

   E. exec

11. Which command will provide you with a summary of inode consumption on your /dev/sda2 partition?

   A. df –i

   B. df –h

   C. df –hT

   D. du –inode

   E. df /dev/sda2

12. The /dev/sda1 partition on your Linux system currently has no volume label. Given that it is an ext4 partition, which command will set the label to "DATA"?

   A. dumpe2fs –L DATA /dev/sda1

   B. tune2fs –L DATA /dev/sda1

   C. lsof /dev/sda1 --label "DATA"

   D. mkfs –t ext4 –L "DATA" /dev/sda1

13. You are concerned about the condition of a hard drive containing a heavily used ext3 disk partition (/dev/sda2). To ensure data integrity, you want to increase the frequency of automatic fsck checks. Which utility should you use to configure this?

   A. dumpe2fs

   B. debugfs

   C. e2fsck

   D. fsck

   E. tune2fs

14. You need to mount an optical disc in /media/dvd. Which command will do this?

   A. mount –t iso9660 /dev/cdrom /media/dvd

   B. mount –t dvd /dev/cdrom /media/dvd

   C. dvdmount –t iso9660 /dev/cdrom /media/dvd

   D. mount –t iso9660 /dev/cdrom ~/dvd

15. You've noticed that a renegade executable has been installed on your Linux server and that it is currently running. You need to (1) identify the process using the file so that you can kill it, and (2) determine which user account is being used to run it. Which fuser command options should you use to do this? (Choose two.)

   A. –a

   B. –k

   C. –i

   D. –u

   E. –p

16. You need to mount a USB flash drive on your Linux system. Given that your Linux system currently has one SATA hard drive installed, which device file represents the flash drive?

   A. /dev/hdb

   B. /dev/usb0

   C. /dev/sdb

   D. /dev/sda

   E. /dev/sdc

17. Which type of backup backs up all files modified since the last full backup and does not flag the files as having been backed up?

   A. Full

   B. Incremental

   C. Differential

   D. Partial

18. You need to create a backup of /etc to a removable hard disk drive mounted at /mnt/USB. Which tar command will do this?

   A. tar –cfv /mnt/USB/backup.tar /etc

   B. tar –xfv ~/backup.tar /etc

   C. tar –xzf /mnt/USB/backup.tar /etc

   D. tar –cfv /mnt/USB/backup.tar ~/etc

19. You want to create a compressed cpio archive of all the files in the Projects directory within your home directory to /mnt/usbdrive/Projectsbackup.cpio.gz. Which command will do this?

   A. cpio –ov ~/Projects | gzip > /mnt/usbdrive/Projectsbackup.cpio.gz

   B. ls ~/ Projects | cpio –ovz | > /mnt/usbdrive/Projectsbackup.cpio.gz

   C. ls ~/ Projects | cpio –ov | gzip > /mnt/usbdrive/Projectsbackup.cpio.gz

   D. cpio –ovz ~/Projects > /mnt/usbdrive/Projectsbackup.cpio.gz

20. Which command can be used to create an image of your /dev/sda2 partition in the /mnt/usb/volback file?

    A. dd if=/dev/sda2 of=/mnt/usb/volback

    B. cp /dev/sda2 /mnt/usb/volback

    C. dd if=/mnt/usb/volback of=/dev/sda2

    D. dd if=/dev/sda of=/mnt/usb/volback

21. You need to create a new GPT partition on the /dev/sdc hard disk drive. You've already entered gdisk /dev/sdc at the shell prompt. Which command should you type to create a new partition that is 100GB in size?

    A. n

    B. p

    C. new –size=100G

    D. t

22. You just added a third 1TB SSD hard disk drive to a Linux server and need to add its storage space to an LVM volume group named DATA on the system. Which command should you enter first to do this?

    A. vgexpand DATA /dev/sdc

    B. pvscan /dev/sdc DATA

    C. pvcreate /dev/sdc

    D. lvextend –L 1T –n DATA

Answers

1. **B.** The **fdisk /dev/sdd** command uses the correct syntax to create an MBR partition for the fourth SATA hard drive in your system.

2. **B.** Type 82 defines a Linux swap partition.

3. **B.** The **mkfs –t ext3 /dev/sdd1** command uses the correct syntax to format the first partition on the fourth SATA drive using the ext3 file system.

4. **B.** The first redundant copy of a partition's superblock is stored on block 32768 by default on an ext4 file system.

5. **A, C.** The **mkswap /dev/sdb1** command is used to create the swap file system, and the **swapon /dev/sdb1** command enables it as a swap partition.

6. **B, C.** Either the **mount –t ext4 /dev/sdb1 /mnt/extraspace/** command or the **mount –a /dev/sdb1 /mnt/extraspace/** command will mount the /dev/sdb1 partition in /mnt/extraspace/.

7. **D.** The **mount –o loop ~/discimage.iso /mnt** command mounts the image file in the /mnt directory.

8. **A, C.** Either the **umount /mnt** command or the **umount /dev/sdb1** command will unmount the partition from the file system.

9. **D.** The /etc/fstab file is used to automatically mount file systems at boot.

10. **B.** The sync option causes pending disk writes to be written immediately.

11. **A.** The **df –i** command displays a summary of inode consumption for all mounted file systems.

12. **B.** The **tune2fs –L DATA /dev/sda1** command will set the volume label to **DATA**.

13. **E.** The **tune2fs** command with the –c option can be used to customize the frequency of automatic fsck checks.

14. **A.** The **mount –t iso9660 /dev/cdrom /media/dvd** command uses the correct syntax on most distributions, assuming a symbolic link named /dev/cdrom has been created that points to /dev/sr0.

15. **B, D.** The –k option for the **fuser** command kills the process, and the –u option shows which user owns the process.

16. **C.** The device will be referenced by /dev/sdb because there is one other drive in the system.

17. **C.** A differential backup backs up all files modified since the last full backup and does not flag the files as having been backed up.

18. **A.** The **tar –cfv /mnt/USB/backup.tar /etc** command uses the correct syntax.

19. **C.** The **ls ~/ Projects | cpio –ov | gzip > /mnt/usbdrive/Projectsbackup.cpio.gz** command will generate a listing of files in the Projects directory, send the list to the **cpio** command to create an archive, and send the archive to gzip for compression.

20. **A.** The **dd if=/dev/sda2 of=/mnt/usb/volback** command creates an image of the /dev/sda2 partition in the /mnt/usb/volback file.

21. **A.** Within gdisk, you type **n** to create a new partition. After doing so, you are prompted to specify its size.

22. **C.** Before you can allocate space from a storage device to a volume group, you must first define it as an LVM physical volume. In this scenario, you do this using the **pvcreate /dev/sdc** command.

Managing Ownership, Permissions, and Quotas

In this chapter, you will learn about:

- Managing file ownership
- Mounting file and directory permissions
- Administering disk quotas

There are two tasks for you to accomplish when managing user access to a Linux system:

- Control who can access the system.
- Define what users can do after they have logged in to the system.

We control who accesses the system by implementing users and groups. In this part of the chapter, we're going to address the second point. We need to define what users can do after they have logged in to the system. Let's begin by discussing file and directory ownership.

Managing Ownership

To effectively control who can do what in the file system, you need to first consider who "owns" files and directories. We're going to discuss the following in this regard:

- How ownership works
- Managing ownership from the command line

Let's start by discussing how ownership works.

How Ownership Works

Any time a user creates a new file or directory, their user account is assigned as that file or directory's "owner." By default, the owner of a directory on a Linux system receives read, write, and execute permissions to the directory. In essence, they can do whatever they want with that directory. Likewise, the owner of a file on a Linux system receives read and write permissions to that file by default. For example, suppose the ksanders user logs in to her Linux system and creates a file named contacts.odt using OpenOffice.org in her home directory. Because she created this file, ksanders is automatically assigned ownership of contacts.odt. By right-clicking this file in the system's graphical user interface and selecting Properties | Permissions, you can view who owns the file. This is shown in Figure 11-1.

Notice in Figure 11-1 that there are actually two owners for contacts.odt. The first is the name of the user who owns the file. In this case, it's ksanders. In addition, the users group owns the file as well. That's because users is the primary group that ksanders belongs to.

You can also view file ownership from the command line using the ls –l command. This has been done in ksanders' home directory in this example:

```
ksanders@openSUSE:~> ls -l
total 40
drwxr-xr-x 2 ksanders users 4096 2011-03-10 16:43 bin
-rw-r--r-- 1 ksanders users    0 2011-03-18 08:02 contacts.odt
drwxr-xr-x 2 ksanders users 4096 2011-03-10 16:44 Desktop
drwxr-xr-x 2 ksanders users 4096 2011-03-10 16:44 Documents
drwxr-xr-x 2 ksanders users 4096 2011-03-10 16:44 Downloads
drwxr-xr-x 2 ksanders users 4096 2011-03-10 16:44 Music
drwxr-xr-x 2 ksanders users 4096 2011-03-10 16:44 Pictures
drwxr-xr-x 2 ksanders users 4096 2011-03-10 16:44 Public
drwxr-xr-x 2 ksanders users 4096 2011-03-10 16:43 public_html
drwxr-xr-x 2 ksanders users 4096 2011-03-10 16:44 Templates
drwxr-xr-x 2 ksanders users 4096 2011-03-10 16:44 Videos
```

Notice that the third column in the output displays the name of the file or directory's owner (ksanders) while the fourth column displays the name of the group that owns it (users). Even though file and directory ownership is automatically assigned at creation, it can be modified. Let's discuss how this is done next.

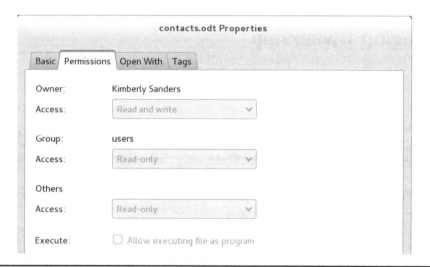

Figure 11-1   Viewing file ownership in the GNOME desktop

Managing Ownership from the Command Line

File and directory ownership isn't a fixed entity. Even though ownership is automatically assigned at creation, it can be modified. You can specify a different user and/or group as the owner of a given file or directory. To change the user who owns a file, you must be logged in as root. To change the group that owns a file, you must be logged in as root or as the user who currently owns the file.

This can be done with either graphical or command-line tools. Staying true to the form of this book, we're going to focus on command-line utilities, including the following:

- Using chown
- Using chgrp

Let's begin by learning how to use chown.

Using chown

The chown utility can be used to change the user or group that owns a file or directory. The syntax for using chown is **chown *user.group file*** or ***directory***. For example, suppose I have a file named myfile.txt in /tmp that is owned by root. If I wanted to change the file's owner to the ksanders user, I would enter **chown ksanders /tmp/myfile.txt**, as shown here:

```
openSUSE:~ # ls -l /tmp/myfile.txt
-rw-r--r-- 1 root root 0 Mar 18 09:38 /tmp/myfile.txt
openSUSE:~ # chown ksanders /tmp/myfile.txt
openSUSE:~ # ls -l /tmp/myfile.txt
-rw-r--r-- 1 ksanders root 0 Mar 18 09:38 /tmp/myfile.txt
```

Notice that this command changed the user who owns the file to ksanders. However, also notice that the group that owns the file is still root. This was assigned when the file was created because root's primary group is named root. If I wanted to change this to the users group, of which ksanders is a member, I would enter **chown .users /tmp/myfile.txt**. Notice that I used a period (.) before the group name to tell chown that the entity specified is a group, not a user account. After this command is executed, the owning group is changed to users, as shown here:

```
openSUSE:~ # chown .users /tmp/myfile.txt
openSUSE:~ # ls -l /tmp/myfile.txt
-rw-r--r-- 1 ksanders users 0 Mar 18 09:38 /tmp/myfile.txt
```

I could have actually changed both the user and the group that owns the file all at once with a single chown command. In this example, I could have entered **chown ksanders.users /tmp/myfile.txt**. This tells chown that the user to change ownership to is ksanders and the group to change ownership to is users.

 NOTE You can use the –R option with chown to change ownership on many files at once, recursively.

Let's also look at the chgrp utility.

Using chgrp

In addition to chown, you can also use chgrp to change the group that owns a file or directory. Simply enter **chgrp** *group file* or *directory*. For example, to change the group ownership of the /tmp/myfile.txt file discussed in the previous examples from root to users, you could enter **chgrp users /tmp/myfile.txt**.

Let's practice managing ownership in the following exercise.

Exercise 11-1: Managing Ownership

In this exercise, you will practice modifying file and directory ownership from the shell prompt of your Linux system. You can perform this exercise using the virtual machine that comes with this book. Run snapshot 11-1 for the correctly configured environment.

 VIDEO Please watch the Exercise 11-1 video for a demonstration on how to perform this task.

Complete the following:

1. Verify that you are logged in to your system.

2. Open a terminal session.

3. If necessary, switch to your root user account with the **su –** command and a password of **student**.

4. Verify that your student user account is a member of the research group by doing the following:

 NOTE The research group was configured in Exercise 9-2 of Chapter 9.

   a. At the shell prompt, enter **cat /etc/group**.

   b. Verify that your student user is a member of the research group.

   c. If your student user is not a member of the research group, add it using the groupmod command.

5. Change to the / directory by entering **cd /** at the shell prompt.

6. Create a new directory named RandD by entering **mkdir RandD** at the shell prompt.

7. At the shell prompt, enter **ls –l**. Notice that the root user account and the root group are the owners of the new directory.

8. Change ownership of the directory to your student user account and the research group by entering **chown student.research RandD** at the shell prompt.

9. Enter **ls –l** again at the shell prompt. Verify that ownership of the RandD directory has changed to your student user account and the research group. This is shown here:

```
openSUSE:/ # ls -l
total 104
drwxr-xr-x    2 student research  4096 Nov 25 17:34 RandD
```

Now that you understand users, groups, and owners, you are finally ready to work with Linux file system permissions. Let's discuss how this is done next.

Managing File and Directory Permissions

Managing ownership represents only a part of what needs to be done to control access to files and directories in the Linux file system. Ownership only specifies who *owns* what. It doesn't say *what* you can or can't do with files and directories. To do this, you need to set up and manage *permissions*. You need to understand the following:

- How permissions work
- Managing permissions from the command line
- Working with default permissions
- Working with special permissions

Let's start by explaining how permissions work.

How Permissions Work

Unlike ownership, permissions are used to specify exactly what a particular user may do with files and directories in the file system. These permissions may allow a user to view a file, but not modify it. They may allow a user to open and modify a file. They may allow a user to even run an executable file. Permissions may be configured to prevent a user from even seeing a file within a directory.

Each file or directory in your Linux file system stores the specific permissions assigned to it. These permissions together constitute the *mode* of the file. Any file or directory can have the permissions shown in Table 11-1 in its mode.

Permission	Symbol	Effect on Files	Effect on Directories
Read	r	Allows a user to open and view a file. Does not allow a file to be modified or saved.	Allows a user to list the contents of a directory.
Write	w	Allows a user to open, modify, and save a file.	Allows a user to add or delete files from the directory.
Execute	x	Allows a user to run an executable file.	Allows a user to enter a directory.

Table 11-1 Linux Permissions

These permissions are assigned to each of three different entities for each file and directory in the file system:

- **Owner** This is the user account that has been assigned to be the file or directory's owner. Permissions assigned to the owner apply only to that user account.
- **Group** This is the group that has been assigned ownership of the file or directory. Permissions assigned to the group apply to all user accounts that are members of that group.
- **Others** This entity refers to all other users who have successfully authenticated to the system. Permissions assigned to this entity apply to these user accounts.

Be aware that permissions are additive. That means it is possible for one user account to receive permissions assigned to more than one entity. For example, suppose I assign the read and write permissions to a file to Owner and the execute permission to Group. If ksanders is the file Owner, users is the Group, and ksanders is a member of users, then ksanders receives *both* the permissions assigned to Owner and Group. Her effective permissions would be rwx!

Also, be very careful about what permissions you assign to Others. Basically, every user on the system belongs to Others; therefore, any permission you grant to Others gets assigned to anyone who successfully authenticates to the system. In some cases, this can be very useful. However, in other cases, it can get you in a lot of trouble! Just ask yourself before assigning permissions, "Do I really want everyone to have this kind of access to this file or directory?"

You can use the ls –l command to view the permissions assigned to each of these entities for any file or directory in the file system. Consider the example shown here:

```
ksanders@openSUSE:~> ls -l
total 48
drwxr-xr-x 2 ksanders users 4096 Nov 25 17:30 bin
drwxr-xr-x 2 ksanders users 4096 Nov 25 18:33 Desktop
drwxr-xr-x 2 ksanders users 4096 Nov 25 18:33 Documents
drwxr-xr-x 2 ksanders users 4096 Nov 25 18:33 Downloads
drwxr-xr-x 2 ksanders users 4096 Nov 25 18:33 Music
drwxr-xr-x 2 ksanders users 4096 Nov 25 18:33 Pictures
-rw-r--r-- 1 ksanders users  123 Nov 25 18:36 Project_design.odt
-rw-r--r-- 1 ksanders users  104 Nov 25 18:36 Project_schedule.odt
drwxr-xr-x 2 ksanders users 4096 Nov 25 18:33 Public
drwxr-xr-x 2 ksanders users 4096 Nov 25 17:30 public_html
drwxr-xr-x 2 ksanders users 4096 Nov 25 18:33 Templates
drwxr-xr-x 2 ksanders users 4096 Nov 25 18:33 Videos
```

The first column displayed is the mode for each file and directory. The first character denotes the file type, which can be a regular file (-), a directory (d), a socket (s), a link (l), a named pipe (p), a block device (b), or character device (c). As you can see, Project_design.odt and Project_schedule.odt are regular files whereas Desktop is a directory.

The next three characters are the permissions assigned to the entry's owner. For example, Project_schedule.odt has rw– assigned to its owner (which is the ksanders user). This means ksanders has read and write permissions to the file, but not execute. Because the file isn't an executable, that permission isn't needed anyway. If the file were an executable and the execute permission were

Table 11-2	Permission	Value
Numeric Values	Read	4
Assigned to	Write	2
Permissions	Execute	1

assigned, an *x* would have replaced the – in this part of the mode. Because the owner has read and write permissions to the file, ksanders can open the file, edit it, and save the changes.

The next three characters are the permissions assigned to the owning group. In this case, it is the users group. Any user on the system who is a member of the users group is granted r– – access to the Project_schedule.odt file. This means they have the read right, allowing them to open a file and view its contents, but they aren't allowed to save any changes to the file.

The last three characters in the mode are the permissions assigned to others, meaning any legitimately authenticated user on the system who isn't the owner and isn't a member of the owning group. In this example, these users are also assigned r– – rights to the Project_schedule.odt file, again, granting them read access.

Before we progress any farther, you should know that permissions for each entity can also be represented numerically. This is done by assigning a value to each permission, as shown in Table 11-2.

Using these values, you can represent the permissions assigned to the Owner, Group, or Others with a single number. Simply add up the value of each permission. For example, suppose Owner is assigned read and write permissions to a file. To determine the numeric value of this assignment, simply add the values of read and write together (4 + 2 = 6). Many times, you will see a file or directory's mode represented by three numbers. Consider the example shown in Figure 11-2.

In this example, the associated file owner has read and write permissions (6), the owning group has the read permission (4), and others also have the read permission (4). Using the ls –l command, this mode would be represented as –rw–r– –r– –.

So what do you do if these permissions aren't correct? You use the chmod utility to modify them! Let's discuss how this is done next.

Managing Permissions from the Command Line

I realize that I'm sounding like a broken record, but, just as with most of the other tasks in this chapter, you can modify permissions either graphically or from the command line. For example, using the file browser in the GNOME desktop environment, you can right-click any file or directory and then select Properties | Permissions. The screen in Figure 11-3 is displayed.

Figure 11-2
Representing permissions numerically

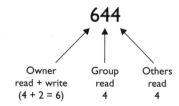

644

Owner	Group	Others
read + write	read	read
(4 + 2 = 6)	4	4

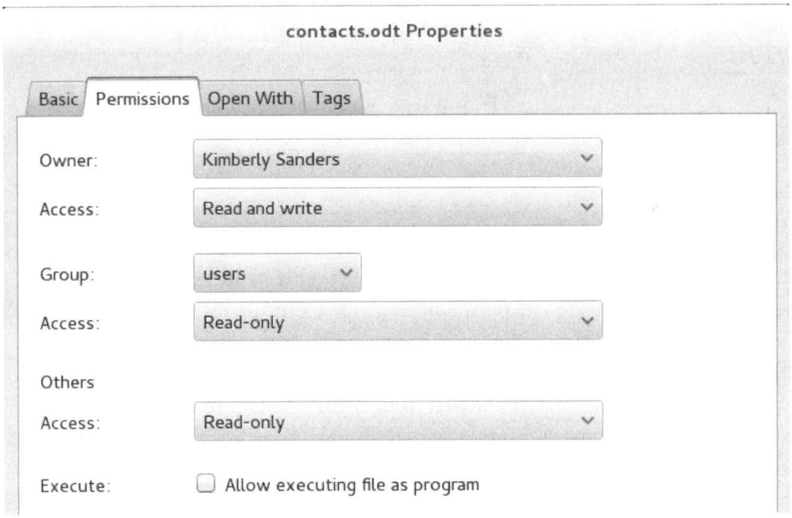

Figure 11-3 Setting permissions in file browser

You then use drop-down lists for Owner, Group, and Others to specify what each entity can do with the file or directory. When you apply the changes, the file or directory's mode is changed to match what you specified.

However, for your LPIC-1/Linux+ exam, you must be able to accomplish this same task using command-line tools. You use chmod to modify permissions. To do this, you must either own the file or be logged in as root. Any other users will not be allowed to do this.

Several different syntaxes can be used with chmod. The first is to enter **chmod** *entity=permissions filename* at the shell prompt. You substitute **u** for Owner, **g** for Group, and **o** for Others in the *entity* portion of the command. You substitute **r**, **w**, and/or **x** for the *permissions* portion of the command. For example, suppose I wanted to change the mode of contacts.odt to –rw–rw–r– – (giving the Owner and Group read and write permissions while giving Others only read access). I would enter **chmod u=rw,g=rw,o=r contacts.odt** at the shell prompt (assuming the file resides in the current directory). After I do so, the mode is adjusted with the permissions assigned by chmod, as shown here:

```
openSUSE:/home/ksanders # chmod u=rw,g=rw,o=r contacts.odt
openSUSE:/home/ksanders # ls -l contacts.odt
-rw-rw-r-- 1 ksanders users 0 Mar 18 08:02 contacts.odt
```

You can also use chmod to toggle a particular permission on or off using the + or – sign. For example, suppose I want to turn off the write permission I just gave to Group for the contacts.odt file. I could enter **chmod g–w contacts.odt** at the shell prompt. When I do, the specified permission is turned off, as shown next:

```
openSUSE:/home/ksanders # chmod g-w contacts.odt
openSUSE:/home/ksanders # ls -l contacts.odt
-rw-r--r-- 1 ksanders users 0 Mar 18 08:02 contacts.odt
```

If I wanted to turn the permission back on, I would enter **chmod g+w contacts.odt**. You can substitute **u** or **o**, respectively, to modify the permission to the file or directory for Owner or Others as well.

Finally, you can also use numeric permissions with chmod. This is the option I use most often. You can modify all three entities at once with only three characters. To do this, enter **chmod** *numeric_permission filename*.

Going back to our earlier example, suppose I wanted to grant read and write permissions to Owner and Group, but remove all permissions from Others. That would mean Owner and Group's permissions would be represented numerically as 6. Because Others gets no permissions, its permissions would be represented by 0. I could implement this by entering **chmod 660 contacts.odt** at the shell prompt. When I do, the appropriate changes are made, as shown here:

```
openSUSE:/home/ksanders # chmod 660 contacts.odt
openSUSE:/home/ksanders # ls -l contacts.odt
-rw-rw---- 1 ksanders users 0 Mar 18 08:02 contacts.odt
```

 TIP You can use the –R option with chmod to change permissions on many files at once, recursively.

Let's practice managing permissions in the following exercise.

Exercise 11-2: Managing Permissions

In this exercise, you will practice modifying permissions from the shell prompt of your Linux system. You will create a design document for your hypothetical Research and Design team and modify its permissions to control access. You can perform this exercise using the virtual machine that comes with this book. Run snapshot 11-2 for the correctly configured environment.

 VIDEO Please watch the Exercise 11-2 video for a demonstration on how to perform this task.

Complete the following:

1. Verify that you are logged in to your system.

2. If necessary, switch to your root user account with the **su –** command and a password of **student**.

3. Change to the /RandD directory by entering **cd /RandD** at the shell prompt.

4. Create a design document for your team and restrict access to it by doing the following:

   a. Create a new file named design_doc.odt by entering **touch design_doc.odt** at the shell prompt.

   b. At the shell prompt, enter **ls –l**. Notice that the root user account and the root group are the owners of the new file.

c. Change ownership of the file to your student user account and the research group using the chown command.

d. Enter **ls –l** again at the shell prompt. Verify that ownership of the file directory has changed to your student user account and the research group. Notice that Owner has rw– permissions to the file, but Group only has r-- permission.

e. Grant Group rw– permissions by entering **chmod g+w design_doc.odt** at the shell prompt.

f. Enter **ls –l** again at the shell prompt. Notice that Owner and Group now both have read/write access to the file.

g. Notice that Others has read access to the file. You need to keep this document confidential, so remove this access by entering **chmod 660 design_doc.odt** at the shell prompt.

h. Enter **ls –l** again. Verify that Others has no permissions to this file.

5. Next, you need to control access to the research directory itself using permissions. Do the following:

a. Enter **cd ..** at the shell prompt.

b. Enter **ls –l** at the shell prompt. Notice that Owner has full access to the RandD directory, but Group is missing the write permission to the directory. Also notice that Others can read the directory contents (**r**) and can enter the directory (**x**).

c. Grant Group full access to the directory and remove Others access to the directory completely by entering **chmod 770 RandD** at the shell prompt.

d. Enter **ls –l** at the shell prompt. Verify that Owner and Group have full access whereas Others has no access.

Next, let's discuss how to work with default permissions.

Working with Default Permissions

You may have noticed as we've worked through exercises and examples in this book that whenever you create a new file or directory in the file system, a default set of permissions is automatically assigned without any intervention on your part.

By default, Linux assigns rw–rw–rw– (666) permissions to every file whenever it is created in the file system. It also assigns rwxrwxrwx (777) permissions to every directory created in the file system. However, these aren't the permissions the files or directories actually end up with. Let's take a look at an example.

Suppose ksanders was to create a new directory named revenue in her home directory and a file named projections.odt in the revenue directory. Based on what we just discussed, the revenue directory should have a mode of rwxrwxrwx and the projections.odt file should have a mode of rw–rw–rw–. However, this isn't the case, as shown here:

```
ksanders@openSUSE:~> ls -l
total 44
drwxr-xr-x 2 ksanders users 4096 2011-03-10 16:43 bin
```

```
-rw-rw---- 1 ksanders users    0 2011-03-18 08:02 contacts.odt
drwxr-xr-x 2 ksanders users 4096 2011-03-10 16:44 Desktop
drwxr-xr-x 2 ksanders users 4096 2011-03-10 16:44 Documents
drwxr-xr-x 2 ksanders users 4096 2011-03-10 16:44 Downloads
drwxr-xr-x 2 ksanders users 4096 2011-03-10 16:44 Music
drwxr-xr-x 2 ksanders users 4096 2011-03-10 16:44 Pictures
drwxr-xr-x 2 ksanders users 4096 2011-03-10 16:44 Public
drwxr-xr-x 2 ksanders users 4096 2011-03-10 16:43 public_html
drwxr-xr-x 2 ksanders users 4096 2011-03-18 11:06 revenue
drwxr-xr-x 2 ksanders users 4096 2011-03-10 16:44 Templates
drwxr-xr-x 2 ksanders users 4096 2011-03-10 16:44 Videos
ksanders@openSUSE:~> ls -l r*
total 0
-rw-r--r-- 1 ksanders users 0 2011-03-18 11:06 projections.odt
```

Notice that the revenue directory has a mode of rwxr–xr–x (755). This means the directory owner has read, write, and execute permissions to the directory. Group and Others have read and execute permissions to the directory. Likewise, notice that the projections.odt file has a mode of rw–r– –r– – (644). The Owner has read and write permissions, whereas Group and Other have only the read permission.

These aren't the default permissions Linux is supposed to assign! Why did this happen? It's because the default permissions are too liberal. Think about it. The default directory mode would allow anyone on the system to enter any directory and delete any files they wanted to! Likewise, the default file mode would allow any user on the system to modify a file you created. What a nightmare!

To increase the overall security of the system, Linux uses a variable called *umask* to automatically remove permissions from the default mode whenever a file or directory is created in the file system. The value of umask is a three-digit number, as shown next (ignoring the first 0):

```
openSUSE:~ # umask
0022
```

For most Linux distributions, the default value of umask is 022. Each digit represents a numeric permission value to be *removed*. The first digit references—you guessed it—Owner, the second references Group, and the last references Other. Because a 0 is listed for Owner, no permissions are removed from the default mode for a file or directory owner. However, because a 2 is listed for Group and Other, the write permission is removed from the default mode whenever a file or directory is created in the file system. The function of umask is shown in Figure 11-4.

Figure 11-4
How umask
works

```
                                     Files
                Default Mode : rw-rw-rw-
          Subtracted by umask : ----w--w-
                                     _____
                         Result: rw-r-r--


                                 Directories
                Default Mode:  rwxrwxrwx
          Subtracted by umask:  ----w--w-
                                     _____
                         Result: rwxr-xr-x
```

The default value of umask works for most Linux admins. However, there may be situations where you need to tighten up or loosen the permissions assigned when a file or directory is created in the file system. To do this, you can change the value assigned to umask.

This can be done in two ways. First, if you only need to make a temporary change to umask, you can enter **umask *value*** at the shell prompt. For example, if you wanted to remove the execute permission that is automatically assigned to Others whenever a new directory is created, you could enter **umask 023**. This would cause the write permission (2) to be removed from Group upon creation as well as write (2) and execute (1) from Others. This will effectively disallow anyone from entering the new directory except for the directory owner or members of the owning group. This is shown here:

```
openSUSE:~ # umask 023
openSUSE:~ # umask
0023
openSUSE:~ # mkdir /home/ksanders/temp
openSUSE:~ # ls -l /home/ksanders
...
drwxr-xr-x 2 ksanders users  4096 Mar 10 16:43 bin
-rw-rw---- 1 ksanders users     0 Mar 18 08:02 contacts.odt
drwxr-xr-x 2 ksanders users  4096 Mar 10 16:43 public_html
drwxr-xr-x 2 ksanders users  4096 Mar 18 11:06 revenue
drwxr-xr-- 2 root     root   4096 Mar 18 11:14 temp
```

Notice that, because the value of umask was changed, the execute permission (x) was removed from Others in the mode when the temp directory was created.

This method for modifying umask works great; however, it isn't persistent. If you were to restart the system, umask would revert to its original value. That's because the value of umask is automatically set each time the system boots using the umask parameter in the /etc/profile file or the /etc/login.defs file, depending on your distribution.

If you want to make your change to umask permanent, simply edit the appropriate configuration file in a text editor and set the value of umask to your desired value.

Next, let's look at special permissions.

Working with Special Permissions

Most of the tasks you will complete with permissions will be with the read, write, and execute permissions. However, there are several other special permissions you can assign to files and directories in your file system. These are shown in Table 11-3.

These special permissions are referenced as an extra digit added to the *beginning* of the file or directory's mode. As with regular permissions, each of these special permissions has a numerical value assigned to it, as shown here:

- SUID: 4
- SGID: 2
- Sticky Bit: 1

You can assign these special permissions to files or directories using chmod. Just add an extra number to the beginning of the mode that references the special permissions you want to associate with the file or directory.

Permission	Description	Effect on Files	Effect on Directories
SUID	Set User ID. Can only be applied to binary executable files (not shell scripts).	When an executable file with the SUID set is run, the user who ran the file temporarily becomes the file's owner.	None.
SGID	Set Group ID. Can be applied to binary executable files (not shell scripts).	When a user runs an executable file with SGID set, the user temporarily becomes a member of the file's owning group.	When a user creates a file in a directory that has SGID set, the file's owner is set to the user's account (as per normal). However, the owning group assigned to the new file is set to the owning group of the parent directory.
Sticky Bit		None.	When the Sticky Bit is assigned to a directory, users can only delete files within the directory for which they are the owner of the file or the directory itself. This negates the effect of having the write permission to a directory, which could allow a user to delete files in a directory that they don't own.

Table 11-3   Special Permissions

For example, suppose you wanted to apply the SUID and SGID permissions to a file named runme that should be readable and executable by Owner and Group. You would enter **chmod 6554 runme** at the shell prompt. This specifies that the file has SUID (4) and SGID (2) permissions assigned (for a total of 6 in the first digit). It also specifies that Owner and Group have read (4) and execute permissions (1) assigned (for a total of 5 in the second and third digits). It also specifies that Others be allowed to read (4) the file, but not be able to modify or run it (for a total of 4 in the last digit).

Let's practice managing default and special permissions in the following exercise.

Exercise 11-3: Managing Default and Special Permissions

In this exercise, you will practice modifying default permissions with umask and creating files. You will also practice adding special permissions to directories. You can perform this exercise using the virtual machine that comes with this book. Run snapshot 11-3 for the correctly configured environment.

 VIDEO   Please watch the Exercise 11-3 video for a demonstration on how to perform this task.

Complete the following:

1. Verify that you are logged in to your system.

2. If necessary, switch to your root user account with the **su –** command and a password of **student**.

3. Change to the /RandD directory by entering **cd /RandD** at the shell prompt.

4. You need to create several Research and Development documents in the RandD directory. However, you need to make sure these documents are secure from prying eyes. Recall from the previous exercise that Others is automatically granted read access to files when you create them. You don't want this to happen. You need Others to have no access at all to any documents created. Do the following:

   a. Change the default permissions by entering **umask 027** at the shell prompt.

   b. Verify the value of umask by entering **umask** at the shell prompt. It should display 0027.

   c. Create a new file named schedule.odt by entering **touch schedule.odt** at the shell prompt.

   d. Enter **ls –l** at the shell prompt. Verify that Owner has rw–, Group has r--, and Others has – – – permissions.

5. In a previous exercise, we granted Owner and Group rwx permissions to the RandD directory. However, having the write permission to the directory allows anyone in the research group to delete any file in the directory. We want to configure the directory so that users in the research group can only delete files they actually own. Do the following:

   a. At the shell prompt, enter **cd /**.

   b. At the shell prompt, add the Sticky Bit permission to the RandD directory by entering **chmod 1770 RandD**.

   c. At the shell prompt, enter **ls –l**. Notice that a *T* has been added to the last digit of the Others portion of the mode of the RandD directory. This indicates that the sticky bit has been set:

   ```
   openSUSE:/ # ls -l
   total 105
   drwxrwx--T   2 tux   research  4096 Mar 18 11:25 RandD
   ...
   ```

6. Experiment with the new permissions you just added by logging in as different users in the system and testing what the permissions will and won't allow you to do.

7. In Exercise 9-1, we created a user named dtracy. However, because we didn't use the –m option when we created him, he doesn't have a home directory. Using what you've learned, do the following:

   a. Create the appropriate home directory for dtracy in /home.

   b. Look at the other home directories and determine the ownership and permissions that should be assigned.

  c. Use command-line utilities to set the ownership and permissions for dtracy's home directory.

  d. Run pwck when you're done to verify that the account is configured correctly.

Let's end this chapter by discussing disk quotas.

Administering Disk Quotas

Disk quotas are a valuable management tool when you're administering a Linux system. The problem here is that, because Linux is a multiuser system, it's possible for one or two users to completely monopolize all the disk space available in the file system. This is especially a problem in today's networked world where users are downloading large music files and even larger movie files from the Internet. How do you keep these users from consuming more than their fair share of disk space? You use disk quotas.

Put simply, disk quotas establish space limitations for users on the system. You can specify that users are each allowed only a certain amount of disk space or inodes (a quota). Users are not allowed to exceed this quota.

To implement quotas on your Linux file system, you first need to install the quota package on your system. Some distributions, especially server distributions, install this package as part of the base installation. Most distributions, however, will require you to install it separately after the system has been set up. To see if quota is already installed on your system, enter **rpm –qi quota** at the shell prompt. If it isn't installed, use rpm or another appropriate package management utility to install it.

Once the package has been installed, complete the following to establish quotas:

  1. Open a terminal session and change to your root user account with su.

  2. Configure your mounted file systems to use quotas by doing the following:

  a. Open your /etc/fstab file in a text editor.

  b. Add the **usrquota** and **grpquota** parameters to the mount options for the file system you want to establish quotas on. In the example that follows, quotas have been established for the **/** file system:

```
/dev/sda2     swap     swap     defaults                       0 0
/dev/sda3     /        ext4     acl,user_xattr,usrquota,grpquota     1 1
/dev/sda1     /boot    ext4     acl,user_xattr     1 2
/dev/sda4     /var     ext4     acl,user_xattr     1 2
```

  c. Save your changes to the file and exit the editor.

  d. Restart your system so that the changes can take effect.

  3. After the system has rebooted, create your quota files by doing the following:

  a. Open a terminal session and switch to your root user account with su.

  b. At the shell prompt, enter **quotacheck –amvug**.

The quotacheck utility is used to scan the file system for disk usages as well as to create quota files. The options used with quotacheck just given do the following:

- **–a**   Checks all mounted file systems
- **–m**   Forces checks on mounted file systems
- **–u**   Checks users
- **–g**   Checks groups
- **–v**   Operates in verbose mode

When quotacheck is complete, two files named aquota.user and aquota.group should have been created in the mount point of your mounted file system, as shown here:

```
openSUSE:/ # ls
RandD           bin    etc    lib64        mnt    root      srv    usr
aquota.group    boot   home   lost+found   opt    sbin      sys    var
aquota.user     dev    lib    media        proc   selinux   tmp
```

4. Enable quotas on your file system by entering **quotaon –av** at the shell prompt.

5. View the current disk space used by your users by entering **repquota –av** at the shell prompt. A report is displayed on the screen showing how much space each user is consuming, as shown here:

```
openSUSE:/ # repquota -av
*** Report for user quotas on device /dev/sda3
Block grace time: 7days; Inode grace time: 7days
                      Block limits                   File limits
User            used    soft    hard  grace    used  soft  hard  grace
----------------------------------------------------------------------
games       --     416      0      0              3     0     0
gdm         --      12      0      0             32     0     0
lp          --      12      0      0              3     0     0
man         --     208      0      0              2     0     0
news        --       4      0      0              1     0     0
polkituser  --      24      0      0              1     0     0
root        -- 4236032      0      0         154678     0     0
uucp        --       4      0      0              1     0     0
ksanders    --    6680      0      0            505     0     0
tux         --  108844      0      0            742     0     0
jsanders    --      52      0      0             14     0     0
rtracy      --      52      0      0             14     0     0
#10000      --    2688      0      0            211     0     0

Statistics:
Total blocks: 8
Data blocks: 1
Entries: 13
Used average: 13.000000
```

Notice in this report that no limits have been configured for any users.

6. Create disk quotas for your users by doing the following:

   a. At the shell prompt, enter **edquota –u** *username*. A screen similar to that shown next for the rtracy user is displayed:

```
Disk quotas for user rtracy (uid 1004):
  Filesystem    blocks      soft      hard     inodes      soft      hard
  /dev/sda3         52         0         0         14         0         0
```

In this example, quotas are being set for rtracy. Notice that the quota file has been opened in the vi editor. Also notice that you can set hard and soft quotas for blocks and for inodes. Soft quotas are those that can be temporarily exceeded. Hard quotas cannot be exceeded. Block quotas specify how many blocks on disk the user can consume. Inode quotas specify how many files the user can own.

b. Use the vi editor to set block and/or inode soft and hard quotas.

c. Save your changes and exit the editor.

d. Repeat this process for each of your users.

TIP You can enter **edquota –p** *source_user destination_user* to copy quotas from one user to another.

7. Create disk quotas for your groups by doing the following:

a. At the shell prompt, enter **edquota –g** *groupname*.

b. Use the vi editor to set block and/or inode soft and hard quotas.

c. Save your changes and exit the editor.

8. In the preceding steps, you created soft quotas for blocks and/or inodes. The default value is to allow users to exceed their soft quotas for a maximum of seven days. This is the *grace period*. You can change this by doing the following:

a. At the shell prompt, enter **edquota –t**. The following is displayed:

```
Grace period before enforcing soft limits for users:
Time units may be: days, hours, minutes, or seconds
  Filesystem                Block grace period      Inode grace period
  /dev/sda3                       7days                   7days
```

b. Edit your grace period settings.

c. Save your changes and exit vi.

9. Check your new quotas by entering **repquota –av** at the shell prompt. You should now see quotas established for your users. In the example that follows, quotas have been established for the rtracy user:

```
openSUSE:/ # repquota -av
*** Report for user quotas on device /dev/sda3
Block grace time: 7days; Inode grace time: 7days
                        Block limits              File limits
User           used    soft    hard  grace    used  soft  hard  grace
-----------------------------------------------------------------------
games     --    416       0       0              3     0     0
gdm       --     12       0       0             32     0     0
lp        --     12       0       0              3     0     0
man       --    208       0       0              2     0     0
news      --      4       0       0              1     0     0
```

```
polkituser --       24        0        0              1      0      0
root        -- 4236028        0        0         154678      0      0
uucp        --        4        0        0              1      0      0
ksanders    --     6680        0        0            505      0      0
tux         --   108856        0        0            745      0      0
jsanders    --       52        0        0             14      0      0
rtracy      --       52    10000    15000             14    800   1000
#10000      --     2688        0        0            211      0      0

Statistics:
Total blocks: 8
Data blocks: 1
Entries: 13
Used average: 13.000000
```

Your system is now protected from disk space hogs! Let's practice establishing disk quotas in the following exercise.

Exercise 11-4: Establishing Disk Quotas

In this exercise, you will practice implementing disk quotas on your Linux system. You can perform this exercise using the virtual machine that comes with this book. Run snapshot 11-4 for the correctly configured environment.

 VIDEO   Please watch the Exercise 11-4 video for a demonstration on how to perform this task.

Complete the following:

1. Verify that you are logged in to your system.

2. If necessary, switch to your root user account with the **su –** command and a password of **student**.

3. Configure your mounted file systems to use quotas by doing the following:

   a. Open your /etc/fstab file in a text editor.

   b. Add the **usrquota** and **grpquota** parameters to the mount options for the / file system.

   c. Save your changes to the file and exit the editor.

   d. Restart your system so that the changes can take effect.

4. After the system has rebooted, create your quota files by doing the following:

   a. Open a terminal session and switch to your root user account using the **su –** command.

   b. At the shell prompt, enter **quotacheck –amvug**.

5. When quotacheck is complete, two files named aquota.user and aquota.groups should have been created in /.

6. Enable quotas on your file system by entering **quotaon –av** at the shell prompt.

7. View the current disk space used by your users by entering **repquota –av** at the shell prompt. A report is displayed on the screen showing how much space each user is consuming. Notice that no limits have been configured for any users.

8. Create disk quotas for your users by doing the following:

   a. At the shell prompt, enter **edquota –u student**.

   b. Use the vi editor to set the following:

      • Block hard quota: 15000

      • Block soft quota: 10000

      • Inode hard quota: 1000

      • Inode soft quota: 800

   c. Save your changes and exit the editor.

   d. Repeat this process for the rest of your users.

9. Check your new quotas by entering **repquota –av** at the shell prompt. You should now see quotas established for your users.

10. Enter **exit** to leave the root user account.

11. Verify that you are logged in as a user account that quotas have been set for.

12. Create a big file by entering **time dd if=/dev/zero of=bigfile.bin bs=1024 count=10000** at the shell prompt. You should see an error indicating the quota has been exceeded.

You are now an expert at working with Linux users, groups, and permissions!

Chapter Review

In this chapter, we discussed ownership, permissions, and quotas. I pointed out that users and groups only control who can access the system. They don't control what the user can do with files or directories in the file system. To do this, we need to implement ownership and permissions.

I pointed out that, whenever a user creates a file or directory, that user is automatically assigned to be its owner. In addition, the group the user belongs to becomes the file or directory's group owner. These defaults can be changed; however, you must be logged in as root to change a file or directory's owner or be logged in as its owner to change its group.

To modify ownership, you use the chown command. This command can change both the user and/or the group that owns a file or directory. If you only want to change the group, you can also use the chgrp command.

I then pointed out that ownership alone can't control user access to files and directories. To fully control access, you need Linux file system permissions. Permissions define what a user can and cannot do with a given file or directory. Linux uses the following permissions:

• Read

• Write

• Execute

Linux assigns permissions to the following entities:

- Owner
- Group
- Others

The permissions assigned to Owner, Group, and Others together constitute a file or directory's mode. I also emphasized that Linux permissions are additive. If a given user is both an owner and member of the owning group, that user receives permissions assigned for a file or directory to Owner and Group.

I then pointed out that permissions can be represented numerically for Owner, Group, and Others using the following values:

- Read: 4
- Write: 2
- Execute: 1

By adding up each permission assigned to a given entity, you can represent all of the permissions assigned with a single number. For example, a value of 7 indicates that all permissions have been assigned. A value of 5 indicates read and execute permissions have been assigned.

We then discussed the chmod tool, which is used to manage permissions from the shell prompt. The chmod utility can use any of the following syntaxes to assign permissions to Owner, Group, and/or Others:

- chmod u=rw,g=rw,o=r *file_or_directory*
- chmod u+rw,g+rw,o+r *file_or_directory*
- chmod 664 file_or_directory

At this point, we began a discussion of default Linux permissions. I pointed out that, by default, Linux automatically assigns new files with rw–rw–rw– permissions and new directories with rwxrwxrwx permissions upon creation. However, to increase security, the umask variable is used to automatically remove some permission. The default umask value is 022, which removes the write permission from Group and Others when a file or directory is created. I pointed out that you can change the value of umask by entering **umask** *value* at the shell prompt.

We also briefly discussed the special permissions you can assign, including the following:

- SUID: 4
- SGID: 2
- Sticky Bit: 1

I pointed out that you assign these permissions with chmod by adding an extra digit before the Owner digit in the command using the values just shown.

We ended the chapter by discussing how to implement disk quotas. I pointed out that disk quotas are used to prevent users from using up too much disk space. To implement quotas, you must first install the quota package on your Linux system. We then reviewed the procedure for setting up quotas for mounted file systems. I pointed out that you can set quotas for the number of blocks a user is allowed to consume (disk space) and/or the number of inodes a user may consume (number of files). For both of these parameters, you can set *hard* and *soft* limits. A user may temporarily exceed soft limits for a time you define as the *grace period*. A user may not exceed a hard limit. You can enter the **repquota –av** command at the shell prompt to view a report displaying hard and soft limits as well as current user space usage.

Accelerated Review

- Ownership defines which user and group owns a particular file or directory in the file system.
- You can use the **ls –l** command to view ownership.
- You can use the chown utility to configure user and group ownership of a file or directory.
- You can use the chgrp utility to change group ownership.
- You must be logged in as root to change user ownership.
- You must be logged in as root or as the file/directory owner to change group ownership.
- Permissions are used to define what users may or may not do with files or directories in the file system.
- Linux uses the read, write, and execute permissions for files and directories.
- Linux permissions are assigned to Owner, Group, and Others.
- Linux permissions are additive.
- The permissions assigned to Owner, Group, and Others constitute the file or directory's mode.
- Permissions can be represented numerically: read=4, write=2, and execute=1.
- Summing up all permissions assigned to an entity, such as Owner, allows you to represent all assigned permissions with a single number.
- You use the chmod utility to modify permissions.
- Linux assigns rw–rw–rw– permissions by default to new files and rwxrwxrwx permissions to new directories.
- These permissions are too relaxed for most situations, so the umask variable is used to subtract specific permissions from the defaults.
- The default value of umask is 022, which subtracts the write permission (2) from Group and Others.
- You can modify the value of umask to change the default permissions assigned upon creation.

- Linux also includes three default special permissions: Sticky Bit, SUID, and SGID.
- You assign special permissions with chmod by adding an additional digit before the Owner digit in the command.
- You can use the quota package to implement disk quotas in the file system.
- Quotas prevent users from consuming too much disk space.
- You can set quotas for the number of blocks a user is allowed to consume (disk space) and the number of inodes a user may consume (number of files).
- You can set hard and soft limits.
- A user may temporarily exceed soft limits for a time you define as the grace period.
- A user may not exceed a hard limit.
- You can enter the **repquota –av** command at the shell prompt to view a report displaying hard and soft limits as well as current user space usage.

Questions

1. You need to change the owner of a file named /var/opt/runme from mireland, who is a member of the users group, to dnelson, who is a member of the editors group. Assuming you want to change both user and group owners, which command will do this?

   A. chown mireland dnelson /var/opt/runme

   B. chown –u "dnelson" –g "editors" /var/opt/runme

   C. chown dnelson /var/opt/runme

   D. chown dnelson.editors /var/opt/runme

2. Which permission, when applied to a directory in the file system, will allow a user to enter the directory?

   A. Read

   B. Write

   C. Execute

   D. Access Control

3. A user needs to open a file, edit it, and then save the changes. What permissions does he need to do this? (Choose two.)

   A. Read

   B. Write

   C. Execute

   D. Modify

4. A file named employees.odt has a mode of rw–r– –r– –. If mhuffman is not the file's owner but is a member of the group that owns this file, what can he do with it?

   A. He can open the file and view its contents, but he can't save any changes.

   B. He can open the file, make changes, and save the file.

   C. He can change ownership of the file.

   D. He can run the file if it's an executable.

5. A file named myapp has a mode of 755. If dnelson doesn't own this file and isn't a member of the group that owns the file, what can she do with it?

   A. She can change the group that owns the file.

   B. She can open the file, make changes, and save the file.

   C. She can change ownership of the file.

   D. She can run the file.

6. You need to change the permissions of a file named schedule.odt so that the file owner can edit the file, users who are members of the group that owns the file can edit it, and users who are not owners and don't belong to the owning group can view it but not modify it. Which command will do this?

   A. chmod 664 schedule.odt

   B. chmod 555 schedule.odt

   C. chmod 777 schedule.odt

   D. chmod 644 schedule.odt

7. Your Linux system's umask variable is currently set to a value of 077. A user named jcarr (who is a member of the users group) creates a file named mythoughts.odt. What can users who are members of the users group do with this file?

   A. They can view the file, but they can't modify or save it.

   B. They can open, modify, and save the file.

   C. They can open, modify, and save the file. They can also execute the file if it is an executable.

   D. They have no access to the file at all.

8. An executable file has the SUID permission set. If this file is run on the system, who owns the file?

   A. The user who created the file remains the owner.

   B. The user who ran the file becomes the file's permanent owner.

   C. The user who ran the file becomes the file's temporary owner.

   D. The root user becomes the file's owner.

9. A directory is owned by the users group and has a mode of rwxrwxr– – permissions assigned to that group. It also has the Sticky Bit permission set. What effect does this have on files within the directory?

A. Users who are members of the users group can only delete files within the directory for which they are the owner.

B. No user is allowed to delete files in this directory.

C. Users who are members of the users group can delete any file within the directory.

D. Others can enter the directory and delete files within the directory for which they are the owner.

10. Which mount options need to be included in /etc/fstab to enable quotas when a file system is mounted? (Choose two.)

A. groupquotas=on

B. usrquota

C. grpquota

D. userquotas=on

E. fsquota

11. With the quota package installed on your Linux system, what parameters can you set quotas for in the file system? (Choose two.)

A. Blocks

B. Permissions

C. Inodes

D. Ownership

E. Number of Users

F. Number of Groups

12. Which command is used to create quota files for the file system where quotas have been enabled?

A. quotacheck –amvug

B. quotaon –av

C. repquota –av

D. edquota –u

Answers

1. **D.** Entering **chown dnelson.editors /var/opt/runme** will change the user and group owners of the runme file to dnelson and editors.

2. **C.** The execute permission allows a user to enter a directory in the file system.

3. **A, B.** The user must have read and write permissions to open and modify a file.

4. **A.** In the mode shown, Group is given the read permission only. Because mhuffman is a member of the group, he can only open and view file contents. He can't modify and save the file.

5. **D.** Because dnelson isn't the owner and isn't a member of the owning group, she is granted the rights assigned to Others, which are read (4) and execute (1). This allows her to run the file.

6. **A.** Entering **chmod 664 schedule.odt** will grant Owner and Group read (4) and write (2) permissions. It will also grant Others read (4) permission.

7. **D.** Because umask is set to 077, all permissions (read=4, write=2, execute=1) are removed from Group and Others. Therefore, members of the owning group have no access to the file.

8. **C.** The SUID permission causes the user who runs the file to temporarily become the file's owner.

9. **A.** The Sticky Bit permission negates the effect of the group write permissions. As a result, users who are members of the users group can only delete files within the directory for which they are the owner.

10. **B, C.** You need to add the usrquota and grpquota options to the mount options for the file system.

11. **A, C.** The quota package can set quotas on blocks and inodes in the file system.

12. **A.** The quotacheck –amvug command is used to create quota files for the file system where quotas have been enabled.

Managing Hardware Under Linux

In this chapter, you will learn about:
- Managing PC hardware
- Working with Linux drivers

This is going to be a fun chapter! As I mentioned earlier in this book, I'm a true techie at heart. I love playing with PC hardware. I spend way too much time scouring hardware vendor catalogs and far too much money ordering new parts. (My local UPS delivery driver and I are on a first-name basis.) Every computer I own is a "Frankenstein" system made of a variety of parts from many different sources.

In this chapter, I'm going to discuss how to manage hardware in your system and configure Linux to support it.

EXAM TIP For your LPIC-1/Linux+ exam, you need to be very comfortable working with PC hardware in a Linux environment. Expect to see several questions about loading kernel modules and installing codecs. Be sure you know where kernel modules are stored in the system and the commands that are used to manage them.

Let's begin this chapter by discussing how to manage PC hardware.

Managing PC Hardware

For your LPIC-1/Linux+ exam, you need to be very familiar with the tasks and procedures associated with managing PC hardware. I'm going to make an assumption at this point that you already have a fairly good understanding of the basics of PC hardware and that I don't need to go into a review of it. For this chapter, I'm going to assume that if I were to open a PC case and show it to you, you could point out the various components that compose the system, including the following:

- Motherboard
- CPU
- RAM

- Hard drive
- Optical drive
- Expansion slots
- Power supply
- Various motherboard connectors
- And so on...

Accordingly, in this chapter we will focus on the hardware skills and tasks specified in the LPIC-1/Linux+ exam objectives. The following topics will be addressed:

- Identifying mass storage devices
- Working with removable hardware interfaces
- Managing system resources
- Managing integrated devices
- Managing systems without external peripherals

Let's begin by learning how to identify the various types of mass storage devices.

Identifying Mass Storage Devices

As you already know, your *random access memory (RAM)* is the place in a computer system where programs and data currently in use on the system are stored. The key benefit of RAM is the fact that it is very fast. Data in RAM can be accessed very quickly because the CPU can directly access any memory location at any time. This makes it an ideal storage device for data that needs to be manipulated by the CPU.

For example, suppose you want to create a word-processing document. The first thing you need to do is open your word-processing application. When you do, the program code for the application is loaded from your hard disk drive into RAM. When you open a word-processing file in the application, the data you are working on is also loaded into RAM.

Although RAM is fast, it does have one key drawback. It has to be constantly refreshed with electricity every few milliseconds. If the system fails to do this, the data and programs stored in RAM are forever lost. The DRAM we use for system memory is really fast, but it isn't *persistent*. To make a PC system truly usable, we need some kind of long-term, persistent storage medium that will retain data even if the power to the system is shut off.

In this topic, we're going to review several storage devices that can do just that. We'll cover the following:

- Hard disk drives
- Solid-state drives
- Optical storage devices
- Flash drives

Let's begin with hard disk drives.

Hard Disk Drives

Hard disk drives are the primary type of persistent storage used in PC systems. Hard disk drives are fast, store huge amounts of data, and are fairly reliable.

Hard disk drives read and write magnetic information to and from spinning aluminum disks called *platters*. These are shown in Figure 12-1.

Most hard disk drives use multiple platters. The platters are coated with a magnetic surface material that allows the hard disk drive heads to read and write magnetic information to and from the drive.

 CAUTION   Don't open a hard disk drive as we did in Figure 12-1. Hard drives are sealed units that contain exceptionally pure air. If you open the drive, you allow dust into the system, which can scratch the surface of the platters and thus render them useless.

Each platter has two heads. One reads the top side of the platter; the other reads the bottom side. The heads themselves don't actually touch the surface of the platters. As the platters spin, a thin cushion of air is created on their surface. The heads actually rest on this cushion of air.

Hard disk platters spin very fast. A low-end drive spins at about 5400 RPM. Most workstation hard drives spin at 7200 RPM. High-end server drives spin at 10,000 RPM or faster. The faster the platters spin, the faster the drive can read or write data.

Figure 12-1   Hard disk drive platters

Every hard disk drive has several parameters that are collectively called the drive's *geometry*. These parameters are used by your system to determine how the drive is to be accessed and where data can be stored. The parameters that compose the drive geometry include the following:

- **Heads**   Refers to the number of read/write heads in the drive.

- **Cylinders**   Refers to the concentric parallel tracks on all sides of all platters in the hard disk drive. Imagine a hollow cylinder that penetrates down through all of the platters in a hard drive. Depending on how wide the cylinder is, you can fit a certain number of progressively wider cylinders, beginning in the center of the platters and working your way outward to the edge, within the drive platters.

- **Sectors Per Track**   Refers to the number of wedges the platters have been divided into. In addition to creating imaginary cylinders in the drive, you can also slice each platter up into imaginary pie-shaped wedges.

Many times, you will hear the drive geometry parameters referred to as simply CHS (cylinders, heads, and sectors per track). Back in the "old" days, we had to manually configure these parameters in the CMOS setup program whenever we added a new drive to the system. Today, this isn't as much of an issue. Your system still needs to know these parameters to be able to address the disk. However, most systems will query the hard drive each time the system boots and automatically update the drive's geometry.

Currently, you have two choices of hard disk drive families that you can use in PC systems: SATA and SCSI. Let's briefly review SATA first.

SATA Hard Disk Drives   Currently, Serial ATA (SATA) hard disk drives are the most common type of mass storage device used in most desktop systems. SATA drives are much faster than earlier types of hard disk drives. This is because each SATA drive in your system has its own dedicated hard disk channel that greatly enhances speed and throughput.

SATA devices connect to the motherboard using a 7-pin connector. SATA devices rely on a serial bus architecture to send and receive information, which requires the use of two channels:

- One signal path to transmit data serially, bit by bit

- A second serial channel to return receipt acknowledgments to the sender

Because SATA uses a point-to-point connection topology, each device has its own cable. Each channel works independent of the others, so there is no contention between drives and no sharing of interface bandwidth. SATA devices can transfer data at rates from 150 MBps (for early devices) up to a current maximum of 1969 MBps.

   TIP   Most modern operating systems, including Linux, will see SATA devices as SCSI devices.

Be aware that the SATA drive connected to the SATA0 connector on the system motherboard will be used as the boot drive by default by your system because it will be assigned an ID of 0.

(The drive connected to the SATA1 connection will have an ID of 1, and so on.) If you want to use a different drive, you'll need to manually specify the drive to boot from.

In addition to ATA drives, you can also use SCSI drives in a PC. Let's talk about SCSI next.

SCSI Hard Disk Drives   SCSI stands for *Small Computer System Interface.* However, in the industry, we just call it "skuzzy." SCSI is a general-purpose interface that can be used to connect a variety of different types of devices to a PC system, including the following:

- Hard disk drives
- Optical drives
- Tape drives
- Scanners
- RAID arrays
- Printers

SCSI is very powerful and very flexible. However, you probably won't encounter many SCSI hard drives in desktop PC systems. That's because SCSI hard disk drives are considerably more expensive than comparable SATA drives. SCSI hard disk implementations are usually reserved for high-end server systems instead.

SCSI implements a communications chain that connects a series of devices together. The SCSI chain runs cabling from device to device to device. These devices can be implemented inside the server and connected together using a ribbon cable, or they can be implemented externally using cables. Either way, the SCSI controller controls all devices in the chain. The SCSI controller is usually implemented as an expansion board in an expansion slot in the motherboard. It usually has two connectors:

- **Internal**   The internal connector is used to connect internal SCSI devices using a SCSI ribbon cable.
- **External**   The external connector is used to connect external SCSI devices to the controller.

Older SCSI controllers supported up to eight devices (including the SCSI controller itself) in the SCSI chain. Many newer SCSI controllers support up to 16 devices (again, including the SCSI controller). The controller determines what data should be sent to which device in the chain using the SCSI ID. Each device in the SCSI chain must have a unique ID number between 0 and 7 (0 and 15 on newer controllers).

Whenever I teach a class that covers SCSI, I always emphasize at this point that the SCSI ID assigned to a device has nothing to do whatsoever with its physical location in the SCSI chain. It's simply a logical number we assign. However, the SCSI ID does perform a crucial function. It defines the priority of the device in the SCSI chain. The higher the SCSI ID assigned to a device, the higher its priority. By default, SCSI controllers are assigned a high-priority SCSI ID of 7. SCSI hard disk drives are usually assigned a lower priority ID of 0 or 1. Optical drives are usually assigned a lower priority SCSI ID of 4 or 5.

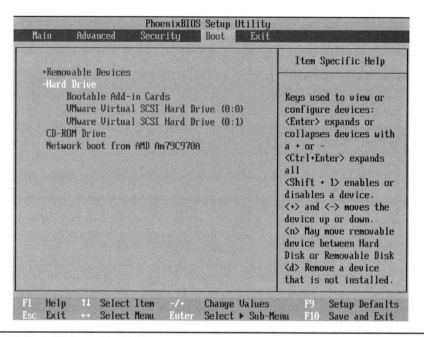

Figure 12-2 SCSI IDs and the BIOS boot order

However, the device ID is also used to determine the boot order, and it works in the opposite fashion. The lower the ID number, the higher the device is in the boot order. For example, if you have a SCSI hard drive with an ID of 0 connected to a SCSI controller and a second hard drive on the same bus assigned an ID of 1, your BIOS will try to boot from the device with an ID of 0 first. This is shown in Figure 12-2.

Notice that each SCSI device has two numbers in its ID: $x{:}n$. The x parameter identifies the ID of the SCSI controller to which the device is connected. The first controller in the system has an ID of 0, the second has an ID of 1, and so on. The n parameter identifies the ID of the device on that controller's bus. Thus, 0:0 indicates the drive is the first SCSI device on the first SCSI controller (and will be the first boot device by default). To change the boot order, you can manually change the boot order or you can change the SCSI ID assigned to the device from which you want to boot.

 TIP   Remember, no two SCSI devices on the same bus can share the same ID number.

The way you set the SCSI ID varies from device to device. Most SCSI hard disk drives use three jumpers to set the ID value. These three jumpers have the following values:

- Jumper 1 = 1
- Jumper 2 = 2
- Jumper 3 = 4

The SCSI ID is determined by adding together the values of all jumpers with shunts installed. For example, if you use no shunts at all (in other words, no jumpers are closed), then the SCSI ID is set to 0 + 0 + 0 = 0. If you put a shunt on jumper 2, then the SCSI ID is set to 0 + 2 + 0 = 2. If you put a shunt on jumpers 2 and 3, then the SCSI ID is set to 0 + 2 + 4 = 6.

 NOTE The SCSI ID may also be set using software, depending on the device.

In addition to SCSI ID, you also need to be concerned with *termination* when setting up a SCSI chain. Each end of the SCSI chain must have a terminating resistor installed to absorb data signals. This prevents the signal from reflecting back down the bus.

Termination can be implemented in a variety of ways on the SCSI chain. Some terminators are implemented by attaching a terminator to the end of the SCSI ribbon cable for internal devices. For external devices, the terminator may be a special plug that is inserted in the second SCSI port on the last external device in the SCSI chain.

Termination can also be implemented on the SCSI devices themselves. This can be done in the following ways:

- **Resistor packs** Resistor packs are inserted in the SCSI device's circuit board to enable termination.

- **Jumpers** A shunted jumper is frequently used to enable termination on the device.

- **Software** SCSI controller boards usually include a software setup program run from the controller board's BIOS that can be used to turn termination off and on.

- **Active termination** Many SCSI devices use active termination. With active termination, the device checks to see if it's the last device on the chain. If it is, it automatically enables the terminating resistor.

When you're configuring SCSI termination, it's important to remember that *both* ends of the SCSI bus must be terminated, but nothing in the middle can be terminated. Any devices after the terminator in the SCSI chain will not be visible to the controller.

 NOTE My experience has been that about 95 percent of problems encountered when working with SCSI are due to misconfigured SCSI IDs or terminators.

Over the years, a wide variety of SCSI standards have been introduced. A thorough review of all the standards is beyond the scope of this topic. It would take an entire chapter devoted to the various SCSI standards to cover all the different flavors of SCSI available. For our purposes here, just make sure that all the devices in your SCSI chain, including the SCSI controller, use the same SCSI standard. For example, if you're using Wide Ultra SCSI III hard disk drives, you need to use a Wide Ultra SCSI III controller.

Be aware that there is a new, high-end SCSI standard that is used almost exclusively in server systems called Serial Attached SCSI (SAS). SAS retains many of the best features of the traditional SCSI standards. However, it also adopts many of the best features of the SATA standard as well. For example, instead of using a SCSI bus, SAS uses a point-to-point connection topology that is very similar to that used by SATA devices. In fact, it is so similar that you can even connect some SATA devices to an SAS connector. Because there is no SCSI bus, there is no longer a need to terminate SAS devices, which eliminates many configuration headaches.

SAS also overcomes device limitations associated with traditional SCSI. Instead of eight or 16 devices, SAS can support (theoretically) up to 65,535 devices. SAS is also faster. It supports data transfer speeds up to 6 Gbps.

Next, we need to look at a new type of mass storage device called a *solid-state drive*.

Solid-State Drives

Recently, solid-state drives (SSDs) have been making inroads into desktop PC systems. A solid-state drive is a storage device that functions much like a standard hard disk drive, using the same block-based I/O operations. However, unlike traditional hard disks, SSDs use flash memory to store data. As discussed earlier in this topic, traditional hard disk drives are mechanical devices that employ electric motors, spinning disks, and movable read/write heads on actuator arms. SSDs, on the other hand, use flash memory and have no moving parts.

Because they have no moving parts, SSDs are less susceptible to damage from physical impact and are much quieter than traditional hard drives. In addition, SSDs are considered to be much faster than typical hard drives. Unfortunately, these benefits come at a cost, as SSDs are also much more expensive than hard drives.

One of the cool features of SSDs is the fact that they use the same SATA interface used by traditional hard disk drives. This makes it very easy to switch to this type of drive in a typical PC system. As such, the same ID number and boot order issues mentioned earlier when I discussed SATA hard disks apply to SSDs as well.

Now that you understand how hard disk drives are implemented, we next need to talk about optical storage devices.

Optical Storage Devices

In addition to hard disks, you can also use optical storage media to store data in a PC system. Currently, you can use CD, DVD, or Blu-ray optical devices in your computer.

Optical storage media stores binary data just like any other storage device. However, the way it stores that data is very different. Unlike hard disks, optical drives do not use magnetism. Instead, they store data in the form of reflected light. The bottom surface of an optical disc is encoded using a series of pits and lands. Pits don't reflect light; lands do. By bouncing a laser beam off the bottom surface of an optical disc, we can reconstruct binary computer data in the form of 0's and 1's by capturing the reflections and non-reflections created by the pits and lands.

Compact Discs (CDs) are 120 mm in diameter and are 1.2 mm thick. A CD can store 650–700MB of binary computer data or 74 minutes of digital audio. Digital Versatile Discs (DVDs) have the same dimensions as a CD. However, because the tracks on a DVD are thinner and closer together, a DVD can store dramatically more data than a CD (4.7GB). Blu-ray discs also have the same physical dimensions as a CD. However, they use a blue-light laser instead of the red-light lasers used by CDs and DVDs. Because the blue-light laser uses higher-frequency, shorter-wavelength light rays, it is able to store dramatically more data in the same physical space (up to 25GB per layer). Some Blu-ray discs implement multiple layers, allowing them to store a very large amount of information.

The key advantages of using optical media to store data in a PC are as follows:

- They can store a relatively large amount of data.
- They are highly portable.
- They are very inexpensive to manufacture.

Optical discs were originally introduced for use in PCs as a read-only media. To encode the pits and lands that store binary PC data, an optical disc had to be pressed at a manufacturing facility. Once the disc was pressed, no more data could be added to it.

Today, that has all changed. In a modern PC system, you can implement writable and re-writable optical drives (usually called *burners*). Optical burner drives implement a second, high-intensity laser in addition to the standard read laser. This second laser is used to write information to the bottom side of a burnable disc. Once-writable discs use a special photo-reactive dye on the bottom side of the disc. When the high-intensity laser in an optical burner strikes this dye, it changes the pigment to a darker color. By doing this, we can encode binary data on the disc using light and dark spots that operate much like the pits and lands found on a factory-pressed optical disc.

With a CD-R, DVD-R, or BD-R optical burner, the data becomes fixed as soon as it is burned. You can't erase or modify the data after that. To be able to do this, you need to use a re-writable optical burner (called a CD-RW, DVD-RW, or BD-RE drive). A re-writable burner uses a high-intensity secondary laser just like a CD-R, DVD-R, or BD-R. However, the bottom surface of an RW or RE disc uses a photo-reactive crystalline coating. These discs can be encoded with light and dark spots just like an -R disc. They can also be erased. Using the right intensity and frequency in the laser, an RW drive can reset the crystals on the bottom surface of the disc back to their original state, allowing you to burn new data.

Flash Drives

The last type of storage device we need to discuss in this chapter is flash storage. Instead of using magnetically encoded platters or optical discs to store data, flash drives use a memory chip. Like an SSD hard drive, flash storage uses flash memory. Flash memory can be electronically erased and reprogrammed. Flash memory is also persistent. Once written, it retains its contents even if the electrical current is turned off.

This combination makes flash drives a very useful and very powerful storage solution for PCs. They can store large amounts of data in a very small package. In fact, most flash drives are so small that they can be carried on a keychain. Many times you will hear flash drives referred to as *thumb drives* due to their small size.

Essentially, a flash drive is little more than a printed circuit board with a flash memory chip installed that is connected to a USB interface. Once a flash drive is plugged in to a USB port on your computer, your system can read information from it or write information to it as if it were a small hard disk drive.

That's it for this topic. We've covered a wide range of PC components. Now we need to cover removable hardware.

Working with Removable Hardware Interfaces

In recent years, new hardware interfaces for PCs have been introduced that have revolutionized the way we connect external devices to the system. Prior to these interfaces, you could still connect external devices to the system using serial ports, parallel ports, keyboard ports, and mouse ports. However, for most of these external devices to work correctly, you had to make sure they were properly connected and turned on (if applicable) before you powered on the PC system itself. If you didn't, the system usually wouldn't recognize that the device was attached. In addition, you couldn't unplug one external device and connect a new one while the system was running. That kind of change usually required a full system reboot.

With removable hardware interfaces, all of that has changed. Now, we can add or remove external devices while the system is running and have the PC automatically recognize the change. In this topic we're going to review the following removable hardware interfaces:

- Universal Serial Bus (USB)
- IEEE 1394 (for example, FireWire)

Let's begin by discussing USB.

Universal Serial Bus

Universal Serial Bus (USB) is a high-speed removable hardware interface that has pretty much replaced serial, parallel, mouse, and keyboard ports on the PC. Most PC systems today include an integrated USB interface in the motherboard. USB can be used to connect a wide variety of external devices, including these:

- External hard drives
- External CD and DVD drives
- Printers
- Scanners
- Digital cameras
- Mice
- Keyboards
- Flash drives

USB connects these devices into a bus. A single USB bus can include up to 127 external devices. All devices on the bus are grouped into one of three categories:

- **Hubs** USB hubs are central connecting points for USB devices. USB uses a star topology. All devices on the bus connect to a USB hub. The USB interface in your PC, whether it is an expansion board or is built in to the motherboard, functions as the root hub in your

USB bus. The cool thing about USB is the fact that you can cascade multiple USB hubs together to connect additional devices to the bus. Simply plugging one USB hub into a USB port on another hub does this. This makes USB extremely scalable.

- **Functions**   Functions are individual external USB devices such as printers, scanners, hard drives, keyboards, and mice.
- **Hub and function**   Some USB devices are both a function and a hub at the same time. For example, many USB keyboards include several USB ports that you can use to connect additional USB devices. This type of device is both a function and a hub.

Because all USB devices eventually connect to the PC through the root hub in your USB interface, USB eliminates the need for multiple interfaces to support multiple external devices. This is a really cool feature of USB. Back in the "old" days of serial and parallel ports, you had to implement a separate interface for each device you wanted to connect. For example, if you wanted to connect two parallel printers to the same PC, you had to purchase and install an additional parallel port interface for the second printer. This isn't an issue with USB. A single USB interface can support many USB devices. Some USB devices, such as a flash drive, can even draw the power they need to run directly from the USB bus. Other USB devices, such as external DVD drives, need their own power supply unit that is plugged into a wall outlet.

In addition, USB devices are self-configuring, self-identifying, and hot-swappable. You can attach a USB device to the system while it is running. When you do, the device will advertise its presence to the PC, which will assign the necessary resources for it to function. When you're done using the device, you can stop the device and disconnect it without halting the system.

USB has been implemented in several different versions. The most important ones to be familiar with are listed here:

- **USB 1.1**   This version of USB is the oldest. It transfers data at a rate of 12 Mbps.
- **USB 2.0**   This version of USB was much faster than USB 1.1 and is still widely used. It can transfer data at 480 Mbps.
- **USB 3.0**   This is the latest version of USB. USB 3.0 is very fast, transferring data at up to 5 Gbps, which is ten times faster than USB 2.0. USB 3.0 is backwards compatible with earlier devices. This means you can plug a USB 2.0 device into a USB 3.0 connector and it will still work. However, it will still run at USB 2.0 speeds.

The important thing to remember is that the overall speed of the entire bus is set to the speed of the slowest device. For example, if you have a USB 2.0 interface and connect a USB 1.1 hard drive to it, the entire system slows down to 12 Mbps.

In addition to USB, a second removable hardware interface called FireWire is commonly used with PCs. Let's review this standard next.

IEEE 1394

IEEE 1394 is very similar to USB. It is designed to support high-speed data transfers between external devices and your PC system. IEEE 1394 was originally developed by Apple. In fact, Apple's Macintosh computer lines were equipped with IEEE 1394 before USB. Today, IEEE 1394 isn't as widely implemented as USB. Most PC systems sold today do not include an IEEE 1394 interface.

To use IEEE 1394 devices, you will probably have to install an IEEE 1394 expansion board in an expansion slot in your system's motherboard.

 NOTE IEEE 1394 is also referred to as FireWire by Apple, i.Link by Sony, and Lynx by Texas Instruments.

Like USB, IEEE 1394 devices are Plug and Play (PnP) compatible and hot-swappable. They are frequently used for the following items:

- External hard drives
- External optical drives
- Digital cameras
- Digital video cameras

IEEE 1394 is very fast. It can transfer data at speeds up to 3.2 Gbps. Unlike USB, IEEE 1394 does not use a star topology. Instead, IEEE 1394 connects devices in true bus fashion by running a cable from device to device to device, forming a chain. A maximum of 63 devices can be connected together in this manner.

With this in mind, let's next look at how you manage system resources used by the various components in a PC system.

Managing System Resources

For your LPIC-1/Linux+ exam, you need to be familiar with the process for managing *system resources*. Every device in a PC system has to be configured with a set of system resources that tell the device what communication channels and addresses it can use. To effectively manage a Linux system, you must have a solid understanding of what these system resources are and how they work. In this part of this chapter, we'll discuss the following:

- Interrupt request channels
- Input/output addresses
- DMA channels
- Plug and Play

Let's begin by discussing interrupts.

Interrupt Request Channels

The first system resource you need to be familiar with is the interrupt request channel. Interrupt request channels are also referred to as *IRQs* or just *interrupts*.

When a device is installed in a PC system, it needs some means of letting the CPU know when it needs attention. Many devices in your PC need lots of CPU time; other devices need the

CPU only on occasion. We need a way to make sure the busy devices get the attention they need without wasting time on devices that don't need as much. This is done through interrupts.

The CPU in your system has one wire on it called the interrupt (INT) wire. If current is applied to this wire, the CPU will stop what it is doing and service the device that placed current on the wire. If no current is present on the wire, the CPU will continue working on whatever processing task has been assigned to it.

The interrupt system in a PC is very similar to a typical classroom. In a classroom setting, the instructor usually presents the material she has prepared to the students. If a student has a question, he can raise his hand and interrupt the instructor's presentation. After the question is answered, the instructor resumes the presentation.

PC interrupts work in much the same manner. Like the instructor, the CPU goes about its business until it is interrupted. Once interrupted, the CPU diverts its attention to the device that raised the interrupt. Once the device's request has been satisfied, the CPU goes back to what it was doing before.

The advantage to using interrupts is that the CPU services system devices only when they need it. It doesn't waste processing time on devices that are idle.

However, the scenario we've just discussed presents a problem. In a typical classroom, there are many students, not just one. Likewise, a PC system has many different devices that all need to get the CPU's attention from time to time. Unlike the hypothetical instructor we just discussed, the CPU has only a single INT wire. That would be sufficient if there were only a single device installed in the system. But this isn't the case. We need some way to allow many different devices to use that same INT wire. This is done using a *programmable interrupt controller (PIC)* chip.

The PIC chip is connected to the INT wire on the CPU as well as the interrupt wires in your motherboard's expansion bus. When a device needs attention, it applies current to its interrupt wire. The PIC is alerted by this event and applies current to the CPU's INT wire. The CPU acknowledges the interrupt, and the PIC then tells the CPU which interrupt number was activated. The CPU can then service the device.

Early PCs had only eight interrupts and a single PIC, as just related. However, a modern PC has many more interrupts. Newer systems use an Advanced Programmable Interrupt Controller (APIC) chip that supports up to 255 IRQ lines.

When working with interrupts, you should keep in mind the following important facts:

- Every device in the PC must be assigned an interrupt.
- Two PCI devices can share interrupts.
- Some system devices have interrupts assigned to them by default. Some of these can be changed or disabled; many cannot:
  - IRQ 0 – System timer
  - IRQ 1 – Keyboard
  - IRQ 3 – COM 2
  - IRQ 4 – COM 1
  - IRQ 5 – LPT 2
  - IRQ 6 – Floppy drive

- IRQ 7 – LPT 1
- IRQ 8 – Real-time clock

- Interrupts 0, 1, and 8 are hardwired. Under no circumstances can you use these interrupts for any other device in the system.

- If a device with a default interrupt assignment isn't installed in the system or is disabled, you can use its interrupt for another device.

In addition to interrupts, devices also require an I/O address to function in a PC system. Let's talk about I/O addresses next.

Input/Output Addresses

Input/output (I/O) addresses go by a variety of names in a PC system. You may hear them referred to as *I/O ports, port addresses,* or simply as *ports.*

I/O addresses allow communications between the devices in the PC and the operating system. I/O addresses are very similar to mailboxes. To send a letter to someone, you must know their mailing address. You write their address on the letter and the mail carrier delivers it to the box with that address. Likewise, the person you wrote to can respond to your letter and leave it in their mailbox for the mail carrier to pick up.

I/O addresses work in much the same manner. They serve as mailboxes for the devices installed in the system. Data can be left for a device in its I/O address. Data from the device can be left in the I/O address for the operating system to pick up.

On a personal computer, there are 65,535 port addresses for devices to use.

 EXAM TIP I/O addresses are written using hexadecimal notation. The decimal numbering system that we use in our everyday work is a base-10 numbering system. When we count, we start at 0 and proceed to 9, and then we start over again at 10. Alternatively, hexadecimal is a base-16 numbering system. Like decimal numbers, hexadecimal starts at 0 and proceeds to 9. However, instead of starting over, hexadecimal continues on with six additional numbers represented by the letters A through F. Therefore, if you were to count in hex, you would say: 0, 1, 2, 3, 4, 5, 6, 7, 8, 9, A, B, C, D, E, F. Because hex and decimal numbers can sometimes be easily mistaken, we usually put an *h* either before or after any hex number.

When working with I/O addresses, you should keep the following important facts in mind:

- All devices must have an I/O address assigned.
- Most devices will use a range of I/O addresses.
- Devices must use unique I/O ports.
- Default I/O port assignments include the following:
  - 0000h – DMA controller
  - 0020h – PIC 1
  - 0030h – PIC 2

- 0040h – System timer
- 0060h – Keyboard
- 0070h – CMOS clock
- 00C0h – DMA controller
- 00F0h – Math co-processor
- 0170h – Secondary IDE hard disk controller
- 01F0h – Primary IDE hard disk controller
- 0200h – Joystick
- 0278h – LPT2
- 02E8h – COM4
- 02F8h – COM2
- 0378h – LPT1
- 03E8h – COM3
- 03F0h – Floppy disk drive controller
- 03F8h – COM1

Direct Memory Access Channels

In addition to interrupts and I/O addresses, some devices also require a direct memory access (DMA) channel. DMA channels are used by high-throughput devices to communicate directly with RAM *without* involving the CPU. Bypassing the CPU can dramatically increase the device's data transfer rate.

Not all devices need DMA. Other devices, however, would be severely handicapped if they couldn't use DMA. These devices include

- Sound boards
- Some hard disk drives

DMA is implemented on the motherboard using the DMA controller chip (DCC). The DCC is very similar to the PIC chip we reviewed earlier. The DCC has four leads that connect it to the memory controller chip (MCC) and the expansion bus slots. Each of these leads is referred to as a *DMA channel.* Data from an expansion slot is routed through the DCC to the MCC, thus allowing direct access to the system memory.

When working with DMA, you should keep the following points in mind:

- No two devices can use the same channel.
- Modern systems use cascaded DMA controllers to increase the number of available DMA channels.

Before we finish talking about system resources, we need to discuss how they are configured on an expansion board. Let's do that next.

Plug and Play

In the "old days" of ISA, we had to manually configure the system resources used by an expansion board in an expansion slot. Most ISA boards had a series of jumpers or DIP switches that you would use to configure the board's interrupt, I/O address, and DMA channel. This doesn't sound too difficult in theory, but in practice it could be very difficult.

The problem was that most expansion boards, to cut manufacturing costs, couldn't be configured to use just any of the available interrupts or port addresses available on the system. Instead, most boards offered the choice of two or three interrupts and I/O address ranges. The issue was that most board manufacturers made the exact same choices of interrupts and I/O address ranges. You could easily run out of resources. For example, you may have had interrupts 2 and 3 available in your system, but the board you wanted to install could only be configured to use interrupts 4, 5, or 7. To implement the board, you would have to manually reconfigure other devices in the system in an attempt to free up an interrupt it could use.

This was all fixed when the Plug and Play (PnP) standard was introduced in the late 1990s. PnP is great! In fact, it's still in use today. The PnP standard is designed to automatically configure the system resources used by your expansion boards for you every time you boot the system. It makes life so much easier for a system administrator. All you have to do is install the board in an available slot and turn on the system—no jumpers, no DIP switches, no misplaced configuration diskettes.

When the system is powered on, the PnP-compatible system negotiates with the PnP expansion board to determine what interrupt, I/O addresses, and DMA channels it will use. If necessary, the operating system can also add its input as to what resources it thinks should be assigned.

NOTE   In the earliest version of PnP, the system didn't always operate correctly. System administrators called it "plug-n-pray."

Next, let's look at managing integrated PC devices.

Managing Integrated Devices

In the old days, the typical PC motherboard was pretty much bare bones in its design. Basically, you had the CPU socket, your chipset components, your expansion slots, and not much else. If you wanted to connect serial or parallel devices to the board, you had to install the appropriate board in an expansion slot. If you wanted to actually see your video output, you likewise had to install a video board in an expansion slot. To connect the system to a network, you had to (you guessed it) install a network interface in an expansion slot. Oh, and by the way, if you wanted to use any kind of hard disk, you also had to install a disk controller board in an expansion slot. Don't even get me started on getting a sound board to work in these old systems.

Today, things are much different. Most motherboards include a plethora of integrated devices on board, including

- I/O ports (including serial, parallel, USB, and FireWire)
- Video interfaces

- Network interfaces

- Sound boards

- Storage controllers

- And so on...

Integrated peripherals are nice. They reduce the overall cost of building the system because you don't have to buy all these devices separately. They make it easier to manage as well because the components (usually) all play nicely together and all the drivers needed to support the devices are included with the board.

However, suppose the video, network, or sound interface integrated into the motherboard in your system isn't up to snuff in your reckoning? Maybe you're a gamer and you need a killer video board to support your habit. Maybe your system will function as a network server and you need a specific network interface installed to support the operating system or application that will be installed on the server.

 NOTE For example, Linux-based VMware ESX and ESXi hypervisors both require very specific network boards and disk controllers to be installed before they can be installed themselves.

In addition, the security requirements used by some organizations (especially governmental organizations) may dictate that some types of peripherals must be disabled. A good example is the USB interface. Although the USB interface can be very handy, it also represents a security nightmare for high-security organizations. Imagine the data that could be carted off if someone with a thumb drive were to gain access to an unattended system!

The good news is that you're not stuck with your integrated peripherals in an enabled state. They can be enabled or disabled quite easily. Once one is disabled, you can install whatever replacement peripheral you want to use in an expansion slot or USB port.

Usually, when you boot a system, you'll see a message indicating which keystroke combination can be used to access the system setup program.

Once in the system setup, you next need to locate the appropriate menu option to access the integrated peripherals menu.

After making the appropriate changes, press the appropriate key indicated (or select the appropriate menu option) to save your changes. Once you are done, the peripherals you modified will be enabled or disabled on the motherboard accordingly.

Be aware that many newer computers no longer use a BIOS chip on the motherboard. Instead, they use the Unified Extensible Firmware Interface (UEFI), which is firmware, like the BIOS. However, it functions in a very different manner. UEFI was designed to address many of the shortcomings of the traditional BIOS, such as memory and hard disk size limitations. It is also designed to prevent unauthorized operating systems from booting on the system. This feature is designed to prevent malware called *rootkits* or *bootkits* from loading on the system. Rootkits and bootkits are an exceptionally sneaky type of malware that inserts itself into the root sector of hard disk drives. This causes them to be loaded before the real operating system loads, which makes it very difficult for your antimalware software to detect them. UEFI won't let an operating system load unless it has been digitally signed, which usually has to be done by the system manufacturer.

This brings up a significant point of frustration where Linux is concerned. It is very common for Linux systems to start out their life as Windows systems. Users blow away the Windows operating system and reinstall Linux in its place. This process worked fine on BIOS-based systems. However, on UEFI-based systems, it causes extreme frustration because the UEFI firmware for a Windows system doesn't have digital certificates for all the various Linux distributions available. On some hardware, you can get around this issue by disabling the SecureBoot option in the UEFI firmware.

Before we move on, we also need to discuss how to manage systems without external peripherals.

Managing Systems Without External Peripherals

Depending on your job role, you may need to manage systems that don't have any external peripherals, not even a keyboard. Many servers are managed in this manner, as are many virtualized systems running on a hypervisor.

You have a couple of options for managing these types of systems. If the system has an integrated management interface (such as is found on high-end server systems), you can usually access this interface using a web browser and perform all kinds of management tasks, including accessing the system display, shutting down the system, and even powering the system on.

If the system doesn't have an integrated management interface, you have two other options:

- **SSH**   Using SSH, you can securely access the shell prompt of the system and run commands as if you were sitting in front of the system. You can also tunnel X server traffic through the SSH connection, which allows you to securely access the graphical desktop of the system.

- **VNC**   You can also use Virtual Network Computing (VNC) to remotely access the graphical desktop of the system. VNC is great, but it lacks the security provided by SSH tunneling, so it is usually used only on secure networks.

We'll discuss configuring SSH in a later chapter. We'll also look at configuring xinetd to enable VNC on a Linux system in a later chapter. For now, just understand that these are options you can use to access a system that doesn't have any external peripherals installed.

With this hardware background in mind, let's look next at how Linux drivers work.

Working with Linux Drivers

Back in the "old" days of Linux, working with hardware was hit or miss at best. If you were installing commonly used hardware from a well-known vendor, it would usually work. However, if you were installing specialty hardware or hardware from a less-visible vendor, chances were that the device wouldn't work under Linux.

Why? The key issue was driver support. Linux wasn't taken seriously in those days, so most hardware vendors didn't invest any time in developing a Linux driver for their hardware. Unless you were capable of writing your own driver, you had to rely on the good graces of a software developer somewhere in the world taking the time to write one that would support your hardware.

Fortunately, things have changed dramatically in today's IT environment. Linux is no longer viewed as a "plaything" for hobbyists. It's quickly gaining acceptance as a reliable, enterprise-level operating system. As a result, Linux driver support is relatively good. It isn't perfect yet, but it's getting better each year. I predict that it won't be much longer before Linux hardware drivers are as ubiquitous as Windows drivers currently are.

If you are going to be responsible for managing Linux systems, it's very important that you understand how drivers work on the operating system. If you've used a Windows system, you're probably already familiar with the process required to load a driver to support a piece of hardware. However, the way drivers work under Linux is somewhat different.

To make sure you are proficient with Linux drivers, we're going to cover the following topics in this part of the chapter:

- What exactly is a driver, anyway?
- How drivers are implemented under Linux
- Managing kernel modules
- Working with hot-plug and cold-plug devices

To effectively manage drivers under Linux, you need to understand what a driver is in the first place. Let's start by defining what a driver is and how drivers work on Linux.

What Exactly Is a Driver, Anyway?

The key idea you need to understand when discussing drivers is the fact that the CPU on your motherboard doesn't natively know how to communicate with other hardware devices installed in your system. It doesn't know how to send video data to the video board, it doesn't know how to save data on your hard drive, and it doesn't know how to send data to the sound board.

To be able to do these things, the CPU needs instructions in the form of software to tell it how to communicate with these devices. For basic devices, such as your system clock and keyboard, basic drivers can be stored in a chip on the motherboard. However, the software for more complex devices, such as network and sound boards, can't be easily stored in a chip on the motherboard. There are so many different makes and models of these types of devices that it is completely unfeasible to store all the software needed for every last device within a motherboard chip. Instead, we store the software on the system's hard drive. As the system boots, the operating system loads the software (called a *driver*) from the hard disk into RAM. Once this is done, the CPU has the instructions it needs to communicate with the associated hardware.

In this chapter, we're primarily concerned with drivers associated with this last category of hardware. Let's discuss how to work with them next.

How Drivers Are Implemented Under Linux

There are two different ways in which Linux can implement a device driver for a particular piece of hardware in your PC system. First of all, the driver can be loaded as a *kernel module*. Once the Linux kernel has been loaded into memory during the boot process we reviewed in the previous

```
root@openSUSE:...top/kernel/drivers                    ✕
File  Edit  View  Search  Terminal  Help
openSUSE:/lib/modules/3.11.10-21-desktop/kernel/drivers # ls
acpi         clocksource  gpu         leds       nfc         rtc       vfio
ata          cpufreq      hid         md         parport     scsi      vhost
atm          crypto       hsi         media      pci         ssb       video
auxdisplay   dca          hv          memstick   pcmcia      staging   virtio
base         dma          hwmon       message    platform    target    vme
bcma         edac         i2c         mfd        power       thermal   wl
block        extcon       infiniband  misc       pps         tty       watchdog
bluetooth    firewire     input       mmc        ptp         uio
cdrom        firmware     ipack       mtd        rapidio     usb
char         gpio         isdn        net        remoteproc  uwb
```

Figure 12-3   Module subdirectories

chapter, it can be configured to load kernel modules, which allow the CPU and operating system to work with the hardware installed in the system.

Kernel modules have a .ko or .o extension and are stored within the /lib/modules/*kernel_version*/ kernel/drivers directory on your Linux system. Within this directory is a series of subdirectories where kernel modules for your hardware devices are actually stored. These are shown in Figure 12-3.

For example, the kernel modules used to support your SATA storage devices are stored in the ata subdirectory, as shown in Figure 12-4.

The second way hardware support can be implemented in Linux is to actually compile the necessary driver support directly within the kernel itself. Doing so requires that you manually

```
root@openSUSE:...kernel/drivers/ata                    ✕
File  Edit  View  Search  Terminal  Help
openSUSE:/lib/modules/3.11.10-21-desktop/kernel/drivers/ata # ls
acard-ahci.ko      pata_cypress.ko    pata_optidma.ko       sata_highbank.ko
ahci_platform.ko   pata_efar.ko       pata_pcmcia.ko        sata_inic162x.ko
ata_generic.ko     pata_hpt366.ko     pata_pdc2027x.ko      sata_mv.ko
ata_piix.ko        pata_hpt37x.ko     pata_pdc202xx_old.ko  sata_nv.ko
pata_acpi.ko       pata_hpt3x2n.ko    pata_piccolo.ko       sata_promise.ko
pata_ali.ko        pata_hpt3x3.ko     pata_radisys.ko       sata_qstor.ko
pata_amd.ko        pata_it8213.ko     pata_rdc.ko           sata_rcar.ko
pata_arasan_cf.ko  pata_it821x.ko     pata_rz1000.ko        sata_sil.ko
pata_artop.ko      pata_jmicron.ko    pata_sc1200.ko        sata_sil24.ko
pata_atiixp.ko     pata_marvell.ko    pata_sch.ko           sata_sis.ko
pata_atp867x.ko    pata_mpiix.ko      pata_serverworks.ko   sata_svw.ko
pata_cmd640.ko     pata_netcell.ko    pata_sil680.ko        sata_sx4.ko
pata_cmd64x.ko     pata_ninja32.ko    pata_sis.ko           sata_uli.ko
pata_cs5520.ko     pata_ns87410.ko    pata_sl82c105.ko      sata_via.ko
pata_cs5530.ko     pata_ns87415.ko    pata_triflex.ko       sata_vsc.ko
pata_cs5535.ko     pata_oldpiix.ko    pata_via.ko
pata_cs5536.ko     pata_opti.ko       pdc_adma.ko
```

Figure 12-4   ATA kernel modules

recompile your kernel from its source code and specify which hardware support you want integrated directly within the kernel in the process. After you do so, kernel modules for those devices are no longer needed because the operating system now has all the software it needs within the kernel itself.

This sounds like a pretty great way to do things, right? So why don't we compile the drivers for all the hardware in the system directly into the kernel? It is a good strategy for some drivers; however, as a general rule of thumb, you should limit the drivers compiled into the kernel to only those drivers the system needs to boot up (keyboard drivers, storage drivers, and so on). The rest should be loaded as kernel modules.

There are a couple of really good reasons for doing things this way. First of all, each driver you compile into the kernel increases the overall size of the kernel. You should try to keep your kernel as lean and clean as possible. Second, configuring a kernel is a more complex operation, requiring in-depth information about the hardware and what each configuration element provides.

Finally, the issue of modularity comes into play. If you never modify, upgrade, or reconfigure your computer system, then compiling more drivers directly into the kernel may make sense. However, it doesn't make sense for PC surgeons like me. I'm constantly adding, removing, and reconfiguring hardware in my PCs. By loading kernel modules, I can add or remove support for hardware devices very quickly from the command line. If I compile them into the kernel, I may end up with a bloated kernel that contains support for hardware that is no longer in the system. Essentially, kernel modules allow your system to be much more dynamic.

We'll be focusing primarily on kernel modules in this chapter. Let's discuss how to manage your kernel modules next.

Managing Kernel Modules

When I first started learning about managing kernel modules back when Linux was young, I was really intimidated. It sounded really difficult. Like many other aspects of Linux, however, it's really pretty easy. In this part of this chapter, we're going to discuss how to manage kernel modules on your system. We'll cover the following topics:

- Viewing installed hardware
- Using shell commands to manage kernel modules

Let's start by discussing how to view the hardware installed on your system.

Viewing Installed Hardware

A key skill you need to have as a Linux system admin is to know how to view currently installed hardware in the system. One of the best tools for doing this is the good old /proc directory. I introduced you to /proc earlier. Remember, the /proc directory doesn't actually exist in the file system. Instead, it's a pseudo file system that is dynamically created whenever it is accessed. As you can see in Figure 12-5, the /proc directory contains a subdirectory for each process running on your system.

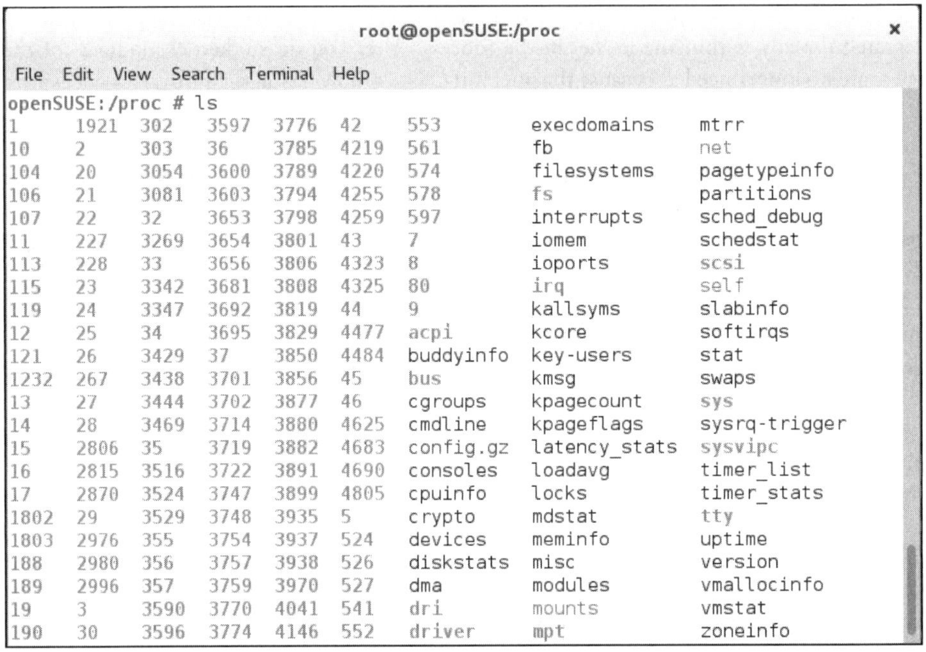

Figure 12-5 Using the /proc directory

However, also notice in Figure 12-5 that /proc contains a number of other files. Here are some of the more useful files:

- **cpuinfo** Contains details about the CPU installed in the system. You can use cat, less, more, or any text editor to view the contents of this file. An example from this file is shown here:

```
processor       : 0
vendor_id       : GenuineIntel
cpu family      : 15
model           : 6
model name      : Intel(R) Pentium(R) D CPU 2.80GHz
stepping        : 2
microcode       : 0xf
cpu MHz         : 2793.072
cache size      : 2048 KB
physical id     : 0
siblings        : 2
core id         : 0
cpu cores       : 2

...
```

- **devices** Contains a list of devices installed in the system.
- **dma** Contains a list of DMA channel assignments in the system.

- **interrupts**   Contains a list of IRQ assignments in the system. A sample is shown here:

```
          CPU0        CPU1
   0:      344           0   IO-APIC-edge      timer
   1:       31         301   IO-APIC-edge      i8042
   3:        1           0   IO-APIC-edge
   4:        0           1   IO-APIC-edge
   6:        7           0   IO-APIC-edge      floppy
   7:        0           0   IO-APIC-edge      parport0
   8:        1           0   IO-APIC-edge      rtc0
   9:        0           0   IO-APIC-fasteoi   acpi
  12:     1589         107   IO-APIC-edge      i8042
  14:        0           0   IO-APIC-edge      ata_piix
  15:     4111        1246   IO-APIC-edge      ata_piix
  16:      659           0   IO-APIC-fasteoi   vmci, Ensoniq AudioPCI
...
```

- **iomem**   Contains a list of I/O port assignments in the system.

- **modules**   Contains a list of all the kernel modules currently being used by the system. A sample is shown here:

```
fuse 75897 3 - Live 0xffffffffa01cc000
p6t_LOG 5898 8 - Live 0xffffffffa020f000
xt_tcpudp 2859 10 - Live 0xffffffffa01f0000
xt_pkttype 1288 3 - Live 0xffffffffa01e3000
ipt_LOG 6067 8 - Live 0xffffffffa00f7000
xt_limit 2559 16 - Live 0xffffffffa00de000
vmsync 4288 0 - Live 0xffffffffa0082000
vmblock 13824 1 - Live 0xffffffffa0065000
...
```

- **version**   Contains the information about the version of the Linux kernel running on the system.

- **/scsi/**   Contains files that hold information about the SCSI devices in your system if you're using a SCSI adapter.

- **/bus/devices**   Contains information about the USB devices in the system.

In addition to /proc, the /sys/ directory also provides information about the hardware installed in the system. The file system is organized in a tree structure grouped by the hardware bus, the hardware devices, and their associated drivers. The top level of the /sys directory contains many subdirectories, including

- **/sys/block**   Contains a symbolic link file for each block device in the system

- **/sys/bus**   Contains a directory for each data bus in the system, including the PCI, SCSI, and USB busses

Each bus directory has two subdirectories—devices and drivers—as shown here:

```
openSUSE:/sys/bus/scsi # ls
devices  drivers  drivers_autoprobe  drivers_probe  uevent
```

The devices subdirectory contains entries for every device on that bus, whereas the drivers directory contains subdirectories for each driver loaded for a device on this bus:

- **/sys/class**   Contains all device classes available
- **/sys/devices**   Contains an entry for every discovered device
- **/sys/module**   Contains subdirectories for each module loaded into the kernel, as shown next:

```
openSUSE:/sys/module # ls
8250            ip6t_LOG            nf_conntrack_ipv6         snd_seq
ac              ip6t_REJECT         nf_conntrack_netbios_ns   snd_seq_device
ac97_bus        ip6table_filter     nf_defrag_ipv4            snd_seq_midi
acpi            ip6table_mangle     parport                   snd_seq_midi_event
apparmor        ip6table_raw        parport_pc                snd_timer
ata_generic     ip_tables           pci_hotplug               soundcore
ata_piix        ipt_LOG             pcie_aspm                 spurious
...
```

Most Linux distributions also include a variety of command-line tools you can use to view information about the hardware in your system. Some of these tools actually pull their information right out of the /proc directory. You can use the following commands:

- **hdparm /dev/*device***   Displays information about your hard drive. Replace *device* with sda, sdb, and so on. An example is shown here:

```
ws1:/proc # hdparm /dev/sdb
/dev/sdb:
 HDIO_DRIVE_CMD(identify) failed: Invalid argument
 readonly     =  0 (off)
 readahead    = 256 (on)
 geometry     = 1044/255/63, sectors = 16777216, start = 0
```

- **sg_scan**   Scans your SCSI bus and lists all the devices connected to your SCSI controller.
- **sginfo –l**   Also lists all connected SCSI devices.
- **lsusb**   Displays information about USB devices connected to your Linux system.
- **hwinfo**   Displays a comprehensive overview of the system hardware. It probes the system hardware and generates a system overview report. An excerpt from a sample report is shown here:

```
    HD 0 type       : none
    HD 1 type       : none
    HD type 48 data: 53760/6/212 C/H/S, precomp 10, lz 0
    HD type 49 data: 273/128/201 C/H/S, precomp 0, lz 7168
    DOS base memory: 640 kB
    Extended memory: 64512 kB (configured), 64512 kB (tested)
    Gfx adapter     : EGA, VGA, ... (with BIOS)
    FPU             : installed
...
```

If you don't specify any options with the command, it can produce a rather long report. However, you can limit the report to a single device subsystem using the *--device* option. See the hwinfo man page to see a list of devices you can use with this option.

- **lspci**   Lists all PCI devices installed in the system. You can use the –k option with this command to see the kernel modules associated with each device.

With this information in hand, you're now ready to learn how to manage kernel modules from the shell prompt. Let's do that next.

Using Shell Commands to Manage Kernel Modules

As with most other operating systems, you can manually list, load, or unload Linux kernel modules. Although many graphical utilities are available that can do this, we're going to focus on accomplishing these tasks from the shell prompt.

To view all currently loaded kernel modules, you can use the lsmod command. This command pulls data from the /proc/modules file and reformats it for display on the screen. To use this command, simply enter **lsmod** at the shell prompt, as shown in the example here:

```
Module              Size   Used by
lp                  10913  0
parport_pc          37547  1
af_packet           23229  0
joydev              11942  0
st                  41564  0
fuse                75897  3
...
```

To view more information about a particular loaded module, you can use the modinfo command. You can first use lsmod to find the name of the module in question and then enter **modinfo** *module_name* at the shell prompt. In the preceding example, one of the modules displayed by lsmod is joydev. This is your system's joystick kernel module. To view more information about this particular module, you can enter **modinfo joydev** at the shell prompt, as shown in the example here:

```
openSUSE:~ # modinfo joydev
filename:       /lib/modules/2.6.34.7-0.7-desktop/kernel/drivers/input/joydev.ko
license:        GPL
description:    Joystick device interfaces
author:         Vojtech Pavlik vojtech@ucw.cz
srcversion:     B57DA6AAEE9B8102A061E91
alias:          input:b*v*p*e*-e*1,*k*2C0,*r*a*m*l*s*f*w*
alias:          input:b*v*p*e*-e*1,*k*130,*r*a*m*l*s*f*w*
alias:          input:b*v*p*e*-e*1,*k*120,*r*a*m*l*s*f*w*
alias:          input:b*v*p*e*-e*3,*k*r*a*6,*m*l*s*f*w*
alias:          input:b*v*p*e*-e*3,*k*r*a*8,*m*l*s*f*w*
alias:          input:b*v*p*e*-e*3,*k*r*a*0,*m*l*s*f*w*
depends:
vermagic:       2.6.34.7-0.7-desktop SMP preempt mod_unload modversions
```

To load a kernel module, you first need to run the **depmod** command from the shell prompt. This command is used to build a file named modules.dep that is stored in /lib/modules/*kernel_version*/, as shown here:

```
openSUSE:/lib/modules/ modules/3.11.10-21-desktop # ls
kernel               modules.builtin.bin  modules.order        systemtap
modules.alias        modules.dep          modules.softdep      vdso
modules.alias.bin    modules.dep.bin      modules.symbols      weak-updates
modules.builtin      modules.devname      modules.symbols.bin
```

Within this file, depmod lists the dependencies between modules. This helps other kernel module management utilities ensure that dependent modules are loaded whenever you load a module.

With the modules.dep file created, you can now go ahead and load kernel modules. You can use one of two different commands to do this. The first is the insmod command. The syntax for insmod is **insmod** *module_filename*. The module filename is usually a kernel module located in a subdirectory of /lib/modules/*kernel_version*/kernel/. For example, if you wanted to load the driver for a standard PC parallel port, you would enter **insmod /lib/modules/*version*/kernel/ drivers/parport/parport_pc.ko** at the shell prompt.

In addition to insmod, you can also use the modprobe command. Most Linux admins prefer modprobe to insmod. The key issue here is that the insmod command doesn't take into account the module dependencies identified by depmod.

The syntax for using modprobe is **modprobe *module_name***. As with insmod, the module you load with modprobe resides in a subdirectory of /lib/modules/*kernel_version*/kernel/. For example, the /lib/modules/*kernel_version*/kernel/drivers/net/ethernet directory contains kernel modules for a variety of network boards, as shown here:

```
ws1:/lib/modules/modules/3.11.10-21-desktop/kernel/drivers/net/ethernet # ls
3c59x.ko      chelsio       hamachi.ko    myri10ge      qlcnic        sunhme.ko
8139cp.ko     cnic.ko       hamradio      natsemi.ko    qlge          tehuti.ko
8139too.ko    cxgb3         hp100.ko      ne2k-pci.ko   r6040.ko      tg3.ko
...
```

If I wanted to load the kernel module for the 3c590 network board, I would enter **modprobe 3c590** at the shell prompt. You're probably wondering, at this point, if the module will be persistent across system restarts after it has been loaded with modprobe. The answer is no, it won't (unless the device is automatically detected during boot). However, modprobe is automatically run every time the kernel loads. It reads the information contained in your /etc/modprobe.conf file to determine what kernel modules should be loaded during startup.

 TIP If the /etc/modprobe.conf file doesn't exist, then modprobe will use the files located in the /etc/modprobe.d directory to determine the kernel modules that will be loaded at boot.

The modprobe.conf file uses the following directives:

- **install *module_name*** Tells modprobe to load the specified module. It can also be used to run any valid shell command, providing you with a high degree of flexibility when loading your modules.
- **alias *alias_name module_name*** Gives a kernel module an alias name that can be used to reference it from the shell prompt.
- **options *module_name options*** Gives modprobe a list of options, such as irq= and io=, that should be used when a particular kernel module loads.

You'll probably notice that there is a big note at the beginning of the file that warns you not to modify /etc/modprobe.conf directly. Instead, if you need to manually specify that a particular kernel module be loaded at system startup, you should enter it in the /etc/modprobe.conf.local file using the modprobe.conf directives just specified.

 NOTE Alternatively, you could also insert the **modprobe** *module_name* command in your rc.local or boot.local file to ensure that the module is loaded at system startup. However, my experience has been that you will rarely need to do this. Most distributions run a hardware detection routine at system boot that scans for new hardware and automatically loads the appropriate kernel module.

If you need to unload a currently loaded kernel module, you can use the **rmmod** *module_name* command at the shell prompt. Be warned that this command won't work if the device serviced by the module is in use. If it is, the command won't remove the module. Like insmod, rmmod doesn't take module dependencies into account and doesn't do anything with them. If you want to remove a module and take dependencies into account, you should use modprobe instead. The syntax for removing a module with modprobe is **modprobe –r** *module_name*.

Let's practice working with kernel modules in the following exercise.

Exercise 12-1: Working with Kernel Modules

In this exercise, you will practice viewing information about kernel modules. You can perform this exercise using the virtual machine that comes with this book. Run snapshot 12-1 for the correctly configured environment.

 VIDEO Please watch the Exercise 12-1 video for a demonstration on how to perform this task.

Complete the following:

1. Boot your Linux system and log in as the **student** user with a password of **student**.

2. Open a terminal session.

3. Switch to your root user account by entering **su** – followed by a password of **student**.

4. View the status of your system's kernel modules by entering **lsmod | less** at the shell prompt.

5. Page through the list of kernel modules. When finished, press Q.

6. View information about the parport kernel module by entering **modinfo parport** at the shell prompt.

7. Create a list of module dependencies by entering **depmod** at the shell prompt.

8. Use the less or more utility to review the dependency file (modules.dep) you just built in /lib/modules/*kernel_version/*.

9. Enter **lsmod | grep joydev** at the shell prompt. You should see a 0 on the output line, indicating the module is loaded but the hardware is not in use.

10. Remove the joydev module by entering **rmmod joydev** at the shell prompt.

11. Verify that the joydev kernel module was unloaded by entering **lsmod | grep joydev** again at the shell prompt. You should see no output listed, indicating the module isn't loaded.

12. Reload the joystick module by entering **modprobe joydev** at the shell prompt.

13. Enter **lsmod | grep joydev** at the shell prompt again. You should again see a 0 on the output line, indicating the module is loaded but the hardware is not in use, as shown here:

```
openSUSE:/etc/modprobe.d # lsmod | grep joydev
joydev                11942   0
```

Working with Hot-Plug and Cold-Plug Devices

When working with PC hardware and kernel modules under Linux, you need to keep in mind that your PC hardware can be grouped into two different categories:

- **Cold-plug devices** Cold-plug devices can be physically connected to or disconnected from the PC system only when it is powered off. PC components such as the CPU, RAM, expansion cards, and storage devices are examples of internal cold-plug devices. Peripherals such as parallel printers and external SCSI devices are examples of external cold-plug devices.

  The key thing to remember about cold-plug devices is the fact that if you plug them in while the system is running, they probably won't be detected and recognized by the system. If you connect them properly while the system is off and then attempt to unplug them while the system is running, you will probably damage the component (or the system itself) electrically. By default, only processes running in the kernel space are allowed to communicate directly with the system hardware.

 NOTE Kernel space processes are part of the kernel itself. User space processes are programs that are run by the end user.

To allow user space processes to access hardware, the /dev directory is provided. As discussed earlier in this book, the hardware in your Linux system is accessed through a device file through /dev. Cold-plug devices (such as your hard disk drive) are accessed in this way.

- **Hot-plug devices** Hot-plug devices, on the other hand, are designed to be connected and disconnected dynamically while the system is up and running. Software on the Linux system detects the changes to the system as these types of devices are attached and detached. The system will recognize the device when it is connected and load the appropriate modules. USB and FireWire devices are examples of hot-plug devices.

  The problem with addressing hot-plug devices lies with how they are accessed. Remember, cold-plug devices are accessed through a device file in /dev. Can hot-plug devices be accessed in this way, too? Yes, but the process needs some help. One option would be to create a device file in /dev for every possible device that could ever be connected to the system. This would allow applications on the system to access hot-plug hardware whenever they were connected to the system through the appropriate device file.

Although this approach works, it's also very messy. A better approach would be to dynamically create a device file in /dev whenever a hot-plug device is connected and then remove it whenever the device is disconnected. For this to work, the new hardware must be recognized by the operating system, the appropriate device files must be created in /dev, and any processes running on the system must be notified that the new hardware is available.

Several Linux components are needed to do this. The first component is sysfs. This component provides the /sys virtual file system we discussed earlier in this chapter. Its job is to export information about system hardware devices (both hot-plug and cold-plug) so that applications and utilities running on the system can access them.

The second component is the Hardware Abstraction Layer (HAL) daemon (hald). This daemon is run automatically at startup. Its job is to provide applications running on the system with information about the hardware (both hot-plug and cold-plug) available in the system.

The next component is the Desktop Bus (dbus). It also runs as a daemon on your Linux system, providing several key functions. For our purposes here, however, you need to remember that it is the dbus daemon that notifies running processes whenever a hot-plug device is connected or disconnected from the system.

Finally, Linux also uses udev. The udev daemon (udevd) creates a virtual file system that is mounted at /dev. It communicates with the Linux kernel through the *uevent* interface. When a hot-plug device has been added or removed, the kernel sends out a uevent message that is picked up by udevd, which does the following, based on the rules defined in the files in the /etc/udev/rules.d directory:

- It initializes the device.
- It creates the appropriate device file in the /dev directory.
- If the new device is a network interface, it configures it using the ifup utility.
- If the new device is a storage device, it mounts it using the information in /etc/fstab.
- It informs running processes about the new device.

Chapter Review

In this chapter, I discussed how to manage hardware in your system and configure Linux kernel modules to support the various installed devices.

I first discussed the various types of storage devices used in a PC system. I reviewed how SATA, SCSI, and solid-state hard disk drives work and how they are configured. I also pointed out how to manipulate the hardware ID assigned to storage devices to configure the boot device. I also discussed how optical and flash memory storage devices work.

I then reviewed removable hardware interfaces that are used to connect external devices to a PC. We first looked at USB. I noted that USB uses hubs to create a cascaded star topology that can connect up to 127 external devices. I then reviewed how IEEE 1394 accomplishes a similar task using a daisy-chained bus topology.

We then looked at managing system resources. I reviewed the role and function of interrupts, I/O addresses, and DMA channels. I also reviewed how the PnP system works, emphasizing that PCI expansion cards use PnP and can be configured to share interrupt channels.

We then turned our attention to managing integrated devices. I pointed out that you can enable or disable integrated devices using the system setup. I pointed out that the keystroke used to access the system setup as well as the exact menu option used to enable or disable integrated devices varies by manufacturer.

We then looked at managing systems that don't have any external peripherals installed, including keyboards or video displays. These types of systems can be managed using either VNC or SSH, with SSH being the more secure option of the two.

Next, you learned how to manage and configure drivers to enable the hardware in your Linux system. I related that drivers are small programs loaded into RAM that enable the CPU to communicate with a particular hardware component. For basic components, this software is stored on a chip on the motherboard. For other components, the driver is stored on the hard disk and must be loaded into RAM by the operating system kernel.

Many newer computers use the Unified Extensible Firmware Interface (UEFI) instead of the traditional BIOS. UEFI was designed to address many of the shortcomings of the traditional BIOS, such as memory size limitations, hard disk size limitations, and rootkit malware infections. Installing Linux on UEFI-based systems can be problematic because the UEFI firmware probably doesn't have a digital certificate for your Linux distribution. On some hardware, you can get around this issue by disabling the SecureBoot option in the UEFI firmware.

On Linux, drivers can be loaded in two ways. First, they can be loaded as kernel modules after the operating system has started. Second, they can be compiled directly into the kernel itself. I related that, as a general rule of thumb, only drivers needed to boot the system should be compiled directly into the kernel. Drivers for other hardware should be loaded as kernel modules. This will keep your kernel lean and trim.

I then reviewed some of the tools you can use to view information about the hardware in your Linux system. Within the /proc directory, you can view hardware information in the following files and directories:

- cpuinfo
- devices
- dma
- interrupt
- iomem
- modules
- version
- /scsi/
- /bus/devices
- /ide/

In addition to /proc, the /sys/ directory also provides information about the hardware installed in the system. The top level of the /sys directory contains many subdirectories, including

- /sys/block
- /sys/bus
- /sys/class
- /sys/devices
- /sys/module

You can also use the following command-line tools to view information about the hardware in your system:

- hdparm /dev/*device*
- sg_scan
- sginfo –l
- hwinfo
- lsusb
- lspci

We then turned our attention to the shell commands you can use to manage kernel modules. These include the following:

- **lsmod**   Views loaded kernel modules
- **modinfo**   Views module information
- **depmod**   Builds a module dependency list
- **insmod**   Installs a kernel module but doesn't factor in module dependencies
- **modprobe**   Installs or removes a kernel module while taking module dependencies into account
- **rmmod**   Removes a kernel module

I pointed out that modprobe is run each time the system boots. It uses /etc/modprobe.conf to determine which kernel modules should be loaded at startup.

I ended this chapter by looking at hot-plug and cold-plug devices. Cold-plug devices can be physically connected to or disconnected from the PC system only when it is powered off. If you plug them in while the system is running, they probably won't be detected and recognized by the system. If you connect them properly while the system is off and then attempt to unplug them while the system is running, you will probably damage the component. Cold-plug devices are accessed through a device file in /dev.

Hot-plug devices, on the other hand, are designed to be connected and disconnected dynamically while the system is up and running. Software on the Linux system detects the changes to the system as these types of devices are attached and detached. The system will recognize the device when it is connected and load the appropriate modules. Several Linux components are needed to do this:

- sysfs
- dbus
- hald
- udev

Accelerated Review

- PC systems need persistent, long-term storage media to store information.
- Hard disks use coated aluminum platters to store data.
- Drive geometry consists of the following parameters:
  - Cylinders
  - Heads
  - Sectors Per Track
- SATA drives are currently the most commonly used type of hard disk drive.
- Each SATA drive in your system has its own dedicated hard disk channel that greatly enhances speed and throughput.
- SATA cabling uses a seven-pin connector.
- SATA devices can transfer data at rates from 150 MBps up to a maximum of 1969 MBps.
- The SATA drive connected to the SATA0 connector on the system motherboard will be used as the boot drive by default because it will be assigned an ID of 0.
- SCSI hard drives are used mostly in server systems.
- SCSI devices are connected in a chain.
- Each SCSI device in the chain is assigned a SCSI ID.
- The lower the SCSI ID, the lower the device's priority.
- The lower the ID number, the higher the device is in the boot order.
- Both ends of the SCSI chain must be terminated and nothing in between.
- Serial Attached SCSI (SAS) combines the best features of SCSI and SATA into a new standard.
- A solid-state drive is a storage device that functions much like a standard hard disk drive, using the same block-based I/O operations.
- SSDs use flash memory to store data.
- SSDs use the same SATA interface used by traditional hard disk drives.
- Optical drives use pits and lands to represent binary 0's and 1's.

- Writable optical discs use a special photo-reactive coating that can be used to encode binary data.
- Flash drives used flash memory to persistently store data.
- USB allows you to connect up to 127 external devices to the PC.
- USB devices are self-configuring and hot-swappable.
- USB hubs can be cascaded.
- IEEE 1394 allows you to connect up to 63 devices.
- IEEE 1394 devices are self-configuring and hot-swappable.
- IEEE 1394 devices are daisy-chained together.
- Interrupts are used to alert the CPU that a device needs attention.
- Every device in the PC must have an interrupt assigned.
- Two PCI devices can share interrupts.
- I/O addresses are like mailboxes for PC devices.
- I/O addresses are written in hex.
- All devices must have an I/O address assigned.
- Most devices will use a range of I/O addresses.
- Devices must use unique I/O ports.
- DMA channels allow a device to communicate directly with the system RAM without using the CPU.
- Devices must use unique DMA channels.
- PnP allows devices to be automatically configured with system resources when the PC is booted.
- Most motherboards include many integrated devices onboard.
- Integrated peripherals can be enabled or disabled quite easily using the system setup.
- Some newer computers use UEFI instead of a traditional BIOS.
- Installing Linux on a UEFI-based system can be problematic because the UEFI firmware probably doesn't have a digital certificate for your distribution.
- You may need to manage systems that don't have any external peripherals, including a keyboard.
- You have a couple of options for managing these types of systems:
  - SSH
  - VNC
- Drivers are small programs that are loaded into RAM that enable the CPU to communicate with a particular hardware component.
- For basic system components, driver software is stored in a chip on the motherboard.

- More complex components require that a driver that is stored on the hard disk be loaded into RAM.
- On Linux, drivers can be loaded in two ways:
  - Loaded as kernel modules after the operating system has started
  - Compiled directly into the kernel itself
- You can view information about your system hardware within the /proc directory.
- You can use the following command-line tools to view information about the hardware in your system:
  - hdparm –a /dev/device
  - sg_scan
  - scsiinfo –l
  - pnpdump
  - lsusb
- You can use the following command-line utilities to manage kernel modules:
  - **lsmod**   Views loaded kernel modules
  - **modinfo**   Views module information
  - **depmod**   Builds a module dependency list
  - **insmod**   Installs a kernel module but doesn't factor in module dependencies
  - **modprobe**   Installs or removes a kernel module while taking module dependencies into account
  - **rmmod**   Removes a kernel module
- modprobe uses the /etc/modprobe.conf file to determine which kernel modules should be loaded at boot.
- Cold-plug devices can be physically connected to or disconnected from the PC system only when it is powered off.
- Hot-plug devices, on the other hand, are designed to be connected and disconnected dynamically while the system is up and running.
- Software on the Linux system detects the changes to the system as these types of devices are attached and detached.
- The system recognizes the device when it is connected and loads the appropriate modules.
- Several Linux components are needed to manage hot-plug devices:
  - sysfs
  - dbus
  - hald
  - udev

Questions

1. Which of the following hard drive parameters refers to a set of concentric, parallel tracks on all sides of all platters in a hard disk drive?

    A. Cylinders

    B. Heads

    C. Sectors Per Track

    D. Write Precompensation

    E. Landing Zone

2. What is the maximum number of devices that can share the same SATA bus?

    A. 1

    B. 2

    C. 4

    D. Varies by manufacturer

3. Which SCSI ID has the highest priority?

    A. 0

    B. 1

    C. 3

    D. 5

    E. 7

4. Suppose you have a SCSI chain with four devices connected on an internal ribbon cable: an internal hard drive (hd0) at the end of the cable followed by a second hard drive (hd1), an internal DVD drive (dvd0), and then the SCSI controller (sc0). Which devices should have termination enabled? (Choose two.)

    A. hd0

    B. hd1

    C. dvd0

    D. sc0

5. Which of the following parameters are used to configure solid-state drives? (Choose two.)

    A. Master

    B. Slave

    C. Primary

    D. Secondary

    E. Cylinders

    F. Sectors Per Track

6. Which USB category includes devices such as printers, scanners, and hard drives?

    A. Hub

    B. Function

    C. Hub and Function

    D. Terminal Device

7. What is the maximum number of USB devices that can be connected to a single USB bus?

    A. 8

    B. 24

    C. 63

    D. 127

    E. 256

8. How fast can FireWire transfer data?

    A. 12 Mbps

    B. 64 Mbps

    C. 128 Mbps

    D. 3.2 Gbps

9. You currently have an external FireWire hard drive connected to the FireWire port in your computer. You need to disconnect the hard drive and connect a FireWire digital video camera to your FireWire port. Can you do this without rebooting the system?

    A. No, you must bring the system down to do this.

    B. No, you can't connect a FireWire digital video camera to a FireWire port used by an external hard drive.

    C. Yes, you can shut down the hard drive and connect the camera.

    D. Yes, but you must use a different port for each device.

10. What is the default assignment for IRQ 0 on an x86 system?

    A. System Timer

    B. Keyboard

    C. COM 1

    D. Floppy Drive

11. Which interrupts are hardwired on a PC system? (Choose two.)

    A. 0

    B. 1

    C. 2

    D. 3

E. 4

F. 5

12. Which I/O address is assigned, by default, to the system timer in a PC system?

    A. 0040h

    B. 0060h

    C. 0170h

    D. 01F0h

13. You've just installed a network board in your Linux system. The kernel did not automatically detect the new device. How can you load a driver for this network board? (Choose two.)

    A. Load the appropriate driver from the BIOS.

    B. Insert the appropriate kernel module.

    C. Recompile the kernel and configure it to support the board.

    D. Load a Windows driver for the board using emulation mode.

    E. Embed the driver within a ROM chip on the board itself.

14. In which directory can you find your kernel modules?

    A. /lib/modules/*version*/kernel/drivers

    B. /lib/modules/*version*/drivers

    C. /boot/

    D. /usr/modules/*version*/drivers/kernel

15. In which directory would you find information about how IRQ channels have been assigned in your system?

    A. /proc/devices

    B. /proc/dma

    C. /proc/interrupt

    D. /proc/iomem

16. You need to get specific information about the SATA hard drive in your system. Which command could you use from the shell prompt to do this?

    A. satadump

    B. lsusb

    C. sg_scan

    D. hdparm

17. Which commands can be used to insert a kernel module? (Choose two.)

   A. insmod

   B. modinfo

   C. modprobe

   D. rmmod

   E. depmod

18. Which command can be used to build a module dependency list?

   A. insmod

   B. modinfo

   C. modprobe

   D. rmmod

   E. depmod

19. In which directory would you find information about how I/O ports have been assigned in your system?

   A. /proc/devices

   B. /proc/dma

   C. /proc/interrupt

   D. /proc/iomem

Answers

1. **A.** Cylinders are composed of concentric, parallel tracks on all sides of all platters in a hard disk drive.

2. **A.** Each SATA devices has its own dedicated data channel to the SATA controller. The controller itself may provide multiple SATA data channels to support multiple devices, however.

3. **E.** The higher the SCSI ID, the higher the device priority.

4. **A, D.** Because the first hard drive and the SCSI controller are located at the ends of the SCSI chain, they must have termination enabled. No devices in between should have termination enabled.

5. **E, F.** Because SSDs are block devices that generally use a SATA interface, they are addressed using the same drive geometry settings (CHS) as mechanical hard disks.

6. **B.** USB functions include end devices, such as printers, scanners, and hard drives, that don't include USB hub functionality. Be aware that manufacturers of some of these devices do include hub functionality, making them a hub and function.

7. **D.** By cascading multiple USB hubs together, you can create a USB bus that can accommodate up to 127 devices. Be aware that the hubs used to create the bus, including the root hub, each count as one device.

8. **D.** A FireWire bus transfers data at speeds up to 3.2 Gbps.

9. **C.** FireWire devices are self-identifying, self-configuring, and hot-swappable.

10. **A.** The system timer is hardwired to interrupt 0 on a PC system.

11. **A, B.** Interrupts 0, 1, and 8 are hardwired on a PC system. They can't be assigned to any other devices.

12. **A.** Port 0040h is assigned to the system timer by default in a PC system.

13. **B, C.** You can insert the appropriate kernel module or you can recompile the kernel and include support for the board.

14. **A.** Your kernel modules are stored in /lib/modules/*version*/kernel/drivers.

15. **C.** Information about IRQ assignments are found in /proc/interrupt.

16. **D.** The hdparm utility can be used to get hard disk information.

17. **A, C.** You can use insmod or modprobe to insert a kernel module.

18. **E.** You can use depmod to build a module dependency list.

19. **D.** You can find information about how I/O ports have been assigned in your system in the /proc/iomem directory.

Managing Linux Processes

In this chapter, you will learn about:

- Understanding Linux processes
- Managing processes
- Scheduling processes

You've learned a great deal about Linux so far in this book. We started off easy, learning about the historical origins of Linux and the different roles it can play in your organization. As we've progressed through each chapter, you've been introduced to increasingly more challenging Linux concepts and skills. In the last chapter, we really ratcheted things up when we talked about managing kernel modules. In this chapter, we're going to look at how the Linux operating system handles executable programs and scripts when they are run. Then we'll spend some time learning how to manage executables while they are running on the system.

 EXAM TIP For your Linux+/LPIC-1 exam, you need to be very familiar with how Linux handles running processes. You need to understand the heredity of Linux processes as well as the difference between user processes and system processes (daemons). You should know how to use shell commands to view processes running on the system. You need to know how to run a process in the foreground and in the background. You should also know how to kill a process from the command line. You also need to know how to tell a process to continue running after the user that started it logs out. Finally, you need to know how to use at and cron to configure a service to run automatically in the future.

Let's begin this chapter by discussing how Linux handles processes.

Understanding Linux Processes

The key to being able to effectively manage Linux processes is to first understand how processes function within the operating system. So, what exactly is a process? For our purposes, a *process* is a program that has been loaded from a long-term storage device, usually a hard disk drive, into system RAM and is currently being processed by the CPU on the motherboard.

Type of Program	Description
Binary executables	These are programs that were originally created as a text file using a programming language such as C or C++. The text file was then run through a compiler to create a binary file that can be processed by the CPU.
Internal shell commands	Some of the commands you enter at the shell prompt are actual binary files in the file system that are loaded and run by the CPU. For example, when you enter **top** at the shell prompt, you load the top binary file into memory. Other commands, however, are not binary executables. Instead, they are commands that are rolled into the shell program itself. For example, if you enter **exit** at a shell prompt, you are actually running an internal shell command. There is no executable file in the file system named "exit." Instead, the computer code associated with the exit function is stored within the shell program code itself.
Shell scripts	These are text files that are executed through the shell itself. You can include commands to run binary executables within the text of any shell script. You will learn how to create shell scripts in a later chapter.

Table 13-1   Linux Programs That Can Create Processes

Many different types of programs can be executed to create a process. On your Linux system, the types of programs listed in Table 13-1 can be loaded into RAM and executed by the CPU.

Remember that the Linux operating system can run many processes "concurrently" on a single CPU. Depending on how your Linux system is being used, it may have only a few processes running at a given point in time or it may have hundreds of processes running concurrently.

In the preceding paragraph, I put the term *concurrently* in quotes because most CPUs can't truly run multiple processes at the same time. Instead, the Linux operating system quickly switches between the various processes running on the CPU, making it appear as if the CPU is working on multiple processes concurrently. However, the CPU actually only executes a single process at a time. All other processes currently "running" wait in the background for their turn. The operating system maintains a schedule that determines when each process is allowed access to the CPU. This is called *multitasking*. Because the switching between processes happens so fast, it appears, to you and me at least, that the CPU is executing multiple processes at the same time.

Be aware, however, that there are two exceptions to this rule. First of all, multicore CPUs can actually execute more than one process at a time because each core in the processor package is a separate CPU. For example, if there are two cores within the CPU, one core can execute one process while the other core works on another. The second exception to this rule is hyperthreading CPUs, which are designed such that a single processor can run more than one process at a time.

The Linux operating system uses several types of processes. Not all processes on your Linux system are the same. Some processes are created by the end user when he or she executes a command from the shell prompt or though the graphical interface. These processes are called *user processes*. User processes are usually associated with some kind of end-user program running on the system.

For example, if you run the LibreOffice suite (using the libreoffice command) from the shell prompt, two user processes for the LibreOffice program are created (oosplash and soffice.bin). These are shown here:

```
rtracy@openSUSE:~> ps -a
  PID TTY          TIME CMD
27913 pts/0    00:00:00 oosplash
27935 pts/0    00:00:04 soffice.bin
28041 pts/2    00:00:00 ps
```

The key point to remember about user processes is that they are called from within a shell and are associated with that shell session.

However, not all processes running on your system are user processes. In fact, most processes executing on a given Linux system will probably be of a different type called *system processes* or *daemons*. Unlike a user process, a system process (usually) does not provide an application or an interface for an end user to use. Instead, it is used to provide a system service, such as a web server, an FTP server, a file service such as Samba, a print service such as CUPS, or a logging service. Such processes run in the background and usually don't provide any kind of user interface.

For example, consider the processes shown in Figure 13-1.

 NOTE Most system processes (but not all of them) are noted with a *d* at the end of the name, which stands for *daemon*.

```
                         rtracy@openSUSE:~                              ✕

 File  Edit  View  Search  Terminal  Help
27290 ?          00:00:00 evolution-sourc
27309 ?          00:00:00 evolution-alarm
27310 ?          00:00:05 tracker-store
27312 ?          00:00:00 deja-dup-monito
27331 ?          00:00:00 tracker-miner-f
27340 ?          00:00:00 evolution-calen
27347 ?          00:00:02 vmtoolsd
27373 ?          00:00:02 libsocialweb-co
27376 ?          00:00:00 obexd
27413 ?          00:00:00 gvfsd-burn
27437 ?          00:00:00 gvfsd-metadata
27501 ?          00:00:02 kworker/u4:2
27649 ?          00:00:00 kworker/1:0
27756 ?          00:00:02 gnome-terminal-
27766 ?          00:00:00 gnome-pty-helpe
27767 pts/0      00:00:00 bash
27913 pts/0      00:00:00 oosplash
27935 pts/0      00:00:05 soffice.bin
27995 ?          00:00:00 sshd
27998 ?          00:00:00 sshd
27999 pts/2      00:00:00 bash
28042 ?          00:00:00 kworker/1:1
28071 pts/0      00:00:00 ps
rtracy@openSUSE:~>
```

Figure 13-1   System processes

Notice that the system has many system processes running. System processes are usually (but not always) loaded by the system itself when it is booted up. Therefore, they are not associated with a particular shell instance. This is another key difference between user processes and system processes. User processes are tied to the particular shell instance they were called from. System processes, on the other hand, are not.

By default, most Linux distributions boot with many daemons configured to automatically start at boot. Some of these daemons are critical to the overall functioning of the system; others are not.

One of the first things I do after implementing a new Linux system, whether as a server or as a workstation, is to turn off all the daemons that aren't needed. Running unnecessary daemons consumes memory and CPU time. More seriously, it can also open up gaping security holes in the system. You need to be very aware of what system services are running on any Linux system you're responsible for. If the service is needed, keep it. If not, get rid of it!

To understand which daemons are critical to the overall function of the system and which aren't, you need to understand the heredity of Linux processes. Let's discuss this next.

How Linux Processes Are Loaded

All Linux process are directly or indirectly loaded by one single process called *init* or *systemd* (depending upon the distribution) that is started by the Linux kernel when the system boots. Understand that any process running on a Linux system can launch additional processes. The process that launched the new process is called the *parent process*. The new process itself is called the *child process*.

This parent/child relationship constitutes the *heredity* of Linux processes. Because any process, including child processes, can launch additional processes, it is possible to have many generations of processes running on a system. This is shown in Figure 13-2.

In Figure 13-2, the first parent process spawned three child processes. Each of these three child processes spawned child processes of their own, making the first parent process a grandparent! Do you see now why we call it a "heredity" of processes?

Figure 13-2
Generations of processes

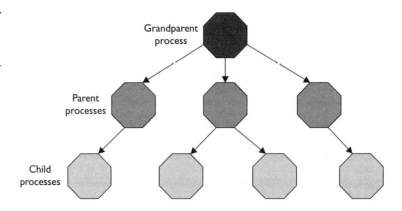

For any process on a Linux system, then, we need to be able to uniquely identify it as well as its heredity. Whenever a process is created on a Linux system, it is assigned two resources:

- **Process ID (PID) number** This is a number assigned to each process that uniquely identifies it on the system.

- **Parent Process ID (PPID) number** This is the PID of the process's parent process (that is, the process that spawned it).

By assigning these two numbers to each process, we can track the heredity of any process through the system. The Linux kernel uses the process table to keep track of the processes running on the system. The process table is maintained in memory by the operating system to facilitate switching between processes, scheduling processes, and prioritizing processes. Each entry in the table contains information about one specific running process, such as the process name, the state of the process, the priority of the process, and the memory addresses used by the process.

Notice in Figure 13-2 that I've depicted a "grandparent" process that spawned all of the other processes. This figure is drawn from a conceptual standpoint to illustrate the nature of the parent/child relationships between processes. However, it also can be used to describe the hierarchy of generations in a Linux system. There really is a "grandparent" process that spawns all other processes. This is the *init* or the *systemd* process (depending upon the distribution).

 NOTE Some distributions still use init, whereas others (such as Fedora and openSUSE) have migrated to systemd. There has actually been a bit of a holy war in the Linux community over the last several years as to which is best. At the time this was written, systemd is slowly starting to win out over init in terms of adoption. For your LPIC-1/Linux+ exam, you need to be familiar with both.

The kernel loads the systemd or init process automatically during bootup. The systemd or init process then launches child processes, such as a login shell, that in turn launch other processes, such as that used by the vi utility, as shown in Figure 13-3.

Figure 13-3
The systemd
process as the
grandparent of all
other processes

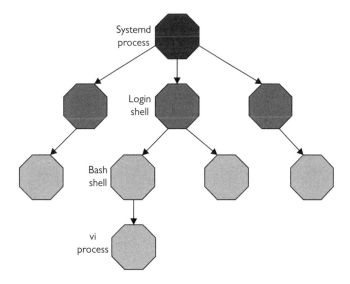

Figure 13-4
The PPID of the systemd process

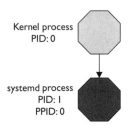

Whereas other processes are assigned a PID randomly from the operating system's table of available PID numbers, the systemd (or the init) process is always assigned a PID of 1. This brings up an interesting point. If the systemd or init process is the first process from which all other processes descend, what then is its PPID? Does it even have one? Actually, it does. Because the systemd or init process is launched directly by the Linux kernel (which always has a PID of 0), the PPID of the systemd process is always 0. This is shown in Figure 13-4.

The systemd (or init) process is responsible for launching all system processes that are configured to automatically start on boot. It also creates a login shell that is used for login.

This brings up an important point. Notice in Figure 13-3 that I've placed a second bash shell beneath the login shell. You might ask, "Couldn't you just run vi from within the login shell? Do you have to launch a second bash shell?"

Actually, in this figure, vi was, in fact, launched from the login shell. Why, then, does it show a second shell between the vi process and the login shell? It's because any time you run a command from within any shell (whether it's a login shell or a standard shell session), a second shell session is created, called a *subshell,* and the process for the command you entered is run within it. The subshell is a separate process in and of itself and has its own PID assigned. The PPID of the subshell is the PID of the shell where the command was entered.

The subshell process remains active for as long as the command that was entered at the shell prompt is in use. The process for the command runs within the subshell and is assigned its own PID. The PPID of the command's process is, of course, the PID of the subshell it's running within. When the command process is complete and has exited, the subshell is terminated and control is returned back to the original shell session. This process of creating a new subshell and running the command process within it is called *forking.*

For example, in Figure 13-5, the user has issued the vi command at the shell prompt of a bash shell. A new subshell is created and the vi process is run within it. When the user exits vi, the subshell is destroyed and control is returned to the original shell instance.

Figure 13-5
Running a process from the shell prompt

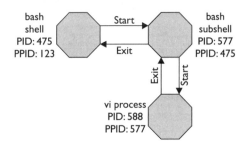

Now that you understand how Linux processes work, you're ready to start managing them. Let's do that next.

Managing Processes

Managing running processes is one of the key tasks you need to complete on the Linux systems you support. In this part of this chapter we're going to review how to do this. We're going to discuss the following topics:

- Starting system processes
- Viewing running processes
- Prioritizing processes
- Managing foreground and background processes
- Ending a running process
- Keeping a process running after logout

Let's begin by learning how to start processes.

Starting System Processes

There are two basic ways to start a process on a Linux system. For a user process, you simply enter the command or script name at the shell prompt. For example, to run the vi program, you simply enter **vi** at the shell prompt. When you do, the vi process is created, as shown here:

```
rtracy@openSUSE:~> ps -a
  PID TTY          TIME CMD
 3719 pts/1    00:00:00 vi
 3729 pts/0    00:00:00 ps
```

For system processes, however, you use either an *init script* or a service file, depending on whether your distribution uses init or systemd. If your distribution uses the init process, an init script is used by the init process to start processes on system boot. These scripts are stored in a specific directory on your Linux system. Which directory they are stored in depends on your Linux distribution. Most Linux distributions use one of two types of init scripts:

- **System V**   Linux distributions that use System V init scripts store them in the /etc/ rc.d directory. Within /etc/rc.d are a series of subdirectories named rc0.d through rc6.d. Each of these directories is associated with a particular runlevel. Within each of these subdirectories are symbolic links that point to the init scripts for your system daemons, which reside in /etc/rc.d/init.d.

- **BSD**   Other Linux distributions use BSD-style init scripts. These scripts reside in the /etc/init.d directory. Within /etc/init.d are a series of directories named rc0.d through rc6.d. As with System V init scripts, these directories are associated with specific runlevels. These directories contain links that point to the init scripts in /etc/init.d.

In addition to using the init process to run these scripts, you can run these scripts from the command prompt. Simply enter **/etc/init.d/***script_name* at the shell prompt (on a BSD-style system) or **/etc/rc.d/init.d/***script_name* (on a System V–style system). If you're not sure of which script name you should use, you can use the ls command to generate a listing of scripts in the script directory. This is shown in Figure 13-6.

The actual scripts in your init directory depend on which services you've installed on your particular system. Whenever you use the rpm utility to install a service on your system, a corresponding init script is automatically installed in your init script directory. Once there, you can execute any script by simply running it from the command prompt. The syntax (on a BSD-style system) is as follows:

```
/etc/init.d/script_name start | stop | restart
```

For example, to run the smb service, you would enter **/etc/init.d/smb start** at the shell prompt. To stop it, you would enter **/etc/init.d/smb stop**. To restart it, you would enter **/etc/init.d/smb restart**.

On some distributions, you can also use the rc script to start, stop, or restart a service process without having to specify the full path to the script file. The syntax is **rc***script_name* **start | stop | restart**. For example, to start the smb service, you could enter **rcsmb start** at the shell prompt. To stop it, you could enter **rcsmb stop**. You could also use the restart option to restart it.

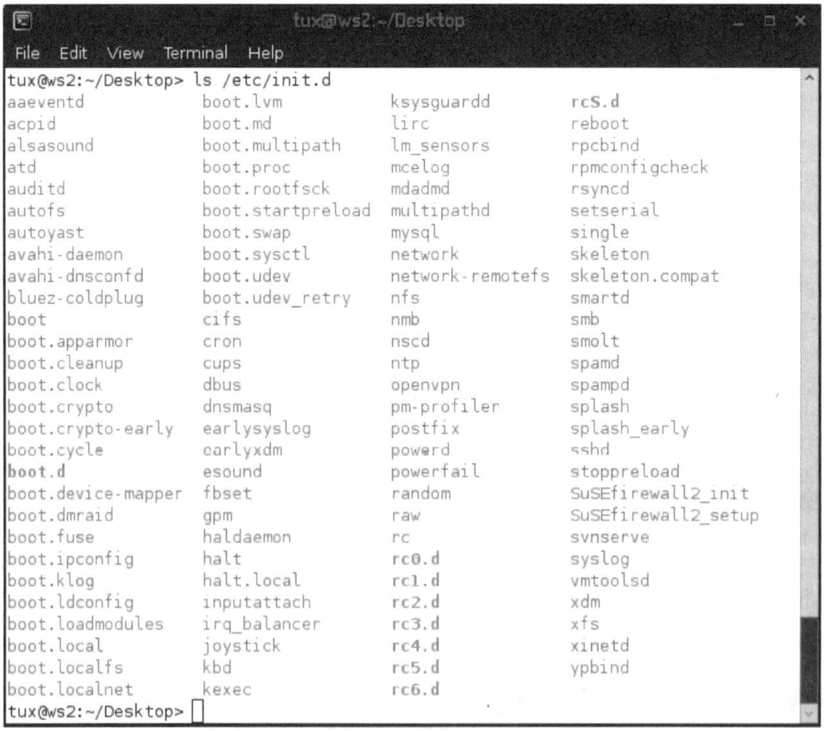

Figure 13-6   Init scripts in /etc/init.d

If your Linux distribution uses the systemd process instead of init, then your system services are managed using service files, which have a .service extension. You use the systemctl command at the shell prompt to start, stop, restart, or check the status of services on the system:

- To start a service, enter **systemctl start** *service_name*.
- To stop a service, enter **systemctl stop** *service_name*.
- To restart a service, enter **systemctl restart** *service_name*.
- To view the status of a service, enter **systemctl status** *service_name*.

For example, to enable the sshd daemon on a distribution that uses systemd, you would enter **systemctl start sshd** at the shell prompt.

Now that you know how to start and stop system processes, let's discuss how you go about viewing your running processes.

Viewing Running Processes

In this part of the chapter, we're going to discuss how to view running processes on your system. We'll cover the following tools:

- Using top
- Using ps
- Using free
- Using pgrep

Let's begin by looking at the top utility.

Using top

Linux provides a wide variety of tools for viewing running processes on your system. One of my favorites is the venerable top utility. You run top by simply entering **top** at the shell prompt. When you do, the interface shown in Figure 13-7 is displayed.

In Figure 13-7, you can see that top displays some of your running processes, one on each line. The following columns are used to display information about each process:

- **PID**   The process ID of the process.
- **USER**   The name of the user who owns the process.
- **PR**   The priority assigned to the process. (We'll discuss process priorities later in this chapter.)
- **NI**   This is the nice value of the process. (We'll talk about what this means later in this chapter.)
- **VIRT**   The amount of virtual memory used by the process.
- **RES**   The amount of physical RAM the process is using (its resident size) in kilobytes.
- **SHR**   The amount of shared memory used by the process.

```
                            root@openSUSE:~                                    ×

 File  Edit  View  Search  Terminal  Help
top - 17:52:43 up 11 min,  3 users,  load average: 0.74, 0.72, 0.43
Tasks: 144 total,   2 running, 142 sleeping,   0 stopped,   0 zombie
%Cpu(s):  4.7 us,  1.7 sy,  0.0 ni, 93.7 id,  0.0 wa,  0.0 hi,  0.0 si,  0.0 st
KiB Mem:   1544012 total,   613836 used,   930176 free,    27880 buffers
KiB Swap:  2103292 total,        0 used,  2103292 free,   248316 cached

  PID USER      PR  NI    VIRT    RES    SHR S  %CPU %MEM     TIME+ COMMAND
  634 root      20   0   68800  17724   7120 S 6.960 1.148   0:26.67 Xorg
 3476 rtracy    20   0  614076 147864  38720 S 4.308 9.577   0:28.47 gnome-she+
 3734 rtracy    20   0  246640  16812  12596 S 0.663 1.089   0:01.25 gnome-ter+
   31 root      20   0       0      0      0 S 0.331 0.000   0:03.49 kworker/1+
 3593 rtracy    20   0   34452  13248  11044 S 0.331 0.858   0:01.04 vmtoolsd
 3886 root      20   0    3636   1236    892 R 0.331 0.080   0:00.33 top
    1 root      20   0    5928   3236   2208 S 0.000 0.210   0:05.99 systemd
    2 root      20   0       0      0      0 S 0.000 0.000   0:00.01 kthreadd
    3 root      20   0       0      0      0 S 0.000 0.000   0:00.05 ksoftirqd+
    5 root       0 -20       0      0      0 S 0.000 0.000   0:00.00 kworker/0+
    6 root      20   0       0      0      0 S 0.000 0.000   0:00.85 kworker/u+
    7 root      rt   0       0      0      0 S 0.000 0.000   0:00.05 migration+
    8 root      -2   0       0      0      0 S 0.000 0.000   0:00.41 rcuc/0
    9 root      -2   0       0      0      0 S 0.000 0.000   0:00.00 rcub/0
   10 root      20   0       0      0      0 S 0.000 0.000   0:01.23 rcu_preem+
   11 root      20   0       0      0      0 S 0.000 0.000   0:00.00 rcu_bh
   12 root      20   0       0      0      0 S 0.000 0.000   0:00.00 rcu_sched
   13 root      rt   0       0      0      0 S 0.000 0.000   0:00.01 watchdog/0
   14 root      rt   0       0      0      0 S 0.000 0.000   0:00.02 watchdog/1
   15 root      -2   0       0      0      0 S 0.000 0.000   0:00.38 rcuc/1
```

Figure 13-7   Using top to view running processes

- **S**   The status of the process. Possible values include the following:
  - **D**   Uninterruptibly sleeping
  - **R**   Running
  - **S**   Sleeping
  - **T**   Traced or stopped
  - **Z**   Zombied

NOTE   A *zombied* process is one where the process has finished executing and exited, but the process's parent didn't get notified that it was finished and hasn't released the child process's PID. A zombied process may eventually clear up on its own. If it doesn't, you may need to manually kill the parent process. We'll talk about how to do this later in the chapter.

- **%CPU**   The percentage of CPU time used by the process.
- **%MEM**   The percentage of available physical RAM used by the process.
- **TIME+**   The total amount of CPU time the process has consumed since being started.
- **COMMAND**   The name of the command that was entered to start the process.

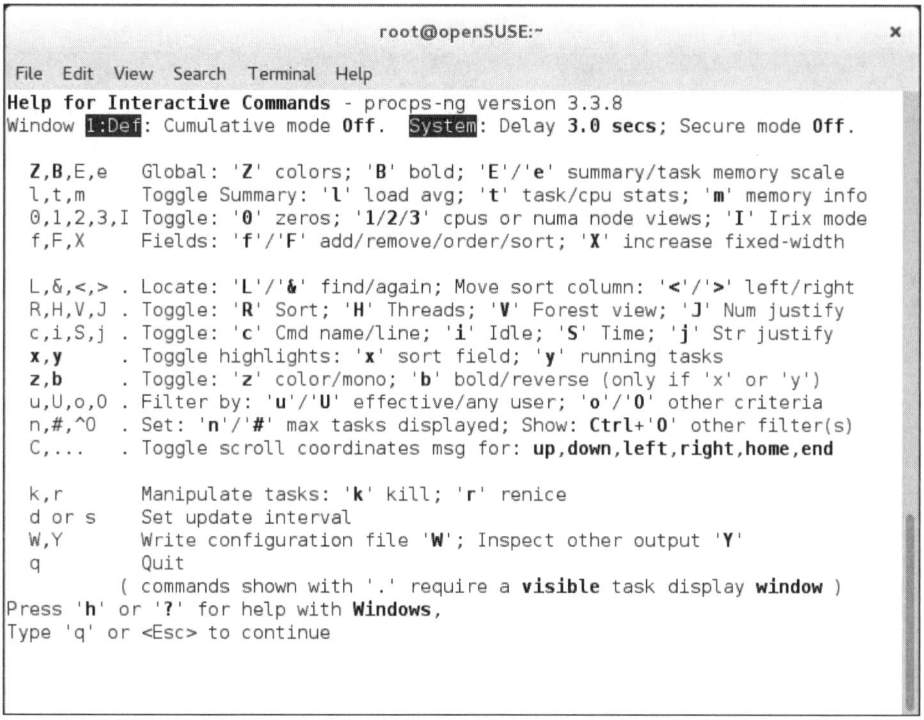

```
                          root@openSUSE:~                                    x

  File  Edit  View  Search  Terminal  Help
 Help for Interactive Commands - procps-ng version 3.3.8
 Window 1:Def: Cumulative mode Off.  System: Delay 3.0 secs; Secure mode Off.

  Z,B,E,e    Global: 'Z' colors; 'B' bold; 'E'/'e' summary/task memory scale
  l,t,m      Toggle Summary: 'l' load avg; 't' task/cpu stats; 'm' memory info
  0,1,2,3,I  Toggle: '0' zeros; '1/2/3' cpus or numa node views; 'I' Irix mode
  f,F,X      Fields: 'f'/'F' add/remove/order/sort; 'X' increase fixed-width

  L,&,<,> . Locate: 'L'/'&' find/again; Move sort column: '<'/'>' left/right
  R,H,V,J . Toggle: 'R' Sort; 'H' Threads; 'V' Forest view; 'J' Num justify
  c,i,S,j . Toggle: 'c' Cmd name/line; 'i' Idle; 'S' Time; 'j' Str justify
  x,y     . Toggle highlights: 'x' sort field; 'y' running tasks
  z,b     . Toggle: 'z' color/mono; 'b' bold/reverse (only if 'x' or 'y')
  u,U,o,O . Filter by: 'u'/'U' effective/any user; 'o'/'O' other criteria
  n,#,^O  . Set: 'n'/'#' max tasks displayed; Show: Ctrl+'O' other filter(s)
  C,...   . Toggle scroll coordinates msg for: up,down,left,right,home,end

  k,r        Manipulate tasks: 'k' kill; 'r' renice
  d or s     Set update interval
  W,Y        Write configuration file 'W'; Inspect other output 'Y'
  q          Quit
             ( commands shown with '.' require a visible task display window )
 Press 'h' or '?' for help with Windows,
 Type 'q' or <Esc> to continue
```

Figure 13-8   Viewing the top help screen

The key thing I like about top is the fact that it's dynamic. The screen is constantly updated to reflect the latest information about each process. You can sort the information as well. By pressing H while top is running, you can display the help screen, which provides you with the keystrokes required to sort by a particular category. This help screen is shown in Figure 13-8.

This screen also shows you how to use other options with top. For example, you can press F to display a list of columns that you can add to the display, as shown in Figure 13-9.

Fields that will be displayed are indicated with an asterisk (*). To add or remove a field, just arrow to it and press SPACEBAR. This will toggle the asterisk on or off to determine whether or not the field is displayed. You can also press U to specify that only the processes associated with a specific user be displayed.

I really like top. The only thing I don't like about it is that it shows only a limited number of processes. There will be times when you need to see everything running on your system. In this situation, top just doesn't cut it. You need to use the ps utility.

Using ps

The ps utility can be used to display running processes on your system. Unlike top, which displays processes dynamically, ps displays a snapshot of the current processes running.

```
root@openSUSE:~                                      ✕

File  Edit  View  Search  Terminal  Help
Fields Management for window 1:Def, whose current sort field is %CPU
    Navigate with Up/Dn, Right selects for move then <Enter> or Left commits,
    'd' or <Space> toggles display, 's' sets sort.  Use 'q' or <Esc> to end!

* PID    = Process Id              SID    = Session Id
* USER   = Effective User Name     nTH    = Number of Threads
* PR     = Priority                P      = Last Used Cpu (SMP)
* NI     = Nice Value              TIME   = CPU Time
* VIRT   = Virtual Image (KiB)     SWAP   = Swapped Size (KiB)
* RES    = Resident Size (KiB)     CODE   = Code Size (KiB)
* SHR    = Shared Memory (KiB)     DATA   = Data+Stack (KiB)
* S      = Process Status          nMaj   = Major Page Faults
* %CPU   = CPU Usage               nMin   = Minor Page Faults
* %MEM   = Memory Usage (RES)      nDRT   = Dirty Pages Count
* TIME+  = CPU Time, hundredths    WCHAN  = Sleeping in Function
* COMMAND= Command Name/Line       Flags  = Task Flags <sched.h>
  PPID   = Parent Process pid      CGROUPS= Control Groups
  UID    = Effective User Id       SUPGIDS= Supp Groups IDs
  RUID   = Real User Id            SUPGRPS= Supp Groups Names
  RUSER  = Real User Name          TGID   = Thread Group Id
  SUID   = Saved User Id           Adj    = oom_adjustment (2^X)
  SUSER  = Saved User Name         Badness= oom_score (badness)
  GID    = Group Id                ENVIRON= Environment vars
  GROUP  = Group Name              vMj    = Major Faults delta
  PGRP   = Process Group Id        vMn    = Minor Faults delta
  TTY    = Controlling Tty         USED   = Res+Swap Size (KiB)
  TPGID  = Tty Process Grp Id
```

Figure 13-9 Adding columns to the top display

By simply entering **ps**, you can view the processes associated with the *current* shell, as shown here:

```
openSUSE:~ # ps
  PID TTY          TIME CMD
 3946 pts/1    00:00:00 su
 3947 pts/1    00:00:00 bash
 3994 pts/1    00:00:00 ps
```

In this example, the following processes are displayed by ps:

- **su** The su utility is in use inside this shell to switch to the root user account.

- **bash** The current bash shell session.

- **ps** Because ps is in use to list current processes, its process is also listed.

Notice that the following information is displayed by default:

- **PID** The process ID of the process.

- **TTY** The name of the terminal session (shell) that the process is running within.

- **TIME** The amount of CPU time used by the process.

- **CMD** The name of the command that was entered to create the process.

Notice that only three processes were listed. On the system where ps was run in the preceding example, many different processes were running. I had top running in a separate shell. In addition, the X server and the GNOME desktop environment were running. Why didn't they show up in the list? By default, ps only shows processes associated with the current shell. Hence, only the shell, su, and ps processes are displayed.

To see all processes running on the system, you need to use the –e option with ps. Here is an example:

```
openSUSE:~ # ps -e
  PID TTY          TIME CMD
    1 ?        00:00:06 systemd
    2 ?        00:00:00 kthreadd
    3 ?        00:00:00 ksoftirqd/0
    5 ?        00:00:00 kworker/0:0H
    7 ?        00:00:00 migration/0
    8 ?        00:00:00 rcuc/0
    9 ?        00:00:00 rcub/0
   10 ?        00:00:01 rcu_preempt
   11 ?        00:00:00 rcu_bh
   12 ?        00:00:00 rcu_sched
   13 ?        00:00:00 watchdog/0
   14 ?        00:00:00 watchdog/1...
```

As you can see in this example, the –e option results in many more processes being displayed by the ps command. Also notice that most of the processes shown have a ? in the TTY column. This indicates the process is a system process. Remember that system processes (daemons) are loaded by the init or systemd process at startup and, therefore, are not associated with any shell. Because of this, a ? is displayed in the TTY column in the output of ps.

Another thing you may notice in the two preceding examples is that the amount of detail displayed by ps is rather limited as compared to top. You can use the –f option with ps to display more detail. In the next example, the –e and –f options have been used together in the ps command to display extended information about every process running on the system:

```
openSUSE:~ # ps -ef
UID        PID  PPID  C STIME TTY          TIME CMD
root         1     0  0 17:41 ?        00:00:06 /sbin/init showopts
root         2     0  0 17:41 ?        00:00:00 [kthreadd]
root         3     2  0 17:41 ?        00:00:00 [ksoftirqd/0]
root         5     2  0 17:41 ?        00:00:00 [kworker/0:0H]
root         7     2  0 17:41 ?        00:00:00 [migration/0]
root         8     2  0 17:41 ?        00:00:00 [rcuc/0]
root         9     2  0 17:41 ?        00:00:00 [rcub/0]
root        10     2  0 17:41 ?        00:00:01 [rcu_preempt]
root        11     2  0 17:41 ?        00:00:00 [rcu_bh]
root        12     2  0 17:41 ?        00:00:00 [rcu_sched]
root        13     2  0 17:41 ?        00:00:00 [watchdog/0]
root        14     2  0 17:41 ?        00:00:00 [watchdog/1]...
```

With the –f option, you can now view additional information, including the following:

- **UID**   The user ID of the process's owner.
- **PPID**   The PID of the process's parent process.

- **C**   The amount of processor time utilized by the process.

- **STIME**   The time that the process started.

If you really want to crank things up, you can also use the –l option with the ps command. The –l option displays the long format of the ps output. Here is an example:

```
openSUSE:~ # ps -efl
F S UID         PID  PPID  C PRI  NI ADDR SZ WCHAN  STIME TTY          TIME CMD
1 S root          2     0  0  80   0 -     0 kthrea 11:09 ?        00:00:00 [kth]
1 S root          3     2  0 -40   - -     0 migrat 11:09 ?        00:00:00 [mig]
1 S root          4     2  0  80   0 -     0 run_ks 11:09 ?        00:00:00 [kso]
5 S root          5     2  0 -40   - -     0 watchd 11:09 ?        00:00:00 [wat]
1 S root          6     2  0 -40   - -     0 migrat 11:09 ?        00:00:00 [mig]
1 S root          7     2  0  80   0 -     0 run_ks 11:09 ?        00:00:00 [kso]
5 S root          8     2  0 -40   - -     0 watchd 11:09 ?        00:00:00 [wat]
1 S root          9     2  0  80   0 -     0 worker 11:09 ?        00:00:00 [eve]
1 S root         10     2  0  80   0 -     0 worker 11:09 ?        00:00:00 [eve]
1 S root         11     2  0  80   0 -     0 worker 11:09 ?        00:00:00 [net]
...
```

With the –l option, you can view the following information about processes running on your system:

- **F**   The flags associated with the process. This column uses the following codes:
  - **1**   Forked, but didn't execute
  - **4**   Used root privileges
- **S**   The state of the process. This column uses the following codes:
  - **D**   Uninterruptible sleep
  - **R**   Running
  - **S**   Interruptible sleep
  - **T**   Stopped or traced
  - **Z**   Zombied
- **PRI**   The priority of the process.
- **NI**   The nice value of the process. (We'll talk about what this means in the next section.)
- **ADDR**   The memory address of the process.
- **SZ**   The size of the process.
- **WCHAN**   The name of the kernel function in which the process is sleeping. You will see a dash (–) in this column if the process is currently running.

Using free

Part of managing processes on your Linux system is knowing how much memory has been used and how much is available. As we discussed earlier, you can use the output of top to view this information.

You can also use the free command to do this. The free command displays the amount of free and allocated RAM and swap memory in your system. You can use the –m option to display memory statistics in megabytes. You can also use the –t option to display totals for each category of information. In the example shown next, the **free –mt** command has been issued to view memory statistics:

```
openSUSE:~ # free -mt
              total       used       free     shared    buffers     cached
Mem:           1507        620        887          4         29        243
-/+ buffers/cache:         347       1160
Swap:          2053          0       2053
Total:         3561        620       2941
```

Using pgrep

The ps command is very useful for viewing process information. However, sometimes the output of ps can be overwhelming, especially if you're just looking for one or two specific processes. One option for managing the volume of output from ps is to pipe the output to the grep command and display only the results that match the criteria you specify.

Another option for doing this is to use the pgrep command. As its name implies, pgrep combines the functionality of the ps and grep commands into a single utility. When you run pgrep, you specify certain selection criteria that you want to look for. Then the command searches through all of the currently running processes and outputs a list of processes that match the criteria you specify. You can use the following options with pgrep to create your selection criteria:

- **-P** *ppid* matches on the specified parent process ID.
- **-f** *name* matches on the specified process name.
- **-u** *user_name* matches on the specified process owner.

Be aware that the output from pgrep lists only the PID of the matching processes by default. If you want to view the name of the process as well as its PID, use the –l option with pgrep command. For example, if you wanted to view a list of all processes owned by the root user, you would use the following command:

```
openSUSE:~ # pgrep -l -u rtracy
3262 systemd
3264 (sd-pam)
3266 gnome-keyring-d
3269 gnome-session
3319 dbus-launch
3320 dbus-daemon
3322 ibus-daemon
3347 gvfsd
...
```

Now that you know how to view running processes, we need to discuss how to prioritize processes running on your system. Let's do that next.

Prioritizing Processes

Recall from the first part of this chapter that Linux is a multitasking operating system. It rotates CPU time between each of the processes running on the system, creating the illusion that all of the processes are running concurrently.

Because Linux is a multitasking operating system, you can specify a priority level for each process. Doing so determines how much CPU time a given process gets in relation to other processes on the system.

By default, Linux tries to equalize the amount of CPU time given to all of the processes on the system. However, there may be times when you need to adjust the priority assigned to a process. Depending on how the system is deployed, you may want a particular process to have a higher priority than other processes. This can be done using several Linux utilities. In this part of the chapter, we'll review the following:

- Setting priorities with nice
- Setting priorities of running processes with renice

Let's begin by learning how to use the nice utility.

Setting Priorities with nice

The nice utility can be used on Linux to launch a program with a different priority level. Recall from our previous discussion of top and ps that each process running on your system has a PR and NI value associated with it. This is shown in Figure 13-10.

```
                              root@openSUSE:~                                    ✕

 File  Edit  View  Search  Terminal  Help
top - 19:45:24 up  2:03,  4 users,  load average: 0.12, 0.04, 0.05
Tasks: 149 total,   2 running, 147 sleeping,   0 stopped,   0 zombie
%Cpu(s):  3.5 us,  1.3 sy,  0.0 ni, 95.2 id,  0.0 wa,  0.0 hi,  0.0 si,  0.0 st
KiB Mem:   1544012 total,   788312 used,   755700 free,    37736 buffers
KiB Swap:  2103292 total,        0 used,  2103292 free,   387936 cached

  PID USER     PR  NI    VIRT    RES    SHR S  %CPU %MEM     TIME+ COMMAND
  634 root     20   0   68800  17724   7120 S  4.631 1.148  0:49.28 Xorg
 3476 rtracy   20   0  620012 154720  38864 S  3.639 10.02  1:32.26 gnome-she+
 3593 rtracy   20   0   34452  13248  11044 S  0.662 0.858  0:16.79 vmtoolsd
 4341 root     20   0    3636   1244    892 R  0.662 0.081  0:00.12 top
 3734 rtracy   20   0  246824  17044  12620 S  0.331 1.104  0:02.06 gnome-ter+
    1 root     20   0    5928   3236   2208 S  0.000 0.210  0:06.18 systemd
    2 root     20   0       0      0      0 S  0.000 0.000  0:00.01 kthreadd
    3 root     20   0       0      0      0 S  0.000 0.000  0:00.06 ksoftirqd+
    5 root      0 -20       0      0      0 S  0.000 0.000  0:00.00 kworker/0+
    7 root     rt   0       0      0      0 S  0.000 0.000  0:00.06 migration+
    8 root     -2   0       0      0      0 S  0.000 0.000  0:00.48 rcuc/0
    9 root     -2   0       0      0      0 S  0.000 0.000  0:00.00 rcub/0
   10 root     20   0       0      0      0 R  0.000 0.000  0:01.42 rcu_preem+
   11 root     20   0       0      0      0 S  0.000 0.000  0:00.00 rcu_bh
   12 root     20   0       0      0      0 S  0.000 0.000  0:00.00 rcu_sched
   13 root     rt   0       0      0      0 S  0.000 0.000  0:00.07 watchdog/0
   14 root     rt   0       0      0      0 S  0.000 0.000  0:00.09 watchdog/1
   15 root     -2   0       0      0      0 S  0.000 0.000  0:00.43 rcuc/1
   16 root     rt   0       0      0      0 S  0.000 0.000  0:00.09 migration+
   17 root     20   0       0      0      0 S  0.000 0.000  0:00.04 ksoftirqd+
```

Figure 13-10 Viewing PR and NI values

The PR value is the process's kernel priority. The higher the number, the lower the priority of the process. The lower the number, the higher the priority of the process. The NI value is the nice value of the process. The nice value is factored into the kernel calculations that determine the priority of the process. The nice value for any Linux process can range between –20 and +19. The lower the nice value, the *higher* the priority of the process.

You can't directly manipulate the priority of a process, but you can manipulate the process's nice value. The easiest way to do this is to set the nice value when you initially run the command that launches the process. This is done using the nice command. The syntax for using nice is **nice –n *nice_level command***.

For example, suppose I wanted to launch the vi program and increase its priority on the system by decreasing its nice level to a value of –5. Before I do so, vi runs on my system with a priority of 80, as shown in this example:

```
openSUSE:~ # ps -el | grep vi
0 S  1000  8435  8425  2  80   0 - 6823 -       pts/0   00:00:00 vi
```

Notice that the vi process has a default nice level of 0. The kernel uses this value to calculate the overall priority of the process, which comes out to a value of 80. I could adjust this process's priority level to a higher level by entering **nice –n –15 vi** at the shell prompt. After doing so, the priority and nice values of the vi process are decreased, thus increasing its priority level on the system. This is shown in the next example:

```
openSUSE:~ # ps -el | grep vi
4 S    0  8488  8455  0  65 -15 - 6533 -       pts/0   00:00:00 vi
```

Notice that the nice value was decreased to a value of –15. This caused the overall priority of the process to be reduced to a value of 65.

Be aware that Linux is hesitant to allow you to reduce the value of nice for processes running on the system. Because Linux is a true multiuser operating system, it's possible for multiple users on the same system to adjust the nice values of their own processes. Naturally, every user on the system thinks that his or her process is much more important than anyone else's and may be tempted to crank that nice value clear down to –20 for just about everything he or she runs.

To keep this from happening, Linux won't let you adjust the nice value of a process below 0 unless you are logged in as root. Basically, if you aren't root, you won't be allowed to use a negative number with the nice command.

The nice command works great for modifying the nice value when you're running a command to start a process. But what can you do if the process you want to modify is already running? You can't use nice in this situation. You have to use the renice command instead. Let's discuss how renice works next.

Setting Priorities of Running Processes with renice

Instead of having to kill a process and restart it with nice to set its nice value, you can use the renice command to adjust the nice value of a process that is currently running on the system. The syntax for using this command is **renice *nice_value PID***.

For example, in the last example, the PID of the vi process is 8488. If I wanted to adjust the priority of the vi process to a lower level without unloading the program, I could enter **renice 4 8488** at the shell prompt, as shown in this example:

```
openSUSE:~ # renice 4 8488
8488: old priority -15, new priority 4
openSUSE:~ # ps -elf | grep vi
4 S root      8488 8455  0 84   4 -  6533 -       08:40 pts/0   00:00:00 vi
```

As you can see in this example, the nice value of the vi process was increased from –15 to 4. This caused the overall priority of the process to go from 65 to 84, thus decreasing the process's overall priority level. Just as with nice, you must be logged in as root to adjust the nice level of a running process to a negative number.

Let's now shift gears and talk about foreground and background processes.

Managing Foreground and Background Processes

In this part of the chapter, we need to discuss running processes in the foreground and background. We'll address the following topics:

- Running processes in the background
- Switching processes between the background and the foreground

Running Processes in the Background

Recall from our earlier discussion of processes that, when you enter any command at the shell prompt, a subshell is created and the process is run within it. As soon as the process exits, the subshell is destroyed. During the time that the process is running, the shell prompt of the parent shell disappears. You can't do anything at the shell prompt unless you open a new terminal session.

This happens because the process runs in the *foreground*. This behavior is even more apparent when running a graphical application from the shell prompt. In Figure 13-11, the LibreOffice application has been launched from the shell prompt using the libreoffice command.

Notice in Figure 13-11 that the cursor in the shell is unavailable. It will remain so until Libre-Office is closed. Only then can additional commands be entered at this shell prompt.

This is the default behavior for all commands entered at the shell prompt, whether the program is a text-based shell program or a graphical program. However, it is possible to run the program in the *background*. If you do this, the program you launch will run normally. However, control will be returned immediately to the shell. You can then use the shell to launch other programs or perform other shell tasks.

Running a program in the background is very easy. All you have to do is append an ampersand (&) character to the command. This tells the shell to run the program in the background. In Figure 13-12, the LibreOffice application has been launched again. However, this time an ampersand was appended to the end of the command, causing it to run in the background.

Notice in Figure 13-12 that two values were displayed on the screen after the process was run in the background. The first value, [1], is the background job ID that was assigned to the

Figure 13-11 Launching a graphical application in the foreground

Figure 13-12 Running an application in the background

background job. The second value is the PID of the process. You can view all background jobs running on the system by entering **jobs** at the shell prompt, like this:

```
rtracy@openSUSE:~> jobs
[1]+   Done                              libreoffice &
```

In this example, the output of the jobs command displays the status of the job as well as the name of the command that was run to create the background job. Let's next discuss how to move jobs from the background to foreground, and vice versa.

Switching Processes Between the Background and the Foreground

Just because a process was started in the background or the foreground doesn't mean it has to stay there. You can switch a process between the foreground and the background while it's running. This is done using the following commands:

- **fg**   This command will move a background process to the foreground. The syntax is **fg** *job_ID*.

- **bg**   This command will move a foreground process to the background. To use this utility, you must first assign the foreground job a background job ID. This is done by pressing CTRL-Z. When you do, you'll see the process stop and a background job ID assigned to the process. You can then enter **bg** *job_ID* to move the process to the background.

In the next example, the vi program was loaded as per normal into the foreground. It was then stopped using CTRL-Z, where it was assigned a job ID of 1. It was then sent to the background using the bg 1 command.

```
rtracy@openSUSE:~> vi

[1]+  Stopped                   vi
rtracy@openSUSE:~> bg 1
[1]+ vi &
```

Let's next discuss how to kill a running process.

Ending a Running Process

To this point in this chapter, we've done just about everything you can think of to processes on a Linux system. We've loaded them, viewed them, prioritized them, and moved them to the background and to the foreground. The one task we've yet to cover is how to end a process that is running on the system.

Normally, you use the exit function that is coded into nearly all programs to end a running process. For example, you enter **:exit** in vi to exit the editor and end its process. Sometimes, however, processes hang and no matter what you do, you can't get them to close properly. In this situation, you may need to manually kill the hung process. This can be done in two ways:

- Using kill and killall
- Using pkill

Let's look at using the kill command first.

Using kill and killall

The kill command is used to terminate a process. The syntax for using kill is **kill** *–signal PID*. The *PID* parameter is the PID of the process you want to kill. You can also send a specific kill signal to the process. This is one of the things about kill that I love. You actually have about 64 different types of kill signals that you can send to the process. Here are the most useful of these:

- **SIGHUP**   This is kill signal 1. This signal restarts the process. After a restart, the process will have exactly the same PID that it had before. This is a very useful option for restarting a service for which you've made changes in a configuration file.

- **SIGINT**   This is kill signal 2. This signal sends a CTRL-C key sequence to the process.

- **SIGKILL**   This is kill signal 9. This is a brute-force signal that kills the process. If the process was hung badly, this option will force it to stop. However, the process may not clean up after itself if this signal is used. The resources allocated to the process may remain allocated until the system is restarted.

- **SIGTERM**   This is kill signal 15. This signal tells the process to terminate immediately. This is the default signal sent by kill if you omit a signal in the command line. This signal allows the process to clean up after itself before exiting.

When using kill, you can use the text of the signal, such as SIGTERM, or you can use the signal's number, such as 15. You will need to use ps or top to first identify the PID of the process before you can use kill to stop it. Here, for example, the vi process is running with a PID of 8312:

```
openSUSE:~ # ps
  PID TTY          TIME CMD
 8278 pts/0    00:00:00 su
 8279 pts/0    00:00:00 bash
 8312 pts/0    00:00:00 vi
 8313 pts/0    00:00:00 ps
openSUSE:~ # kill -SIGTERM 8312
openSUSE:~ #
```

In this example, I've entered **kill –SIGTERM 8312** to kill the vi process. I could have also entered **kill –15 8312** and accomplished exactly the same task. Because the SIGTERM signal allows the process to return its resources before exiting, the vi process ends cleanly.

This brings up a mistake I've seen many new Linux admins make when working with kill. They frequently "go for the jugular" before trying less forceful signals first. Yes, using SIGKILL will work, but it's best if you try other, cleaner signals first. Only if these signals fail should you try a harsher signal. If you experience a hung process that needs to be killed, I suggest you use the following sequence:

1. Send a SIGINT first. If it doesn't respond, then go on to step 2.

2. Send a SIGTERM. Usually, this will fix the problem and allow the process to exit cleanly. If it doesn't, then go on to step 3.

3. Send a SIGKILL.

In addition to kill, you can also use killall to kill processes. The killall command is very similar to the kill command. The syntax is almost the same. The key difference is that killall uses the command name of the process to be killed instead of its PID. For example, if I wanted to kill the vi process in the preceding example with killall instead of kill, I would have entered **killall –15 vi**. This command sends the SIGTERM signal to the process named vi.

I strongly suggest that you spend some time reviewing the man page for killall. It's quite extensive and contains excellent information. For example, it will show you how to use the –u option with killall to end processes owned by a specific user.

Using pkill

In addition to kill and killall, you can also use the pkill command to stop a running process. The pkill command is a cousin of the pgrep command we looked at earlier. In fact, they use exactly the same options and even share the same man page.

Using pkill, you can search for processes that match the search criteria you specify and then send them a certain kill signal. For example, suppose I want to search through all of the running processes for those named "vi" and then send them the SIGTERM signal. To do this, I would enter **pkill -SIGTERM -f vi** at the shell prompt.

Keeping a Process Running After Logout

The last topic we will address in this objective is how to keep a process you've started running after you log out from the system. As we've discussed previously, signals can be sent to running processes to indicate that a system event has occurred and that the process needs to respond.

A very commonly used signal is the hang-up signal (SIGHUP). Linux keeps track of which processes are being run by which terminal session, as we've previously discussed in this chapter. When a user logs out of the terminal session, Linux sends a SIGHUP signal to all the programs associated with that terminal session.

Normally, each process will respond as it is supposed to when it receives a SIGHUP. However, a process can also be told to ignore SIGHUP signals, which will allow it to remain running even if you log out of your shell session. This is done by using the nohup utility to run the program. This causes the process created by the command to ignore all SIGHUP signals.

For example, suppose you've created a shell script called updatemydb that automatically updates a database with information from an external data source. This script takes a long time to run (usually overnight), and you don't want to leave your system logged in while it runs. You could enter **nohup updatemydb &** at the shell prompt and then log out. If the command generates output that is usually sent to the stdout, nohup will redirect the output to the ~/nohup.out file.

It's important to note that a command run under nohup is only immune to SIGHUP signals. All other kill signals still work. For example, you could terminate the program while it's running using the SIGTERM signal with kill.

A similar command you can use is the screen command. The screen command is an interesting utility that is particularly useful if you are accessing a Linux system remotely through an SSH connection. The key benefit of screen is that it allows you to use multiple shell windows from within a single SSH session. For example, suppose you were to run top remotely in an SSH session. Because of the way the SSH client works, you can't enter any other commands until top is stopped and you return to the shell prompt, unless you open up multiple SSH sessions.

Using screen, however, you can keep top running while you access the shell prompt through the SSH connection and enter additional commands. This is especially beneficial because it can keep an SSH shell active even if the network goes down. You can even use screen to disconnect and reconnect to a shell session from multiple locations without having to stop and then restart whatever process you were working on.

Before you can use screen, you first need to make sure it has been installed on your system. Most distributions include it by default, but some don't.

Once screen has been installed, you run it by simply entering **screen** at the shell prompt. When you do, a splash screen with license and usage information is displayed that you must navigate through. After doing so, you'll see the shell prompt displayed. It doesn't appear any differently. However, it is different because you are now inside of a window within screen. This window functions just like a normal shell session. You can run commands and interact with programs just as you would from any other shell prompt.

However, if you press CTRL-A, then whatever you type after it is sent to the screen command instead of to the shell. Here are some examples:

- Pressing CTRL-A and then ? causes the screen help to be displayed.

- Pressing CTRL-A and then C causes a new screen window to be created. The old window you were working in remains active along with any processes that were running within it. For example, suppose you had top running in a screen window within an SSH session. You need to check your email, but you don't want to stop running top. To do this, you can open a new window and access your mail. As you do, top stays running in the first window.

- Pressing CTRL-A and then N toggles between open windows in screen.

- Pressing CTRL-A and then D detaches your screen window and drops you back at your original shell prompt. However, whatever you had running in the window remains running. In fact, you can log completely out of the server and everything will keep working within the detached window.

- Entering **screen –r** reattaches you to a detached screen window. If you have multiple detached screen windows, you'll be prompted to specify which one you want to reattach to.

Let's practice working with Linux processes in the following exercise.

Exercise 13-1: Working with Linux Processes

In this exercise, you will practice using shell commands to manage processes running on your system. You can perform this exercise using the virtual machine that comes with this book. Run snapshot 13-1 for the correctly configured environment.

VIDEO   Please watch the Exercise 13-1 video for a demonstration on how to perform this task.

Complete the following:

1. Boot your Linux system and log in as a standard user.

2. Open a terminal session.

3. Switch to your root user account by entering **su –** followed by a password of **student**.

4. Practice starting system processes by doing the following:

   a. At the shell prompt, enter **systemctl status atd**. What's the status of your at daemon? (For most distributions, the atd daemon is not configured to run by default.)

   b. Start the atd daemon by entering **systemclt start atd** at the shell prompt.

   c. Enter **systemctl status atd** again at the shell prompt. The atd service should now be shown as running.

5. Practice using top by doing the following:

   a. At the shell prompt, enter **top**.

   b. View your running processes.

   c. Press H to access the top help screen. Which keystroke will sort the display by CPU stats?

   d. Press T to sort the display by CPU stats. Which processes are using the most CPU time on your system?

   e. Press M to sort the display by memory usage. Which processes are using the most memory?

   f. Add columns by pressing F.

   g. Add the PPID column to the display by pressing B and then SPACEBAR. You should now see the PPID of each process added to the display.

   h. Exit top by pressing Q.

6. Practice using the ps utility to view processes by doing the following:

   a. At the shell prompt, enter **ps**. What processes are associated with the current shell session?

   b. View all running processes on the system by entering **ps –ef | more** at the shell prompt.

   c. Press SPACEBAR until you find the atd service. What username does atd run under? (On most distributions, it should run under the at user.)

   d. At the shell prompt, enter **ps –el | less**.

   e. Locate the Status (S) column.

   f. Press SPACEBAR until you find the atd service. What is the status of the service? (Because it isn't being used at the moment, it's probably sleeping.)

7. Practice managing process priorities by completing the following:

    a. At the shell prompt, enter **top**.

    b. What are the priority (PR) and nice (NI) values associated with the top process? (For most distributions, these values should be 16 and 0.)

    c. Press Q to stop the top process.

    d. At the shell prompt, enter **nice –n –20 top**. Now what are the PR and NI values for the top process?

    e. Note the PID for the top process.

    f. Open a new terminal window and su to root.

    g. At the shell prompt, adjust the nice value of the top process while it's running by entering **renice 1** *top_PID*.

    h. Switch back to the first terminal session where top is running. What are its PR and NI values now?

    i. Press Q to exit top.

8. Practice switching processes between the foreground and the background by doing the following:

    a. Load top again by entering **top** at the shell prompt.

    b. In the terminal where top is running, press CTRL-Z.

    c. Note the background job ID number assigned to the process.

    d. At the shell prompt, enter **bg** *background_job_ID*. The output from top disappears while the process runs in the background.

    e. Press CTRL-C.

    f. At the shell prompt, enter **fg** *background_job_ID*. The output from top reappears as the process now runs in the foreground.

9. Practice killing processes by completing the following:

    a. Ensure that top is still running.

    b. Switch to your other terminal session where you're logged in as root.

    c. At the shell prompt, enter **ps –e | grep top**.

    d. Note the PID of the top process.

    e. At the shell prompt, enter **kill –SIGTERM** *top_PID*.

    f. Switch back to the terminal session where top was running. Verify that top has exited.

    g. Load **top** again at the shell prompt.

    h. Switch back to your other terminal session where you're logged in as root.

    i. Kill the top process by entering **killall –15 top**.

    j. Switch back to your first terminal window and verify that top has exited.

10. Practice using screen by doing the following:

   a. If necessary, enter **exit** to return to your standard user account.

   b. Press ENTER to exit the splash screen.

   c. At the shell prompt in the screen window, enter **top**.

   d. Press CTRL-A and then C to create a new window.

   e. At the shell prompt in the new window, enter **pgrep –l –f top**. Top should still be running and its PID displayed.

   f. Press CTRL-A and then N. You should be toggled back to the window where top is running.

   g. Press CTRL-A and then D to detach the current window.

   h. Reattach to the window where top is running by entering **screen –r** at the shell prompt. You should see the top window displayed again.

   i. Exit out of top by pressing ESC, and then exit out of screen by entering **exit**.

It's time to make a quantum leap and change topics! We next need to discuss how to schedule processes on your Linux system.

Scheduling Processes

So far in this chapter, you've learned how to execute and manage processes on a Linux system from the shell prompt. However, there will be many occasions when you need a process to run automatically without any intervention on your part. Backups are a good example. One of the key problems with backups is not that system administrators perform them incorrectly; it's that they forget to perform them at all! One of the worst things you can do in your backup strategy is to rely on a human being to remember to run them.

Instead, you can configure your Linux system to run programs for you automatically. This removes the human element from the equation and ensures that the specified programs execute regularly and on time. Two key utilities can be used to schedule processes to run in the future. We'll discuss the following in this part of the chapter:

- Using the at daemon
- Using the cron daemon
- Using anacron

Let's begin by learning how to use the at daemon.

Using the at Daemon

Using at is a great way to schedule a process to run once sometime in the future. The at service is a system daemon (called *atd*) that runs in the background on your system. Most Linux distributions install this service for you during the initial installation of the system. If not, you may need to install it manually from your installation repository using the rpm utility.

If your distribution uses init, then the startup script used to start the atd daemon is located in your init script directory, which should be either /etc/init.d or /etc/rc.d/init.d, depending on your particular distribution. The name of the script is atd.

Before attempting to use at, you need to make sure the atd daemon is running. You can do this by entering **rcatd start** at the shell prompt. You can also run the script file with its full path followed by **start** at the shell prompt to accomplish the same task. Make sure the atd daemon will start automatically on boot using the insserv or chkconfig command.

If your distribution uses systemd instead of init, you start the atd daemon by entering **systemctl start atd** at the shell prompt as root.

At this point, you need to specify which users can and which users cannot create at jobs. This can be done by editing the following files:

- **/etc/at.allow** Users listed in this file are allowed to create at jobs.

- **/etc/at.deny** Users listed in this file are not allowed to create at jobs.

To use at to schedule a command to run at a future time, complete the following:

1. At the shell prompt enter **at** *time*. The at daemon is very flexible as to how you specify the *time* value in this command. Observe the syntax shown in Table 13-2.

Type of Reference	Syntax	Description
Fixed	HH:MM	Specifies the exact hour and minute when the commands should be run. The at daemon assumes that the hour and minute specified is today unless that time has already passed; then it assumes it is tomorrow. You can also add **am** or **pm** to the value to specify morning or afternoon.
	Noon	Specifies that a command be run at 12:00 P.M.
	Midnight	Specifies that a command be run at 12:00 A.M.
	Teatime	Specifies that a command be run at 4:00 P.M.
	MMDDYY or MM/DD/YY or MM.DD.YY	Specifies the exact month, date, and year when a command is to be run.
	HH:MM MMDDYY	Specifies the exact month, date, year, and time when a command is to be run.
Relative	now	Specifies that the command be run immediately.
	now + value	Specifies that the command be run at a certain time in the future. For example, you could enter any of the following: **now + 5 minutes** **now + 2 hours** **now + 3 days**
	today	Specifies that the command be run today. You can mix this value with a fixed value from one of the preceding types, such as **2 pm today**.
	tomorrow	Specifies that the command be run tomorrow. You can also mix this value with a fixed value, such as **2 pm tomorrow**.

Table 13-2 The at Command Time Syntax Options

After you enter the at command and a time value from Table 13-2, the at> prompt is displayed, as shown here:

```
openSUSE:~ # at now +10 minutes
warning: commands will be executed using /bin/sh
at>
```

2. At the at> prompt, enter the command(s) you want at to run for you. It's important to note that if your commands display output on the screen from the shell prompt, you won't see the output when the commands are run by at. You have two different options for viewing the output. First of all, if you don't specify any alternative, at will e-mail the output to your local user account.

Alternatively, you can also redirect the output to a file. You learned how to do this earlier in this book. For example, if you wanted to run the tail /var/log messages command in the future with at, you could enter **tail /var/log/messages > ~/atoutput.txt** at the at> prompt to send the output from the command to a text file named atoutput.txt in your home directory.

3. Press ENTER if you want to add additional commands. You can run multiple commands within the same job. Each command should be on its own line.

4. When you're done entering commands, press CTRL-D. When you do, the at> prompt will disappear, the job will be scheduled, and a job number will be assigned, as shown here:

```
openSUSE:~ # at now +10 minutes
warning: commands will be executed using /bin/sh
at> tail /var/log/messages > ~/atoutput.txt
at> <EOT>
job 3 at 2011-04-02 08:57
openSUSE:~ #
```

Once you've configured the job, you can use the atq command to view a list of pending at jobs. This is shown next:

```
openSUSE:~ # atq
3       2011-04-02 08:57 a root
```

If you are logged in as a regular user, the atq command will display only the jobs associated with the current user account. If you're logged in as root, then atq will display all pending jobs for all users. If you need to remove a pending job from the list, you can use the **atrm** *job_number* command.

In addition to the at daemon, you can also use the cron daemon to schedule future jobs. Let's discuss how this is done next.

Using the cron Daemon

The at daemon is great; however, it has one key drawback. It can only schedule a job to run once in the future. That's not a problem if you only want the job to run once. However, there will be many times when you want a job to run in the future on a regular schedule. For example, you may need to run a process, such as a backup utility, every day at a certain time. In this situation, the at daemon doesn't cut it. You need a tool that can handle repetitious schedules.

The cron daemon can do just that. Unlike at, cron can run commands on a schedule you specify. It's a very powerful, very useful service. I use at occasionally. However, cron is a service that I use all of the time. In fact, I would have a hard time getting my work done without it. Most of my clients' offices are many miles from my office. Making rounds just to run backups for all of my clients each day would take up all my time. Of course, I don't dare trust my clients' administrative personnel to make sure backups occur each day. Instead, I set up the cron daemon to run the backups for me. That way, I know that backups are occurring on a regular schedule and that the correct command has been issued to create them.

In this part of the chapter, we'll discuss the following:

- How cron works
- Using cron to manage scheduled system jobs
- Using cron to manage scheduled user jobs

Let's begin by learning how the cron service works.

How cron Works

The cron daemon is a service that runs continuously in the background on your system and checks a special file called a *crontab* file once every minute to see if there's a scheduled job it should run. If your distribution uses init, then the cron daemon is managed using the cron init script in your init directory. If your distribution uses systemd, you use the systemctl command to manage the cron daemon.

By default, the cron daemon is configured to run automatically every time the system boots on most Linux distributions. If not, you'll need to start it manually using the cron init script in your system's init directory.

You can configure cron to run system jobs or user-specific jobs. Let's talk about running system jobs first.

Using cron to Manage Scheduled System Jobs

Using cron to run scheduled system jobs is an extremely useful tool for a Linux system administrator. You can configure your systems to perform a wide variety of tasks on a regular schedule automatically, thus saving you a ton of time and effort.

Remember when I mentioned the problems with running regular backups? Creating a system job in cron that runs a backup on a regular schedule saves me tons of time. If I don't have time to visit a client site on a particular day, I don't have to worry. I know that cron will run a backup at the preconfigured time. All I have to do is drop by now and then to verify that everything is still working properly and to perhaps rotate the backup media. I love cron!

To run system jobs, the cron service uses the /etc/crontab file, shown next, to configure what jobs to run:

```
openSUSE:/etc # cat ./crontab
SHELL=/bin/sh
PATH=/usr/bin:/usr/sbin:/sbin:/bin:/usr/lib/news/bin
MAILTO=root
#
# check scripts in cron.hourly, cron.daily, cron.weekly, and cron.monthly
#
-*/15 * * * *   root  test -x /usr/lib/cron/run-crons &&
/usr/lib/cron/run-crons >/dev/null 2>&1
```

As you can see in this example, the /etc/crontab file contains commands that are used to run scripts found in four different directories:

- **/etc/cron.hourly**   Contains cron scripts that are run every hour
- **/etc/cron.daily**   Contains cron scripts that are run every day
- **/etc/cron.weekly**   Contains cron scripts that are run once a week
- **/etc/cron.monthly**   Contains cron scripts that are run once a month

All scripts found in any of these directories are automatically run by cron according to the specified schedule. For example, the /etc/cron.daily directory contains a variety of scripts that are used to clean up your system and rotate your logs once each day. These scripts are shown here:

```
openSUSE:/etc/cron.daily # ls
logrotate                     suse-clean_catman         suse.de-backup-rpmdb
mdadm                         suse-do_mandb             suse.de-check-battery
packagekit-background.cron    suse.de-backup-rc.config  suse.de-cron-local
```

If you have a system task that needs to be run on one of these four schedules, you can simply create a script file and copy it into the appropriate cron directory in /etc.

What do you do, however, if your system job needs to run on a schedule other than one of the four used by the cron directories? No problem. The cron daemon has got you covered. In addition to the four directories just presented, there's a fifth directory in /etc/ called cron.d.

If you need a system job to run on a custom schedule, you can create a crontab file in this directory where it will be read and run by the cron daemon.

How do you create a crontab file? It looks difficult but it really isn't. A crontab file is simply a text file that uses one line per job. Each line has six fields, separated by tabs, as detailed in Table 13-3.

Many times, you will see an asterisk (*) in one or more fields in a given crontab file. This wildcard means "match everything."

For example, suppose I wanted to run the tar command to back up the /home directory using the **tar –cvf /media/usb/backup.tar /home** command every day of every month, except Sundays, at 11:05 P.M. I could create a crontab file in /etc/crontab.d and add the following line:

```
5       23      *       *       1-6     /bin/tar -cvf /media/usb/backup.tar /home
```

Table 13-3	Field	Description
The crontab File Fields	1	Minutes. This field specifies the minutes past the hour that the command should be run.
	2	Hour. This field specifies the hour of the day when the command should be run. The cron daemon prefers military time, so you should use a value of 0 to 23 in this field.
	3	Day. This field specifies the day of the month that the command should be run.
	4	Month. This field specifies the month of the year when the command should be run.
	5	Day of the week. Sunday is 0 and Saturday is 6.
	6	The name of the command, including the full path, to be run.

This line in the crontab file specifies that the command be run at 5 minutes after 11:00 P.M. (23) every day (*) of every month (*) on Monday (1) through Saturday (6).

 NOTE System cron jobs run as the root user!

In addition to system cron jobs, individual users can also create their own cron jobs. Let's review how this is done next.

Using cron to Manage Scheduled User Jobs

Users on your system can create their own schedules using a crontab file that is associated with their user account. Unlike system crontab files, which are saved in /etc, user crontab files are stored in /var/spool/cron/tabs. If a user has created a crontab file, it will be saved under his or her username in this directory.

Before proceeding, I should point out that not all Linux system administrators want to allow their users to do this. If allowing users to make their own crontab files and run programs on a schedule makes you nervous, you can lock the system to prevent them from doing so. To do this, you use an approach similar to that used when working with the at daemon.

The cron daemon will read the /etc/cron.allow and /etc/cron.deny files when it starts up to determine who can and who can't create crontab schedules. By default, only the /etc/cron.deny file is created automatically, and it contains only one restriction by default for the guest user account. All other users are allowed to create crontab files to schedule jobs. If you create an /etc/cron.allow file, then *only* the users in that file will be allowed to create crontab files; all others will be denied.

With that out of the way, let's discuss how users can create their own crontab files. To do this, they can use the **crontab –e** command. After this command has been entered, the vi editor is opened with a new, blank crontab file loaded.

In this file, the user simply adds lines for each job they want to run using the syntax we reviewed previously. For example, in Figure 13-13, the tar command is run at 5:10 P.M. every day to back up the user's home directory to a file named ~/homebak.tar.

The file is edited using standard vi commands and keystrokes, which you learned earlier in this book. (I told you knowing how to use vi would come in handy!) When you're done, exit vi and save the file. After doing so, a new crontab file for the user is created in /var/spool/cron/tabs,

```
                    crontab.wwzr9t + (/tmp) – VIM                              ✕

File   Edit   View   Search   Terminal   Help
10        17      *       *       *        /bin/tar -cvf ~/homebak.tar ~
~
~
~
```

Figure 13-13   Creating a user crontab file

as shown in the next example. In addition, the cron service is reloaded so the new configuration can be applied.

```
openSUSE:/ # ls /var/spool/cron/tabs/
rtracy
openSUSE:/ # cat /var/spool/cron/tabs/rtracy
# DO NOT EDIT THIS FILE - edit the master and reinstall.
# (/tmp/crontab.wwzr9t installed on Tue Dec  2 22:31:44 2014)
# (Cronie version 4.2)
10      17     *        *         *          /bin/tar -cvf ~/homebak.tar ~
```

In this example, I used the cat command to view the tux user's crontab file. However, you can also use the **crontab –l** command to display your user's crontab file. In addition, you can use the **crontab –r** command to remove your user's crontab file.

Let's practice working with Linux processes in the following exercise.

Exercise 13-2: Scheduling Linux Processes

In this exercise, you will practice using the cron and at commands to schedule processes to run in the future on your system. You can perform this exercise using the virtual machine that comes with this book. Run snapshot 13-2 for the correctly configured environment.

 VIDEO   Please watch the Exercise 13-2 video for a demonstration on how to perform this task.

Complete the following:

1. Boot your Linux system and log in as a standard user.

2. Open a terminal session.

3. Switch to your root user account by entering **su –** followed by a password of **student**.

4. Practice using the at daemon by doing the following:

   a. At the shell prompt, enter **systemctl status atd**.

   b. Verify that the at daemon is running. If it isn't, enter **systemctl start atd** at the shell prompt.

   c. At the shell prompt, enter **at now +5 minutes**.

   d. At the at prompt, enter **ps –ef > ~/psoutput.txt**.

   e. Press CTRL-D.

   f. Generate a listing of pending at jobs by entering **atq**. You should see the job you just created.

   g. Wait for the pending at job to complete.

   h. Use the cat command to check the ~/psoutput.txt file and verify that the output from the ps command was generated correctly.

    i. At the shell prompt, enter **at 2 pm tomorrow**.

    j. At the at prompt, enter **ps –ef > ~/psoutput.txt**.

    k. Press ENTER.

    l. Press CTRL-D.

    m. Generate a listing of pending at jobs by entering **atq**. You should see the job you just created. Note its job number.

    n. Remove the pending job by entering **atrm** *job_number*.

    o. Enter **atq** again. The pending job should be gone.

5. Practice using cron by completing the following:

    a. Log out of your root user account by entering **exit**.

    b. At the shell prompt, enter **crontab –e**.

    c. Press INSERT.

    d. Configure your system to create a backup of your user's home directory every day at 5:05 P.M. by entering the following:

```
05    17    *    *    *       /bin/tar –cvf ~/mybackup.tar ~/
```
       If you don't want to wait until 5:05 p.m., you could instead specify a time value that is only two or three minutes in the future.

    e. Press ESC.

    f. Enter **:exit**. You should see a message on the screen indicating that a new crontab has been installed.

    g. Enter **crontab –l** and verify that the job was created correctly.

    h. Wait until the time you specified in the crontab file; then check your user's home directory and verify that the mybackup.tar file was created.

    i. Remove your user's crontab file by entering **crontab –r** at the shell prompt.

Using anacron

Some distributions use anacron along with cron to automate the running of tasks. The two services work in pretty much the same manner. The key difference is that cron assumes that your computer system will remain up and running 24 hours a day, 7 days a week. That's fine for some systems, such as servers and desktops, but not for others. For example, a notebook system is very likely to be off or asleep during certain periods of the day. If a system is not powered on when a scheduled cron job should run, it is skipped.

The anacron service attempts to work around this issue. If a job is scheduled in anacron, but the system is off, then the missed job will automatically run when the system comes back up.

Just as cron uses the /etc/crontab file, anacron uses the /etc/anacrontab file. This file uses the following fields:

```
period   delay   job-identifier   command
```

The first field specifies the recurrence period (in days). For example, you could use any one of the following values in this field:

- **1**   The task recurs daily.
- **7**   The task recurs weekly.
- **30**   The task recurs monthly.

The second field specifies the delay (in minutes) anacron should wait before executing a skipped job after the system starts up.

The third field contains the job identifier. This is the name that will be used for the job's time-stamp file and must be unique for each anacron job. This file is created in the /var/spool/anacron directory and contains a single line with a timestamp that indicates the last time the particular job was run. The fourth field specifies the command or script that should be run.

Consider the following example in which anacron is configured to run the /usr/bin/updatedb.sh script once a day. If the system is down when the anacron job is supposed to run, the script will be executed 30 minutes after the system comes back up.

```
openSUSE:/ # cat /etc/anacrontab
1       30      updatedbtime.log      /usr/bin/updatedb.sh
```

Notice that this file does not specify the exact time when the job will run. This is configured by the START_HOURS_RANGE variable in the /etc/anacrontab file. In the following example, the start range is set to 3-22, which specifies a time range from 3 A.M. to 10 P.M.

```
openSUSE# cat /etc/anacrontab
...
START_HOURS_RANGE=3-22
```

It's important to note that anacron also adds a random number of minutes to whatever value you specified in the second field of the anacrontab file. The number of minutes that can be added is constrained by the RANDOM_DELAY variable within the /etc/anacrontab file. By default, this variable is set to a value of 45, which causes anacron to add a random number of minutes between 0 and 45 to the delay time in the anacrontab file. This is shown here:

```
openSUSE# cat /etc/anacrontab
...
RANDOM_DELAY=45
```

Well done! You now know how to manage Linux processes on your system! Not many can make that claim. Let's now review what you learned in this chapter.

Chapter Review

In this chapter, you learned how to manage Linux processes. We began this chapter by reviewing what a process is. We established that whenever you run a command from the shell prompt or when a daemon is loaded, a process is created on the system as the associated program's code is loaded into RAM and the code is executed by the CPU.

I pointed out that Linux is a multitasking operating system. Even though the CPU can only run one process at a time, Linux continually switches CPU time among many processes loaded into RAM, making it appear that the CPU is processing many processes concurrently.

I also pointed out that when a daemon is loaded, a system process is created. When an end user enters a command at the shell prompt, a user process is created. User processes are associated with a shell session; system processes are not.

We then discussed the heredity of Linux processes. I pointed out that Linux processes can spawn other Linux processes. The process that spawned another process is called the *parent.* The new process that was created by the first process is called the *child.* Every Linux process has a parent process. All Linux processes can trace their heredity back to the init process or the systemd process (depending on your distribution), which is the first process loaded by the kernel on system boot.

Every Linux process is assigned a process ID (PID) that uniquely identifies the process on the system. Processes are also assigned a PPID, which is the PID of the process's parent process. Whenever you run a command from the shell prompt, a new shell (called a *subshell)* is created and the command is run within it. When the process is complete, the subshell is destroyed and control is returned to the original shell.

We then turned our attention to managing Linux processes. We first discussed how you go about creating processes. User processes are created by simply entering commands at the shell prompt. On distributions that use init, system processes are created by running a daemon startup script from your system's init directory. Some distributions use System V init scripts, which are stored in /etc/rc.d/init.d. Other distributions use BSD init scripts, which are stored in /etc/init.d. Distributions that use systemd use the systemctl command to start and stop services.

We next discussed how to view running processes. The first utility we looked at was the top utility. You load top by entering **top** at the shell prompt. You can press the H key while top is running to view a help screen that will show you how to sort by a specific column or even add columns of data to the display.

You can also use the ps command to view running processes. By default, the ps command only displays running processes associated with the current shell session. To view all running processes, use the –e option with the ps command. You can also use the –f and –l options with ps to view extended process information. We also looked at the pgrep command, which can be used to search for specific processes based on a set of criteria you configure.

Next, we discussed how to prioritize processes on your system. A process's overall priority is heavily influenced by its nice value. Nice values can range from –20 to +19. The lower the nice value, the higher the priority of the process. To adjust the nice value of a process when it's loaded, you can use the nice command. The syntax is **nice –n** *nice_value command*. You can't use a nice value lower than 0 unless you are logged in as root. You can also adjust the nice value of a running process without unloading it. This is done using the renice command. The syntax is **renice** *nice_value PID*.

Then we discussed how to run processes in the foreground and the background. By default, processes you launch from the shell prompt run in the foreground. In this situation, the shell prompt is locked until the process is complete. You can also run a process in the background. In this situation, the program runs, but it does so in the background and control is returned to the shell prompt, allowing you to run additional commands. This is done by simply appending the

& character to the end of the command. When you do, the background process is assigned a job ID number.

You can move a process that is running in the background to the foreground by entering **fg** *job_ID* at the shell prompt. You can also move a foreground process into the background. To do this, first press CTRL-Z to stop the process. The process will then be assigned a job ID number. You can then enter **bg** *job_ID* to move the process to the background.

Finally, we discussed how to kill a running process from the shell prompt. You can use the kill command or the killall command to do this. Both of these commands use a variety of kill signals. Some of the most useful signals include

- SIGHUP (1)
- SIGINT (2)
- SIGKILL (9)
- SIGTERM (15)

The syntax for kill is **kill** *–signal PID*. The syntax for killall is **killall** *–signal process_name*. When working with a hung process, you should try less aggressive kill signals, such as SIGINT and SIGTERM, before using more aggressive kill signals such as SIGKILL. The pkill command can also be used to search for and kill specific processes based on search criteria you configure. I also pointed out that you can run a process using the nohup command to cause it to ignore the SIGHUP signal that is sent when a user logs out. This allows the process to continue running even though the user is no longer logged in to the system. You can also use the screen command to create windows that can be detached, which allows you to log out but leave processes running.

At this point in the chapter, we shifted gears and discussed how to schedule processes to run automatically in the future. If you only need the process to run once in the future, you can use the at daemon. Before you can use at, you need to make sure the atd daemon is running on your system. Then, you can enter **at** *time* at the shell prompt. The time value can be a fixed time, such as **10:00**, or a relative time, such as **tomorrow**. You will then be presented with an at> prompt, where you can enter a list of commands to be run. Press CTRL-D when you're done. You can use the atq command to view a list of pending at jobs. You can also use the atrm command to remove a pending at job.

If you need to schedule a process to run on a recurring basis, you need to use the cron daemon instead of at. The cron daemon can run system jobs or user jobs. System cron jobs are created by adding script files to one of the following directories:

- /etc/cron.hourly
- /etc/cron.daily
- /etc/cron.weekly
- /etc/cron.monthly

You can also create a crontab file and save it in the /etc/cron.d directory. A crontab file contains one line for each command that is to be run. Each line contains six fields:

- **1** Minutes
- **2** Hour
- **3** Day
- **4** Month
- **5** Day of the week
- **6** Command to be run

In addition to system jobs, you can also use cron to create user jobs. User cron jobs are stored in /var/spool/cron/tabs. You can create a crontab file by entering **crontab –e** at the shell prompt. You then create one line for each scheduled command using the syntax just described. After creating the crontab file, you can use the **crontab –l** command to view your crontab file. You can also use the **crontab –r** command to remove your crontab file.

You can use anacron in addition to cron to automatically run jobs on a schedule. The anacron daemon keeps track of jobs that should have run but couldn't because the system was off. It will run them when the system comes back up after a specified delay time.

Accelerated Review

- Whenever you run a command from the shell prompt, a process is created on the system.
- When a process loads, the program's code is loaded into RAM and is executed by the CPU.
- Linux is a multitasking operating system.
- Most CPUs can only run one process at a time.
- Linux continually switches CPU time among the many processes loaded into RAM, making it appear that the CPU is processing many processes concurrently.
- When the init process or the systemd process loads a daemon, a system process is created.
- When an end user enters a command at the shell prompt, a user process is created.
- User processes are associated with a shell session; system processes are not.
- Linux processes can spawn other Linux processes.
- The process that spawned another process is called the *parent.*
- The new process that was created by the first process is called the *child.*
- Every Linux process has a parent process.
- All Linux processes can trace their heredity back to the init process or the systemd process (depending on the distribution), which is the first process loaded by the kernel on system boot.
- Every Linux process is assigned a process ID (PID) that uniquely identifies the process on the system.
- Processes are assigned a PPID value, which is the PID of the process's parent process.
- Whenever you run a command from the shell prompt, a subshell is created and the command is run within it.

- When the process is complete, the subshell is destroyed and control is returned to the original shell.

- User processes are created when you enter commands at the shell prompt.

- Some distributions use System V init scripts, which are stored in /etc/rc.d/init.d.

- Some distributions use BSD init scripts, which are stored in /etc/init.d.

- For distributions that use systemd, you use the systemctl command to start and stop system services.

- You can use the top utility to view system processes. You load top by entering **top** at the shell prompt.

- You can press the H key while top is running to view a help screen that will show you how to configure the data displayed by top.

- You can use the ps command to view running processes.

- By default, the ps command only displays running processes associated with the current shell session.

- You can use the –e option with the ps command to view all running processes.

- You can use the –f and –l options with ps to view extended process information.

- You can use the pgrep command to search for specific processes running on your system.

- Linux allows you to prioritize processes running on your system.

- A process's overall priority is heavily influenced by its nice value.

- Nice values can range from –20 to +19.

- The lower the nice value, the higher the priority of the process.

- You can use the nice command to adjust the nice value of a process as it's loaded.

- To use nice, you enter **nice –n** *nice_value command*.

- You can't assign a nice value lower than 0 unless you are logged in as root.

- You can also adjust the nice value of a running process without unloading it using the renice command.

- The syntax for using renice is **renice** *nice_value PID*.

- By default, processes you launch from the shell prompt run in the foreground.

- Foreground processes lock the shell prompt until the process is complete.

- You can run Linux processes in the background.

- Background processes return control to the shell prompt.

- You can run a process in the background by appending an **&** character to the end of the command.

- When you load a process into the background, the process is assigned a job ID number.

- You can move a process that is running in the background to the foreground by entering **fg** *job_ID* at the shell prompt.

- You can move a foreground process into the background by pressing CTRL-Z to stop the process and then entering **bg** *job_ID* to move the process to the background.

- You can use the kill or the killall command to kill a running process.

- There are many kill signals that can be sent using kill or killall; some of the most useful include
  - SIGHUP (1)
  - SIGINT (2)
  - SIGKILL (9)
  - SIGTERM (15)

- To kill a process with kill, enter **kill** *–signal PID* at the shell prompt.

- To kill a process with killall, enter **killall** *–signal process_name*.

- You should use less aggressive kill signals, such as SIGINT and SIGTERM, before attempting to use more forceful kill signals such as SIGKILL.

- You can use the pkill command to search for and kill specific processes based on search criteria you configure.

- You can load a program using the nohup command to cause the process to ignore the SIGHUP command that is sent when the user logs out, thus allowing the process to continue running.

- You can use the screen command to create windows that can be detached, thus allowing processes to continue to run even though you log out from the system.

- If you only need a process to run once in the future, you should use the at daemon.

- You need to load the atd daemon before you can use at.

- You can load atd by entering **rcatd start** or **systemctl start atd** at the shell prompt.

- To schedule a command to run in the future with at, enter **at** *time* at the shell prompt.

- The at time value can be a fixed time, such as
  - HH:MM
  - Noon
  - Midnight
  - Teatime
  - MMDDYY, MM/DD/YY, or MM.DD.YY

- The at time value can also be a relative time, such as
  - now
  - now +*x* minutes, hours, or days
  - today
  - tomorrow

- At the at> prompt, enter a list of commands to be run; press CTRL-D when you're done.

- If you don't redirect output from your commands to a file, the output will be e-mailed to your local user account.
- You can use the atq command to view a list of pending at jobs.
- You can use the atrm command to remove a pending at job.
- If you need to schedule a process to run on a recurring basis, you should use the cron daemon instead of at.
- The cron daemon can run system jobs or user jobs.
- System cron jobs are created by adding script files in the following directories:
  - /etc/cron.hourly
  - /etc/cron.daily
  - /etc/cron.weekly
  - /etc/cron.monthly
- You can also define system cron jobs by creating a crontab file in the /etc/cron.d directory.
- A crontab file contains one line for each command that is to be run; each line contains six fields:
  - **1** Minutes
  - **2** Hour
  - **3** Day
  - **4** Month
  - **5** Day of the week
  - **6** Command to be run
- You can use cron to create user jobs.
- User cron jobs are stored in /var/spool/cron/tabs.
- A user can create a crontab file by entering **crontab –e** at the shell prompt.
- After creating the crontab file, you can use the **crontab –l** command to view your crontab file contents.
- You can use the **crontab –r** command to remove your crontab file.
- You can use anacron to make sure jobs that were missed because the system was powered off get run when the system comes back up.

Questions

1. Which of the following best describes a multitasking operating system?
   A. An operating system that can run multiple tasks concurrently on multiple CPUs
   B. An operating system that can run a single task concurrently across multiple CPUs
   C. An operating system that runs multiple tasks concurrently on a single CPU
   D. An operating system that constantly switches CPU time between loaded processes

2. You just entered **vi** at the shell prompt. What type of process was created on your Linux system?

    A. User

    B. System

    C. Daemon

    D. System V

3. Your current shell session has a PID of 3456. You run the su command to change to the root user account. The su process has a PID of 3457. You then run vi from the shell prompt as root. The vi process has a PID of 3458. What is the PPID of the vi process?

    A. 3456

    B. 3457

    C. 3458

    D. 3459

4. Which process could be the grandparent of all processes running on a Linux system? (Choose two.)

    A. bash

    B. init

    C. sh

    D. ps

    E. systemd

5. You're running a Fedora Linux system that uses System V init scripts. Where are these scripts stored in your file system?

    A. /etc/init.d

    B. /etc/rc.d/init.d

    C. /etc/sysv/init.d

    D. /etc/init.d/rc.d

6. You want to use ps to display extended information about only the processes associated with your current terminal session. Which command will do this?

    A. ps

    B. ps –e

    C. ps –f

    D. ps –ef

7. What is a zombied process?

    A. A process that has finished executing but whose parent process hasn't released the child process's PID

    B. A process that has stopped executing while waiting for user input

C. A process that is being traced by another process

D. A process that has gone to sleep and can't be interrupted

8. Which ps option can be used to display all currently running processes?

A. –c

B. –e

C. –f

D. –l

9. The myapp process has a nice value of 1. Which of the following nice values would increase the priority of the myapp process? (Choose two.)

A. –15

B. 5

C. 19

D. 0

E. 2

10. Which of the following shell commands will load the myapp program with a nice value of –5?

A. myapp –n –5

B. nice –5 myapp

C. renice –5 myapp

D. nice –n –5 myapp

11. The myapp process (PID 2345) is currently running on your system. Which of the following commands will reset its nice value to –5 without unloading the process?

A. myapp –n –5 –p 2345

B. renice –n –5 2345

C. renice –5 2345

D. nice –n –5 2345

12. You want to load the myapp program from the shell prompt and run it in the background. Which command will do this?

A. myapp –b

B. myapp &

C. myapp –bg

D. load myapp into background

13. Which kill signal sends a CTRL-C key sequence to a running process?

   A. SIGHUP

   B. SIGINT

   C. SIGKILL

   D. SIGTERM

14. You need to kill a hung process. You know its process name, but you don't know its PID. Which utilities could you use? (Choose two.)

   A. killall

   B. kill

   C. hangup

   D. SIGKILL

   E. pkill

15. You want to run the rsync command to synchronize your home directory with another server on the network. You know this command will take several hours to complete and you don't want to leave your system logged in during this time. Which commands could you use to leave rsync running after your logout? (Choose two.)

   A. SIGHUP

   B. nohup

   C. stayalive

   D. kill –NOHUP

   E. screen

16. It's currently 1:00 in the afternoon. You want to schedule the myapp program to run automatically tomorrow at noon (12:00). Which of the following at commands could you use? (Choose two.)

   A. at 12 pm tomorrow

   B. at tomorrow –1 hour

   C. at now +1 day

   D. at today +23 hours

   E. at now +23 hours

17. Which of the following crontab lines will cause the /usr/bin/myappcleanup process to run at 4:15 A.M. on the first of every month?

   A. 15   4   1   *   *   /usr/bin/myappcleanup

   B. 15   4   *   1   *   /usr/bin/myappcleanup

   C. 1   4   15   *   *   /usr/bin/myappcleanup

   D. 4   1   *   *   15   /usr/bin/myappcleanup

Answers

1. **D.** A multitasking operating system constantly switches CPU time between loaded processes, creating the impression that the CPU is actually executing processes concurrently.

2. **A.** Because the command was entered from the shell prompt, a user process was created.

3. **A.** Because the command was entered from the shell prompt, its parent process is the bash process, which has a PID of 3456.

4. **B, E.** On some distributions, the init process is the grandparent of all other Linux processes on the system. Other distributions use the systemd process instead. All other processes can trace their heredity to init or systemd, depending on the distribution.

5. **B.** The init scripts for distributions that use System V init scripts are stored in /etc/rc.d/init.d.

6. **C.** The ps –f command will display extended information about processes associated with the current shell session.

7. **A.** A zombied process is one where the process has finished executing, but the parent process wasn't notified and, therefore, hasn't released the child process's PID.

8. **B.** The **ps –e** command can be used to display a list of all running processes on the system.

9. **A, D.** The lower the nice value, the higher the priority of the process. Therefore, nice values of 0 and –15 will increase the priority of the myapp process.

10. **D.** The **nice –n –5 myapp** command will load myapp with a nice value of –5.

11. **C.** The **renice –5 2345** command will reset the nice value of the myapp process while it's running.

12. **B.** The **myapp &** command will cause myapp to run in the background.

13. **B.** The SIGINT kill signal sends a CTRL-C key sequence to the specified process.

14. **A, E.** The killall utility uses the process name in the command line and can be used to kill the process in this scenario. You could also use the –f option with the pkill command to search for and kill the hung process by its name.

15. **B, E.** The nohup command can be used to load a program so that it will ignore the SIGHUP signal that is sent when the user logs out, thus allowing the process to remain running. Alternatively, you could use the screen command to create a window and detach it. This would also allow the process to remain running.

16. **A, E.** You can enter **at 12 pm tomorrow** or **at now +23 hours** to cause the atd daemon to run the specified command at 12:00 on the following day.

17. **A.** The 15 4 1 * * /usr/bin/myappcleanup crontab line will cause the myappcleanup process to be run at 4:15 A.M. on the first day of every month no matter what day of the week it is.

## CHAPTER 14

Writing Shell Scripts

In this chapter, you will learn about:
- Working with shell scripts
- Creating simple shell scripts
- Using control structures in scripts
- Processing text streams
- Using command substitution and shell functions

One of the cool things about Linux is the fact that it allows you to create your own powerful *shell scripts* that you can run right from your shell prompt. A shell script is a text file that contains a series of commands that are executed by the shell. Shell scripts can be used to run multiple commands at once. They can also be used to read input from the end user or from shell commands, and make decisions based on the input.

 EXAM TIP Shell scripts range from very simple to extremely complex. For your Linux+/LPIC-1 exam, you don't need to be a scripting guru, but you do need to know how to create a script from scratch, use control structures within the script, and process text streams within a script. If you master the topics we cover here, you should be in good shape for your exam.

Let's begin by discussing how shell scripts work.

Working with Shell Scripts

To understand how shell scripts work, you need to know the following:

- The components of a shell script
- How shell scripts are executed

Let's begin by discussing the components of a shell script.

The Components of a Shell Script

As mentioned, a shell script is a simple text file that contains a series of commands that are executed from top to bottom. Here is a sample shell script named runme:

```
#!/bin/bash
#A simple script that displays the current date and time
echo "The current date and time is:"
date
exit 0
```

Notice that this script contains several parts:

- **#!/bin/bash**   The first line of any shell script should specify which shell the script is written to run under. In this case, the /bin/bash shell is specified. When a script is run, a subshell will be created using the shell specified here and the script contents will be processed within it.

- **#A simple script that** . . . .   This part of the script is a comment that describes what the script does. Notice that this part of the script begins with a # character to indicate that the text that comes after it is a comment. Because it is a comment, this part of the script is not displayed on the screen when it is run. Comments are optional. The script will run just fine without them. However, it's considered good form to include a comment at the beginning of your scripts right after the shell declaration that describes what the script does and, optionally, who wrote it.

- **echo, date**   These elements in the script are simple commands that are typically used at the shell prompt. The echo command is used to display text on the screen. The date command is used to display the current date and time on the screen.

- **exit 0**   This part of the script is its end. It tells the shell what to do after it is done running the commands in the script. In this case, it tells the shell to exit the script.

When we run this script, the output shown in Figure 14-1 is displayed on the screen.

Notice that this script first displayed the text specified by the echo command. Then the next command was processed, which directed the shell to run the date command. When the script was done, the shell exited the script and returned us to the command prompt.

How Shell Scripts Are Executed

Notice in Figure 14-1 that, to run the script, I had to call the shell (/bin/bash) and then tell it what script to execute (./runme). This is one option for running a script. However, there's a second

Figure 14-1   Running the simple shell script

option (and a better one in my opinion) for running shell scripts. Remember in an earlier chapter when we talked about permissions? Recall that one of the file permissions you could assign to a file is named *execute*. With the execute permission assigned, any file, including a text file, can be allowed to execute from the shell prompt. This is a great option for making scripts easy for end users to run.

To do this, simply enable the execute attribute for Owner, Group, and/or Others. As you learned earlier, this is done using the chmod command. In the example we're working with here, I can configure the runme file to be executed by the file Owner by entering **chmod u+x runme** at the shell prompt. Then I can run the runme script by simply entering its name at the shell prompt, just as I would with any other system command. This is shown in the next example:

```
rtracy@openSUSE:~> chmod u+x runme
rtracy@openSUSE:~> ls -l runme
-rwxr--r-- 1 rtracy users 118 Dec 11 10:50 runme
rtracy@openSUSE:~> ./runme
The current date and time is:
Thu Dec 11 11:07:08 MST 2014
```

If necessary, I could have also given the execute permission to Group and/or Others as well.

There is one other issue you need to be aware of when working with scripts, and that is the issue of paths. Notice in the preceding example that I had to enter **./runme** at the shell prompt. Even though the file resided in the current directory (in this case, /home/rtracy), this directory is not in my PATH environment variable.

If you're creating scripts for yourself, this probably doesn't pose a problem. By now, you should be familiar enough with Linux to understand why you have to specify the path to the file at the shell prompt and know how to do it. However, if you're creating a script for your end users to run, this may present a problem. To save yourself frustration, you should consider putting the script in a directory that is part of the PATH or adding the directory to your existing PATH.

One option you can use is the ~/bin directory in each user's home directory. Most Linux distributions automatically create a directory named /bin for each user. Then, one of the bash configuration files, discussed in an earlier chapter, is used to automatically add ~/bin to the PATH environment variable when a shell is started. This is shown here:

```
rtracy@openSUSE:~> echo $PATH
/usr/lib/mpi/gcc/openmpi/bin:/home/rtracy/bin:/usr/local/bin:/usr/bin:
/bin:/usr/bin/X11:/usr/X11R6/bin:/usr/games
```

Because it's in the PATH, any files you put in ~/bin can be run from the shell prompt without specifying the full path to the file. You could also, of course, create your own directory and manually edit your bash configuration files to add it to your user's PATH environment variable.

With this background in mind, let's spend some time discussing how to create a basic shell script.

Creating a Basic Script

As mentioned earlier, shell scripts can range from extremely basic to extremely complex. The example we reviewed earlier was a very simple script. It echoed text on the screen and ran one command. For your Linux+/LPIC-1 exam, you need to be able to create scripts that are much more complex than this. Therefore, in this part of the chapter, we're going to cover the following topics:

- Displaying text on the screen
- Adding commands to a script
- Reading input from the user

Let's begin by discussing how to display text on the screen in a shell script.

Displaying Text on the Screen

This task is pretty easy. As you saw in the earlier examples we reviewed, you can display text on the screen in a shell script using the echo command. The syntax for using echo is to simply enter **echo "***text_to_be_displayed***"** in the script file.

In the simple script example we looked at earlier, I entered **echo "The current date and time is:"** to display the associated text on the screen. Because the shell script simply calls and runs the echo command, you can use all of the options you would use if you were to run echo at the shell prompt. Check out the man page for echo to see what's available.

In addition to displaying text on the screen, you can also run commands from the script. Let's review how this is done next.

Adding Commands to a Script

To run a shell command from within a script, simply enter the appropriate command in the script with all of the options you want to include with it. In the simple script example we looked at earlier, I used the date command to display the current date and time. You can include just about any command you want in your shell scripts. Just remember to put each command on a separate line unless you are using pipes to move data between commands.

Let's make things a little more interesting by discussing how to gather input from the user in a script.

Reading Input from the User

Up to this point, our scripts have been non-interactive, meaning that the user simply types the command at the shell prompt and the script does whatever it has been written to do.

However, you can make your scripts more flexible by making them interactive, meaning that you can have your scripts ask the user a question and then capture their input for processing. This is done using the echo command discussed previously in conjunction with the read command. The echo command is used to present the user with a question. The read command is used to pause the script, present a prompt on the screen, and read the information the user supplies into a variable you define. Consider this example:

```
#!/bin/bash
#A script for adding a directory to the PATH environment variable
echo "What directory do you want to add to the PATH?"
read MYNEWPATH
echo "You want to add " $MYNEWPATH
exit 0
```

In this script, the user is prompted for the name of the directory he or she wants to add to the PATH environment variable. The read command provides the user with a prompt to enter the directory name. When the user presses the ENTER key, the value he or she typed is assigned to the variable named MYNEWPATH.

Once the variable is stored in memory, the echo command is used a second time to display the value of MYNEWPATH on the screen. Now, we didn't actually modify the PATH variable yet. To do this, we need to add some more commands to the shell script. The best way to approach this is to ask yourself, "If I were doing this from the shell prompt, what commands would I need?" Then enter the commands in the script and try it out.

In this example, we need to add the directory specified by the user to PATH and then export PATH. This could be done using the commands shown in this example:

```
#!/bin/bash
#A script for adding a directory to the PATH environment variable
echo "What directory do you want to add to the PATH?"
read MYNEWPATH
echo "Adding the " $MYNEWPATH " directory to PATH."
PATH=$PATH:$MYNEWPATH
export PATH
echo "Your PATH environment variable is now:"
echo $PATH
exit 0
```

If you've done any programming, you probably noticed that we didn't have to declare the MYNEWPATH variable anywhere in the script. With many scripting and programming languages, you have to first declare a variable, set its size, and specify what type of information (text string, real number, integer, Boolean value, and so on) it will contain. The bash shell is a little more forgiving. The bash shell will create the variable in memory dynamically for you from the read command and assign the user's input as its value.

Of course, bash does let you declare and type the variable if you want to. This is done using the declare command in the script. This can be useful if you want to have the user enter numbers in a read command. The issue here is that the bash shell interprets anything entered at the read command as *text*, even if the user enters a number. Consider this script:

```
#!/bin/bash
#A script that adds variables together.
echo "Enter a number:"
read NUM1
echo "Enter a second number:"
read NUM2
TOT=$NUM1+$NUM2
echo "The sum of these numbers is " $TOT
exit 0
```

When run, this script asks the user for two numbers, adds them together, assigns the result to a variable named TOT, and echoes the value of TOT on the screen. Notice what happens when the script is run:

```
rtracy@openSUSE:~> ./addnum
Enter a number:
1
```

```
Enter a second number:
3
The sum of these numbers is  1+3
```

Because we didn't declare the NUM1, NUM2, and TOT variables, bash treated them all as simple text. No arithmetic took place; the text values of each variable were concatenated together into a single text string. However, if we declare these variables and type them as integers, something very different will happen. Consider a revised version of this script, shown here:

```
#!/bin/bash
#A script that adds variables together.
declare -i NUM1
declare -i NUM2
declare -i TOT
echo "Enter a number:"
read NUM1
echo "Enter a second number:"
read NUM2
TOT=$NUM1+$NUM2
echo "The sum of these numbers is " $TOT
exit 0
```

Notice that NUM1, NUM2, and TOT are declared at the beginning of the script using the –i (integer) option. Now the bash shell will interpret the user's input as a whole number, not as text. When we use the + operator on the variables in the script, they are actually added, not just concatenated, as shown next:

```
rtracy@openSUSE:~> ./addnum
Enter a number:
1
Enter a second number:
3
The sum of these numbers is  4
```

You're doing great! We've gone from relatively simple scripts to ones that are a little more complex. Let's ratchet things up a notch and add some control structures to our scripts.

Using Control Structures in Scripts

In addition to interactivity, it can also be very beneficial to add control structures to your shell scripts. Our scripts, to this point, have executed straight through from beginning to end. This works fine, but what if we need the script to make some decisions? Based on user input or output from a command, you may want the script to determine a course of action. This is done by implementing control structures in the script. We're going to discuss the following about this type of script element:

- Using if/then/else structures
- Using case structures
- Using looping structures

Let's begin by reviewing if/then statements.

Using if/then Structures

Using an if/then/else structure within your shell script gives your script the ability to execute different commands based on whether a particular condition is true or false. The structure appears as follows:

```
if condition then
        commands
else
        commands
fi
```

The **if** part of the structure tells the shell to determine if the specified condition evaluates to *true* or *false*. If it is true, the commands under the **then** part of the structure are run. If the condition evaluates to false, the commands under the **else** part of the structure are run.

For example, in the script we've been working with so far in this part of the chapter, we've asked the user to enter the name of a directory he or she wants to add to the PATH environment variable. When we add the directory to PATH, the shell doesn't check to see if the directory the user entered actually exists. It would be beneficial to run a quick test and verify that the specified directory exists. If it does, we should go ahead and add it to the PATH variable. If not, we should post an error message on the screen telling the user what happened. The script shown in this next example does this very thing:

```
#!/bin/bash
#A script for adding a directory to the PATH environment variable
echo "What directory do you want to add to the PATH?"
read MYNEWPATH
if [ -d "$MYNEWPATH" ]; then
        echo "The " $MYNEWPATH " directory exists."
        echo "Adding the " $MYNEWPATH " directory to PATH."
        PATH=$PATH:$MYNEWPATH
        export PATH
        echo "Your PATH environment variable is now:"
        echo $PATH
else
        echo $MYNEWPATH " doesn't exist."
fi
exit 0
```

In this example, the [**–d "$MYNEWPATH"**] condition calls a utility called *test* and directs it to check and see if the directory contained in the MYNEWPATH variable exists (as specified by the –d option).

If test returns a value of TRUE, the steps immediately under the if statement are executed. However, if the test program returns a value of FALSE, the statements under the else portion of the structure are executed. In this case, an error message will be displayed indicating that the directory doesn't exist. When we run this script and supply a valid directory, the following output is displayed:

```
rtracy@openSUSE:~> ./addpath
What directory do you want to add to the PATH?
/tmp
The  /tmp  directory exists.
Adding the  /tmp  directory to PATH.
```

```
You PATH environment variable is now:
/usr/lib/mpi/gcc/openmpi/bin:/home/rtracy/bin:/usr/local/bin:/usr/bin:
/bin:/usr/bin/X11:/usr/X11R6/bin:/usr/games:/tmp
```

In addition to using the –d option in the if/then/else structure to test a condition, you can also use the test command itself. You can use the following options with test:

- **–d**   Checks to see if the specified file exists and if it is a directory.

- **–e**   Checks to see if the specified file exists. However, it does not differentiate between files and directories.

- **–f**   Checks to see if the specified file exists and if it is a regular file.

- **–G**   Checks to see if the specified file exists and is owned by a specified group.

- **–h or –L**   Checks to see if the specified file exists and if it is a symbolic link.

- **–O**   Checks to see if the specified file exists and if it is owned by the specified user ID.

- **–r**   Checks to see if the specified file exists and if the read permission is granted.

- **–w**   Checks to see if the specified file exists and if the write permission is granted.

- **–x**   Checks to see if the specified file exists and if the execute permission is granted.

For example, the following structure tests to see if a file named myfile in the /home/rtracy directory exists:

```
if test -f /home/rtracy/myfile; then
      echo "myfile exists"
else
      echo "myfile does not exist"
fi
```

You can do more than test whether files exist with the test command. Some sample conditions you can evaluate with test are shown next.

True if the text is the same:

```
test "text1" = "text2"
```

True if strings are not equal:

```
test "text1" != "text2"
```

True if both numbers are the same:

```
test num1 -eq num2
```

True if num1 is less than num2:

```
test num1 -lt num2
```

True if num1 is greater than num2:

```
test num1 -gt num2
```

You can also use a related structure in your scripts called case. Let's discuss how to use it next.

Using case Structures

The case statement is really just a glorified if/then statement. The if/then statement works perfectly if we have a condition that can be evaluated in one of two ways. In the preceding examples, the condition could be evaluated as true or false. However, what do you do if you have a condition that could be evaluated in many different ways, but you still want your script to take certain actions based on how it evaluates? You use the case statement instead.

 TIP You could also use a whole series of if/then statements instead of a case statement. However, it can get really messy and is considered poor form. If you have a condition that can be evaluated to return more than two responses, you should use a case statement.

The syntax for using a case structure is as follows:

```
case variable in
     response_1 ) commands
                   ;;
     response_2 ) commands
                   ;;
     response_3 ) commands
                   ;;
esac
```

Essentially, the case statement compares the value of the variable listed to the list of responses within the case statement. If a match is found, the commands associated with that response are run. Commands for all other list items are ignored.

For example, we could write a script that asks users what month they were born in. Based on the response they give, you could cause the script to provide a customized response using a case statement. Here is a sample script that does this:

```
#!/bin/bash
#A simple script to demonstrate the case structure.
echo "What month were you born in?"
read MYMONTH
case $MYMONTH in
     December | January | February ) echo "Being born in" $MYMONTH",
     you were born during the winter in the Northern Hemisphere."
     ;;
     March | April | May ) echo "Being born in" $MYMONTH",
     you were born during the spring in the Northern Hemisphere."
     ;;
     June | July | August ) echo "Being born in" $MYMONTH",
     you were born during the summer in the Northern Hemisphere."
     ;;
     September | October | November ) echo "Being born in" $MYMONTH",
     you were born during the fall in the Northern Hemisphere."
     ;;
     * ) echo "Sorry, I'm not familiar with that month!"
     ;;
esac
exit 0
```

This script asks users what month they were born in and then determines the season of their birth using a case structure. Five options are provided:

- December, January, or February
- March, April, or May
- June, July, or August
- September, October, or November
- *

Notice that the different terms on the same line are separated with a pipe character (|). This means "or." If the user's response matches one of the terms, the command associated with its line is executed. In the following example, the script has been run and the user has responded with a birth month of June:

```
rtracy@openSUSE:~> ./casetest
What month were you born in?
June
Being born in June, you were born during the summer in the Northern Hemisphere.
```

Because the value of the MYMONTH variable matched the line in the case statement for *June,* the echo command for the June, July, or August response was run. Notice that we added one extra response at the end of the case statement using an asterisk (*). This option allows us to provide users with feedback in the event that the response they supply doesn't match any of the other items listed in the case statement.

Using Looping Structures

The if/then/else and case structures are called *branching structures.* Depending on how a condition evaluates, the script branches in one direction or another. You can also use *looping* control structures within a shell script. Looping structures come in three varieties: the *while loop,* the *until loop,* and the *for loop.* A while loop executes over and over until a specified condition is no longer true. The structure of a while loop is as follows:

```
while condition
do
      script commands
done
```

A while loop will keep processing over and over and over until the condition evaluates to false.

In addition to a while loop, you can also use an until loop in your script. It works in the opposite manner. An until loop runs over and over as long as the condition is false. As soon as the condition is true, it stops. The structure for an until loop is as follows:

```
until condition
do
      script commands
done
```

You can also use a for loop, which operates in a different manner than until or while loops. The until and while loops keep looping indefinitely until the specified condition is met. A for loop, on the other hand, loops a specific number of times.

It is very common to use the seq command within a for loop to create the sequence of numbers to determine how many times it will loop. There are three options for creating a number sequence with seq:

- If you specify a single value, the sequence starts at one, increments by one, and ends at the specified value.

- If you specify two values, the sequence starts at the first value, increments by one, and ends at the second value.

- If you specify three values, the sequence starts at the first value, increments by the second value, and ends at the third value.

Consider the following example:

```
seq 5 15
```

This command creates a sequence of numbers that starts at 5, increments by 1, and ends at 15. Here is an example of using seq in a for loop:

```
for i in 'seq 15'
     do
             echo "The current number in the sequence is $i."
     done
exit 0
```

The biggest danger with looping structures is that it is possible to get stuck in an infinite loop. This happens when the condition never changes to a value that will break the loop. In this situation, the script gets "hung" because it keeps running the same loop structure over and over and over and will continue to do so until you manually break out of it using CTRL-C.

Let's practice working with basic shell scripts in the following exercise.

Exercise 14-1: Creating a Basic Shell Script

In this exercise, you will practice creating a basic shell script. This script will ask the user for a series of three numbers. It will then ask the user if he or she wants to sum the three numbers or average them. You will also add the execute permission to the file to allow the file owner to run it.

You can perform this exercise using the virtual machine that comes with this book. Run snapshot 14-1 for the correctly configured environment.

 VIDEO   Please watch the Exercise 14-1 video for a demonstration on how to perform this task.

Complete the following:

1. If necessary, boot your Linux system and log in as a standard user.

2. Change to the ~/bin directory.

3. At the shell prompt, enter **vi domath**.

4. Enter the following script:

```
#!/bin/bash
#A script to do some simple math.
clear
declare -i A
declare -i B
declare -i C
declare -i ANSWER
echo "Enter the first number:"
read A
echo "Enter the second number:"
read B
echo "Enter the third number:"
read C
echo "What would you like to do with these numbers?"
echo "P: Add them up!"
echo "V: Average them!"
echo "Enter your choice:"
read CHOICE
case $CHOICE in
        p | P ) ANSWER=A+B+C
        ;;
        v | V ) ANSWER=A+B+C
                ANSWER=$ANSWER/3
        ;;
esac
echo "Your answer is" $ANSWER "."
exit 0
```

5. Save your changes to the script and exit vi.

6. Make the script executable by the file owner by entering **chmod u+x domath** at the shell prompt.

7. Test the script by entering **domath** at the shell prompt.

8. Test the script and verify that it works.

Processing Text Streams

When you're processing text streams within a script or when piping output at the shell prompt, there may be times when you need to filter the output of one command so that only certain portions of the text stream are actually passed along to the stdin of the next command. You can use a variety of tools to do this. In the last part of this chapter, we'll look at using the following commands:

- cut
- expand and unexpand
- fmt
- join and paste
- nl
- od
- pr

- sed and awk

- sort

- split

- tr

- uniq

- wc

Let's begin by looking at the cut command.

cut

The cut command is used to print columns or fields that you specify from a file to the standard output. By default, the tab character is used as a delimiter. The following options can be used with cut:

- **–b***list*   Select only these bytes.

- **–c***list*   Select only these characters.

- **–d***delim*   Use the specified character instead of tab for the field delimiter.

- **–f***list*   Select only the specified fields. Print any line that contains no delimiter character, unless the –s option is specified.

- **–s**   Do not print lines that do not contain delimiters.

For example, you could use the cut command to display all group names from the /etc/group file. Remember, the name of each group is contained in the first field of each line of the file. However, the group file uses colons as the delimiter between fields, so you must specify a colon instead of a tab as the delimiter. The command to do this is **cut –d: –f1 /etc/group**. An example is shown in Figure 14-2.

Let's next look at the expand and unexpand commands.

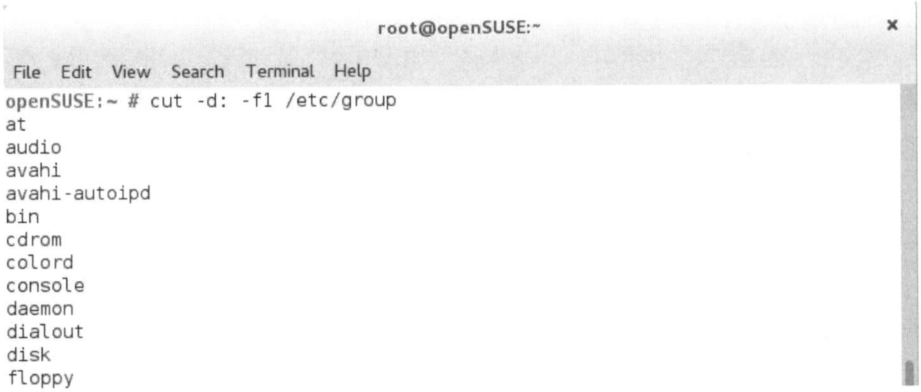

```
root@openSUSE:~                                               ×
File  Edit  View  Search  Terminal  Help
openSUSE:~ # cut -d: -f1 /etc/group
at
audio
avahi
avahi-autoipd
bin
cdrom
colord
console
daemon
dialout
disk
floppy
```

Figure 14-2   Using the cut command to extract a field from /etc/group

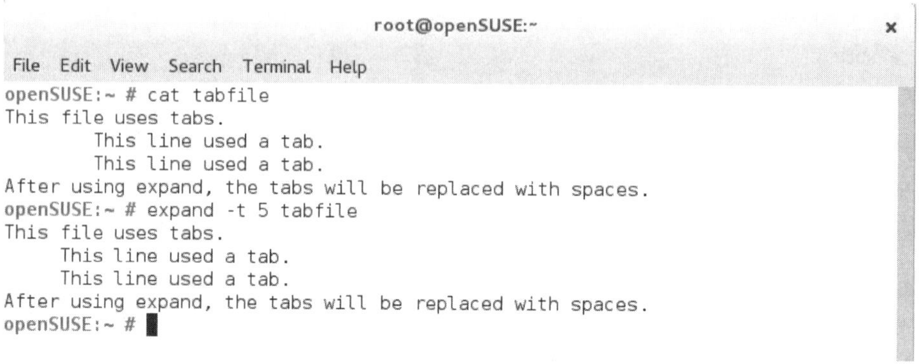

```
                        root@openSUSE:~                              ✕

 File  Edit  View  Search  Terminal  Help
 openSUSE:~ # cat tabfile
 This file uses tabs.
         This line used a tab.
         This line used a tab.
 After using expand, the tabs will be replaced with spaces.
 openSUSE:~ # expand -t 5 tabfile
 This file uses tabs.
      This line used a tab.
      This line used a tab.
 After using expand, the tabs will be replaced with spaces.
 openSUSE:~ # █
```

Figure 14-3   Using expand to replace tabs with spaces

expand and unexpand

The expand command is used to process a text stream and remove all instances of the tab character and replace them with the specified number of spaces (the default is eight). You can use the **–t** *number* option to specify a different number of spaces. The syntax is **expand –t** *number filename*. In Figure 14-3, the tab characters in the tabfile file are replaced with five spaces.

You can also use the unexpand command. The unexpand command works in the opposite manner as the expand command. It converts spaces in a text stream into tab characters. By default, eight contiguous spaces are converted into tabs. However, you can use the –t option to specify a different number of spaces.

It's important to note that, by default, unexpand will only convert leading spaces at the beginning of each line. To force it to convert all spaces of the correct number to tabs, you must include the –a option with the unexpand command. In Figure 14-4, the five spaces at the beginning of the second and third lines of the tabfile file that we created with the expand command are converted back to tab characters using the unexpand command.

Next, let's look at reformatting text with the fmt command.

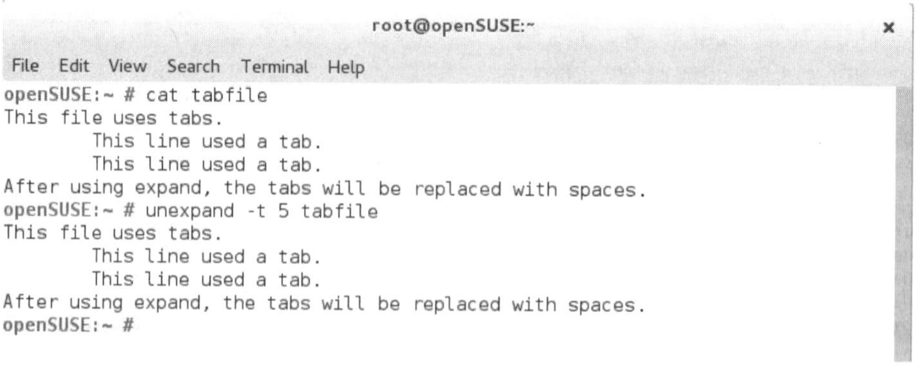

```
                        root@openSUSE:~                              ✕

 File  Edit  View  Search  Terminal  Help
 openSUSE:~ # cat tabfile
 This file uses tabs.
         This line used a tab.
         This line used a tab.
 After using expand, the tabs will be replaced with spaces.
 openSUSE:~ # unexpand -t 5 tabfile
 This file uses tabs.
         This line used a tab.
         This line used a tab.
 After using expand, the tabs will be replaced with spaces.
 openSUSE:~ #
```

Figure 14-4   Converting spaces into tabs with the unexpand command

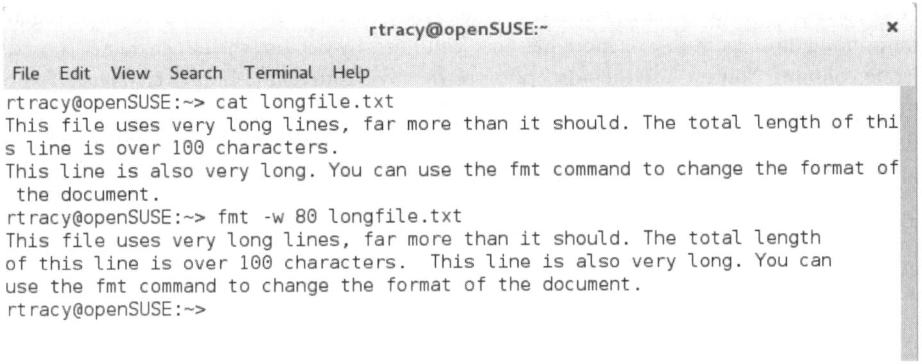

```
                          rtracy@openSUSE:~                          ✕

 File  Edit  View  Search  Terminal  Help
 rtracy@openSUSE:~> cat longfile.txt
 This file uses very long lines, far more than it should. The total length of thi
 s line is over 100 characters.
 This line is also very long. You can use the fmt command to change the format of
  the document.
 rtracy@openSUSE:~> fmt -w 80 longfile.txt
 This file uses very long lines, far more than it should. The total length
 of this line is over 100 characters.  This line is also very long. You can
 use the fmt command to change the format of the document.
 rtracy@openSUSE:~>
```

Figure 14-5   Using fmt to change the number of columns in a text file

fmt

You can use the fmt command to reformat a text file. It is commonly used to change the wrapping of long lines within the file to a more manageable width. The syntax for using fmt is **fmt** *option filename*.

For example, you could use the –w option with the fmt command to narrow the text of a file to 80 columns by entering **fmt –w 80 *filename***. An example is shown in Figure 14-5.

Let's look at the join and paste commands next.

join and paste

The join command prints a line from each of two specified input files that have identical join fields. The first field is the default join field, delimited by white space. You can specify a different join field using the **–j** *field* option.

For example, suppose you have two files. The first file (named firstnames) contains the following content:

```
1 Mike
2 Jenny
3 Joe
```

The second file (named lastnames) contains the following content:

```
1 Johnson
2 Doe
3 Jones
```

You can use the join command to join the corresponding lines from each file by entering **join –j 1 firstnames lastnames**. This is shown here:

```
rtracy@openSUSE:~> join -j 1 firstnames lastnames
1 Mike Johnson
2 Jenny Doe
3 Joe Jones
```

The paste command works in much the same manner as the join command. It pastes together corresponding lines from one or more files into columns. By default, the tab character is used to separate columns. You can use the –d*n* option to specify a different delimiter character. You can also use the –s option to put the contents of each file into a single line.

For example, you could use the paste command to join the corresponding lines from the firstnames and lastnames files by entering **paste firstnames lastnames**. An example is shown here:

```
rtracy@openSUSE:~> paste firstnames lastnames
1 Mike    1 Johnson
2 Jenny   2 Doe
3 Joe     3 Jones
```

Next, let's look at the nl command.

nl

The nl command determines the number of lines in a file. When you run the command, the output is written with a line number added to the beginning of each line in the file. The syntax is **nl** *filename*.

For example, in the example shown here, the nl command is used to add a number to the beginning of each line in the tabfile.txt file:

```
rtracy@openSUSE:~> nl tabfile.txt
     1 This file uses tabs.
     2          This line used a tab.
     3          This line used a tab.
     4 After using expand, the tabs will be replaced with spaces.
```

od

The od (octal dump) command is used to dump a file, including binary files. This utility can dump a file in several different formats, including octal, decimal, floating point, hex, and character format. The output from od is simple text, so you can use the other stream-processing tools we've been looking at to further filter it.

The od command can be very useful. For example, you can perform a dump of a file to locate stray characters in a file. Suppose you created a script file using an editor on a different operating system (such as Windows) and then tried to run it on Linux. Depending on which editor you used, there may be hidden formatting characters within the script text that aren't displayed by your text editor. However, they will be read by the bash shell when you try to run the script, thus causing errors. When you look at the script in an editor, everything seems fine.

You could use the od command to view a dump of the script to isolate where the problem-causing characters are located in the file. The syntax for using od is **od** *options filename*. Some of the more commonly used options include the following:

- **–b** Octal dump
- **–d** Decimal dump
- **–x** Hex dump
- **–c** Character dump

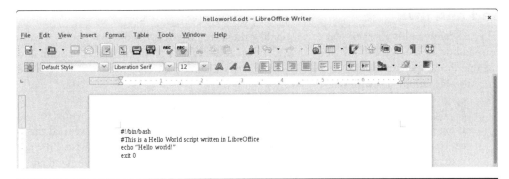

Figure 14-6 Creating a script in OpenOffice.org

For example, in Figure 14-6 a simple "Hello World" script has been created in the LibreOffice word processor and saved as an .odt file. As such, it has a myriad of hidden characters embedded in the text.

These characters obviously cannot be viewed from within LibreOffice. However, they can be viewed using the **od –c helloworld.odt** command. This is shown in Figure 14-7.

Next, let's review the pr command.

pr

The pr command is used to format text files for printing. It formats the file with pagination, headers, and columns. The header contains the date and time, filename, and page number. You can use the following options with pr:

- **–d** Double-space the output.
- **–l** *page_length* Set the page length to the specified number of lines. The default is 66.
- **–o** *margin* Offset each line with the specified number of spaces. The default margin is 0.

Next, we need to look at sed and awk.

```
rtracy@openSUSE:~
File  Edit  View  Search  Terminal  Help
rtracy@openSUSE:~> od -c helloworld.odt
0000000   P   K 003 004 024  \0  \0  \b  \0  \0   U   % 214   E   ^ 306
0000020   2  \f   '  \0  \0  \0   '  \0  \0  \0  \b  \0  \0  \0   m   i
0000040   m   e   t   y   p   e   a   p   p   l   i   c   a   t   i   o
0000060   n   /   v   n   d   .   o   a   s   i   s   .   o   p   e   n
0000100   d   o   c   u   m   e   n   t   .   t   e   x   t   P   K 003
0000120 004 024  \0  \0  \b  \0  \0  \0   U   % 214   E 231 225 002 375 266
0000140  \a  \0  \0 266  \a  \0  \0 030  \0  \0  \0   T   h   u   m   b
0000160   n   a   i   l   s   /   t   h   u   m   b   n   a   i   l   .
0000200   p   n   g 211   P   N   G  \r  \n 032  \n  \0  \0  \0  \r   I
0000220   H   D   R  \0  \0  \0 306  \0  \0 001  \0  \b 002  \0  \0  \0
0000240   g   ? 236 027  \0  \0  \a   }   I   D   A   T   x 234 355 332
0000260 333 213   M 377 037 307 361   q 026 243 344 020   ! 027   3   r
```

Figure 14-7 Creating a character dump with od

sed and awk

The sed command is a *stream* text editor. Unlike the interactive text editors that you've already learned how to use in this book, such as vi, a stream editor takes a stream of text as its stdin and then performs operations on it that you specify. Then, sed sends the results to stdout. You can use the following commands with sed:

- **s** Replaces instances of a specified text string with another text string. The syntax for using the s command is **sed s/*term1*/*term2*/**. For example, in Figure 14-8, I've used the cat command to display a file in the tux user's home directory named lipsum.txt. I then use cat to read lipsum.txt and then pipe the stdout to the stdin of the sed command and specify that the term "ipsum" be replaced with "IPSUM."

- **d** Deletes the specified text. For example, to delete every line of text from the stdin that contains the term "eos," you would enter **sed /eos/d**.

Remember, sed doesn't actually modify the source of the information—in this case, the lipsum .txt file. It takes its stdin, makes the changes, and sends it to the stdout. If you want to save the changes made by sed, you need to redirect its stdout to a file using >. For example, I could redirect the output from the command in Figure 14-8 to a file named lipsum_out.txt by entering **cat lipsum.txt | sed s/ipsum/IPSUM/ > lipsum_out.txt** at the shell prompt.

 NOTE The sed and awk commands discussed in this chapter are quite powerful. We only have space here to cover the basics you need for your Linux+/LPIC-1 exam. You should review the man page for both of these commands and use this information to explore the possibilities available.

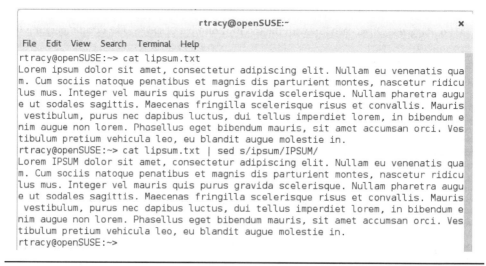

Figure 14-8 Using sed to replace text

Record	Field1	Field2	Field3	Field4	Field5	Field6	Field7	Field8	Field9	Field10	Field11
1	Lorem	ipsum	dolor	sit	amet,	consectetur	adipisicing	elit,			
2	sed	do	eiusmod	tempor	incididunt	ut	labore	et	dolore	magna	aliqua.

Table 14-1 Viewing a Text File as a Database

In addition to sed, you can also use awk to manipulate output. Like sed, awk can be used to receive output from another command as its stdin and manipulate it in a manner you specify. However, the way awk does this is a little bit different. The awk command treats each line of text it receives as a record. Each word in the line, separated by a space or tab character, is treated as a separate field within the record.

For example, consider the following text file:

```
Lorem ipsum dolor sit amet, consectetur adipisicing elit,
sed do eiusmod tempor incididunt ut labore et dolore magna aliqua.
Ut enim ad minim veniam, quis nostrud exercitation ullamco laboris
nisi ut aliquip ex ea commodo consequat. Duis aute irure dolor in
reprehenderit in voluptate velit esse cillum dolore eu fugiat nulla pariatur.
Excepteur sint occaecat cupidatat non proident, sunt in culpa qui officia
deserunt mollit anim id est laborum
```

According to awk, this file has seven records because it has seven separate lines of text. Each line of text has a carriage return/linefeed character at the end that creates a new line. This is the character awk uses to define the end of a record. The first record has eight fields, the second record has 11 fields, and so on. These are shown in Table 14-1.

Notice that white space, not punctuation, delimits the fields. Each field is referenced as $*field_ number*. For example, the first field of any record is referenced as $1, the second as $2, and so on.

Using awk, we can specify a field in a specific record and manipulate it in some manner. The syntax for using awk is **awk '*pattern* {*manipulation*}'**. For example, we could enter **cat lipsum2 .txt | awk '{print $1,$2,$3}'** to print out the first three words ("fields") of each line ("records"). Because we didn't specify a pattern to match on, awk simply prints out the first three words of every line. This is shown in Figure 14-9.

```
rtracy@openSUSE:~                                            ×

File  Edit  View  Search  Terminal  Help
rtracy@openSUSE:~> cat lipsum2.txt | awk '{print $1,$2,$3}'
Lorem ipsum dolor
sed do eiusmod
Ut enim ad
nisi ut aliquip
reprehenderit in voluptate
Excepteur sint occaecat
deserunt mollit anim
rtracy@openSUSE:~>
```

Figure 14-9 Using awk to print the first three fields of each record

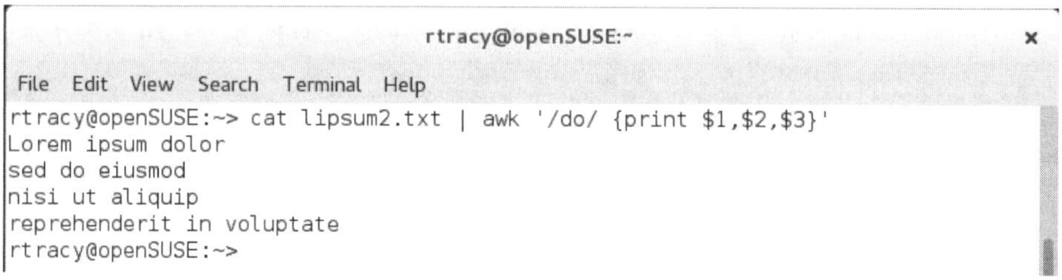

Figure 14-10 Using search patterns in an awk command

You can also include a pattern to specify exactly which records to search on. For example, suppose we only wanted to display the first three fields of any record that includes the text "do" somewhere in the line. To do this, you add a pattern of **/do/** to the command. This is shown in Figure 14-10.

You can also add your own text to the output. Just add it to the manipulation part of the command within quotes. In fact, you can also add control characters to output as well. Use the following:

- **\t** Inserts a tab character
- **\n** Adds a newline character
- **\f** Adds a form feed character
- **\r** Adds a carriage return character

For example, in Figure 14-11, I've entered

```
cat lipsum.txt | awk '/do/ {print "Field 1: "$1"\t", "Field 2: "$2"\t",
"Field 3: "$3"\t"}'
```

which causes each field to be labeled Field 1, Field 2, and Field 3. It also inserts a tab character between each field. As with sed, awk doesn't modify the original file. It sends its output to stdout (the screen). If you want to send it to a file, you can redirect it using >.

With this in mind, let's next look at the sort command.

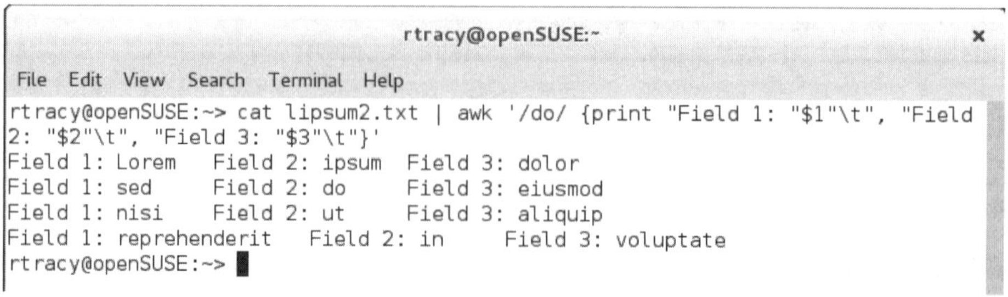

Figure 14-11 Adding text to the output of awk

sort

The sort command sorts the lines of a text file alphabetically. The output is written to the standard output. Some commonly used options for the sort command include the following:

- **–f** Fold lowercase characters to uppercase characters.
- **–M** Sort by month.
- **–n** Sort numerically.
- **–r** Reverse the sort order.

For example, the **sort –n –r firstnames** command sorts the lines in the firstnames file numerically in reverse order. This is shown here:

```
rtracy@openSUSE:~> sort -n -r firstnames
3 Joe
2 Jenny
1 Mike
```

The sort command can be used to sort the output of other commands (such as ps) by piping the standard output of the first command to the standard input of the sort command.

Next, let's look at the split command.

split

The split command splits an input file into a series of files (without altering the original input file). The default is to split the input file into 1,000-line segments. You can use the –n option to specify a different number of lines.

For example, the **split –1 firstnames outputfile_** command can be used to split the firstnames file into three separate files, each containing a single line. This is shown in Figure 14-12.

Next, let's look at the tr command.

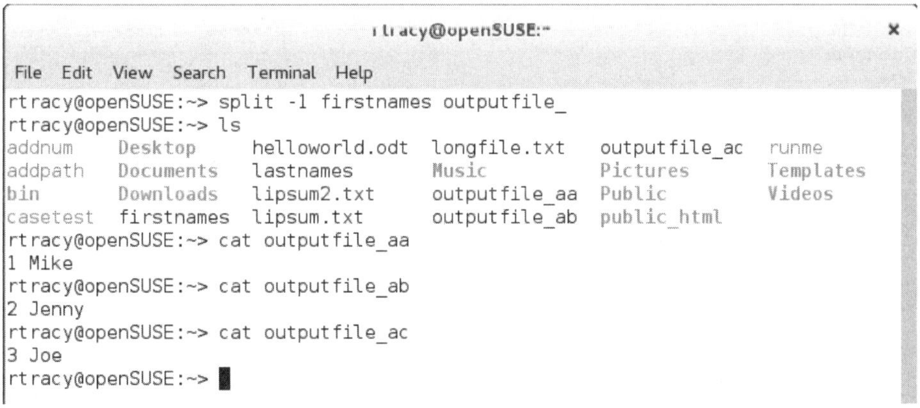

Figure 14-12 Splitting a file

tr

The tr command is used to translate or delete characters. However, be aware that this command does not work with files. To use it with files, you must first use a command such as cat to send the text stream to the standard input of tr. The syntax is **tr** *options X Y*. Some commonly used options for the tr command include the following:

- **–c** Use all characters not in X.
- **–d** Delete characters in X; do not translate.
- **–s** Replace each input sequence of a repeated character that is listed in X with a single occurrence of that character.
- **–t** First truncate X to the length of Y.

For example, to translate all lowercase characters in the lastnames file to uppercase characters, you could enter **cat lastnames | tr a-z A-Z**, as shown in this example:

```
rtracy@openSUSE:~> cat lastnames | tr a-z A-Z
1 JOHNSON
2 DOE
3 JONES
```

Next, let's look at the uniq command.

uniq

The uniq command reports or omits repeated lines. The syntax is **uniq** *options input output*. You can use the following options with the uniq command:

- **–d** Only print duplicate lines.
- **–u** Only print unique lines.

For example, suppose our lastnames file contained duplicate entries:

```
1 Johnson
1 Johnson
2 Doe
3 Jones
```

You could use the **uniq lastnames** command to remove the duplicate lines. This is shown in the following example:

```
rtracy@openSUSE:~> uniq lastnames
1 Johnson
2 Doe
3 Jones
```

Be aware that the uniq command only works if the duplicate lines are adjacent to each other. If the text stream you need to work with contains duplicate lines that are not adjacent, you can use the sort command to first make them adjacent and then pipe the output to the standard input of uniq.

Finally, let's look at the wc command.

wc

The wc command prints the number of newlines, words, and bytes in a file. The syntax is **wc** *options files*. You can use the following options with the wc command:

- **–c**   Print the byte counts.
- **–m**   Print the character counts.
- **–l**   Print the newline counts.
- **–L**   Print the length of the longest line.
- **–w**   Print the word counts.

For example, to print all counts and totals for the firstnames file, you would use the **wc firstnames** command, as shown in this example:

```
rtracy@openSUSE:~> wc firstnames
  3 6 21 firstnames
```

Let's practice processing text streams in the following exercise.

Exercise 14-2: Processing Text Streams

In this exercise, you will practice processing text streams. You can perform this exercise using the virtual machine that comes with this book. Run snapshot 14-2 for the correctly configured environment.

 VIDEO   Please watch the Exercise 14-2 video for a demonstration on how to perform this task.

Complete the following:

1. If necessary, boot your Linux system and log in as a standard user.

2. At the shell prompt, use the ls command to verify that the test.txt file exists in your home directory.

   This file contains the following text:

   ```
   Usu agam legere delicata ut, per democritum scriptorem an. Nec
   te zzril possim tincidunt, at qui probo mucius gubergren. Ea mei
   paulo cetero oportere, at pertinax liberavisse pri.
   ```

3. Use sed to replace the word "oportere" with the word "democritum" and send the output to a new file named testsed.txt by completing the following:

   a. At the shell prompt, enter **cat ~/test.txt | sed s/oportere/democritum/ 1>testsed.txt**.

   b. Use the cat command to verify that the word was replaced in the testsed.txt file.

4. Use awk to print the second word in each line of the test.txt file that has the characters "us" in it. Enter **cat ~/test.txt | awk '/us/ {print $2}'** at the shell prompt.

5. Which line matched and which word was subsequently printed on the screen?

Using Command Substitution and Shell Functions

Let's end this chapter by discussing the following features of the bash shell environment:

- Using command substitution
- Using shell functions

Using Command Substitution

The bash shell allows you to use *command substitution*, which means you can run a command and have its output pasted back on the command line as an argument for another command. Essentially, command substitution allows you to perform multiple tasks at once.

Command substitution works by first creating a child process that runs the first command. The stdout from this command is then piped back to the bash shell. The shell parses the output from the first command into words separated by white space. After the pipe from the first command closes (indicating the first command is done running), the shell starts another child process to run the second command using the stdout from the first command as arguments.

For example, suppose you wanted to use the tail command to view the last few lines of all the files in /etc that contained the text "192.168". You could use the following command substitution:

```
tail $(fgrep -l 192.168 /etc/*)
```

First, the **fgrep –l** command is run to search through all the files in the /etc directory for the text string "192.168". Using the –l option with fgrep causes the command to return a list of filenames only, not the actual matching text. This list of files is then piped to the tail command, which then displays the last few lines of each file it receives.

You can use the xargs command within the bash shell to accomplish a similar task. For example, it's possible that command substitution could fail if the first command pipes too many results back to the second command. In this situation, you end up with a "too many arguments" error, as shown here:

```
Argument list too long
```

Due to a limit imposed by the Linux kernel, the maximum length of a bash command line is 128KB. If this is the case, you can use xargs instead of command substitution. The xargs command breaks down a long command line into 128KB chunks and passes each chunk as an argument to the command listed within the xargs command line. For example, suppose you wanted to delete all the backup files (which usually end with a ~ character) from your home directory. You could use the following command:

```
find ~/ -name "*~" | xargs rm
```

The find command first generates a list of matching files and then pipes it to the input of the xargs command, which then processes the text stream 128KB at a time and sends it to the stdin of the rm command.

Let's end this chapter by looking at using shell functions.

Using Shell Functions

The bash shell allows you to define functions that can be used from the shell prompt or from within a script. When you define a function, you essentially define a new "command" that you can call and use as if it were a standard internal or external command. The function contains a list of commands you want to run, just like the scripts we discussed earlier. However, a function is not saved in a file; it only exists in memory. That means it will go away if you close the current shell session. Of course, you can add the function definition to one of your bash configuration files to make it persistent. The syntax for a function is shown here:

```
function_name()
{
  command1
  command2
  command3
}
```

Let's look at a simple function example at the shell prompt. This function doesn't do much; it simply displays the contents of a directory you specify as an argument for the function:

```
rtracy@openSUSE:~> show ()
> {
> ls -l $1
> }
rtracy@openSUSE:~> show /tmp
total 84
drwx------ 2 rtracy users  4096 2011-04-30 04:00 keyring-eiVJ50
drwx------ 2 rtracy users  4096 2011-06-24 11:40 keyring-rGEjnD
drwx------ 2 gdm    gdm    4096 2011-06-24 11:40 orbit-gdm
```

Notice that the first argument I specified on the command line when I called the show function was passed as the $1 variable to the ls –l command. If I had specified multiple arguments when I called the function, they would have been passed to the appropriately numbered variable ($1, $2, $3, and so on).

Functions can also be defined within a shell script. Functions are a great timesaver when used in this manner for tasks within a script that occur repeatedly. Instead of rewriting the same code multiple times, you simply define the function once at the beginning of the script and then call it by name wherever it is needed throughout the rest of the script.

For example, you could declare a function at the beginning of a script that checks to see if a file exists. An example is shown here:

```
function isitthere ()
{
   if [ -s $1 ]
     then
        echo $1 "file exists!"
     else
       echo $1 "file does not exist!"
   fi
}
```

Then you could call the isitthere function anywhere needed throughout the rest of the script. For example, you could use a read statement to prompt the user for a filename and write the input to a variable named MYFILE. You could then pass that variable to the function using this statement:

```
isitthere $MYFILE
```

The function would then read the value of MYFILE, pass it to $1, and then use its if/then/else statement to see if the file exists.

If you really get into script writing, you will likely find yourself reusing a lot of the same functions over and over in many different scripts. Instead of redefining them over and over in each script file, you can define a commonly used function once in its own separate file. The function can then be loaded from the file into whatever script you are currently working on. When you do, the script will read the file, load the function, and execute it. Essentially, you are creating script libraries that can be reused, hence, saving a lot of time.

For example, we could take the commands that we defined earlier for the isitthere function, and put them in a separate script file named isitthere.sh:

```
#!/bin/bash
isitthere ()
{
    if [ -s $1 ]
      then
          echo $1 "file exists!"
      else
          echo $1 "file does not exist!"
   fi
}
```

Now we can call and use the isitthere() function from the isitthere.sh file in different scripts, using the source command. The syntax is **source *filename arguments***. As before, we could use a read statement in the script to prompt the user for a filename, and write the input to a variable named MYFILE. We could then load the isitthere() function from the isitthere.sh file and pass the value of the variable to the function. This could be done using the following statement in the script:

```
source isitthere.sh $MYFILE
```

Of course, this example assumes the isitthere.sh file is located in a directory that is contained in the PATH environment variable. If it isn't, then the full path to the file in the source statement must be specified.

You are now an experienced bash shell user! Let's review what you learned in this chapter.

EXAM TIP You can also include environment variables in your scripts. For example, you could include the **MAILTO=root** line in your script to have notification events or other conditional events mailed to the root superuser account. You could even define a custom PATH environment variable by adding **PATH=** to your script followed by a list of paths.

Chapter Review

In this chapter, you learned how to create basic shell scripts on a Linux system. A shell script is a text file that is interpreted and run by the bash shell. A shell script contains a series of commands that automate tasks and process information for you. A shell script is composed of the following parts:

- #!/bin/bash
- #Comments
- shell commands
- exit 0

Shell scripts can be created and edited with any text editor. They can be executed in one of two ways:

- Entering **/bin/bash** *script_filename*
- Adding the execute permission to the script file using the chmod utility and then entering the filename of the script at the shell prompt

In addition, you can also add the path to the script file to your users' PATH environment variables so they won't have to remember the full path to the file to use it. Alternatively, you can also move the script file to a directory that is already in the users' PATH environment variable, such as ~/bin.

In addition to running commands from a script, you can also read input from the user and assign it to a variable using the **read** *variable_name* command in a script. Script variables don't need to be declared if you are going to read text into them. However, if you want to read numbers into a variable that will be actually treated as numbers (so that you can perform arithmetic functions, for example), you need to declare them first using the **declare −i** *variable_name* command in the script.

You can also use control structures in your scripts. Control structures allow you to configure your scripts so that they branch or loop based on conditions that you supply. To make a script that branches in two directions, you can use an if/then/else structure in your script. If the condition you specify in the structure is true, then one set of commands (under then) is executed. If the condition is false, then the commands under the else portion of the structure are executed. The syntax for using if/then/else structures in a script is as follows:

```
if condition then
      commands
else
      commands
fi
```

You can use the test command in an if/then/else structure to test a condition. You can use the following options with test:

- **−d**   Checks to see if the specified file exists and if it is a directory.
- **−e**   Checks to see if the specified file exists. It doesn't care whether it is a file or directory.
- **−f**   Checks to see if the specified file exists and if it is a regular file.

- **–G**   Checks to see if the specified file exists and is owned by a specified group.
- **–h or –L**   Checks to see if the specified file exists and if it is a symbolic link.
- **–O**   Checks to see if the specified file exists and if it is owned by the specified user ID.
- **–r**   Checks to see if the specified file exists and if the read permission is granted.
- **–w**   Checks to see if the specified file exists and if the write permission is granted.
- **–x**   Checks to see if the specified file exists and if the execute permission is granted.

If you want more than two branches in your script, you can use the case structure. The case structure is an advanced if/then/else statement. With a case structure, you can evaluate multiple conditions and execute commands based upon which condition is true. The case structure is a handy way to replace multiple if/then/else statements in a script. The syntax for using the case structure is as follows:

```
case variable in
      condition_1 ) commands
      ;;
      condition_2 ) commands
      ;;
      condition_3 ) commands
      ;;
esac
```

You can also use looping control structures within a shell script. Looping structures come in three varieties: the *while* loop, the *until* loop, and the *for* loop.

The structure of a while loop is as follows:

```
while condition
do
      script commands
done
```

A while loop will keep processing over and over and over until the condition evaluates to false.

You can also use an until loop in your script. An until loop runs over and over as long as the condition is false. As soon as the condition is true, it stops. The structure for an until loop is as follows:

```
until condition
do
      script commands
done
```

You can also use a for loop, which loops a specific number of times. It is very common to use the seq command within a for loop to create the sequence of numbers to determine how many times it will loop. There are three options for creating a number sequence with seq:

- If you specify a single value, the sequence starts at one, increments by one, and ends at the specified value.

- If you specify two values, the sequence starts at the first value, increments by one, and ends at the second value.

- If you specify three values, the sequence starts at the first value, increments by the second value, and ends at the third value.

We then discussed how to process text streams to manipulate and modify text within a script or within a pipe. We looked at the following utilities:

- **cut**   The cut command is used to print columns or fields that you specify from a file to the standard output. By default, the tab character is used as a delimiter.

- **expand and unexpand**   The expand command is used to process a text stream and remove all instances of the tab character and replace them with the specified number of spaces (the default is eight). The unexpand command works in the opposite manner as the expand command. It converts spaces in a text stream into tab characters.

- **fmt**   You can use the fmt command to reformat a text file.

- **join and paste**   The join command prints a line from each of two specified input files that have identical join fields. The first field is the default join field, delimited by white space. The paste command works in much the same manner as the join command. It pastes together corresponding lines from one or more files into columns. By default, the tab character is used to separate columns.

- **nl**   The nl command determines the number of lines in a file. When you run the command, the output is written with a line number added to the beginning of each line in the file.

- **od**   The od (octal dump) command is used to dump a file, including binary files. This utility can dump a file in several different formats, including octal, decimal, floating point, hex, and character format.

- **pr**   The pr command is used to format text files for printing. It formats the file with pagination, headers, and columns. The header contains the date and time, filename, and page number.

- **sed and awk**   The sed utility is a stream editor. It can be used to edit text coming from another command's stdout. You can use command-line options to search and replace, or delete text and display it on screen or write it to a file. The awk command can also be used to manipulate a stream of text. The awk utility views each line arriving at its stdin as a record. Each word in the line is treated as a field. You can use awk to reference a specific field (word) in a specific record (line).

- **sort**   The sort command sorts the lines of a text file alphabetically.

- **split**   The split command splits an input file into a series of files (without altering the original input file).

- **tr**   The tr command is used to translate or delete characters.

- **uniq**   The uniq command reports or omits repeated lines.

- **wc**   The wc command prints the number of newlines, words, and bytes in a file.

We ended this chapter by discussing command substitution and functions. I related that the bash shell allows you to run a command and have its output pasted back on the command line as an argument for another command. This is called command substitution. In situations where too much data is sent from the first command to the second command, you can use the xargs command to parse the output into manageable 128KB chunks for processing.

We also looked at functions. The bash shell allows you to define functions that can be used from the shell prompt or from within a script. When you define a function, you define a new command that you can call and use as if it were a standard internal or external command. The function contains a list of commands you want to run. You can use script structures (such as if/then/else) within a function.

Accelerated Review

- Shell scripts are text files that contain a variety of commands that can be used to automate tasks and process information.

- All shell scripts begin with **#!/bin/bash** to specify that the bash shell should be used to run the script.

- You should include a comment at the beginning of each script that describes what it does.

- Your shell scripts should end with **exit 0** to tell the script to exit.

- You can run shell scripts by running **/bin/bash** *script_filename* or by adding the execute permission to the script file.

- You can read user input in a script using **read** *variable_name* in a script.

- To make your scripts more powerful, you can add branching structures in a script.

- Control structures allow you to configure your scripts so that they branch or loop according to conditions that you supply.

- To make a script that branches in two directions, you can use an if/then/else structure in your script.

- If the condition you specify in the structure is true, then one set of commands (under then) is executed.

- If the condition is false, then the commands under the else portion of the structure are executed.

- You can use the test command in an if/then/else structure to test a condition.

- If you want more than two branches in your script, you can use the case structure.

- With a case structure, you can evaluate multiple conditions and execute a series of commands that are executed according to which condition is true.

- You can also use looping control structures within a shell script.

- Looping structures come in three varieties: the while loop, the until loop, and the for loop.

- A while loop executes over and over until a specified condition is no longer true.

- You can also use an until loop in your script.

- An until loop runs over and over as long as the condition is false. As soon as the condition is true, it stops.

- You can also use a for loop, which loops a specific number of times.

- It is very common to use the seq command within a for loop to create the sequence of numbers to determine how many times it will loop.

- There are three options for creating a number sequence with seq:

  - If you specify a single value, the sequence starts at one, increments by one, and ends at the specified value.

  - If you specify two values, the sequence starts at the first value, increments by one, and ends at the second value.

  - If you specify three values, the sequence starts at the first value, increments by the second value, and ends at the third value.

- You can process text streams to manipulate and modify text within a script or within a pipe.

- You can use the following utilities to process a text stream:

  - cut

  - expand

  - unexpand

  - fmt

  - join

  - paste

  - nl

  - od

  - pr

  - sed

  - awk

  - sort

  - split

  - tr

  - uniq

  - wc

- Command substitution allows you to run a command and have its output pasted back on the command line as an argument for another command.

- You can use the xargs command to parse the output into manageable 128KB chunks for processing.

- You can define your own functions that can be used from the shell prompt or from within a script.

- Defining a function creates a new command that you can call and use as if it were a standard internal or external command.

Questions

1. Which of the following elements must be included at the beginning of every shell script?

   A. #Comment

   B. #!/bin/bash

   C. exit 0

   D. #begin script

2. You've created a shell script in your home directory named myscript. How can you execute it? (Choose two.)

   A. Enter **/bin/bash ~/myscript** at the shell prompt.

   B. Enter **myscript** at the shell prompt.

   C. Select Computer | Run in the graphical desktop; then enter **~/myscript** and select **Run**.

   D. Enter **run ~/myscript** at the shell prompt.

   E. Enter **chmod u+x ~/myscript**; then enter **~/myscript** at the shell prompt.

3. Which command will create a new variable named TOTAL and set its type to be "integer"?

   A. variable –i TOTAL

   B. declare –i TOTAL

   C. declare TOTAL –t integer

   D. TOTAL=integer

4. You need to display the text "Hello world" on the screen from within a shell script. Which command will do this?

   A. echo "Hello world"

   B. read Hello world

   C. writeln "Hello world"

   D. print "Hello world"

5. From within a shell script, you need to prompt users to enter their phone number. You need to assign the value they enter into a variable named $PHONE. Which command will do this?

   A. read "What is your phone number?" $PHONE

   B. read $PHONE

    C. read PHONE

    D. ? "What is your phone number?" PHONE

6. Which command can be used from within an if/then/else structure to evaluate whether or not a specified condition is true?

    A. eval

    B. ==

    C. test

    D. <>

7. Which command will evaluate to True within an if/then/else structure in a shell script if the variable num1 is less than the variable num2?

    A. eval num1 < num2

    B. test num1 < num2

    C. test num1 –lt num2

    D. test "num1" != "num2"

    E. eval "num1" != "num2"

8. In a shell script, you need to prompt the user to select from one of seven different options presented with the echo command. Which control structure would best evaluate the user's input and run the appropriate set of commands?

    A. while loop

    B. for loop

    C. until loop

    D. if/then/else

    E. case

9. Which control structure will keep processing over and over until a specified condition evaluates to false?

    A. while loop

    B. for loop

    C. until loop

    D. if/then/else

    E. case

10. Which control structures are considered to be branching structures? (Choose two.)

    A. while loop

    B. for loop

    C. until loop

    D. if/then/else

    E. case

11. Which control structure will keep processing over and over as long as the specified condition evaluates to false?

    A. while loop

    B. for loop

    C. until loop

    D. if/then/else

    E. case

12. Which control structure will process a specified number of times?

    A. while loop

    B. for loop

    C. until loop

    D. if/then/else

    E. case

13. Consider the following use of the seq command: **seq 3 9**. What sequence of numbers will this command generate?

    A. 3, 4, 5, 6, 7, 8, 9

    B. 3, 6, 9

    C. 1, 4, 7, 10, 13, 16, 19, 22, 25

    D. 9, 18, 27

14. Which command can be used to print columns or fields that you specify from a file to the standard output using the tab character as a delimiter?

    A. cut

    B. pr

    C. fmt

    D. sort

15. Which command can be used to process a text stream and remove all instances of the tab character and replace them with eight spaces?

    A. cut

    B. replace –t 8

    C. expand

    D. unexpand

16. Which command can process a file or text stream and add a number to the beginning of each new line?

    A. join

    B. paste

C. fmt

D. nl

17. You want to send the contents of the logfile.txt file in the current directory to the sort command to sort them alphabetically and display them on the screen. Which commands will do this? (Choose two.)

    A. sort < logfile.txt

    B. sort logfile.txt

    C. sort < logfile.txt –o "screen"

    D. sort < logfile.txt > screen

    E. sort –n logfile.txt

18. You want to display on screen the sixth, seventh, and eighth words in any line of /var/log/ messages that has the term "syslog" in it. Which of the following commands will do this?

    A. cat /var/log/messages | awk '/syslog/ {print $6,$7,$8}'

    B. cat /var/log/messages | awk '/syslog/ {print 6,7,8}'

    C. cat /var/log/messages | awk /syslog/ {print $6,$7,$8}

    D. cat /var/log/messages | awk 'syslog {print 6,7,8}'

19. Your word processing application has left hundreds of backup files in various locations on your hard drive. These files are no longer needed and are consuming a lot of disk space. Because there are so many of them, you don't want to delete them one at a time. You tried using the find command to send a list of backup files (that all end with a ~ character) to the rm command, but the list of files was too long. What should you do?

    A. Pipe the output from find to the xargs command.

    B. Delete the files one at a time using rm.

    C. Pipe the output from find to the del command instead of rm.

    D. Pipe the output from find to the rmdir command instead of rm.

20. You need to search for and replace the word "June" with the word "July" in a file named proj_sched.txt in your home directory and send the output to a new file named new_ proj_sched.txt. Which command will do this?

    A. cat ~/ proj_sched.txt | sed s/June/July/

    B. cat ~/ proj_sched.txt | awk s/June/July/

    C. cat ~/ proj_sched.txt | awk s/June/July/ 1> new_proj_sched.txt

    D. cat ~/ proj_sched.txt | sed s/June/July/ 1> new_proj_sched.txt

Answers

1. **B.** The **#!/bin/bash** element must be included at the beginning of every bash shell script.

2. **A, E.** You can enter **/bin/bash ~/myscript** or **chmod u+x ~/myscript** to make the script execute.

3. **B.** The **declare –i TOTAL** command will create the TOTAL variable and type it as integer.

4. **A.** The **echo "Hello world"** command will display the text "Hello world" on the screen from within a shell script.

5. **C.** The **read PHONE** command in a shell script will assign the value entered by the user into a variable named $PHONE.

6. **C.** The **test** command can be used from within an if/then/else structure to evaluate whether or not a specified condition is true.

7. **C.** The **test num1 –lt num2** command will evaluate to True within an if/then/else structure if the variable num1 is less than the variable num2.

8. **E.** The case structure is the best option presented to evaluate the user's choice of multiple selections and run the appropriate set of commands as a result.

9. **A.** A while loop will keep processing over and over until the specified condition evaluates to false.

10. **D, E.** The if/then/else and case structures are considered to be branching structures because they branch the script in one of several directions based on how a specified condition evaluates.

11. **C.** The until loop control structure will keep processing over and over as long as the specified condition evaluates to false.

12. **B.** The for loop control structure will process a specified number of times.

13. **A.** The **seq 3 9** command will generate the following sequence of numbers: 3, 4, 5, 6, 7, 8, 9. The first number specifies the starting number, whereas the second number specifies the ending number in the sequence. Because an increment is not specified, the sequence increments by 1.

14. **A.** The **cut** command can be used to print columns or fields that you specify from a file to the standard output using the tab character as a delimiter.

15. **C.** The **expand** command can be used to process a text stream and remove all instances of the tab character and replace them with eight spaces.

16. **D.** The **nl** command can be used to process a file or text stream and add a number to the beginning of each new line.

17. **A, B.** The **sort < logfile.txt** command and the **sort logfile.txt** command will both send the contents of the logfile.txt file to the sort command to sort its lines alphabetically and display them on the screen.

18. **A.** The **cat /var/log/messages | awk '/syslog/ {print $6,$7,$8}'** command will find instances of "syslog" in the stdout of cat and print the sixth, seventh, and eighth words in each matching line.

19. **A.** The xargs command can be used in this situation to break the data down into 128KB chunks before sending it to the rm command, which is small enough for the shell to process.

20. **D.** The **cat ~/ proj_sched.txt | sed s/June/July/ 1> new_proj_sched.txt** command will search the proj_sched.txt file for the word "June" and replace all instances with the word "July." The output from sed will be written to a file named new_proj_sched.txt.

## CHAPTER 15

Managing Linux Network Settings

In this chapter, you will learn about:

- Understanding IP networks
- Configuring network addressing parameters
- Troubleshooting network problems

Up to this point in the book, we've focused on configuring and using Linux as a stand-alone computer system. However, Linux can also be configured to function in a networked environment. Unlike many operating systems, Linux was designed from the ground up with networking in mind.

One of the things I love about Linux is the fact that you can take just about any distribution and configure it to fill a wide variety of roles on your network—all for little or no cost. For example, you can configure a Linux system as any of the following:

- A networked workstation
- A file and print server
- A database server
- A DHCP server
- A DNS server
- A web server
- An e-mail server
- A domain controller
- An LDAP directory server
- A gateway router
- A packet-filtering, stateful, or application-level firewall

Isn't Linux fantastic? With other operating systems, you have to pay a lot of money to get this kind of functionality. With Linux, you've got just about everything you need to set up a very complex network. In this chapter, we're going to focus on enabling basic networking on your Linux system. In the next chapter, we'll discuss how to set up a variety of Linux services.

EXAM TIP   Be sure you are very comfortable with Linux networking basics before taking your Linux+/LPIC-1 exam. The exam assumes you have a solid understanding of the Internet Protocol (IP). Be sure you understand how IP addressing works with both IPv4 and IPv6. You should be able to look at any given IP address and identify it as a class A, B, or C address. You should also be able to identify the network and node portions of the address using the subnet mask. You should know what the DNS server and default gateway router addresses are used for when configuring network settings on a Linux system.

You should also know how to install a network interface in the system, including an Ethernet card and a modem. You should know how to use the ifconfig command to manage the network interfaces installed in your system. You should also know how to use commands such as dig, ping, netstat, and traceroute to troubleshoot your network configuration.

Let's begin this chapter by reviewing how the IP protocol can be used to enable communications between networked systems.

Understanding IP Networks

Before you can configure your Linux system to participate on a computer network, you have to first install some kind of network interface and then configure it to work on your particular network. Back in the early days of networking, you could choose from a variety of network interfaces and network protocols. However, most of the networks you will work with today will be Ethernet networks using the IP protocol. In light of this situation, the Linux+/LPIC-1 exam is heavily focused on using Ethernet boards configured with the IP protocol in Linux systems. We're going to spend the first part of this chapter learning how to do this.

For your Linux+/LPIC-1 exam, you need to be proficient with the IP protocol (both versions 4 and 6). You need to know how to configure the protocol such that a system can participate on the network. To make sure you have the information you need, we're going to briefly review IP addressing in this part of this chapter. We'll cover the following topics:

- What is a protocol?
- How IPv4 addresses work
- How IPv4 subnet masks work
- Specifying the DNS server and default gateway router addresses
- Using IPv6

Let's begin by discussing what a protocol is.

What Is a Protocol?

So what exactly is a protocol? Strictly speaking, a *protocol* is a set of rules, and in the context of networking, a protocol is the set of rules that govern communication between two systems. A good analogy for a protocol is a human language. Before two people can communicate, they must speak the same language; otherwise, no information can be transferred between them. For example, suppose you were to call someone on the phone who doesn't speak your language. Even though they have picked up the receiver and are listening to the information you are sending, they don't understand what you are saying. Why? Because you don't share a common language.

The same holds true with computer systems. Before they can share information, they must be configured to use the same protocol. The protocol specifies how the information is encoded and sent on the network so that that receiving system can interpret it and reconstruct the data that was originally sent.

As discussed previously, there are many different protocols you can use on a computer network. However, for your Linux+/LPIC-1 exam, you need to be familiar with the IP protocol, which is the networking protocol used on the Internet. IP works in conjunction with other protocols, such as the Transmission Control Protocol (TCP) or the User Datagram Protocol (UDP) to divide information being transmitted on the network into chunks.

 NOTE The two versions of the IP protocol are called IPv4 and IPv6. We're going to be discussing IPv4 first in this chapter and then we will explore IPv6.

To understand how this process works, you need to have a solid understanding of the OSI Reference Model. The OSI Reference Model was designed by delegates from major computer and telecom companies back in 1983. The goal was to design a network communications model that was modular so that products from different vendors could interoperate. Prior to this, networking solutions tended to be proprietary, forcing implementers to purchase all of their components from the same vendor. By defining the OSI Reference Model, the industry created a standard that allows you to pick and choose components from a variety of vendors.

The OSI Reference Model divides the communication process between two hosts into layers. This is shown in Figure 15-1.

Figure 15-1
The OSI Reference Model

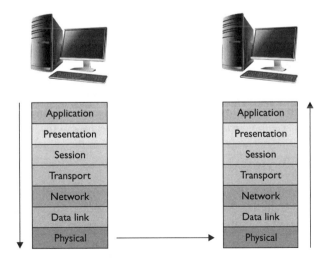

These layers break down the overall communication process into specific tasks. Information flows down through the layers on the sending system and then is transmitted on the network medium. The information then flows up the layers on the receiving side.

The OSI Reference Model has seven layers:

- **Physical**   Transmits electrical signals between hosts.

- **Data Link**   Defines the rules and procedures for accessing the physical layer. It defines how hosts are identified on the network and how the network medium is accessed. It also specifies how to verify that the data received from the physical layer doesn't have any errors. Information received from upper layers is organized into *datagrams.*

- **Network**   Enables the routing of the data. It specifies how to recognize the address of neighboring nodes and routers. It also specifies how to determine the next network point to which a packet should be forwarded toward its destination. The Internet Protocol (IP) operates at this layer, as does the Internet Control Message Protocol (ICMP).

- **Transport**   On the sending host, the Transport layer receives information from the upper layers of the OSI model and divides it into small, transmittable chunks called *packets.* On the receiving host, the Transport layer reassembles packets from datagrams received from lower layers of the OSI model. The Transport layer provides error-checking mechanisms to ensure that data arrives at the destination host intact. The Transmission Control Protocol (TCP) and User Datagram Protocol (UDP) operate at this layer.

- **Session**   Responsible for establishing and maintaining connections between source and destination network hosts. These connections are called *sessions.*

- **Presentation**   Responsible for ensuring that information passing through the OSI layers is formatted correctly for the application on the destination system.

- **Application**   Responsible for providing applications with a way to access the network.

The IP protocol itself is used only to make sure each packet arrives at the destination system. The TCP or UDP protocol is used with IP to fragment the data from the sending host and then reassemble and resequence it when it arrives at the destination system. This is shown in Figure 15-2.

The Internet Protocol (IP) is the protocol used on the Internet. It is a connectionless protocol designed to ensure data arrives at its destination host. The IP protocol relies on information being broken down into transmittable chunks (packets) by the TCP or UDP protocol. Each packet is treated by IP as an independent data unit, independent of other data units. The key thing to remember about IP is the fact that it isn't concerned with fragmentation or resequencing. It's only concerned with making sure each packet arrives at the destination.

The job of keeping track of individual packets belongs to the Transmission Control Protocol (TCP). TCP is one of the two original components of the IP protocol suite. The entire suite is commonly referred to as TCP/IP, but that isn't technically correct because UDP may be used with IP as well.

The TCP protocol ensures data is reliably exchanged directly between two network hosts. It does this by requiring acknowledgment of each packet sent from the sender to the receiver. Because of the way the IP protocol works, packets can be lost, duplicated, or delivered out of

Figure 15-2

Transferring data with the IP protocol

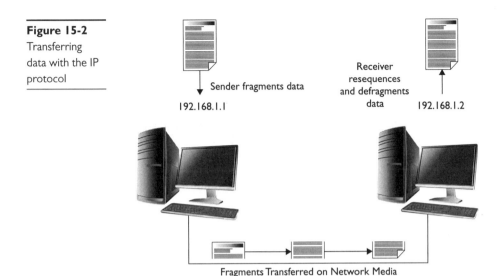

Sender fragments data

192.168.1.1

Receiver resequences and defragments data

192.168.1.2

Fragments Transferred on Network Media

sequence. TCP detects these problems, requests retransmission of lost packets, and resequences packets received out of order. Essentially, TCP ensures the final reassembled data on the receiving system is a perfect copy of the data originally transmitted.

Using TCP with IP is kind of like using signature confirmation with a shipping company. When you send a package, the shipper requires the receiver to sign for the package, allowing the sender to verify that the package was received correctly. TCP/IP works in much the same manner.

The TCP protocol is used by upper-layer applications that require a high degree of data integrity, including

- Web servers
- E-mail servers
- FTP servers

However, the data fidelity offered by TCP comes at a cost, primarily in the form of latency. TCP requires a fair amount of network and processing overhead. Not all network applications actually require the high degree of data fidelity provided by TCP. Some upper-layer applications require less latency and can tolerate less reliability. These applications use the User Datagram Protocol (UDP) protocol instead of TCP.

UDP functions in a manner similar to TCP; however, it is a *connectionless* protocol. With UDP, IP packets are sent unacknowledged. UDP is usually implemented with applications that send very small amounts of data at a time. It assumes that error checking and correction is either not necessary or will be performed by the application, thus avoiding the processing overhead.

In this respect, UDP is similar to sending someone a postcard through the mail. A postcard doesn't contain much data, and the receiver doesn't have to sign for it. Essentially, the sender assumes that the mail carrier is reasonably reliable and that the information on the postcard isn't important enough to require the receiver to sign for it. UDP works in much the same way. Some upper-layer applications that make use of UDP include

- Streaming audio and video
- VoIP

In addition to IP, TCP, and UDP, you also need to be familiar with the Internet Control Message Protocol (ICMP) for your Linux+/LPIC-1 exam. ICMP is another core protocol in the IP protocol suite. It differs in purpose from TCP and UDP, which are transport protocols. The primary role of ICMP is to test and verify network communications between hosts.

For example, to test network connectivity, the ping utility will send ICMP Echo Request packets to a remote host. If the host receives them, it will respond with an ICMP Echo Response packet to the sender. If the ICMP Echo Response packet is received, the sender knows that a viable network connection exists between the sender and receiver and that the receiver is responding to network requests. If an ICMP Echo Response packet is not received, the sender knows something is wrong and can begin troubleshooting communications.

For your Linux+/LPIC-1 exam, you also need to understand the concept of IP ports, which are provided by both the TCP and UDP protocols at the Transport layer. In essence, a *port* is a logical connection provided by TCP and UDP for upper-layer protocols. Ports allow a single host with a single IP address to provide multiple network services. Each service uses the same IP address but operates using a different TCP or UDP port number.

For example, suppose you have a network server with an IP address of 192.168.1.1 assigned to it. You could configure both a web server and an FTP server to run at the same time on this server. Each service will listen for requests on the interface assigned an IP address of 192.168.1.1. However, the web server runs on port 80, whereas the FTP server runs on ports 20 and 21. Requests sent to port 80 are handled by the web service, whereas information sent to ports 20 and 21 is handled by the FTP service.

 NOTE The FTP service is somewhat unique in that it uses two ports. One is for the control connection (port 21) and the other (port 20) is used for actually transferring data. Most services use only a single port.

You should become familiar with the various categories used to organize IP ports. Port numbers can range from 0 to 65536. The way these ports are used is regulated by the Internet Corporation for Assigned Names and Numbers (ICANN). IP ports are lumped into three different categories:

- **Well-known ports** Reserved for specific services, well-known ports are those numbered from 0 to 1023. Here are some examples:
  - Ports 20 and 21: FTP
  - Port 22: Secure Shell (SSH)
  - Port 23: Telnet
  - Port 25: SMTP
  - Port 53: DNS

- Port 80: HTTP
- Port 110: POP3
- Port 119: NNTP (news)
- Port 123: NTP (time synchronization)
- Ports 137, 138, 139: NetBIOS
- Port 143: IMAP
- Port 161: SNMP
- Port 162: SNMP Traps
- Port 389: LDAP
- Port 443: HTTPS
- Port 465: SMTP using TLS/SSL (SMTPS)
- Port 514: Syslog remote logging
- Port 636: Secure LDAP
- Port 993: IMAP using TLS/SSL (IMAPS)
- Port 995: POP3 using TLS/SSL (POP3S)

- **Registered ports**   ICANN has reserved ports 1024 through 49151 for special implementations. Organizations can create their own network service and then apply for a registered port number to be assigned to it.
- **Dynamic ports**   Dynamic ports are also called *private ports*. Ports 49152 through 65535 are designated as dynamic ports. They are available for use by any network service. They are frequently used by network services that need to establish a temporary connection. For example, the service may negotiate a dynamic port with the client. It will then use that port during the session. When the session is complete, the port is closed.

To make all of this work, you need to assign each host on the network an IP address. Let's discuss how this is done next.

How IPv4 Addresses Work

Every host on an IP-based network must have a unique IP address. An IP address is a Network layer (3) address that is logically assigned to a network host. Because the IP address is a logical address, it's not permanent. It can be changed at any time.

The IP address is different from the MAC address. The MAC address is a Data Link layer (2) hardware address that is burned into a ROM chip on every network board sold in the world. The MAC address is hard-coded and can't be changed.

 NOTE   The Address Resolution Protocol (ARP) is used to map logical IP addresses assigned to systems to their hard-coded MAC addresses.

An IP address consists of four numbers, separated by periods. Examples of valid IP addresses include

- 12.34.181.78
- 192.168.1.1
- 246.270.3.8

 NOTE   IPv4 addresses are sometimes called "dotted quad" addresses.

In decimal notation, each number must be between 0 and 255. For example, 192.168.1.1 is a valid IP address. Here are some examples of *invalid* IP addresses:

- **256.78.1.3**   Can't use a value greater than 255
- **10.3.4**   Must use four values

Each number in the address is actually an eight-bit binary number called an *octet.* Because each octet is a binary number, it can be represented as 0's and 1's. For example, the address 192.168.1.1 can be represented in binary form as

`11000000.10101000.00000001.00000001`

There are several simple ways to convert between the eight-bit binary address and the three-digit decimal version of an IP address. One option is to use the calculator software that comes with most Linux distributions (and even Windows) in Scientific mode. To convert a decimal IP address number to binary, enter the decimal version and then click the Bin option.

You can also go the other direction by entering a binary number in Bin mode and then switching to Dec mode, which will convert the binary number to its decimal equivalent.

If you're the mathematical type, you can also perform the conversion manually. Use the following to determine the value of each bit in a binary number:

- Bit 1 = 128
- Bit 2 = 64
- Bit 3 = 32
- Bit 4 = 16
- Bit 5 = 8
- Bit 6 = 4
- Bit 7 = 2
- Bit 8 = 1

For example, 11000000 = 128 + 64 = 192.

Some IP addresses are reserved and can't be assigned to a host. For example, the last octet in a host IP address can't be a 0. This is reserved for the address of the network segment itself that the host resides on. For example, the network address for the host assigned an IP address of 192.168.1.1 is 192.168.1.0.

In addition, the last octet of an IP address assigned to a host can't be 255. This is reserved for sending a broadcast to all hosts on the segment. In the preceding example, the broadcast address for a host with an IP address of 192.168.1.1 would be 192.168.1.255.

It's critical that you understand that every host on an IP-based network must have a *unique* IP address assigned to it. No two hosts on the same IP network can have the same IP address assigned. If the host resides on a public network, such as the Internet, it must use a *globally* unique IP address. You can apply to the Internet Assigned Numbers Authority (IANA) for a block of registered IP addresses. Once an IP address is assigned, no one else in the world can use it on a public network.

This actually introduces a key problem with IP version 4. The 32-bit addressing scheme used by IPv4 allows for a maximum of four billion possible unique addresses. This seemed like a lot of addresses back when IPv4 was originally defined. However, today this finite amount of available addresses has been almost completely allocated.

One way to get around this shortage of IPv4 addresses is to use private networks with network address translation (NAT). With network address translation, you can use a NAT router to present a single registered IP address to a *public* network while using *private* IP addresses on the network behind it. This is shown in Figure 15-3.

Using a NAT router has many advantages. Key among these is the fact that you can hide a huge private network behind a public interface (or a couple of public interfaces). This allows a large organization to implement its network and only need a relatively small number of globally unique public IP addresses.

Within each class of IP address are blocks of addresses called *private* or *reserved* IP addresses. These addresses are unallocated and can be used by anyone who wants to use them. This allows you to use private addresses on your local network and still be able to connect to public networks, such as the Internet. All traffic from your private network appears to be originating from the registered IP address configured on the public side of the NAT router.

The private IP address ranges are

- 10.0.0.0–10.255.255.255 (Class A)

- 172.16.0.0–172.31.255.255 (Class B)

- 192.168.0.0–192.168.255.255 (Class C)

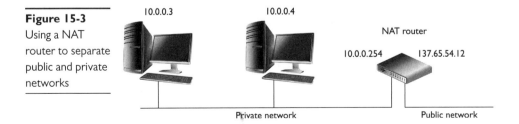

Figure 15-3
Using a NAT router to separate public and private networks

These are nonroutable addresses, meaning that if you try to use them on a public network, such as the Internet, IP routers won't forward data to or from them. This is handled by network address translation to a public IP address by a NAT router. This allows anyone in the world to use these private IP address ranges without worrying about conflicts, even if multiple instances are used. NAT makes this all possible!

In addition to assigning an IP address, you also need to assign a subnet mask when configuring the IP protocol on a Linux system. Let's discuss how this is done next.

How IPv4 Subnet Masks Work

If you've ever configured a system with an IP address, you probably noticed that you also had to assign a *subnet mask.* Have you ever wondered what this parameter is? Well, now is the time to learn.

To understand how a subnet mask works, you first need to understand that IP addresses are divided into two parts:

- Network address
- Node address

Part of an IPv4 address is used to identify the network the host resides on. The rest uniquely identifies a particular host (node) on the network. The key thing to remember is that every system on the same network segment must have exactly the same numbers in the network portion of the address. However, they each must have a unique node portion. This is shown in Figure 15-4.

How much of the address is used for the network and how much is used for the node is defined by the subnet mask. Default subnet masks include the following:

```
255.0.0.0
255.255.0.0
255.255.255.0
```

Any subnet mask octet with a 255 in it identifies a portion of the IP address that is used for the network address. Remember that the operating system sees IP addresses in binary notation. It also sees subnet masks in binary notation. If you have an IP address of 192.168.1.1 and a subnet mask of 255.255.255.0, the subnet mask specifies that the first three octets of the address are network and the last octet is node. This is shown in Figure 15-5.

IP addresses are divided into five different classes. Each address class has its own default subnet mask. For our purposes here, we only need to be concerned with the first three address classes:

- **Class A** The decimal value of the first octet must be between 1 and 126. In a Class A address, the first octet is the network address and the last three octets are the node address. Therefore, the default subnet mask is 255.0.0.0. Class A allows 126 total possible networks (that's not a lot), but they do offer 16.7 million possible node addresses per network (that is a lot!).

Figure 15-4

Network vs. node in an IP address

192.168.1.1

Network | Node

Figure 15-5

Using the subnet mask to define the network and node portions of an IP address

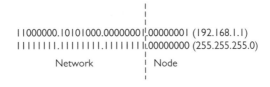

11000000.10101000.00000001.00000001 (192.168.1.1)
11111111.11111111.11111111.00000000 (255.255.255.0)

            Network   Node

- **Class B** The decimal value of the first octet must be between 128 and 191. In a Class B address, the first two octets are the network address and the last two octets are the node address. Therefore, the default subnet mask is 255.255.0.0. Using Class B addressing allows 16,384 possible networks with 65,534 million possible nodes each.

- **Class C** The decimal value of the first octet must be between 192 and 223. In a Class C address, the first three octets are the network address while the last octet is the node address. Therefore, the default subnet mask is 255.255.255.0. Because so much of the address is used for the network address, a huge number of Class C networks are available (2,097,152 possible networks). However, only a limited number of hosts (254 maximum) can exist on any given Class C network.

Subnet masks are sometimes noted using a type of shorthand called *CIDR notation*. This is done by adding a slash (/) and the number of bits used in the mask after the IP address (for example, 192.168.1.1/24). The /24 parameter indicates 24 bits are used for the subnet mask, which would be written out in longhand as 255.255.255.0. When using CIDR notation, the number of bits used in the mask is called the *prefix*.

You don't have to use these default subnet masks. You could define a subnet mask of 255.255.0.0 for a Class A address, for example. You can also use only part of an octet for the network address. This is called *partial subnetting* or *variable-length subnet masking* (VLSM). Using VLSM, we ignore the default subnet mask boundaries and specify a custom number of subnet mask bits. For example, suppose we defined a subnet mask of 255.255.252.0 for hosts on our network. In addition to the first and second octets, this mask would also include the first six of the eight bits in the third octet to be used for the network portion of the address. In essence, bits are "stolen" from the available node addresses to be used for network address, adding additional subnets. This allows you to create additional networks, but reduces the number of host addresses available on each.

For example, suppose your network is composed of four separate physical network segments connected by routers. This network uses the 10.0.0.0 private IP addressing scheme, so you want to divide the 10.0.0.0 network into four separate networks. By default, this network uses a Class A address (10.0.0.0). This means the first octet is used for the network address whereas and the last three octets are used for node addresses.

However, you can create four additional networks (subnets) by configuring the subnet mask to include the first two bits of the second octet in the network address to create additional networks. Instead of using the default Class A subnet mask of 11111111.00000000.00000000.000 00000 (255.0.0.0), you would use a subnet mask of 11111111.11000000.00000000.00000000

Subnet Address	Subnet Mask	Available Addresses	Broadcast Address
10.0.0.0	255.192.0.0	10.0.0.1–10.63.255.254	10.63.255.255
10.64.0.0	255.192.0.0	10.64.0.1–10.127.255.254	10.127.255.255
10.128.0.0	255.192.0.0	10.128.0.1–10.191.255.254	10.191.255.255
10.192.0.0	255.192.0.0	10.192.0.1–10.255.255.254	10.255.255.255

Table 15-1   Creating Subnets with a 10-bit Subnet Mask

(255.192.0.0). Using CIDR notation, you would specify a prefix of /10 to indicate you are using 10 bits for the subnet mask. There are four possible values for these two bits:

- 00 = 0
- 01 = 64
- 10 = 128
- 11 = 192

This will create the four subnets shown in Table 15-1.

The important thing to remember is that for two hosts on the same network segment to communicate, they need to have *exactly* the same network address, which means they must have *exactly* the same subnet mask. For example, suppose you have three systems, as shown in Figure 15-6.

Host 1 and Host 2 both have the exact same network address and subnet mask. These two hosts can communicate on the IP network segment. However, Host 3 uses a subnet mask of 255.255.252.0 instead of 255.255.255.0. Therefore, Host 3 has a different network address than Host 1 and Host 2 and won't be able to communicate with them without the use of a network router.

Next, let's discuss the DNS server address and the default gateway router address.

Figure 15-6
Hosts with wrong
subnet masks

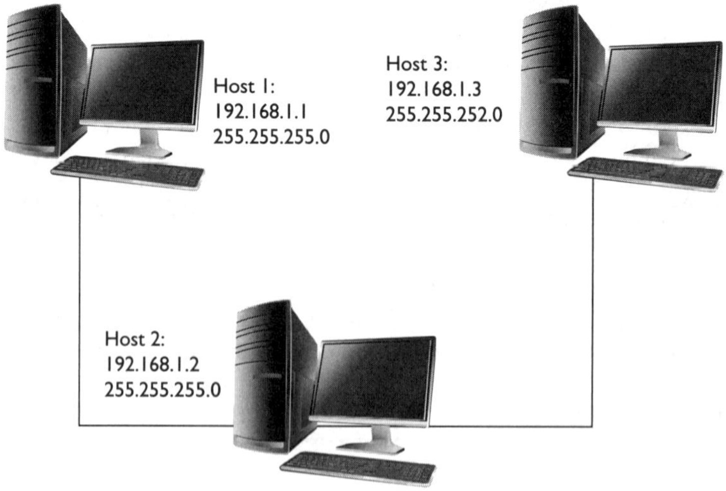

Host 1:
192.168.1.1
255.255.255.0

Host 3:
192.168.1.3
255.255.252.0

Host 2:
192.168.1.2
255.255.255.0

Specifying the DNS Server and Default Gateway Router Addresses

So far, we've discussed the IP address and subnet mask parameters that you need to specify when configuring the IP stack on a Linux system. However, you should also specify the DNS server address and the default gateway router address.

If you've used the Internet, you know that you can use domain names, such as www.google .com, to navigate to particular hosts on the Web. However, your system actually can't work with alphanumeric domain names. It has no idea where www.google.com is or what it has to offer.

To make this work, your local system needs to resolve domain names into IP addresses. One of the ways this can be done is to submit the domain name to a DNS server. When a DNS server receives a name resolution request, it matches the domain name submitted with an IP address and returns it to the requesting system. Then your system can contact the specified host using its IP address. For example, in Figure 15-7, the domain name www.google.com has been resolved to an IP address of 74.125.239.144 by the DNS server.

To make this system work, you need to provide your system with the IP address of the DNS server you want it to use. We'll spend more time working with DNS later in this chapter.

In addition, you also need to specify the IP address of your network's default gateway router. The IP protocol was designed from the ground up with internetworking in mind. In an internetwork,

```
                          student@openSUSE:~                                  ✕

 File  Edit  View  Search  Terminal  Help
student@openSUSE:~> dig www.google.com

; <<>> DiG 9.9.4-rpz2.13269.14-P2 <<>> www.google.com
;; global options: +cmd
;; Got answer:
;; ->>HEADER<<- opcode: QUERY, status: NOERROR, id: 60141
;; flags: qr rd ra; QUERY: 1, ANSWER: 5, AUTHORITY: 0, ADDITIONAL: 1

;; OPT PSEUDOSECTION:
; EDNS: version: 0, flags:; udp: 512
;; QUESTION SECTION:
;www.google.com.                        IN      A

;; ANSWER SECTION:
www.google.com.         146     IN      A       74.125.239.144
www.google.com.         146     IN      A       74.125.239.145
www.google.com.         146     IN      A       74.125.239.147
www.google.com.         146     IN      A       74.125.239.146
www.google.com.         146     IN      A       74.125.239.148

;; Query time: 36 msec
;; SERVER: 192.168.2.1#53(192.168.2.1)
;; WHEN: Tue Feb 03 13:29:32 MST 2015
;; MSG SIZE  rcvd: 123
```

Figure 15-7   Resolving a domain name into an IP address

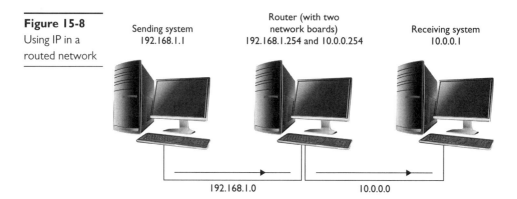

Figure 15-8
Using IP in a
routed network

Sending system
192.168.1.1

Router (with two
network boards)
192.168.1.254 and 10.0.0.254

Receiving system
10.0.0.1

192.168.1.0

10.0.0.0

multiple network segments are connected together using routers. If a system on one segment tries to send data to a host that doesn't reside on the same network, the IP protocol will redirect the packets to the default gateway router for its segment. The router will then use a variety of routing protocols to determine where the packets should be sent to get them to their destination. This is shown in Figure 15-8.

In Figure 15-8, the sending system (192.168.1.1) is sending data to 10.0.0.1. However, 10.0.0.1 resides on the 10.0.0.0 network segment, not the 192.168.1.0 network segment. Therefore, the IP stack on the sending system redirects the data to the router connecting the two segments together. The routing software on the router knows where the 10.0.0.0 network segment resides and forwards the packets on to that network, where they are delivered to the receiving system.

This system is very powerful. It's what allows you to connect to the Internet and pull down web pages from a server somewhere else in the world. However, for it to work, your local system needs to know the IP address of the router to which it should forward packets if they are addressed to a system that doesn't reside on the local network segment. You need to configure this parameter whenever you configure network settings on a Linux system. If you don't, the system will be able to communicate only with systems on the same local network segment.

Using IPv6

Earlier in this chapter, I mentioned that the world's supply of registered IP addresses is nearly exhausted. To address this issue, most organizations reduce the number of registered IP addresses that they need by implementing a NAT router. However, using a NAT router is a short-term solution. To fully address this issue, a new version of the IP protocol is needed that can handle the number of IP addresses the modern computing world needs.

To accomplish this, IP version 6 (IPv6) is being rolled out throughout the world. IPv6 is expected to completely replace IPv4 over the next decade. Instead of 32 bits, IPv6 defines 128-bit IP addresses. This allows for a maximum of 3.4×10^{38} total unique IP addresses. (Hopefully, this will be enough!) Most Linux distributions support both IPv4 and IPv6.

IPv6 addresses are composed of eight four-character hexadecimal numbers (called *quartets*), separated by colons instead of periods. Each quartet is represented as a hexadecimal number between 0 and FFFF. For example, a valid IPv6 address could be 35BC:FA77:4898:DAFC:200C :FBBC:A007:8973. This 128-bit address contains two parts:

- **Prefix**   The prefix is the first 64 bits. The prefix includes the network and subnet addresses. This is equivalent to an IPv4 network address. In fact, we reference the prefix in IPv6 using CIDR notation, just we did for IPv4 addresses. Because IPv6 prefixes are 64-bits long, we specify **/64**.

- **Interface ID**   The interface ID is the last 64 bits. This is the unique address assigned to a network host. This is equivalent to an IPv4 host address.

 NOTE   Because IPv6 addresses are so long, you will frequently see them abbreviated. If the address contains a long string of multiple zeros, we can omit them by specifying **::**. For example, if you had an IPv6 address of 2001:1db8:3a4c:1115:0000:0000:1a2f:1a2b, you could omit all the extra zeros using a shorthand notation of 2001:1db8:3a4c:1115::1a2f:1a2b.

There are three major types of IPv6 addresses you need to be familiar with:

- Global unicast
- Unique local
- Link local

Let's look at global unicast addresses first.

Global Unicast Addresses

Global unicast IPv6 addresses function in a manner similar to public IPv4 addresses. Typically, an organization that wishes to deploy IPv6 will be assigned a registered, unique *global routing prefix* (which is equivalent to an IPv4 network address). Every global routing prefix must be unique throughout the entire Internet. This ensures that every IPv6 address assigned to individual network hosts is globally unique as well.

The global routing prefix is assigned by your ISP and is usually 48 bits long (/48). This allows you to use the remaining 16 bits in the global routing prefix to create your own internal subnets. Because of the size of the prefix (/64), you can define up to 2^{16} subnets. That's a huge number! All subnets within the same organization will use the same global routing prefix that was assigned by the ISP, but will use a different value in the subnet portion of the prefix.

When deploying IPv6, you don't actually have to use global unicast addresses. If appropriate, you could implement unique local addressing instead.

Unique Local Addresses

Unique local addresses are similar to private IPv4 addresses and are normally used for networks that are not connected to a public network (such as the Internet). Unique local addresses are not registered, so they cannot be used on a public network without network address translation.

The first eight bits of unique local addresses use a prefix that always begins with **FC** or **FD**. The next 40 bits are used for the *global ID*, which is a randomly generated number that is intended to create a high probability of uniqueness. Therefore, unique local addresses are actually designed to be globally unique, even though they can't be used on the Internet. The remaining 16 bits in the prefix after the Global ID are used for creating subnets, just as we saw with globally unique addressing. The rest of the address is used for the interface IDs that are assigned to individual network hosts.

Before we end, we also need to look at link-local addresses.

Link-Local Addresses

IPv6 also uses special unicast addresses called link-local addresses that are used just for communications within a local network segment. Routers never forward packets addressed to link-local addresses on other subnets. As such, link-local addresses cannot be used for communications between hosts on different network segments. Link-local addresses are used for specific purposes, including the following:

- Automatic address configuration
- Neighbor discovery
- Routerless subnets

The prefix used by link-local addresses begins with **FE8**, **FE9**, **FEA**, or **FEB**. When working with IPv6, you will notice that every IPv6 host has at least one link-local address that is automatically assigned when the system comes up.

With this background in mind, let's now discuss how to configure an Ethernet interface in a Linux system.

Configuring Network Addressing Parameters

Probably the most common network interface you will work with in a Linux system is an Ethernet interface. Be aware that, under Linux, when we refer to a "network interface," we are referring to

- The physical network interface card (NIC) hardware installed in the system
- The kernel modules (drivers) loaded to support the physical NIC
- The IP networking configuration parameters assigned to the interface

To install an Ethernet network interface in your system, you need to complete the following tasks:

- Installing the Ethernet board
- Configuring IPv4 parameters
- Configuring routing parameters
- Configuring name resolver settings
- Configuring IPv6

Let's begin by discussing how to install an Ethernet board in your system.

Installing the Ethernet Board

Obviously, the first thing you need to do when configuring an Ethernet interface is to install the NIC hardware in the system. To do this, complete the following:

1. Power off your system.

2. Install your Ethernet board in an available expansion slot.

3. Connect the Ethernet board to your network switch or hub with the appropriate drop cable.

4. Power your system back on. If you installed a modern Ethernet board, your Linux operating system will probably detect it as it boots and automatically load the required kernel modules. If not, you may have to download the appropriate module from the board manufacturer's website and load it manually.

After the system has booted, you should check your module configuration file and verify that the appropriate kernel module has been loaded and that an alias has been created for the new board. The file to check depends on your distribution. Some distributions use the /etc/modprobe. conf or /etc/modules.conf file, whereas others use a configuration file in /etc/modprobe.d. For example, my openSUSE system (which is installed in a VMware virtual machine) uses the /etc/ modprobe.d/50-vmnics.conf file, as shown in Figure 15-9.

The alias used for your network interface will depend on your distribution. Older distributions that use init will assign the Ethernet adapters in your Linux system the following aliases:

- **eth0** The first Ethernet adapter in your system

- **eth1** The second Ethernet adapter in your system

- **eth2** The third Ethernet adapter in your system, and so on...

Newer distributions that use systemd no longer use these aliases. They worked great, unless you happened to have multiple network adapters in the system. Occasionally, we saw situations where interface aliases got swapped between network adapters. For example, a given interface could be eth0 on one boot, but end up being assigned eth1 on the next boot. As you can imagine, this situation could really mess up your network services, routing tables, and firewall rules.

To address this issue, systemd uses *predictable network interface names*. One of the key benefits of doing this is the fact that specific aliases can be permanently assigned to specific

```
root@openSUSE:/etc/modprobe.d                           ✕
File  Edit  View  Search  Terminal  Help
openSUSE:/etc/modprobe.d # cat 50-vmnics.conf
install pcnet32 /sbin/modprobe -q --ignore-install vmxnet; /sbin/modprobe -q --i
gnore-install pcnet32 $CMDLINE OPTS; /bin/true;
```

Figure 15-9 A kernel module configuration file for an Ethernet board

network interfaces. Predictable network interface device names are assigned based on one of the following parameters. The preferred order is as follows:

- For an onboard network adapter, the index number provided by the system firmware (or BIOS) is used to construct the alias. A commonly assigned alias created using this parameter is **eno1**. The elements of this name are as follows:
  - **en**   Ethernet interface
  - **o1**   Onboard device index number (in this case, device number **1**)
- If the network adapter is plugged into a PCI-E hot-plug slot instead of being integrated into the motherboard, then systemd will use the index number of the slot itself, as provided by the firmware (or BIOS), to construct the alias. A commonly assigned alias created using this parameter is **ens1**. The elements of this name are as follows:
  - **en**   Ethernet interface
  - **s1**   Hot-plug slot index number (in this case, slot number **1**)
- If the preceding options are not applicable, then systemd will try to construct an alias using the name of the physical connector the interface is connected to, such as a USB connector. A commonly assigned alias created using this parameter is **enp2s0**. The elements of this name are as follows:
  - **en**   Ethernet interface
  - **p2**   Bus number (in this case, USB bus number **2**)
  - **s0**   Slot number on the bus (in this case, slot number **0**)
- If all else fails, then systemd will try to use the interface's MAC address to construct an alias. The format is **enx** followed by the MAC address.

Notice in the preceding list that every sample interface name started with **en**. That's because we're assuming you are working with standard Ethernet interfaces. Other types of interfaces use different naming conventions:

- **en**   Used for Ethernet adapters
- **sl**   Used for serial line IP interfaces
- **wl**   Used for WLAN interfaces

At this point, your network interface is loaded and active. However, before you can use it, you have to configure it with the IP protocol. Let's discuss how this is done next.

Configuring IPv4 Parameters

Remember that you need to configure your network interface with four parameters in order for the system to participate on an IP-based computer network. These include the following:

- IP address
- Subnet mask

Option	Description	Advantages	Disadvantages
Static address assignment	In this configuration, you manually configure a network host with IP address parameters.	The address used by a particular host never changes. This option is generally used by servers in the network.	The host consumes the address regardless of whether the system is powered on or off. This strategy also requires a lot of legwork on the part of the system administrator. He or she has to visit each computer in the network and manually specify IP parameters.
Dynamic address assignment	In this configuration, a network host contacts a Dynamic Host Configuration Protocol (DHCP) server when it boots. The DHCP server dynamically assigns an IP address to the host for a specified period of time called a lease.	This option makes configuring IP parameters for a large number of network hosts very easy. Just power the system on, and it gets its IP address information. It also conserves IP address usage. Addresses used by systems that are powered off can be reassigned to other network hosts.	You must have a DHCP server installed and configured before you can use this option. In addition, the address assigned to a particular host can change frequently, making it an unsuitable option for network infrastructure systems such as servers. Because of this, this option is generally used for workstations.

Table 15-2 IP Address Assignment Options

- Default gateway router address
- DNS server address

There are two different ways to do this, as discussed in Table 15-2.

If you want to statically assign IP address parameters to a Linux system, you can use the ifconfig command. If **ifconfig** is entered without any options, it displays the current status of all network interfaces in the system, as shown in Figure 15-10.

```
root@openSUSE:/
File Edit View Search Terminal Help
openSUSE:/ # ifconfig
ens32     Link encap:Ethernet  HWaddr 00:0C:29:B0:9F:B5
          inet addr:10.0.0.83  Bcast:10.0.0.255  Mask:255.255.255.0
          inet6 addr: fe80::20c:29ff:feb0:9fb5/64 Scope:Link
          UP BROADCAST RUNNING MULTICAST  MTU:1500  Metric:1
          RX packets:92 errors:0 dropped:0 overruns:0 frame:0
          TX packets:71 errors:0 dropped:0 overruns:0 carrier:0
          collisions:0 txqueuelen:1000
          RX bytes:13685 (13.3 Kb)  TX bytes:12624 (12.3 Kb)

lo        Link encap:Local Loopback
          inet addr:127.0.0.1  Mask:255.0.0.0
          inet6 addr: ::1/128 Scope:Host
          UP LOOPBACK RUNNING  MTU:65536  Metric:1
          RX packets:8 errors:0 dropped:0 overruns:0 frame:0
          TX packets:8 errors:0 dropped:0 overruns:0 carrier:0
          collisions:0 txqueuelen:0
          RX bytes:544 (544.0 b)  TX bytes:544 (544.0 b)
```

Figure 15-10 Using ifconfig to view network interface information

NOTE When you run ifconfig, you'll notice that your system probably has two or more interfaces listed, not just one. The extra interface labeled **lo** is the loopback interface and is usually assigned a special IP address of 127.0.0.1. This is a virtual interface, not an actual hardware interface. It's used for internal communications, for diagnostics, and so on.

Notice in Figure 15-10 that two network interfaces are displayed: ens32 and lo. The ens32 interface is the Ethernet network interface installed in the system. The lo interface is the local loopback virtual network interface. The lo interface is required for many Linux services to run properly, so don't tinker with it. Notice in Figure 15-10 that ifconfig also displays extensive information about each network interface. Some of the more important parameters include those shown in Table 15-3.

In addition to displaying information about a particular network interface, ifconfig can also configure the network interface with the IP address parameters discussed earlier. The syntax for using ifconfig is **ifconfig** *interface ip_address* **netmask** *subnet_mask* **broadcast** *broadcast_ address*. For example, suppose I want to assign the ens32 interface an IP address of 192.168.1.1, a subnet mask of 255.255.255.0, and a broadcast address of 192.168.1.255. I would enter **ifconfig ens32 192.168.1.1 netmask 255.255.255.0 broadcast 192.168.1.255** at the shell prompt.

It's important to remember that this IP address assignment isn't persistent. If you reboot the system, it will be lost. To make it persistent, you need to configure a special file in the /etc/sysconfig/network directory. For example, the file used to configure the Ethernet interface on my system is named ifcfg-ens32.

NOTE On some distributions, this file will be named using the MAC address of the NIC. For example, ifcfg-eth-id-00:0c:29:d1:52:d4 would be the configuration file for the Ethernet interface in the system with a MAC address of 00:0C:29:D1:52:D4, which will be the first interface if there is only one NIC installed. Other distributions will name this file using the alias assigned to the interface, such as eth0, ens1, and so on.

ifconfig Parameter	Description
HWaddr	The MAC address of the network board
inet addr	The IP address assigned to the interface
Bcast	The broadcast address of the network segment
Mask	The subnet mask assigned to the interface
RX packets	Statistics for received packets
TX packets	Statistics for transmitted packets
Collisions	The number of Ethernet collisions detected
RX bytes	The number of bytes of data received by the interface since it was brought up
TX bytes	The number of bytes of data transmitted by the interface since it was brought up

Table 15-3 ifconfig Output

This file is used to configure the interface when the system is powered on. Sample parameters for this interface are shown here:

```
openSUSE:~ # cat /etc/sysconfig/network/ifcfg-ens32
BOOTPROTO='dhcp'
BROADCAST=''
ETHTOOL_OPTIONS=''
IPADDR=''
MTU=''
NAME='82545EM Gigabit Ethernet Controller (Copper)'
NETMASK=''
NETWORK=''
REMOTE_IPADDR=''
STARTMODE='auto'
USERCONTROL='no'
```

Some of the configuration options you can use in this configuration file are listed in Table 15-4.

Option	Description	Other Possible Values
BOOTPROTO="static"	This option specifies that the interface use a static IP address assignment.	Set to **dhcp** to dynamically assign an address.
STARTMODE="auto"	This option specifies that the interface be brought online when the system is booted.	Set to **manual** to manually start the interface. Some distributions use **onboot** instead of **auto**.
IPADDR="192.168.1.81/24"	Assigns an IP address of 192.168.1.10 to the interface with a subnet mask of 255.255.255.0.	
NETMASK="subnet_mask"	If the prefix isn't assigned using CIDR notation in the IPADDR parameter, you can use NETMASK= to assign a subnet mask to the interface.	
NETWORK="192.168.1.0"	Specifies the network address of the segment that the interface is connected to.	
BROADCAST="192.168.1.255"	Specifies the broadcast address of the segment the interface is connected to.	
REMOTE_IPADDR=	Specifies the IP address of the remote node in a peer-to-peer type of connection.	
MTU=	Specifies the size of the Maximum Transmission Unit (which is 1500 by default on an Ethernet network).	If your network uses jumbo frames, you can set this parameter to **9000**.
ETHTOOL_OPTIONS=	Specifies command arguments used by the ethtool utility.	
LABEL_0='0' IPADDR_0='2607:f 0d0:1002:0011:0000:0000:0000:0003' PREFIXLEN_0='64'	These parameters are used to assign an IPv6 address to the eth0 interface.	

Table 15-4 Configuring Persistent Parameters for a Network Interface

The lines for IPADDR, NETMASK, NETWORK, and BROADCAST are not required if BOOTPROTO is set to "dhcp". The /etc/hostname file configures your Linux system's hostname.

After making any changes to these files, you will need to restart your network interface to apply the changes. To do this, simply enter **ifdown** *interface* followed by **ifup** *interface*, where *interface* is the alias of the interface, such as ens32.

This is all well and good if you want to use a static address assignment, but what if you want to get an address dynamically from a DHCP server? You can configure your network interface to do this using the dhclient command at the shell prompt. The syntax for using this command is **dhclient** *interface*. For example, you could enter **dhclient ens32** to specify that your interface get its IP address information dynamically from a DHCP server. This is shown in Figure 15-11.

Notice in Figure 15-11 that the dhclient utility broadcasted a DHCPREQUEST packet on the ens32 interface. In response, the DHCP server with an IP address of 10.0.0.1 sent a DHCPACK packet back with an IP address of 10.10.0.83 that was assigned to the ens32 interface.

Another utility you can use to manage IP addressing on a Linux system is the ip command. For example, to view your current configuration, you can enter **ip addr show** at the shell prompt, as shown here:

```
openSUSE:/ # ip addr show
1: lo: <LOOPBACK,UP,LOWER_UP> mtu 65536 qdisc noqueue state UNKNOWN
    link/loopback 00:00:00:00:00:00 brd 00:00:00:00:00:00
    inet 127.0.0.1/8 brd 127.255.255.255 scope host lo
       valid_lft forever preferred_lft forever
    inet6 ::1/128 scope host
       valid_lft forever preferred_lft forever
2: ens32: <BROADCAST,MULTICAST,UP,LOWER_UP> mtu 1500 qdisc pfifo_fast
state UP qlen 1000
    link/ether 00:0c:29:b0:9f:b5 brd ff:ff:ff:ff:ff:ff
    inet 10.0.0.83/24 brd 10.0.0.255 scope global ens32
       valid_lft forever preferred_lft forever
    inet6 fe80::20c:29ff:feb0:9fb5/64 scope link
       valid_lft forever preferred_lft forever
```

```
                            root@openSUSE:/                                    ✕

  File  Edit  View  Search  Terminal  Help
 openSUSE:/ # dhclient ens32 -v
 Internet Systems Consortium DHCP Client 4.2.5-P1
 Copyright 2004-2013 Internet Systems Consortium.
 All rights reserved.
 For info, please visit https://www.isc.org/software/dhcp/

 Listening on LPF/ens32/00:0c:29:b0:9f:b5
 Sending on   LPF/ens32/00:0c:29:b0:9f:b5
 Sending on   Socket/fallback
 DHCPDISCOVER on ens32 to 255.255.255.255 port 67 interval 3
 DHCPOFFER from 10.0.0.1
 DHCPREQUEST on ens32 to 255.255.255.255 port 67
 DHCPACK from 10.0.0.1
 bound to 10.0.0.83 -- renewal in 41783 seconds.
```

Figure 15-11   Using dhclient to obtain an IP address lease

To use the ip command to configure IP addressing parameters, enter **ip addr add *ip_address* dev *interface*** at the shell prompt. For example, to set the IP address assigned to my ens32 network interface to 10.0.0.84, I would enter **ip addr add 10.0.0.84 dev ens32**. To remove an IP address from an interface, just enter **ip addr del *ip_address* dev *interface*** at the shell prompt.

You can also use the ip command to disable and enable a network interface in the system. To disable an interface, enter **ip link set *interface* down** at the shell prompt. To bring a disabled interface back online, enter **ip link set *interface* up** at the shell prompt.

In addition to the command-line utilities discussed here, most Linux distributions provide some kind of graphical interface you can use to configure your network interfaces. For example, on SUSE Linux, you can use the Network Settings YaST module to configure your network board as well as the IP address information assigned to it. This module is shown in Figure 15-12.

Let's practice working with the ifconfig command in the following exercise.

Figure 15-12 Using the YaST Network Settings module

Exercise 15-1: Working with Network Interfaces

In this exercise, you will practice using the ifconfig command to manage your network interface. You can perform this exercise using the virtual machine that comes with this book. Run snapshot 15-1 for the correctly configured environment.

 VIDEO   Please watch the Exercise 15-1 video for a demonstration on how to perform this task.

Complete the following:

1. Boot your Linux system and log in as your student user with a password of **student**.

2. Open a terminal session.

3. Switch to your root user account by entering **su** – followed a password of **student**.

4. At the shell prompt, enter **ifconfig**. Record the following information about your Ethernet interface:

   - MAC address

   - IP address

   - Broadcast address

   - Subnet mask

5. At the shell prompt, use the **cd** command to change to the /etc/sysconfig/network directory.

6. Use the **ls** command to identify the configuration file for your network board.

7. Use the **cat** command to view the contents of the configuration file for your Ethernet network interface board.

8. Bring your interface down by entering **ifdown** *interface_name* at the shell prompt.

9. Bring your interface back up by entering **ifup** *interface_name* at the shell prompt.

10. Change the IP address assigned to your Ethernet network interface to 192.168.1.100 by entering **ifconfig** *interface_name* **192.168.1.100 netmask 255.255.255.0 broadcast 192.168.1.255** at the shell prompt.

11. Enter **ifconfig** again and verify that the change was applied.

12. Use the **ifconfig** command again to change your IP configuration parameters back to their original values.

13. If you have a DHCP server on your network segment, modify your network interface configuration to use DHCP and then dynamically assign an IP address to your Ethernet board by entering **dhclient** *interface_name* at the shell prompt.

Configuring Routing Parameters

You may have noticed that we didn't configure two important IP parameters in the preceding topics in this chapter: the default gateway router address and the DNS server address.

Using the IP protocol, routers do just what their name implies: they route data across multiple networks to deliver information to a destination host. Routers operate at the Network layer and are used to connect various networks together.

Routers are usually implemented in conjunction with a gateway. The router hardware itself may be as simple as a computer system with two NICs installed, or it may be a specialized hardware appliance dedicated to routing.

One of the key jobs performed by routers is to determine the best way to get information to the right destination host. To do this, a router maintains a routing table of available routes. Routers use an algorithm that evaluates distance, cost, and network status to determine the best route to the destination host. Even if it isn't configured as a router, every Linux system maintains a routing table in RAM that it uses to determine where to send data on a network.

When you're configuring networking parameters on a Linux system, one of the key tasks you need to perform is to configure the default router address. The default router is the default location packets are sent to if they are addressed to a host that doesn't reside on the local network segment. Your default gateway router address is stored in the /etc/sysconfig/network/routes file, shown here:

```
openSUSE:/ # cat /etc/sysconfig/network/routes
default 10.0.0.1 - ens32
```

The syntax for specifying the default route in this file is **default *router_IP_address***. Notice in the preceding example that the default gateway router address is set to 10.0.0.1.

TIP   If you have more than one NIC installed and each interface needs its own routing configuration (for example, if each NIC is connected to a different network), you can define an additional routing configuration file in /etc/sysconfig/network/ named ifroute-*interface_name*.

The syntax for adding a route to the routes file is shown next:

```
DESTINATION        GATEWAY        NETMASK    INTERFACE    [TYPE]
```

The first column contains the route's destination. It may contain the IP address or DNS hostname of a network or host. Entering **default** in this column indicates the route is the default route.

NOTE   I recommend you use IP addresses, not DNS names, in this file. If your DNS server were to go down or become unreachable, routing would be gone!

The second column contains the IP address of the router through which the specified host or a network can be reached. In this column, specify the IP address of a router that can route the information to the remote network or host.

The third column contains the netmask for the network or host behind the router. The fourth column applies the route to a specific interface. If nothing is specified, the route applies to all interfaces.

NOTE If you want to leave a column in this file blank, be sure to enter a dash (-).

The fifth column is optional. It is used to specify the route type. You can enter one of the following:

- **unicast** The route specifies a real path to the destination route.
- **local** The destination is the localhost. Packets sent to this route are looped back and delivered to the local machine.
- **broadcast** The destination is a broadcast address. Packets sent to this route are sent as link broadcasts.
- **multicast** Used for multicast routing. This type of route is not typically used with most routing tables.
- **unreachable** Configures the route destination as unreachable. Packets sent to this route are silently dropped.

Here is a sample entry in a routes file:

```
207.68.156.51     207.68.145.45     255.255.255.0     ens32
```

After making any changes to the routes file, you will need to restart your network interface by entering **ifdown** *interface* followed by **ifup** *interface*.

For your LPIC-1/CompTIA Linux+ exam, you also need to be familiar with how to manage routes with the route command at the shell prompt. You use the route command to display or modify the routing table on the Linux host. If you enter **route** without options, it simply displays the current routing table, as shown in this example:

```
openSUSE:/ # route
Kernel IP routing table
Destination    Gateway      Genmask          Flags Metric Ref    Use Iface
default        10.0.0.1     0.0.0.0          UG    0      0        0 ens32
10.0.0.0       *            255.255.255.0    U     0      0        0 ens32
loopback       *            255.0.0.0        U     0      0        0 lo
```

You can add routes to the host's route table by entering **route add –net** *network_address* **netmask** *netmask* **gw** *router_address*. For example, suppose you need to add a route to the 192.168.2.0/24 network through the router with an IP address of 10.0.0.254. You could do this by entering **route add –net 192.168.2.0 netmask 255.255.255.0 gw 10.0.0.254** at the shell prompt.

You can also remove existing routes from the routing table on a Linux host using the route command. This is done by entering **route del –net** *network_address* **netmask** *netmask* **gw** *router_address* at the shell prompt. For example, suppose you want to remove the route just added in the preceding paragraph. You could do this by entering **route del –net 192.168.2.0 netmask 255.255.255.0 gw 10.0.0.254** at the shell prompt.

You can also use route to set the default route. This is done by entering **route add default gw** *router_address* at the shell prompt. For example, if you want to add 10.0.0.254 as your default gateway router, you would enter **route add default gw 10.0.0.254** at the shell prompt.

TIP   Changes made with the route command are not persistent! If you want the route changes to be persistent across reboots, you need to add them to your /etc/sysconfig/network/routes file.

You can also use the ip command at the shell prompt to manage routing. For example, to view the routing table, you can enter **ip route show** at the shell prompt, as shown here:

```
openSUSE:/ # ip route show
default via 10.0.0.1 dev ens32
10.0.0.0/24 dev ens32  proto kernel  scope link  src 10.0.0.83
127.0.0.0/8 dev lo  scope link
```

You can also use the ip command to add a static route to the routing table. This is done by entering **ip route add** *network/prefix* **via** *router_ip_address* **dev** *interface* at the shell prompt. In the following example shown, I've added a route to the 192.168.5.0/24 network through a router with an IP address of 10.0.0.254:

```
openSUSE:/ # ip route add 192.168.5.0/24 via 10.0.0.254 dev ens32
openSUSE:/ # ip route show
default via 10.0.0.1 dev ens32
10.0.0.0/24 dev ens32  proto kernel  scope link  src 10.0.0.83
127.0.0.0/8 dev lo  scope link
192.168.5.0/24 via 10.0.0.254 dev ens32
```

You can also remove a route from the routing table by entering **ip route del** *network/prefix* at the shell prompt. For example, to remove the 192.168.5.0/24 route I just added, I would enter **ip route del 192.168.5.0/24**.

Configuring Name Resolver Settings

When configuring IP settings for a network interface, you also need to specify the system's host-name and the IP address of your DNS server. Because you are most likely a savvy Internet user, you know that you can use domain names to navigate to particular hosts on the Web. However, your Linux system (or any other operating system, for that matter) actually can't work with the alphanumeric domain names that we are used to.

For example, when you open a browser window and enter **http://www.google.com** in the URL field, your browser, IP stack, and operating system have no clue where to go to get the requested information. To make this work, your local system needs to first resolve these domain names into IP addresses.

In the old days, basic hostname-to-IP-address resolution was performed by the /etc/hosts file, which contains IP-address-to-hostname mappings.

NOTE   The /etc/hosts file still exists on Linux systems. In fact, it is the first name resolver used by default. Only if a record for the requested domain name doesn't exist in the hosts file will the operating system then try to resolve the hostname using DNS. Because of this, you have to manage your hosts file very carefully. Many network hacks exploit this function of the operating system. A malicious website or malware may try to rewrite your hosts file with name mappings that point you to fake websites on the Internet that look like your favorite auction or banking site but instead are elaborate phishing websites designed to steal your personal information.

The hosts file contains one line per host record. The syntax is

```
IP_address host_name alias
```

For example, consider the following hosts file entry:

```
192.168.1.1 mylinux.mydom.com mylinux
```

This record resolves either the fully qualified DNS name of mylinux.mydom.com or the alias (CNAME) of mylinux to an IP address of 192.168.1.1. Usually this file only contains the IP address and hostname of the local system, but you can add other entries too.

Using the hosts file to resolve hostnames works just fine; however, it really isn't feasible as the sole means of name resolution. The file would have to be huge in order to resolve all the domain names used by hosts on the Internet. In addition, you would have to manually add, remove, and modify hostname mappings in the file whenever a domain name changed on the Internet. What a nightmare! Can you imagine trying to manage this type of hosts file for an entire network of users?

A better option is to submit the domain name to a DNS server. When a DNS server receives a name resolution request, it matches the domain name submitted with an IP address and returns it to the requesting system. Your system can then contact the specified host using its IP address. Here's how it works:

1. The system needing to resolve a hostname sends a request to the DNS server it has been configured to use on IP port 53. If the DNS server is authoritative for the zone where the requested hostname resides, it responds with the appropriate IP address. If not, the process continues on to step 2.

 NOTE   A DNS server is considered to be authoritative if it has a record for the domain name being requested in its database of name mappings.

2. The DNS server sends a request to a root-level DNS server. There are 13 root-level DNS servers on the Internet. Every DNS server is automatically configured with the IP addresses of these servers. These root-level DNS servers are configured with records that resolve to authoritative DNS servers for each top-level domain (.com, .gov, .edu, .au, .de, .uk, .ca, and so on).

3. The root-level DNS server responds to your DNS server with the IP address of a DNS server that is authoritative for the top-level domain of the domain name you are trying to resolve.

4. Your DNS server sends the name resolution query to the DNS server that is authoritative for the hostname's top-level domain (such as .com).

5. The top-level domain DNS server responds to your DNS server with the IP address of a DNS server that's authoritative for the DNS zone of the hostname you need to resolve.

6. Your DNS server sends a name resolution request to the DNS server that's authoritative for the zone where the hostname you are trying to resolve resides.

7. The authoritative DNS server responds to your DNS server with the IP address for the hostname.

8. Your DNS server responds to your system with the IP address mapped to the hostname, and the respective system is contacted using this IP address.

 NOTE Once this process happens for a particular name mapping, most DNS servers will cache the mapping for a period of time. That way, if a resolution request for the same hostname is received again, they can respond directly to the client without going through this whole process again.

Therefore, to make this system work, you must provide your system with the IP address of the DNS server you want it to use. This is configured in the /etc/resolv.conf file. This file defines the search prefix and the name servers to use. Here is some sample content from my openSUSE system's resolv.conf file:

```
search mydom.com
nameserver 8.8.8.8
nameserver 8.8.4.4
nameserver 192.168.2.1
```

As you can see in this example, the file contains two types of entries:

- **search** Specifies the domain name that should be used to fill out incomplete hostnames. For example, if you were to try to resolve a hostname of WS1, the name will be automatically converted to the fully qualified domain name of WS1.mydom.com. The syntax is **search *domain*.**

- **nameserver** Specifies the IP address of the DNS server you want to use for name resolution. You can configure up to three DNS servers. If the first server fails or is otherwise unreachable, the next DNS server is used. The syntax is **nameserver *DNS_ server_IP_address*.**

You can use the /etc/nsswitch.conf (name service switch) file to define the order in which services will be used for name resolution. Here are the two lines of the file you need to be concerned with:

```
hosts:        files dns
networks:     files dns
```

These two entries specify that the /etc/hosts file (files) is consulted first for name resolution. If there is no applicable entry, the query is then sent to the DNS server (dns) specified in the resolv.conf file.

 TIP You can use the hostname command at the shell prompt to show or set the system's hostname. You can also use the dnsdomainname command to show the system's DNS domain name.

Configuring IPv6

Before we move on in this chapter, we need to spend some time discussing IPv6 address configuration. There are actually several configuration options when it comes to IPv6 addressing. The first is to use static assignment. As with IPv4, static IPv6 address assignments require you to manually assign the entire 128-bit IPv6 address and prefix to the host. This can be done from the shell prompt using a command-line utility such as ifconfig or ip. Alternatively, you can manually enter the address and prefix in the appropriate interface configuration file in /etc/sysconfig/network.

Another configuration option is to use *static partial assignment*. Using this method, the prefix is statically assigned, but the interface ID portion of the address is automatically generated using the host's MAC address.

Another configuration option is to use *stateless address auto-configuration*, which is affectionately called SLAAC. Using SLAAC, we allow IPv6 hosts to automatically generate their own interface ID, but we require them to obtain a correct prefix and default gateway address from a network router (usually the default gateway) using the Neighbor Discovery Protocol (NDP). NDP uses the following messages for autoconfiguration:

- Router solicitation (RS) messages are sent from network hosts requesting that any listening router respond.

- Router advertisement (RA) messages are sent by the router in response to RS messages received from network hosts. These messages inform the network hosts of the correct IPv6 prefix they should use, along with the default gateway address.

NDP is also used by network hosts to discover the MAC address of other interfaces on the network, thus completely replacing the ARP when using IPv6. However, NDP cannot provide network hosts with the address of your DNS server. It can only provide the network prefix and the default gateway address.

The final IPv6 address configuration option is to use DHCP. As with IPv4, IPv6 address assignments can be made automatically using an updated version of DHCP called DHCPv6. Because IPv6 has so many more configuration options than IPv4, DHCPv6 operates in a different manner. There are two different modes:

- **Stateful DHCPv6**   Configures the DHCP server to provide each IPv6 DHCP client with an IP address, the default gateway address, and the DNS server IP address. The DHCP server tracks the status of each IPv6 DHCP client, hence the name *stateful*.

- **Stateless DHCPv6**   Does not assign IPv6 addressees to IPv6 clients, nor does not track their status. In this configuration, the DHCPv6 server simply assigns the DNS server IP address to network hosts. Obviously, stateless DHCPv6 does not provide a complete addressing solution. Instead, it must be used in conjunction with other IPv6 address assignment schemes, such as SLAC.

When an IPv6 host boots up, it follows the process described next to configure an address on its network interface:

1. The host automatically generates an IPv6 link-local address using the link-local prefix (which usually starts with **FE80**) combined with an interface ID derived from its MAC address.

2. The host sends a neighbor solicitation (NS) message addressed to its own link-local address to make sure another host on the network isn't already using it.

3. The host sends out a multicast RS message, which should be received by all routers on the same network segment. If no routers respond, the host attempts to use stateful DHCPv6 to receive an IPv6 address.

4. If a router receives the RS message, it then sends a multicast RA message to all hosts on the network segment. The RA message identifies how the IPv6 address is to be configured. Possible options include the following:

   - Obtain all IPv6 configuration information from a DHCPv6 server. If this is the case, the host sends out a REQUEST message to any listening DHCPv6 server.

   - Use stateless autoconfiguration to get the prefix and default gateway from the RA message and to generate the interface ID portion of its address automatically. The address of the DNS must then be obtained from a DHCPv6 server.

5. If a static IPv6 address has been configured or if stateful autoconfiguration has been used, the host sends an NS message to make sure no one else is using its address.

With this in mind, let's next look at some of the tools you can use to troubleshoot networking issues on Linux.

Troubleshooting Network Problems

Getting your network interface installed is only half the battle. To enable communications, you need to use a variety of testing and monitoring tools to make sure the network itself is working properly. We'll discuss how to do this in this part of the chapter. We'll cover the following topics:

- Using a standardized troubleshooting model
- Using ping
- Using netstat
- Using traceroute
- Using nc
- Using name resolution tools

Let's begin by discussing how to use a standardized troubleshooting model.

Using a Standardized Troubleshooting Model

Being a good troubleshooter is a key part of being an effective Linux system administrator. I've been teaching new system administrators for nearly two decades now, and this is one of the hardest skills for some to master. Some new admins just seem to have an intrinsic sense for how to troubleshoot problems; others don't. The reason for this, in my opinion, is that troubleshooting is part art form. Just as it's difficult for some of us (me included) to learn how to draw, sculpt, or paint, it's also difficult for some of us to learn how to troubleshoot.

However, I've noticed that, with a little training and a lot of practice, most new administrators can eventually learn how to troubleshoot effectively. There are three keys to doing this:

- Using a solid troubleshooting procedure
- Obtaining a working knowledge of troubleshooting tools
- Gaining a lot of experience troubleshooting problems

The last point is beyond the scope of this book. The only way to gain troubleshooting experience is to spend a couple of years in the field. However, we can work with the first two points. In the last part of this chapter, we'll focus specifically on troubleshooting network issues. However, the procedure we will discuss here can be broadly applied to any system problem.

Network problems can be caused by a wide array of issues, and I can't even begin to cover them all here. Instead, I want to focus on using a standardized process for troubleshooting network issues. By using a standardized process, you can adapt to, confront, and resolve a broad range of network problems. The model I'm going to present here is by no means all-inclusive. You may need to add, remove, or reorganize steps to match your particular situation. However, I hope it gives you a good base to start from.

Many new system administrators make a key mistake when they troubleshoot system or network problems. Instead of using a methodical troubleshooting approach, they go off half-cocked and start trying to implement fixes before they really know what the problem is. I call it "shotgun troubleshooting." The administrator tries one fix after another, hoping that one of them will repair the problem.

This is a very dangerous practice. I've watched system administrators do this and cause more problems than they solve. Sometimes they even cause catastrophic problems. Case in point: Several years ago I was setting up several servers in a network. One of the servers was misconfigured and was having trouble synchronizing information with the other systems. While I was trying to figure out the source of the problem, my coworker (let's call him Syd) started implementing one fix after another in shotgun fashion trying to get the server to sync with the other servers. In the process, he managed to catastrophically mess up all of them! The actual issue was relatively minor and would have required only about 20 minutes to fix. Instead, we had to spend the rest of the day and part of the night reinstalling each server from scratch and restoring their data.

Instead of using shotgun troubleshooting, you should use a standardized troubleshooting model. The goal of a troubleshooting model is to concretely identify the source of the problem *before* you start fixing things. I know that sounds simple, but many system administrators struggle with this concept. Here's a suggested troubleshooting model that you can use to develop your own personal troubleshooting methodology:

Step 1. *Gather information.* This is a critical step. You need to determine exactly what has happened. What are the symptoms? Were any error messages displayed? What did they say? How extensive is the problem? Is it isolated to a single system, or are many systems experiencing the same problem?

Step 2. *Identify what has changed.* In this step, you should identify what has changed in the system. Has new software been installed? Has new hardware been installed? Did a user change something? Did you change something?

Step 3. *Create a hypothesis.* With the information gathered in the preceding steps, develop several hypotheses that could explain the problem. To do this, you may need to do some research. You should check FAQs and knowledgebases available on the Internet. You should also consult with peers to validate your hypotheses. Using the information you gain, narrow your results down to the one or two most likely causes.

Step 4. *Determine the appropriate fix.* The next step is to use peers, FAQs, knowledgebases, and your own experience to identify the steps needed to fix the problem. As you do this, be sure to identify the possible ramifications of implementing the fix and account for them. Many times, the fix may have side effects that are as bad as or worse than the original problem.

Step 5. *Implement the fix.* At this point, you're ready to implement the fix. Notice that in this troubleshooting model, we did a ton of research before implementing a fix! Doing so greatly increases the likelihood of success. After implementing the fix, be sure to verify that the fix actually repaired the problem and that the issue doesn't reappear.

Step 6. *Ensure user satisfaction.* This is a key mistake made by many system administrators. I like to teach students the adage "If the user ain't happy, you ain't happy." We system admins are notoriously poor communicators. If the problem affects users, you need to communicate the nature of the problem with them and make sure they are aware that it has been fixed. If applicable, you should also educate them as to how to keep the problem from occurring in the future. You should also communicate with your users' supervisors and ensure they know that the problem has been fixed.

Step 7. *Document the solution.* Finally, you need to document the solution to your problem. That way, when it occurs again a year or two down the road, you or other system administrators can quickly identify the problem and how to fix it.

If you use this methodology, you can learn to be a very effective troubleshooter as you gain hands-on experience in the real world.

In addition to using a troubleshooting methodology, you also need to know how to use a variety of network troubleshooting tools for your Linux+/LPIC-1 exam. Let's first discuss how to use the ping utility.

Using ping

The ping utility is my best friend. It is one of the handiest tools in my networking virtual tool-box. I use ping all the time to test connectivity between hosts through the network. Ping works by sending an ICMP echo request packet from the source system to the destination system. The destination system then responds with an ICMP echo response packet. This process is shown in Figure 15-13.

If the ICMP echo response packet is received by the sending system, you know three things:

- Your network interface is working correctly.

- The destination system is up and working correctly.

- The network hardware between your system and the destination system is working correctly.

Figure 15-13

Using ping

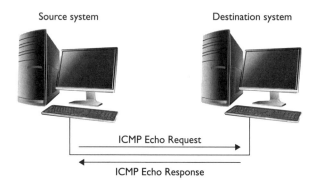

NOTE Be warned that many host-based firewalls used by many operating systems are configured by default to not respond to ICMP echo request packets. This is done to prevent a variety of denial of service (DoS) attacks that utilize a flood of ping requests. This configuration can give the false impression that the destination system is down. It's actually up and running just fine; it's just that the firewall on the host is stopping the ping packets from reaching the operating system.

That is valuable information to know! The basic syntax for using ping is **ping** *destination_ IP_address*. This causes ICMP echo request packets to be sent to the specified host. For example, you could enter **ping 192.168.2.1** to ping a host with this address. This is shown in Figure 15-14.

Notice in Figure 15-14 that the results of each ping sent are shown on a single line. Each line displays the size of the echo response packet (64 bytes), who it came from (192.168.2.1), its time-to-live value (63), and the round-trip time (4.25 ms to 1.01 ms).

NOTE The time-to-live (TTL) value specifies the number of routers the packet is allowed to cross before being thrown away.

```
                              root@openSUSE:/                            ×
 File  Edit  View  Search  Terminal  Help
openSUSE:/ # ping 192.168.2.1
PING 192.168.2.1 (192.168.2.1) 56(84) bytes of data.
64 bytes from 192.168.2.1: icmp_seq=1 ttl=63 time=4.25 ms
64 bytes from 192.168.2.1: icmp_seq=2 ttl=63 time=2.52 ms
64 bytes from 192.168.2.1: icmp_seq=3 ttl=63 time=1.01 ms
64 bytes from 192.168.2.1: icmp_seq=4 ttl=63 time=1.07 ms
64 bytes from 192.168.2.1: icmp_seq=5 ttl=63 time=1.09 ms
```

Figure 15-14 Pinging a host by IP address

```
root@openSUSE:/                                    ✕

File  Edit  View  Search  Terminal  Help
openSUSE:/ # ping www.google.com
PING www.google.com (74.125.239.144) 56(84) bytes of data.
64 bytes from nuq05s02-in-f16.1e100.net (74.125.239.144): icmp_seq=1 ttl=54 time=30.7 ms
64 bytes from nuq05s02-in-f16.1e100.net (74.125.239.144): icmp_seq=2 ttl=54 time=31.2 ms
64 bytes from nuq05s02-in-f16.1e100.net (74.125.239.144): icmp_seq=3 ttl=54 time=30.9 ms
64 bytes from nuq05s02-in-f16.1e100.net (74.125.239.144): icmp_seq=4 ttl=54 time=31.5 ms
64 bytes from nuq05s02-in-f16.1e100.net (74.125.239.144): icmp_seq=5 ttl=54 time=29.5 ms
```

Figure 15-15   Pinging by hostname

By default, the ping utility will continue sending ping requests to the specified host until you press CTRL-C to stop it. You can use the –c option with the ping command to specify a number of times to ping. For example, you can enter **ping –c 10 192.168.2.1** to ping ten times and then exit.

You can also ping by hostname instead of IP address. As long as you've configured your system with a valid DNS server address, ping will resolve the hostname into an IP address and send ping requests to it. This is shown in Figure 15-15.

Pinging with a hostname can be a valuable troubleshooting tool. It lets you know if there is a problem with the DNS server. For example, if pinging by IP address works but pinging by hostname does not work, then you know that your basic network configuration and connectivity is working properly but there is a problem with the DNS server.

You can also test IPv6 communications using ping as well. However, you must use the **ping6** command instead of ping.

In addition to ping, you should also be familiar with the netstat command. Let's look at it next.

Using netstat

The netstat utility is another powerful tool in your virtual toolbox. This utility can do the following:

- List network connections
- Display your routing table
- Display information about your network interface

The syntax for using netstat is to enter **netstat** *option* at the shell prompt. You can use the options listed in Table 15-5.

In addition to netstat, you should also be familiar with traceroute. Let's look at this utility next.

Table 15-5	netstat Option	Description
netstat Options	–a	Lists all listening and nonlistening sockets
	–i	Displays statistics for your network interfaces
	–l	Lists listening sockets
	–s	Displays summary information for each protocol
	–r	Displays your routing table

Using traceroute

The traceroute utility is really cool. Remember that if you try to send information to an IP host that doesn't reside on your local network segment, the packets will be sent to your default gateway router. This router will then use a variety of routing protocols to figure out how to get the packets to the destination system. In the process, the packets may have to be transferred from router to router to router to get them there. This is shown in Figure 15-16.

This is one of the beauties of an IP-based network. You can connect multiple networks together using routers and transfer data between them. It's this functionality that allows the Internet to exist. You can use a web browser to send http request packets to a web server located somewhere in the world and have it respond with the web page you want to view. The routing protocols used by routers dynamically determine the best route for packets to take based on system load. The route taken can change as network conditions change.

The traceroute utility can be used to trace the route a packet must traverse through these routers to arrive at its destination. It does this using the same ICMP echo request and ICMP echo response packets used by the ping utility, but it manipulates the TTL parameter of those packets. As a result, an ICMP echo response packet is sent back to the source system from each router your packets cross as they work their way through the network to the destination host, providing you with a list that shows the route between the source and destination systems.

Figure 15-16
Routing in an IP
network

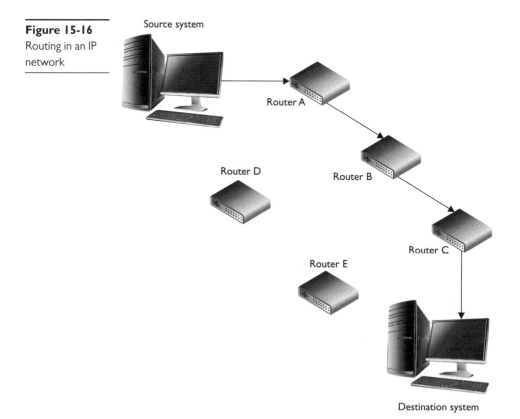

```
                              Terminal                         _ □ ×
File   Edit   View   Terminal   Help
ws1:/ # traceroute www.google.com
traceroute to www.google.com (74.125.93.99), 30 hops max, 40 byte packets using UDP
 1   192.168.1.1 (192.168.1.1)   0.748 ms    0.375 ms    0.178 ms
 2   192.168.0.1 (192.168.0.1)   1.678 ms    1.375 ms    1.478 ms
```

Figure 15-17   Using traceroute

This utility can be a very useful tool if you're experiencing communication problems between networks. The traceroute utility can help you track down which router in the route isn't working correctly. The syntax for using this utility is **traceroute** *destination_hostname_or_IP_address*. When you run it, traceroute creates one line for each router your packets cross as they make their way to the destination system. This is shown in Figure 15-17.

As you can see in Figure 15-17, the IP address of the router is displayed along with round-trip time statistics. As with the ping command, you can also use the traceroute command with the IPv6 protocol. To do this, you run **traceroute6** instead of traceroute.

 NOTE   You can also use the tracepath command to trace the route to a remote network host. The syntax, functionality, and output are almost identical to traceroute. As with traceroute, you can run tracepath6 to use the IPv6 protocol with this command.

Using nc

The netcat command (nc) is a very useful tool for testing network communications between hosts. It goes one step beyond the ping command and actually establishes a TCP or UDP connection between two network hosts. One way to use this command is to open a listening TCP or UDP socket on one host, and then connect to that socket from another host. In the following example, I first open a TCP listening socket on one of the hosts being tested:

```
openSUSE:/ # nc -l 2388
```

The –l option tells netcat to listen for incoming connections instead of trying to establish a connection with another computer. Because I didn't specify a protocol, TCP is used by default. If I wanted to use UDP, I would need to include the –u option with the command. I also specified the IP port to listen on (2388).

With a listening socket established on one system, I can then connect to it from another system and establish a TCP (or UDP) connection using the nc command again. This time, I enter the following:

```
[root@fs5 ~]# nc 10.0.0.83 2388
```

This command tells nc the IP address of the host to connect to and which IP port to use. Once the connection is established, I can type text at the prompt of the second system and see if it appears on the screen of the second system, as shown here:

```
[root@fs5 ~]# nc 10.0.0.83 2388
This is a test.
openSUSE:/ # nc -l 2388
This is a test.
```

If this test works, you know that TCP or UDP connections between those two hosts can be established.

> **NOTE** You must open the appropriate ports in the firewalls of both systems; otherwise, this test won't work!

Let's next look at several tools you can use to test name resolution on your network.

Using Name Resolution Tools

Using DNS for name resolution works great—unless it doesn't work correctly, that is. Then it can be a royal inconvenience for you because your end users won't be able to check their stock prices or manage their fantasy baseball team. Fortunately, there are several tools you can use to troubleshoot name resolution on your network:

- dig
- host
- getent

dig

You can use the Domain Information Groper (dig) utility to perform a DNS lookup on your DNS server and display detailed information about the hostname being resolved and about the DNS server itself. If you don't specify a particular DNS server with the dig command, the DNS servers configured in the resolv.conf file will be used. The syntax is **dig @*dns_server hostname***. An example is shown in Figure 15-18.

The output from dig is considerably more extensive than that displayed by other DNS trouble-shooting tools such as nslookup and host. The dig command returns the IP address associated with the hostname in the ANSWER SECTION. It also lists the authoritative name server for the hostname and zone in the AUTHORITY SECTION. You can use the following options with dig:

- **a** Resolve A record information
- **ptr** Resolve a PTR record
- **cname** Resolve CNAME record information
- **in** Resolve Internet record information
- **mx** Resolve MX record information
- **soa** Resolve start of authority information

host

You can also use the host command to resolve hostnames. Whereas the dig command provides extensive name resolution information, host provides simple, quick information. The syntax is similar to that used with dig. You enter **host *hostname DNS_server*** at the shell prompt. Again, if

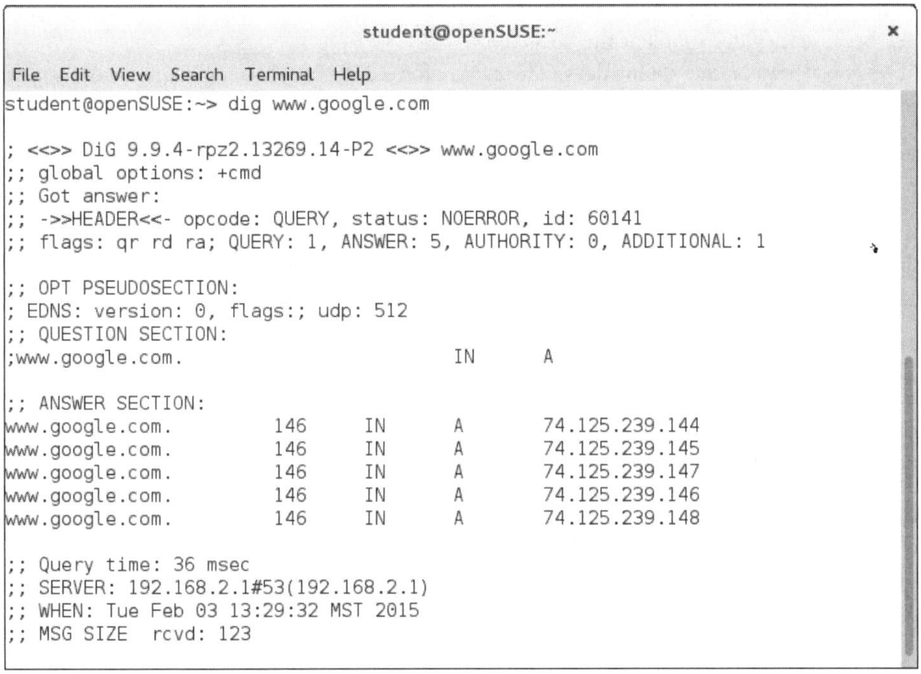

Figure 15-18 Using dig to resolve a hostname

you don't specify a DNS server, the default DNS server specified in /etc/resolv.conf will be used. An example of using host is shown here:

```
openSUSE:/ # host www.google.com
www.google.com has address 74.125.239.49
www.google.com has address 74.125.239.48
www.google.com has address 74.125.239.50
www.google.com has address 74.125.239.52
www.google.com has address 74.125.239.51
www.google.com has IPv6 address 2607:f8b0:4005:800::1011
```

getent

In addition to host and dig, you can also use getent to test your name resolution system. One of the weaknesses of the host and dig commands is that they don't actually follow the same process for name resolution as applications and services running on your system do. If an application such as a web browser needs to resolve a hostname to an IP address, it first queries your /etc/hosts file. If an entry for the host in question can't be found there, it uses the DNS server you configured to resolve the hostname.

However, the dig and host commands don't do this. They skip the hosts file completely and go directly to your DNS server to test name resolution. This is an issue of concern! Many phishing and pharming attacks exploit the hosts file to redirect URLs to malicious websites where users' personal information can be gleaned. As you can see, using host or dig will not reveal such an attack because they don't look at the hosts file.

The good news is that getent does. The syntax for using getent to test name resolution is to enter **getent hosts *hostname*** at the shell prompt. An example is shown next:

```
openSUSE:/ # getent hosts router1
10.0.0.1        router1
```

In this example, an entry for the router1 hostname exists in the hosts file, so getent was able to grab it and display it on the screen. If the hosts file doesn't have an entry for the hostname specified, it will try to resolve it via DNS, just like a regular application would. An example is shown next:

```
openSUSE:/ # getent hosts www.nebo-tech.com
98.139.135.199  sbsfe-p11.geo.mf0.yahoodns.net www.nebo-tech.com
```

 TIP The getent command can query any data configured in your /etc/nsswitch.conf file. For example, you can enter **getent passwd** at the shell prompt to pull entries out of your passwd file.

Let's practice working with network commands in the following exercise.

Exercise 15-2: Working with Network Commands

In this exercise, you will practice using network commands to manage and troubleshoot your network interface. This exercise assumes that you have a connection to the Internet. You can perform this exercise using the virtual machine that comes with this book. Run snapshot 15-1 for the correctly configured environment.

 VIDEO Please watch the Exercise 15-2 video for a demonstration on how to perform this task.

Complete the following:

1. Boot your Linux system and log in as your student user.

2. Open a terminal session.

3. Switch to your root user account by entering **su –** followed by a password of **student**.

4. Test connectivity by entering **ping www.google.com** at the shell prompt. Your system should resolve the hostname into an IP address and send ICMP echo request packets to it. (If your system isn't connected to the Internet, this step won't work.)

 NOTE If you are unable to ping the remote website, verify that an IP address has been assigned using the ifconfig command. If an address has not been assigned, enter **systemctl restart network** to reload the network configuration.

5. Display summary information about your network interface by entering **netstat –s |** **more** at the shell prompt. Review the information displayed.

6. Trace the route to www.google.com by entering **traceroute www.google.com** at the shell prompt. Note the various routers crossed as your packets traverse the Internet to www .google.com.

7. Generate extended name resolution about www.google.com by entering **dig www.google** **.com** at the shell prompt.

Chapter Review

In this chapter, you learned how to set up networking on your Linux system. I first pointed out that you will most likely work with Ethernet network boards and the IP protocol in most modern organizations. I pointed out that a protocol is a common networking "language" that must be configured in order for two hosts to communicate.

I pointed out that the Internet Protocol (IP) works in conjunction with the Transmission Control Protocol (TCP) or the User Datagram Protocol (UDP) to fragment, transmit, defragment, and resequence network data to enable communications between hosts. We also looked at the Internet Control Message Protocol (ICMP), which is another core protocol in the IP protocol suite. It differs in purpose from TCP and UDP, which are transport protocols. The primary role of ICMP is to test and verify network communications between hosts.

I reviewed the role and function of the OSI Reference Model. I related that the OSI Reference Model layers break down the overall communication process into specific tasks. Information flows down through the layers on the sending system and then is transmitted on the network medium. The information then flows up the layers on the receiving side. The OSI Reference Model has seven layers:

- Physical
- Data Link
- Network
- Transport
- Session
- Presentation
- Application

I then discussed the concept of IP ports. Ports are provided by both the TCP and UDP protocols at the Transport layer. In essence, a port is a logical connection provided by TCP and UDP for upper-layer protocols. Ports allow a single host with a single IP address to provide multiple network services. Each service uses the same IP address but operates using its own different TCP or UDP port number. Port numbers can range from 0 to 65536. The way these ports are used is regulated by the Internet Corporation for Assigned Names and Numbers (ICANN). There are three different categories that IP ports are lumped into:

- Well-known ports
- Registered ports
- Dynamic ports

We then looked at how IPv4 addressing works. Each host on the network must have a correctly configured, unique IP address assigned to it. It must also have the correct subnet mask assigned. The subnet mask defines how much of a given host's IP address is the network address and how much is the IP address. When viewed in binary form, any bit in the subnet mask that has a 1 in it represents a network address bit in the IP address. Any bit with a 0 in it represents the host address. IP addresses are categorized into several classes. The first three classes each have a default subnet mask assigned:

- **Class A**   255.0.0.0
- **Class B**   255.255.0.0
- **Class C**   255.255.255.0

You don't have to use these default subnet masks. You can also use only part of an octet for the network address. This is called *partial subnetting* or *variable-length subnet masking (VLSM)*. Using VLSM, we ignore the default subnet mask boundaries and specify a custom number of subnet mask bits.

Hosts on the same network segment must have the same network address for them to communicate. Therefore, the same subnet mask must be assigned to each host.

To resolve domain names into IP addresses, your Linux system must also be configured with the IP address of your organization's DNS server. In addition, you must also configure it with the IP address of your network segment's default gateway router for it to communicate with hosts on other network segments.

We also looked at the concept of public and private IP addressing. Public networks use globally unique, registered IP addresses. Private networks use nonroutable, nonregistered, nonunique IP addresses. You can use a NAT router to hide a private network behind one or more public interfaces. This allows you to implement their network using only a relatively small number of globally unique public IP addresses. Within each class of IP address are blocks of addresses called *private* or *reserved* IP addresses. These addresses are unallocated and can be used by anyone who wants to use them. The private IP address ranges are

- 10.0.0.0–10.255.255.255 (Class A)
- 172.16.0.0–172.31.255.255 (Class B)
- 192.168.0.0–192.168.255.255 (Class C)

We also looked at IPv6. IPv6 addresses are composed of eight four-character hexadecimal numbers, separated by colons instead of periods. For example, a valid IPv6 address could be 35BC :FA77:4898:DAFC:200C:FBBC:A007:8973. This 128-bit address contains two parts:

- The *prefix* is the first 64 bits. It includes the network and subnet address.
- The *interface ID* is the last 64 bits. This is the unique address assigned to a network host.

There are three types of IPv6 addresses you need to be familiar with:

- Global unicast
- Unique local
- Link local

I then shifted gears and discussed how to configure an Ethernet network interface in a Linux system. The first task you need to complete is to install the network board in the system and connect it to your network. Then you need to load the appropriate kernel modules for the board. For newer boards, this happens automatically. For older or uncommon network boards, you may have to do this manually. Once this is done, the network board should have an alias created for it. If your distribution uses init, then the first interface in the system will be named eth0. Subsequent network boards should have the following aliases created for them: eth1, eth2, eth3, and so on.

Distributions that use systemd no longer use this naming convention for network interfaces. Instead, they use predictable network interface names. This allows specific aliases to be permanently assigned to specific network interfaces. Predictable network interface device names are assigned based on one of the following parameters. The preferred order is as follows:

- For an onboard network adapter, the index number provided by the system firmware (or BIOS) is used to construct the alias.

- If the network adapter is plugged into a PCI-E hot-plug slot instead of being integrated into the motherboard, then systemd will use the index number of the slot itself, as provided by the firmware (or BIOS), to construct the alias.

- If the preceding options are not applicable, then systemd will try to construct an alias using the name of the physical connector the interface is connected to, such as a USB connector.

- If all else fails, then systemd will try to use the interface's MAC address to construct an alias.

Once the board is installed, you need to use the ifconfig command or dhclient command to configure the network interface with the appropriate IP configuration parameters. When you enter **ifconfig** at the shell prompt without any parameters, the details of your installed network interfaces are displayed. To assign IP information, enter **ifconfig *interface ip_address* netmask *subnet_mask* broadcast *broadcast_address*** at the shell prompt. To make the assignment persistent, you need to enter your IP configuration parameters in the appropriate file located within the /etc/sysconfig/network directory.

You can also use the ip command to manage your network interfaces. This command can be used to

- View your current IP configuration.

- Configure IP addressing parameters.

- Disable or enable a network interface.

To assign the DNS server address or the default gateway router address, you need to edit several configuration files:

- **DNS server address**   /etc/resolv.conf
- **Default gateway router address**   /etc/sysconfig/network/routes

To bring a network interface down, you can enter **ifdown** at the shell prompt. To bring it up, enter **ifup**. To use a DHCP server to dynamically assign IP address information to a Linux host, enter **dhclient *interface*** at the shell prompt.

We then spent some time looking at configuring the IPv6 protocol. IPv6 addresses are assigned using processes that are quite different from those used for IPv4 addresses. You can use

- Static address assignments
- Static partial assignment
- Stateless auto configuration
- DHCPv6 configuration

I ended this chapter by discussing several command-line utilities you can use to test and monitor the network. You can use the ping command to test connectivity between systems. The syntax is **ping *destination_host***. You can use the netstat command to view a variety of network interface information using the –a, –i, –l, –s, and –r options. To use ping with IPv6, you run the ping6 command. You can also use the traceroute utility to trace the route your packets must follow to reach a remote system. The syntax for using traceroute is **traceroute *destination_host***. To use traceroute with IPv6, you run the traceroute6 command.

To test TCP or UDP communications, you use the nc command, which stands for netcat. This utility can be used to establish a TCP or UDP connection between two network hosts. First, you open a listening TCP or UDP socket on one host, and then you connect to that socket from another host. If this test works, you know that TCP or UDP connections between those two hosts can be established.

We also looked at tools you can use to test name resolution, including dig, host, and getent. The dig and host commands are used to verify that your DNS server is resolving IP addresses correctly. The getent command first tests name resolution using your hosts file. If it can't find an entry there, it will query your DNS server to resolve the name.

Accelerated Review

- You will most likely work with Ethernet network boards and the IP protocol when managing Linux systems.
- A protocol is a common networking language that must be configured for network hosts to communicate.
- The Internet Protocol (IP) works in conjunction with TCP or UDP to fragment, transmit, defragment, and resequence network data.
- The Internet Control Message Protocol (ICMP) is used to test and verify network communications between hosts.
- The OSI Reference Model is composed of layers that break down the overall communication process into specific tasks:
  - Physical
  - Data Link
  - Network
  - Transport

- Session
- Presentation
- Application
- Ports are provided by both the TCP and UDP protocols at the Transport layer.
- A port is a logical connection provided by TCP and UDP for upper-layer protocols.
- Ports allow a single host with a single IP address to provide multiple network services.
- There are three different categories that IP ports are lumped into:
  - Well-known ports
  - Registered ports
  - Dynamic ports
- Each host on an IPv4 network must have a unique IP address assigned as well as the correct subnet mask.
- The subnet mask defines how much of a given host's IP address is the network address and how much is the IP address.
- IP addresses are categorized into several classes, each of which has a default subnet mask assigned:
  - **Class A**   255.0.0.0
  - **Class B**   255.255.0.0
  - **Class C**   255.255.255.0
- Using VLSM, you can ignore the default subnet mask boundaries and specify a custom number of subnet mask bits.
- Hosts on the same network segment must have the same subnet mask and must be assigned to each host.
- A network host must be configured with the IP address of a DNS server to resolve domain names into IP addresses.
- A network host must be configured with the IP address of the segment's default gateway router for it to communicate with hosts on other network segments.
- IPv6 addresses are composed of eight four-character hexadecimal numbers, separated by colons instead of periods.
- The 128-bit IPv6 addresses are divided into two parts:
  - The *prefix* is the first 64 bits.
  - The *interface ID* is the last 64 bits.
- There are three types of IPv6 addresses you need to be familiar with:
  - Global unicast
  - Unique local
  - Link local

- Public networks use globally unique, registered IP addresses.

- Private networks use nonroutable, nonregistered, and nonunique IP addresses.

- Within each class of IP address are blocks of addresses called private or reserved IP addresses:
  - 10.0.0.0–10.255.255.255 (Class A)
  - 172.16.0.0–172.31.255.255 (Class B)
  - 192.168.0.0–192.168.255.255 (Class C)

- You can use a NAT router to hide a private network behind one or more public interfaces.

- To install an Ethernet interface in a Linux system, you first need to install the network board in the system and connect it to the network medium.

- Next, you need to load the appropriate kernel modules for the board.

- If your distribution uses init, the first network board should have an alias created for it named eth0.

- Additional boards will have aliases of eth1, eth2, and so on assigned.

- Distributions that use systemd use predictable network interface names.

- You can enter **ifconfig** at the shell prompt to view the details of your installed network interfaces.

- To assign an IP address to a network interface, enter **ifconfig** *interface ip_address* **netmask** *subnet_mask* **broadcast** *broadcast_address* at the shell prompt.

- To make IP address assignments persistent, enter them in the appropriate file within the /etc/sysconfig/network directory.

- You can also use the ip command to manage your network interfaces.

- Enter your organization's DNS server address in the /etc/resolv.conf file.

- Enter your segment's default gateway router address in the /etc/systconfig/network/routes file.

- Enter **ifdown** at the shell prompt to bring a network interface down.

- Enter **ifup** to bring a network interface back up.

- To dynamically assign an IP address to a Linux host, enter **dhclient** *interface* at the shell prompt.

- IPv6 addresses are assigned using one of the following processes:
  - Static address assignments
  - Static partial assignment
  - Stateless auto configuration
  - DHCPv6 configuration

- Linux includes a variety of command-line utilities you can use to test and monitor the network.

- Use ping to test connectivity between systems. The syntax is **ping** *destination_host*.

- Use ping6 to test IPv6 communications between hosts.

- Use the netstat command to view a variety of network interface information using the –a, –i, –l, –s, and –r options.

- Use the traceroute utility to trace the route your packets follow to reach a remote system. The syntax is **traceroute** *destination_host*.

- Use traceroute6 to test IPv6 routing between hosts.

- Use the route command or the netstat –r command to view your system's route table.

- To test TCP or UDP communications, use the nc command.

- Use the route command to add or remove routes from the route table.

- You can use the dig, host, and getent commands to test DNS name resolution.

Questions

1. Which of the following are true of the MAC address? (Choose two.)

   A. It's hard-coded in the network board.

   B. It's logically assigned by the operating system.

   C. MAC addresses are globally unique.

   D. The network administrator can configure its value.

   E. It is used by the DNS server to resolve domain names.

2. Which transport protocol is used by network applications that need very low latency and can tolerate a certain degree of unreliability?

   A. User Datagram Protocol

   B. Transmission Control Protocol

   C. Internet Protocol

   D. Internet Control Message Protocol

3. Which layer of the OSI model enables the routing of data?

   A. Data Link

   B. Network

   C. Transport

   D. Session

   E. Application

4. You've just set up an e-mail server on your Linux system and enabled the SMTP and POP3 daemons to allow users to send and receive mail. Which ports must be opened in your system's host firewall to allow this? (Choose two.)

    A. 20

    B. 21

    C. 25

    D. 110

    E. 119

    F. 80

5. Which of the following are valid IP addresses that can be assigned to a network host? (Choose two.)

    A. 192.168.254.1

    B. 11.0.0.0

    C. 257.0.0.1

    D. 192.345.2.1

    E. 10.200.0.200

6. Which of the following is the default subnet mask for a Class B network?

    A. 255.255.0.0

    B. 255.0.0.0

    C. 255.255.255.0

    D. 255.255.255.252

7. You've configured three hosts on your network with the following IP addresses and subnet masks:

    • **Host A** IP = 23.0.0.1, Mask = 255.0.0.0

    • **Host B** IP = 23.0.0.3, Mask = 255.255.0.0

    • **Host C** IP = 23.0.0.4, Mask =255.255.0.0

    Is this network configured properly?

    A. Yes, this network is configured properly.

    B. No, the 23.0.0.1 IP address used by Host A is a reserved IP address.

    C. No, Host A uses the wrong subnet mask.

    D. No, Host B and Host C must use the default Class A subnet mask.

8. Your network interface has been assigned an IP address of 10.0.0.1. What is this binary equivalent of this decimal address?

   A. 10001010.00000000.00000000.00000001

   B. 00001010.00000001.00000001.00000001

   C. 10100000.00000000.00000000.00000001

   D. 00001010.00000000.00000000.00000001

9. Which files can you check on some distributions to verify that a kernel module has been loaded and an alias created for a newly installed network board? (Choose two.)

   A. /etc/sysctl.conf

   B. /etc/modprobe.conf

   C. /etc/modules.conf

   D. /etc/drivers

   E. /etc/aliases

10. You just installed a second Ethernet board in an older Linux system. What alias is assigned to this interface by default?

    A. eth0

    B. eth1

    C. eth2

    D. eth3

11. You need to use ifconfig to assign an IP address of 176.23.0.12 and a subnet mask of 255.255.0.0 to your eth0 interface. Which of the following commands will do this?

    A. ifconfig eth0 176.23.0.12 netmask 255.255.0.0

    B. ifconfig 176.23.0.12 netmask 255.255.0.0

    C. ifconfig eth0 176.23.0.12 mask 255.255.0.0

    D. ifconfig dev=eth0 ipaddr=176.23.0.12 subnetmask=255.255.0.0

12. You need to make a permanent, static IP address assignment for your eth0 network interface, which has a MAC address of 00:0C:29:B1:50:A4. Which file do you need to edit to do this, depending on your particular distribution? (Choose two.)

    A. /etc/sysconfig/network/eth0/ifcfg-eth-id-00:0C:29:B1:50:A4

    B. /etc/sysconfig/network/00:0C:29:B1:50:A4/eth0

    C. /etc/sysconfig/network/ifcfg-eth0

    D. /etc/sysconfig/network/ifcfg-eth-id-00:0C:29:B1:50:A4

    E. /etc/sysctl/network/ifcfg-eth-id-00:0C:29:B1:50:A4

13. Which option in your eth0 network interface configuration file should you use to configure the NIC to get its IP address information dynamically from a DHCP server?

    A. STARTMODE

    B. BOOTPROTO

    C. IPADDR

    D. DHCP

14. Which parameters in your network interface configuration file are required to assign an IPv6 address to the host? (Choose two.)

    A. ETHTOOL_OPTIONS

    B. PREFIXLEN

    C. IPADDR

    D. MTU

    E. REMOTE_IPADDR

    F. USERCONTROL

15. You've opened your /etc/sysconfig/network/routes file in the vi editor. You want to specify a default gateway router address of 10.200.200.254. Which of the following directives would you enter in this file to do this?

    A. default 10.200.200.254

    B. gw_addr 10.200.200.254

    C. gateway 10.200.200.254

    D. router 10.200.200.254

16. You've opened your /etc/sysconfig/network/resolv.conf file in the vi editor. You want to specify a DNS server address of 10.200.200.1. Which of the following directives would you enter in this file to do this?

    A. host 10.200.200.1

    B. resolver 10.200.200.1

    C. dnsserver 10.200.200.1

    D. nameserver 10.200.200.1

17. You want to use your organization's DHCP server to dynamically assign an IP address to your ens1 network interface. Which of the following commands would you enter at the shell prompt to do this?

    A. dhcp ens1

    B. dhclient ens1

    C. get address dynamic ens1

    D. ip address=dhcp dev= ens1

18. You want to temporarily disable the second interface in an older Linux system. Which of the following commands would you enter at the shell prompt to do this?

    A. ifdown eth1

    B. ifdown eth0

    C. ifdown eth2

    D. ifconfig disable dev eth1

19. You need to verify that a remote host with a hostname of fs1.mycorp.com is up and running. Which of the following commands would you enter at the shell prompt to do this?

    A. finger fs1.mycorp.com

    B. ping fs1.mycorp.com

    C. netstat –s fs1.mycorp.com

    D. verify fs1.mycorp.com

20. Your users can't access your organization's e-mail server, which is hosted by a third-party vendor. You suspect that a router may be down somewhere within your organization. Given that the hostname of the e-mail server is pop.mymail.com, which of the following commands would you enter at the shell prompt to test this? (Choose two.)

    A. traceroute pop.mymail.com

    B. netstat –r pop.mymail.com

    C. finger pop.mymail.com

    D. verify pop.mymail.com

    E. tracepath pop.mymail.com

21. Which of the following commands will add a default gateway router address of 10.200.200.254 to your route table?

    A. route 10.200.200.254

    B. route add default gw 10.200.200.254

    C. netstat –a default 10.200.200.254

    D. gateway 10.200.200.254

22. Consider the following IPv4 address that uses CIDR notation: **10.0.0.5/12**. Which of the following subnet masks corresponds to the CIDR prefix used in this address?

    A. 255.0.0.0

    B. 255.240.0.0

    C. 255.224.0.0

    D. 255.252.0.0

23. A workstation on your network has just sent several packets to a host that does not reside on the current network segment. The packets are sent to the default gateway router for the network segment. What happens next?

   A. The packets are dropped.

   B. The packets are translated from private IP addresses used on the internal network to the public IP address configured on the router.

   C. The default gateway router checks its routing table to determine where to send the packets next.

   D. The default gateway router performs a DNS lookup to determine the IP address of the target host.

Answers

1. **A, C.** MAC addresses are hard-coded into the firmware of every Ethernet network board. Theoretically, no two network boards in the world should have the same MAC address. However, a few types of network boards actually do allow you to manually configure the MAC address.

2. **A.** The User Datagram Protocol is an unacknowledged, connectionless protocol that sends packets without requesting a confirmation of receipt. This makes it ideal for network applications that need very low latency but can tolerate a certain degree of unreliability, such as streaming video.

3. **B.** The Network layer of the OSI model enables the routing of data between networks. In an IP network, this functionality is provided by the Internet Protocol (IP itself).

4. **C, D.** The SMTP daemon uses port 25 by default, whereas the POP3 daemon uses port 110 by default.

5. **A, E.** 192.168.254.1 and 10.200.0.200 are both valid IP addresses that can be assigned to network hosts.

6. **A.** 255.255.0.0 is the default subnet mask for a Class B network.

7. **C.** The network isn't configured properly because Host A uses the wrong subnet mask.

8. **D.** The binary equivalent of the first octet (10) is 00001010. The binary equivalent of the second and third octets (0) is 00000000 each. The binary equivalent of the fourth octet (1) is 00000001.

9. **B, C.** You can check the /etc/modprobe.conf file or the /etc/modules.conf file on some distributions to verify that the correct module has been loaded and an alias has been created.

10. **B.** The second Ethernet board in an older Linux system that uses init is assigned an alias of eth1 by default.

11. **A.** The **ifconfig eth0 176.23.0.12 netmask 255.255.0.0** command will assign the IP address and subnet mask to the eth0 interface.

12. **C, D.** Depending on which distribution you're using, you can make persistent IP address assignments using either the /etc/sysconfig/network/ifcfg-eth0 file or the /etc/sysconfig/network/ifcfg-eth-id-00:0C:29:B1:50:A4 file.

13. **B.** The BOOTPROTO option is used to specify whether the interface uses a static or dynamic IP address assignment.

14. **B, C.** The PREFIXLEN and IPADDR directives are used along with the LABEL directive in a network interface configuration file to assign an IPv6 address to a NIC that also has an IPv4 address assigned.

15. **A.** The default 10.200.200.254 directive specifies a default gateway router address of 10.200.200.254.

16. **D.** The nameserver 10.200.200.1 directive specifies a DNS server with an IP address of 10.200.200.1.

17. **B.** The dhclient ens1 command will configure the ens1 interface with IP address information from a DHCP server.

18. **A.** The **ifdown eth1** command will disable the second Ethernet interface in an older Linux system that uses init instead of systemd.

19. **B.** The **ping fs1.mycorp.com** command will test communications between your system and the specified host.

20. **A, E.** The **traceroute pop.mymail.com** and **tracepath pop.mymail.com** commands will list all the routers between the source and destination hosts, allowing you to identify a router that isn't working correctly.

21. **B.** The **route add default gw 10.200.200.254** command will add the specified IP address as the default gateway router.

22. **B.** A CIDR IP address of 10.0.0.5/12 specifies a 12-bit prefix length. The subnet mask for this address is therefore 12-bits long (11111111.11110000.00000000.00000000). In decimal notation, this would be a subnet mask of 255.240.0.0.

23. **C.** Because the packets are being sent to a host that does not reside on the current network segment, they are automatically forwarded to the default gateway router configured on the segment. The default gateway router checks its routing table to determine where to send the packets next.

Managing Network Services on Linux

In this chapter, you will learn about:
- Configuring printing with CUPS
- Maintaining system time
- Managing an MTA
- Managing SQL data

In this chapter, I'm going to teach you how to configure a variety of network services on your Linux system. In my opinion, this is where Linux really shines. You can take just about any Linux distribution and enable network services on it to configure it to fill a variety of powerful roles in your network. Do you need a web server? No problem! Linux can do that. Do you need a Windows domain controller? Linux can do that as well. How about a network firewall? Again, Linux can fill that role. Need a database server? You got it! Need a hypervisor for running virtual machines? Linux excels at this.

These roles are made possible using Linux daemons. To enable a service on your system, you need to first install the appropriate daemon from your distribution's installation media using the installation utility of your choice, such as yum or rpm. Once it is installed, you can then use a text editor to modify the daemon's configuration file, usually saved in /etc/, to configure how it behaves. If your distribution uses the init daemon, you can start, stop, or reload the service using the appropriate init script in the /etc/init.d or /etc/rc.d/init.d directory on your system. If your distribution uses systemd, you can use the systemctl command to start, stop, or reload the service.

Be warned that we need to cover a lot of topics in this chapter. Therefore, I'm not going to go into great depth on any one of them. Most of the network services I'm going to cover in this chapter are quite complex. Entire books have been written about most of them. We don't have the time or space to do that here. To get you ready for your Linux+/LPIC-1 exam, I'm going to introduce you to each topic and then teach you how to perform a basic configuration.

EXAM TIP Try not to be overwhelmed by this chapter! We're going to cover a lot of network services, but you don't have to be an expert with them. Just familiarize yourself with the basics of each of the services covered here (printing, time, e-mail, and SQL databases).

Let's begin this chapter by discussing how to configure printing on your Linux system.

Configuring Printing with CUPS

No matter what operating system you're using, one of the most important services it offers is the ability to send print jobs to a printer. If you don't believe me, just unplug your office's printer for an hour and observe the mayhem that results. Okay, don't really unplug your office's printer. Your coworkers may inflict bodily harm upon you.

The point is that printing is vital to most users. Because of this, you need to be very familiar with Linux printing. In this part of this chapter, we're going to cover the following topics:

- How Linux printing works
- Installing CUPS
- Configuring CUPS
- Using the Line Printer Daemon (lpd)
- Troubleshooting printing issues

Let's begin by discussing how Linux printing works.

How Linux Printing Works

The most common Linux printing system in use today is the Common UNIX Printing System (CUPS). CUPS was designed from the ground up to make Linux printing as easy as possible, whether printing to a locally attached printer or to a remote network printer. The CUPS service is provided by the cupsd daemon, which automatically announces the availability of its print queues on the local network. CUPS client systems listen to these announcements, allowing the user to select the printer he or she wants with little networking knowledge. In addition, CUPS supports network printing over the *Internet Printing Protocol (IPP)* on port 631. The CUPS system is composed of several component parts.

The first is the *CUPS scheduler*, which is a web server that is used solely to handle IPP printing requests from CUPS clients. Because the CUPS scheduler runs on IP port 631, it can coexist with the Apache web server running on the same system. In fact, the CUPS configuration file even looks like the Apache web server's configuration file. In addition to processing print jobs, the CUPS scheduler also functions as a typical web server, providing documentation as well as a CUPS administration tool in a browser interface.

The next components you need to be familiar with are the CUPS filters. Modern printers use a variety of different *page description languages (PDLs)*. In a Linux system, most applications generate print jobs using Adobe's PostScript PDL. This works well if you have a PostScript-compatible printer. However, not all printers include PostScript support due to the fact that the printer manufacturer must pay licensing fees to Adobe, which can dramatically increase the price of the unit. Instead, many printer manufacturers, such as Hewlett-Packard, use the Printer Control Language (PCL) PDL. Other manufacturers, such as Epson, use the ESC/P PDL.

If your printer isn't PostScript compatible, you use CUPS filters to convert print jobs from PostScript into the appropriate format using the PDL of the printer to which they are being sent. These filters are located in /usr/lib/cups/filter.

The next components you need to know about are the CUPS backends. Backends are responsible for providing the interface between the scheduler and the actual printer hardware. The CUPS backends are located in /usr/lib/cups/backend. CUPS provides backends for a variety of different printer interfaces, including parallel, serial, USB, and so on. Each time cupsd starts, it queries each backend installed on the system. The backends respond to the daemon, reporting whether or not a printer is connected. If a printer is connected, they report information about the printer, such as the make and model.

The next CUPS components you need to be familiar with are the PPD (PostScript Printer Description) files. PPDs are used by cupsd to determine the capabilities of your printer. These PPD files are stored in /etc/cups/ppd.

The last CUPS component you need to be familiar with is the web-based administration utility. The CUPS scheduler provides the web-based administrative interface. The CUPS administration utility can be used to set up printers and manage print jobs. To access the CUPS web-based administration utility, just open a web browser and navigate to http://*your_server_address*:631. When you do, the screen in Figure 16-1 is displayed.

When a print job is submitted to a CUPS server, the process depicted in Figure 16-2 occurs.

First, an application on the client system generates a print job and sends it to the cupsd daemon on the server. The daemon saves the job in the spooling directory. Print queue and filter information from the print job are saved in /var/spool/cups. The file is named with a *c,* concatenated with a print job number assigned by cupsd. The document to be printed is also saved in /var/spool/cups. This time, however, the file is named with a *d,* concatenated with the print job number assigned by cupsd.

Figure 16-1   Using the CUPS administration utility

Figure 16-2
Sending a
print job

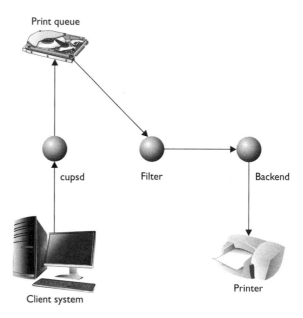

Next, the print job is sent to the filter for conversion to the appropriate PDL. Once that's done, the converted print job is sent from the filter to the backend, which forwards the job to its connected printer. After sending the job to the printer, the backend notifies the cupsd daemon and the print job is deleted from the print queue.

Now that you know how CUPS printing works, I need to discuss how to install the service on your Linux system. Let's do that next.

Installing CUPS

Unlike the services we reviewed earlier in this chapter, there's a pretty good chance that your Linux distribution installed the packages required to provide CUPS printing by default. As stated earlier, CUPS is the default printing system used by most modern Linux distributions.

If your distribution didn't install CUPS for some reason, use the package installation utility of your choice to install the following packages (along with any dependent packages):

- cups
- cups-client (optional)
- gutenprint (Contains printer drivers for cups.)
- cups-libs
- libgnomecups (optional)

NOTE The actual list of packages you end up installing may vary depending on your distribution.

```
boot.clock           cron          powerfail      syslog
boot.crypto         [cups  ]       random         vboxadd
boot.crypto-early    dbus          raw            vmtoolsd
boot.d               dnsmasq       rc             xdm
boot.device-mapper   dvb           rc0.d          xdm.orig
boot.dmraid          earlysyslog   rc1.d          xfs
boot.fuse            earlyxdm      rc2.d          xinetd
boot.ipconfig        fbset         rc3.d          ypbind
boot.klog            gpm           rc4.d
linux:/etc/init.d #
```

Figure 16-3 The cups init script

After the packages are installed, the binary that provides the CUPS service is the cupsd executable located in /usr/sbin. If your distribution uses the init daemon to manage processes, the CUPS service is started and stopped using the cups init script in /etc/init.d or /etc/rc.d/init.d, shown in Figure 16-3. If your distribution is based on systemd, the CUPS service is started and stopped using the /usr/lib/systemd/system/cups.service file.

Once the CUPS packages are installed on your system, you're ready to configure and start the CUPS service on your server. Let's discuss how to do that next.

Configuring CUPS

The CUPS service appears complicated, and under the hood, it is. Fortunately, the developers who wrote CUPS made it very easy for you and me to configure and manage. In this part of this chapter, you're going learn how to configure CUPS by learning about the following topics:

- Configuring the CUPS service
- Configuring a CUPS printer
- Using command-line tools to manage CUPS

Let's begin by discussing how to configure the cupsd daemon.

Configuring the CUPS Service

The CUPS service is configured using several text files within the /etc/cups directory. The /etc/cups/cupsd.conf file is the main configuration file you will use to configure the cupsd daemon (called the scheduler). Remember that cupsd is also an HTTP server, like Apache. Accordingly, the cupsd.conf file is very similar to the Apache web server configuration file. A sample cupsd.conf file is shown in Figure 16-4.

Figure 16-4 only shows a very small portion of the cupsd.conf file, which is quite long. The cupsd.conf file is composed of many server directives, which specify how cupsd operates. We don't have the time or space in this book to cover all the configuration options in cupsd.conf. I'm just going to cover the most important ones here. For more information, see the man page for cupsd.conf. You can also open http://localhost:631/help/ in a browser on your Linux system

Figure 16-4

Using the cupsd.
conf file to config-
ure CUPS

```
#
# "$Id: cupsd.conf.in 9407 2010-12-09 21:24:51Z mike $"
#
# Configuration file for the CUPS scheduler.  See "man cupsd.conf" for a
# complete description of this file.
#

# Log general information in error_log - change "warn" to "debug"
# for troubleshooting...
LogLevel warn

# Administrator user group...
SystemGroup sys root

# Only listen for connections from the local machine.
Listen localhost:631
Listen /var/run/cups/cups.sock

# Show shared printers on the local network.
Browsing On
BrowseOrder allow,deny
BrowseAllow all
BrowseLocalProtocols CUPS
--More--(10%)
```

to see an extensive list of cupsd.conf directives, or you can visit http://www.cups.org/documen-
tation.php/ref-cupsd-conf.html. Some of the more useful cupsd.conf directives include those
shown in Table 16-1.

The way you configure cupsd.conf will largely depend on the particular network you are
implementing the system in. The good news is that you don't need to do much with cupsd.conf
to configure a basic implementation that provides local printing.

However, if you want other Linux systems to be able to print through your CUPS printer,
you must enable BrowseAddress or else CUPS won't announce its printers on the network. This
directive is *not* enabled by default on many distributions. Sample configurations for this directive
include the following:

```
BrowseAddress 255.255.255.255:631
BrowseAddress 192.168.1.255:631
BrowseAddress mydom.com:631
BrowseAddress @LOCAL
```

The BrowseAddress directive is usually set to a value of @LOCAL. This causes CUPS to send
printer announcement broadcasts to all local network interfaces in the system. You can set this
directive to @IF(*interface_name*) to limit broadcasts to a specific network interface.

After making any changes to cupds.conf, be sure to restart the cupsd daemon. After configuring your cupsd.conf file, you next need to set up a Linux user account that will be used as the
CUPS administrator. CUPS does not use the same user accounts that your Linux system uses.
Instead, CUPS is configured to use the /etc/cups/passwd.md5 file to store user accounts. To create
an administrative user in the passwd.md5 file named root that is a member of the CUPS administration group named sys, you would enter **lppasswd –g sys –a root**.

Now that you've configured an administrative user, your next task is to configure a CUPS
printer and queue. Let's discuss how to do that next.

Directive	Description
ServerName	Specifies the server name that is announced to CUPS clients.
ServerAdmin	Specifies the e-mail address users can use to contact the CUPS administrator.
DocumentRoot	Specifies the directory where documents cupsd serves to clients are located. By default, this is /usr/share/doc/packages/cups.
LogLevel	Specifies the level of detail stored in log files. Some of the values you can use include the following: • **none** No logging • **error** Log errors only • **warn** Log errors and warnings • **info** Log errors, warnings, and print requests (default) • **debug** Log nearly all cupsd messages • **debug2** Log all cupsd messages
MaxCopies	Sets a limit on the number of copies for a single print job. The default is 100.
MaxJobsPerUser	Limits the number of active print jobs per user.
User	Specifies the user cupsd runs as. By default, cupsd runs as lp.
Group	Specifies the cupsd group. By default, this is the lp group.
MaxClients	Sets a limit on the number of concurrent client connections. By default, this is set to 100.
Browsing	Specifies whether or not cupsd will announce its printers using broadcasts on the network. The default value is on.
BrowseAddress	Specifies the broadcast address cupsd should use to announce its printers. You should set this directive to the broadcast address of your network segment. This directive may be disabled by default on some distributions. Until you enable it, cupsd won't announce its printers. If your clients can't see your CUPS printers, this directive should be the first thing you check.
BrowseAllow and BrowseDeny	Specifies where incoming printer information packets will be accepted or denied from. You can specify one of the following values: • all • none • hostname.domain_name • *.domain_name • IP_address/netmask • @LOCAL
BrowseInterval	Specifies the interval between printer announcements. The default is 30 seconds.

Table 16-1   cupsd.conf Configuration Directives

Configuring a CUPS Printer

All CUPS printers are defined in the /etc/cups/printers.conf file. Although you can manually edit this file, you really should use the CUPS web-based administration utility instead. Configuring a CUPS printer is a snap with it. You can either configure CUPS to service a locally attached printer (and optionally make it available to other network users) or connect to a CUPS printer over the network. For example, to configure CUPS to use a locally attached printer, do the following:

1. On your Linux system, start a web browser and navigate to **http://localhost:631**.

2. Select **Administration**. The screen in Figure 16-5 is displayed.

3. Under Printers, select **Add Printer**.

4. When prompted, log in as the administrative user you created previously. The screen in Figure 16-6 is displayed.

5. Select a locally attached printer type under Local Printers and then select **Continue**. A screen similar to that shown in Figure 16-7 is displayed.

TIP You could also select a network printer in this screen. All broadcasting CUPS printers on other network hosts are listed under Discovered Network Printers. To send print jobs to one of these printers, just select it.

6. In the Name field, enter a name for the printer.

7. In the Description field, enter a description of the printer.

8. In the Location field, enter a location for the printer.

9. If you want to share the printer with other network users, mark **Share This Printer**.

10. Select **Continue**. The screen in Figure 16-8 is displayed.

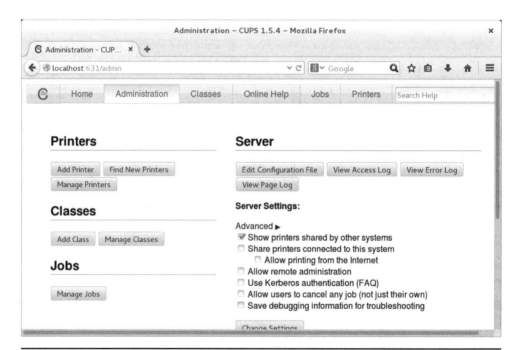

Figure 16-5 The CUPS administration screen

Add Printer

Local Printers: ○ SCSI Printer
○ Forward print job data like a pipe to another command
○ HP Printer (HPLIP)
○ LPT #1
○ HP Fax (HPLIP)

Discovered Network Printers:

Other Network Printers: ○ Internet Printing Protocol (ipp)
○ LPD/LPR Host or Printer
○ AppSocket/HP JetDirect
○ Internet Printing Protocol (http)
○ Backend Error Handler
○ Windows Printer via SAMBA

Continue

Figure 16-6 Selecting a printer type

Figure 16-7
Adding a new
CUPS printer

Add Printer

Name: [   ]
(May contain any printable characters except "/", "#", and space)

Description: [   ]
(Human-readable description such as "HP LaserJet with Duplexer")

Location: [   ]
(Human-readable location such as "Lab 1")

Connection: parallel:/dev/lp0

Sharing: ☐ Share This Printer

Continue

Figure 16-8
Configuring the
printer make
and model

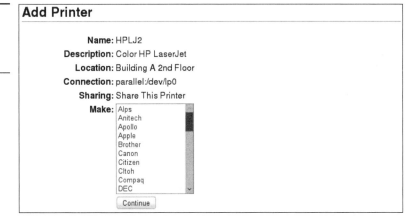

Add Printer

Name: HPLJ2
Description: Color HP LaserJet
Location: Building A 2nd Floor
Connection: parallel:/dev/lp0
Sharing: Share This Printer
Make: Alps
Anitech
Apollo
Apple
Brother
Canon
Citizen
Cltoh
Compaq
DEC

Continue

11. Select the printer manufacturer; then select **Continue**.

12. In the Model field, select your printer model; then select **Add Printer**.

13. Configure your default options for the printer, such as paper size, color model, media source, print quality, two-sided printing, and so on. When complete, select **Set Default Options**.

At this point, a page is displayed indicating your printer has been added. The current status of your printer is displayed, similar to that shown in Figure 16-9.

From the Printer Status page, you can manage your CUPS printer. You can send a test page, stop the printer, kill a print job, modify the printer configuration, or delete the printer altogether.

At this point, you can send print jobs to the printer. If you're using a graphical X application, you can simply select **File | Print**; then select the printer and click **OK**. You can also send print jobs from the command line to the printer. This is done using the lp command, which will send a specified file to the printer. The syntax for using lp is **lp –d *printer_name filename***. For example, if I wanted to print the myfiles file in the current directory to the HPLJ2 printer I just created, I would enter **lp –d HPLJ5 ./myfiles** at the shell prompt, as shown here:

```
openSUSE:~ # lp -d HPLJ2 ./myfiles
request id is HPLJ2-2 (1 file(s))
```

As you can see in this example, the job is created and assigned an ID (in this case, HPLJ2-2). The job is added to the print queue and sent to the printer. The lp utility includes a variety of options besides –d that you can use to create print jobs, including the following:

- **–n *x*** Prints *x* number of copies

- **–m** E-mails a confirmation message to my local user account when the job is finished printing

Figure 16-9 Viewing the printer status

- **–q** *x*   Sets the priority of the print job to *x*
- **–o landscape**   Prints the file landscape instead of portrait
- **–o sides=2**   Prints the file double-sided on a printer that supports duplexing

You can also configure other Linux systems to print to the CUPS printer. Simply configure a new printer, but specify that it listen for CUPS announcements. The CUPS printer you configured should be displayed within 30 seconds. After you select it, all print jobs sent to that printer will be redirected over the network connection to your CUPS printer.

In addition, if you've installed Samba on your system, your CUPS printers are automatically shared. You can connect to them from Windows workstations and submit print jobs. Now that's cool!

Let's next discuss how to use command-line tools to manage your CUPS printers.

Using Command-Line Tools to Manage CUPS

In addition to the CUPS web-based administration utility, you can also use a variety of command-line tools to configure CUPS. To view CUPS printer information, you can use the lpstat utility. One of the most useful options you can use with **lpstat** is **–t**.

This will cause lpstat to display all information about all CUPS printers on the system, as this next example shows:

```
openSUSE:~ # lpstat -t
scheduler running
no system default destination
device for HPLJ2: parallel:/dev/lp0
HPLJ2 accepting requests since Fri 13 May 2011 10:57:13 AM MDT
printer HPLJ2 is idle.  enabled since Fri 13 May 2011 10:57:13 AM MDT
        Printer is now online.
```

This shows the default CUPS printer (HPLJ2), how it's connected (/dev/lp0), the print job currently being processed (if any), and a list of pending print jobs.

To cancel a pending print job, you can use the cancel command. The syntax is **cancel** *job_ID*. For example, suppose I sent a huge print job (a Linux user manual from /usr/share/doc/manual/) and it was assigned a print ID of HPLJ2-4. While printing, I decided that this was a real waste of paper. I could kill the job and remove it from the print queue by entering **cancel HPLJ2-4** at the shell prompt. This can also be done from within the CUPS web-based administration utility. Just go to the Jobs tab and select Show Active Jobs. Locate the job that needs to be canceled and select Cancel Job, as shown in Figure 16-10.

If you have more than one CUPS printer connected, you can use the **lpoptions –d** *printer* command to specify the default printer. For example, to set the HPLJ5 printer as the default, I would enter **lpoptions –d HPLJ5**. This sets the default printer for all users on the system. Individual users can override this setting, however, by creating a file named .lpoptions in their home directory and adding the following directive:

```
default printer_name
```

If you want to view your printer's configuration settings, you can enter **lpoptions –l** at the shell prompt.

Figure 16-10 Canceling a print job from within the CUPS administration tool

In addition to the lpoptions command, you can also use the **cupsaccept** *printer_name* or **cupsreject** *printer_name* command to enable or disable a printer's print queue. For example, I could enter **cupsreject HPLJ2** at the shell prompt to disable the printer's print queue, as shown in this example:

```
openSUSE:~ # cupsreject HPLJ2
openSUSE:~ # lpstat is -t
scheduler is running
system default destination: HPLJ2
device for HPLJ2: parallel:/dev/lp0
HPLJ2 not accepting requests since Fri 13 May 2011 11:03:07 AM MDT -
      Rejecting Jobs
printer HPLJ2 is idle.  enabled since Fri 13 May 2011 11:03:07 AM MDT
      Rejecting Jobs
```

The printer itself will continue processing queued print jobs, but cupsd will not allow any new jobs to enter the queue. The cupsdisable command also includes the --hold option, which stops printing after the current job is complete. To enable the queue again, I would enter **cupsaccept HPLJ2** at the shell prompt.

To disable the printer itself, not the queue, I could enter **cupsdisable HPLJ2** at the shell prompt, as this example shows:

```
openSUSE:~ # cupsdisable HPLJ2
openSUSE:~ # lpstat is -t
scheduler is running
system default destination: HPLJ2
device for HPLJ2: parallel:/dev/lp0
HPLJ2 accepting requests since Fri 13 May 2011 11:15:28 AM MDT
printer HPLJ2 disabled since Fri 13 May 2011 11:15:28 AM MDT -
      Paused
```

The print queue will continue to accept jobs, but none of them will be printed until I enter **cupsenable HPLJ2** at the shell prompt. The cupsenable command also includes the --release option to release pending jobs for printing.

Using the Line Printer Daemon (lpd)

By far, CUPS is the preferred printing system for modern Linux distributions. Many years ago, however, the preferred printing system was the *Line Printer Daemon (lpd)*. You probably won't work much with lpd, but the LPIC-1/Linux+ exam still expects you to know some of the commands used to manage this daemon. Most of the lpd commands have functionality similar to that offered by a CUPS command, as shown in Table 16-2.

As an interesting side note, these commands will also work with cupsd. For example, you can enter **lpc status** at the shell prompt and it will return the status of your CUPS printers, if CUPS is installed instead of lpd.

Troubleshooting Printing Issues

Ask any system administrator what type of user complaints they receive most often and I'll bet 90 percent of them will list two main issues:

- I can't log in.
- I can't print.

To manage Linux systems, you need to be able to troubleshoot a wide variety of printing issues. Obviously, we don't have the time or space to cover all possible printing problems here. Instead, I'm going to give you some key insights that I have gained over the years supporting users and their print jobs. My experience is that these insights will cover 80 to 90 percent of the issues you will encounter. Let's take a look:

- Always use the standardized troubleshooting model presented in the previous chapter. Yes, it applies to printing as well as to networking. Don't go off half-cocked trying multiple resolutions before you have a solid understanding of what is wrong and what the scope of the problem is. Recall that the model I suggested you use consists of the following steps:

  1. *Gather information.* This is a critical step. You need to determine exactly what has happened. What are the symptoms? Were any error messages displayed? What did they say? How extensive is the problem? Is it isolated to a single system, or are many systems experiencing the same problem?

Table 16-2	Task	lpd Command-Line Utility
lpd Commands	Print a document.	lpr –P *printer_name filename*
	View printer status.	lpc status
	View pending print jobs.	lpq
	Delete a pending print job from the queue.	lprm *job_number*

2. *Identify what has changed.* In this step, you should identify what has changed in the system. Has new software been installed? Has new hardware been installed? Did a user change something? Did you change something?

3. *Create a hypothesis.* With the information gathered in the preceding steps, develop several hypotheses that could explain the problem. To do this, you may need to do some research. You should check FAQs and knowledgebases available on the Internet. You should also consult with peers to validate your hypotheses. Using the information you gain, narrow your results down to the one or two most likely causes.

4. *Determine the appropriate fix.* The next step is to use peers, FAQs, knowledgebases, and your own experience to identify the steps needed to fix the problem. As you do this, be sure to identify the possible ramifications of implementing the fix and account for them. Many times, the fix may have side effects that are as bad as or worse than the original problem.

5. *Implement the fix.* At this point, you're ready to implement the fix. Notice that in this troubleshooting model, we did a ton of research before implementing a fix! Doing so greatly increases the likelihood of success. After implementing the fix, be sure to verify that the fix has actually repaired the problem and that the issue doesn't reappear.

6. *Ensure user satisfaction.* You need to communicate the nature of the problem with users and make sure they are aware that it has been fixed. You should also educate them as to how to keep the problem from occurring in the future. In addition, communicate with your users' supervisors and ensure they know that the problem has been fixed.

7. *Document the solution.* Finally, you need to document the solution to your problem. That way, when it occurs again a year or two down the road, you or other system administrators can quickly identify the problem and how to fix it.

- Document the flow of print jobs. Where do they originate from? Are they sent over a network connection, or are they sent locally? How do they eventually arrive at the printer?

- Check the obvious first:

  - Is the printer out of paper? (Yes, this happens all of the time!)

  - Is the printer turned on?

  - If it's a networked printer, is it connected to the network? Is the network up? Can you ping the printer from the user's workstation?

  - Did the user select the correct printer when sending the print job? This is actually the number-one cause of user printing problems in my experience. If a user has multiple printers configured, they may not understand the difference between them or simply not pay attention to which printer they are sending the job to. When the job doesn't show up on their printer, they call you. You'll likely discover that they just sent 80 duplicate copies of a 100-page document to someone else's printer.

  - Has the correct printer driver been configured for the printer? Using the wrong driver will result in hundreds of pages of gibberish being sent to the printer.

With this in mind, let's practice configuring CUPS in the following exercise.

Exercise 16-1: Configuring Cups

In this exercise, you will install and configure CUPS on your Linux system. This exercise assumes you have a stand-alone Linux system (*not* a virtual machine) with an Ethernet network board installed and configured. It also assumes you have a printer available to connect to a USB or parallel port in the system.

 VIDEO   Please watch the Exercise 16-1 video for a demonstration on how to perform this task.

Complete the following:

1. Power down your Linux system and physically connect your printer.

2. Boot your Linux system and log in as a standard user.

3. Open a terminal session.

4. Switch to your root user account by entering **su –** followed by your root user's password.

5. Use the **rpm –q** command to verify that the cups packages appropriate for your distribution have been installed on your system.

6. Create a CUPS administrative user by completing the following:

    a. At the shell prompt, enter **lppasswd –g sys –a root**.

    b. When prompted for a password, enter **M3linux273**.

7. Create a CUPS printer by completing the following:

    a. Open a web browser and navigate to **http://localhost:631**.

    b. Select **Administration**.

    c. Under Printers, select **Add Printer**.

    d. When prompted to authenticate, log in as **root** with a password of **M3linux273**.

    e. Under Local Printers, select your printer type; then select **Continue**.

    f. In the Name field, enter a name for your printer.

    g. In the Location field, enter a location for your printer.

    h. In the Description field, enter a description of your printer.

    i. Share the printer on your network by marking **Share This Printer**; then select **Continue**.

    j. In the Make field, select your printer's manufacturer; then select **Continue**.

    k. In the Model field, select your printer's model; then select **Continue**. Your printer should be created at this point.

8. Send a print job to the printer by doing the following:

   a. Open a terminal session and generate a list of files in your user's home directory.

   b. Select a text file for printing.

   c. At the shell prompt, enter **lp –d** *printer_name filename*.

   d. Verify that the document is printed on your printer.

Now that you know how to set up printing on your Linux system, we need to shift gears and talk about keeping your system time in sync. Let's do that next.

Maintaining System Time

Recall that when you initially set up your Linux system, you were prompted to configure your system time and your time zone. You may have not considered these settings as terribly critical to the overall functioning of the system. I work with many system administrators who feel they same way. The time on their systems is always out of whack and it drives me nuts!

However, when you're working with Linux, it is actually quite important that you maintain the correct system time, especially if the system is providing network services. You need to ensure that file timestamps are accurate. If your system is participating in some type of directory service or is a database server, then maintaining the correct system time is absolutely critical. For example, each change submitted to a database server from client systems must have an accurate timestamp. Image what problems could arise if database modifications get applied out of sequence because the timestamps are inaccurate. The integrity of your data is toast!

In Chapter 5, we discussed how to set your time zone when we looked at managing locale settings. In this chapter, we'll address the following topics:

- Setting the hardware clock with hwclock
- Synchronizing time with netdate
- Synchronizing time with NTP

Let's begin by discussing how to manage time with hwclock.

Setting the Hardware Clock with hwclock

Recall from Chapter 5 that two time sources are used on a Linux system:

- **Hardware clock** This clock is integrated into the CMOS chip on your Linux system's motherboard. It runs all the time, even when the system is powered off.
- **System time** This clock runs via software inside the Linux kernel itself. It is driven by an ISA timer interrupt. System time is measured as the number of seconds since 00:00:00 January 1, 1970, UTC.

The key thing to remember is that the hardware clock and the system time may not be the same. When managing a Linux system, we are more concerned with the system time than the time reported by the hardware clock. The role of the hardware clock is pretty basic. Its job is to keep time when the system is powered off. The system time is synchronized to the hardware clock time when the Linux operating system starts. After booting, Linux only uses system time. The hardware clock is ignored.

To manage the hardware clock on your system, you can use the hwclock command at the shell prompt. It can do the following:

- Display the current time.
- Set the hardware clock time.
- Synchronize the hardware clock to the system time.
- Synchronize the system time to the hardware clock.

 NOTE You can also view the current time of the hardware clock on some Linux distributions by viewing the contents of the /proc/driver/rtc file.

You can use the options shown in Table 16-3 with hwclock on most Linux distributions.

As you can see, the scope of hwclock's functionality is limited to the local computer system. On a network, you may need to ensure that the system time on your Linux systems is synchronized. One tool you can use to do this is netdate. Let's look at how this is done next.

Synchronizing Time with netdate

You can use the netdate command to synchronize time on the local system with the time on a time server over the network. The syntax is **netdate *time_server***, where *time_server* is the IP address or DNS name of another Linux system on the network that is running the time service, which is configured to listen on UDP port 37 by default for time requests. The time server could be an internal provider on your local LAN, or it could be an Internet-based time provider.

hwclock Option	Description
–r or --show	Reads the current time from the hardware clock and displays it on the screen.
--set --date=*date_string*	Sets the hardware clock to the time specified by the --date option. For example, **hwclock --set --date="9/16/11 08:00:00"** will set the date to September 16, 2001, and the time to 8:00 A.M. The argument is in local time, even if you keep your hardware clock in Universal Time Coordinated.
–s or --hctosys	Sets the system time to the current time of the hardware clock.
–w or --systohc	Sets the hardware clock to the current system time.
--utc or --localtime	Specifies that the hardware clock time is configured to use either UTC or local time.

Table 16-3 hwclock Command Options

NOTE You can actually specify multiple time servers with the netdate command. If you do, the time returned from the various time servers will be compared. The time value most commonly returned will be considered to be the most accurate and the one applied to the system time.

After syncing the system time with netdate, you may want to synchronize the system time with your hardware clock using the hwclock --systohc command discussed earlier.

It's important to note that netdate only syncs time once. If your system time drifts (and it will), you may need to run netdate (and possibly hwclock --systohc) on a regular schedule to keep time in sync. This can be done automatically using a cron job. However, it's really not the best option. A better way to keep time synchronized on a regular schedule is to use the Network Time Protocol (NTP). Let's review how NTP works next.

Synchronizing Time with NTP

The key problem with using netdate in a cron job to keep time synchronized is the fact that net-date adjusts the time abruptly. It doesn't gradually adjust time to reach a point of synchronization. Whatever time it is on the time server is the time the system time on the local system is set to. In addition, netdate may adjust the time backward and forward, depending on how your local system clock has drifted. This really messes up timestamps on your local files and can cause some Linux services to completely freak out.

A better option for network time synchronization is to use the Network Time Protocol (NTP) to sync time with a network time provider. NTP manages time in a much cleaner fashion than netdate. NTP adjusts time in a much gentler manner. If there is a time differential between the time provider and the time consumer (your local system), it adjusts time gradually in small incre-ments until time is eventually synchronized.

NTP is also widely supported by most operating systems. The netdate option only works with the time service on a Linux/UNIX time provider. NTP, on the other hand, allows time to be synchronized among systems in a heterogeneous network environment. It's supported by the following operating systems:

- Linux
- Windows
- OSX
- UNIX

NTP is a little more complex than netdate. Therefore, to implement NTP, you need to be familiar with the following:

- How NTP works
- Configuring NTP

Let's begin by discussing how NTP works.

How NTP Works

You can use the ntpd daemon on Linux to synchronize time with another NTP time provider. In fact, a system running ntpd can function as both a *time consumer* and a *time provider* at the same time. The NTP protocol operates over IP port 123. The time consumer sends a time synchronization request to the time provider on port 123. The time provider sends its time to the consumer, and the system time on the consumer is adjusted according to the NTP algorithm.

TIP   Because NTP is designed to synchronize time across global networks, it assumes all systems involved are configured to use UTP time.

Here are several key NTP concepts you need to be familiar with:

- **Stratum**   NTP uses the concept of *stratum* to define a hierarchy of NTP servers:
  - **Stratum 1**   Stratum 1 time servers get their time from a reference time source, such as the Naval atomic clock. (See tycho.usno.navy.mil for more information.)
  - **Stratum 2**   Time servers that get their time from stratum 1 servers.
  - **Stratum 3**   Time servers that get their time from stratum 2 servers.
  - **Stratum *n***   NTP servers can continue to a depth of 256 strata.

  Although they are available on the Internet, you probably won't be allowed access to a Stratum 1 server. However, many Stratum 2 servers are publicly available. To reduce the load on these public time sources, you should configure a very limited number of systems on your internal network to sync time with the public time provider. In fact, many organizations configure only a single Stratum 3 server on their network that gets its time from a public Stratum 2 server on the Internet. They then configure all their internal hosts to get their time from that server. On a larger network, you may need to configure several Stratum 4 servers and configure them to get time from your Stratum 3 server and then configure the rest of your network hosts to get time from the Stratum 4 servers. This is shown in Figure 16-11.

- **Stepping and slewing**   The NTP protocol initially syncs time between the time consumer and the time provider about once per minute. However, the interval increases gradually to once every 17 minutes once time is closely synced between the provider and consumer. Essentially, large adjustments occur relatively quickly, but then only small adjustments are made across a longer time interval.

  If the time difference between the provider and the consumer is small (less than 128 milliseconds), NTP adjusts the time on the consumer gradually. This is called *slewing*. If, on the other hand, the time difference between provider and consumer is relatively large, the time adjustments are made more quickly on the consumer. This is called *stepping*.

- **Insane time**   If the time difference between the provider and consumer is more than 17 minutes off, the NTP daemon (ntpd) considers time to be "insane" and will not adjust it.

Figure 16-11
NTP stratums

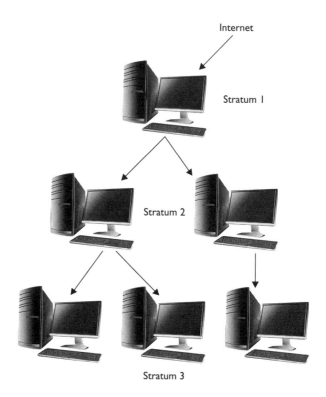

- **Drift** NTP measures and corrects for incidental clock frequency errors (called *drift*). It writes the current frequency value to the ntp.drift file in the /var/lib/ntp/drift/ directory. If you stop and then restart the NTP daemon, it initializes the clock frequency using the value in this file. This prevents ntpd from having to relearn the frequency error associated with the system clock on your system. Here is a sample ntp.drift file:

```
openSUSE:/var/lib/ntp/drift # cat ./ntp.drift
0.000
```

- **Jitter** Jitter is the estimated time difference between the consumer and the provider since the last time poll.

With this background in mind, let's discuss how you configure a system to use NTP to get time from a time provider.

Configuring NTP

In order to use NTP to configure system time with an NTP time provider, you must first install the ntpd daemon on your Linux system. You can use the **rpm –q ntp** command at the shell prompt to do this, like so:

```
openSUSE:~ # rpm -q ntp
ntp-4.2.6p5-15.5.1.i586
```

NTP is usually installed by default on most Linux systems. If it hasn't been, you can use the software package management utility of your choice to install it. Once this is done, you need to next edit the /etc/ntp.conf file in a text editor. The first thing you need to do is ensure that the following entries exist for the local clock, which is used if the time server is not available:

```
server 127.127.1.0 # local clock (LCL)
fudge 127.127.1.0 stratum 10 # LCL is unsynchronized
```

These directives tell the ntpd daemon to get time from the local clock in the event it can't reach any of the configured NTP time providers.

Next, you need to add entries to the file for network time providers you want your system to sync time with. Here is the syntax:

```
server time_server_IP_address_or_DNS_name
```

You can specify the IP address or DNS name of any NTP time provider you want to use. It could be any of the following:

- **An NTP time provider on your network**
- **A public NTP time provider on the Internet**   You can visit http://support.ntp.org/bin/view/Servers/WebHome to view a list of publicly available NTP time providers on the Internet. If you wish, you can use an *NTP pool time server.* The pool.ntp.org domain uses DNS round robin to make a random selection from a pool of time providers who have volunteered to be in the pool. That way, no one public NTP server is overloaded with time synchronization requests. To use this, simply add the following server directive in addition to the local clock server directive just discussed:

```
server pool.ntp.org
```

When you're done, save your changes and then close the file. Before you actually start the ntpd daemon, however, you need to do a quick, one-time synchronization with your NTP time provider. The issue here is insane time. If your system time is already more than 17 minutes off from the time on the NTP time provider, you must get the two systems within this time window before NTP will work.

 TIP   In my experience, insane time is the number-one problem Linux admins have when configuring NTP. They install the NTP software and configure it correctly, but then they can't figure out why time never synchronizes when they start the daemon.

You can eliminate insane time issues by entering **ntpdate *address_of_time_provider*** at the shell prompt. This will perform an initial synchronization to get time close before you start the daemon. You may actually need to run the command multiple times if the times are really far apart between your system and the NTP time provider.

 TIP   The ntpd daemon must be stopped before you run the ntpdate command!

Newer versions of NTP on newer Linux distributions also allow you to use the ntptimeset option with the ntpd daemon itself to accomplish the same thing. Instead of specifying start, stop, or restart with the daemon init script, you enter (on an system that uses init) **/etc/init.d/ntp ntptimeset** or **rcntp ntptimeset** at the shell prompt. When you do, a quick time sync takes place with the time provider, as in this example:

```
ws1:/ # rcntp ntptimeset
Time synchronized with pool.ntp.org
```

Once this is done, you can then start the ntpd daemon using its init script in the appropriate init script directory used by your distribution. If your system uses rc scripts, you can simply enter **rcntp start** at the shell prompt, like this:

```
ws1:/ # rcntp start
Time synchronized with pool.ntp.org
Starting network time protocol daemon (NTPD)                              done
```

You should configure the ntpd daemon to start every time the system boots using the **insserv ntp** command. After starting the daemon, you can check the ntp log file with the tail command to verify that no errors occurred.

If your distribution uses systemd, you start and stop ntpd using the systemctl command. For example, to start the ntpd daemon, you would enter **systemctl start ntp** at the shell prompt. You can verify that it started correctly by entering **systemctl status ntp** at the shell prompt. The status of the daemon is displayed, as shown in Figure 16-12.

```
openSUSE:/etc # systemctl status ntp
ntp.service - LSB: Network time protocol daemon (ntpd)
   Loaded: loaded (/etc/init.d/ntp)
  Drop-In: /run/systemd/generator/ntp.service.d
           └50-insserv.conf-$time.conf
   Active: active (running) since Thu 2014-12-18 12:34:35 MST; 3min 28s ago
  Process: 4963 ExecStart=/etc/init.d/ntp start (code=exited, status=0/SUCCESS)
   CGroup: /system.slice/ntp.service
           └4982 /usr/sbin/ntpd -p /var/run/ntp/ntpd.pid -g -u ntp:ntp -i /v...

Dec 18 12:34:35 openSUSE ntpd[4982]: ntp_io: estimated max descriptors: 102...16
Dec 18 12:34:35 openSUSE ntpd[4982]: Listen and drop on 0 v4wildcard 0.0.0....23
Dec 18 12:34:35 openSUSE ntpd[4982]: Listen and drop on 1 v6wildcard :: UDP 123
Dec 18 12:34:35 openSUSE ntpd[4982]: Listen normally on 2 lo 127.0.0.1 UDP 123
Dec 18 12:34:35 openSUSE ntpd[4982]: Listen normally on 3 ens32 10.0.0.83 U...23
Dec 18 12:34:35 openSUSE ntpd[4982]: Listen normally on 4 lo ::1 UDP 123
Dec 18 12:34:35 openSUSE ntpd[4982]: Listen normally on 5 ens32 fe80::20c:2...23
Dec 18 12:34:35 openSUSE ntpd[4982]: peers refreshed
Dec 18 12:34:35 openSUSE ntpd[4982]: Listening on routing socket on fd #22 ...es
Dec 18 12:34:35 openSUSE systemd[1]: Started LSB: Network time protocol dae...).
Hint: Some lines were ellipsized, use -l to show in full.
openSUSE:/etc # 
```

Figure 16-12 Viewing the status of the NTP daemon

Once the NTP daemon has been started, you can use two commands to keep track of how the ntpd daemon is working:

- **ntpq –p**   This command queries the status of the ntpd daemon. Here is an example:

```
openSUSE:~ # ntpq -p
     remote          refid      st t when poll reach   delay   offset  jitter
==============================================================================
*LOCAL(0)        .LOCL.          10 l   14   64    3   0.000    0.000   0.001
 helium.constant 18.26.4.105      2 u   12   64    1  96.614  -31.777   0.001
```

The columns in the output include the following:

- **remote**   Specifies the hostname or IP address of the time provider.
- **refid**   Specifies the type of the reference source.
- **st**   Specifies the stratum of the time provider.
- **when**   Specifies the number of seconds since the last time poll.
- **poll**   Specifies the number of seconds between two time polls.
- **reach**   Displays whether or not the time server was reached in the last poll. Each successful poll increments this field by 1.
- **delay**   Specifies the time (in milliseconds) that it took for the time provider to respond to the request.
- **offset**   Specifies the time difference between the local system clock and the time provider (in milliseconds).
- **jitter**   Specifies the size of time discrepancies (in milliseconds).

- **ntptrace**   The ntptrace utility traces how the time consumer is receiving time from the provider. It lists the time provider's name, its stratum, and its time offset from the system clock on the local system.

Let's practice working with NTP in the following exercise.

Exercise 16-2: Configuring NTP

In this exercise, you will practice configuring NTP to get time from us.pool.ntp.org. For this exercise to work, your Linux system must have Internet access. You can perform this exercise using the virtual machine that comes with this book. Run snapshot 16-2 for the correctly configured environment.

   VIDEO   Please watch the Exercise 16-2 video for a demonstration on how to perform this task.

Complete the following:

1. Open a terminal session and **su –** to your root user account.
2. At the shell prompt, verify that the ntp package has been installed on your system by entering **rpm –q ntp** at the shell prompt.

3. At the shell prompt, enter **vi /etc/ntp.conf**.

4. Scroll down to the lines that read

```
server      127.127.1.0 #local clock (LCL)
fudge       127.127.1.0 stratum 10 #LCL is unsynchronized
```

5. Press INSERT and then remove the comment character (#) from the beginning of these two lines.

6. Add a new line below the fudge line.

7. Add the following directive on the new line:

```
server us.pool.ntp.org
```

   This directive is used to configure the ntp service to synchronize your local computer's time with the time on a public NTP server on the Internet.

8. Press ESC and then enter **:exit**.

9. Perform a one-time synchronization by entering **ntpdate us.pool.ntp.org** at the shell prompt.

10. Start the ntp service by entering **systemctl start ntp** at the shell prompt.

11. Configure the ntp daemon to automatically start at system boot by entering **systemctl enable ntp** at the shell prompt.

12. Check the status of the ntp daemon by entering **systemctl status ntp** at the shell prompt.

That's it for NTP. Let's next discuss how you manage e-mail on Linux.

Managing an MTA

In most modern organizations, e-mail has become the backbone of communications. If you have any doubt, just visit any organization where the mail server has gone down. All productive work grinds to a halt.

Because e-mail has become such an integral component of most networks, you need to know how to manage a mail server. In addition, many Linux services, such as cron, rely on a local mail server to send messages to local users. Accordingly, you need to be familiar with managing a Mail Transfer Agent (MTA) on Linux systems for your Linux+/LPIC-1 exam. In this part of this chapter, we'll look at the following topics:

- How e-mail works
- Using MTA management commands on Linux

Let's begin by discussing how e-mail works.

How E-mail Works

To understand how an MTA works and how to deploy it, you must first understand how the e-mail process itself works.

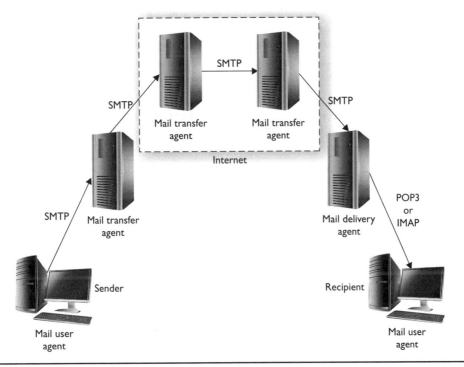

Figure 16-13 The e-mail process

The first thing you must understand is the fact that an e-mail system is composed of several modular components. Each component plays a different role in delivering messages from the sender to the recipient. The following steps occur as an e-mail message is sent from the sender to the recipient. These are shown in Figure 16-13.

1. The user composes a message using an e-mail client. The e-mail client software is called the *mail user agent (MUA)*. Common MUAs include Evolution, Mozilla Thunderbird, and Mutt. The key thing to remember is that the MUA has no idea how to get the message to the final recipient. Instead, it's configured to send outgoing messages to a mail server.

2. When the user selects Send, the MUA sends outgoing messages to a configured e-mail mail server using the Simple Mail Transfer Protocol (SMTP). SMTP is an upper-layer, IP-based protocol that runs on port 25. The sole purpose of SMTP is to transfer e-mail messages between e-mail agents.

3. The message is transferred from the MUA to the *mail transfer agent (MTA)* on the mail server. The MTA then decides what to do with the message. If it's intended for another user in the same organization, the message is held by the local MTA for delivery to the recipient's MUA. However, if it's intended for a recipient in a different domain, the MTA forwards the message via SMTP through the Internet to the MTA used by the message's recipient.

4. The destination MTA transfers the e-mail message to the *message delivery agent* (*MDA,* also called the *Message Store*) for the system where the recipient resides. The MDA's job is to store the message until the MUA of the recipient requests it.

5. The recipient uses e-mail client software (another MUA) to connect to the Message Store and pulls down the message. To do this, it can use either the Post Office Protocol (POP) version 3 or the Internet Message Access Protocol (IMAP). Both protocols are supported by most MDAs and MUAs. POP3 downloads the message using port 110, and the message is deleted from the Message Store. IMAP does the same thing over port 143. However, IMAP has several advantages over POP3. First, IMAP allows you to download the entire message or only the message headers. IMAP also allows you to keep a copy of your messages in the Message Store. In addition, it allows you to create custom folders in the Message Store for organizing messages.

NOTE   Most Linux MTAs do not include any POP3 or IMAP functionality. To use most Linux MTAs with end-user MUAs, you must install and configure a POP3/IMAP daemon that grabs messages from the MTA and delivers them via the appropriate protocol to the MUA.

All Linux distributions include an MTA that runs by default on the system. Several MTAs are commonly implemented on Linux:

- **sendmail**   The sendmail daemon is the oldest MTA used on Linux, but it's still the default MTA used by many distributions. It's been widely used for many years. The key thing to remember about sendmail is the fact that it's noncomponentized; instead, it's a single executable. However, when compared with other Linux MTAs, sendmail can be somewhat difficult to configure.

- **postfix**   The postfix daemon is a popular MTA that has replaced sendmail on many Linux distributions. One of the key advantages of postfix over sendmail is the fact that it is modular, meaning that it is composed of multiple programs instead of one single executable. Each program has its own tasks that it is responsible for. It uses the master daemon in conjunction with multiple worker daemons that are only started when they are needed. When their tasks are complete, the master daemon automatically shuts them down. In effect, the master daemon and the worker daemons function together as a unit to process e-mail messages through the MTA. The process is shown in Figure 16-14.

Figure 16-14
Processing
messages
through postfix

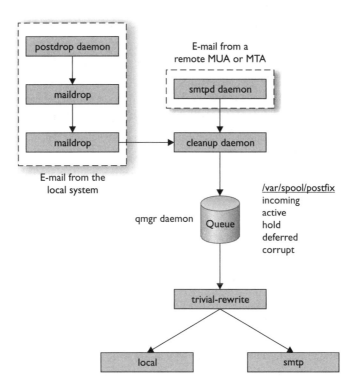

1. If an e-mail message is sent to the Postfix MTA by a remote MTA or remote MUA, it is accepted into the system by the smtpd worker daemon. The smtpd daemon forwards the message to the cleanup daemon.

2. If an e-mail message is sent to the Postfix MTA by a user using the shell prompt on the local system, the following occurs:

    a. It is accepted into the system by the postdrop daemon, which is also a postfix worker daemon.

    b. The postdrop daemon places the e-mail message in the maildrop directory in /var/spool/postfix.

    c. The pickup daemon transfers the message from the maildrop directory and forwards it to the cleanup daemon.

3. The e-mail message, regardless of whether it originated remotely or on the local system, is then processed by the cleanup daemon.

4. The cleanup daemon places the e-mail message in the incoming queue, which is also /var/spool/postfix.

5. The cleanup daemon notifies the Queue Manager daemon (qmgr) that a message has been added to the incoming queue.

6. The qmgr daemon moves the e-mail message to one of five message queues, all of which are located in /var/spool/postfix:

- **incoming**   This queue contains incoming messages that have been processed by the cleanup daemon.

- **active**   This queue contains messages that arrived intact, were processed correctly, and are ready to be forwarded on to the next MTA or MDA.

- **hold**   This queue contains messages whose delivery, for some reason, has been put on hold.

- **deferred**   This queue contains messages that could not be delivered on the first attempt. The qmgr daemon will wait a while; then it will make several more delivery attempts.

- **corrupt**   This queue contains messages that were damaged somewhere in transit and are no longer readable.

7. The qmgr daemon then invokes the trivial-rewrite daemon, which identifies the next MTA or MDA to which the message should be sent.

8. The qmgr daemon then passes the message to the appropriate delivery agent. If the message is intended for a local user account, the local agent is used. If the message is intended for another MTA or an MDA, the smtp agent is used.

9. The selected agent transfers the e-mail message to the appropriate system:

- **qmail**   The qmail MTA is also a modular MTA daemon that is frequently used as a replacement for sendmail. The qmail MTA is unique in that it was designed from the ground up with security in mind. Essentially, its modular architecture is composed of mutually untrusting components. This means each module in the MTA (such as the SMTP listener) will use a set of credentials that are unique to it. No two modules use the same credentials. Many administrators consider qmail, like postfix, easier to manage than sendmail. However, it's not the default MTA used by any Linux distribution because it has components that are covered by a proprietary licensing agreement. In spite of this, qmail is greatly loved by those who use it. My niece is married to a system admin, and he swears by qmail. You need to be aware that two additional mail protocols are implemented by qmail:

  - **Quick Mail Queuing Protocol (QMQP)**   Allows the sharing of e-mail queues among different MTAs

  - **Quick Mail Transport Protocol (QMTP)**   A transmission protocol similar to SMTP, but considered to be faster

- **Exim**   For your LPIC-1/Linux+ exam, you also need to be familiar with the Exim MTA. Exim is a nonmodular MTA, composed of only a single program (similar to sendmail). However, it is considered to be much easier to configure and manage than sendmail. A limited number of Linux distributions use Exim as the default MTA.

As mentioned earlier, these MTAs can be used to receive sent e-mail messages from MUAs via SMTP. However, they can't download messages to e-mail clients via POP3 or IMAP. To do this, you must install the imap package on your system using the software management utility of your choice. This package installs IMAP and POP3 daemons that you can use to transfer messages from your MTA to your e-mail client software.

Both of these daemons are managed using the xinetd daemon. You can enable these daemons using the /etc/xinetd.d/imap file. Once this is done, restart the xinetd daemon.

> **NOTE** We'll discuss xinetd in more detail in the next chapter.

If your distribution uses init, you manage your MTA daemon using the appropriate init script in your init directory. For example, the postfix init script is appropriately named *postfix,* whereas the sendmail init script is *sendmail.* If your distribution uses systemd, you use the systemctl command to start, stop, or reload the appropriate service file for the MTA installed on your system.

Now that you understand how e-mail works and the role of the MTA, let's next look at commands you can use to manage MTAs on Linux.

Using MTA Management Commands on Linux

Let's first look at reading messages stored in your local MTA. When you log in to a shell session, you will receive a notification if there are mail messages waiting for you. You can read messages for local users from the local MTA directly from the command line using the mail command at the shell prompt. When you do, a list of messages is displayed. An example is shown in Figure 16-15.

> **NOTE** Some services running on Linux are configured to send notification messages to the root user.

These messages are stored in your user's mail queue, which is located in the /var/spool/mail/ directory. The mail utility reads your messages directly out of your user's queue file. Because you're running the mail utility on the same system where your queue resides, you don't need POP3 or IMAP support configured. You can enter the mail commands shown in Table 16-4 at the ? prompt.

An example of viewing a received message with the t command is shown in Figure 16-16.

To send a message, you can also enter **mail *recipient_address*** at the shell prompt. You can then enter a subject line and the text of your message. Press CTRL-D when you're done to actually send the message. When you do, the message is delivered to the other user's mail queue by your local MTA.

To view a list of unread messages in your mail queue, you can enter **mailq** at the shell prompt.

Figure 16-15

Reading mail from the shell prompt

```
rtracy@ws1:~> mail
Heirloom mailx version 12.2 01/07/07.  Type ? for help.
"/var/spool/mail/rtracy": 1 message 1 new
>N  1 root@ws1.mydomain. Mon May 16 14:10   18/601    Greetings Robb
?
```

Mail Command	Description
t	To read a message, enter **t *message_number*** at the ? prompt.
d	You can delete a message by entering **d *message_number*** at the ? prompt.
u	You can undelete a message by entering **u *message_number*** at the ? prompt.
n	Enter **n** to display the next message in the queue.
e	Enter **e *message_number*** to edit a message.
R	You can reply to the message sender by entering **R *message_number*** at the ? prompt.
r	You can reply to all recipients by entering **r *message_number*** at the ? prompt.
m	You can send a new message by entering **m *recipient*** at the ? prompt.
q	Enter **q** to quit mail.

Table 16-4 Mail Commands

In addition to mail, many other packages are available that you can install to read mail from the shell prompt. The key thing to remember is that the user must run the mail command from the *local* shell prompt. If the user isn't using the local computer system, they must ssh into the system to read mail.

 NOTE We'll discuss ssh (Secure Shell) in Chapter 18.

```
rtracy@ws1:~> mail
Heirloom mailx version 12.2 01/07/07.  Type ? for help.
"/var/spool/mail/rtracy": 1 message 1 new
>N  1 root@ws1.mydomain. Mon May 16 14:10    18/601    Greetings Robb
? t 1
Message  1:
From root@ws1.mydomain.com  Mon May 16 14:10:39 2011
X-Original-To: rtracy
Delivered-To: rtracy@ws1.mydomain.com
Date: Mon, 16 May 2011 14:10:39 -0600
To: rtracy@ws1.mydomain.com
Subject: Greetings Robb
User-Agent: Heirloom mailx 12.2 01/07/07
MIME-Version: 1.0
Content-Type: text/plain; charset=us-ascii
Content-Transfer-Encoding: 7bit
From: root@ws1.mydomain.com (root)

This is a message for Robb.

?
```

Figure 16-16 Viewing a message in the mail queue

You can also configure aliases for the MTA running on your Linux system. Mail aliases redirect mail addressed to one user to another user's account. You use the /etc/aliases file to configure aliases. This file defines one alias per line. The alias you define must point to an existing e-mail address. The syntax for this file follows:

```
alias:  list of real e-mail addresses (separated by commas)
```

For example, the following two aliases must be present in this file on most Linux distributions:

```
postmaster:  root
mailer-daemon:     postmaster
```

These aliases cause any e-mail messages sent to the postmaster to be automatically redirected to the root user. Likewise, any e-mail messages sent to mailer-daemon will be redirected to postmaster (which will then be redirected to root). Depending on your distribution, you will probably find that many aliases are defined for you by default. Here is an example:

```
# General redirections for pseudo accounts in /etc/passwd.
administrator:      root
daemon:             root
lp:          root
news:        root
uucp:        root
games:       root
man:         root
at:          root
postgres:    root
mdom:        root
amanda:      root
ftp:         root
wwwrun:      root
squid:       root
msql:        root
gnats:       root
nobody:      root
# "bin" used to be in /etc/passwd
bin:         root
```

Of course, you can enter your own custom aliases if needed. Just open the aliases file in a text editor and add the appropriate aliases, one per line. When done configuring aliases, you must run the **newaliases** command at the shell prompt as root to enable them.

You can also use the ~/.forward file in your user's home directory to configure forwarding. Most Linux MTAs check for the existence of this file in the user's home directory to configure forwarding of messages. You can open/create the file in a text editor and enter the e-mail address to which you want to forward e-mail. If you are forwarding to a local user, just enter the username. If you're forwarding to a remote user account, enter ***username@domain*.com**. If you need to forward messages to multiple recipients, separate them with a comma.

 NOTE   The MTA will treat the addresses you enter in this file as an alias. This causes all e-mail to be forwarded to the forwarding e-mail address. Messages will *not* be delivered to the original user's mailbox.

Now that you are familiar with managing e-mail on a Linux system, let's finish this chapter by talking about managing SQL server data.

Managing SQL Data

For your Linux+/LPIC-1 exam, you need to be familiar with how to manage data within an SQL database. Implementing and managing an SQL database is a huge topic, much larger than we have time or space to delve into here. However, I will give you some basic installation steps and also show you how to add information to the database as well as how to retrieve information from it. To accomplish this, the following topics will be addressed in this part of the chapter:

- How databases work
- Installing MySQL
- Managing data in the SQL server

Let's begin by discussing how SQL databases work.

How Databases Work

A *database* is a collection of information organized so that data can be quickly selected and retrieved based on a search query that you create. In the past 20 years, databases have become the backbone of commerce, communications, and government around the world. Instead of maintaining huge rooms full of paper documents, databases allow us to store huge amounts of information in an itty-bitty amount of physical space.

Database services run on a client/server model. You usually install the client and server pieces on the database server. You can then install the client software on client systems that will be used to access the information in a database. Two database services are commonly implemented on Linux:

- MySQL
- PostgreSQL

By installing one of these database services, you install the software needed to run, operate, and manage the database using SQL (Structured Query Language), which is a standard language for accessing and manipulating databases. SQL defines statements that can be used to retrieve and update data in a database, such as SELECT, UPDATE, DELETE, INSERT, and WHERE.

Both of these database services are relational databases, which are hierarchical in nature. Relational databases are specialized to organize and store huge amounts of data. They are also designed to be highly scalable, allowing them to grow over time.

A relational database is organized using fields, records, and tables. A *field* is a single piece of information. A *record* is one complete set of fields, and a *table* is collection of records. Each table is identified by a name, such as Customers. Each table contains records (each one a single row) that contain one or more fields that in turn contain the actual database data. For example, suppose you were to define a table called Customers and create the following three records:

```
Last        First       Address                 City        State       Zip
Tracy       Leah        1234 W. Longfellow      Bone        Idaho       83401
Morgan      Ken         3456 W. 100 S.          Rigby       Idaho       83442
```

Using the SQL language, you could create queries that select and retrieve specific data from the database. For example, suppose you were to compose the following query:

```
SELECT Last FROM Customers
```

The database would return the following data:

```
Last
Tracy
Morgan
```

You can use the following commands to manage data in an SQL database:

- **SELECT**   Retrieves information from a table
- **UPDATE**   Modifies information in a table
- **DELETE**   Removes information from a table
- **INSERT INTO**   Adds new data to a table
- **CREATE TABLE**   Creates a new table
- **ALTER TABLE**   Modifies an existing table
- **DROP TABLE**   Deletes and existing table

A key feature of relational databases is the fact that you can create *relationships* between tables, which allows you to create interrelated data sets.

With this in mind, let's look at how you install an SQL database on your Linux system.

Installing MySQL

Although there are several different SQL database services you can install on Linux, we're going to focus on using MySQL Community Server in this chapter. MySQL is an open source SQL database server that's included on the installation media of most distributions. It's also relatively easy to install and to get started creating databases with.

MySQL may or may not be installed by default on your Linux distribution. If it's not installed on your system, use the package management utility of your choice to install the following packages:

- mysql-community-server
- mysql-community-server-client
- mysql-community-server-tools

NOTE The actual packages you install depend on which Linux distribution you are using and which version of MySQL you are installing.

After installing your MySQL packages, you next need to set up your MySQL server's grant tables. All MySQL access controls are managed from within the MySQL service itself. It's important to understand that MySQL has its own unique set of user accounts defined in its grant tables; it doesn't use the accounts defined on your Linux system. Five tables are implemented within the MySQL database to do this:

- **user** Specifies whether a user is allowed to connect to the MySQL server
- **db** Defines which databases a user is allowed to access
- **host** Specifies which hosts are allowed to access a particular database
- **tables_priv** Defines access privileges for a given table
- **columns_priv** Specifies access privileges for specific columns of data for a given table

These tables must be initialized before you can use MySQL. This is done by changing to the /usr/bin directory and running the **mysql_install_db** command at the shell prompt. The grant tables are ready to go after you do so. You only need to run mysql_install_db once after you initially install MySQL. The command creates two MySQL user accounts named *root* and *anonymous-user.*

With the grant tables created, you next need to start the database service. If your distribution uses init, you can use the mysql init script located in your init script directory. Then you can use the insserv or chkconfig command to ensure the database service starts every time the system boots. If your distribution uses systemd, you can use the systemctl command to enable and start the mysql service.

To verify that the server is running, you can enter the **mysqladmin version** command at the shell prompt. You should see output similar to the following:

```
openSUSE:/usr/bin # mysqladmin version
mysqladmin  Ver 8.42 Distrib 5.6.12, for Linux on i686
Copyright (c) 2000, 2013, Oracle and/or its affiliates. All rights reserved.

Oracle is a registered trademark of Oracle Corporation and/or its
affiliates. Other names may be trademarks of their respective owners.
Server version          5.6.12
Protocol version        10
Connection              Localhost via UNIX socket
UNIX socket             /var/run/mysql/mysql.sock
Uptime:                 40 sec
Threads: 1  Questions: 2  Slow queries: 0  Opens: 70  Flush tables: 1
Open tables: 63  Queries per second avg: 0.050
```

With the service started, you can now execute several tests to verify that the MySQL server is functioning correctly. For example, you can view the databases currently on the server by entering **mysqlshow** at the command prompt. You should see the databases shown here:

```
openSUSE:~ # mysqlshow
+--------------------+
|     Databases      |
+--------------------+
| information_schema |
| mysql              |
| performance_schema |
| test               |
+--------------------+
```

You can also view the tables within any of the databases shown in the output using the **mysqlshow** *table_name* command.

Now that MySQL is running properly, you need to assign passwords to your MySQL user accounts. After you run msql_install_db, your root database user account has been created but has no password assigned. To remedy this, enter **mysqladmin –u root password** *'your_new_password'* at the shell prompt. Then restrict root access to the system where MySQL is running by entering **mysqladmin –u root –h** *system_hostname* **password** *mysql_root_user_password* at the shell prompt.

At this point, your MySQL server system is up and running. You can now use it to manage SQL data! Let's talk about how this is done next.

Managing Data in the SQL Server

In order to manage data on the MySQL server, you must connect to it using some type of SQL client. You can choose from a plethora of different clients. However, for your Linux+/LPIC-1 exam, it's best that you be familiar with the command-line-based MySQL client. If you can manipulate SQL server data with this utility, all the other clients will be a piece of cake for you to use.

The command-line MySQL client is run by entering **mysql** at the shell prompt. The syntax is **mysql –h** *host_name* **–u** *user_name* **–p**. For example, to connect to the MySQL service running on the local Linux system as root, you would enter **mysql –h localhost –u root –p**. This is shown next:

```
openSUSE:/usr/bin # mysql -h localhost -u root -p
Enter password:
Welcome to the MySQL monitor.  Commands end with ; or \g.
Your MySQL connection id is 7
Server version: 5.6.12 openSUSE package
Copyright (c) 2000, 2013, Oracle and/or its affiliates. All rights reserved.
Oracle is a registered trademark of Oracle Corporation and/or its
affiliates. Other names may be trademarks of their respective owners.
Type 'help;' or '\h' for help. Type '\c' to clear the current input statement.
mysql>
```

At this point you are connected to the database and can execute any supported SQL command construct. Let's practice doing so in the following exercise.

Exercise 16-3: Managing SQL Data

In the scenario for this exercise, you will create a new database called customers and populate it with data. You can perform this exercise using the virtual machine that comes with this book. Run snapshot 16-3 for the correctly configured environment.

 VIDEO Please watch the Exercise 16-3 video for a demonstration on how to perform this task.

Complete the following (the semicolons must remain in the commands):

1. Switch to root using the **su–** command.

2. Set up your MySQL server's grant tables by changing to the /usr/bin directory and running the **mysql_install_db** command at the shell prompt.

3. Start the MySQL service by entering **servicectl start mysql** at the shell prompt.

4. Verify that the server is running by entering the **mysqladmin version** command at the shell prompt.

5. Assign a password to your MySQL root user account by entering **mysqladmin –u root password '*your_new_password*'** at the shell prompt.

6. Connect to the MySQL server from the command line by entering **mysql –h localhost –u root –p** at the shell prompt. When prompted, enter the root password you just specified.

7. At the mysql prompt, enter **CREATE DATABASE customers;**. You should be prompted that the database was created.

8. To use the new database, enter **USE customers;** at the mysql prompt.

9. To view the tables that were defined by default in the new database, enter **SHOW TABLES;** at the mysql prompt. You should see that no tables are defined. At this point, things get a little more complex. You need to use the **CREATE TABLE** command to create the table, but you will also need to define your table's columns in the command. Therefore, you first need to define the fields you want to include in each record in the table. You also need to decide what kind of data will be stored in each field as well as how long the table will be. In the table we're building here, we'll need four columns:

    first
    last
    phone
    lastcontact

    We know that the 'first' and 'last' fields will contain alphabetical characters of varying length. The 'phone' field will contain ten digits with two hyphens (*area_code-prefix-number*). The 'lastcontact' column will contain the date of each customer's last purchase.

10. Create a new table in the database by entering **CREATE TABLE active (first VARCHAR(15), last VARCHAR(15), phone CHAR(12), lastcontact DATE);** at the mysql prompt.

11. Verify that the table and columns were created correctly by entering **DESCRIBE active;** at the mysql prompt. You should see that the active table and its fields were created, as shown here:

```
mysql> DESCRIBE active;
+-------------+-------------+------+-----+---------+-------+
| Field       | Type        | Null | Key | Default | Extra |
+-------------+-------------+------+-----+---------+-------+
| first       | varchar(15) | YES  |     | NULL    |       |
| last        | varchar(15) | YES  |     | NULL    |       |
| phone       | char(12)    | YES  |     | NULL    |       |
| lastcontact | date        | YES  |     | NULL    |       |
+-------------+-------------+------+-----+---------+-------+
4 rows in set (0.01 sec)
```

With the table defined, you can now insert data into it.

12. To add a record for a customer named Robb Tracy, enter **INSERT INTO active VALUES ('Robb','Tracy','801-756-5555','2015-07-01');**.

13. To view the data just added to the table, you use the following syntax:

```
SELECT field(s) FROM table [WHERE conditions] [ORDER BY field]
```

For example, to view everything in the active table, you would enter **SELECT * FROM active;** at the mysql prompt. You should see the following data:

```
mysql> SELECT * FROM active;
+-------+-------+--------------+-------------+
| first | last  | phone        | lastcontact |
+-------+-------+--------------+-------------+
| Robb  | Tracy | 801-756-5555 | 2015-07-01  |
+-------+-------+--------------+-------------+
1 row in set (0.01 sec)
```

You could also enter **SELECT first,phone FROM active;** to view just certain fields from each record. Another example would be **SELECT * FROM active WHERE last='Tracy';** to view just records containing the string "Tracy" in the last field.

You can also delete data from the table. Here is the syntax:

```
DELETE FROM table WHERE conditions
```

For example, to delete the Robb Tracy record from the table, you could enter **DELETE FROM active WHERE last='Tracy';** at the mysql prompt. Before deleting, however, you should use the equivalent SELECT command first to see what exactly you'll be deleting! For example, first run **SELECT FROM active WHERE last='Tracy';** and then run **DELETE FROM active WHERE last='Tracy';**.

You can also modify existing data using the UPDATE command. The syntax is as follows:

```
UPDATE table_name SET column = new_value WHERE condition
```

You can use the GROUP BY statement to consolidate the results from a SELECT statement by one or more columns. It is commonly used with the SUM() statement. For example, suppose the active table contains two additional columns named quantity and custid and you use this information to record individual orders. In this situation, each customer may have multiple records in the table—one for each order placed. The command **SELECT custid,SUM(quantity) AS "Total" FROM active GROUP BY custid;** would aggregate a single result for each unique customer ID displaying the total quantity purchased for each (in a new column named "Total").

 TIP You can also use the JOIN command to merge fields from two different tables.

Chapter Review

In this chapter, we looked at several different network services that can be implemented on Linux. First we looked at configuring printing using CUPS. The CUPS service is provided using the cupsd daemon. CUPS can announce the availability of its printers on the local network. Other Linux systems can listen for these announcements, connect to the CUPS service, and send print jobs to its printers. The CUPS system is made up of the following components:

- CUPS scheduler
- CUPS filters
- CUPS backends
- PPD files
- Web-based configuration utility
- Print queue (/var/spool/cups)

The CUPS service is configured using the /etc/cups/cupsd.conf file. One of the tasks you need to complete when setting up CUPS is to configure a CUPS administrator. To do this, enter **lppasswd –g sys –a** *user_name* at the shell prompt. After doing so, you can use the web-based configuration utility to create your printers. You do this by opening a web browser and navigating to http://localhost:631.

After creating your printer, you can send print jobs by selecting **File | Print** in your graphical Linux applications. You can also send print jobs from the shell prompt using the lp command. You can use the following command-line utilities to manage your CUPS system:

- **lpstat –t**   Displays information about CUPS printers on the system
- **cancel**   Cancels a print job
- **lpoptions –d**   Sets the default printer for the system
- **cupsaccept/cupsreject**   Enables or disables a CUPS print queue
- **cupsenable/cupsdisable**   Enables or disables a CUPS printer

You can also manage Linux printing using the Line Printer Daemon (lpd). You can use lpd commands to do the following:

- **lpr –P** *printer_name filename*   Print a document.
- **lpc status**   View a printer's status.

- **lpq**   View pending print jobs.
- **lprm** *job_number*   Delete a pending print job from the queue.

These commands also work with CUPS printers and print queues.

I also reviewed a standardized process you can use to troubleshoot printing problems. We also looked at some commonly encountered printing problems and how to resolve them.

We then shifted gears and looked at managing time on Linux. I first reviewed the difference between the hardware clock and the system time on Linux and how each is used. We then looked at how you can use the hwclock command to manage the hardware clock.

To synchronize time between networked Linux systems, you can use the netdate command at the shell prompt. The syntax is **netdate** *time_server*, where *time_server* is the IP address or DNS name of another Linux system on the network that is running the time service on UDP port 37. After syncing the system time with netdate, you may want to synchronize the system time with your hardware clock using the **hwclock --systohc** command.

The netdate command works reasonably well to synchronize time on a network. However, a better way to keep time synchronized on a regular schedule is to use the Network Time Protocol (NTP). NTP manages time in a much cleaner fashion than netdate. NTP adjusts time in a much gentler manner. If there is a time differential between the time provider and the time consumer (your local system), NTP adjusts time gradually in small increments until it is eventually synchronized. NTP is also widely supported by most operating systems.

You can use the ntpd daemon on Linux to synchronize time with another NTP time provider. A system running ntpd can function as both a time consumer and a time provider at the same time. The NTP protocol operates over IP port 123. The time consumer sends a time synchronization request to the time provider on port 123. The time provider sends its time to the consumer, and the system time on the consumer is adjusted according to the NTP algorithm.

Several key NTP concepts you need to be familiar with are listed next:

- Stratum
- Stepping and slewing
- Insane time
- Drift
- Jitter

Once NTP is installed on your system, you can edit the /etc/ntp.conf file in a text editor to specify which system it should get time from. The syntax is as follows:

```
server time_server_IP_address_or_DNS_name
```

If desired, you can use an NTP pool time server. The pool.ntp.org domain uses DNS round robin to make a random selection from a pool of time providers who have volunteered to be in the pool.

Before you actually start the ntpd daemon, you need to do a quick, one-time synchronization with your NTP time provider to avoid insane time issues. This is done by entering **ntpdate** *address_of_time_provider* at the shell prompt. This will perform an initial synchronization to get time close before you start the daemon. You may actually need to run the command multiple times if the time is really far apart between your system and the NTP time provider. Once this is done, you can then start the ntpd daemon using its init script in the appropriate init script directory used by your distribution.

Once the NTP daemon has been started, you can use two commands to keep track of how the ntpd daemon is working:

- ntpq –p
- ntptrace

With NTP under our belts, we then looked at managing Linux MTAs. I started by reviewing how e-mail works. We looked at the roles of the MUA, MTA, and MDA as well as the IMAP and POP3 daemons. We then looked at several commonly used Linux MTAs:

- sendmail
- postfix
- qmail
- Exim

These MTAs can be used to receive sent e-mail messages from MUAs via SMTP. However, they can't download messages to e-mail clients via POP3 or IMAP. To do this, you must install the imap package on your system.

We then looked at the mail command-line utility that you can use to read e-mail stored in the local MTA at the shell prompt. To send a message, you can enter **mail *recipient_address*** at the shell prompt. To view a list of unread messages in your mail queue, you can enter **mailq** at the shell prompt.

You can also configure aliases for the MTA running on your Linux system. Mail aliases redirect mail addressed to one user to another user's account. You use the /etc/aliases file to configure aliases. This file defines one alias per line. The alias you define must point to an existing e-mail address. Here is the syntax for this file:

```
alias: list of real e-mail addresses
```

When done configuring aliases, you must run the **newaliases** command at the shell prompt as root to enable them.

You can also use the ~/.forward file in your user's home directory to configure forwarding. Most Linux MTAs check for the existence of this file in the user's home directory to configure the forwarding of messages. You can open/create the file in a text editor and enter the e-mail address to which you want to forward e-mail.

At this point, we shifted our attention to managing SQL data. I began by discussing how databases work to store information. Two database services are commonly implemented on Linux:

- MySQL
- PostgreSQL

SQL defines statements that can be used to retrieve and update data in a database, such as SELECT, UPDATE, DELETE, INSERT, and WHERE. A relational database is organized using fields, records, and tables. A *field* is a single piece of information. A *record* is one complete set of fields, and a *table* is a collection of records. Each table is identified by a name, such as Customers. Each table contains records (each one a single row) that contain one or more fields that in turn contain the actual database data. You can use the following commands to manage data in an SQL database:

- SELECT
- UPDATE
- DELETE
- INSERT INTO
- CREATE TABLE
- ALTER TABLE
- DROP TABLE

I then reviewed how to implement the MySQL database service on Linux. Once it is installed, you can use an SQL client to manage the data in the SQL server. I reviewed how to do this using the mysql command at the shell prompt. The syntax is **mysql –h *host_name* –u *user_name* –p**. I then discussed how to use the following commands within the mysql client:

- CREATE DATABASE
- USE
- SHOW TABLES
- CREATE TABLE
- DESCRIBE
- SELECT
- FROM
- WHERE
- DELETE
- UPDATE
- JOIN

Accelerated Review

- Most Linux distributions use CUPS to provide local and network printing.
- The CUPS service is provided by the cupsd daemon.
- CUPS can announce the availability of its printers on the local network.

- Other Linux systems can listen for these announcements, connect to the CUPS service, and send print jobs to its printers.
- The CUPS system is made up of the CUPS scheduler, CUPS filters, CUPS backends, PPD files, the web-based configuration utility, and the Print queue (/var/spool/cups).
- The CUPS service is configured with the /etc/cups/cupsd.conf file.
- To enable other Linux systems to print through your CUPS printers, you must uncomment the BrowseAddress directive in the /etc/cups/cupsd.conf file.
- Use the **lppasswd –g sys –a *user_name*** command at the shell prompt to create a CUPS administrative user.
- You use the web-based configuration utility to configure your printers. It is accessed at http://localhost:631.
- After creating your CUPS printer, you can send print jobs by selecting **File | Print** in a graphical Linux application.
- You can send print jobs from the shell prompt using the lp command.
- You can use the following command-line utilities to manage your CUPS system:
  - lpstat –t
  - cancel
  - lpoptions –d
  - cupsaccept/cupsreject
  - cupsenable/cupsdisable
- You can also manage Linux printing using the Line Printer Daemon (lpd).
- You can use lpd commands to do the following:
  - Use **lpr –P *printer_name filename*** to print a document.
  - Use **lpc status** to view the printer status.
  - Use **lpq** to view pending print jobs.
  - Use **lprm *job_number*** to delete a pending job from the print queue.
- You should use a standardized process to troubleshoot printing problems.
- You should document the flow of print jobs to help you troubleshoot printing problems.
- Commonly encountered printing problems include the following:
  - Is the printer out of paper?
  - Is the printer turned on?
  - If it's a networked printer, is it connected to the network?
  - Is the network up?
  - Can you ping the printer from the user's workstation?
  - Did the user select the correct printer when sending the print job?
  - Has the correct printer driver been configured for the printer?

- You can use the hwclock command to manage the hardware clock.

- To synchronize time between networked Linux systems, you can use the netdate command at the shell prompt.

- The syntax is **netdate *time_server*** where *time_server* is the IP address or DNS name of another Linux system on the network that is running the time service on UDP port 37.

- After syncing the system time with netdate, you may want to synchronize the system time with your hardware clock using the **hwclock --systohc** command.

- A better way to keep time synchronized on a regular schedule is to use the Network Time Protocol (NTP).

- NTP manages time in a much cleaner fashion than netdate.

- If there is a time differential between the time provider and the time consumer (your local system), NTP adjusts the time gradually in small increments until it is eventually synchronized.

- NTP is widely supported by most operating systems.

- A system running ntpd can function as both a time consumer and a time provider simultaneously.

- The NTP protocol operates over IP port 123. The time consumer sends a time synchronization request to the time provider on port 123.

- The time provider sends its time to the consumer, and the system time on the consumer is adjusted according to the NTP algorithm.

- Key NTP concepts that you need to be familiar with include the following:
  - Stratum
  - Stepping and slewing
  - Insane time
  - Drift
  - Jitter

- You can edit the /etc/ntp.conf file in a text editor to specify which system it should get time from.

- The pool.ntp.org domain uses DNS round robin to make a random selection from a pool of time providers who have volunteered to be in the pool.

- Before you actually start the ntpd daemon, you need to do a quick, one-time synchronization with your NTP time provider to avoid insane time issues by entering **ntpdate *address_of_time_provider*** at the shell prompt.

- You can start the ntpd daemon using its init script in the appropriate init script directory used by your distribution.

- E-mail messages are created and transferred using the MUA, MTA, and MDA as well as the IMAP or POP3 daemons.

- Commonly used Linux MTAs include the following:
  - sendmail
  - postfix
  - qmail
  - Exim
- MTAs can't download messages to e-mail clients via POP3 or IMAP.
- To do this, you must install the imap package on your system.
- You can use the mail command-line utility to read e-mail stored in the local MTA at the shell prompt.
- To send a message, you can enter **mail *recipient_address*** at the shell prompt.
- To view a list of unread messages in your mail queue, you can enter **mailq** at the shell prompt.
- You can configure aliases for the MTA running on your Linux system.
- Mail aliases redirect mail addressed to one user to another user's account.
- You use the /etc/aliases file to configure aliases.
- This file defines one alias per line.
- The alias you define must point to an existing e-mail address.
- When done configuring aliases, you must run the **newaliases** command at the shell prompt as root to enable them.
- You can also use the ~/.forward file in your user's home directory to configure forwarding.
- Most Linux MTAs check for the existence of this file in the user's home directory to configure the forwarding of messages.
- You can open/create the file in a text editor and enter the e-mail address to which you want to forward e-mail.
- Two database services commonly implemented on Linux are
  - MySQL
  - PostgreSQL
- SQL defines statements that can be used to retrieve and update data in a database, such as SELECT, UPDATE, DELETE, INSERT, and WHERE.
- A relational database is organized using fields, records, and tables.
- A field is a single piece of information.
- A record is one complete set of fields, and a table is a collection of records.
- Each table is identified by a name, such as Customers.

- Each table contains records (each one a single row) that contain one or more fields that in turn contain the actual database data.

- You can use the following commands to manage data in an SQL database:
  - SELECT
  - UPDATE
  - DELETE
  - INSERT INTO
  - CREATE TABLE
  - ALTER TABLE
  - DROP TABLE

- You can use the mysql command at the shell prompt to connect to a MySQL database.

- The syntax is **mysql –h** *host_name* **–u** *user_name* **–p**.

- You can use the following commands within the mysql client:
  - CREATE DATABASE
  - USE
  - SHOW TABLES
  - CREATE TABLE
  - DESCRIBE
  - SELECT
  - FROM
  - WHERE
  - DELETE
  - UPDATE
  - JOIN

Questions

1. Which of the following commands will print two copies of the /home/tux/employees.txt file to a CUPS printer named MIN2300W?

    A. lp –d MIN2300W –n 2 /home/tux/employees.txt

    B. lp –p MIN2300W –c 2 /home/tux/employees.txt

    C. lp /home/tux/employees.txt

    D. lp –d MIN2300W /home/tux/employees.txt

2. Which of the following commands sets the default printer on a Linux system to a printer named MIN2300W?

   A. lpoptions MIN2300W

   B. lpstat –d MIN2300W

   C. lp default = MIN2300W

   D. lpoptions –d MIN2300W

3. Which CUPS component handles IPP printing requests from CUPS clients?

   A. CUPS Scheduler

   B. PDLs

   C. CUPS Backends

   D. PPDs

4. Your Linux system has an IP address of 192.168.1.20. What URL should you use in a browser to access the CUPS web-based administration utility?

   A. http://192.168.1.20

   B. https://192.168.1.20

   C. http://192.168.1.20:631

   D. http://192.168.1.20/cups

5. Which directive in the /etc/cups/cupsd.conf file specifies whether or not cupsd will announce its printers using broadcasts on the network?

   A. BrowseAddress

   B. BrowseAllow

   C. Broadcast

   D. Browsing

6. Which command can be used to set the hardware clock on a Linux system to the system time?

   A. hwclock –w

   B. hwclock –s

   C. hwclock –set

   D. hwclock –r

7. You want to use the netdate command to synchronize your local system time with a time server whose DNS name is time.mydom.com. Which command will do this?

   A. netdate time.mydom.com

   B. netdate –utc time.mydom.com

   C. netdate –u time.mydom.com

   D. netdate --sync time.mydom.com

8. Which IP port does the NTP daemon use to synchronize time?

    A. 636

    B. 80

    C. 443

    D. 123

    E. 25

9. Which NTP concept refers to gradual time adjustments that occur when the time difference between the provider and the consumer is less than 128 milliseconds?

    A. Stratum

    B. Stepping

    C. Slewing

    D. Drift

10. Which NTP concept refers to situations where the time on the consumer and the time on the provider are more than 17 minutes apart?

    A. Insane time

    B. Slewing

    C. Drift

    D. Jitter

11. Which component is used in the e-mail process to create or read an e-mail message?

    A. MTA

    B. MDA

    C. MUA

    D. Message Store

12. Which postfix daemon accepts an e-mail message that is sent to the Postfix MTA by a user using the shell prompt on the local system?

    A. postdrop

    B. pickup

    C. cleanup

    D. qmgr

13. Which qmail protocol allows for the sharing of e-mail queues between multiple MTAs?

    A. QMTP

    B. QSNMP

    C. QPOP

    D. QMQP

    E. QMTA

14. Where are your users' mail queues stored on a Linux system running postfix?

   A. /var/queues/mail

   B. /opt/postfix/mail/queues

   C. /var/mail/queues

   D. /var/spool/mail

15. You need to send a message to the ksanders user on your Linux system. Given that your user account and the ksanders account both reside on the same system, what command can you use to do this?

   A. mail ksanders

   B. send ksanders

   C. mailq ksanders

   D. newmail ksanders

16. Which file is used to configure e-mail aliases?

   A. /etc/mail/aliases

   B. /var/spool/mail/aliases

   C. /etc/aliases

   D. /etc/postfix/aliases

17. Which SQL command can be used to retrieve information from a database table?

   A. QUERY

   B. SELECT

   C. FIND

   D. UPDATE

18. Which command can be used to view all the databases defined on a MySQL server?

   A. mysqlshow

   B. mysqladmin

   C. mysql_install_db

   D. mysqldatabase

19. You want to query a MySQL database table named clients and find all records whose last name (contained in the last column) is Jones. Which SQL command will do this?

   A. SELECT * FROM clients WHERE last='Jones';

   B. SELECT * FROM clients last='Jones';

   C. QUERY * FROM clients WHERE last='Jones';

   D. SELECT last='Jones' FROM clients;

20. You want to delete all records from a MySQL database table named clients whose status is Inactive (contained in the status column). Which SQL command will do this?

    A. DELETE * FROM clients;

    B. DELETE FROM clients status='Inactive';

    C. DELETE * status='Inactive' FROM clients;

    D. DELETE FROM clients WHERE status='Inactive';

Answers

1. **A.** The **lp –d MIN2300W –n 2 /home/tux/employees.txt** command will print two copies of the /home/tux/employees.txt file to a CUPS printer named MIN2300W.

2. **D.** The **lpoptions –d MIN2300W** command will set the default printer on a Linux system to a printer named MIN2300W.

3. **A.** The CUPS Scheduler handles IPP printing requests from CUPS clients.

4. **C.** The http://192.168.1.20:631 URL can be used to access the CUPS administration utility on a Linux system with an IP address of 192.168.1.20.

5. **D.** The Browsing directive in the /etc/cups/cupsd.conf file specifies whether cupsd will announce its printers using broadcasts on the network.

6. **A.** The **hwclock –w** command can be used to set the hardware clock on a Linux system to the system time.

7. **A.** The **netdate time.mydom.com** command can be used to synchronize your local system time with a time server whose DNS name is time.mydom.com.

8. **D.** Port 123 is used by the NTP daemon to synchronize time.

9. **C.** The NTP concept of slewing refers to gradual time adjustments that occur when the time difference between the provider and the consumer is less than 128 milliseconds.

10. **A.** The NTP concept of insane time refers to situations where the time on the consumer and the time on the provider are more than 17 minutes apart.

11. **C.** The Mail User Agent refers to the e-mail client software used in the e-mail process to create or read an e-mail message.

12. **A.** The postdrop daemon accepts an e-mail message that is sent to the Postfix MTA by a user using the shell prompt on the local system.

13. **D.** The QMQP qmail protocol allows for the sharing of e-mail queues between multiple MTAs.

14. **D.** Your users' mail queues on a Linux system running postfix are stored in /var /spool/mail.

15. **A.** The **mail ksanders** command can be used to send a message to the ksanders user on your Linux system.

16. **C.** The /etc/aliases file is used to configure e-mail aliases.

17. **B.** The **SELECT** command can be used to retrieve information from an SQL database table.

18. **A.** The **mysqlshow** command can be used to view all the databases defined on a MySQL server.

19. **A.** The **SELECT * FROM clients WHERE last='Jones';** SQL command can be used to query a MySQL database table named *clients* and find all records whose last name (contained in the *last* column) is Jones.

20. **D.** The **DELETE FROM clients WHERE status='Inactive';** SQL command can be used to delete all records from a MySQL database table named *clients* whose status is Inactive (contained in the *status* column).

Securing Linux

In this chapter, you will learn about:
- Securing the system
- Controlling user access
- Defending against network attacks
- Managing system logs
- Configuring xinetd and inetd

In today's world, security is a key issue in nearly every organization. As a Linux system administrator, you need to be very aware of the security issues affecting your implementation. In this chapter, I'm going to spend some time discussing how you can increase the security of your Linux systems and network.

 EXAM TIP Computer and network security are evolving, ever-changing topics. The security issues of last year are ancient history today. You will see this reflected in your Linux+/LPIC-1 exam. Don't be overly concerned with specific security threats. Instead, focus on key security principles and practices.

Let's begin this chapter by discussing how to physically secure your Linux system.

Securing the System

One of the most important, and most frequently overlooked, aspects of Linux security is securing the system itself. I'll address the following topics here:

- Securing the physical environment
- Securing access to the operating system

Let's begin by discussing how to secure the physical environment.

Securing the Physical Environment

As a consultant, I work with a variety of different clients. In any given week, I may visit three or four different organizations to help them with their network or to help them develop training materials for computing products (such as this book). In this capacity, I've had the opportunity to observe a wide range of system implementations. One of the most common mistakes I see over and over is the failure to properly secure physical access to the organization's computer systems.

Most of the larger organizations I work with are very security conscious and properly secure access to their systems. However, many of the smaller organizations I work with do not. You would be surprised how many organizations place computer systems that contain sensitive or mission-critical data in areas that are easily accessible.

For example, one client I did work for a few years ago kept their server in an unoccupied cubicle in the back of the office where it was "out of the way." There was no door to the cubicle. Anyone with access to the office could have simply picked up the server and walked out the door with it. Because it was kept in an out-of-the-way location, no one in the organization would have ever seen the perpetrator walking off with the server. No firewall in the world can protect you from this kind of threat.

As a Linux administrator, one of the most important things you can do is to limit who can access your systems. The level of access depends on the type of system involved. Keep the following points in mind:

- **Servers** The server should have the highest degree of physical security. No one (and I mean *no one*) from the general public should have physical access to your organization's servers. In fact, only a very limited number of employees within the organization should have access to your servers. Servers should not be kept in an unoccupied cubicle or on the network administrator's desk. Instead, they should be kept in a locked server room that only the system administrator and very few other people have access to.

  You should evaluate your situation and see how hard it would be for someone to get access to your servers. I've heard of instances where intruders have dressed up as copier technicians, plumbers, electricians, and even vending machine repairmen to gain access to an organization. Once inside, they had free run of the place and were able to walk off with critical computing equipment. Because they looked official, no one questioned what they were doing.

  The key idea is that an intruder should have to defeat several layers of security to get at the server system. At a minimum, someone should have to get through a secured front door, past a receptionist or security guard, and through a locked door to get to your servers. Most of the larger organizations I work with use a proximity lock that requires an ID card to enter their server rooms, limiting access to specific people in the organization.

  I walked into a small store recently and the door to the (unoccupied) server room in the back was wide open. Even worse, the server room door was right next to the rear emergency exit. If I had wanted to, I could have grabbed the server and ran out the emergency exit before anyone in the store could have known what was going on.

- **Workstations** Securing access to workstations is much more difficult. The key problem is the broad use of cubicles in the modern working environment. If you've ever worked in a sea of cubicles, you can probably already guess what the issue is. Yep, you're right. There are no doors in cubicles. Anyone with access to the office has access to everyone's computer system. As with servers, this allows an intruder to fake their way into the office and walk out with a workstation system. If done correctly, they won't even be challenged as they walk out the front door. The best you can do is to secure access to the office itself. Again, proximity locks and ID cards work well in this scenario. Only someone with an authorized card should be able to gain physical access to the work area.

 NOTE Some cool biometric systems are available that scan retinas, fingerprints, or even your voice to control access to a room.

In addition to controlling access to the office, you can further protect your organization's workstations and servers by securing access to the operating system.

Securing Access to the Operating System

After you have physically secured access to your computer systems, your next line of defense is the access controls built into the Linux operating system itself. Of course, Linux uses user accounts and passwords to control who can do what with the system. This is a very good thing. In fact, we'll talk about managing passwords later in this chapter.

However, there is a key problem that occurs daily in most organizations. During the course of the day, users constantly come and go from their cubicles or offices. It's very common to find one or more workstations logged in and left unattended at any given point in the day. Users have meetings, take breaks, go to lunch, and use the restroom. During these times, the data on their systems is highly vulnerable. An intruder who managed to get access into the office (remember the copier tech and vending machine repairmen mentioned earlier) now has access to everything the given user account has access to on the system and the network. This window of opportunity may last only a few minutes or several hours. It doesn't take long to copy a lot of critical, sensitive data to a flash drive! Even worse, the intruder could load any one of a number of programs onto the system that compromise security, such as key-logging software or a virus.

So what can you do to protect your systems? First of all, you can implement screensaver passwords. This will require an intruder to supply a password to gain access to the system console. This helps, but it still leaves the system vulnerable for a period of time, depending on how long the screensaver inactivity period is set for.

Better yet, you should train your users to log out or lock their workstations before leaving them for even the shortest period of time. Most Linux graphical desktop environments provide the option of locking the operating system. For example, within KDE, you can select K Menu | Lock Session to lock the system. You must then re-authenticate before you can use the system again. This is shown in Figure 17-1.

 NOTE You should never leave a server logged in. I see system admins do this all the time! If you're not using the server console, log out!

If you're using a text-based environment, your users should log out when they leave their desks and then log back in when they return. Many users, especially software developers, like to take a

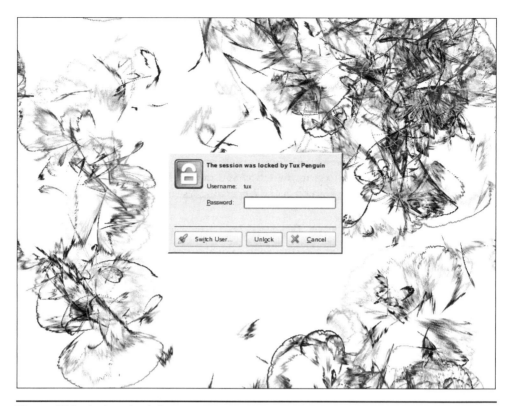

Figure 17-1   Locking the desktop

break while the Linux system is working on a big task, such as compiling a program, downloading a database update, and so on. If the user logs out from the shell prompt while these processes are running, they will be automatically stopped. To allow the user to log out and leave without killing an important process, you can use the nohup command to initially load it. Any process loaded by nohup will ignore any hang-up signals it receives, such as those sent when logging out from a shell prompt. The syntax for using nohup is **nohup *command* &**. For example, in Figure 17-2, the **find –name named &** command has been loaded using nohup, allowing it to run even if the shell were logged out.

```
root@openSUSE:~                                              ✕
File  Edit  View  Search  Terminal  Help
openSUSE:~ # nohup find / -name named &
[1] 2658
nohup: ignoring input and appending output to 'nohup.out'
```

Figure 17-2   Using nohup

My experience has been that this issue comes down to end-user training. There's only so much you can do as the system administrator to secure individual workstations. If the end user doesn't cooperate, it won't make much difference. Educate your users as to the danger and teach them how to mitigate it.

Along these lines, you also need to configure user access controls to secure your Linux systems. Let's discuss how this is done next.

Controlling User Access

A key aspect of both Linux workstation and Linux server security is to implement and use user access controls to constrain what users can do with the system. Earlier in this book, we discussed how to create and manage users, groups, and permissions to do this. However, you can take additional measures to increase the security of your systems. In this part of the chapter, we'll review the following:

- To root or not to root?
- Implementing a strong password policy
- Configuring user limits
- Disabling user login
- Auditing files

Let's begin by discussing the proper care and feeding of the root user account.

To root or Not to root?

As we discussed earlier in this book, every Linux system, whether a workstation or a server, includes a default superuser account named root. This account has full access to every aspect of the system. As such, it should be used with great care. In this part of this chapter, we'll discuss the following:

- Proper use of the root user account
- Using su
- Using sudo

Let's begin by discussing the proper way to use the root user account.

Proper Use of the root User Account

One of the key mistakes made by new Linux users is excessive use of the root user account. There's a time and a place when the root user account should be used. However, most of your work on a Linux system should be done as a non-root user account. The rule of thumb that you should follow is this: only use root when absolutely necessary. If a task can be completed as a non-root user, then it should be done so.

Why is the proper use of the root user account of concern? A few pages back, we discussed the risks of leaving a logged-in system unattended. Imagine the havoc an intruder could wreak if they were to happen upon an unattended system that was logged in as root! All of the data on the system could be accessed and copied. Major configuration changes could be made to the daemons running on the system. Heaven only knows what kind of malware could be installed.

In a nutshell, a system logged in as root represents a serious security risk. Leaving such a system unattended represents a critical security risk. Everyone, including the system administrator (that's you!), should have a standard user account that they *always* use to log in to the system.

If you find that you need root-level access while working on the system, you can use the su command to temporarily gain root-level privileges to the system. Let's discuss how this is done next.

Using su

By now, you should already know how su works. We've used it countless times in this book's exercises. This command allows you to change to a different user account at the shell prompt. The syntax for using su is **su** *options user_account*. If no user account is specified in the command, su assumes you want to switch to the root user account. Some of the more useful options you can use with su include the following:

- **–**   Loads the user's environment variables. Notice that we've always used the su – command to switch to the root user account. This changes to root and loads root's environment variables.

- **–c** *command*   Switches to the user account and runs the specified command.

- **–m**   Switches to the user account but preserves the existing environment variables.

The su command will be your best friend as a Linux administrator. However, there are times when other users may need root-level access. You can use sudo to give them limited root access. Let's discuss how sudo works next.

Using sudo

Suppose you have a power user on your Linux system. This user may be a programmer, a project manager, or a database administrator. Users in this category may frequently need to run some root-level commands. But do you really want to give them your root password? Probably not. You want them to be able to run a limited number of commands that require root privileges, but you don't want them to have full root access. This can be done using sudo.

The sudo command allows a given user to run a command as a different user account. As with su, it could be any user account on the system; however, it is most frequently used to run commands as root. The sudo command uses the /etc/sudoers file to determine what user is authorized to run which commands. This file uses the following aliases to define who can do what:

- **User_Alias**   Specifies the users who are allowed to run commands
- **Cmnd_Alias**   Specifies the commands that users are allowed to run
- **Host_Alias**   Specifies the hosts users are allowed to run the commands on
- **Runas_Alias**   Specifies the usernames that commands may be run as

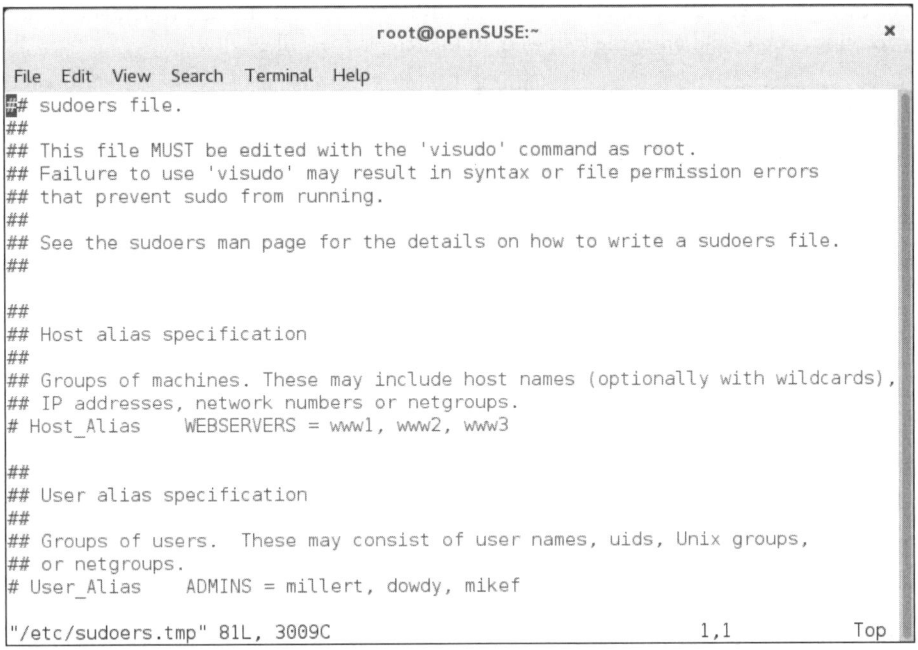

Figure 17-3   Editing /etc/sudoers with visudo

To edit your /etc/sudoers file, you need to run the **visudo** command as your root user. The /etc/sudoers file is loaded in your default editor, which is usually vi. Your changes are written to /etc/sudoers.tmp until committed. This is shown in Figure 17-3.

On most distributions, the sudoers file is configured by default such that users must supply the root password when using sudo. Obviously, this configuration doesn't accomplish anything. If the user already knows the root password, what's the point of configuring sudo? This configuration is specified by the following lines in sudoers:

```
# In the default (unconfigured) configuration, sudo asks for the root password.
# This allows use of an ordinary user account for administration of a freshly
# installed system. When configuring sudo, delete the two
# following lines:
Defaults targetpw   # ask for the password of the target user i.e. root
ALL      ALL=(ALL) ALL   # WARNING! Only use this together with 'Defaults
targetpw'!
```

To fix this, comment out the two lines specified here in the sudoers file. Then you can begin your sudoers configuration in the file. First, you need to use User_Alias to define an alias containing the user accounts (separated by commas) you want to allow to run commands. The syntax is

```
User_Alias alias = users
```

For example, to create an alias named PWRUSRS that contains the tux, rtracy, and ksanders user accounts, you would enter the following in the /etc/sudoers file:

```
User_Alias PWRUSRS = student, ksanders, rtracy
```

 TIP All alias names must start with a capital letter!

You next need to use Cmnd_Alias to define an alias that contains the commands (using the full path) that you want the users you just defined to be able to run. Separate multiple commands with commas. For example, if your users are programmers who need to be able to kill processes, you could define an alias named KILLPROCS that contains your kill command, as shown here:

```
Cmnd_Alias KILLPROCS = /bin/kill, /usr/bin/killall
```

Then you need to use Host_Alias to specify what systems the users can run the commands on. For example, to let them run the commands on a system named WS1, you would use the following:

```
Host_Alias MYHSTS = openSUSE
```

Finally, you need to glue these aliases together to define exactly what will happen. The syntax is

```
User_Alias Host_Alias = (user) Cmnd_Alias
```

Using the aliases just defined, you could allow the specified users to run the specified commands on the specified hosts as root by entering

```
PWRUSRS     MYHSTS = (root) KILLPROCS
```

To exit the editor, press ESC and then enter **:exit**. The visudo utility will check your syntax and inform you if you've made any errors. At this point, the users you defined can execute the commands you specified as root by entering **sudo *command*** at the shell prompt. For example, the rtracy user could kill a process named vmware-toolbox (owned by root) by entering **sudo killall vmware-toolbox** at the shell prompt. After the rtracy user supplies his password, the process will be killed.

In addition to using the root user account properly, you also should implement a strong password policy. Let's discuss how this is done next.

Implementing a Strong Password Policy

Another serious security weakness I've observed over the years is the use of weak passwords. A weak password is one that can be easily guessed or cracked. Here are some examples:

- Your last name
- Your spouse's name
- Your mother's maiden name

- Your child's name

- Your birthday

- Your pet's name

- Any word that can be found in the dictionary

- Using "password" for your password

- Single-character passwords

- Blank passwords

You would be surprised how often users use these types of passwords. Not good! You need to train your users to use stronger passwords. A strong password uses

- Six or more characters (the longer the better!)

- A combination of numbers and letters

- Upper- and lowercase letters

- Words not found in the dictionary

- (Optionally) non-alphanumeric characters such as punctuation marks

For example, a password such as M3n0v3l273 is a relatively strong password because it meets the preceding criteria. The password management utilities that come with most Linux distributions are configured by default to check your user passwords to make sure they meet the criteria for strong passwords. For example, if you try to use a weak password with the passwd command, you are prompted to use a stronger one, as shown here:

```
openSUSE:~ # passwd ksanders
New Password:BAD PASSWORD: it is WAY too short
BAD PASSWORD: is too simple
Retype new password:
```

In addition to using strong passwords, you should also configure your user accounts such that passwords expire after a certain period of time. This is called *password aging*. Why age passwords? The longer a user has the same password, the more likely it is to be compromised. By forcing users to periodically rotate passwords, you keep intruders guessing. Even if they do manage to get a user's password, it will be rendered useless at some point. The length of time allowed for a given password varies from organization to organization. More security-minded organizations may mandate a password age of 30 days or less. Less paranoid organizations may use an age of 60 or even 90 days.

You can configure aging for your passwords using the chage command. The syntax for using chage is **chage *option user***. You use the following options with chage:

- **−m *days*** Specifies the minimum number of days between password changes

- **−M *days*** Specifies the maximum number of days between password changes

- **−W *days*** Specifies the number of warning days before a password change is required

```
                         root@openSUSE:~                                    ×

  File  Edit  View  Search  Terminal  Help
 openSUSE:~ # chage -m 5 -M 90 -W 7 ksanders
 openSUSE:~ # █
```

Figure 17-4   Using chage to set password aging

For example, in Figure 17-4, the chage command has been used to specify a minimum password age of five days, a maximum password age of 90 days, and seven warning days for the ksanders user.

In addition, your Linux systems should *not* be configured to store passwords within the /etc/passwd file. Many processes running in a Linux system need access to /etc/passwd to complete various tasks. Storing your passwords in that file exposes them to these processes and opens a serious security hole. Most system implementers realize that storing passwords within /etc/passwd is a very bad idea, so you probably won't run into many systems configured this way anymore. However, if you do run into such a system, you can use the **pwconv** command to move user passwords out of /etc/passwd and into /etc/shadow.

You should also train your users to use good common sense when working with passwords. One security breach I see all too often is users writing their password on a sticky note and sticking it somewhere on their desk. I've even seen system passwords written on a sticky note right on the monitor or keyboard. I know the thought of passwords written down and displayed in plain sight makes you cringe, but I see it over and over and over. Some users try to hide their sticky note under the keyboard or in a drawer, but it's still a significant security issue. All the intruder has to do is watch the user at login and note where she has hidden her password, making his job a cakewalk. We had a recent issue at my child's middle school where this very thing happened. The attendance secretary kept her password on a sticky note next to her keyboard. A student noticed this and, one day after school, logged in to her computer and used the school's attendance tracking software to send out automated prank phone calls to the parents of all students in the school. This "exploit" was fairly innocuous, but it gives you an idea of just how easy it is to defeat the most complex security systems if users write down their passwords and leave the note in plain sight.

The "sticky note phenomenon" is yet another reason for enforcing good physical security. A ne'er-do-well can gain easy access to corporate information using a password that's posted in plain sight. Once done, it can be very difficult to trace the breach back to the intruder.

Finally, you should train your users how to deal with social engineering attempts. This is actually one of the easiest and most effective tools in the intruder's toolbox. Social engineering exploits human weaknesses instead of technical weaknesses in the system. Here's how a typical social engineering exploit works.

The intruder calls an employee of an organization posing as another employee. The intruder tells the employee that he is "Fred" from Sales and is on the road at a client site. He needs to get a very important file from the server and can't remember his password. He then asks the employee if he can use their password "just this once" to get the files he needs.

Most employees want to be team players and help out in an emergency. They are all too willing to hand out their password, granting the intruder easy access to the system. Some social engineering attempts are less direct. Instead of calling and asking for passwords, the intruder sifts through the company garbage looking for little yellow sticky notes with users' passwords written on them. Some social engineering attempts are more "in your face." The intruder sifts through the trash to find the name of a high-ranking person in the company. He then calls an employee posing as that person and demands that the employee divulge their password, threatening to fire them if they don't comply. Pretty sneaky, huh?

In addition, you need to be diligent against the flood of *phishing e-mails* that have been plaguing organizations for the last several years. Phishing e-mails are drafted such that they appear to have come from a legitimate organization, such as a bank, social media, or e-commerce website. They convince the user to click a link that takes them to a malicious website where they are tricked into revealing sensitive information.

Phishing emails are a low-tech but very popular exploit because they are extremely successful. This type of attack has resulted in devastating security breaches on the part of several large corporations in recent years. All they take to be successful is a handful of employees who are unwise enough to open the message and follow the instructions therein.

To detect phishing e-mails, you need to learn to recognize several key characteristics. They may look legitimate, but there are several key attributes that identify them as a scam. For example, it's common for the source address of the message to not match the domain of the company it claims to be coming from. In addition, the message typically tries to create a sense of urgency. For example, it may warn that your bank account will be frozen, that your credit card has been stolen, or even that you will be subject to arrest if you don't follow the instructions in the message. The key giveaway is the fact that the hyperlinks in the message go to websites that are not associated with the organization the message claims to be coming from. If you hover your mouse over a link (*without* clicking it) you can see where the link actually leads. If it isn't pointing to the organization's URL, there's a pretty good chance the message is an exploit.

The best way to combat social engineering is to, again, train your users. Teach them to not write down passwords. Teach them to not throw sensitive data in the trash—shred it instead! Teach them about social engineering phone calls and how to deal with them. Most organizations simply tell their employees to forward any calls asking for a password to the help desk (that's you). Chances are, all they will hear is a click on the other end. Teach them how to recognize a phishing e-mail and how to respond properly.

In addition to configuring password aging, you can also increase the security of your Linux systems by limiting logins and resources. Let's review how this is done next.

Configuring User Limits

You can impose limits on how many times users may log in, how much CPU time they can consume, and how much memory they can use on a Linux system. This can be done in two ways:

- Using pam_limits to restrict access to resources
- Using ulimit to restrict access to resources

Using pam_limits to Restrict Access to Resources

You can limit user access to Linux system resources using a Pluggable Authentication Modules (PAM) module called pam_limits, which is configured using the /etc/security/limits.conf file. This file contains resource limits that you can configure using the following syntax:

```
domain      type      item      value
```

This syntax is described here:

- **domain** Describes the entity to which the limit applies. You can use one of the following values:
  - **user** Identifies a specific Linux user
  - **@group_name** Identifies a specific Linux group
  - * Specifies all users
- **type** Defines a **hard** or **soft** limit. A hard limit cannot be exceeded. A soft limit can be temporarily exceeded.
- **item** Specifies the resource being limited. You can use the values shown in Table 17-1.
- **value** Specifies a value for the limit.

For example, to configure the rtracy user with a soft CPU limit of 15 minutes, you would open the /etc/security/limits.conf file in a text editor and then enter the following:

```
rtracy     soft     cpu      15
```

This limit could be useful if the user is running a CPU-intensive program that is hogging cycles away from other users. Likewise, you could also limit the rtracy user to a maximum of two concurrent logins by entering the following in the file:

```
rtracy     hard     maxlogins     2
```

This would prevent any logins to the system as the rtracy user after two initial logins were successful.

In addition to using pam_limits, you can also limit user access to system resources using the ulimit command. Let's look at how this is done next.

	Resource	Description
Table 17-1	core	Restricts the size of core files (in KB)
Configuring	data	Restricts the size of a program's data area in RAM (in KB)
Resource Limits	fsize	Restricts the size of files created by the user (in KB)
	nofile	Restricts the number of data files a user may have open concurrently
	stack	Restricts the stack size (in KB)
	cpu	Restricts the CPU time of a single process (in minutes)
	nproc	Restricts the number of concurrent processes a user may run
	maxlogins	Sets the maximum number of simultaneous logins for user
	priority	Sets the priority to run user processes with
	locks	Sets the maximum number of locked files
	nice	Sets maximum nice priority a user is allowed to raise a process to

Using ulimit to Restrict Access to Resources

You can also use the ulimit command to configure limits on system resources. However, be aware that the limits you configure with ulimit are applied only to programs launched from the shell prompt. The syntax for using ulimit is **ulimit *options limit*.** You can use the following options with ulimit:

- **−c** Sets a limit on the maximum size of core files in blocks. If you set this limit to a value of **0**, core dumps on the system are disabled.

- **−f** Sets a limit on the maximum size (in blocks) of files created by the shell.

- **−n** Sets a limit on the maximum number of open file descriptors.

- **−t** Sets a limit on the maximum amount of CPU time (in seconds) a process may use.

- **−u** Sets a limit on the maximum number of processes available to a single user.

- **−d** Sets a limit on the maximum size (in KB) of a process's data segment in RAM.

- **−m** Sets a limit on the maximum resident size (in KB) of a process in RAM.

- **−s** Sets a limit on the maximum stack size (in KB).

- **−H** Sets a hard resource limit.

- **−S** Sets a soft resource limit.

You can use the –a option with the ulimit command to view the current value for all resource limits. This is shown in Figure 17-5.

You can also use ulimit to set resource limits. For example, to set a soft limit of 50 processes, you would enter **ulimit –S –u 50** at the shell prompt. The current user could then own no more than 50 concurrent shell processes.

```
                               root@openSUSE:~                              ✕

  File  Edit  View  Search  Terminal  Help
openSUSE:~ # ulimit -a
core file size          (blocks, -c) 0
data seg size           (kbytes, -d) unlimited
scheduling priority             (-e) 0
file size               (blocks, -f) unlimited
pending signals                 (-i) 11889
max locked memory       (kbytes, -l) 64
max memory size         (kbytes, -m) unlimited
open files                      (-n) 1024
pipe size            (512 bytes, -p) 8
POSIX message queues     (bytes, -q) 819200
real-time priority              (-r) 0
stack size              (kbytes, -s) 8192
cpu time               (seconds, -t) unlimited
max user processes              (-u) 11889
virtual memory          (kbytes, -v) unlimited
file locks                      (-x) unlimited
```

Figure 17-5 Viewing current resource limits with ulimit

```
                        root@openSUSE:~                              ✕

 File  Edit  View  Search  Terminal  Help
openSUSE:~ # w
 19:05:56 up 29 min,  4 users,  load average: 0.51, 0.28, 0.26
USER     TTY      FROM        LOGIN@   IDLE    JCPU   PCPU WHAT
rtracy   :0       console     18:43    ?xdm?   2:57   0.31s /usr/lib/gdm/gd
rtracy   console  :0          18:43    29:13   0.00s  0.31s /usr/lib/gdm/gd
rtracy   pts/0    :0          18:43    4.00s   0.78s  1.70s /usr/lib/gnome-
ksanders pts/1    10.0.0.60   19:05    27.00s  0.17s  0.17s -bash
```

Figure 17-6   Generating a list of logged-in users

Disabling User Login

From time to time, you may need to completely disable all logins to your Linux system. For example, you have a serious issue that needs to be resolved and you need to keep everyone out for a period of time. To do this, you first need to log out all current users. You can use the **w** command to view a list of all currently logged-in users. For example, in Figure 17-6, two users are currently logged in: ksanders and rtracy.

Now that you know who's logged in, you can use the **pkill –KILL –u** *user_name* command to brute-force log out each user. For example, in Figure 17-7, the pkill command has been used to log off the ksanders user.

At this point you can disable all future logins. This is actually very easy to do. All you need to do is create a file in /etc named **nologin**. As long as this file exists, no one but root is allowed to log in. In addition, any text you enter in the nologin file will be displayed if a user does try to log in. In the example shown in Figure 17-8, the text "The system is currently unavailable for login." has been entered in the /etc/nologin file. Thus, when a user tries to log in, this is the error message that is displayed.

```
                        root@openSUSE:~                              ✕

 File  Edit  View  Search  Terminal  Help
openSUSE:~ # w
 19:05:56 up 29 min,  4 users,  load average: 0.51, 0.28, 0.26
USER     TTY      FROM        LOGIN@   IDLE    JCPU   PCPU WHAT
rtracy   :0       console     18:43    ?xdm?   2:57   0.31s /usr/lib/gdm/gd
rtracy   console  :0          18:43    29:13   0.00s  0.31s /usr/lib/gdm/gd
rtracy   pts/0    :0          18:43    4.00s   0.78s  1.70s /usr/lib/gnome-
ksanders pts/1    10.0.0.60   19:05    27.00s  0.17s  0.17s -bash
openSUSE:~ # pkill -KILL -u ksanders
openSUSE:~ # w
 19:10:10 up 33 min,  3 users,  load average: 0.13, 0.17, 0.21
USER     TTY      FROM        LOGIN@   IDLE    JCPU   PCPU WHAT
rtracy   :0       console     18:43    ?xdm?   3:21   0.31s /usr/lib/gdm/gd
rtracy   console  :0          18:43    33:27   0.00s  0.31s /usr/lib/gdm/gd
rtracy   pts/0    :0          18:43    2.00s   0.79s  2.16s /usr/lib/gnome-
```

Figure 17-7   Forcing a user to log off

Figure 17-8

Login denied
message from
/etc/nologin

This behavior is actually configured in the /etc/pam.d/login file, shown here:

```
openSUSE:~ # cat /etc/pam.d/login
#%PAM-1.0
auth      requisite      pam_nologin.so
auth      [user_unknown=ignore success=ok ignore=ignore auth_err=die
default=bad]pam_securetty.so
auth      include         common-auth
account   include         common-account
password  include         common-password
session   required        pam_loginuid.so
session   include         common-session
session   required        pam_lastlog.so   nowtmp
session   optional        pam_mail.so standard
session   optional        pam_ck_connector.so
```

The line that reads **auth requisite pam_nologin.so** causes PAM to check whether a file named nologin exists in /etc. If it does, PAM does not allow regular users to log in. When you're done, you can re-enable logins by deleting or renaming the nologin file. For example, you could rename it by entering **mv /etc/nologin /etc/nologin.bak** at the shell prompt.

Let's next discuss how to audit files to locate files with the SUID or SGID permission set.

Auditing Files

In addition to disabling user login, another user security-related issue you need to be familiar with is auditing files that have SUID root permissions set. As you learned in Chapter 11, SUID stands for *Set User ID*. When an executable file with the SUID permission set is run, the process is granted access to the system as the user who owns the executable file, not on the user who actually ran the command. This is a serious issue if the file is owned by root. When the root user owns a file with the SUID permission set, it allows the process created by the file to perform actions as root, which the user who started it is probably not allowed to do. The same issue applies to files owned by the root group that have the SGID permission set.

Be aware that a small number of files owned by root on a Linux system do need to have these permissions set. However, other files owned by root/root that have the SUID/SGID permission set represent a security vulnerability on your system. Many exploits are facilitated using files with this permission set. A file that has the SUID permission set appears as follows when listed with the ls command at the shell prompt:

```
-rwSr-xr-x
```

A file that has the SGID permission sets appears as follows when listed with the ls command at the shell prompt:

```
-rw-r-Sr-x
```

Therefore, you should consider running periodic audits to identify any files owned by root that have either of these permissions set. Any files beyond the minimal necessary files should be scrutinized carefully to make sure they aren't part of some type of exploit. You can search for files on your Linux system that have SUID permissions set using the following command at the shell prompt as your root user:

```
find / -type f -perm -u=s -ls
```

Here is an example:

```
openSUSE:/etc # find / -type f -perm -u=s -ls
 36406    32 -rwsr-xr-x  1 root     root        31848 Sep  5  2009 /bin/su
 30659    36 -rwsr-xr-x  1 root     root        35796 May  3  2007 /bin/ping
 84596    20 -rwsr-xr-x  1 root     audio       20252 Jun 16  2006 /bin/eject
 85643   324 -rwsr-xr-x  1 root     root       330420 Sep  5  2009 /bin/mount
 30661    36 -rwsr-xr-x  1 root     root        35716 May  3  2007 /bin/ping6
 85644   120 -rwsr-xr-x  1 root     root       121111 Sep  5  2009 /bin/umount
```

The –perm option tells **find** to match files that have the specified permission assigned to the mode; in this case, the S permission is assigned to user. You can also identify any files with the SGID permission set using the following command:

```
find / -type f -perm -g=s -ls
```

When you do, a list of all files with the SGID permission set is displayed. Here is an example:

```
openSUSE:~ # find / -type f -perm -g=s -ls
 94451    12 -rwxr-sr-x  1 root     tty         10588 May 18  2007 /opt/gnome/lib/vte/
                                                                    gnome-pty-helper
 85710    12 -rwxr-sr-x  1 root     tty         10404 Sep  5  2009 /usr/bin/wall
  5867    12 -rwxr-sr-x  1 root     shadow       8800 Jun 16  2006 /usr/bin/vlock
 85713    12 -rwxr-sr-x  1 root     tty          9024 Sep  5  2009 /usr/bin/write
 93913    12 -rwxr-sr-x  1 root     maildrop    11300 Sep  5  2009usr/sbin/postdrop
 93919    12 -rwxr-sr-x  1 root     maildrop    11668 Sep  5  2009 /usr/sbin/postqueue
 26192     8 -rwxr-sr-x  1 root     tty          7288 Jun 16  2006 /usr/sbin/utempter
 35720    24 -rwxr-sr-x  1 root     shadow      20672 Sep  5  2009 /sbin/unix_chkpwd
```

Let's practice controlling user access to a Linux system in the following exercise.

Exercise 17-1: Managing User Access

In this exercise, you will practice setting age limits on user passwords. You also configure sudo to allow a standard user to kill processes on the system as the root user. You can perform this exercise using the virtual machine that comes with this book. Run snapshot 17-1 for the correctly configured environment.

 VIDEO Please watch the Exercise 17-1 video for a demonstration on how to perform this task.

Complete the following:

1. Boot your Linux system and log in as your **student** user with a password of **student**.

2. Open a terminal session.

3. Switch to your root user account by entering **su –** followed by a password of **student**.

4. Practice configuring age limits by completing the following:

   a. Use the cat or less utility to view the /etc/passwd file. Identify a user on the system that you want to configure password age limits for.

   b. Set the minimum password age to three days, the maximum password age to 60 days, and the number of warning days before expiration to seven by entering **chage –m 3 –M 60 –W 7 *username*** at the shell prompt.

5. Configure sudo to allow a user on your system to kill processes as the root user by doing the following:

   a. Identify a user on your system to whom you want to grant the ability to kill processes as root.

   b. As your root user, enter **visudo** at the shell prompt. You should see the /etc/sudoers file loaded in the vi text editor.

   c. Press INS.

   d. Scroll down to the lines shown in the example that follows and comment them out by inserting a # character at the beginning of each one.

   ```
   Defaults targetpw   # ask for the password of the target user i.e. root
   ALL     ALL=(ALL) ALL   # WARNING! Only use this together with 'Defaults
   targetpw'!
   ```

   e. Add the following lines to the end of the sudoers file:

   ```
   User_Alias PWRUSRS = your_user
   Cmnd_Alias KILLPROCS = /bin/kill, /usr/bin/killall
   Host_Alias MYHSTS = openSUSE
   PWRUSRS MYHSTS = (root) KILLPROCS
   ```

   f. Press ESC and then enter **:exit** to save the changes to the sudoers file.

   g. Run **top** at the shell prompt as your root user.

   h. Open a new terminal session and (as your standard user) enter **ps –elf | grep top**. You should see a top process running that is owned by the root user.

   i. Kill that process as your standard user by entering **sudo killall top** at the shell prompt.

   j. When prompted, enter your user's password.

   k. Enter **ps –elf | grep top** at the shell prompt again. You should see that the top process that was owned by the root user has been killed.

Now that you've got your users secured, let's next discuss how to defend against network attacks.

Defending Against Network Attacks

It would be nice if we lived in a world where we could connect networks together and be able to trust others to respect our systems. Unfortunately, such a world doesn't exist. If your Linux systems are connected to a network, you need to be very concerned about network attacks. If your network is connected to a public network, such as the Internet, you need to be extremely concerned about network attacks.

As with most of the topics discussed in this book, network security is a huge topic that can fill many volumes. We really don't have the time or space here to do the topic justice. Instead, I'm going to discuss some basic things you can do to defend against network attacks. I'll discuss the following:

- Mitigating network vulnerabilities
- Implementing a firewall with iptables

Let's begin by discussing some things you can do to mitigate network vulnerabilities.

Mitigating Network Vulnerabilities

The good news is that there are some simple things you can do to mitigate the threat to your Linux systems from network attacks. These include the following:

- Staying abreast of current threats
- Unloading unneeded services
- Installing updates

Let's first discuss staying abreast of current network threats.

Staying Abreast of Current Threats

One of the biggest problems with network security threats is the fact that we're always one step behind the guys wearing black hats. No sooner do we implement a fix to protect our systems from the latest exploit than they hit us with a new one. Therefore, it's critical that you stay up to date with the latest network threats. You'll soon see that they change week to week, and sometimes even day to day! The only way you can keep your systems safe is to be aware of what the current threats are.

The best way to do this is to visit security-related websites on a regular basis. These sites inform you of the latest exploits and how to defend yourself against them. One of the best sites to visit is www.cert.org, which is maintained by the Computer Emergency Response Team (CERT) at the Carnegie Mellon Software Engineering Institute. The CERT website contains links to the latest security advisories.

Another excellent resource is www.us-cert.gov. Maintained by the United States government's Computer Emergency Readiness Team, the US-CERT website provides tons of information about current cyber-attacks.

Of course, there are hundreds of other security-related websites out there. However, those I've listed here are among the most authoritative sites around. Most of the other security-related websites derive their content from these sites. If you visit these sites religiously, you can stay abreast of what's happening in the security world and hopefully prevent an attack on your systems.

In addition to staying current with these sites, you should also review your systems to see if all the services they provide are really necessary. Let's talk about how to do that next.

Unloading Unneeded Services

One of the easiest things you can do to mitigate the threat from a network attack is to simply unload network services running on your system that aren't needed. Depending on your distribution and how you installed it, you probably have a number of services running on your

```
                              root@openSUSE:~                                    ✕

  File  Edit  View  Search  Terminal  Help
 openSUSE:~ # chkconfig
 after.local      off
 alsasound        on
 autofs           off
 avahi-daemon     on
 avahi-dnsconfd   off
 before.local     off
 chargen          off
 chargen-udp      off
 cifs             off
 cron             on
 cups             on
 cups-lpd         off
 cvs              off
 daytime          off
 daytime-udp      off
 dbus             on
 discard          off
 discard-udp      off
 echo             off
 echo-udp         off
 esound           off
 gpm              off
 inputattach      off
```

Figure 17-9   Viewing installed services

system that you didn't know were there and that you don't need. You can view a list of installed services and whether or not they are running by entering **chkconfig** at the shell prompt. This command will list each service and its status, as shown in Figure 17-9.

NOTE   The chkconfig utility is not available on all distributions. It was originally a Red Hat utility and has been ported to many other distributions, such as SUSE Linux. If you're using Debian, however, you'll likely find that it isn't available.

As a word of caution, however, don't disable a service unless you know what it actually does. Some daemons are required for the system to run properly. If you don't know what a particular service is, use the man utility, the info utility, or the Internet to research it and determine whether or not it is necessary.

In addition to chkconfig, you can also use the nmap command to view open IP ports on your Linux system. This information is really useful. Each port that is open on your Linux system represents a potential vulnerability. Some open ports are necessary. Others, however, may not be necessary. You can close the port by unloading the service that is using it.

NOTE   You need to install the nmap package before you can use the nmap command.

```
root@openSUSE:~                                        ✕

File  Edit  View  Search  Terminal  Help
openSUSE:~ # nmap -sT 10.0.0.3

Starting Nmap 6.40 ( http://nmap.org ) at 2015-01-20 19:33 MST
Nmap scan report for 10.0.0.3
Host is up (0.0011s latency).
Not shown: 982 filtered ports
PORT       STATE   SERVICE
22/tcp     open    ssh
80/tcp     open    http
113/tcp    closed  ident
139/tcp    open    netbios-ssn
389/tcp    open    ldap
427/tcp    open    svrloc
443/tcp    open    https
445/tcp    closed  microsoft-ds
524/tcp    open    ncp
631/tcp    open    ipp
636/tcp    open    ldapssl
5801/tcp   open    vnc-http-1
5901/tcp   open    vnc-1
5989/tcp   open    wbem-https
6901/tcp   open    jetstream
8008/tcp   open    http
8009/tcp   open    ajp13
```

Figure 17-10 Using nmap to scan for open ports

The syntax for using nmap is **nmap –sT *host_IP_address*** for a TCP port scan and **nmap –sU *host_IP_address*** for a UDP port scan. In Figure 17-10, the nmap utility has been used to scan for open TCP ports.

As you can see in this figure, a number of services are running on the host that was scanned. You can use this output to determine what should and shouldn't be left running on the system. To disable a service, you can use its init script in your init directory to shut it down. You should also use the chkconfig or systemctl command to configure the service to not automatically start.

 TIP You should run nmap both locally and from a different system against the same host. This will tell you what ports are open on your system and which services are allowed through your host's firewall.

In addition to the nmap utility, you can also use the netstat utility to scan for open ports. The netstat utility is another powerful tool in your virtual toolbox. The syntax for using netstat is to enter **netstat *option*** at the shell prompt of the system you want to scan. You can use the options listed in Table 17-2.

An example of using netstat with the –l option to view a list of listening sockets on a Linux host is shown in Figure 17-11.

In addition to unloading unneeded services, you should also install operating system updates. Let's discuss how this is done next.

Table 17-2	netstat Option	Description
netstat Options	–a	Lists all listening and nonlistening sockets
	–i	Displays statistics for your network interfaces
	–l	Lists listening sockets
	–s	Displays summary information for each protocol
	–r	Displays your routing table

Installing Updates

One of the most important things you can do to defend against network attacks is to regularly install operating system updates. A simple fact of life that we have to deal with in the IT world is that software isn't written perfectly. Most programs and services have some defects. Even your Linux kernel has defects in it. Some of these defects are inconsequential, some are just annoying, and others represent serious security risks.

As software is released and used, these defects are discovered by system administrators, users, and (unfortunately) hackers. As they are discovered, updates are written and released that fix the defects. With most distributions, you can configure the operating system to automatically go out on the Internet and periodically check for the availability of updates. For example, with SUSE Linux, you

```
                                root@openSUSE:~                                    ✕

 File   Edit   View   Search   Terminal   Help
openSUSE:~ # netstat -l
Active Internet connections (only servers)
Proto Recv-Q Send-Q Local Address          Foreign Address        State
tcp        0      0 *:59082                *:*                    LISTEN
tcp        0      0 *:ssh                  *:*                    LISTEN
tcp        0      0 localhost:ipp          *:*                    LISTEN
tcp        0      0 localhost:smtp         *:*                    LISTEN
tcp        0      0 *:mysql                *:*                    LISTEN
tcp        0      0 *:ssh                  *:*                    LISTEN
tcp        0      0 localhost:ipp          *:*                    LISTEN
tcp        0      0 *:44472                *:*                    LISTEN
tcp        0      0 localhost:smtp         *:*                    LISTEN
udp        0      0 *:43439                *:*
udp        0      0 *:35268                *:*
udp        0      0 *:ipp                  *:*
udp        0      0 10.0.0.83:ntp          *:*
udp        0      0 localhost:ntp          *:*
udp        0      0 *:ntp                  *:*
udp        0      0 *:mdns                 *:*
udp        0      0 *:10123                *:*
udp        0      0 *:dhcpv6-client        *:*
udp        0      0 *:59465                *:*
udp        0      0 fe80::20c:29ff:feb0:ntp *:*
udp        0      0 localhost:ntp          *:*
```

Figure 17-11 Using netstat to view a list of listening sockets

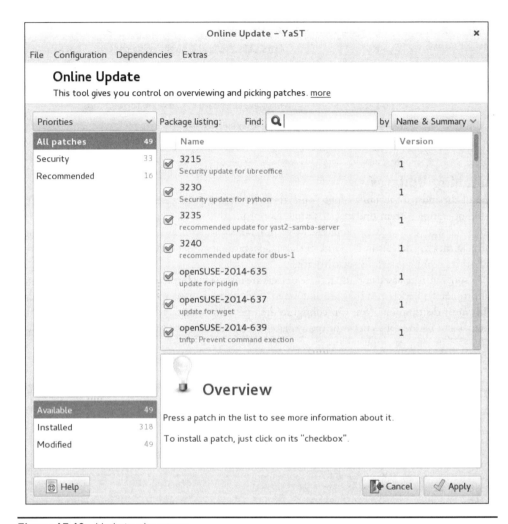

Figure 17-12 Updating the system

can use the YaST Online Update module, shown in Figure 17-12, to do this. You can configure the system to either automatically install them for you or prompt you to install them. The tool you use to update your system will vary depending on which Linux distribution you are using.

TIP Another thing you should do to protect network communications is use OpenSSH to encrypt sensitive data being transferred from system to system. Using OpenSSH is a big topic, so we'll address it in more detail in the next chapter.

You should also implement a host-based firewall to protect your Linux system. Let's discuss how this is done next.

Implementing a Firewall with iptables

Today, most organizations connect their corporate networks to the Internet. Doing so enhances communications and provides access to a wealth of information. Unfortunately, it also exposes their network to a serious security threat. If users can go out on the Internet, an uninvited person from the Internet can also get into the network, unless measures are taken to keep this from happening. To do this, the organization needs to implement a network firewall as well as host-based firewalls on each system.

A network firewall is very different from a host-based firewall. A *host-based firewall* controls traffic in and out of a single computer system. A *network firewall,* on the other hand, is used to control traffic in and out of a network segment or an entire network.

In this part of the chapter, we're going to spend some time learning how to use Linux in both capacities. We'll discuss the following topics:

- How firewalls work
- Implementing a packet-filtering firewall

Let's begin by discussing how firewalls work.

How Firewalls Work

So what exactly is a firewall? A *firewall* is a combination of hardware and software that acts like a gatekeeper between your network and another network. Usually, a firewall has two or more network interfaces installed. One is connected to the internal network; the other, connected to the public network, acts much like a router. However, a firewall is not a router (although it may be implemented in conjunction with one).

The job of a firewall is to monitor the traffic that flows between the networks, both inbound and outbound. You configure the firewall with rules that define the type of traffic that is allowed through. Any traffic that violates the rules is not allowed, as shown in Figure 17-13.

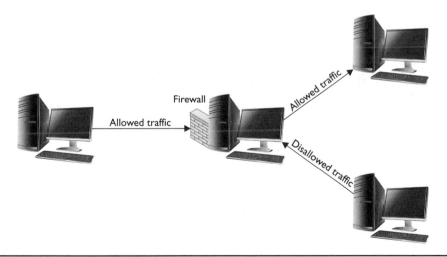

Figure 17-13   How a firewall works

Firewalls can be implemented in a variety of ways. One of the most common types is a *packet-filtering firewall,* where all traffic moving between the private and public networks must go through the firewall. As it does, the firewall captures all incoming and outgoing packets and compares them against the rules you've configured.

The firewall can filter traffic based on the origin address, the destination address, the origin port, the destination port, the protocol used, or the type of packet. If a packet abides by the rules, it is forwarded on to the next network. If it doesn't, it is dropped, as shown in Figure 17-14.

Packet-filtering firewalls don't necessarily have to be implemented between your network and the Internet. They can also be implemented between a network segment and a backbone segment to increase your internal network security.

To use a packet-filtering firewall, you must be familiar with which port numbers are used by default by specific services. IP ports 0 through 1023 are assigned by the IANA organization to network services and are called *well-known ports.* Some of the more common port assignments that you need to be familiar with are shown in Table 17-3.

Packet-filtering firewalls are widely used. They cost less than other types of firewalls. They also require relatively little processing. Data moves through very quickly, making them much faster than other firewalls.

 TIP   You can also implement stateful firewalls as well as application-level gateways, both of which operate higher up in the OSI model. Unfortunately, we don't have the time or space to address how they work here.

With this background in mind, let's review how to implement a packet-filtering firewall on Linux.

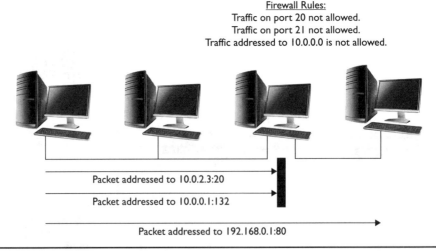

Figure 17-14   Using a packet-filtering firewall

Table 17-3	**Port**	**Service**
Common Port	20, 21	FTP
Assignments	22	OpenSSH
	23	Telnet
	25	SMTP
	53	DNS
	80, 443	HTTP and HTTPS
	110	POP3
	119	NNTP
	137, 138, and 139	SMB and NetBIOS (used by Samba)
	143	IMAP
	161 and 162	SNMP
	177	X Display Manager Control Protocol (xdmcp)
	389, 636	LDAP (insecure and secure)
	631	IPP

Implementing a Packet-Filtering Firewall

Just as Linux can act as a router, it can also be configured to function as a firewall. In fact, it can be used to configure a very robust, very powerful firewall. Currently, there are many firewall appliances on the market based on the Linux operating system. There are also many downloadable Linux ISOs, such as from Untangle, that you can install on standard PC hardware to turn it into a router. For our purposes here, we're going to focus on creating a basic packet-filtering firewall using iptables.

The first step in setting up a packet-filtering firewall on a Linux system is to design your implementation. You should answer the following questions when designing in your firewall:

- Will you allow all incoming traffic by default, establishing rules for specific types of traffic that you don't want to allow in?

- Will your firewall deny all incoming traffic except for specific types of traffic that you want to allow?

- Will you allow all outgoing traffic by default, blocking only specific types or destinations?

- Will you block all outgoing traffic except for specific types or destinations?

- What ports must be opened on the firewall to allow traffic through from the outside? For example, are you going to implement a web server that needs to be publicly accessible behind the firewall? If so, you will need to open up ports 80 and probably 443 on your boundary firewall.

How you decide to configure your firewall depends on your organization's security policy. However, I recommend that you err on the side of caution. Given a choice, I'd rather deal with a user who's upset because the firewall won't let him share bootlegged music files over the Internet than deal with a major attack that has worked its way deep into my network.

Once your firewall has been designed, you're ready to implement it. After installing and configuring the required network boards, you can configure a firewall on your Linux system using the iptables utility. Many Linux distributions include graphical front ends for iptables that you can use to build your firewall. These front ends are usually not as flexible as the command-line utility, but they make the setup process much faster and easier!

The heart of the Linux firewall is the iptables package. Most distributions include it. If yours didn't, it can be downloaded from www.netfilter.org. Versions of the Linux kernel prior to 2.4 used ipfwadm or ipchains instead of iptables. If you visit The Linux Documentation Project at www.tldp.org, you'll see that many of the firewall HOWTOs are still written to help with these older packages.

NOTE   The iptables package will be replaced in the future by a new package called nftables.

The Linux kernel itself completes packet-filtering tasks on Linux. In order to use iptables, your kernel must comply with the netfilter infrastructure. The netfilter infrastructure is included by default when most distributions are installed.

The netfilter infrastructure uses the concept of "tables and chains" to create firewall rules. A *chain* is simply a rule that you implement to determine what the firewall will do with an incoming packet. The netfilter infrastructure uses the *filter table* to create packet-filtering rules. Within the filter table are three default chains:

- **FORWARD**   The FORWARD chain contains rules for packets being transferred between networks through the Linux system.
- **INPUT**   The INPUT chain contains rules for packets that are being sent to the local Linux system.
- **OUTPUT**   The OUTPUT chain contains rules for packets that are being sent from the local Linux system.

If you don't explicitly specify a table name when using the iptables utility, it will default to the filter table. Each chain in the filter table has four policies that you can configure:

- ACCEPT
- DROP
- QUEUE
- REJECT

You can use iptables to create rules within a chain. A chain can contain multiple rules. Each rule in a chain is assigned a number. The first rule you add is assigned the number 1. The iptables utility can add rules, delete rules, insert rules, and append rules. The syntax for using iptables is **iptables –t** *table command chain options*. You can use the following commands with iptables:

- **–L** Lists all rules in the chain
- **–N** Creates a new chain

You can work with either the default chains listed previously or create your own chain. You create your own chain by entering **iptables –N** *chain_name*. You can add rules to a chain by simply using the **–A** option. You can also use one of the other options listed here:

- **–I** Inserts a rule into the chain
- **–R** Replaces a rule in the chain
- **–D** Deletes a rule from the chain
- **–F** Deletes all the rules from the chain (called *flushing*)
- **–P** Sets the default policy for the chain

You can also use the following options with iptables:

- **–p** Specifies the protocol to be checked by the rule. You can specify all, tcp, udp, or icmp. If you specify tcp or udp, you can also use the following extensions for matching:
  - **--sport** Specifies a single port to match on
  - **--dport** Specifies a single destination port to match on
  - **--sports** Specifies multiple source ports to match on
  - **--dports** Specifies multiple destination ports to match on
- **–s** *ip_address/mask* Specifies the source address to be checked. If you want to check all IP addresses, use 0/0.
- **–d** *ip_address/mask* Specifies the destination address to be checked. If you want to check all IP addresses, use 0/0.
- **–j** *target* Specifies what to do if the packet matches the rule. You can specify ACCEPT, REJECT, DROP, or LOG actions.
- **–i** *interface* Specifies the interface where a packet is received. This only applies to INPUT and FORWARD chains.
- **–o** *interface* Specifies the interface where a packet is to be sent. This applies only to OUTPUT and FORWARD chains.

 NOTE The options presented here represent only a sampling of what you can do with iptables. To see all the options available, see the iptables man page.

iptables Command	Function
iptables –L	Lists existing rules
iptables –D FORWARD 1	Deletes the first rule in the FORWARD chain
iptables –t filter –F	Deletes all rules from the filter table
iptables –P INPUT DROP	Sets a default policy for the INPUT chain that drops all incoming packets
iptables –P FORWARD DROP	Configures your FORWARD chain to drop all packets
iptables –A INPUT –s 0/0 –p icmp –j DROP	Configures the firewall to disregard all incoming PING packets addressed to the local Linux system
iptables –A FORWARD –p tcp –s 0/0 --sport 80 –j ACCEPT	Configures the firewall to allow HTTP traffic
iptables –A INPUT –i eth0 –s 192.168.2.0/24 –j DROP	Configures the firewall to accept all incoming packets on eth0 coming from the 192.168.2.0 network

Table 17-4   Some iptables Commands

The best way to learn how to use iptables is to look at some examples. Table 17-4 has some sample iptables commands that you can start with.

You can use iptables to create a sophisticated array of rules that control how data flows through the firewall. Most administrators use the –P option with iptables to set up the firewall's default filtering rules. Once the default is in place, you use iptables to configure exceptions to the default behavior needed by your particular network.

Remember that any rules you create with iptables are not persistent. If you reboot the system, they will be lost by default. To save your rules, you use the iptables-save command to write your tables out to a file. You can then use the iptables-restore command to restore the tables from the file you created.

Let's practice implementing network security measures on a Linux system in the following exercise.

Exercise 17-2: Implementing Network Security Measures on Linux

In this exercise, you will practice scanning for open IP ports and implementing a simple host-based firewall. You will need a second system to test your firewall configuration with.

You can perform this exercise using the virtual machine that comes with this book. Run snapshot 17-1 for the correctly configured environment.

 VIDEO   Please watch the Exercise 17-2 video for a demonstration on how to perform this task.

Complete the following:

1. Boot your Linux system and log in as your student user.

2. Open a terminal session.

3. Switch to your root user account by entering **su –** followed by a password of **student**.

4. Scan your system for open ports by completing the following steps:

   a. At the shell prompt, enter **nmap –sT** *your_IP_address*. What TCP/IP ports are in use on your system?

   b. At the shell prompt, enter **nmap –sU** *your_IP_address*. What UDP/IP ports are in use on your system?

5. Configure a simple firewall with iptables by doing the following:

   a. From a remote system, ping your Linux system and verify that it responds.

   b. Open a terminal session.

   c. At the shell prompt, **su –** to root.

   d. Configure the kernel to use the iptables filter by entering **modprobe iptable_filter** at the shell prompt.

   e. List the current rules for the filter table by entering **iptables –t filter –L** at the shell prompt.

   f. At the shell prompt, enter **iptables –t filter –A INPUT –s 0/0 -p icmp –j DROP**.

      This command creates a rule that will drop all incoming packets using the ICMP protocol from any source destined for the local system.

   g. View your new rule by entering **iptables –t filter –L** at the shell prompt. You should see the following rule added to your INPUT chain:

      ```
      DROP       icmp -- anywhere            anywhere
      ```

   h. Using your remote system, ping your Linux system's IP address. The packets should be dropped, as shown in this sample output:

      ```
      Pinging 192.168.1.10 with 32 bytes of data:
      Request timed out.
      Request timed out.
      Request timed out.
      Request timed out.
      ```

Now that you understand how to defend your network, let's spend some time learning how to manage your system logs.

Managing System Logs

Log files are a gold mine of information for the system administrator. You can use your log files to detect intruders into your system. Log files can also be used to troubleshoot problems with your system. In this part of the chapter, I'll teach you how to manage and use your system log files. I'll cover the following topics:

- Configuring log files
- Using log files to troubleshoot problems
- Using log files to detect intruders

Let's begin by discussing how to configure your log files.

```
                        root@openSUSE:/var/log                            ✕

  File  Edit  View  Search  Terminal  Help
openSUSE:/var/log # ls
NetworkManager    btmp          mail.err          pm-powersave.log
Xorg.0.log        cups          mail.info         samba
Xorg.0.log.old    faillog       mail.warn         speech-dispatcher
Xorg.1.log        firewall      messages          warn
YaST2             gdm           messages-20141222.xz  wpa_supplicant.log
acpid             hp            mysql             wtmp
alternatives.log  krb5          news              zypp
apparmor          lastlog       ntp
audit             localmessages pbl.log
boot.log          mail          pk backend zypp
```

Figure 17-15   Contents of the /var/log directory

Configuring Log Files

Your system log files are stored in the /var/log directory, shown in Figure 17-15.

Notice in this figure that there are a number of subdirectories in /var/log where system daemons, such as mysql, apparmor, audit, and cups, store their log files. Some of these log files are simple text files that can be read with text manipulation utilities. Others are binary files that require the use of a special utility, such as lastlog. As you can see in Figure 17-15, there are quite a number of files within /var/log and its subdirectories. As with anything, some log files are much more useful than others. Table 17-5 contains a list of some of the more important log files.

Log File	Description
boot.log	Contains log entries from daemons as they were started during bootup.
boot.msg	Contains all the messages displayed onscreen during system boot. This can be a very valuable troubleshooting tool when you're trying to rectify startup problems. The messages displayed onscreen usually fly by too quickly to be read.
faillog	Contains failed authentication attempts.
firewall	Contains firewall log entries.
lastlog	Contains the last login information for users.
mail	Contains messages generated by the postfix and sendmail daemons.
messages	Contains messages from most running processes. This is probably one of the most useful of all log files. You can use it to troubleshoot services that won't start, services that don't appear to work properly, and so on.
warn	Contains warning messages.
wtmp	Contains a list of users who have authenticated to the system.
xinetd.log	Contains log entries from the xinetd daemon.

Table 17-5   Useful Log Files

> **NOTE**   The files shown in Table 17-5 are the log files used on a SUSE Linux system. Other distributions may use different files by default. You can customize your logging using the syslog.conf file, discussed next.

How logging is implemented on Linux depends on which distribution you are using. For your Linux+/LPIC1 exam, you need to be familiar with the following logging implementations:

- syslogd
- journald

syslogd

Logging on a Linux system that uses init is usually handled by the syslogd daemon. Instead of each daemon maintaining its own individual log file, most of your Linux services are configured to write log entries to /dev/log by default. This device file is maintained by the syslogd daemon. When a service writes to this socket, the input is captured by syslogd. The syslogd daemon then uses the entries in the /etc/syslog.conf file, shown in Figure 17-16, to determine where the information should go.

> **NOTE**   Some Linux distributions use syslog-ng or rsyslogd instead of syslogd to manage logging. The logging daemon your system uses is configured in /etc/sysconfig/syslog by the SYSLOG_DAEMON= directive.

```
# Log all kernel messages to the console.
# Logging much else clutters up the screen.
#kern.*                                                 /dev/console

# Log anything (except mail) of level info or higher.
# Don't log private authentication messages!
*.info;mail.none;authpriv.none;cron.none               /var/log/messages

# The authpriv file has restricted access.
authpriv.*                                             /var/log/secure

# Log all the mail messages in one place.
mail.*                                                 -/var/log/maillog


# Log cron stuff
cron.*                                                 /var/log/cron

# Everybody gets emergency messages
*.emerg                                                *

# Save news errors of level crit and higher in a special file.
uucp,news.crit                                         /var/log/spooler
./syslog.conf
```

Figure 17-16   The /etc/syslog.conf file

The syntax for the syslog.conf file is

```
facility.priority          file
```

A *facility* refers to a subsystem that provides a message. Each process on your Linux system that uses syslog for logging is assigned to one of the following facilities:

- **authpriv**   Facility used by all services associated with system security or authorization
- **cron**   Facility that accepts log messages from cron and at
- **daemon**   Facility that can be used by daemons that do not have their own facility
- **kern**   Facility used for all kernel log messages
- **lpr**   Facility that handles messages from the printing system
- **mail**   Facility for log messages from the mail MTA (such as postfix or sendmail)
- **news**   Facility for log messages from the news daemon
- **syslog**   Facility for internal messages from the syslog daemon itself
- **user**   Facility for user-related log messages (such as failed login attempts)
- **uucp**   Facility for log messages from the uucp daemon
- **local0–local7**   Facilities you can use to capture log messages from your own applications that you develop

In addition to facilities, the syslogd daemon also provides *priorities* that you can use to customize how logging occurs on your system. Prioritization is handled by the klogd daemon on most distributions, which runs as a client of syslogd. You can use the following priorities with syslogd:

- **debug**   All information
- **info**   Informational messages
- **notice**   Issues of concern, but not yet a problem
- **warn**   Noncritical errors
- **err**   Serious errors
- **crit, alert, or emerg**   Critical errors

For example, in Figure 17-16, the syslog.conf file directs messages of all priority levels (*) from the cron facility to the /var/log/cron file. If desired, you could customize your syslog.conf file to split messages of different priority levels to different files.

Your Linux distribution should also include a utility named logrotate. The logrotate utility is run daily, by default, by the cron daemon on your system. You can customize how your log files are rotated using the /etc/logrotate.conf file, shown in Figure 17-17.

 NOTE   Some distributions use the logrotated daemon to manage log file rotation.

Figure 17-17

Configuring log
file rotation in
/etc/logrotate.
conf

```
# see "man logrotate" for details
# rotate log files weekly
weekly

# keep 4 weeks worth of backlogs
rotate 4

# create new (empty) log files after rotating old ones
create

# use date as a suffix of the rotated file
dateext

# uncomment this if you want your log files compressed
#compress

# comment these to switch compression to use gzip or another
# compression scheme
compresscmd /usr/bin/bzip2
uncompresscmd /usr/bin/bunzip2

# former versions had to have the compressext set accordingly
#compressext .bz2

# RPM packages drop log rotation information into this directory
include /etc/logrotate.d

# no packages own wtmp and btmp -- we'll rotate them here
#/var/log/wtmp {
#    monthly
#    create 0664 root utmp
#        minsize 1M
#    rotate 1
#}
#
# /var/log/btmp {
#   missingok
#    monthly
#    create 0600 root utmp
#    rotate 1
#}
/etc/logrotate.conf lines 1-41/43 93%
```

This file contains default global parameters used by logrotate to determine how and when log files are rotated. However, these defaults can be overridden for specific daemons using the configuration files located in the /etc/logrotate.d/ directory. For example, in Figure 17-18, the /etc/logrotate.d/apache2 file is used to customize logging for the apache2 daemon.

In this figure, the /var/log/apache2/access_log file will be compressed. It can have a maximum age of 365 days, after which it will be removed (**maxage 365**). Old versions of the file will be archived using a date extension (**dateext**). The log file will go through 99 rotations before being removed (**rotate 99**). If the file grows larger than 4096KB, it will be rotated (**size=+4096k**). The file will not be rotated if it is empty (**notifempty**). No error message will be generated if the file is missing (**missingok**). The file will be created with 644 permissions, will have the root user as owner, and will be owned by the root group (**create 644 root root**). After a log file is rotated, the /etc/init.d/apache2 reload command will be run (**postrotate /etc/init.d/apache2 reload**).

NOTE Many other directives can be used in a logrotate configuration file. See the logrotate man page for more information.

Figure 17-18

Configuring
Apache web
server logging

```
/var/log/apache2/access_log {
    compress
    dateext
    maxage 365
    rotate 99
    size=+4096k
    notifempty
    missingok
    create 644 root root
    postrotate
      /etc/init.d/apache2 reload
    endscript
}

/var/log/apache2/error_log {
    compress
    dateext
    maxage 365
    rotate 99
    size=+1024k
    notifempty
    missingok
    create 644 root root
    postrotate
      /etc/init.d/apache2 reload
apache2 lines 1-25/69 38%
```

One of the cool features of the syslogd daemon is that it supports logging to a remote host. Moving your log files from the local system to a different computer on the network can be a very valuable administrative and security measure. For example, you could redirect all logging by Linux systems on your network to a single log host. Then, if a user calls with a problem, you have instant access to their log files on the log host.

In addition, remote logging increases the security of your systems. Inexperienced intruders tend to leave footprints all over in your log files. However, savvy intruders will try to erase their tracks by altering the log files after accessing the system, making it very difficult to detect the intrusion. If you redirect your logging, however, the intruder can't cover their tracks nearly so easily. To redirect logging, complete the following:

1. Open a terminal session and **su –** to root.

2. Open /etc/syslog.conf in a text editor.

3. Add the following line to the beginning of the file:

   ```
   *.*            @IP_address_of_loghost
   ```

   For example, to redirect all messages to a log server host with an IP address of 192.168.1.10, you would enter

   ```
   *.*            @192.168.1.10
   ```

4. Save the file and exit your editor.

5. Restart the syslogd daemon.

6. To configure the log server host to receive log messages from the other systems, complete the following:

   a. In a text editor, open /etc/sysconfig/syslog.

   b. Locate to the SYSLOGD_PARAMS directive.

    c. Set the value of the SYSLOGD_PARAMS directive to **–r**.

    d. Save the changes and exit the file.

    e. Restart syslogd.

 TIP You can test your logging configuration using the logger utility. This command-line tool allows you to manually make entries in your logging system. The syntax is **logger –p** *facility.priority "log_message"*.

journald

Newer Linux distributions that use the systemd daemon use the journald daemon for logging instead of syslogd. The journald daemon maintains a system log called the *journal* (located in /var/log/journal/). You view the journal using the **journalctl** command. If you enter this command at the shell prompt with no parameters, the entire journal is displayed, as shown in Figure 17-19.

One of the neat features of the journald daemon is the fact that you can use it to also view your system boot messages. To do this, you enter **journalctl –b** at the shell prompt. The messages from the most recent system boot are displayed. In addition, you can use journalctl to view messages from previous system boots as well. This can be done in two different ways:

- Specifying –b with the command followed by a positive number will look up the messages from the specified system boot starting from the beginning of the journal. For example, entering **journalctl –b 1** will display messages created during the first boot found at the beginning of the journal.

```
                          root@openSUSE:~                                      ✕

 File  Edit  View  Search  Terminal  Help
-- Logs begin at Thu 2015-01-22 16:56:49 MST, end at Thu 2015-01-22 17:08:25 MST
Jan 22 16:56:49 openSUSE systemd-journal[227]: Runtime journal is using 276.0K (
Jan 22 16:56:49 openSUSE systemd-journal[227]: Runtime journal is using 280.0K (
Jan 22 16:56:49 openSUSE kernel: Initializing cgroup subsys cpuset
Jan 22 16:56:49 openSUSE kernel: Initializing cgroup subsys cpu
Jan 22 16:56:49 openSUSE kernel: Initializing cgroup subsys cpuacct
Jan 22 16:56:49 openSUSE kernel: Linux version 3.11.10-21-desktop (geeko@buildho
Jan 22 16:56:49 openSUSE kernel: Disabled fast string operations
Jan 22 16:56:49 openSUSE kernel: e820: BIOS-provided physical RAM map:
Jan 22 16:56:49 openSUSE kernel: BIOS-e820: [mem 0x0000000000000000-0x0000000000
Jan 22 16:56:49 openSUSE kernel: BIOS-e820: [mem 0x000000000009f800-0x0000000000
Jan 22 16:56:49 openSUSE kernel: BIOS-e820: [mem 0x00000000000ca000-0x0000000000
Jan 22 16:56:49 openSUSE kernel: BIOS-e820: [mem 0x00000000000dc000-0x0000000000
Jan 22 16:56:49 openSUSE kernel: BIOS-e820: [mem 0x0000000000100000-0x000000005f
Jan 22 16:56:49 openSUSE kernel: BIOS-e820: [mem 0x000000005fef0000-0x000000005f
Jan 22 16:56:49 openSUSE kernel: BIOS-e820: [mem 0x000000005feff000-0x000000005f
Jan 22 16:56:49 openSUSE kernel: BIOS-e820: [mem 0x000000005ff00000-0x000000005f
Jan 22 16:56:49 openSUSE kernel: BIOS-e820: [mem 0x00000000e0000000-0x00000000ef
Jan 22 16:56:49 openSUSE kernel: BIOS-e820: [mem 0x00000000fec00000-0x00000000fe
Jan 22 16:56:49 openSUSE kernel: BIOS-e820: [mem 0x00000000fee00000-0x00000000fe
Jan 22 16:56:49 openSUSE kernel: BIOS-e820: [mem 0x00000000fffe0000-0x00000000ff
Jan 22 16:56:49 openSUSE kernel: NX (Execute Disable) protection: active
Jan 22 16:56:49 openSUSE kernel: SMBIOS 2.4 present.
lines 1-23
```

Figure 17-19 Viewing the journal with journalctl

- Specifying –b with the command followed by a negative number will look up the messages from the specified system boot starting from the end of the journal. For example, entering **journalctl –b -2** will display system messages created two boots ago.

The journalctl command can also be used to display only log entries related to a specific service running on the system. The syntax is **journalctl –u** *service_name*. For example, to view all journal entries related to the SSH daemon running on the system, you would enter **journalctl –u sshd** at the shell prompt. An example is shown in Figure 17-20.

The behavior of the journal daemon is configured using the /etc/systemd/journald.conf file. This file has many parameters you can configure. Some of the more useful ones are listed here:

- **MaxFileSec**   Specifies the maximum amount of time to store entries in the journal file before starting a new file.

- **MaxRetentionSec**   Specifies the maximum amount of time to store journal entries. Any entries older than the specified time are automatically deleted from the journal file.

- **ForwardToSyslog**   Configures journald to forward its log messages to the traditional syslog daemon.

- **MaxLevelStore**   Controls the maximum log level of messages stored in the journal file. All messages equal to or less than the log level specified are stored, whereas any messages above the specified level are dropped. This parameter can be set to one of the following values:

  - emerg (0)
  - alert (1)
  - crit (2)
  - err (3)
  - warning (4)
  - notice (5)
  - info (6)
  - debug (7)

```
root@openSUSE:~                                                    ✕
File  Edit  View  Search  Terminal  Help
openSUSE:~ # journalctl -u sshd
-- Logs begin at Thu 2015-01-22 17:37:48 MST, end at Thu 2015-01-22 17:49:00 MST
Jan 22 17:38:53 openSUSE systemd[1]: Starting OpenSSH Daemon...
Jan 22 17:38:53 openSUSE systemd[1]: Started OpenSSH Daemon.
Jan 22 17:38:54 openSUSE sshd[2811]: Server listening on 0.0.0.0 port 22.
Jan 22 17:38:54 openSUSE sshd[2811]: Server listening on :: port 22.
Lines 1-5/5 (END)
```

Figure 17-20   Viewing sshd journal events

NOTE If your distribution uses systemd, but you are longing for the functionality of syslogd, you can install syslog-ng. The syslog-ng daemon works with systemd, but is configured in much the same manner as syslog.

With this background in mind, let's next discuss how to actually view and use your log files.

Using Log Files to Troubleshoot Problems

As mentioned earlier in this chapter, your log files can be an invaluable resource when you're troubleshooting Linux problems. If the kernel or a service encounters a problem, it will be logged in a log file. Reviewing these log files can provide you with a wealth of information that may not necessarily be displayed on the screen.

Some log files are binary files that must be read with a special utility. However, most of your log files are simple text files that you can view with standard text manipulation utilities. Earlier in this book, you learned how to use the cat, less, and more utilities to view text files on a Linux system. These utilities can, of course, be used to view text-based log files as well. However, there's a problem with these utilities: log files are usually far too long to be viewed effectively with these utilities.

For example, the /var/log/messages file may have 10,000 or more lines in it. That's a lot of text! The less utility displays only 24 lines at a time. You're going to have to press the SPACEBAR a lot of times to get to the end of the file.

You can use two strategies to get around this. The first is to redirect the output of the cat command to the grep command to filter out a specific term within a log file. For example, suppose you wanted to locate information within /var/log/messages related to logins. You could enter **cat /var/log/messages | grep login | more** at the shell prompt. Then, only entries containing the term "login" would be displayed. If your system uses systemd and a journal, you can do the same thing with the journalctl command. Just pipe the output from journalctl to grep and specify what term you are looking for.

In addition to grep, you can also use the head and tail utilities to view log file entries. Understand that most log files record entries chronologically, usually oldest to newest. If you want to view the beginning of a log file, you can enter **head** *filename* at the shell prompt to display the first lines of the file. For example, in Figure 17-21, the beginning of the /var/log/messages file has been displayed with head.

The tail utility works in a manner opposite of head. Instead of displaying the first lines of a file, it displays the last lines. This is very useful. Usually, when troubleshooting, you need to see only the last few lines of a log file. To do this, enter **tail** *filename* at the shell prompt. In Figure 17-22, the /var/log/messages file is being viewed using tail.

The tail utility provides the –f option, which I use all of the time when troubleshooting. When you use the –f option, tail will display the last lines of a log file as per normal. However, it doesn't exit after it initially displays the text on the screen. Instead, it monitors the file being displayed and displays new lines as they are added to the log file. For example, you could use the **tail –f /var/log/ messages** command to monitor your system log file for error messages as you troubleshoot a system.

The tail command monitors the /var/log/messages file waiting for new lines to be added. If something happens on the system that generates messages, such as stopping and then restarting

```
                          root@openSUSE:~                              ✕

 File  Edit  View  Search  Terminal  Help
openSUSE:~ # head /var/log/messages
2014-12-22T16:00:10.536035-07:00 openSUSE logrotate: ALERT exited abnormally wit
h [1]
2014-12-22T16:00:10.546737-07:00 openSUSE logrotate: error: skipping "/var/log/m
ysql/mysqld.log" because parent directory has insecure permissions (It's world w
ritable or writable by group which is not "root") Set "su" directive in config f
ile to tell logrotate which user/group should be used for rotation.
2014-12-22T16:00:10.549918-07:00 openSUSE logrotate: compress_ext is /usr/bin/xz
2014-12-22T16:00:10.551164-07:00 openSUSE logrotate: compress_ext was changed to
 .xz
2014-12-22T16:00:30.106794-07:00 openSUSE org.freedesktop.PackageKit[534]: Downl
oadProgressReportReceiver::start():http://download.opensuse.org/update/13.1/ --l
ibksba8;1.3.0-5.4.1;i586;repo-update
2014-12-22T16:00:33.767476-07:00 openSUSE org.freedesktop.PackageKit[534]: Downl
oadProgressReportReceiver::start():http://download.opensuse.org/update/13.1/ --n
tp;4.2.6p5-15.13.1;i586;repo-update
2014-12-22T16:00:58.500998-07:00 openSUSE /USR/SBIN/CRON[4257]: pam_unix(crond:s
ession): session closed for user root
2014-12-22T16:01:25.144933-07:00 openSUSE systemd[1]: Stopping Session 2 of user
 rtracy.
2014-12-22T16:01:25.157079-07:00 openSUSE systemd[1]: Stopped Session 2 of user
rtracy.
2014-12-22T16:01:25.213964-07:00 openSUSE systemd[1]: Stopping Stop Read-Ahead D
ata Collection 10s After Completed Startup.
```

Figure 17-21   Using head to view a log file

```
                          root@openSUSE:~                              ✕

 File  Edit  View  Search  Terminal  Help
openSUSE:~ # tail /var/log/messages
2015-01-22T20:15:01.401866-07:00 openSUSE systemd[1]: Started Session 13 of user
 root.
2015-01-22T20:15:01.797227-07:00 openSUSE /USR/SBIN/CRON[4534]: pam_unix(crond:s
ession): session closed for user root
2015-01-22T20:22:38.598946-07:00 openSUSE gdm-password]: gkr-pam: unlocked login
 keyring
2015-01-22T20:23:54.017323-07:00 openSUSE systemd[1]: Mounting Arbitrary Executa
ble File Formats File System...
2015-01-22T20:23:54.089089-07:00 openSUSE systemd[1]: Mounted Arbitrary Executab
le File Formats File System.
2015-01-22T20:30:01.831200-07:00 openSUSE /usr/sbin/cron[4587]: pam_unix(crond:s
ession): session opened for user root by (uid=0)
2015-01-22T20:30:01.855247-07:00 openSUSE systemd[1]: Starting Session 14 of use
r root.
2015-01-22T20:30:01.858679-07:00 openSUSE systemd[1]: Started Session 14 of user
 root.
2015-01-22T20:30:02.096318-07:00 openSUSE /USR/SBIN/CRON[4587]: pam_unix(crond:s
ession): session closed for user root
2015-01-22T20:30:53.766809-07:00 openSUSE gdm-password]: gkr-pam: unlocked login
 keyring
```

Figure 17-22   Using tail to view a log file

a network interface, the results are instantly displayed on the screen without you having to run tail again. You can quit monitoring the file by pressing CTRL-C.

If your system uses the journald daemon to managing logging, you can do the same thing with the journalctl command. If you run journalctl –f at the shell prompt, the last few entries in the journal are displayed. The journalctl command then monitors the journal and prints new entries as they are added.

You can check one of the system log files listed previously in Table 17-5 to troubleshoot problems. However, the files in Table 17-5 are the default log files used with SUSE Linux. On other distributions, such as Fedora, you may need to look at other log files, including

- **cron**   Contains entries from the cron daemon
- **dmesg**   Contains hardware detection information
- **maillog**   Contains entries generated by the sendmail daemon
- **secure**   Contains information about access to network daemons
- **rpmpkgs**   Contains a list of installed rpm packages

To troubleshoot problems associated with an application or service, you may need to check for a log file maintained specifically for that service. For example, you would check the mail, mail.err, mail.info, and mail.warn files on a SUSE Linux system or the maillog file on a Fedora system to troubleshoot problems with the postfix or sendmail daemon. If you were having trouble with the mysqld daemon, you would look in the mysqld.log file within the /var/log/mysql directory. To troubleshoot problems with the Apache web server, you would investigate the various log files within the /var/log/apache2 directory.

In addition to using log files to troubleshoot problems on your Linux system, you can also use them to detect unauthorized intrusion attempts. Let's look at how this is done next.

Using Log Files to Detect Intruders

Detecting intruders involves looking for clues they left behind in the system. One of your best resources in this regard is the log files your Linux system maintains for you. Much like a CSI detective, you need practice and experience to develop an intuitive sense that lets you know when something looks suspicious. The best way to develop this intuition is to spend a lot of time reviewing your log files. This will help you develop a feel for what is "normal" for your system. Once you know what is normal, you can spot that which is not normal.

With this in mind, let's look at several log files you can analyze to identify suspicious activities. The first is the /var/log/wtmp file. This log file contains a list of all users who have authenticated to the system. The file is saved in binary format. You can't use cat, less, or a text editor such as vi to view it. Instead, you must use the **last** command at the shell prompt. Output from the last utility is shown in Figure 17-23.

The last utility displays the user account, login time, logout time, and where users authenticated from. When you review this file, look for anything that appears unusual—for example, logins that occurred in the middle of the night when no one is at work are suspicious.

```
                              root@openSUSE:~                                    ✕

 File  Edit  View  Search  Terminal  Help
openSUSE:~ # last
rtracy     pts/0       :0                Thu Jan 22 17:48    still logged in
rtracy     console     :0                Thu Jan 22 17:42    still logged in
rtracy     :0          :0                Thu Jan 22 17:42    still logged in
reboot     system boot 3.11.10-21-deskt  Thu Jan 22 17:37 - 20:48   (03:10)
(unknown   :0          :0                Thu Jan 22 17:39 - crash   (00:-1)
reboot     system boot 3.11.10-21-deskt  Thu Jan 22 17:37 - 20:48   (03:10)
rtracy     pts/0       :0                Thu Jan 22 17:07 - 17:36   (00:28)
rtracy     console     :0                Thu Jan 22 16:59 - 17:36   (00:36)
rtracy     :0          :0                Thu Jan 22 16:59 - 17:36   (00:36)
reboot     system boot 3.11.10-21-deskt  Thu Jan 22 16:56 - 17:36   (00:40)
(unknown   :0          :0                Thu Jan 22 16:58 - crash   (00:-1)
reboot     system boot 3.11.10-21-deskt  Thu Jan 22 16:56 - 17:36   (00:40)
root       pts/2       :0.0              Tue Jan 20 19:39 - 19:58   (00:18)
root       pts/2       :0.0              Tue Jan 20 19:27 - 19:31   (00:03)
rtracy     pts/1       10.0.0.60         Tue Jan 20 19:13 - down    (01:17)
ksanders   pts/1       10.0.0.60         Tue Jan 20 19:05 - 19:10   (00:04)
```

Figure 17-23 Using last to review login history

You can also view the /var/log/faillog file. This log file contains a list of failed authentication attempts. This file is very effective at detecting *dictionary attacks,* which run through a list of dictionary terms, trying them as passwords for user accounts. Like wtmp, faillog is a binary file. To view it, you need to use the faillog utility. This utility displays the user who tried to authenticate, how many times that user failed to log in, and when the last unsuccessful attempt occurred. You can use the –u option to view login attempts for a specific user account—for example: faillog –u rtracy.

When reviewing this log file, look at unusual login attempts, such as an abnormally high number of failed logins, especially if they occurred late at night. You can also use the faillog utility to specify how the system handles failed login attempts. This is done using the following options with the faillog command:

- **–l** *seconds* Locks the account for the specified number of seconds after a failed login attempt

- **–m** *number* Sets the maximum number of failed login attempts before the user account is disabled

The next log file is /var/log/lastlog. This file contains a list of all the users in the system and when they last logged in. As with the other log files we've looked at, you can't view lastlog with less, cat, or a text editor. To view lastlog, you must use the lastlog utility from the shell prompt, as shown in Figure 17-24.

The last type of log files you can use to detect intrusion attempts are /var/log/messages and your journal (if your distribution uses it). As mentioned earlier, these log files contain messages from all services running on the system. As such, they contain a lot of data that may or may not be related to intrusion attempts. You can use grep to isolate the relevant entries. For example, you

```
root              tty1                          Fri Jan  2 15:25:03 -0700 2015
rtkit                                           **Never logged in**
scard                                           **Never logged in**
srvGeoClue                                      **Never logged in**
sshd                                            **Never logged in**
statd                                           **Never logged in**
svn                                             **Never logged in**
tftp                                            **Never logged in**
usbmux                                          **Never logged in**
uucp                                            **Never logged in**
wwwrun                                          **Never logged in**
dtracy                                          **Never logged in**
ksanders          pts/1    10.0.0.60            Tue Jan 20 19:05:29 -0700 2015
rtracy            :0       console              Thu Jan 22 17:42:15 -0700 2015
student           pts/1    10.0.0.60            Tue Nov 25 17:27:58 -0700 2014
mysql             _                             **Never logged in**
```

Figure 17-24   Using lastlog to view last login times

could use the **cat /var/log/messages | grep login | more** command to view login-related entries in the files. You could do the same thing with the journalctl command.

In addition to viewing log files, you can also use a variety of command-line tools to see who is currently using the system. The first is the **who** command. You can use who to see who is currently logged in to your system. In Figure 17-25, you can see that the rtracy and ksanders users are logged in to the system. The rtracy user is logged in to the first X server session (**:0**) and has a terminal session open console. The ksanders user is logged in using an SSH connection from a host with an IP address of 10.0.0.60. You can also use the finger utility to see who's currently logged in to the system, as shown in Figure 17-25.

Next, we need to look at configuring xined and inetd.

```
                               root@openSUSE:~                               ✕

File  Edit  View  Search  Terminal  Help
openSUSE:~ # who
rtracy    :0          Jan 22 17:42 (console)
rtracy    console     Jan 22 17:42 (:0)
rtracy    pts/0       Jan 22 17:48 (:0)
ksanders  pts/1       Jan 22 20:58 (10.0.0.60)
openSUSE:~ # finger
Login       Name                  Tty        Idle  Login Time   Where
ksanders    Kimberly Sanders      pts/1       -        Thu 20:58 10.0.0.60
rtracy      Robb Tracy            *:0         -        Thu 17:42 console
rtracy      Robb Tracy            *console   3:21      Thu 17:42 :0
rtracy      Robb Tracy            pts/0       -        Thu 17:48 :0
openSUSE:~ # ▮
```

Figure 17-25   Using who and finger

Configuring xinetd and inetd

In this part of this chapter, you learn how to configure Linux "super-daemons." Most Linux distributions install a wide variety of network services during the system installation process. Most of these services, such as Telnet, are very handy and provide a valuable service. However, they aren't needed most of the time. We need a way to provide these services when requested but then unload them when they aren't needed, saving memory, reducing CPU utilization, and increasing the overall security of the system.

Depending on your distribution, there are two ways to do this. The following options are discussed here:

- Configuring xinetd
- Configuring inetd

Configuring xinetd

Many Linux distributions include a special daemon called xinetd that can be used to manage a number of different network services. In this part of this chapter, you learn how to configure and use xinetd. We'll discuss the following topics:

- How xinetd works
- Configuring xinetd network services
- Using TCP Wrappers

Let's begin by discussing how the xinetd daemon works.

How xinetd Works

The xinetd daemon is a super-daemon. It's called a super-daemon because it acts as an intermediary between the user requesting network services and the daemons on the system that provide the actual service. This is shown in Figure 17-26.

When a request for one of the network services managed by xinetd arrives at the system, it is received and processed by xinetd, not the network daemon being requested. The xinetd daemon then starts the daemon for the requested service and forwards the request to it. When the request has been fulfilled and the network service is no longer needed, xinetd unloads the daemon from memory.

Some of the network services managed by xinetd include the following:

- chargen
- daytime
- echo
- ftp
- pop3
- rsync
- smtp

Figure 17-26
How xinetd works

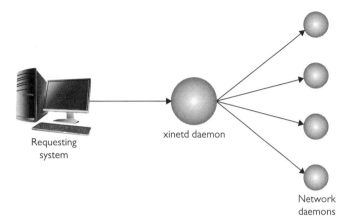

Requesting
system

xinetd daemon

Network
daemons

- telnet
- tftp
- time
- vnc

Let's discuss how you configure services managed by xinetd next.

Configuring xinetd Network Services

As with all the network services I've discussed, the xinetd configuration files are stored in /etc. The xinetd daemon itself is configured using the /etc/xinetd.conf file. Generally speaking, you won't need to make many changes to this file. The default configuration usually works very well. At the end of this file you will notice a directive that reads

```
includedir /etc/xinetd.d
```

This line tells the xinetd daemon to use the configuration files in /etc/xinetd.d. These files tell xinetd how to start each service when requested. Each of these files is used to configure the startup of a particular service managed by xinetd. For example, the vsftpd file in /etc/xinetd.d is used to configure the vsftpd FTP server daemon. The xinetd configuration settings for vsftpd in this file are shown here:

```
service ftp
{
        socket_type             = stream
        protocol                = tcp
        wait                    = no
        user                    = root
        server                  = /usr/sbin/vsftpd
#        server_args            =
#        log_on_success         += DURATION USERID
#        log_on_failure         += USERID
#        nice                   = 10
        disable                 = yes
}
```

This file doesn't configure the daemon itself. It only tells xinetd how to start up the daemon. The actual configuration file for the vsftpd daemon itself is in /etc/vsftpd.conf. One of the most important parameters in the /etc/xinetd.d/vsftpd file is the **disable** directive. This directive specifies whether or not xinetd is allowed to start the daemon when requested. In the preceding example, this directive is set to **yes**, which means the daemon will not be started when requested. The daemon to actually start is specified by the **server =** directive. In the example, xinetd will start the /usr/sbin/vsftpd daemon. To enable this daemon, you need to edit this file and change the disable parameter to a value of **no**. After changing a value in any of the files in /etc/xinetd.d, you need to restart the xinetd daemon using its init script in /etc/rc.d/init.d or /etc/init.d.

 TIP If you enable a service provided by xinetd, you'll need to create an exception in your Linux system's host firewall to allow traffic for the IP port used by the daemon.

Using TCP Wrappers

If you enable a particular service using its configuration file in the /etc/xinetd.d/ directory, any host can connect to it through xinetd. However, depending on how your system is deployed, you may need to control access to these network services. You may want to limit access to only a specific set of hosts and deny access to everyone else. If this is the case, you need to configure these services to use TCP Wrappers, which are used by xinetd to start and run the network services using a set of configuration files that specify who can and who can't access the service.

To use TCP Wrappers, you first need to enable the functionality in each service's configuration file in /etc/xinetd.d. Do the following:

1. Verify that the tcpd package has been installed on your Linux system.

2. Open the appropriate configuration file in a text editor.

3. Comment out the existing server = line from the file.

4. Add the following line:

   ```
   server     = /usr/sbin/tcpd
   ```

   This will cause xinetd to start the tcpd daemon instead of the service daemon itself.

5. Add the following line:

   ```
   server_args      = path_to_daemon
   ```

   This tells the tcpd daemon to then run the requested network daemon. In the example shown here, the /etc/xinetd.d/telnet file has been configured to run the vsftpd daemon within a TCP Wrapper:

   ```
   service ftp
   {
           socket_type              = stream
           protocol                 = tcp
           wait                     = no
           user                     = root
   #        server                   = /usr/sbin/vsftpd
           server                   = /usr/sbin/tcpd
           server_args              = /usr/sbin/vsftpd
   #        log_on_success           += DURATION USERID
   ```

```
#       log_on_failure          += USERID
#       nice                    = 10
        disable                 = no
}
```

6. Save the file and restart the xinetd daemon.

Next, you need to create your access controls. The tcpd daemon uses the /etc/hosts.allow and /etc/hosts.deny files to specify who can access the services it manages. Entries in /etc/hosts.allow are allowed access; hosts in /etc/hosts.deny are not allowed access. The syntax for both of these files is

```
service: host_addresses
```

As these files are processed, the search stops as soon as a matching condition is found in a file. Files are no longer processed after this occurs. The following steps occur in the order shown:

- Access will be granted if a matching entry is found in the /etc/hosts.allow file.
- If not, access will be denied if a matching entry is found in the /etc/hosts.deny file.
- If this does not occur, access will be granted.

For example, suppose you needed to configure the /etc/hosts.allow file to allow access to the vsftpd daemon for just a few specific hosts. The following entry grants access to the vsftpd service to hosts with the IP addresses of 192.168.1.10 and 192.168.1.102.

```
vsftpd:     192.168.1.10, 192.168.1.102
```

Some distributions use the inetd daemon instead of xinetd. This daemon works in much the same manner as xinetd. Let's learn how it works next.

Configuring inetd

The inetd daemon is a super-daemon like xinetd, but it is typically used on older Linux distributions. Like xinetd, the inetd daemon acts as a mediator for connection requests to network services running on the Linux host. It accepts connection requests from client systems, starts the requested service, and then forwards the requests from clients to the newly started daemon. When the transaction is complete and the connection from the client is terminated, the daemon is stopped on the Linux host.

As we discussed with xinetd, managing the network services on your Linux host in this way has advantages and disadvantages. Key among these is the fact that it conserves system memory and CPU resources. The network daemon is started only when it is needed. When it isn't needed, it's removed from memory until it is requested again. However, this benefit comes at a cost in terms of latency. When a service is requested by a client, the client must wait for a short period of time while the necessary daemon is loaded and the connection established. Therefore, inetd (and xinetd) should only be used to manage network services that are needed only occasionally on the system.

The inetd daemon is configured using the /etc/inetd.conf file. Unlike the xinetd daemon, all the services managed by inetd are configured in this single configuration file. Each line in this file configures a single service to be managed by inetd. The syntax used in inted.conf is shown here:

```
service_name socket_type protocol flags user executable arguments
```

Configuration Parameter	Description
service_name	Specifies the name of the service to be managed, as contained in the /etc/services file. The /etc/services file maps port numbers and protocols to specific service names. The service_name parameter in inetd.conf then maps one of these service names to a specific daemon.
	By default, inetd listens for requests for the specified service on all active network interfaces. If you want to limit access to the service to just one interface, add that interface's IP address to the service name (separated by a colon). For example, to limit vsftp requests to the network interface with an IP address of 192.168.1.10, you would use a service name of 192.168.1.10:vsftpd.
socket_type	Specifies the type of network socket. This parameter is usually set to a value of **stream** for most network services.
protocol	Specifies the protocol used by the daemon being started, as specified in /etc/protocols. This parameter is usually set to a value of **tcp** or **udp** for most network services.
flags	Specifies the appropriate flags for the protocol specified. If you specified the TCP protocol, you can use a value of **nowait** for this parameter. If you specified the UDP protocol, you can use a value of **wait** for this parameter.
user	Specifies the user and group the service will run as. Use a syntax of **user.group**.
executable	Specifies the filename (including the full path) of the executable that inetd will run when a connection request is made for the specified service.
arguments	Specifies arguments that will be passed to the service when it is started by inetd.

Table 17-6   The inetd Configuration File Parameters

Each of the parameters in this line is described in Table 17-6.

Here is a sample entry in inetd.conf for the vsftpd daemon:

```
ftp stream tcp nowait ftp /usr/sbin/tcpd vsftpd
```

Notice in this example that you can use TCP Wrappers with inetd just as you did with xinetd. In this example, when a client tries to establish an FTP connection with this Linux host, the inetd daemon will start the tcpd daemon and pass to it the name of the actual daemon to be started (vsftpd) as a server argument. As with xinetd, using TCP Wrappers with inetd allows you to control access to the network services running on the host using the /etc/hosts.allow and /etc/hosts.deny files.

Let's practice configuring super-daemons in the following exercise.

Exercise 17-3: Configuring xinetd

In this exercise, you'll practice working with xinetd by enabling one of the several services managed by this super-daemon. You can perform this exercise using the virtual machine that comes with this book. Run snapshot 17-1 for the correctly configured environment.

 VIDEO   Please watch the Exercise 17-3 video for a demonstration on how to perform this task.

You will enable the time service on your Linux host via xinetd. Once this is done, your Linux host can function as a time provider to time clients. Complete the following:

1. Boot your Linux system and log in as a standard user.

2. Open a terminal session.

3. Switch to your root user account by entering **su –** followed by your root user's password.

4. At the shell prompt, use the cd command to change to the /etc/xinetd.d directory.

5. At the shell prompt, enter **vi ./time-udp** to open the xinetd configuration file for the time service. You should see configuration settings that are similar to the following:

```
service time
{
        type            = INTERNAL UNLISTED
        id              = time-dgram
        socket_type     = dgram
        protocol        = udp
        user            = root
        wait            = yes
        disable         = no
        port            = 37
        FLAGS           = IPv6 IPv4
}
```

 TIP There are two different configuration files for the time service. The time file configures time to use TCP, whereas time-udp configures time to use UDP. Be sure you are editing the correct version of the file! Notice that the type parameter indicates that the time service is an *internal* service. This means the time service is part of the xinetd daemon itself. There is no external executable file for this daemon.

6. Press INS; then set the value of the disable parameter to **no**.

7. Press ESC; then enter **:exit** to save your changes to the file.

8. Restart the xinetd daemon by entering **systemctl restart xinetd** at the shell prompt.

Wow! You know a lot know about securing Linux now! Let's review what you learned in this chapter.

Chapter Review

In this chapter, you were introduced to a variety of security issues affecting Linux systems. I started this chapter by discussing the importance of physically securing your Linux system. I pointed out that many organizations overlook this very important issue. Many organizations leave their systems in unsecured areas, allowing an intruder to easily snatch the system and walk away.

I pointed out that servers need the highest degree of physical security. Servers should be locked in a server room. Access to the server room should be strictly controlled. Workstations, by their very nature, demand a higher degree of access than servers. Access to the work area itself should be secured to prevent unauthorized persons from accessing users' workstations.

I then discussed measures you can take to secure the operating system itself. One of the problems with workstations in most organizations is that users tend to leave them logged in while the system is unattended. To prevent unauthorized access, you should consider implementing screensaver passwords. You should also train your users to lock their workstations or log out completely before leaving their systems. To facilitate this, users can use the nohup command to load processes. This will allow the processes to continue running even if the user logs out from the shell prompt.

I then discussed user access controls you can use to constrain what users can and can't do in the system. Users, groups, and permissions are the main means of controlling access to the system. However, there are other things you can do to increase the security of the system. First of all, you need to use your root user account judiciously. The root user should be used only to complete root tasks. All other tasks should be completed using a standard user account. The system should never be left unattended while the root user is logged in. You can use the su command to switch to the root user account when you need to complete tasks that require root-level access. You can use the exit command to switch back to your regular user account when done.

If you have users who occasionally need to run commands as root but you don't want to give them your root password, you can use the sudo command. You use the /etc/sudoers file to specify which users can run which commands as root. You edit this file using the visudo utility. This utility will load the /etc/sudoers file in the vi editor. When you exit vi, it will check your syntax to make sure you didn't make syntax errors in the file.

Next, I talked about implementing a strong password policy. Users need to be trained to avoid using passwords that can be easily guessed, such as spouses' names, children's names, or pets' names. Users need to be trained to use strong passwords, which use

- Six or more characters
- Numbers in addition to letters
- Upper- and lowercase letters
- Words not found in the dictionary

You should also configure password aging with the chage command. You can specify the minimum number of days between password changes, the maximum number of days between password changes, and the number of warning days before a password change is required.

You should also verify that your Linux systems use shadow passwords. Storing passwords in /etc/passwd is highly insecure. You can use the pwconv command to migrate passwords from /etc/passwd to /etc/shadow.

In addition, you need to train your users to follow proper security procedures. You should not allow them to write their passwords down. You should also train them how to handle social engineering attempts. Specifically, they should be trained how to recognize phishing attacks. Users should also shred important documents rather than just throw them in the common trash.

We then looked at configuring user limits. You can impose limits on how many times users may log in, how much CPU time they can consume, and how much memory they can use on a Linux system. One way to do this is to use the pam_limits module with the Pluggable Authentication Modules (PAM) system. Limits are configured in the /etc/security/limits.conf file using the following syntax:

```
domain type item value
```

For example, you could limit the rtracy user to a maximum of two concurrent logins by entering the following in the file:

```
rtracy hard maxlogins 2
```

You can also use the ulimit command to configure limits on system resources that are applied to programs launched from the shell prompt. The syntax for using ulimit is

```
ulimit options limit
```

You can use the following options with ulimit:

- **–c**   Sets a limit on the maximum size of core files in blocks
- **–f**   Sets a limit on the maximum size (in blocks) of files created by the shell
- **–n**   Sets a limit on the maximum number of open file descriptors
- **–t**   Sets a limit on the maximum amount of CPU time (in seconds) a process may use
- **–u**   Sets a limit on the maximum number of processes available to a single user
- **–d**   Sets a limit on the maximum size (in KB) of a process's data segment in RAM
- **–m**   Sets a limit on the maximum resident size (in KB) of a process in RAM
- **–s**   Sets a limit on the maximum stack size (in KB)
- **–H**   Sets a hard resource limit
- **–S**   Sets a soft resource limit

I then reviewed how you can completely disable user logins to the Linux system. You can use the **w** command to view a list of all currently logged-in users. You can then use the **pkill –KILL –u *user_name*** command to brute-force log out each user. At this point, you can disable all future logins by creating a file in /etc named nologin. As long as this file exists, no one but root is allowed to log in.

In addition to disabling user login, another user security–related issue you need to be familiar with is auditing files that have SUID or SGID root permissions set. You can search for files on your Linux system that have SUID permissions set using the following command at the shell prompt as your root user:

```
find / -type f -perm -u=s -ls
```

You can also identify any files with the SGID permission set using the following command:

```
find / -type f -perm -g=s -ls
```

I then shifted our focus to the threat from network attacks. I pointed out that connecting your network to the Internet exposes your Linux systems to a host of network attacks. To mitigate these threats, you need to stay abreast of current threats. Two excellent resources to do this include the www.cert.org and www.us-cert.gov websites.

You should also check your system to see if any unneeded daemons are running. You can do this using the chkconfig and nmap utilities. Unnecessary services can be easily unloaded using the appropriate init script. You should also use chkconfig or systemctl to prevent the unneeded services from being loaded at system boot.

To further protect your system from network attacks, you should regularly install operating system updates that patch security holes. Most distributions provide some type of online update functionality that you can use to automate the task.

I then took a giant leap forward and discussed how to implement a simple packet-filtering firewall with iptables. I pointed out that firewalls are a critical security component in your network. A firewall sits between your network and another network. It captures all network traffic and compares it against a set of rules that you define. If the traffic meets the conditions in the rules, it is allowed through. If it doesn't, it is denied. Rules can be based on the origin address, the destination address, the origin port, the destination port, the protocol used, or the type of packet.

I then discussed how you can use a Linux system to implement a firewall. The first step is to design how it will work. Once you've determined what type of traffic will be allowed and what traffic will be denied, you can implement the firewall using the netfilter infrastructure, which is usually compiled into your Linux kernel by default. The netfilter infrastructure uses the concepts of tables, chains, and rules. The filter table is used to create packet-filtering rules. The filter table includes the FORWARD, INPUT, and OUTPUT chains. Each chain in the filter table can be configured with ACCEPT, DROP, QUEUE, and REJECT policies. This is done using the iptables command. The general practice when creating a firewall with iptables is to use the –P option to set the default rules, which are usually quite restrictive. Then you use iptables to configure exceptions to the default rules.

In addition to baselines, you can also use system log files to troubleshoot problems with your system. Your system log files are stored in /var/log. Some of the more important log files in this directory include

- boot.log
- boot.msg
- faillog
- firewall
- lastlog
- mail
- messages
- warn
- wtmp
- xinetd.log
- cron
- dmesg
- maillog
- secure
- rpmpkgs

Not all distributions will use the same log files. If your distribution uses the init daemon, then logging is usually handled by the syslogd daemon. The way syslogd manages log files can be customized using the /etc/syslog.conf file. Most Linux distributions are configured to automatically rotate your log files periodically, preventing them from growing too large. The cron daemon periodically runs the logrotate utility to do this. How logrotate rotates specific log files is configured using the /etc/logrotate.conf file and the configuration files for individual services located in /etc/logrotate.d/. You can configure syslogd to send all logging events to a syslogd daemon running on a different Linux system. Many administrators will set up a single system in their network to function as a log host where all Linux administrators will send their log files. Doing so centralizes your log files and also makes it harder for intruders to modify log files to cover their tracks. You configure remote logging by adding the following command to the beginning of your /etc/syslog.conf file:

```
*.*    @IP_address_of_loghost
```

You also need to set the value of the SYSLOGD_PARAMS directive in the /etc/sysconfig/ syslog file on the log host to **–r**.

If your distribution uses systemd, it probably uses the journald daemon to manage logging. The journald daemon maintains a system log called the *journal* (located in /var/log/journal/). You view the journal using the **journalctl** command. The behavior of the journal daemon is configured using the /etc/systemd/journald.conf file. If your distribution uses systemd, but you prefer the functionality of syslogd, you can use syslog-ng instead of journald. The syslog-ng daemon works with systemd, but is configured in much the same manner as syslog.

I then discussed the utilities that can be used to view text-based log files. Although you can use less, cat, and more, the tail and head utilities can be used to view log files more effectively. The tail utility displays the last few lines of a file. The head utility will display the first few lines of a file. You can also use grep to search for content within a log file. You can use the –f option with tail or with journalctl to monitor a log file for new entries.

I then discussed how to detect intrusion attempts using your Linux log files. You should periodically review your log files, looking for anomalies that indicate an intrusion attempt. The log files best suited to this task include

- /var/log/wtmp
- /var/log/faillog
- /var/log/lastlog
- /var/log/messages

You can also use the who and finger utilities to see who is currently using the Linux system.

I ended the chapter by discussing how to configure xinetd and inetd. Both xinetd and inetd are super-daemons. They manage other network service daemons on the system. When a network service is requested, the xinetd (or inetd) daemon starts the service and forwards the request to it. When the request has been completed and the service is no longer needed, xinetd (or inetd) unloads it from memory.

The xinetd daemon is configured using the /etc/xinetd.conf file. Individual services managed by xinetd can be enabled or disabled using the appropriate configuration file located in the /etc/ xinetd.d directory.

To add additional security, you can use TCP Wrappers to control access to your network services. Using TCP Wrappers, the xinetd daemon runs the tcpd daemon instead of the network service itself. The tcpd daemon checks the /etc/hosts.deny and /etc/hosts.allow files to determine if the requesting host is allowed to use the service. If it is, tcpd loads the requested daemon.

The inetd daemon is configured using the /etc/inetd.conf file. All the services managed by inetd are configured in this single configuration file. Each line in this file configures a single service to be managed by inetd. The syntax used in inetd.conf is shown here:

```
service_name socket_type protocol flags user executable arguments
```

You can use TCP Wrappers with inetd just as you did with xinetd. This allows you to control access to the network services running on the host using the /etc/hosts.allow and /etc/hosts.deny files.

Accelerated Review

- Many organizations overlook physical security and leave their systems in unsecured areas.
- Servers need the highest degree of physical security and should be locked in a server room where physical access is strictly controlled.
- Workstations require a higher degree of access than servers.
- Access to the work area itself should be secured to prevent unauthorized persons from accessing users' workstations.
- Because users tend to leave workstations logged in while the system is unattended, you should implement screensaver passwords.
- You should train your users to lock their workstations or log out completely before leaving their systems.
- You can use the nohup command to load processes and allow them to continue running even if you log out from the shell prompt.
- Users, groups, and permissions are the main means of controlling access to the system.
- The root user should be used only to complete root tasks; all other tasks should be completed using a standard user account.
- The system should never be left unattended while the root user is logged in.
- You can use the su command to switch to the root user account when you need to complete tasks that require root-level access.
- You can use the exit command to switch back to your regular user account.
- You can use the sudo command to allow specific users to run commands as root without giving them your root password.
- You use the /etc/sudoers file to specify which users can run what commands as root.
- You edit /etc/sudoers using the visudo utility, which will check your syntax to make sure you didn't make syntax errors in the file.
- Users need to be trained to avoid using passwords that can be easily guessed.

- Users should be trained to use strong passwords, which use
  - Six or more characters
  - Numbers in addition to letters
  - Upper- and lowercase letters
  - Words not found in the dictionary
- You can configure password aging with the chage command.
- The chage utility allows you to specify the minimum number of days between password changes, the maximum number of days between password changes, and the number of warning days before a password change is required.
- Verify that your Linux systems use shadow passwords.
- Storing passwords in /etc/passwd is highly insecure.
- You can use the pwconv command to migrate passwords from /etc/passwd to /etc/shadow.
- You should not allow users to write their passwords down.
- You should train users how to handle social engineering attempts.
- Users should shred important documents rather than throw them in the common trash.
- You can impose limits on how many times users may log in, how much CPU time they can consume, and how much memory they can use with the pam_limits module.
- Limits are configured in the /etc/security/limits.conf file.
- You can also use the ulimit command to configure limits on system resources that are applied to programs launched from the shell prompt.
- The syntax for using ulimit is **ulimit *options limit***.
- You can completely disable user logins to the Linux system.
- First, use the **w** command to view a list of all currently logged-in users; then use the **pkill –KILL –u *user_name*** command to brute-force log out each user.
- At this point you can disable all future logins by creating a file in /etc named nologin.
- As long as this file exists, no one but root is allowed to log in.
- You can search for files on your Linux system that have SUID permissions set using the **find / –type f –perm –u=s –ls** command at the shell prompt as your root user.
- You can also identify any files with the SGID permission set using the **find / –type f –perm –g=s –ls** command.
- Connecting your network to the Internet exposes your Linux systems to a number of network attacks, so you need to stay abreast of current threats.
- You should regularly visit the www.cert.org and www.us-cert.gov websites to see the latest issues.
- You should check your system to see if any unneeded daemons are running using the chkconfig and nmap utilities.

- Unnecessary services can be unloaded using the appropriate init script.

- You should also use chkconfig or systemctl to prevent the unneeded services from being loaded at system boot.

- You should regularly install operating system updates to patch security holes.

- Most distributions provide some type of online update functionality that you can use to automatically install patches.

- Firewalls are a critical security component in your network.

- A firewall sits between your network and another network.

- A firewall captures all network traffic and compares it against a set of rules that you define.

- If the traffic meets the conditions in the rules, it is allowed through; if the traffic doesn't meet the rules, it is denied.

- Rules can be based on the origin address, the destination address, the origin port, the destination port, the protocol used, or the type of packet.

- You should first design how the firewall will work.

- You can implement the firewall on Linux using the netfilter infrastructure, which is usually compiled into your Linux kernel by default.

- The netfilter infrastructure uses the concepts of tables, chains, and rules.

- The filter table is used to create packet-filtering rules. It includes the FORWARD, INPUT, and OUTPUT chains.

- Each chain in the filter table can be configured with ACCEPT, DROP, QUEUE, and REJECT policies using the iptables command.

- The general practice when creating a firewall with iptables is to use the –P option to set the default rules and then configure exceptions to the default rules.

- You can use your system log files (stored in /var/log) to troubleshoot problems with your system.

- Some of the more important log files in this directory include boot.log, boot.msg, faillog, firewall, lastlog, mail, messages, warn, wtmp, xinetd.log, cron, dmesg, maillog, secure, and rpmpkgs.

- Not all distributions use the same log files.

- On older distributions, logging is handled by the syslogd daemon, which can be customized using the /etc/syslog.conf file.

- Most Linux distributions are configured to automatically rotate your log files periodically, preventing them from growing too large.

- The cron daemon periodically runs the logrotate utility to rotate log files.

- How logrotate rotates specific log files is configured using the /etc/logrotate.conf file and the configuration files for individual services located in /etc/logrotate.d/.

- You can configure syslogd to send all logging events to a syslogd daemon running on a different Linux system.

- Many administrators will set up a single system in their network to function as a log host where all Linux administrators will send their log files.

- Newer distributions use the journald daemon to manage logging.

- You can view the journal using the journalctl command.

- Although you can use less, cat, and more, the tail and head utilities can be used to view log files more effectively.

- The tail utility displays the last few lines of a file.

- The head utility will display the first few lines of a file.

- You can also use grep to search for content within a log file.

- You can use the –f option with tail or journalctl to monitor a log file for new entries.

- Linux log files can be used to detect intrusion attempts.

- You should periodically review the following log files, looking for anomalies that indicate an intrusion attempt:

  - /var/log/wtmp

  - /var/log/faillog

  - /var/log/lastlog

  - /var/log/messages

- You can use the who and finger utilities to see who is currently using the Linux system.

- Both xinetd and inetd daemons are super-daemons that manage other network service daemons on the system.

- When a network service is requested, the xinetd (or inetd) daemon starts the service and forwards the request to it.

- When the request has been completed and the service is no longer needed, xinetd (or inetd) unloads it from memory.

- The xinetd daemon is configured using the /etc/xinetd.conf file.

- Individual services managed by xinetd can be enabled or disabled using the appropriate configuration file located in the /etc/xinetd.d directory.

- You can use TCP Wrappers to control access to your network services.

- With TCP Wrappers, the xinetd daemon runs the tcpd daemon instead of the network service.

- The tcpd daemon checks the /etc/hosts.deny and /etc/hosts.allow files to determine if the requesting host is allowed to use the service. If it is, tcpd loads the requested daemon.

- The inetd daemon is configured using the /etc/inetd.conf file.

- All the services managed by inetd are configured using this single configuration file.

- Each line in this file configures a single service to be managed by inetd.
- You can use TCP Wrappers with inetd just as you did with xinetd. This allows you to control access to the network services running on the host using the /etc/hosts.allow and /etc/hosts.deny files.

Questions

1. Which of the following would be the most secure place to locate a Linux server?
   A. On the receptionist's front desk
   B. In the CIO's office
   C. In an unoccupied cubicle
   D. In a locked room

2. Which of the following can be used to secure users' workstations? (Choose two.)
   A. Screensaver password
   B. Session lock
   C. Long screensaver timeout period
   D. Passwords written on sticky notes and hidden in a drawer
   E. Easy-to-remember passwords

3. Which of the following commands will load the updatedb process and leave it running even if the user logs out of the shell?
   A. updatedb
   B. updatedb &
   C. updatedb –nohup
   D. nohup updatedb &

4. Which of the following commands can be used to switch to the root user account and load root's environment variables?
   A. su –
   B. su root
   C. su root –e
   D. su –env

5. Which of the following is a strong password?
   A. Bob3
   B. TuxP3nguin
   C. penguin
   D. Castle

6. You need to set password age limits for the ksanders user account. You want the minimum password age to be one day, the maximum password age to be 45 days, and the user to be warned five days prior to password expiration. Which command will do this?

   A. usermod –m 1 –M 45 –W 5 ksanders

   B. useradd –m 1 –M 45 –W 5 ksanders

   C. chage –M 1 –m 45 –W 5 ksanders

   D. chage –m 1 –M 45 –W 5 ksanders

7. You need to scan a Linux system with an IP address of 10.200.200.1 to determine what ports are currently open on it. What commands could you use at the shell prompt to do this? (Choose two.)

   A. nmap –sT 10.200.200.1

   B. scan 10.200.200.1 –TCP

   C. scan 10.200.200.1 –UDP

   D. nmap –sU 10.200.200.1

   E. nmap 10.200.200.1 –scan

8. You need to configure your /etc/hosts.allow file to allow only the linux1, linux2, and linux3 systems to access the vsftpd daemon on your system. Which of the following lines in the file will do this?

   A. vsftpd: ALL

   B. vsftpd: linux1, linux2, linux3

   C. vsftpd: ALL EXCEPT linux1, linux2, linux3

   D. vsftpd linux1, linux2, linux3

9. You need to configure your Linux firewall to allow all network traffic addressed to the DNS service on the local system. Which command will do this?

   A. iptables –t filter –A INPUT –s 0/0 –p tcp –dport 53 –j DROP

   B. iptables –t filter –A OUTPUT –s 0/0 –p tcp –dport 53 –j ACCEPT

   C. iptables –t filter –A INPUT –s 0/0 –p tcp –dport 80 –j DROP

   D. iptables –t filter –A INPUT –s 0/0 –p tcp –dport 53 –j ACCEPT

10. Which log file contains a list of all users who have authenticated to the Linux system, when they logged in, when they logged out, and where they logged in from?

   A. /var/log/faillog

   B. /var/log/last

   C. /var/log/wtmp

   D. /var/log/login

11. Which log file contains a list of failed login attempts?

    A. /var/log/faillog

    B. /var/log/last

    C. /var/log/wtmp

    D. /var/log/login

12. Which log file contains messages from all services running on the system?

    A. /var/log/faillog

    B. /var/log/messages

    C. /var/log/wtmp

    D. /var/log/services

13. Which utility can you use to view your /var/log/lastlog file?

    A. cat

    B. last

    C. grep

    D. lastlog

14. You need to view the first few lines of the /var/log/boot.msg file. Which of the following commands will do this? (Choose two.)

    A. head /var/log/ boot.msg

    B. tail /var/log/ boot.msg

    C. grep –l 10 /var/log/boot.msg

    D. less /var/log/boot.msg

    E. cat /var/log/boot.msg

15. You're configuring the /etc/logrotate.d/ntp file to customize logging from the Network Time Protocol daemon on your system. You want old, archived logs to be saved using the current date in the filename extension. Which directive in the ntp file will do this?

    A. notifempty

    B. dateext

    C. rotate

    D. create

16. Which option, when used with the tail command, will cause the journalctl utility to monitor a log file for new entries?

    A. –

    B. –l

    C. –m

    D. –f

17. Which of the following directories contains configuration files that the xinetd daemon uses to manage network daemons (by default)?

    A. /var/lib/xinetd.d

    B. /etc/xinetd.d

    C. /etc/xinetd

    D. /srv/xinetd.d

18. You need to scan your Linux file system to locate all files that have either the SUID or SGID permission set. Which commands can you use to do this? (Choose two.)

    A. find / –type f –perm –u=s –ls

    B. find / –type f –perm –g=s –ls

    C. audit –p=SUID

    D. audit –p=SGID

    E. find / –p=s

    F. find / -p=g

19. The existence of which file prevents all users except root from logging in to a Linux system?

    A. /root/nologin

    B. /etc/nologin

    C. /var/log/nologin

    D. /tmp/nologin

    E. /usr/sbin/nologin

20. You want to configure limits on the system resources your Linux users are allowed to consume using the pam_limits PAM module. Which file do you need to edit to set these limits?

    A. /etc/limits.conf

    B. /etc/pam_limits.conf

    C. /etc/security/limits.conf

    D. /etc/security/pam_limits.conf

    E. /etc/sysconfig/limits.conf

Answers

1. **D.** A locked room would be the most secure place to locate a Linux server.

2. **A, B.** Screensaver passwords and the session lock function offered by KDE and GNOME can be used to secure users' workstations.

3. **D.** The **nohup updatedb &** command will load the updatedb process and leave it running even if the user logs out of the shell.

4. **A.** The **su –** command switches to the root user account and loads root's environment variables.

5. **B.** The **TuxP3nguin** password meets the basic requirements for a strong password.

6. **D.** The **chage –m 1 –M 45 –W 5 ksanders** command will set the minimum password age to be one day, the maximum password age to be 45 days, and the user to be warned five days prior to password expiration.

7. **A, D.** The **nmap –sT 10.200.200.1** command scans for open TCP ports. The **nmap –sU 10.200.200.1** command scans for open UDP ports.

8. **B.** The **vsftpd: linux1, linux2, linux3** line in /etc/hosts.allow will configure the tcpd daemon to allow only these hosts access to the vsftpd daemon.

9. **D.** The **iptables –t filter –A INPUT –s 0/0 –p tcp –dport 53 –j ACCEPT** command configures your Linux firewall to allow all network traffic addressed to the DNS service on the local system.

10. **C.** The /var/log/wtmp log file contains a list of all users who have authenticated to the Linux system, when they logged in, when they logged out, and where they logged in from.

11. **A.** The /var/log/faillog log file contains a list of failed login attempts.

12. **B.** The /var/log/messages log file contains messages from all services running on the system.

13. **D.** The **lastlog** command can be used to view your /var/log/lastlog file.

14. **A, D.** The **head /var/log/boot.msg** and **less /var/log/boot.msg** commands will display the first few lines of the file onscreen.

15. **B.** The **dateext** directive will cause old, archived log files to be saved using the current date in the filename extension.

16. **D.** The –f option, when used with journalctl, will cause it to monitor a file for changes and display them on the screen.

17. **B.** The /etc/xinetd.d directory contains the configuration files that the xinetd daemon uses to manage network daemons.

18. **A, B.** The **find / –type f –perm –u=s –ls** command locates all files that have the SUID permission set. The **find / –type f –perm –g=s –ls** command locates all files that have the SGID permission set.

19. **B.** The existence of the /etc/nologin file prevents all users except root from logging in to the Linux system.

20. **C.** User limits enforced by the pam_limits module are configured in the /etc/security/limits.conf file.

Using Encryption

In this chapter, you will learn about:

- How encryption works
- Encrypting remote access with OpenSSH
- Encrypting Linux files

As mentioned at the beginning of the preceding chapter, information security is a key issue in nearly every organization. If it isn't, it should be. Twenty-five years ago, we in the IT industry just didn't worry all that much about information security. That's because society in general didn't worry all that much about information security. Let me give you two examples. First, when I was an undergraduate in the late 1980s and early 1990s, it was common for my professors to post exam scores in the hallway outside their office using students' Social Security numbers. I chuckle when I recall the reason why; it was to protect students' privacy. Heaven forbid we should associate a name with a test score, so let's just use their SSNs!

State and federal governments were not immune to this type of practice either. Again, when I was in college, my home state used Social Security numbers as driver's license numbers. They printed it right on the license itself. Therefore, every time you used your driver's license for ID, you were revealing your SSN. What's worse, we used checks a lot more back then than we do now. Guess what every store clerk wrote on each check? Yep, they recorded the customer's driver's license number. That means each check I wrote in college had my SSN and my bank account number recorded on it. Sheesh!

Today, we think doing something like this would be crazy. Back then, we didn't think anything of it. That has all changed in today's security-conscious world. Folks who wear black hats have figured out that a minimal amount of information can yield huge profits, and they will stop at nothing to get it. As a result, we who wear white hats have to be almost obsessive about information security.

Information security is focused on protecting the valuable electronic information of organizations and users. Therefore, the demand for IT professionals who know how to secure networks and computers is at an all-time high. As a Linux system administrator, you need to be very aware of the security issues affecting your implementation. In the preceding chapter, we spent some time looking at several policies and practices you can put in place to help secure your systems. In this chapter, we're going to expand on what you learned in the last chapter and discuss how you can use encryption to increase the security of your Linux systems and network.

TIP Information security is a huge topic that we can't adequately address in this book. I highly recommend that you enhance your knowledge by getting your Security+ certification from CompTIA. The IT world has become the modern equivalent of the Wild West from American history. You need to know how to thoroughly protect your data from malicious black hats!

Let's begin by discussing how encryption works.

How Encryption Works

Harken back with me, if you will, to your elementary school days. Did you ever pass notes to your friends? I know that in the modern era of mobile devices and text messaging, this may seem archaic; however, when I was a kid, notes were a vital means of communication at school. After all, you had important business to conduct, right?

If your school was like mine, these extracurricular forms of communication were strictly forbidden in class. If a teacher intercepted a poorly handled note pass, you could be sure it would be read in front of the class, which could be a fate worse than death (especially if the note contained information about who currently likes whom).

To prevent this, my buddies and I developed codes to encrypt our notes. If one of them was intercepted, we could rest assured that the teacher wouldn't be able to read it to the rest of the class. As fourth graders, our encoding mechanisms were primitive. For the most part, we used two codes. The first one involved skewing the alphabet down a letter or two, as shown here:

```
ZABCDEFGHIJKLMNOPQRSTUVWXY
ABCDEFGHIJKLMNOPQRSTUVWXYZ
```

 NOTE This simple encryption technique is called a *letter shift*.

We would use the bottom line for the clear text and the top line for the cipher text. For example, the clear text "JAKE LIKES PAM" would come out "IZJD KHJFR OZL" when encoded. Eventually, our teacher started getting wise to this code and figured out how to crack it. Therefore, we switched to a different code using numbers and letters, as shown here:

```
26 1 2 3 4 5 6 7 8 9 10 11....
A  B C D E F G H I J  K  L ....
```

Using this code, my friend Jake's name would be encoded as 9 26 10 4. This basic concept of using keys to scramble and descramble messages can be used to encode network communications as well. In today's security-conscious world, the need to encrypt the contents of network communications is preeminent. Using network monitoring tools (such as nmap, discussed in the preceding chapter), it is relatively easy for a mischievous individual to sniff out network transmissions and read them. If these transmissions contain sensitive information, such as usernames, passwords, financial data, credit card numbers, or personal information, we could have a real problem on our hands.

To protect this information, we need to encrypt critical network communications. Unlike the simple codes I used in the fourth grade, network cryptography today uses much more sophisticated encoding mechanisms. There are two general approaches to doing this:

- Symmetric encryption
- Asymmetric encryption

Let's first look at using symmetric encryption.

Symmetric Encryption

For my fourth-grade encryption system to work, my buddies and I all had to have exactly the same key to encrypt and decrypt our messages. Using the wrong key on either the sending or receiving end would result in gibberish. This system is called *symmetric encryption.* With symmetric encryption, the key used to encrypt a message is the same key used to decrypt the message. That means the sender and the receiver must both have the exact same key. This is shown in Figure 18-1.

 NOTE Symmetric encryption is sometimes called *secret key* encryption.

Symmetric encryption works very well. One of its key advantages is speed. It is much faster than asymmetric encryption (discussed later). However, one of the difficulties associated with symmetric encryption is how to securely distribute the key to all the parties that need to communicate with each other. For example, if you've ever configured a security key on a wireless network, you know that you must create the key on the wireless access point, copy it to a USB thumb drive, sneaker-net it to each wireless client, and paste the key in the configuration of the wireless NIC. Examples of cryptographic standards that use symmetric encryption include the following:

- **Triple Data Encryption Standard (3DES)** 3DES is commonly used by many Linux services. 3DES encrypts data in three stages. It uses either a 112-bit or a 168-bit key.
- **Advanced Encryption Standard (AES)** AES is an improved version of 3DES. It supports 128-bit, 192-bit, and 256-bit keys.
- **Blowfish** Blowfish uses variable key lengths up to 448 bits.

Figure 18-1
Symmetric
encryption

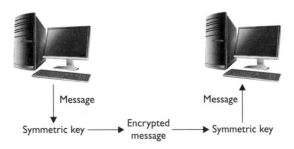

Message   Message

Symmetric key ──────▶ Encrypted ──────▶ Symmetric key
                       message

An important factor to keep in mind when selecting any encryption scheme is the number of bits used to encode the data. Older encryption schemes used only 40 or 56 bits to encode data. In today's computing world, this simply isn't strong enough. A fast PC from your local discount retail store can crack 40-bit encryption in a relatively short amount of time. When selecting an encryption scheme, you should pick one that supports a minimum of 128 bits. Basically, the longer the key, the more secure the data is.

Because of the difficulties associated with key distribution, another encryption mechanism is commonly used today called *asymmetric encryption*. Let's look at how it works next.

Asymmetric Encryption

Unlike symmetric encryption, asymmetric encryption uses two keys instead of one: the public key and the private key. Data that has been encoded with the public key can be decoded only with the private key. Data that has been encoded with the private key can only be decoded with the public key. For this reason, asymmetric encryption is frequently referred to as *public key cryptography*. Rivest Shamir Adleman (RSA) and the Digital Signature Algorithm (DSA) are examples of cryptographic standards that use asymmetric encryption.

 NOTE Private/public key pairs should be much longer than those used for symmetric encryption. They should be 1024 bits or longer.

This type of encryption is used to encrypt the contents of network communications as well as generate digital signatures. In a digital signature, the contents of a message aren't encrypted. Instead, the private key is used by the sender to create an encrypted hash of the message. This hash is sent along with the message to the recipient. The recipient generates its own hash of the message. Then it uses the public key to decrypt the hash sent with the message. If the hashes are the same, the recipient can be assured that the message arrived without being altered en route.

Because of its flexibility, public key cryptography is widely used method for encrypting data. It allows you to easily scramble and send sensitive information over a public network, such as the Internet. If you've ever bought anything online from an e-commerce website, you've used public key cryptography. When you send your credit card number, the retailer's website should have encrypted your data and sent it using HTTPS so that prying eyes will be unable to read it.

One of the key disadvantages of asymmetric encryption is speed. Symmetric encryption is much faster than asymmetric encryption. Hence, you will frequently see implementations that use a combination of both mechanisms. Asymmetric encryption is used for an initial key exchange to securely copy a secret key to both parties in a session. Once that is done, both parties have the same key and can switch to symmetric encryption for the remainder of the session.

Another problem associated with public key cryptography is the issue of how to verify that the public key is legitimate. To do that, we use a *certificate authority (CA)*. The CA is a network service that is responsible for issuing and managing encryption keys. When a key pair is requested from a CA, it generates a public key and a private key simultaneously, using a specified encryption scheme, such as RSA or DSA.

The private key in the pair is given only to the requesting entity. It is not shared with anyone else. The public key in the pair, on the other hand, can be made available to anyone who needs it.

The primary role of the CA is to verify that parties involved in an encrypted exchange are who they say they are. A CA accomplishes this by issuing *public key certificates.* A public key certificate is a digital message signed with the private key that provides a cryptographic binding between the public key and the organization that owns the private key. A certificate contains the following information:

- The name of the organization
- The public key of the organization
- The expiration date of the certificate
- The certificate's serial number
- The name of the CA that signed the certificate
- A digital signature from the CA

There are two types of CAs that you need to be familiar with:

- **Internal CA** An internal CA is one that is maintained by an organization for internal use. On most Linux distributions, the OpenSSL package is installed automatically and is used to create a CA on your system. This CA is used to create keys and issue certificates for services running on the server. However, this CA is not a *trusted* CA. If other systems connect to a service on your system via secure connection, users on a remote system will be issued a warning in their client software. This message will indicate that the certificate it received was valid but it didn't come from a trusted CA. That's because the certificate came from the CA on your own system. For internal communications, this doesn't represent a serious issue. We trust ourselves. If you're going to be dealing with external parties, however, an internal CA won't suffice.

- **External CA** External parties need assurance from a trusted, objective third party that the certificates they are receiving are legitimate and that you are who you say you are. This is done by using an external CA, such as VeriSign or GTECyberTrust. These organizations perform the same functions as an internal CA. However, they are globally trusted. For example, suppose you were to access a secure website on the Internet using the Firefox web browser. If the site is using an external CA, you won't be presented with the warning that you see when using your internal CA. That's because your browser has been preconfigured with a list of trusted CAs, as shown in Figure 18-2.

Let's look at an example to see how public key cryptography works. Suppose you're using a web browser to visit www.mydomain.com and you've found some product that you just can't live without. You've put it in your shopping cart and are in the process of checking out from the online store. The process shown in Figure 18-3 occurs as you submit your credit card information to the e-commerce web server.

1. Your browser requests the public key for www.mydomain.com from the external CA.
2. The CA returns the public key to the browser, which then uses that key to encrypt the message.

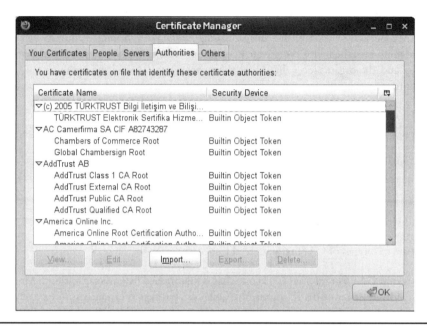

Figure 18-2 Trusted CAs

3. The browser sends the encrypted message to www.mydomain.com.

4. The web server at the other end then uses its private key to decrypt the transmission.

The whole reason this process works is because only the private key can decrypt a message encoded by the public key. For example, a hacker could easily intercept the public key used in the transaction in Figure 18-3. But that's not a problem because it can't be used to decrypt information encrypted with the same public key (in this case, the credit card submission). That can only be done by the private key, which is kept safe on the web server and is never transmitted openly.

Figure 18-3
How public key
encryption works

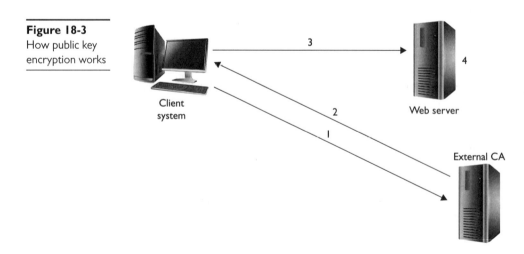

Because your Linux system installed its own CA when you initially installed the system, you can use it to mint your own certificates and use them to encrypt both network transmissions and files in the file system. Let's review how this is done next.

Encrypting Remote Access with OpenSSH

In the early days of UNIX/Linux, we used a variety of tools to establish network connections between systems. You could access the shell prompt of a remote system using Telnet, rlogin, or rshell. You could copy files back and forth between systems using rcp or FTP. However, these utilities had one glaring weakness. Network services such as Telnet, rlogin, rcp, rshell, and FTP transmit data as clear text. Anyone running a sniffer could easily capture usernames and passwords along with the contents of the transmissions.

For example, suppose I remotely accessed my Linux system via Telnet. After authenticating to the remote system, I decided that I needed to switch to root using the su command to complete several tasks. If someone were sniffing the network wire while I was doing this, they would be able to easily grab the following information:

- My username and password
- The root user password

This is not a good thing! The attacker would have everything he needs to gain unfettered access to my Linux system.

To prevent this from happening, you can use the OpenSSH package to accomplish these same management tasks using encryption. In this part of the chapter, you will learn how to use OpenSSH. The following topics are addressed:

- How OpenSSH works
- Configuring OpenSSH
- Tunneling traffic through SSH
- Configuring SSH to use public key authentication

Let's begin by discussing how OpenSSH works.

How OpenSSH Works

OpenSSH provides the functionality of Telnet, rlogin, rsh, rcp, and FTP, but it does so using encryption. To do this, OpenSSH provides the following encryption-enabled components:

- **sshd**   This is the ssh daemon that allows remote access to the shell prompt.
- **ssh**   This is the ssh client used to connect to the sshd daemon on another system.
- **scp**   This utility can be used to securely copy files between systems.
- **sftp**   This utility can be used to securely FTP files between systems.
- **slogin**   This utility can also be used to access the shell prompt remotely.

To establish a secure connection, OpenSSH actually uses both private/public key encryption along with secret key encryption. First, the SSH client creates a connection with the system where the SSH server is running on IP port 22. The SSH server then sends its public keys to the SSH client. The SSH server uses the host key pair to store its private and public keys, which identify the host where the SSH server is running. The keys are stored in the following files:

- **Private key** /etc/ssh/ssh_host_key
- **Public key** /etc/ssh/ssh_host_key.pub

The client system receives the public key from the SSH server and checks to see if it already has a copy of that key. The SSH client stores keys from other systems in the following files:

- /etc/ssh/ssh_known_hosts
- ~/.ssh/known_hosts

By default, if it doesn't have the server's public key in either of these files, it will ask the user to add it. Having done this, the client now trusts the server system and generates a 256-bit secret key. It then uses the server's public key to encrypt the new secret key and sends it to the server. Because the secret key was encrypted with the public key, the server can decrypt it using its private key. Once this is done, both systems have the same secret key and can now use symmetric encryption during the duration of the SSH session. The user is presented with a login prompt and can now authenticate securely because everything she types is sent in encrypted format.

 NOTE In SSH version 2, several things are a little different. First of all, the host key files used on the server are different. The /etc/ssh/ssh_host_rsa_key and /etc/ssh/ssh_host_dsa_key files are used (along with their associated public keys) instead of /etc/ssh/ssh_host_key. The key pair used depends on which encryption mechanism (RSA or DSA) the client and server have been configured to use. In addition, the secret key is not actually transmitted from the client to the server system. A *Diffie-Hellman key agreement* is used instead to negotiate a secret key to be used for the session without actually sending it over the network medium.

After this secure channel has been negotiated and the user has been authenticated through the SSH server, data can be securely transferred between both systems.

Now that you understand how SSH connections are established, you need to learn how to configure OpenSSH.

Configuring OpenSSH

To use ssh, you must first install the openssh package on your system from your distribution media. This package includes both the sshd daemon and the ssh client. OpenSSH is usually installed by default on most Linux distributions. You can use the package management utility of your choice to verify that it has been installed on your system.

The process of configuring OpenSSH involves configuring both the SSH server and the SSH client. You configure the sshd daemon using the /etc/ssh/sshd_config file. The ssh client, on the other hand, is configured using the /etc/ssh/ssh_config file or the ~/.ssh/ssh_config file.

Let's look at configuring the SSH server (sshd) first. There are many directives within the /etc/ssh/sshd_config file. The good news is that after you install the openssh package, the default parameters work very well in most circumstances. To get sshd up and running, you shouldn't have to make many changes to the sshd_config file. Some of the more useful parameters in this file include those shown in Table 18-1.

The ssh client on a Linux system is configured using the /etc/ssh/ssh_config file. The /etc/ssh/ssh_config file is used to specify default parameters for all users running ssh on the system. A user can override these defaults using the ~/.ssh/ssh_config file in his or her home directory. The precedence for ssh client configuration settings are as follows:

1. Any command-line options included with the ssh command at the shell prompt

2. Settings in the ~/.ssh/ssh_config file

3. Settings in the /etc/ssh/ssh_config file

As with the sshd daemon, the default parameters used in the ssh_config file usually work without a lot of customization. However, some of the more useful parameters that you can use to customize the way the ssh client works are listed in Table 18-2.

Of course, before you can connect to an SSH server, you must open up port 22 in the host-based firewall of the system where sshd is running. For example, in Figure 18-4, the YaST Firewall module has been loaded on a SUSE Linux Enterprise Server 10 system and configured to allow SSH traffic through.

Option	Description
AllowUsers	Restricts logins to the SSH server to only the users listed. Specify a list of users separated by spaces.
DenyUsers	Prevents the users listed from logging in through the SSH server. Specify a list of users separated by spaces.
HostKey	Specifies which private host key file should be used by SSH. As discussed previously, the default private key file for SSH version 1 is /etc/ssh/ssh_host_key for protocol version 1, whereas SSH version 2 can use the /etc/ssh/ssh_host_rsa_key and /etc/ssh/ssh_host_dsa_key files. You can configure sshd to use multiple host key files. Be aware that if a key file has read or write permissions assigned to group or others, sshd will refuse to use it.
ListenAddress	If the host where sshd is running has multiple IP addresses assigned, you can restrict sshd to only listening on specific addresses using this parameter. The syntax is **ListenAddress *IP_address:port***.
PermitRootLogin	Specifies whether you can authenticate through the SSH server as root.
Port	Specifies the port on which the sshd daemon will listen for SSH requests.
Protocol	Specifies which version of SSH to use. Specify one of the following: • **1** Configures SSH version 1 • **2** Configures SSH version 2 • **2,1** Configures sshd to support both SSH versions, but preference is given to version 2

Table 18-1 Options in the sshd_config File

Option	Description
Port	Specifies the port number to connect to on the SSH server system to initiate an SSH request.
Protocol	Specifies which version of SSH to use. Use one of the following: • **1** Configures SSH version 1 • **2** Configures SSH version 2 • **2,1** Configures the ssh client to support both SSH versions, but preference is given to version 2
StrictHostKeyChecking	The SSH server sends the SSH client its public key when you initiate an SSH connection. By default, the first time you connect to a given SSH server, you are prompted on the client end to accept the server's public key. However, you can change this behavior using the StrictHostKeyChecking parameter in the ssh_config file. If you set it to a value of **yes**, the client can establish connections only to SSH servers whose public key has already been added to either the ~/.ssh/known_hosts or the /etc/ssh/ssh_known_hosts file. Be aware that if you do this and then want to connect to a new SSH server, you must manually add that server's key to one of the aforementioned files.
User	Specifies the user to log in to the SSH server as.

Table 18-2 Options in the ssh_config File

After configuring your firewall, you can load the ssh client on your local computer and connect to the sshd daemon on the remote Linux system by entering **ssh –l** *user_name ip_address*.

> **TIP** Don't forget the –l parameter. If you don't, the SSH client will attempt to authenticate you to the remote system using the same credentials you used to authenticate to the local system. If the credentials are the same on both the client and server systems, you'll still be able to authenticate. But if they aren't, you won't be able to authenticate.

For example, if I wanted to connect to a remote Linux system with a hostname of fedora (which has an IP address of 10.0.0.85) as the user student using the ssh client on a local computer system, I would enter **ssh –l student fedora** at the shell prompt. This is shown in Figure 18-5.

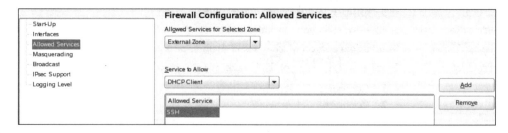

Figure 18-4 Configuring the firewall to allow ssh traffic

```
rtracy@openSUSE:~> ssh -l student fedora
The authenticity of host 'fedora (10.0.0.85)' can't be established.
RSA key fingerprint is 03:8f:61:c0:ba:3f:fc:00:3b:f1:03:1e:5f:f5:18:42.
Are you sure you want to continue connecting (yes/no)? yes
Warning: Permanently added 'fedora,10.0.0.85' (RSA) to the list of known hosts.
student@fedora's password:
Last login: Fri Jan 23 20:11:46 2015
[student@fedora ~]$ █
```

Figure 18-5   Connecting remotely via SSH

Notice in Figure 18-5 that I was prompted to accept the public key from the fedora host because this was the first time I connected to this particular SSH server. Once done, I was authenticated to the remote system as the student user (notice the change in the shell prompt). At this point, I have full access to the shell prompt on fedora and I can complete any task that I could if I were sitting right at the console of the remote system. To close the connection, I just enter **exit** at the shell prompt.

TIP   Windows workstations don't provide an ssh client. You can download the PuTTY.exe SSH client from the Internet and use it to connect to a Linux SSH server from a Windows workstation.

Let's practice working with SSH in the following exercise.

Exercise 18-1: Working with SSH

In this exercise, you will set up the sshd daemon on your Linux system and then connect to it using the SSH client on another Linux system.

NOTE   You'll need at least two Linux systems for this and the remaining exercises in this chapter. You can use two live Linux systems, two Linux virtual machines, or a mixture of both.

VIDEO   Please watch the Exercise 18-1 video for a demonstration on how to perform this task.

Complete the following:

1. Configure the SSH server system by doing the following:

    a. Boot the Linux system that you want to function as an SSH server and log in as a standard user.

    b. Open a terminal session.

    c. Switch to your root user account by entering **su** – followed by your root user's password.

d. At the shell prompt, use the package management utility of your choice to ensure the openssh package has been installed.

e. At the shell prompt, enter **vi /etc/ssh/sshd_config**.

f. Locate the PermitRootLogin setting. If it has been commented out, remove the # character from the beginning of the line.

g. Press INS; then set PermitRootLogin to a value of **no**.

h. Press ESC; then enter **:exit** to save your changes and exit the editor.

i. At the shell prompt, enter **service sshd restart** to restart the SSH service and apply the change.

j. If necessary, open port 22 in the host firewall of the system where the SSH server is running. The steps for doing this will depend on your particular distribution.

2. Create an SSH connection from a client system by doing the following:

a. Start your second system, which will function as an SSH client, and log in as a standard user.

b. Open a terminal session.

c. Open an SSH session with the first Linux system by entering **ssh –l** *user_name IP_address_of_SSH_server* at the shell prompt. For example, to connect to a system with an IP address of 192.168.1.125 as the student user on that system, I would enter **ssh –l student 192.168.1.125** at the shell prompt.

d. If prompted, enter **yes** to accept the public key from the SSH server.

e. Enter the password for the user you specified on the SSH server system.

f. Enter **exit** at the shell prompt to log off from the remote system.

3. Practice working with SSH utilities from your client system by doing the following:

a. Run the ifconfig command on the remote system using SSH by entering **ssh –l** *user_name IP_address_of_SSH_server* **/sbin/ifconfig** at the shell prompt.

b. Enter the password of the remote user when prompted. You should see the networking configuration assigned to the various interfaces on the remote system. Notice that the connection automatically closed once the command finished running.

c. Copy a file using a secure SSH connection by doing the following:

i. Create a new file in your user's home directory by entering **echo "This is my new file." > ~/mytestfile.txt** at the shell prompt.

ii. Copy this new file to the home directory for your remote user account on your SSH server system by entering **scp ~/mytestfile.txt** *user_name@ IP_address_of_SSH_server*: at the shell prompt.

iii. Enter the remote user's password when prompted. You should see that the file was copied.

    iv. Use the ssh command to establish an SSH connection again with your SSH server system using the same username you entered previously to copy the file.

    v. Verify that the file exists in the remote user's home directory.

    vi. Enter **exit** to close the connection.

  d. Use the sftp command to copy the mytestfile.txt file down from the SSH server system to the local /tmp directory by doing the following:

    i. At the shell prompt of your workstation system, enter **sftp user_name@ IP_address_of_SSH_server**.

    ii. Enter the remote user's password when prompted.

    iii. At the sftp> prompt, enter **get mytestfile.txt /tmp/**.

    iv. At the sftp> prompt, enter **exit**.

    v. At the shell prompt, enter **ls /tmp**. You should see the mytestfile.txt file that was copied down from the SSH server system.

Now that you know how to use the SSH server and SSH client, you're ready to advance your knowledge by learning how to tunnel unencrypted traffic through an SSH connection.

Tunneling Traffic Through SSH

One of the key security issues you must deal with as a system administrator is the fact that many commonly used network protocols transfer information as clear text. Good examples of this are the POP3 and IMAP daemons we discussed in the preceding chapter. We noted that for your Linux MTA to download e-mail messages to client systems, you must first enable either your POP3 or IMAP daemon via xinetd. Once done, end users can use an e-mail client to connect to the MTA and download their mail using the appropriate protocol. The problem, however, is the fact that both of these daemons transfer data as clear text by default. That means the usernames and passwords users send to authenticate to the MTA are sent as clear text along with all the contents of their e-mail messages. This allows anyone with a sniffer to capture packets and view the contents of the transmissions.

The good news is SSH can be used to encrypt clear-text traffic by tunneling it through an SSH connection. When client software for the tunneled protocol (such as an e-mail client using POP3) establishes a connection with the local SSH client, the traffic is encrypted using SSH and tunneled through to the SSH server. On the SSH server end, the traffic is decrypted and then forwarded to the appropriate target service (in this case, the POP3 daemon). This is great, because the information is encrypted before being transmitted, even though the original protocol (in this case, POP3) doesn't support encryption.

Let's walk through an example of how you can use SSH to tunnel POP3 traffic:

1. Make sure the ssh client is installed on the local system where the e-mail client will run.

2. Make sure the sshd daemon is installed and running on the POP3 server.

3. Ensure IP port 22 is open on the server where sshd is running.

4. On the system where sshd is running, switch to root and edit the /etc/ssh/sshd_config file.

5. Locate the AllowTcpForwarding parameter, uncomment it if necessary, and then set it to a value of **yes**. An example is shown here:

```
AllowTcpForwarding yes
```

6. Save your changes to the file and exit the editor.

7. Restart the sshd daemon by entering **systemctl restart sshd** at the shell prompt (as root).

8. Switch to the client system.

9. Create a local ssh tunnel from a local high IP port (in this example, port 2345) to port 110 on the POP3 server using the following command (enter the remote user's password when prompted):

```
ssh -f -N -L 2345:pop3_host_address:110 user_name@pop3_host_address
```

The options specified in this command do the following:

- **–N and –f**   Tell ssh not to execute a command remotely on the server and to run in the background after prompting for the remote user's password

- **–L**   Specifies three things:

    - The local port to be used for the client end of the tunnel (in this case, 2345)

    - The hostname or IP address of the remote POP3 server

    - The port on the remote server that will be used for the server end of the tunnel (in this case, 110)

    You don't have to use port 2345. You can use the same port on both ends if desired. However, be aware that you will need to switch to the root user if you want to use a port number less than 1024 on the client side of the tunnel. These are called *privileged* ports.

10. With the tunnel established, configure the local e-mail client program to retrieve mail from the local system on the port you configured for the client end of the SSH tunnel. In this example, you would configure it to get mail from the local system's IP address on port 2345. An example of how to do this with the Evolution e-mail client is shown in Figure 18-6. Note that I used the hostname of the local host, not the POP3 server, in the Server field. I also added the port number of the workstation end of the tunnel to the end of the hostname.

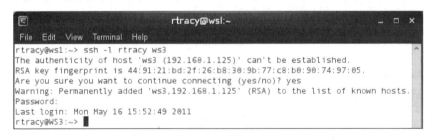

Figure 18-6   Configuring Evolution to use an SSH tunnel

At this point, when the client uses the POP3 protocol to download new messages, the SSH client on the local system will encrypt the request and forward it to the SSH server through the SSH tunnel you established. The SSH server will receive the request, decrypt it, and then pass the data on to the local port 110, where the POP3 daemon is listening. The cool thing about this process is that it is completely transparent to the e-mail client software. As far as it's concerned, it's retrieving e-mail from a local POP3 server.

You can test the tunnel you created using the telnet command from the client end of the tunnel. The syntax is **telnet localhost** *client_tunnel_port*. Here's an example:

```
telnet localhost 2345
```

When you do this, you should see a connection established with the remote system where the POP3 daemon is running. An example is shown in Figure 18-7.

You can also tunnel your X server traffic to remote X clients using an SSH connection. This is important because unencrypted X traffic provides an attacker with a gold mine of information that he or she can use to compromise your systems.

To configure a remote X client *without* encryption, you can use the following procedure:

1. On the remote X client, enter **xhost +***X_server_hostname*. This tells the client to accept connections from the X server.

2. On the X server, enter **DISPLAY=***X_client_hostname***:0.0** and then enter **export DISPLAY**. This tells the X server to display its output on the remote X client.

3. From the X client, use the ssh client to access the shell prompt on the X server and then run the graphical application you want displayed on the X client. For example, you could enter **gedit** at the shell prompt to remotely display the gedit text editor. You could also enter **office** at the shell prompt to remotely display the OpenOffice.org suite.

This procedure works, but all the X traffic is transmitted unencrypted. This isn't good. Instead, you should use SSH to tunnel the X server traffic between the X server and the X client. You can do this using one of the following options:

- Use the –X option with the ssh client program.
- Set the ForwardX11 option to a value of **yes** in the /etc/ssh/ssh_config file on the X client system.

Once this is done, you then need to set the X11Forwarding option to **yes** in the /etc/ssh/sshd_config file on the X server system.

Let's practice working with SSH tunneling in the following exercise.

Figure 18-7

Testing an SSH tunnel with telnet

```
rtracy@ws1:~> telnet localhost 2345
Trying ::1...
Connected to localhost.
Escape character is '^]'.
+OK ready  <28591.1307038747@WS3.mydom.com>
```

Exercise 18-2: Tunneling X Traffic with SSH

In this exercise, you will set up the sshd daemon and ssh client to tunnel X traffic from the server to the client.

 NOTE You'll need at least two Linux systems for this exercise. You can use two live Linux systems, two Linux virtual machines, or a mixture of both.

 VIDEO Please watch the Exercise 18-2 video for a demonstration on how to perform this task.

Complete the following:

1. Configure the client system by doing the following:
   a. Log in to your client system as a standard user.
   b. Open a terminal session.
   c. At the shell prompt, enter **xhost +*X_server_IP_address***. This tells the client to accept connections from the X server (where sshd is running).
2. Configure the server system by doing the following:
   a. Log in to your server system as a standard user.
   b. Open a terminal session and switch to root using the **su –** command.
   c. At the shell prompt, enter **DISPLAY=*X_client_IP_address*:0.0** and then enter **export DISPLAY**. This tells the X server to display its output on the remote X client.
   d. Edit the /etc/ssh/sshd_config file and set the X11Forwarding option to **yes**. Save your changes to the file and exit the editor.
3. Switch back to your client system.
4. At the shell prompt of the client system, enter **ssh –X –l *user_name IP_address_of_SSH_server***.
5. When prompted, enter the remote user's password. Notice that you are now logged in to the server system.
6. At the shell prompt, enter **gedit** to start the gedit text editor. Notice that even though you were logged in to the remote server system, the X application is displayed on the local desktop. An example is shown in Figure 18-8. Because you used the –X option, all the X traffic is encrypted as it passes between systems.

Before we finish discussing SSH, we need to look at configuring SSH to use public key authentication instead of usernames and passwords. Let's review how this is done next.

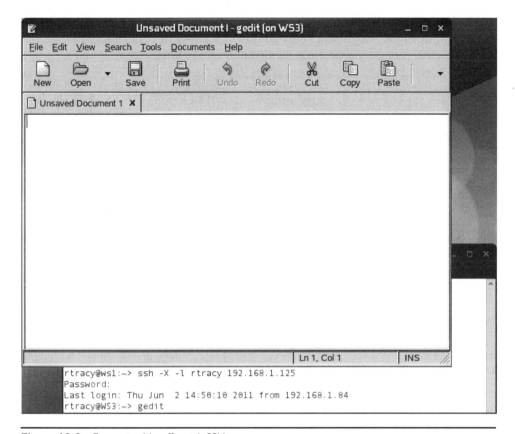

Figure 18-8 Encrypting X traffic with SSH

Configuring SSH to Use Public Key Authentication

In addition to authenticating to the SSH server with a username and password combination, you can also configure your sshd daemon to allow authentication using an RSA or DSA public key. For this to work, the public key of the user on the client system must be stored in the ~/.ssh/ authorized_keys file in the home directory of the user on the server system that you will authenticate as. To do this, you need to securely copy the public key from the client system to the server system. The private key, of course, remains on the client system.

If you configure the SSH server to use public key authentication, the SSH client tells the SSH server which public key should be used for authentication when the SSH session is initially established. The SSH server then checks to see if it has that client's public key; if it does, it will generate a random number and encrypt it with that public key. It then sends the encrypted number to the client, which decrypts it using the private key associated with the public key. The client then calculates an MD5 checksum of the number it received from the server. It sends the checksum back over the SSH server system, which then calculates its own MD5 checksum of the number it originally sent. If the two checksums match, the user is automatically logged in.

To configure public key authentication, the first thing you need to do is create the public/private key pair on the client system so that you can send the public key to the SSH server. This can be done using the ssh-keygen command. Complete the following:

1. At the shell prompt of the client system, enter **ssh-keygen –t rsa** or **ssh-keygen –t dsa**, depending on which encryption method your SSH server supports. To be safe, you can simply use both commands to make two key pairs—one for RSA encryption and the other for DSA encryption.

2. When prompted for the file in which the private key will be saved, press ENTER to use the default filename of ~/.ssh/id_rsa or ~/.ssh/id_dsa. The associated public key will be saved as ~/.ssh/id_rsa.pub or ~/.ssh/id_dsa.pub, respectively.

3. When prompted, enter a passphrase for the key. It is important that you use a passphrase. If you don't, then anyone who manages to get a copy of your key files could authenticate to the SSH server without being required to enter a passphrase. Assigning a passphrase to the key renders the key useless if someone doesn't know it.

At this point, your key pair is created. An example of creating an RSA key pair is shown here:

```
rtracy@ws1:~> ssh-keygen -t rsa
Generating public/private rsa key pair.
Enter file in which to save the key (/home/rtracy/.ssh/id_rsa):
Enter passphrase (empty for no passphrase):
Enter same passphrase again:
Your identification has been saved in /home/rtracy/.ssh/id_rsa.
Your public key has been saved in /home/rtracy/.ssh/id_rsa.pub.
The key fingerprint is:
ba:14:48:14:de:fd:42:40:f2:4b:c8:8b:03:a4:6d:fc rtracy@ws1
The key's randomart image is:
+--[ RSA 2048]----+
|  .   +oo        |
|oo + = o         |
|o + = + o        |
| o + + o .       |
|  o E o S .       |
|     .   o .     |
|       o         |
|      . .        |
|        .        |
+-----------------+
rtracy@ws1:~>
```

The next thing you need to do is to copy the public key you just created to the SSH server. An easy (and secure) way to do this is to use the scp command you learned about earlier in this chapter. The syntax is

```
scp ~/.ssh/key_name.pub user_name@address_of_SSH_server:filename
```

In the example shown here, the RSA public key for the local rtracy user on WS1 is copied to the home directory of the rtracy user on WS3 and saved in a file named keyfile:

```
rtracy@ws1:~> scp ~/.ssh/id_rsa.pub ws3:keyfile
Password:
```

```
id_rsa.pub                           100%  392     0.4KB/s   00:00
rtracy@ws1:~>
```

At this point, the contents of the key file you just copied need to be appended to the end of the ~/.ssh/authorized_keys file in the home directory of the user you will connect to the SSH server as. An easy way to do this is to connect to the SSH server system using a standard (password-authenticated) SSH session and then use the cat command to append the contents of the key file to the end of the ~/.ssh/authorized_keys file in the user's home directory. An example of how to do this is shown here:

```
rtracy@ws1:~> ssh -l rtracy ws3
Password:
Last login: Thu Jun  2 15:05:34 2011 from 192.168.1.84
rtracy@WS3:~> mkdir ~/.ssh
rtracy@WS3:~> cat keyfile >> ~/.ssh/authorized_keys
rtracy@WS3:~>
```

In this example, I logged in to the WS3 system via an SSH connection as the remote rtracy user and then created the hidden .ssh directory in that user's home directory. I had to create the directory because it didn't exist yet. If the .ssh directory already exists, you can skip this step and just append the contents of the key file to the end of the authorized_keys file. Notice in the example that I used the cat command with the >> redirection characters to add the contents of the file named keyfile to the end of the authorized_keys file.

In this example, the authorized_keys file didn't exist yet, so the redirection process automatically created it for me. Because of this, I could have actually just used a single > redirection character because the file didn't exist.

If, on the other hand, the authorized _keys file does already exist, it's very important that you remember to use the >> redirection characters instead of >. Remember, using >> will *append* the output of the command to the end of the specified file. Using a single redirection > character will *overwrite* the entire file with the output of the command. That wouldn't be a good thing if the authorized_keys file already had several keys in it that you wanted to keep.

You can now test the configuration to see if public key authentication works. If you're still logged in to an SSH session with the SSH server, exit out of it. Then establish a new SSH session with the server. You should be prompted for the key file's passphrase instead of a username and password, as shown in Figure 18-9.

Figure 18-9
Supplying the key file's passphrase

Once you enter the passphrase, you will be authenticated to the SSH server. Notice in the next example that no password was requested to establish the SSH session:

```
rtracy@ws1:~> ssh -l rtracy ws3
Last login: Thu Jun  2 16:13:39 2011 from 192.168.1.84
rtracy@WS3:~>
```

If desired, you can use the ssh-agent command to eliminate the need to enter the passphrase every time you establish an SSH connection. Complete the following:

1. At the shell prompt of your client system, enter ssh-agent bash.

2. At the shell prompt, enter **ssh-add ~/.ssh/id_rsa** or **ssh-add ~/.ssh/id_dsa**, depending on which key file you have created.

3. When prompted, enter the key file's passphrase. When you do, you should be prompted that the identity has been added. An example follows:

```
rtracy@ws1:~> ssh-agent bash
rtracy@ws1:~> ssh-add ~/.ssh/id_rsa
Enter passphrase for /home/rtracy/.ssh/id_rsa:
Identity added: /home/rtracy/.ssh/id_rsa (/home/rtracy/.ssh/id_rsa)
rtracy@ws1:~>
```

Once this is done, the ssh-agent process stores the passphrase in memory. It then listens for SSH requests and automatically provides the key passphrase for you when requested.

Let's practice configuring SSH to use public key authentication in the following exercise.

Exercise 18-3: Configuring Public Key Authentication

In this exercise, you will generate an RSA key pair on your client system and copy the public key to the SSH server to enable public key authentication.

NOTE You'll need at least two Linux systems for this remaining exercise. You can use two live Linux systems, two Linux virtual machines, or a mixture of both.

VIDEO Please watch the Exercise 18-3 video for a demonstration on how to perform this task.

Complete the following:

1. Generate an RSA key pair on your client system by doing the following:

   a. Log in to your client system as a standard user.

   b. Open a terminal session.

   c. At the shell prompt, enter **ssh-keygen –t rsa**.

   d. When prompted for the file in which the private key will be saved, press ENTER to use the default filename of ~/.ssh/id_rsa.

   e. When prompted, enter a passphrase for the key.

2. Configure the server system to use public key authentication by doing the following:

   a. Copy the public key you just created to your SSH server system by entering **scp ~/.ssh/id_rsa.pub** *user_name@address_of_SSH_server:***mykeyfile**.

   b. Enter the remote user's password when prompted.

   c. Establish an SSH session with the remote system as the user you intend to authenticate as using public key authentication. Use the following command: **ssh –l** *user_name address_of_SSH_server*.

   d. Enter the remote user's password when prompted.

   e. At the shell prompt of the remote system, check to see if the .ssh hidden directory already exists by entering **ls –la** at the shell prompt. If the .ssh directory doesn't exist, create it using the **mkdir ~/.ssh** command. Otherwise, go on to the next step.

   f. At the shell prompt of the remote system, enter **cat mykeyfile >> ~/.ssh/ authorized_keys**.

   g. Enter **exit** at the shell prompt to close the SSH session.

3. Test the new configuration by doing the following:

   a. At the shell prompt of your client system, enter **ssh –l** *user_name address_of_ SSH_server*.

   b. When prompted, enter the passphrase you assigned to your RSA private key. At this point, you should be automatically authenticated to the SSH server.

   c. Close the session by entering **exit** at the shell prompt.

4. Configure ssh-agent to remember your private key passphrase by doing the following:

   a. At the shell prompt of your client system, enter **ssh-agent bash**.

   b. At the shell prompt, enter **ssh-add ~/.ssh/id_rsa**.

   c. When prompted, enter the key file's passphrase. When you do, you should be prompted that the identity has been added.

   d. At the shell prompt of your client system, enter **ssh –l** *user_name address_of_ SSH_server*. You should be automatically authenticated to the SSH server without being prompted for the private key passphrase.

Great work! You're an SSH pro now! Before we end this chapter, there's one more encryption-related topic we need to address: encrypting files. Let's do that next.

Encrypting Linux Files

Just as you can encrypt network transmissions between Linux systems using OpenSSH, you can also use encryption to protect files in the Linux file system. You can use a wide variety of tools to do this. Some are open source; others are proprietary. For your Linux+/LPIC-1 exam, you need to know how to use the open source GNU Privacy Guard (GPG) utility to encrypt files. Therefore, that's the tool we will use here. We'll discuss the following:

- How GPG works
- Using GPG to encrypt files

Let's begin by discussing how GPG works.

How GPG Works

GNU Privacy Guard (GPG) is an open source implementation of the OpenPGP standard (RFC 4880). It allows you to encrypt and digitally sign your data and communications. For example, you can encrypt files in your Linux file system. You can also encrypt and digitally sign e-mail messages.

GPG provides a cryptographic engine that can be used directly from the shell prompt using the **gpg** command-line utility. It can also be called from within shell scripts or other programs running on the system. For example, GPG support has been integrated into several popular Linux e-mail clients such as Evolution and KMail. It has also been integrated into instant messaging applications such as Psi.

A variety of graphical front ends are available for GPG as well. Some of the more popular front ends include KGPG and Seahorse. However, for your Linux+/LPIC-1 exam, you need to know how to use GPG from the shell prompt, so that's what we'll focus on in this chapter.

GPG functions in a manner similar to OpenSSH in that it uses both asymmetric and symmetric cryptography. GPG first generates a random symmetric key and uses it to encrypt the message to be transferred. The symmetric key itself is then encrypted using the recipient's public key and sent along with the message that was encrypted using the symmetric key. When the recipient receives a message, GPG first decrypts the symmetric key using the user's private key. GPG then uses the decrypted symmetric key to decrypt the rest of the message.

GPG supports many encryption algorithms, including the following:

- Symmetric encryption:
    - AES
    - 3DES
    - Blowfish
- Asymmetric encryption:
    - Elgamal
    - RSA
- Hashes:
    - MD5
    - SHA-1 and -2
    - RIPEMD-160

- Digital signatures:
  - DSA
  - RSA

Now that you understand how GPG works, let's review how you can use GPG to encrypt files.

Using GPG to Encrypt Files

To encrypt a file using GPG, do the following:

1. Use GPG to generate your keys. To do this, enter **gpg --gen-key** at the shell prompt. An example is shown here:

```
rtracy@openSUSE:~> gpg --gen-key
gpg (GnuPG) 2.0.22; Copyright (C) 2013 Free Software Foundation, Inc.
This is free software: you are free to change and redistribute it.
There is NO WARRANTY, to the extent permitted by law.

Please select what kind of key you want:
    (1) RSA and RSA (default)
    (2) DSA and Elgamal
    (3) DSA (sign only)
    (4) RSA (sign only)
Your selection?
```

2. Select the type of key you want to create. Usually you will use the default option (1), which uses RSA and RSA. You are prompted to specify the size of the key, as shown here:

```
RSA keys may be between 1024 and 4096 bits long.
What keysize do you want? (2048)
```

3. Specify the size of key you want to create. Using the default size of 2048 bits is usually sufficient. You are prompted to configure the key lifetime, as shown here:

```
Please specify how long the key should be valid.
         0 = key does not expire
      <n>  = key expires in n days
      <n>w = key expires in n weeks
      <n>m = key expires in n months
      <n>y = key expires in n years
Key is valid for? (0)
```

4. Specify when the key will expire. As shown in step 3, you can specify that the key expire in a certain number of days, weeks, months, or years.

5. Construct your user ID for the key. The first parameter you need to specify is your real name. The name you specify is very important because it will be used later during the encryption process. In the next example, I entered **rtracy** for my real name:

```
GnuPG needs to construct a user ID to identify your key.
Real name: rtracy
```

6. When prompted, enter your e-mail address.

7. When prompted, enter a comment of your choosing. You are prompted to confirm the user ID you have created for the key. An example is shown here:

```
You selected this USER-ID:
    "rtracy <rtracy@openSUSE>"

Change (N)ame, (C)omment, (E)mail or (O)kay/(Q)uit?
```

8. If the information is correct, enter **O** to confirm the ID. You are prompted to enter a passphrase for the key, as shown in Figure 18-10.

9. Enter a unique passphrase for the key. After doing so, you are prompted to perform various actions on the system while the key is generated. An example is shown here:

```
We need to generate a lot of random bytes. It is a good idea to perform
some other action (type on the keyboard, move the mouse, utilize the
disks) during the prime generation; this gives the random number
generator a better chance to gain enough entropy.
.+++++.+++++++++++++++++++++++++++++++.+++++.+++++++++++++++++++++++++++++++++
+++.++++++++++.++++++++++.++++++++++.++++++++++..+++++.++++++++++>++++++++++
.......................................>+++++............................<+++++.
.................................>+++++..........<+++++.......+++++
```

10. Move the mouse, type characters on your keyboard, or open and close your optical disc drive door. GPG uses these actions to generate random numbers to create your key. Be aware that if you're not doing enough, you'll be prompted to increase your activity to generate enough entropy to create the key. An example is shown here:

```
Not enough random bytes available.  Please do some other work to give
the OS a chance to collect more entropy! (Need 137 more bytes)
```

At this point, your key pair has been generated! The key files are stored in the ~/.gnupg directory in your user's home directory. The following files are created in this directory:

- **secring.gpg** This file is the GPG secret keyring.
- **pubring.gpg** This file is the GPG public keyring.
- **trustdb.gpg** This file is the GPG trust database.

Before going any further, you should seriously consider creating a backup of your private key in case it gets corrupted. This is very important because if you encrypt files with your key pair and then lose your key, you will never be able to decrypt them. They are toast! Even if you re-create

Figure 18-10
Providing a GPG
passphrase

your key pair, you will not be able to decrypt the files because they were encrypted with a different key pair.

To create a backup of your gpg key pair, enter **gpg --export-secret-keys --armor** *key_owner_ email_address* **>** *filename***.asc** at the shell prompt. This is shown in the following example:

```
gpg --export-secret-keys --armor rtracy@openSUSE > rtracy-privatekey.asc
rtracy@openSUSE:~> ls
addnum          firstnames        mytestfile.txt        rtracy-privatekey.asc
```

For security reasons, you probably shouldn't leave this file on your hard disk. Instead, consider burning it to an optical disc or copying it to a USB flash drive and locking it away in a file cabinet somewhere. This will allow you to restore your private key should the original copy on the hard drive get mangled.

You can now use your key pair to encrypt files and messages. For example, if you wanted to encrypt a file in your Linux file system, you would do the following:

1. At the shell prompt, enter **gpg –e –r** *key_user_name filename*. In the example shown here, I'm encrypting the mytestfile.txt file using the key I generated previously. The –e option tells gpg to encrypt the specified file. Remember that I specified a key username of rtracy when I created the key user ID, so that's what I entered here.

   ```
   rtracy@openSUSE:~> gpg -e -r rtracy mytestfile.txt
   ```

2. At the shell prompt, use the ls command to view the new encrypted version of the file gpg created. The original file is left intact. The new file will have the same filename as the original file with a ".gpg" extension added. In the example here, the name of the new file is mytestfile.txt.gpg. In Figure 18-11, the differences between the original file and the encrypted file are shown.

Once the file has been encrypted, it can then be decrypted using the gpg command. The syntax is **gpg --output** *output_filename* **--decrypt** *encrypted_filename*. For example, to decrypt

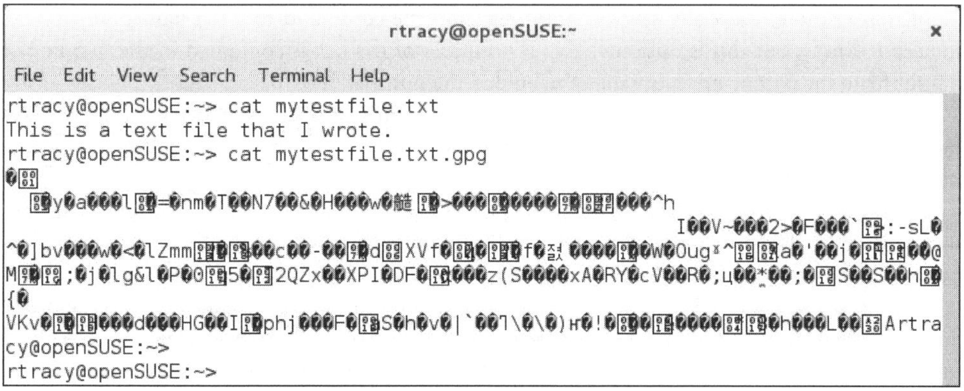

Figure 18-11   Viewing a file encrypted with gpg

the mytestfile.txt.gpg file I created earlier, I would enter **gpg --output mytestfile.txt.decrypted --decrypt mytestfile.txt.gpg**. This is shown in the example here:

```
rtracy@openSUSE:~> gpg --output mytestfile.txt.decrypted --decrypt
mytestfile.txt.gpg

You need a passphrase to unlock the secret key for
user: "rtracy (<rtracy@openSUSE>"
2048-bit RSA key, ID FB8BF16C, created 2015-01-24 (main key ID 9DF54AB2)

gpg: encrypted with 2048-bit RSA key, ID FB8BF16C, created 2015-01-24
      "rtracy (<rtracy@openSUSE>"
rtracy@openSUSE:~> cat mytestfile.txt.decrypted
This is a text file that I wrote.
rtracy@openSUSE:~>
```

At this point, you are able to encrypt and decrypt files on your local system. But what do you do if you want to be able to exchange encrypted files with someone else and both of you be able to decrypt them? To do this, you must exchange and install gpg public keys on your systems. There are two ways to do this.

The first option is to copy your public keys to a public key server on the Internet. This is done by entering **gpg --keyserver hkp://subkeys.pgp.net --send-key *key_ID*** at the shell prompt. Notice that this command requires you to know the ID number associated with your gpg public key. This number is actually displayed when you initially create your gpg key pair, but if you're like me, you probably didn't take note of it. That's not a problem because you can generate it again from the command line. To do this, enter **gpg --fingerprint *key_owner_email***. An example is shown here:

```
rtracy@openSUSE:~> gpg --fingerprint rtracy@openSUSE > key_ID.txt
rtracy@openSUSE:~> cat key_ID.txt
pub   2048R/9DF54AB2 2015-01-24
      Key fingerprint = AF46 4AB3 1397 B88E BC6A  FBDA 465F 82C4 9DF5 4AB2
uid                  rtracy       <rtracy@openSUSE>
sub   2048R/FB8BF16C 2015-01-24
```

In this example, I actually saved the output from the command to a file named key_ID.txt to keep it handy, but this is optional. The ID number of the key is contained in the first line of output from the command. Note that I've bolded the number needed.

Once you have the ID number, you can then copy your gpg public key to a public key server on the Internet. Using the preceding information for my system, I would enter **gpg --keyserver hkp://subkeys.pgp.net --send-key 9DF54AB2** at the command prompt.

This option works great if you want to be able to exchange keys with a large number of other users. However, if you are only concerned about doing this with a limited number of people, you can also just directly exchange keys between systems.

To do this, you (and the other users) can export your public keys and send them to each other. To do this, you enter **gpg --export --armor *key_owner_email* > *public_key_filename*** at the shell prompt. For example, to export the public key to a file named gpg.pub from the key pair I created earlier, I would enter the following:

```
rtracy@openSUSE:~> gpg --export rtracy@openSUSE > gpg.pub
```

Each user can then copy their key file to the other users. For example, if I wanted to send my key to the student user account on another Linux host named fedora, I would enter the following:

```
rtracy@openSUSE:~> scp gpg.pub student@fedora:
```

Once this is done, each user should import the other users' public keys into their GPG keyring using the **gpg --import** *public_key_filename* command at the shell prompt. In the example shown next, I first used scp to copy the public key file from the openSUSE system to the fedora system. I then used gpg to import the public key.

```
[student@fedora ~]$ gpg --import gpg.pub
gpg: key 9DF54AB2: public key "rtracy <rtracy@openSUSE>" imported
gpg: Total number processed: 1
gpg:               imported: 1  (RSA: 1)
[student@fedora ~]
```

Remember, each user needs to repeat this process. Then they can use each other's gpg keys to encrypt and decrypt files. You can view the keys in your GPG keyring using the **gpg --list-keys** command, as shown in the following example:

```
[student@fedora ~]$ gpg --list-keys
/home/student/.gnupg/pubring.gpg
--------------------------------
pub   2048R/9DF54AB2 2015-01-24
uid                  rtracy <rtracy@openSUSE>
sub   2048R/FB8BF16C 2015-01-24
[student@fedora ~]$
```

In this example, you can see that the public key I created earlier on openSUSE is now imported into the student user's GPG keyring on fedora. The keyring file itself is located in the ~/.gnupg/ directory within my home directory and is named pubring.gpg.

 NOTE   The gpg.conf file is also located in the ~/.gnupg directory. You can use this file to customize the way gpg works on your system.

I would then need to do the same thing in reverse. I should import the public key from the student user on the fedora system to my system (openSUSE). With the public keys imported, we could exchange encrypted files and be able to decrypt them. The syntax for doing this is **gpg --output** *output_filename* **--symmetric** *encrypted_filename*. For example, if I sent the mytestfile.txt.gpg encrypted document from my openSUSE system to my fedora system, I would enter the following command to decrypt it:

```
[student@fedora ~]$ gpg --output mytestfile.txt.decrypted --symmetric
mytestfile.txt.gpg
[student@fedora ~]$ ls
Desktop     Music       Pictures         Documents        mykeyfile
Templates   Downloads   mytestfile.txt.decrypted          Videos
gpg.pub     mytestfile.txt.gpg           Public
[student@fedora ~]$
```

When I do, I am prompted to enter the passphrase I assigned to the private key when I initially generated it. Once this is done, the decrypted version of the file is created and is accessible to the local user.

Before we end this chapter, we need to discuss the topic of *key revocation*. From time to time, you may need to revoke a key, which withdraws it from public use. This should be done if the key becomes compromised, gets lost, or if you forget the passphrase associated with the key.

 NOTE Forgetting the passphrase associated with the key pair is a very common problem that results in key revocation.

To revoke a key, you create a *key revocation certificate*. As a best practice, you should create a key revocation certificate immediately after initially creating your key pair. This is done in case something gets corrupted and the revocation certificate can't be created should it be required for some reason later on. Here's a key thing to remember: creating the key revocation certificate doesn't actually revoke the key pair. Only when you actually issue the key revocation certificate does the key get revoked. Basically, you create the key revocation certificate and save it in a secure location just in case it's needed later.

To create (not issue) the key revocation certificate, enter **gpg --output revoke.asc --gen-revoke key_ID** at the shell prompt. Remember, you can use the --fingerprint option with the gpg command to view the key ID number. In the example that follows, I create a key revocation certificate for the gpg key pair I generated for the student user on my fedora system:

```
[student@fedora ~]$ gpg --fingerprint student@fedora
pub   2048R/899AB9E6 2015-01-24
      Key fingerprint = A469 942C F5C9 555A B4A4  F975 1B3A CB26 899A B9E6
uid                  student <student@fedora>
sub   2048R/A86F1A4B 2015-01-24
[student@fedora ~]$ gpg --output revoke.asc --gen-revoke 899AB9E6
sec  2048R/899AB9E6 2015-01-24 student <student@fedora>
Create a revocation certificate for this key? (y/N) y
Please select the reason for the revocation:
  0 = No reason specified
  1 = Key has been compromised
  2 = Key is superseded
  3 = Key is no longer used
  Q = Cancel
(Probably you want to select 1 here)
Your decision? 1
Enter an optional description; end it with an empty line:
> This key has been compromised
>
Reason for revocation: Key has been compromised
This key has been compromised
Is this okay? (y/N) y
You need a passphrase to unlock the secret key for
user: "student <student@fedora>"
2048-bit RSA key, ID 899AB9E6, created 2015-01-24
ASCII armored output forced.
Revocation certificate created.
Please move it to a medium which you can hide away; if Mallory gets
access to this certificate he can use it to make your key unusable.
```

```
It is smart to print this certificate and store it away, just in case
your media become unreadable.  But have some caution:  The print system of
your machine might store the data and make it available to others!
```

Notice in this example that I had to specify a reason why the key is to be revoked along with a more detailed description. I also had to provide the passphrase that was used when the key pair was originally created. Also notice the warning message at the end of the command output. You probably should avoid keeping the key revocation certificate on your system's hard disk. Instead, burn it to the same optical disc or copy it to the same flash drive as your key pair backup and lock it away! If someone were to get a hold of this file, they could revoke your certificate without your knowledge or consent, which would be a bad thing.

 TIP The output of the command says to print out the key revocation certificate. I think that is a cumbersome way to archive it. If you ever needed to issue it, you would have to type the revocation certificate in manually. Yuck! I much prefer copying it to a flash drive that I keep locked in a cabinet. Don't forget to delete the file off the hard disk, no matter what archival mechanism you choose to use.

So what should you do if your certificate actually does get compromised and you end up needing to revoke it? The process is actually pretty easy. All you have to do is import the revocation certificate in the same manner we talked about for standard certificates. You enter **gpg --import** *revocation_certificate_filename* at the shell prompt. An example is shown here:

```
[student@fedora ~]$ gpg --import revoke.asc
gpg: key 899AB9E6: "student <student@fedora>" revocation certificate imported
gpg: Total number processed: 1
gpg:     new key revocations: 1
gpg: 3 marginal(s) needed, 1 complete(s) needed, PGP trust model
gpg: depth: 0  valid:   1  signed:   0  trust: 0-, 0q, 0n, 0m, 0f, 1u
```

Once this is done, you can verify that the key was revoked by entering **gpg --list-keys** *key_ID* at the shell prompt. You should see that the revoked key is now gone from your keyring. If you used the manual method discussed earlier in this chapter to distribute your public key, you must import the key revocation certificate on any other systems where your public key was imported.

If you are using a public key server on the Internet to distribute your keys to other users, you would need to issue the key revocation certificate there as well. Enter **gpg --keyserver** *public_key_server_URL* **--send** *key_ID* at the shell prompt. This lets everyone who is using your public key know that the key has been compromised and should no longer be used.

Let's practice working with GPG in the following exercise.

Exercise 18-4: Using GPG to Encrypt Files

In this exercise, you will use GPG to encrypt a file and send it to a second Linux system. You will then export your public key, copy it to the second Linux system, and then use that key to decrypt the file that was sent.

 NOTE You'll need at least two Linux systems for this exercise. You can use two live Linux systems, two Linux virtual machines, or a mixture of both.

VIDEO   Please watch the Exercise 18-4 video for a demonstration on how to perform this task.

Complete the following:

1. Generate your GPG key pair by following these steps:

    a. Boot your first Linux system and log in as a standard user.

    b. Open a terminal session.

    c. Enter **gpg --gen-key** at the shell prompt.

    d. When prompted to select the type of key you want to create, press ENTER to use the default option (1), which uses RSA and RSA.

    e. When prompted to specify the size of the key, press ENTER to use the default size of 2048 bits.

    f. When prompted to specify when the key will expire, press ENTER to select the default option (0), which specifies that the key never expires.

    g. Enter **y** when prompted to confirm this selection.

 NOTE   We're doing this for demonstration purposes. In the real world, you should configure your keys to expire after a certain length of time. That way, if your key ever gets compromised, it will become invalid after a period of time.

    h. Construct the user ID for the key by first specifying a username that is at least five characters long. Write down the username you entered because you will need it later.

    i. When prompted, enter your e-mail address. Write down the e-mail address you entered because you will need it later.

    j. When prompted, enter your full name as a comment.

    k. When prompted to confirm the user ID you created for the key, enter **O** (the letter O) to confirm it.

    l. When prompted to enter a passphrase for the key, enter a unique passphrase.

    m. When prompted, move the mouse, type characters on your keyboard, or open and close your optical disc drive door. After you have done this, your key pair is been generated!

2. Encrypt a file with GPG by doing the following:

    a. At the shell prompt, enter **gpg –e –r *key_user_name* mytestfile.txt**. Replace *key_user_name* with the real name you entered when creating your key. You created the mytestfile.txt file in Exercise 18-1. If you don't have this file, create a new one with this name.

    b. At the shell prompt, use the ls command to verify that the mytestfile.txt.gpg file was created.

3. Decrypt the file you just created by doing the following:

   a. Enter **gpg --output mytestfile.txt.decrypted --decrypt mytestfile.txt.gpg** at the shell prompt to decrypt the file.

   b. Use the cat command to display the contents of the mytestfile.txt.decrypted file and verify that it matches the content of the original file.

4. Send the encrypted file to a different system and decrypt it there by doing the following:

   a. Boot your second Linux system and log in as a standard user.

   b. Use the ping command to verify that it can communicate over the network with the first Linux system, where you create the GPG key pair.

   c. Switch back to your first Linux system.

   d. From the shell prompt of your first Linux system, export your key by entering **gpg –export --armor** *key_owner_email* **> gpg.pub**.

   e. Use the scp command to copy the gpg.pub and mytestfile.txt.gpg files from your first Linux system to your second Linux system.

   f. Switch over to your second Linux system.

   g. Verify that the gpg.pub file was copied to your user's home directory.

   h. Import the public key from your first Linux system into the GPG keyring by entering **gpg --import ~/gpg.pub** at the shell prompt.

   i. Verify that the public key was imported by entering **gpg --list-keys** at the shell prompt.

   j. Decrypt the encrypted file you copied over from the first Linux system by entering **gpg --output mytestfile.txt.decrypted --symmetric mytestfile.txt.gpg** at the shell prompt.

   k. When prompted, enter the passphrase you assigned to the GPG key when you created it on the first system.

   l. Use the cat command to display the contents of the mytestfile.txt.decrypted file and verify that it matches the content of the original file on the first Linux system.

5. Perform maintenance tasks on your GPG key pair by doing the following:

   a. Create a backup of your GPG key pair by entering **gpg --export-secret-keys --armor** *key_owner_email_address* **> gpgkey.asc** at the shell prompt.

   b. Create a key revocation certificate by entering **gpg --output revoke.asc --gen-revoke** *key_ID* at the shell prompt. Remember, you can use the --fingerprint option with the gpg command to view the key ID number.

You did it! You're now an SSH and GPG expert! Let's review what you learned in this chapter.

Chapter Review

In this chapter, you learned how to use encryption to secure data on a Linux system. We first looked at encrypting network communications with OpenSSH, and then we looked at using GPG to encrypt Linux files.

I began this chapter by reviewing how encryption works. The first type of encryption we looked at was symmetric encryption. With symmetric encryption, the key used to encrypt a message is the same key used to decrypt the message. That means the sender and the receiver must both have the exact same key. One of the key advantages of using symmetric encryption is speed. It processes much faster than asymmetric encryption. One of the difficulties associated with symmetric encryption is how to securely distribute the key to all the parties that need to communicate with each other. Examples of cryptographic standards that use symmetric encryption include

- 3DES
- AES
- Blowfish

When selecting an encryption scheme, you should pick one that supports a minimum of 128 bits. The longer the key, the more secure the data is.

We then turned our attention to asymmetric encryption. Asymmetric encryption uses two keys instead of one: the public key and the private key. Data that has been encoded with the public key can be decoded only with the private key. Data that has been encoded with the private key can only be decoded with the public key. Asymmetric encryption is frequently referred to as *public key cryptography*. Commonly used asymmetric encryption mechanisms include

- RSA
- DSA

Private/public key pairs should be much longer than those used for symmetric encryption. They should be 1024 bits or longer.

You will frequently see implementations that use a combination of both symmetric and asymmetric encryption. Asymmetric encryption is used for an initial key exchange to securely copy a secret key to both parties in a session. Once this is done, both parties have the same key and can switch to symmetric encryption for the remainder of the session.

A certificate authority is responsible for issuing and managing encryption keys. When a key pair is requested from a CA, it generates a public key and a private key simultaneously, using a specified encryption scheme, such as RSA or DSA. The private key in the pair is given only to the key owner. The public key, on the other hand, can be made available to anyone who needs it. The primary role of the CA is to verify that parties involved in an encrypted exchange are who they say they are. You need to be familiar with two types of CAs:

- Internal CA
- External CA

Because your Linux system installed its own internal CA when you installed the operating system, we can use it to mint our own certificates and use them to encrypt both network transmissions and files in the file system.

I then discussed how you can use OpenSSH to encrypt remote access sessions between Linux systems. Early Linux network services such as Telnet, rlogin, rcp, rshell, and FTP transmit data as clear text, which exposes usernames, passwords, and other sensitive data to sniffers. OpenSSH, on the other hand, provides a suite of utilities that you can use to encrypt these data transfers:

- sshd
- ssh
- scp
- sft
- slogin

OpenSSH uses private/public key encryption along with secret key encryption. First, the SSH client creates a connection with the system where the SSH server is running on IP port 22. The SSH server then sends its public key to the SSH client. The client system receives the public key from the SSH server and checks to see if it already has a copy of that key. By default, if it doesn't have the server's public key in either of these files, it will ask the user to add it. Once this is done, the client now trusts the server system and generates a 256-bit secret key. It then uses the server's public key to encrypt the new secret key and sends it to the server. The server decrypts it using its private key. Once this is done, both systems can now use symmetric encryption for the session. In SSH version 2, the secret key is not actually transmitted from the client to the server system. A Diffie-Hellman key agreement is used instead to negotiate a secret key to be used for the session without actually sending it over the network.

The process of configuring OpenSSH involves configuring both the SSH server and the SSH client. You configure the sshd daemon using the /etc/ssh/sshd_config file. The ssh client is configured using the /etc/ssh/ssh_config file or the ~/.ssh/ssh_config file. Before you can connect to an SSH server, you must open up port 22 in the host-based firewall of the system where sshd is running.

You can load the ssh client on your local computer and connect to the sshd daemon on the remote Linux system by entering **ssh –l** *user_name ip_address*.

Next, we looked at ways you can tunnel network traffic that is unencrypted by default securely through an SSH tunnel. When client software for the tunneled protocol (such as an e-mail client using POP3) establishes a connection with the local SSH client, the traffic is encrypted using SSH and tunneled through to the SSH server. On the SSH server end, the traffic is decrypted and then forwarded to the appropriate target service (such as a POP3 e-mail daemon). The information is encrypted before being transmitted, even though the original protocol (such as POP3) doesn't support encryption.

To configure an SSH tunnel, you have to first edit the /etc/ssh/sshd_config file on the system where sshd is running and set the AllowTcpForwarding parameter to a value of **yes**. Then you create a local ssh tunnel from a local high IP port to the port on the remote server that the desired service is listening on (such as port 110 for a POP3 server). This is done using the following command:

```
ssh -f -N -L high_port:remote_host_address:port user_name@remote_host_address
```

You can test the tunnel using the telnet command from the client end of the tunnel. Enter **telnet localhost *client_tunnel_port*** at the shell prompt.

You can also tunnel your X server traffic to remote X clients using an SSH connection. To do this, you must configure the client system to accept connections from the X server using the **xhost +*X_server_hostname*** command. Then you configure the X server to redirect its graphical display to the client system by setting the DISPLAY environment variable. The syntax is **DISPLAY=*X_client_hostname*:0.0**. Then you export the new value of the variable.

Next, you need to set the X11Forwarding option to **yes** in the /etc/ssh/sshd_config file on the X server system. At the shell prompt of the client system, enter **ssh –X –l *user_name IP_address_of_X_server*** and log in to the remote system. Then enter the appropriate command to start a graphical application. When you do, the application will run on the X server system but be securely displayed on the client system's desktop.

I wrapped up our discussion of SSH by discussing how to configure it to use public key authentication instead of usernames and password. To do this, the public key of the user on the client system must be stored in the ~/.ssh/authorized_keys file in the home directory of the user on the server system that you will authenticate as.

In this configuration, the SSH client tells the SSH server which public key should be used for authentication when the SSH session is initially established. The SSH server then checks to see if it has that client's public key; if it does, it will generate a random number and encrypt it with that public key. It then sends the encrypted number to the client, which decrypts it using the private key associated with the public key. The client then calculates an MD5 checksum of the number it received from the server. It sends the checksum back over the SSH server system, which then calculates its own MD5 checksum of the number it originally sent. If the two checksums match, the user is automatically logged in.

To configure public key authentication, you must do the following:

1. Create the public/private key pair on the client system using the ssh-keygen command.

2. Copy the public key you just created to the SSH server using the scp command.

3. Append the contents of the key file you just copied to the end of the ~/.ssh/authorized_keys file in the home directory of the user you will connect to the SSH server as. This can be done by redirecting (>>) the output of the cat command to the authorized_keys file.

Once this is done, you can connect to the remote SSH server from the client system. Instead of entering a username and password to authenticate, you'll be prompted to provide the passphrase of the private key. If desired, you can use the ssh-agent command to eliminate the need to enter the passphrase every time you establish an SSH connection.

At this point, I shifted topics to encrypting files in the Linux file system. For your Linux+/LPIC-1 exam, you need to know how to use the open source GNU Privacy Guard (GPG) utility to encrypt files. GPG is an open source implementation of the OpenPGP standard (RFC 4880) that allows you to encrypt and digitally sign your data and communications.

GPG uses both asymmetric and symmetric cryptography. GPG first generates a random symmetric key and uses it to encrypt the message to be transferred. The symmetric key itself is then encrypted using the recipient's public key and sent along with the message that was encrypted using the symmetric key. When the recipient receives a message, GPG first decrypts the symmetric key using the user's private key. GPG then uses the decrypted symmetric key to decrypt the rest of the message. GPG supports many encryption algorithms, including the following:

- Symmetric encryption:
  - AES
  - 3DES
  - Blowfish
- Asymmetric encryption:
  - Elgamal
  - RSA
- Hashes:
  - MD5
  - SHA-1 and -2
  - RIPEMD-160
- Digital signatures:
  - DSA
  - RSA

To encrypt a file using GPG, do the following:

1. Generate your keys using the **gpg --gen-key** command at the shell prompt.
2. Encrypt the file using the **gpg –e –r** *key_user_name filename* command at the shell prompt.

Once the file has been encrypted, it can then be decrypted using the **gpg --output** *output_filename* **--decrypt** *encrypted_filename* command at the shell prompt.

If you want to be able to exchange encrypted files with someone else and both of you be able to decrypt them, you must exchange and install gpg public keys on your systems. There are two ways to do this:

- The first option is to copy your public keys to a public key server on the Internet. This is done by entering **gpg --keyserver hkp://subkeys.pgp.net --send-key** *key_ID* at the shell prompt.
- The second option is to manually exchange keys with the other user. To do this, you enter **gpg --export --armor** *key_owner_email* > *public_key_filename* at the shell prompt. Once this is done, each user should import the other user's public keys into their GPG keyring using the **gpg --import** *public_key_filename* command at the shell prompt.

You can view the keys in your GPG keyring using the **gpg --list-keys** command. With the public key imported, you can decrypt files sent to you from the user who encrypted them using the **gpg --output** *output_filename* **--symmetric** *encrypted_filename* command.

You may need to revoke a key if it becomes compromised, gets lost, or if you forget the passphrase associated with the key. To revoke a key, you create a key revocation certificate. As a best practice, you should create a key revocation certificate immediately after initially creating your key pair. To create the key revocation certificate, enter **gpg --output revoke.asc --gen-revoke** *key_ID* at the shell prompt. To revoke a key, you must import the revocation certificate by entering **gpg --import** *revocation_certificate_filename* at the shell prompt. If you used the manual method to distribute your public key, you must import the key revocation certificate on any other systems where your public key was imported. If you are using a public key server on the Internet to distribute your keys to other users, you would need to issue the key revocation by entering **gpg --keyserver** *public_key_server_URL* **--send** *key_ID* at the shell prompt.

Accelerated Review

- With symmetric encryption, the key used to encrypt a message is the same key used to decrypt the message.
- The sender and the receiver must both have the exact same key.
- Symmetric encryption processes much faster than asymmetric encryption.
- One of the difficulties associated with symmetric encryption is how to securely distribute the key to all the parties that need to communicate with each other.
- Symmetric encryption standards include
  - 3DES
  - AES
  - Blowfish
- The longer the key, the more secure the data is.
- Asymmetric encryption uses two keys instead of one: the public key and the private key.
- Data that has been encoded with the public key can be decoded only with the private key.
- Data that has been encoded with the private key can be decoded only with the public key.
- Asymmetric encryption is frequently referred to as public key cryptography.
- Commonly used asymmetric encryption mechanisms include
  - RSA
  - DSA
- Private/public key pairs should be at least 1024 bits in length.
- You will frequently see implementations that use a hybrid of both symmetric and asymmetric encryption.
  - Asymmetric encryption is used for an initial key exchange to securely copy a secret key to both parties in a session.

- Once this is done, both parties have the same key and can switch to symmetric encryption for the remainder of the session.
- A certificate authority (CA) is responsible for issuing and managing encryption keys.
- When a key pair is requested from a CA, it generates a public key and a private key simultaneously, using a specified encryption scheme, such as RSA or DSA.
- The private key is given only to the key owner.
- The public key can be made available to anyone who needs it.
- The primary role of the CA is to verify that parties involved in an encrypted exchange are who they say they are.
- Early Linux network services such as Telnet, rlogin, rcp, rshell, and FTP transmit data as clear text, which exposes usernames, passwords, and other sensitive data to sniffers.
- OpenSSH provides a suite of utilities that you can use to encrypt these data transfers:
  - sshd
  - ssh
  - scp
  - sft
  - slogin
- OpenSSH uses private/public key encryption along with secret key encryption:
  - The SSH client first creates a connection with the system where the SSH server is running on IP port 22.
  - The SSH server then sends its public key to the SSH client.
  - The client system receives the public key from the SSH server and checks to see if it already has a copy of that key.
  - If it doesn't have the server's public key in either of these files, it will ask the user to add it.
  - The client generates a 256-bit secret key, uses the server's public key to encrypt it, and sends it to the server.
  - The server decrypts the secret key using the private key.
  - Both systems can now use symmetric encryption for the session.
- You can load the ssh client on your local computer and connect to the sshd daemon on the remote Linux system by entering **ssh –l *user_name ip_address*** at the shell prompt.
- You can tunnel unencrypted network traffic securely through an SSH tunnel.
  - When client software for the tunneled protocol establishes a connection with the local SSH client, the traffic is encrypted using SSH and tunneled through to the SSH server.
  - On the SSH server end, the traffic is decrypted and then forwarded to the appropriate target service.

- To configure an SSH tunnel, you have to
  - Edit the /etc/ssh/sshd_config file on the system where sshd is running and set the AllowTcpForwarding parameter to a value of **yes**.
  - Create a local ssh tunnel from a local high IP port to the port on the remote server that the desired service is listening on.
- You can test the tunnel using the telnet command from the client end of the tunnel.
- You can also tunnel your X server traffic to remote X clients using an SSH connection by doing the following:
  - Configure the client system to accept connections from the X server.
  - Configure the X server to redirect its graphical display to the client system using the DISPLAY environment variable.
  - Export the new value of the variable.
  - Set the X11Forwarding option to **yes** in the /etc/ssh/sshd_config file on the X server system.
  - At the shell prompt of the client system, use the –X option with the ssh command to log in to the remote system.
  - Enter the appropriate command to start a graphical application.
- You can configure SSH to use public key authentication instead of usernames and password.
- To do this, the public key of the user on the client system must be stored in the ~/.ssh/authorized_keys file in the home directory of the user on the server system that you will authenticate as.
- To configure public key authentication, you must do the following:
  - Create the public/private key pair on the client system using the ssh-keygen command.
  - Copy the public key you just created to the SSH server using the scp command.
  - Append the contents of the key file you just copied to the end of the ~/.ssh/authorized_keys file in the home directory of the user you will connect to the SSH server as.
- If desired, you can use the ssh-agent command to eliminate the need to enter the passphrase every time you establish an SSH connection.
- For your Linux+/LPIC-1 exam, you need to know how to use the open source GNU Privacy Guard (GPG) utility to encrypt files.
- GPG uses both asymmetric and symmetric cryptography:
  - GPG first generates a random symmetric key and uses it to encrypt the message to be transferred.

- The symmetric key itself is then encrypted using the recipient's public key and sent along with the message that was encrypted using the symmetric key.

- When the recipient receives a message, GPG first decrypts the symmetric key using the user's private key.

- GPG then uses the decrypted symmetric key to decrypt the rest of the message.

- To encrypt a file using GPG, do the following:

  - Generate your keys using the **gpg --gen-key** command.

  - Encrypt the file using the **gpg –e –r** *key_user_name filename* command.

- Once the file has been encrypted, it can then be decrypted using the **gpg --output** *output_filename* **--decrypt** *encrypted_filename* command.

- If you want to send the encrypted file to others, you can export your public key and send it to them:

  - Enter **gpg --export --armor** *key_user_email* > *public_key_filename*.

  - Send this key file to the user who you want to be able to open your encrypted files.

  - The user can import your public key into their GPG keyring using the **gpg –import** *public_key_filename* command.

  - You can view the files in your GPG keyring using the **gpg --list-keys** command.

  - With the public key imported, you can decrypt files sent to you using the **gpg --output** *output_filename* **--symmetric** *encrypted_filename* command.

- You can copy your public keys to a public key server on the Internet by entering **gpg --keyserver hkp://subkeys.pgp.net --send-key** *key_ID* at the shell prompt.

- You should create a key revocation certificate immediately after initially creating your key pair by entering **gpg --output revoke.asc --gen-revoke** *key_ID* at the shell prompt.

- To revoke a key, you must import the revocation certificate by entering **gpg --import** *revocation_certificate_filename* at the shell prompt.

- If you are using a public key server on the Internet to distribute your keys to other users, you would need to issue the key revocation by entering **gpg --keyserver** *public_key_server_URL* **--send** *key_ID* at the shell prompt.

Questions

1. Which of the following are true of symmetric encryption? (Choose two.)

    A. It uses a private/public key pair.

    B. Both the sender and the recipient must have a copy of the same key.

    C. RSA is a form of symmetric encryption.

    D. Blowfish is a form of symmetric encryption.

    E. The private key is sent to the recipient to decrypt information encrypted with the public key.

2. Which of the following are true of asymmetric encryption? (Choose two.)

    A. The private key is sent to the recipient.

    B. The public key is sent to the recipient.

    C. Information encrypted with the public key can only be decrypted with the private key.

    D. Information encrypted with the public key can be decrypted with the public key.

    E. Information encrypted with the private key can be decrypted with the private key.

3. Which host key files store the private keys used by the SSH version 2 server? (Choose two.)

    A. /etc/ssh/ssh_host_key

    B. /etc/ssh/ssh_host_key.pub

    C. /etc/ssh/ssh_known_hosts

    D. /etc/ssh/ssh_host_rsa_key

    E. /etc/ssh/ssh_host_dsa_key

4. Which parameter in the /etc/ssh/sshd_config file specifies which version of SSH the sshd daemon should use?

    A. HostKey

    B. Protocol

    C. SSHVersion

    D. ListenAddress

5. Which parameter in the /etc/ssh/ssh_config file configures the ssh client to only establish connections with SSH servers whose public key has already been added to either the ~/.ssh/known_hosts or the /etc/ssh/ssh_known_hosts file?

    A. StrictHostKeyChecking

    B. HostKey

    C. Protocol

    D. User

6. Which port does the sshd daemon listen on by default for incoming SSH connections?

    A. 20

    B. 22

    C. 389

    D. 631

    E. 80

    F. 443

7. Which of the following shell commands will load the ssh client and connect as the ksanders user to an SSH server with an IP address of 10.0.0.254?

   A. sshd –l ksanders 10.0.0.254

   B. ssh –u ksanders 10.0.0.254

   C. ssh –l ksanders 10.0.0.254

   D. ssh user=ksanders 10.0.0.254

8. You want to configure an SSH tunnel between a POP3 mail server running the sshd daemon and your local ssh client system running the Mozilla Thunderbird e-mail client. Which parameter in the /etc/ssh/sshd_config file must be set to a value of **yes** to enable the tunnel?

   A. AllowTcpForwarding

   B. AllowTcpTunneling

   C. AllowSSHTunnel

   D. AllowPop3Tunnel

   E. AllowPop3ImapForwarding

9. You want to establish a secure SSH tunnel for X server traffic. Which parameter in the /etc/ssh/ssh_config file on the X client system and in the /etc/ssh/sshd_config file on the X server system can be used to enable this functionality?

   A. AllowTcpForwarding

   B. AllowX11Tunnel

   C. ForwardX11

   D. AllowSSHTunnel

10. You want to configure your SSH server to use public key authentication. Which command can you use at the shell prompt of the SSH client system to create an RSA private/public key pair for this purpose?

    A. ssh-keygen –t rsa

    B. ssh-keygen –t dsa

    C. ssh-rsakeygen

    D. rsakeygen –ssh

11. You've just created a DSA private/public key pair for use with SSH public key authentication. What is the name of the public key file?

    A. ~/.ssh/id_rsa

    B. ~/.ssh/id_dsa

    C. ~/.ssh/id_rsa.pub

    D. ~/.ssh/id_dsa.pub

    E. ~/ssh_host_key.pub

12. You've copied your RSA public key to the home directory of a user on an SSH server. Which file do you need to add the public key to in order to enable public key authentication?

   A. ~/.ssh/authorized_keys

   B. /etc/ssh/authorized_keys

   C. ~/.ssh/id_rsa

   D. ~/ssh_host_key.pub

   E. /etc/ssh/ssh_host_rsa_key.pub

13. You want to use GPG to encrypt files. Which command should you use to create your GPG private/public key pair?

   A. gpg –e –r key_user_name filename

   B. gpg --gen-key

   C. gpg --export key_user_name > public_key_filename

   D. gpg --import public_key_filename

14. You need to import another user's GPG public key into your keyring so that you can decrypt files she sends you. Which command will do this?

   A. gpg –gen-key

   B. gpg --import *public_key_filename*

   C. gpg --list-keys

   D. gpg --export *key_user_name > public_key_filename*

15. An associate has just sent you a GPG-encrypted file, and you need to decrypt it. Assuming you've already imported this associate's GPG key into your keyring, which command can you use to decrypt the file?

   A. gpg --output *output_filename* --symmetric *encrypted_filename*

   B. gpg --export *encrypted_filename > output_filename*

   C. gpg --output *output_filename* --decrypt *encrypted_filename*

   D. gpg --import *encrypted_filename output_filename*

16. You just created a new GPG key pair. You want to now create a key revocation certificate just in case the key gets compromised at some point in the future. Which command should you use?

   A. gpg --output *filename* --gen-revoke *key_ID*

   B. gpg --export *encrypted_filename > output_filename*

   C. gpg --output *output_filename* --decrypt *encrypted_filename*

   D. gpg --import *filename*

Answers

1. **B, D.** With symmetric encryption, both the sender and the recipient must have a copy of the same key. Blowfish is a form of symmetric encryption.

2. **B, C.** With asymmetric encryption, the public key is sent to the recipient. Information encrypted with the public key can only be decrypted with the private key.

3. **D, E.** The private keys used by the SSH version 2 server are stored in /etc/ssh/ssh_host_ rsa_key and /etc/ssh/ssh_host_dsa_key.

4. **B.** The Protocol parameter in the /etc/ssh/sshd_config file specifies which version of SSH the sshd daemon should use.

5. **A.** The StrictHostKeyChecking parameter in the /etc/ssh/ssh_config file configures the ssh client to only establish connections with SSH servers whose public key has already been added to either the ~/.ssh/known_hosts or the /etc/ssh/ssh_known_hosts file.

6. **B.** The sshd daemon listens on port 22 by default for incoming SSH connections.

7. **C.** The **ssh –l ksanders 10.0.0.254** command will load the ssh client and connect as the ksanders user to an SSH server with an IP address of 10.0.0.254.

8. **A.** The AllowTcpForwarding parameter in the /etc/ssh/sshd_config file must be set to a value of **yes** to enable an SSH tunnel between the SSH client and the SSH server.

9. **C.** The ForwardX11 parameter in the /etc/ssh/ssh_config file on the X client system and in the /etc/ssh/sshd_config file on the X server system can be used to enable a secure SSH tunnel for X server traffic.

10. **A.** The **ssh-keygen –t rsa** command can be used at the SSH client to create an RSA private/public key pair for SSH public key authentication.

11. **D.** The ~/.ssh/id_dsa.pub file is the DSA public key that can be used for SSH public key authentication.

12. **A.** You need to add the public key to the ~/.ssh/authorized_keys file in the home directory of the user you want to authenticate as using public key authentication.

13. **B.** The **gpg --gen-key** command is used to create a GPG private/public key pair.

14. **B.** The **gpg --import** *public_key_filename* command can be used to import another user's GPG public key into your keyring so that you can decrypt files she sends you.

15. **A.** The **gpg --output** *output_filename* **--symmetric** *encrypted_filename* command can be used to decrypt a file sent to you by someone else (assuming you've already imported this person's GPG key into your keyring).

16. **A.** The **gpg --output** *filename* **--gen-revoke** *key_ID* command can be used to create a key revocation certificate just in case the key gets compromised at some point in the future.

Pre-Assessment Test

Instructions

Prior to completing the practice items in the chapters of this book, you should first complete this pre-assessment test to identify key areas that you need to focus on as you study for your Linux+/LPIC-1 exams.

In this activity, you will be presented with 50 assessment items that mirror the type of items you are likely to see on the real exam. The weighting of objective domains used in the real exams is approximated in this activity.

To make this experience as realistic and accurate as possible, you should allocate 45 minutes of uninterrupted time to complete these items. Turn off your phone, computer, TV, and music player; then find a comfortable place to work. Set a timer for 45 minutes and then begin this activity. Allowing yourself more than 45 minutes to complete this experience will yield inaccurate results. Be sure you work through all the questions in this activity before you check your answers. Again, this pre-assessment should mimic a real testing environment as much as possible. Wait until you have answered every question before checking the answers.

When you are done, you can use the "Quick Answer Key" along with the "In-Depth Answer Explanations" sections to evaluate your responses. Keep track of the number of questions you answer correctly and compare this number with the table found in the "Analyzing Your Results" section. This table will give you valuable feedback based on the number of correct answers you gave. You should also compare the answers you missed with the domain maps at the end of this activity to identify areas that you need to focus on as you study.

Ready? Set your timer for 45 minutes and begin!

Questions

1. Which bash configuration files are used for non-login bash shell sessions? (Choose two.)

   A. /etc/profile

   B. /etc/bashrc

   C. ~/.bashrc

   D. ~/.profile

   E. ~/.bash_profile

2. You need more information on the ls command. Which commands can be used to learn how to use this utility? (Choose two.)

   A. man ls

   B. help ls

   C. ls /help

   D. info ls

   E. ls –man

3. You've opened the /var/opt/myapp/settings.txt file in the vi editor. You need to enter new text into the file. Which keys will switch you to Insert mode? (Choose two.)

   A. INSERT

   B. ESC

   C. CTRL-E

   D. I

   E. ALT-R

4. You've opened a configuration file on your Linux system in the vi text editor. You've made a number of typing mistakes and want to close the file without saving any changes and start over. Which command will do this?

   A. :q

   B. :quit

   C. :exit!

   D. :q!

5. You need to create a new directory in your user's home directory named MyFiles. Which command can be used to do this?

   A. mkdir ~/myfiles

   B. mkdir ~/MyFiles

   C. md ~/myFiles

   D. mkdir ~ MyFiles

   E. md ~/MyFiles

6. Which command can be used to display information about your Linux kernel, such as version number and release number?

   A. ver

   B. uname

   C. msinfo

   D. sysconfig

   E. info

7. Which vi command-line mode commands can be used to save changes to the current file being edited and close the vi editor? (Choose two.)

   A. :exit

   B. :wq

   C. :q

   D. :q!

   E. :e!

8. You need to change the permissions of a file named widgets.odt such that the file owner can edit the file, but no other users on the system will be allowed to view or modify it. Which command will do this?

   A. chmod 660 widgets.odt

   B. chmod 640 widgets.odt

   C. chmod 777 widgets.odt

   D. chmod 600 widgets.odt

9. You need to change the permissions of a file named projectx.odt such that the file owner can edit the file, users who are members of the group that owns the file can view and edit it, and users who are not owners and don't belong to the owning group can't view or modify it. Which command will do this?

   A. chmod 660 projectx.odt

   B. chmod 640 projectx.odt

   C. chmod 777 projectx.odt

   D. chmod 644 projectx.odt

10. Which usermod command options must be used to add user accounts as members of a secondary group? (Choose two.)

   A. –a

   B. –R

   C. –g

   D. –p

   E. –G

11. Which control structure processes over and over as long as a specified condition evaluates to false?

   A. while

   B. until

   C. for

   D. case

12. You are designing the implementation of a new Linux server in your company's network. This server will function as an internal file and print server for your organization. Employees will save their work-related files in shared storage locations on the server. Print jobs for shared printers will be managed by the server as well. What services should be included in your specifications? (Choose two.)

   A. Apache

   B. MySQL

   C. Samba

   D. Telnet

   E. Pure-FTP

   F. CUPS

13. You need more information on the chgrp command. Which commands can be used to learn how to use this utility? (Choose two.)

   A. man chgrp

   B. help chgrp

   C. chgrp /help

   D. info chgrp

   E. chgrp –man

14. Which bash shell configuration files contain parameters that are applied system-wide? (Choose two.)

   A. /etc/bash.bashrc

   B. ~/.profile

   C. ~/.bashrc

   D. /etc/profile

   E. /etc/environment

15. You've logged in to your Linux system through the GNOME graphical desktop environment. You've opened a terminal session within GNOME to complete several command-line tasks. Which bash configuration files were used to configure the bash environment within the shell session? (Choose two.)

   A. /etc/profile

   B. ~/.profile

   C. /etc/bashrc

   D. ~/.bashrc

   E. ~/.bash_profile

16. In your user's home directory are four hidden bash shell configuration files: ~/.bash_profile, ~/.bash_login, ~/.bashrc, and ~/.profile. Which file will be used by default for bash login shells?

    A. ~/.bash_profile

    B. ~/.bash_login

    C. ~/.profile

    D. ~/.bashrc

17. Which configuration files are used to store your X server configuration settings? (Choose two.)

    A. /etc/X11/XF86Config

    B. /etc/sysconfig/windowmanager

    C. /etc/sysconfig/displaymanager

    D. /etc/X11/xorg.conf

    E. /etc/X11/xinit

18. When you are using local authentication on a Linux system, which file contains the passwords for your user accounts?

    A. /etc/passwd

    B. /etc/passwords

    C. /etc/gshadow

    D. /etc/shadow

19. Consider the following entry from the /etc/passwd file: `kmorgan:x:1001:100:Ken Morgan:/home/kmorgan:/bin/bash`. What user ID (UID) has been assigned to this user account?

    A. kmorgan

    B. 1001

    C. 100

    D. Ken Morgan

20. Consider the following entry from the /etc/shadow file: `kmorgan:$2a$05 $KL1DbTBqpSEMiL.2FoI3ue4bdyR.eL6GMKs7MU6.nZl5SCC7/ REUS:15043:1:60:7:5::`. In how many days will this account be disabled after the user's password has expired?

    A. One day

    B. Seven days

    C. Five days

    D. Null value (never)

21. Where is the UID number range that can be assigned to new user accounts defined?

   A. /etc/login.defs

   B. /etc/default/useradd

   C. /etc/skel

   D. /etc/passwd

22. You need to create a new user account for a user named Kimberly Sanders on your Linux system. You want to specify a username of ksanders, a full name of Kimberly Sanders, a default shell of /bin/bash, and that a home directory be created. Which command will do this?

   A. useradd –c "Kimberly Sanders" –m –s "/bin/bash" ksanders

   B. useradd –c "Kimberly Sanders" –m –s "/bin/bash" –u ksanders

   C. usermod –c "Kimberly Sanders" –m –s "/bin/bash" ksanders

   D. useradd –c "Kimberly Sanders" –s "/bin/bash" ksanders

23. The stracy user has recently married and changed her last name to Marsden. Which command can be used to update her user account with her new last name?

   A. usermod –l stracy –c "Sandy Marsden" smarsden

   B. usermod –l smarsden –c "Sandy Marsden " –u stracy

   C. usermod –l smarsden –c "Sandy Marsden " stracy

   D. usermod–c "Sandy Marsden " stracy

24. Where is the GID number range that can be assigned to new groups defined?

   A. /etc/login.defs

   B. /etc/default/useradd

   C. /etc/skel

   D. /etc/default/groupadd

25. You need to add the aebbert user to the secondary dbusers group. Which command can be used to do this?

   A. useradd –g dbusers aebbert

   B. usermod –g dbusers aebbert

   C. groupadd –U "aebbert" dbusers

   D. usermod –aG dbusers aebbert

26. You're writing a script that will require the end user to enter the name of his or her supervisor. Which of the following lines will input the user's response into a variable named SUP?

   A. read SUP

   B. input SUP

   C. prompt SUP

   D. query SUP

27. You've just created a new script in your home directory named runme.sh. When you try to run your script while in your home directory using the ./runme.sh command from the shell prompt, you see the following error: `bash: ./runme.sh: Permission denied`. Which resolution will fix this issue?

    A. Copy the file to the ~/bin directory.

    B. Add your home directory to the PATH environment variable.

    C. Enter chmod u+x runme.sh at the shell prompt.

    D. Change the she-bang line of the script to #!/bin/sh.

28. You need to assign a numeric value to a variable named TOT in a script so that you can perform mathematical operations on it. Which line can you add to your script to do this?

    A. declare –i TOT

    B. type TOT integer

    C. declare –r TOT

    D. declare –f TOT

29. You need to write an if/then/else statement in a script that will test to see if a file named /var/opt/mydb/mydb exists and has the write permission assigned for the user running the script. Which statement will do this?

    A. if test –e /var/opt/mydb/mydb; then…

    B. if test –w /var/opt/mydb/mydb; then…

    C. if test –f /var/opt/mydb/mydb; then…

    D. if test –x /var/opt/mydb/mydb; then…

30. You need to implement a for loop in a script. You want to use the seq command to generate a sequence of numbers that starts at 1, increments by 1, and stops at 100. Which statements will do this? (Choose two.)

    A. for i in `seq 1 5 100`

    B. for i in `seq 100`

    C. for i in `seq 1 1 100`

    D. for i in `seq 1-100`

    E. for i in `seq 1..100`

31. Which script structure executes over and over until a specified condition is no longer true?

    A. For loop

    B. Case

    C. While loop

    D. Until loop

32. Which protocols operate at the Network layer of the OSI model? (Choose two.)

   A. IP

   B. TCP

   C. UDP

   D. ICMP

   E. HTTP

33. Which IP addresses are private addresses? (Choose two.)

   A. 11.23.5.254

   B. 172.17.8.1

   C. 10.254.254.1

   D. 192.169.1.10

   E. 137.65.5.5

34. Consider the following IP address: 172.17.8.10/22. Which subnet mask is assigned to this address?

   A. 255.255.252.0

   B. 255.255.0.0

   C. 255.255.255.0

   D. 255.255.255.252

35. You need to assign the ens32 interface an IP address of 172.17.8.1 with a subnet mask of 255.255.0.0 and a broadcast address of 172.17.255.255. Which command will do this?

   A. ifconfig ens32 172.17.8.1 mask 255.255.0.0 bcast 172.17.255.255

   B. ifconfig 172.17.8.1 netmask 255.255.0.0 broadcast 172.17.255.255

   C. ifconfig ens32 172.17.8.1 subnetmask 255.255.0.0 bcast 172.17.255.255

   D. ifconfig ens32 172.17.8.1 netmask 255.255.0.0 broadcast 172.17.255.255

36. Which directive in /etc/sysconfig/network/ifcfg-eth0 is used to specify whether the interface is automatically enabled when the system is booted?

   A. STARTMODE

   B. BOOTPROTO

   C. IPADDR

   D. USERCONTROL

37. One of your Linux workstations has been configured with an incorrect default gateway router address. Which file do you need to edit to correct this?

   A. /etc/sysconfig/network/routes

   B. /etc/sysconfig/network/ifcfg-eth0

   C. /etc/hostname

   D. /etc/resolv.conf

38. For security reasons, you want your Linux system to always try to resolve hostnames using your DNS server before trying to resolve them using the /etc/hosts file. Which file can you use to configure the name resolver order?

   A. /etc/resolv.conf

   B. /etc/sysconfig/network/ifcfg-eth0

   C. /etc/nsswitch.conf

   D. /etc/sysconfig/services

39. The /etc/sudoers file on your Linux system is configured by default such that users must supply the root password when using sudo. You want to change this such that they only must supply their own password to use sudo. Which directives in the /etc/sudoers file must be commented out to do this? (Choose two.)

   A. Defaults env_keep

   B. root ALL=(ALL) ALL

   C. Defaults env_reset

   D. Defaults targetpw

   E. ALL ALL=(ALL) ALL

40. Which syslog facility can be used to capture log messages from an application you programmed yourself?

   A. user

   B. authpriv

   C. daemon

   D. local1

41. To secure the sshd service running on your Linux system from hackers, you decide to configure it to listen for SSH requests on a port other than the default of 22. Which directive in your etc/ssh/sshd_config file can you use to do this?

   A. Port

   B. BindAddress

   C. Protocol

   D. Tunnel

42. You want to write the stdout from the ps command to a file named myprocesses in the /tmp directory without overwriting the existing contents of that file. Which command will do this?

   A. ps 3 > /tmp/myprocesses

   B. ps 1 > /tmp/myprocesses

   C. ps 2 >> /tmp/myprocesses

   D. ps 1 >> /tmp/myprocesses

43. Which Linux runlevel puts the system in multiuser mode with networking enabled and a command-line interface?

    A. 1

    B. 2

    C. 3

    D. 5

44. You need to configure the GRUB2 bootloader such that it will boot the first operating system in the boot menu by default unless the end user manually selects an operating system within the timeout period. Which directive should you add to the /etc/default/grub configuration file to do this?

    A. GRUB_DEFAULT=0

    B. GRUB_SAVED DEFAULT=true

    C. GRUB_HIDDEN_TIMEOUT_QUIET=true

    D. GRUB_CMDLINE_LINUX=saved

45. Your Linux distribution uses systemd. It is currently running in a graphical environment. You want to switch to a multiuser text-based environment. Which commands could you use to do this? (Choose two.)

    A. systemctl isolate runlevel3.target

    B. systemctl rescue.target

    C. systemclt isolate multi-user.target

    D. systemctl isolate runlevel5.target

    E. systemctl isolate graphical.target

46. You just added a third SATA hard disk drive to your Linux system and need to create a GPT partition on it. Which command should you use to do this?

    A. fdisk /dev/sdb

    B. gdisk /dev/sdc

    C. gdisk /dev/sdd

    D. fdisk /dev/sdc

47. You are implementing an LVM volume on a Linux system with 16GB of RAM. You've added two SATA hard disks (/dev/sdb and /dev/sdc) to the system and created a partition on each one. You also defined both of these partitions as LVM physical volumes. Now you need to add both physical volumes to a new volume group named DATA. Which command should you use?

    A. lvscan –v

    B. vgcreate DATA /dev/sdb1 /dev/sdc1

    C. pvcreate /dev/sdb1

    D. lvcreate -L 700G -n research DATA

    E. pvcreate /dev/sdc1

48. Your Linux distribution currently uses the LightDM display manager with the Unity greeter. You want to reconfigure it to use the Qt greeter. Which parameter must you change in the LightDM configuration to do this?

   A. user-session

   B. greeter-session

   C. allow-guest

   D. greeter-show-manual-login

49. You installed a new Linux system about a week ago. Three days ago, you compiled and installed a new application from source code. Now, the Ethernet interface in the system sporadically goes offline. You need to see the boot messages generated by the system when it was in a pristine state shortly after being installed. Given that your system uses systemd instead of the init daemon, which command should you use?

   A. journalctl –b 2

   B. logger –p 2

   C. journalctl –b

   D. journalctl –b -2

50. Your organization uses private IP addresses using the 192.168.0.0 addressing scheme. You need to divide your IP address space into multiple subnets, so you decide to use a 26-bit subnet mask instead of the default Class C subnet mask. Which of the following is a valid address that could be assigned to a host on the second subnet created using this subnet mask?

   A. 192.168.0.66/26

   B. 192.168.0.91/24

   C. 192.168.0.60/26

   D. 192.168.0.138/26

Quick Answer Key

1. B, C	9. A
2. A, D	10. A, E
3. A, D	11. B
4. D	12. C, F
5. B	13. A, D
6. B	14. A, D
7. A, B	15. C, D
8. D	16. A

17.	A, D	34.	A
18.	D	35.	D
19.	B	36.	A
20.	C	37.	A
21.	A	38.	C
22.	A	39.	D, E
23.	C	40.	D
24.	A	41.	A
25.	D	42.	D
26.	A	43.	C
27.	C	44.	A
28.	A	45.	A, C
29.	B	46.	B
30.	B, C	47.	B
31.	C	48.	B
32.	A, D	49.	A
33.	B, C	50.	A

In-Depth Answer Explanations

1. ☑ **B** and **C** are correct. Both /etc/bashrc and ~/.bashrc are used to configure non-login shell sessions, although other files may be used on some distributions.
☒ **A, D**, and **E** are incorrect. The /etc/profile, ~/.profile, and ~/.bash_profile files are used to configure login shell sessions.

2. ☑ **A** and **D** are correct. The man and info utilities can be used to view documentation on the ls command.
☒ **B, C**, and **E** are incorrect. There is no help shell command in Linux. The /help and –man options are not valid with the ls command. However, you could use the --help option with ls to view a summary of how to use the command.

3. ☑ **A** and **D** are correct. You can press INSERT or I to enter Insert mode in the vi editor.
☒ **B, C**, and **E** are incorrect. The ESC key is used to return to Normal mode from Insert mode in the vi editor. The CTRL-E and ALT-R keystrokes aren't used by the vi editor.

4. ☑ **D** is correct. Entering :q! in Normal mode in the vi editor will discard all changes to the file since the last save and exit the editor.
☒ **A, B**, and **C** are incorrect. The :q and :quit commands will only quit the editor if no changes have been made to the file. The :exit! Command will exit the editor but will also save any changes made to the file.

5. ☑ **B** is correct. The mkdir command is used to create new directories in the file system (in this case, ~/MyFiles).

   ☒ **A** is incorrect because it uses the wrong case for the directory name. **C** and **E** are incorrect because they use the incorrect command for creating new directories (md). **D** is incorrect because it omits the (/) character after the tilde.

6. ☑ **B** is correct. The uname command displays information about your Linux kernel, including version numbers.

   ☒ **A**, **C**, **D**, and **E** are incorrect. The ver, msinfo, and sysconfig commands are not used on Linux. The info command is used to view help files for Linux commands and applications.

7. ☑ **A** and **B** are correct. Both the :exit and :wq commands will save any changes to the current file and then close the vi editor.

   ☒ **C**, **D**, and **E** are incorrect. The :q command will close the current file and exit the editor without saving changes. The :q! command will discard any changes made to the current file, close it, and then exit the editor. The :e! command discards any changes made to the current file since the last write operation.

8. ☑ **D** is correct. The chmod 600 widgets.odt command grants the owner rw- permissions, but takes away permissions from all other users.

   ☒ **A** is incorrect because it allows the file owner to edit the file, but also grants access to the group. **B** is incorrect because it grants the group the write (w) permission. **C** is incorrect because it grants the owner, group, and others all permissions to the file.

9. ☑ **A** is correct. The chmod 660 projectx.odt command grants the owner rw- permissions, the group rw- permissions, and others --- permissions.

   ☒ **B** is incorrect because it fails to grant the group the write (w) permission. **C** is incorrect because it grants the owner, group, and others all permissions to the file. **D** is incorrect because it fails to grant the group the write (w) permission and it grants others read (r) permission to the file.

10. ☑ **A** and **E** are correct. The usermod –aG command adds the users you specify as members of the specified group.

    ☒ **B**, **C**, and **D** are incorrect. The –R option is not used by the usermod command. The –g option assigns the user's primary group. The –p option changes the password assigned to the user.

11. ☑ **B** is correct. An until loop runs over and over as long as the condition is false. As soon as the condition is true, it stops.

    ☒ **A**, **C**, and **D** are incorrect. A while loop executes over and over until a specified condition is no longer true. A for loop processes a specific number of times. A case statement is not a looping structure.

12. ☑ **C** and **F** are correct. The Samba service provides file sharing. CUPS is used to manage printing.

    ☒ **A**, **B**, **D**, and **E** are incorrect. The Apache web server is frequently implemented on Linux in conjunction with the MySQL database server to develop web-based applications. Telnet is an older service that was formerly used for remote access. Pure-FTP provides an FTP service.

13. ☑ **A** and **D** are correct. The man and info utilities can be used to view documentation on the chgrp command.

    ☒ **B**, **C**, and **E** are incorrect. There is no help shell command in Linux. The /help and –man options are not valid with the chgrp command. However, you could use the --help option with chgrp to view a summary of how to use the command.

14. ☑ **A** and **D** are correct. Either /etc/bash.bashrc or /etc/profile (depending on the type of bash shell) is used to provide default configuration parameters for the bash shell that are applied system-wide.

    ☒ **B** and **C** are incorrect because they contain bash configuration parameters that are unique to the current user. **E** is incorrect because it contains configuration parameters used by the pam_env module.

15. ☑ **C** and **D** are correct. Because the terminal session is a non-login shell, the /etc/bashrc (or /etc/bash.bashrc) and ~/.bashrc files are used to configure the bash shell environment.

    ☒ **A**, **B**, and **E** are incorrect. Each of these files is used on various distributions to configure the login shell environment. Because the terminal session opened here is a non-login shell, these files are not used.

16. ☑ **A** is correct. By default, when a login shell session is started, bash will search for the ~/.bash_profile, ~/.bash_login, or ~/.profile file, in this order. It uses the first file it finds and ignores all the rest.

    ☒ **B**, **C**, and **D** are incorrect. By default, when a login shell session is started, bash will search for the ~/.bash_profile, ~/.bash_login, or ~/.profile file, in this order. It uses the first file it finds and ignores all of the rest. The ~/.bashrc file is only used for non-login shells.

17. ☑ **A** and **D** are correct. If your distribution uses X.org, then the X server configuration settings are saved in /etc/X11/xorg.conf. If your distribution uses XFree86, then the X server configuration settings are saved in /etc/X11/XF86Config.

    ☒ **B**, **C**, and **E** are incorrect. The /etc/sysconfig/windowmanager file is used to specify which window manager (such as GNOME or KDE) your system uses. The /etc/sysconfig/displaymanager file specifies which X server your system has implemented. The /etc/X11/xinit file is an executable that is run by the startx script to initialize an X session from the command prompt.

18. ☑ **D** is correct. The /etc/shadow file contains passwords for your user accounts.

    ☒ **A**, **B**, and **C** are incorrect. The /etc/passwd file contains your user accounts. The /etc/passwords file is not used for local authentication and is a distracter. The /etc/gshadow file contains passwords for your groups.

19. ☑ **B** is correct. The third field in each user entry in /etc/passwd specifies the user's ID number (UID). In this case, it's 1001.

    ☒ **A** is incorrect because it specifies the username. **C** is incorrect because it specifies the group ID (GID) of the user's primary group. **D** is incorrect because it specifies the user's full name.

20. ☑ **C** is correct. The seventh field in each record in /etc/shadow specifies the number of days to wait after a password has expired to disable the account.

☒ **A** is incorrect because it specifies the minimum number of days (one) required before a password can be changed. **B** is incorrect because it specifies the number of days prior to password expiration before the user will be warned of the pending expiration. **D** is incorrect because it is assigned to the eighth field, which specifies the number of days since January 1, 1970, after which the account will be disabled.

21. ☑ **A** is correct. The /etc/login.defs file contains values that can be used for the GID and UID parameters when creating an account with useradd. It also contains defaults for creating passwords in /etc/shadow.

☒ **B, C,** and **D** are incorrect. The /etc/default/useradd file contains defaults used by the useradd utility. The /etc/skel directory contains default directories and files that are automatically copied to the home directory of newly created users. The /etc/passwd file contains user account records.

22. ☑ **A** is correct. The useradd –c "Kimberly Sanders" –m –s "/bin/bash" ksanders command creates a new user account for a user named Kimberly Sanders with a username of ksanders, a full name of Kimberly Sanders, a default shell of /bin/bash, and a home directory.

☒ **B** is incorrect because it uses incorrect syntax for the useradd command. **C** is incorrect because it uses an incorrect command (usermod). **D** is incorrect because it omits the –m option, which is required to create a home directory.

23. ☑ **C** is correct. The usermod –l smarsden –c "Sandy Marsden" stracy command changes the full name and the username of the user account.

☒ **A** is incorrect because it reverses the old username and new username parameters. **B** is incorrect because it uses the –u option incorrectly (it is used to change the UID assigned to the account). **D** is incorrect because it fails to change the user's username (although it does change the user's full name).

24. ☑ **A** is correct. The default parameters for new group accounts, including the GID number, are contained in the /etc/login.defs file.

☒ **B, C,** and **D** are incorrect. The /etc/default/useradd file contains defaults used by the useradd utility. The /etc/skel directory contains default directories and files that are automatically copied to the home directory of newly created users. The /etc/default/groupadd file isn't used and is a distracter.

25. ☑ **D** is correct. The usermod –aG dbusers aebbert command can be used to add the aebbert user account to the secondary dbusers group.

☒ **A, B,** and **C** are incorrect. The useradd and groupadd commands can't be used to add a user to a group. The usermod –g command is used to set the primary group for a user.

26. ☑ **A** is correct. The read command is used to pause the script and prompt the user to provide some type of input, which is assigned to the specified variable.

☒ **B, C,** and **D** are incorrect. The input, prompt, and query commands can't be used to read user input.

27. ☑ **C** is correct. The error shown is caused by not having the execute permission set for the user trying to run the script. The chmod u+x runme.sh command will allow the user who owns the file to run it.

☒ **A** and **B** are incorrect because they resolve path-related problems, which aren't an issue in this scenario. **D** is incorrect because it changes the command interpreter to the sh shell, which isn't necessary in this scenario.

28. ☑ **A** is correct. The declare –i TOT statement specifies that the TOT variable contains integers.

☒ **B**, **C**, and **D** are incorrect. Although declaring a variable is sometimes called "typing" a variable, type is not a valid shell command. The declare –r statement creates a read-only variable that can't be changed (essentially, it becomes a constant). The declare –f statement is used to define a function.

29. ☑ **B** is correct. The test –w command checks to see if the specified file exists and if the write permission is granted.

☒ **A**, **C**, and **D** are incorrect. The test –e command only checks to see if the specified file exists. The test –f command checks to see if the specified file exists and if it is a regular file. The test –x command checks to see if the specified file exists and if the execute permission is granted.

30. ☑ **B** and **C** are correct. If you specify a single value with seq, the sequence starts at one, increments by one, and ends at the specified value. If you specify three values, the sequence starts at the first value, increments by the second value, and ends at the third value.

☒ **A** is incorrect because it increments by five instead of one. **D** and **E** are incorrect because they use incorrect syntax for the seq command.

31. ☑ **C** is correct. A while loop executes over and over until a specified condition is no longer true.

☒ **A**, **B**, and **D** are incorrect. A for loop executes a specific number of times. A case statement evaluates only once. An until loop runs over and over as long as the condition is false. As soon as the condition is true, it stops.

32. ☑ **A** and **D** are correct. The IP and ICMP protocols operate at the Network layer of the OSI model.

☒ **B**, **C**, and **E** are incorrect. The TCP and UDP protocols operate one layer up from the IP and ICMP protocols at the Transport layer of the OSI model. The HTTP protocol operates at the highest layer (Application) of the OSI model.

33. ☑ **B** and **C** are correct. The reserved class B range of IP addresses is 172.16.0.0–172.31.255.255, while the reserved class A range is 10.0.0.0–10.255.255.255.

☒ **A**, **D**, and **E** are incorrect. Each of these responses contains a public IP address that must be registered if the associated host is connected to a public network.

34. ☑ **A** is correct. The /22 prefix length indicates the first two octets of the subnet mask (16 bits) are populated plus six additional bits in the third octet.

☒ **B**, **C**, and **D** are incorrect. The prefix length for 255.255.0.0 would be /16. The prefix length for 255.255.255.0 would be /24. The prefix length for 255.255.255.252 would be /30.

35. ☑ **D** is correct. This command will assign the eth0 interface an IP address of 172.17.8.1 with a subnet mask of 255.255.0.0, and a broadcast address of 172.17.255.255.

☒ **A** and **C** are incorrect because they use incorrect parameters for setting the subnet mask and broadcast address. **B** is incorrect because it omits the network interface being configured.

36. ☑ **A** is correct. STARTMODE determines whether the interface is started automatically at system boot or must be manually enabled.

☒ **B**, **C**, and **D** are incorrect. The BOOTPROTO parameter can be set to a value of STATIC to use static IP address assignments or to DHCP to configure dynamic IP addressing. IPADDR assigns an IP address to the interface but only works if BOOTPROTO is set to STATIC. USERCONTROL determines whether standard user accounts are allowed to manage the interface.

37. ☑ **A** is correct. All of your routes are configured in the /etc/sysconfig/network/ routes file.

☒ **B** is incorrect because it is used to configure IP addressing information but doesn't contain routing information. **C** is incorrect because it is used to configure the system's hostname. **D** is incorrect because it is used to configure your name server IP address.

38. ☑ **C** is correct. You can use the /etc/nsswitch.conf (name service switch) file to define the order in which services will be used for name resolution.

☒ **A** is incorrect because it is used to configure the IP address of the DNS server but doesn't configure the name service order. **B** is incorrect because it is used to configure IP addressing information but doesn't contain name resolution information. **D** is incorrect because it is used to configure how services will behave after they are updated.

39. ☑ **D** and **E** are correct. These two directives must be commented out in the /etc/ sudoers file; otherwise, users must know the root password to use sudo run commands as root.

☒ **A**, **B**, and **C** are incorrect. The Defaults env_keep and Defaults env_reset directives are used to manage environment variables when using sudo. The root ALL=(ALL) ALL directive is used to define root user privileges.

40. ☑ **D** is correct. The local0–local7 facilities can be used to capture log messages from applications you develop yourself.

☒ **A**, **B**, and **C** are incorrect. The user facility is used for user-related log messages. The authpriv facility is used by all services associated with system security or authorization. The daemon facility is used by daemons that do not have their own dedicated facility.

41. ☑ **A** is correct. The Port directive specifies the port on which the sshd daemon will listen for SSH requests.

☒ **B**, **C**, and **D** are incorrect. The BindAddress directive is used to specify the address on the local machine to be used as the source address of the connection. The Protocol directive specifies the protocol versions SSH should support. The Tunnel directive is used to set up forwarding between the SSH client and the SSH server.

42. ☑ **D** is correct. The ps 1 >> /tmp/myprocesses command writes the stdout from the ps command to a file named myprocesses in the /tmp directory without overwriting the existing contents of that file.

☒ **A** is incorrect because it tries to use the stdin file descriptor for redirecting output, which can't be done. It also overwrites the contents of the file. **B** is incorrect because it redirects the stdout, but it also overwrites the contents of the file. **C** is incorrect because it redirects the stderr to the file.

43. ☑ **C** is correct. Runlevel 3 puts Linux in multiuser mode with networking enabled. The command-line interface is used.

☒ **A**, **B**, and **D** are incorrect. Runlevel 1 uses a command-line interface but puts the system in single-user mode. Runlevel 2 also uses a command-line interface and runs in multiuser mode; however, it also disables networking. Runlevel 5 runs Linux in multiuser mode with networking enabled and a graphical user interface.

44. ☑ **A** is correct. The GRUB_DEFAULT =0 directive causes GRUB2 to use the first menu entry by default, regardless of what operating system was selected on the last boot.

☒ **B**, **C**, and **D** are incorrect. If you set GRUB_SAVED DEFAULT to true, then GRUB will automatically select the last selected operating system from the menu as the default operating system to be used on the next boot. This parameter could conflict with the GRUB_DEFAULT parameter. Therefore, you can use either one, but not both. The GRUB_HIDDEN_TIMEOUT_QUIET=true directive causes no countdown timer to be displayed. The GRUB_CMDLINE_LINUX directive is used to pass options to the kernel.

45. ☑ **A** and **C** are correct. Both systemctl isolate runlevel3.target and systemclt isolate multiuser.target are used to switch the system into a text-based, multiuser environment comparable to runlevel 3 on an init-based system.

☒ **B**, **D**, and **E** are incorrect. To switch to the systemd equivalent of runlevel 5, you could enter either systemctl isolate runlevel5.target or systemctl isolate graphical.target. The systemctl rescue.target command switches the system to a rescue environment equivalent to runlevel 2.

46. ☑ **B** is correct. To create a GPT partition on the third SATA hard disk in a Linux system, you must first switch to your root user and then enter gdisk /dev/sdc at the shell prompt.

☒ **A** and **D** are incorrect because the fdisk command only supports MBR partitions. **C** is incorrect because it manages partitions on the fourth hard disk in the system (/dev/sdd) instead of the third (/dev/sdc).

47. ☑ **B** is correct. You use the vgcreate command to define a new volume group and assign physical partitions to it (/dev/sdb1 and /dev/sdc1 in this case). The vgcreate command is used after you define the physical volumes with pvcreate.

☒ **A**, **C**, **D**, and **E** are incorrect. You use the pvcreate command to define a partition (or even an entire disk) as an LVM physical volume. The lvscan command is used to view the logical volumes defined on the system. The lvcreate command is used to define logical volumes on the system.

48. ☑ **B** is correct. You can change which greeter LightDM uses by creating the appropriate file in /etc/lightdm/lightdm.conf.d/ and using greeter-session=*file_name* to specify the name of a greeter file (which has a .desktop extension) that you want to use in /usr/share/xgreeters.

    ☒ **A, C,** and **D** are incorrect. The user-session directive changes the default session type used by LightDM. The allow-guest directive enables or disables guest logins to the system. The greeter-show-manual-login directive allows users to manually specify a user account to use for authentication.

49. ☑ **A** is correct. The journalctl –b 2 command displays messages created during the second boot event found at the beginning of the journal. This should contain boot messages from the system's pristine state required by the scenario.

    ☒ **B, C,** and **D** are incorrect. The journalctl –b -2 command displays system messages that were logged two boot events ago. The logger command is used to send test log events to the logging daemon. The journalctl –b command displays boot messages that were logged in the most recent boot event.

50. ☑ **A** is correct. Using a 26-bit subnet mask allows you to divide this Class C network into four subnets. The valid host address range for the second subnet is 192.168.0.65–192.168.0.126.

    ☒ **B** is incorrect because it uses the default Class C subnet mask, instead of the custom 26-bit mask required in the scenario. **C** is incorrect because it is a valid address for the first subnet. **D** is incorrect because it is a valid address for the third subnet.

Analyzing Your Results

Now that you're done, let's analyze your results! You can use this information to identify two things:

- What resources you should use to prepare for your exams
- Domains that you may need to spend some extra time studying

First, use the following table to determine what tools and resources you should use to prepare for your exams:

Number of Answers Correct	Recommended Course of Study
1–12	If this had been the actual Linux+/LPIC-1 exams, you wouldn't have passed. Considerable study is necessary before taking the real exams. It is recommended that you review each chapter in this book in detail. You should set up the Linux virtual machine included with this book and practice completing the tasks covered in this book.
13–25	If this had been the actual Linux+/LPIC-1 exams, you most likely wouldn't have passed. Additional study is necessary before taking the real exams. It is recommended that you review each chapter in this book in detail. You should set up the Linux virtual machine included with this book and practice completing the tasks covered in this book.

Number of Answers Correct	Recommended Course of Study
26–37	If this had been the actual Linux+/LPIC-1 exams, you probably wouldn't have passed. Additional study and targeted review is recommended. At this level, you should make a list of each item you missed on a piece of paper. As you read this book, be sure to spend extra time studying the topics you missed. You should set up the Linux virtual machine included with this book and practice completing the tasks covered in this book.
38–50	Congratulations! If this had been the actual Linux+/LPIC-1 exams, there is a good chance you would have passed. But don't get cocky! The Linux+/LPIC-1 exams are very difficult. You could still easily fail. You should still work through all the chapters included in this book to ensure you are familiar with all the possible content you could potentially be tested on during the actual exams. One of the best ways to do this is to practice on a live system. You should set up the Linux virtual machine included with this book and practice everything covered in this book.

With the recommendations in the table above in mind, you can now use the following tables to determine which domains you need to focus your study efforts on:

Certification Exam 1 Objectives: LX0-103

Official Exam Domain	Question Number
101 System Architecture	43, 45
102 Linux Installation and Package Management	12, 44, 47
103 GNU and Unix Commands	2, 3, 4 ,5, 6, 7, 13, 42
104 Devices, Linux File Systems, Filesystem Hierarchy Standard	8, 9, 46

Certification Exam 2 Objectives: LX0-104

Official Domain Objective	Question Number
105 Shells, Scripting, and Data Management	1, 11, 14, 15, 16, 26, 27, 28, 29, 30, 31
106 User Interfaces and Desktops	17, 48
107 Administrative Tasks	10, 18, 19, 20, 21, 22, 23, 24, 25
108 Essential System Services	40, 49
109 Networking Fundamentals	32, 33, 34, 35, 36, 37, 38, 50
110 Security	39, 41

About the DVD

The DVD included with this book comes complete with Total Tester practice exam software loaded with simulated LX0-103/101-400 and LX0-104/102-400 exam questions, a virtual machine, videos, and a PDF copy of the book. The exam questions loaded into the Total Tester practice exam software are also provided as paper & pencil tests and available for download.

System Requirements

The Total Tester software requires Windows XP or higher and 30MB of hard disk space for full installation, in addition to a current or prior major release of Chrome, Firefox, Internet Explorer, or Safari. To run the software, you must set the screen resolution to 1024×768 or higher.

To install and configure the virtual machine, you must have at least 4GB of memory, at least 8–10GB of free disk space, and be using one of the following operating systems: Windows, OS X, Linux, or Solaris. The videos are in the MPEG-4 video file format and can be viewed with a number of media players, including Microsoft Windows Media Player, Apple QuickTime Player, VideoLAN VLC Media Player, and MPlayer. All PDF files require Adobe Acrobat, Adobe Reader, or Adobe Digital Editions to be viewed.

Total Tester Premium Practice Exam Software

Total Tester provides you with a simulation of the actual CompTIA Linux+/LPIC-1 exams. You can also create custom exams by exam domain and further customize the number of questions and time allowed.

The exams can be taken in either Practice Mode or Exam Mode. Practice Mode provides an assistance window with hints, references to the book, explanations of the correct and incorrect answers, and the option to check your answers as you take the exam. Exam Mode provides a simulation of the actual exam. The number of questions, the types of questions, and the time allowed are intended to be an accurate representation of the exam environment. Both Practice Mode and Exam Mode provide an overall grade and a grade broken down by exam domain.

To take an exam, launch the program and select either LX0-103/101-400 or LX0-104/102-400 from the Installed Question Packs list. You can then select Practice Mode, Exam Mode, or Custom Mode. After making your selection, click Start Exam to begin.

Installing and Running Total Tester Premium Practice Exam Software

From the DVD's main screen you may install Total Tester by clicking the Install Total Tester Practice Exams link. This will begin the installation process and place an icon on your desktop and in your Start menu. To run Total Tester, navigate to Start | (All) Programs | Total Seminars, or double-click the icon on your desktop.

To uninstall Total Tester, go to Start | Settings | Control Panel | Add/Remove Programs (XP) or Programs And Features (Vista/7/8), and then select the Total Tester program. Select Remove, and Windows will completely uninstall the software.

Paper & Pencil Tests

The exam questions loaded into the Total Tester practice exam software are also provided as paper & pencil tests in PDF and available for download.

You can download the paper & pencil tests from the McGraw-Hill Professional Media Center. To access the McGraw-Hill Professional Media Center, visit the following URL and enter the ISBN provided and your e-mail address. You will then receive an e-mail message with a download link to a .zip file. In addition to the paper & pencil tests, the .zip file will also include the virtual machine and videos.

- http://mhprofessional.com/mediacenter
- 9780071841719

Virtual Machine

The virtual machine included on the DVD can be used to set up a lab environment that you can use to practice working with Linux. Most of the exercises featured in this book can be completed using this virtual machine. For each of the applicable exercises, a customized Linux environment has been prepared and saved in a virtual machine snapshot. Prior to starting a particular exercise, you should first restore the snapshot specified for that exercise and then boot the Linux virtual machine. Each exercise and its corresponding snapshot are listed in Table B-1.

Installing and Configuring the Virtual Machine

With the DVD in hand, to install and configure the virtual machine, you will need to do the following:

1. Ensure your workstation meets the minimum requirements as noted in the "System Requirements" section.

2. Save the openSUSE_vm_files.zip file to a folder on your workstation's hard drive and extract it. If you're using a Windows workstation, you can right-click the .zip file and select Extract All. On a Linux workstation, you can use the gunzip command from the command prompt or the Files utility within the graphical environment to unzip the file.

Exercise	Snapshot Name
Exercise 2-1: Working with Linux Shells	Snapshot 2-1
Exercise 2-2: Using Linux Commands	Snapshot 2-1
Exercise 2-3: Using Command History	Snapshot 2-1
Exercise 2-4: Using Command Completion	Snapshot 2-1
Exercise 2-5: Using man Pages	Snapshot 2-1
Exercise 2-6: Using info	Snapshot 2-1
Exercise 2-7: Working with Environment Variables	Snapshot 2-1
Exercise 2-8: Working with Aliases	Snapshot 2-1
Exercise 2-9: Redirecting Input and Output	Snapshot 2-1
Exercise 2-10: Using Pipes	Snapshot 2-1
Exercise 3-1: Using the vi Editor	Snapshot 3-1
Exercise 4-1: Using Linux Search Tools	Snapshot 4-1
Exercise 4-2: Navigating the File System	Snapshot 4-1
Exercise 4-3: Managing Files and Directories	Snapshot 4-1
Exercise 4-4: Using grep	Snapshot 4-1
Exercise 5-1: Installing a Linux System	None
Exercise 6-1: Working with GRUB	Snapshot 6-1
Exercise 6-2: Working with GRUB2	Snapshot 6-2
Exercise 6-3: Working with Linux Runlevels	None
Exercise 6-4: Working with Linux Boot Targets	Snapshot 6-2
Exercise 7-1: Working with Accessibility Settings	Snapshot 7-1
Exercise 8-1: Using Web Resources to Obtain Linux Software	Snapshot 8-1
Exercise 8-2: Installing RPM Packages	Snapshot 8-2
Exercise 8-3: Uninstalling RPM Packages	Snapshot 8-3
Exercise 8-4: Managing RPM Packages	Snapshot 8-4
Exercise 8-5: Building Software from Source Code	Snapshot 8-5
Exercise 8-6: Working with Shared Libraries	Snapshot 8-6
Exercise 9-1: Managing User Accounts from the Command Line	Snapshot 9-1
Exercise 9-2: Managing Groups from the Command Line	Snapshot 9-2
Exercise 10-1: Managing Linux Partitions	Snapshot 10-1
Exercise 10-2: Backing Up Data	Snapshot 10-2
Exercise 11-1: Managing Ownership	Snapshot 11-1
Exercise 11-2: Managing Permissions	Snapshot 11-2
Exercise 11-3: Managing Default and Special Permissions	Snapshot 11-3
Exercise 11-4: Establishing Disk Quotas	Snapshot 11-4
Exercise 12-1: Working with Kernel Modules	Snapshot 12-1

Table B-1   Exercises and Their Corresponding Snapshot (*continued*)

Exercise	Snapshot Name
Exercise 13-1: Working with Linux Processes	Snapshot 13-1
Exercise 13-2: Scheduling Linux Processes	Snapshot 13-2
Exercise 14-1: Creating a Basic Shell Script	Snapshot 14-1
Exercise 14-2: Processing Text Streams	Snapshot 14-2
Exercise 15-1: Working with Network Interfaces	Snapshot 15-1
Exercise 15-2: Working with Network Commands	Snapshot 15-1
Exercise 16-1: Configuring CUPS	None
Exercise 16-2: Configuring NTP	Snapshot 16-2
Exercise 16-3: Managing SQL Data	Snapshot 16-3
Exercise 17-1: Managing User Access	Snapshot 17-1
Exercise 17-2: Implementing Network Security Measures on Linux	Snapshot 17-1
Exercise 17-3: Configuring xinetd	Snapshot 17-1
Exercise 18-1: Working with SSH	None
Exercise 18-2: Tunneling X Traffic with SSH	None
Exercise 18-3: Configuring Public Key Authentication	None
Exercise 18-4: Using GPG to Encrypt Files	None

Table B-1   Exercises and Their Corresponding Snapshot

3. Install VirtualBox on your workstation by doing the following:

   a. On your workstation, open a web browser and navigate to https://www.virtualbox
      .org/wiki/Downloads.

   b. Download the version of VirtualBox appropriate for your workstation's operating
      system.

   c. Install VirtualBox on your workstation using the instructions found in the VirtualBox
      documentation (available from https://www.virtualbox.org/manual/UserManual.html).

4. Import the openSUSE virtual machine you extracted from the .zip file into VirtualBox
   by doing the following:

   a. Launch VirtualBox on your workstation.

   b. Click **Machine** | **Add**.

   c. Browse to the folder where you extracted the .zip file and select the
      openSUSE.vbox file.

5. To restore a specific snapshot, do the following:

   a. Click **Snapshots**.

   b. Right-click the snapshot you want to use and then click **Restore Snapshot**.

   c. When prompted to restore the snapshot, click **Restore**.

   d. Click **Start** to launch the virtual machine.

   e. Wait while the virtual machine boots.

Alternatively, you can download the openSUSE_vm_files.zip file from the McGraw-Hill Professional Media Center in the manner noted in the "Paper & Pencil Tests" section.

Videos

Also included on the DVD are videos that showcase a select number of the exercises included in the book. If you prefer, you can download the video files from the McGraw-Hill Professional Media Center in the manner noted in the "Paper & Pencil Tests" section.

PDF Copy of the Book

The entire contents of the book are provided in PDF on the DVD. This file is viewable on your computer and many portable devices. Adobe Acrobat, Adobe Reader, or Adobe Digital Editions is required to view the file on your computer. A link to Adobe's website, where you can download and install Adobe Reader, has been included on the DVD.

 NOTE For more information on Adobe Reader and to check for the most recent version of the software, visit Adobe's website at www.adobe.com and search for the free Adobe Reader or look for Adobe Reader on the product page. Adobe Digital Editions can also be downloaded from the Adobe website.

To view the PDF copy of the book on a portable device, copy the PDF file to your computer from the DVD, and then copy the file to your portable device using a USB or other connection. Adobe offers a mobile version of Adobe Reader, the Adobe Reader mobile app, which currently supports iOS and Android. For customers using Adobe Digital Editions and an iPad, you may have to download and install a separate reader program on your device. The Adobe website has a list of recommended applications, and McGraw-Hill Education recommends the Bluefire Reader.

Technical Support

Technical support information is provided in the following sections by feature.

Total Seminars Technical Support

For questions regarding the Total Tester software or operation of the DVD, visit www.totalsem.com or e-mail support@totalsem.com.

McGraw-Hill Education Content Support

For questions regarding the PDF copy of the book, e-mail techsolutions@mhedu.com or visit http://mhp.softwareassist.com.

For questions regarding the book content, virtual machine, and videos, e-mail customer .service@mheducation.com. For customers outside the United States, e-mail international_cs@ mheducation.com.

INDEX